# Knowledge, Nature, and Norms

# Knowledge, Nature, and Norms

**MARK TIMMONS**
University of Arizona

**DAVID SHOEMAKER**
Bowling Green State University

WADSWORTH
CENGAGE Learning™

Australia • Brazil • Japan • Korea • Mexico • Singapore • Spain • United Kingdom • United States

WADSWORTH
CENGAGE Learning™

**Knowledge, Nature, and Norms**
**Mark Timmons and**
**David Shoemaker**

Acquisitions Editor: Worth Hawes

Development Editor: Ian Lague

Assistant Editor: Patrick Stockstill

Editorial Assistant: Kamillah Lee

Technology Project Manager:
Julie Aguilar

Marketing Manager: Christian Shea

Marketing Assistant: Mary Anne
Payumo

Marketing Communications
Manager: Darlene Amidon-Brent

Project Manager, Editorial
Production: Matt Ballantyne

Creative Director: Rob Hugel

Art Director: Maria Epes

Print Buyer: Linda Hsu

Permissions Editor: Roberta Broyer

Production Service:
Aaron Downey, Matrix
Productions Inc.

Copy Editor: Cheryl Smith

Cover Designer: Yvo

Cover Image: Bruno Mallart/
Images.com

Compositor: Macmillan Publishing
Solutions

For product information and technology assistance, contact us at
**Cengage Learning Customer & Sales Support, 1-800-354-9706**

For permission to use material from this text or product,
submit all requests online at **cengage.com/permissions**
Further permissions questions can be e-mailed to
**permissionrequest@cengage.com**

Library of Congress Control Number: 2007938834

ISBN-13: 978-0-495-09722-8

ISBN-10: 0-495-09722-5

**Wadsworth Cengage Learning**
10 Davis Drive
Belmont, CA 94002-3098
USA

Cengage Learning products are represented in Canada by
Nelson Education, Ltd.

For your course and learning solutions, visit **academic.cengage.com**

Purchase any of our products at your local college store
or at our preferred online store **www.ichapters.com**

Printed in the United States of America
1 2 3 4 5 6 7 12 11 10 09 08

*To my stepdaughters, Kristin and Ashley,
for keeping me pseudo-hip on student life
and language, and also allowing me to exploit
their lives for my best classroom examples*
—D. S.

*For Betsy*
—M. T.

# Contents

# Preface

Our primary purpose in putting together this text is to provide introductory philosophy students with an *affordable* and *compact* anthology consisting of carefully chosen, well-edited readings on several of the most important topics in philosophy, paired with clear and informative introductions to the essential ideas presented in those readings. We were motivated to assemble such a text because of our frustration with numerous shortcomings of the "monster" anthologies currently available to introductory students. First, these texts are typically quite expensive, causing some students to be irritated with philosophy prior to even entering the classroom. Second, because of the large number of selections such texts usually include, it is very difficult for students to read, or for instructors to teach, much more than a small fraction of the material in the text. This leaves students frustrated as well at the fact that so much material in their very expensive text has been ignored. Third, many individual selections in these big anthologies are included in their entirety, despite the fact that most instructors discuss (as we do) only certain well-traveled portions of them in class. So once again students become frustrated at having to read long, difficult selections, the bulk of which are left unexplored. Finally, most of the big texts have either unhelpful or nonexistent introductory material, and often lack topic introductions to motivate the issues, lay out relevant distinctions, summarize readings, and demonstrate the relevance of the issues to students' lives.

To address these problems, we incorporate the following features in this anthology, all of which are intended to benefit students in one way or another (and, incidentally, also to benefit instructors):

- *Six essential topics.* The text is divided into six chapters (in addition to an introductory chapter), each focusing on a significant problem or central topic in philosophy. These are the topics most often taught in introductory philosophy courses, and for good reason: they are not only central to the discipline, but they also provide a well-rounded

introduction to philosophy. The topics we have chosen to cover are
personal identity and immortality, the mind-body problem, free will and
responsibility, the existence of God, knowledge, skepticism and belief,
and ethics. Each chapter includes between six and nine individual
readings. We have deliberately kept the number of readings small in order
to produce a more affordable text and also to allow for a greater per-
centage of the selections to be read and taught.

■ *Careful editing.* Most of the included readings have been carefully (and in
some cases heavily) edited to focus on the main points, the points most
often worth discussing in an introductory philosophy classroom. This
keeps most of the readings short and to the point, and allows students to
zero in on what is most important in the selection without being side-
tracked or confused by the caveats and corollary arguments endemic to
scholarly debate.

■ *Literary selections.* Each chapter's readings begin with a literary selection to
provide students with an entrée into the topic that is accessible and
fun. These include science fiction stories, such as Pohl and Kornbluth's
"The Meeting," Terry Bisson's "They're Made Out of Meat," and John
Pollock's "A Brain in a Vat," as well as literary philosophical pieces
including the "Rebellion" sequence from Dostoevsky's *The Brothers
Karamazov,* and the ring of Gyges story from Plato's *Republic.* For us,
discussion of these sorts of stories in class, before students plunge into the
philosophical texts, offers a chance to draw out the relevant issues of the
chapter in a more informal and lively fashion.

■ *Chapter introductions.* At the very beginning of each chapter, we have
included a basic but detailed introduction to the issues, pitched directly
to introductory undergraduate students. Each chapter introduction starts
with a "motivation" section, designed to show students the importance
and relevance of the particular topics. The introduction goes on to lay
out the various issues in the readings, introducing key concepts and
drawing essential distinctions along the way. The idea is that if students
have read through the introduction carefully, they will be well prepared
to read and get a basic grasp of the selections that follow.

■ *Selection introductions.* In order to aid students' understanding, each reading
selection is preceded by a short introduction to the author and the
content of the selection.

■ *Reading questions.* Following each reading, we have included substantive
reading comprehension questions. These questions are intended to get
the students thinking like philosophers about the readings and about their
own lives. The questions challenge students to identify, analyze, and
critically evaluate philosophical arguments, as well as to begin offering
and defending their own views on these topics. The questions should also
provide instructors with points of focus in class discussion, in writing
assignments, or on exams. We have provided sample answers and hints on

the course website, to enhance student comprehension and provide immediate feedback.

- *An introduction to philosophy primer.* To prepare students for the work ahead, we have written a general introduction to the text, which provides a primer on philosophy and philosophical arguments. It includes a discussion on how to identify and critically evaluate arguments in a text and a list of common fallacies and argumentative failures. Each of the fallacies and failures is illustrated with examples from the text as well as from everyday public discourse. We urge students to return to this introduction as they work their way through the text and the reading comprehension questions. Again, the idea is to provide students with the tools to start thinking like philosophers (and for them to see the value of doing so as well).

- *Glossary.* To facilitate reference, we have included a glossary of terms that are introduced and defined in the general introduction and chapter introductions. Each term in the glossary appears in boldface type when it is first introduced and explained.

There is no "right" agenda to follow when approaching these philosophical topics, and the chapters can be taught in any order. One of us takes Descartes' *Meditations* as a model for the structure of his introductory class, starting off with skepticism (Chapter 6), then moving on to the nature of the self and personal identity (Chapter 2), followed by the existence of God and the problem of evil (Chapter 5), and concluding with free will and moral responsibility (Chapter 4). The other of us likes to begin with ethics (Chapter 7), and then proceeds to the topics of free will and moral responsibility (Chapter 4), followed by personal identity and immortality (Chapter 2), and concluding with the mind-body problem (Chapter 3). We have simply tried to provide a text that will reveal the joys of philosophical inquiry no matter how one approaches it.

While both of us have done our share of scholarly philosophical work, we remain committed to, and have a great love for, *teaching* philosophy, and together we have well over thirty years of experience, in several different kinds of institutions and with a wide range of introductory philosophy students. Our anthology represents a meeting of pedagogical minds, and we have tried to include here what has worked, and worked well, for us.

For help in putting this volume together, we have many people to thank. For his assistance in gathering together a number of possible articles for inclusion, as well as for tracking down many in the public domain, we thank Steve Weimer. For his persistent encouragement, advice, and much-needed hectoring, we thank Ian Lague at Wadsworth. We are also grateful to Worth Hawes, Patrick Stockstill, and the rest of the good folks at Wadsworth. Thanks also to Aaron Downey at Matrix Productions for his friendly help in the final stages of this project. For their proofreading expertise, we thank Nathan Ballantyne, Michael Bukoski, Jacob Caton, and Daniel Sanderman. David Shoemaker would like to thank the Center for Ethics and Public Affairs (Murphy Institute, Tulane University) for providing a generous research fellowship, during which time he worked on this book. We are thankful for the terrific advice we received from several reviewers, including Karen Adkins, Torin Alter, Benjamin F. Armstrong Jr., Leonard Berkowitz, James Buchanan, Matthew Burnstein, Eric M. Cave, Deen Chatterjee, Sharon Crasnow, Steven Doty, William Eaton, Ronald Endicott, James Heffernan, John Holmes, Rob Hull, Peter Hutcheson, Erik Jackiw, Todd Jones, Errol Katayama, David A. Keith, John L. King, Ian MacKinnon, Chad Mohler, Nathan Nobis, Csaba Nyiri, David Pitt, Frederick Rauscher, Franklin E. Robinson, Priscilla Sakezles, Joseph Shay, Ed Slowick, Michael Thune, Andrea Veltman, and David Wisdo. Finally, special thanks to Terry Horgan for his advice and to Chris Brown for help with the instructor's manual.

# 1

# Introduction

## WHAT IS PHILOSOPHY?

This book features a collection of essays on philosophy. But what *is* philosophy? What is it about? How do philosophers go about doing philosophy? This introductory chapter addresses these questions. Our aim is to help beginning students—especially students who have never taken a philosophy course or who have never been otherwise exposed to philosophy—get an idea of what they will encounter in the chapters to follow.

The word *philosophy* derives from the Greek words "philo" and "sophia" which, when put together, mean "love of wisdom." And while this love of wisdom is something that many philosophers feel and express, it isn't a very revealing statement about the precise nature of the enterprise. When asked what philosophy is, the famous British philosopher Bertrand Russell (1872–1970) would take people to his library and point at the shelves, saying "It's what all these books here are about." This was Russell's way of indicating that the field of philosophy is vast, covering many topics, and that it is hard if not impossible to give a short answer to the question that would be adequate. Indeed, trying to give a short but informative answer to this question without conveying some idea of what all those books include would be like trying to give a short but informative answer to the question, "What is science?" to someone who had no familiarity with physics, or chemistry, or biology, or psychology, or any of the other sciences. Any short and informative answer to these questions must be preceded by some indication of their subject matters.

With this in mind, we can follow Russell's lead and consider the sorts of topics that we find in philosophy books—what philosophy as a discipline is all about. Philosophers are interested in answering questions about various topics. So, let's consider a sampling of these questions and the associated topics, after which we can return to our question about philosophy.

1. Are you who you think you are? As you read these words, you probably assume (right now) that you are the same person who bought this book a week ago, played softball that evening, got up the next day and cleaned your apartment, and so on and on. (Readers are asked to fill in details that fit their memories about the past week.) How about going back two weeks? A year? Ten years? How about going back to the day on which a certain infant was born whose picture your mom has in a frame on her desk at home with your name on it? If you answer "yes" to any or all of these questions, ask yourself what facts make it true that you are the same person as a certain series of persons stretching back into the past? And, of course, your answer to this question will bear importantly on another: Will *you* survive your physical death—are you immortal? Such questions comprise the topic of *personal identity and immortality* that one encounters in Chapter 2.

2. Do you have a mind? The answer to this one is a no-brainer. Right? But what is the mind supposed to be? Is it supposed to be some spiritual, nonphysical substance that is not spatially extended? If so, how is the mind (or mental phenomena such as feelings and thoughts) related to your body in general and your brain (or events in your brain) in particular? Maybe what we call the mind just *is* your brain; then it would not be a no-brainer. These and related questions concern what is called the *mind-body problem,* the topic of Chapter 3.

3. Are you free? Here you are, reading these sentences. You probably assume that you could be doing something else right now, were you to choose to do so. "It's really up to me" (you think), "I'm in control; right now, I have the freedom to keep on reading or to do something else." But your actions are events. And don't we know from science that all events are caused and thus determined by events that precede them in time? When you move your body, there is a complicated network of physical *events* in your brain and central nervous system that terminate in action. Suppose you now think: "OK, right now I'm going to close this book and show that I'm in control here. And my making this *decision*—something mental—is what starts the chain of physical events that lead to my act of closing the book. So, there you go, I'm free." But your making this decision is a mental event, so isn't it too caused by other mental events—such as *wanting* to prove a point? The same goes for your wanting to prove a point, which in turn is caused by some prior event. But if all physical and mental events are caused, how can anything you do (an event) be an act of freedom? And if you aren't free, then how can you be responsible for what you do? These questions comprise the topic of *free will, determinism, and responsibility,* which will occupy us in Chapter 4.

But enough about you. Here, briefly, are some further questions and corresponding topics that occupy the attention of philosophers and that are featured in this book.

4. Does God exist? What reasons are there (if any) for thinking that God does or does not exist? This is the problem of *the existence of God,* the topic of Chapter 5. Theists are those who believe that God does exist, and some theists think that there are arguments that prove God's existence. If so, then those proofs can be used to *know* that God exists. Atheists deny the claim that God exists. Agnostics on the other hand claim that it not possible to know one way

or the other and so refuse to either affirm or deny God's existence. The position of the agnostic raises questions not only about religious knowledge, but about knowledge generally.

5. Can we have knowledge? Some propositions are true and others are false. But that doesn't guarantee that we can know which are which. What does it take to really know that some claim is true? Can we meet those standards? If not, we must embrace skepticism about knowledge. So which is it, knowledge or skepticism? Furthermore, are there ethical obligations regarding what beliefs one holds? Chapter 6, on *knowledge, skepticism,* and *belief,* takes up these questions.

6. What should we do? Tom is very hungry, out of work, and wandering around. One day, he happens to find a wallet containing $20 lying on the sidewalk near an ATM at a bank. Would it be ethical for him to take the money? If not, why not? If so, why? What makes an act ethical or unethical? Questions about the nature of ethical and unethical behavior—questions of *ethics*—are taken up in the readings of our final chapter.

These six questions represent some of the most basic philosophical questions one can ask. Collectively they concern the nature of things (including ourselves), the possibility of knowledge, and norms of ethically correct behavior: nature, knowledge, and norms. Inquiry into these (and other basic) questions is what philosophy is all about: the really Big Questions. If one had to sum up in a single sentence the answer to our question, "What is philosophy?" one could say (given what has just been said about the topics in philosophy), *philosophy is an area of inquiry that raises questions about knowledge, nature, and norms as described above and tries to give reasoned answers to them.* It should be noted that the subject matter of philosophy is not restricted to these questions. But these six questions are representative of what philosophy is all about. Many of the books Russell would point to in his library are books that raise one or more of the sorts of questions just mentioned.

So far, the focus of this chapter has been about the topics that concern philosophy—its *subject matter.* But the italicized one-liner about what philosophy is also mentions the attempt to give reasoned answers to philosophical questions. More needs to be said about this aspect of philosophy. The attempt to give answers based on reasons—indeed, good reasons—has to do with the *method* of doing philosophy. So philosophy has a subject matter and method, and the rest of this introduction is occupied with philosophical method. Put very briefly, the method of philosophy involves putting forward what one takes to be good reasons in support of whatever claim one is attempting to support. In giving reasons for some claim—in giving what philosophers call an argument—one is engaged in what we might call the *constructive aim* of philosophy, the aim of trying to construct good arguments that really do support some philosophical claim. But this means that the philosophical method also involves critically evaluating arguments, putting them to the test to see if they are any good. Call this the *critical aim* of philosophy. The critical aim of philosophy is at the service of the constructive aim. Both are crucial to philosophical method.

Arguments, then, are at the heart of philosophical method. But what is an argument? What makes an argument good? How can arguments be evaluated to determine whether they are good? These are the questions that will occupy us for the rest of the introduction.

## WHAT ARE PHILOSOPHICAL ARGUMENTS?

The word *argument* has different meanings in English. Two people shouting at one another are having an argument, but they are probably not giving what philosophers call arguments. An **argument** consists of a series of statements, called **premises**, intended to provide support for another statement, called the **conclusion**. The first task in reading an argumentative essay is to identify what the actual arguments are. One helpful tip is that the following words or phrases usually indicate that a premise is about to appear: "because," "since," "for," and "for the reason that." On the other hand, the following words or phrases usually indicate that a conclusion is about to appear: "therefore," "thus," "and so," "consequently," "necessarily," "hence," "it follows that," and "for that reason."

Generally, it is useful to distinguish two types of arguments: deductive and inductive. The difference between them has to do with the support relationship between premises and conclusions.

A **deductive argument** involves the attempt to prove a conclusion—to provide in the premises the strongest possible support for the conclusion—giving a logical guarantee. When a deductive argument is done correctly, *if the premises are true, the conclusion must be true as well.* This is the type of argument most often used in philosophy, and it is the domain of formal logic.

One very common type of deductive argument is the **syllogism**, in which a conclusion is inferred from two premises. Here is the classic example of a syllogism:

1. All human beings are mortal.
2. Socrates is a human being.
3. Thus, Socrates is mortal.

One very helpful way of analyzing and evaluating philosophical arguments, then, is to try to put them in syllogistic form like this (although one may need to use more than two premises). While doing so may oversimplify the argument, it at least allows one to visualize its overall structure in a clear way, so that one is in a position to evaluate the argument. (Strategies for evaluating arguments are addressed in the next section of this chapter.)

While a deductive argument purports to offer reasons that establish its conclusion beyond doubt, an **inductive argument** is less ambitious. In an inductive argument the premises are meant to provide strong support for the conclusion, even though the support they provide does not establish the conclusion beyond doubt. For example, a common form of inductive argument called **inductive generalization** is one that moves from what is called a "sample" to a general conclusion about a population. (The term "population" here refers to anything at all—persons, pencils, plays, etc.—that this kind of argument is about.) This is the form of most scientific arguments and is the kind of argument with which you are likely very familiar. So, for example, suppose I decide to identify the color of every swan I can, and after five years of investigation, I present the following argument:

1. Swan #1 was white.
2. Swan #2 was white.
3. [And so on for all ten thousand swans I have seen.]
4. Therefore, (probably) all swans are white.

I am inferring something that is highly likely to be true about the population of swans, based on my very large sample size, but it remains possible that there's a non-white swan out there I just didn't run across. This is what the inserted "probably" makes clear: the relation between the premises and the conclusion is one of probability. By contrast, in a deductive argument, one may insert the word "necessarily" to make the intended relation between premises and conclusion clear.

Another common type of inductive argument worth calling attention to is **argument by analogy**. An analogy is a comparison between two or more things, meant to be in some way illuminating. "Life is like a beanstalk" is an example. One would expect anyone who made this analogy to say more about the ways in which life and a beanstalk are similar. An argument by analogy is one in which, for example, two or more things are compared in order to draw a conclusion about one of them. People reason this way all the time in making all sorts of practical decisions. Here is an everyday example:

> The course in Philosophy of Religion being taught next semester by
> Professor Smith is probably going to be very entertaining. I took
> Philosophy of Science and Ethics from this professor last year, and both
> of them were very entertaining.

The speaker is drawing a conclusion about a future course (that it will be entertaining) based on its similarity to other courses (its being a philosophy course taught by a particular instructor). This above argument can be set forth as follows:

1. The courses in Philosophy of Science, Ethics, and Philosophy of Religion are all philosophy courses that have been or will be taught by Professor Smith.
2. The courses in Philosophy of Science and Ethics were entertaining.
3. Therefore, (probably) the Philosophy of Religion course will also be entertaining.

Let us call the items that are mentioned in the premises but not in the conclusion the *comparison base,* and let us call the item (it may be more than one) mentioned in the conclusion—the item the inference is about—the *target item.* An analogical argument, then, attempts to call attention to similarities between the items in the comparison base and the target item as a basis for attributing some further property to the target.

One finds arguments by analogy in philosophy. For instance, one of the most famous arguments for the existence of God compares nature to a watch. A watch has a watchmaker. And so, if the analogy between nature and a watch is a good one, then we may conclude that in all probability there is a being who created all of nature, God. Of course, whether this argument by analogy is a good argument brings us to the question about how one is to evaluate arguments. But before turning to this topic, let us sum up the basic points that have been made in this section:

- The method of philosophy involves giving and evaluating arguments for philosophical conclusions.
- An argument is a set of statements, some of which—the premises—are being used in an attempt to provide support for another member of the set—the conclusion.

- It is useful to distinguish deductive from inductive arguments. The main difference between these two types of argument has to do with the intended support relation between the premises and conclusion of the argument. A deductive argument is intended to provide the strongest possible support for its conclusion: the truth of the premises is supposed to guarantee the truth of the conclusion. An inductive argument is intended to provide strong, but not conclusive, support for its conclusion.

- There are two common sorts of inductive argument: argument by inductive generalization, in which specific instances are used to support a generalization, and argument by analogy, in which two or more items are compared for their similarities in drawing a conclusion about one of the items.

## HOW DOES ONE EVALUATE ARGUMENTS?

Once you have identified and articulated an argument, and once you have determined whether or not it is deductive or inductive (by identifying the intended strength of the connection between its premises and its conclusion), your next step will be to critically evaluate it. Because most philosophical arguments are deductive in form, we will focus on evaluating them, although at the end of this section, we will offer some suggestions for evaluating inductive arguments. You should also be aware that some of this material may be difficult to comprehend completely on first reading, so we invite you to revisit it in tandem with the relevant comprehension questions at the end of each reading in the text. You will occasionally be asked to evaluate an argument in the reading, and you ought to do so in light of the following considerations.

In evaluating deductive arguments, you need to ask the following three questions, and it will be most helpful to ask them in this particular order:

- Is the argument *valid,* that is, do the premises logically guarantee the truth of the conclusion?

- Are the terms in the premises *clear?*

- Are the premises (fairly obviously) true? (A valid argument with all true premises is called *sound*).

Only once you've gotten a "yes" answer to a question should you move on to address the next.

### Validity

To say that a deductive argument is **valid** is to say that the rules of inference have been applied correctly, so that *if* the premises are true, then the conclusion *must* also be true. So a valid argument is an argument that has followed the rules of logic correctly. A valid argument's conclusion may be true *or false,* depending on the truth of its premises. An invalid argument's conclusion may *also* be true or false. The preceding Socrates argument was an example of a valid argument, as is the following:

1. All college students are 20 years old.
2. The president of the United States is a college student.
3. Thus, the president of the United States is 20 years old.

In this example, both premises 1 and 2 are false. But the argument is still valid, because *if* the premises *were* true, then the conclusion (#3) would necessarily be true. It may surprise you to be told that the premises and the conclusion of a valid argument may all be false. This is probably due to the fact that in ordinary English, the term "valid" is often used to mean the same thing as "true," as when someone says that someone has made a valid point (has said something true). So it may help to realize that what makes an argument valid (in the technical sense of valid used by philosophers) is its logical form. Both the Socrates argument and the argument about college students share the same form, namely:

1.  All Xs are Ys.
2.  Z is an X.
3.  Therefore, Z is a Y.

One can see that *any* argument having this form will be such that *if* its premises were true (maybe as a matter of fact they are, but maybe they aren't), then the conclusion would have to be true (though as a matter of fact, the conclusion may not be true). The fact that validity has to do with the form of an argument is why the study of deductive arguments is called *formal logic.*

There are many ways for a deductive argument to fail to be valid, and exploring these ways is what's usually done in a critical thinking or introduction to logic course. For our purposes, though, there is a fairly easy intuitive test to run on an argument to see if it's valid. Simply ask yourself, "Granting the truth of the premises, is there *any way*—no matter how wild or crazy—for the conclusion to be false?" If the answer is no—there's no way for the premises to be true and the conclusion to be false—then you've got a valid argument. If the answer is yes—if you can come up with a scenario in which the premises are true but the conclusion is false—then you've got an invalid argument. And if the argument is invalid, then your evaluative work is done: the conclusion does not follow from the premises, and so the argument fails. If, however, the argument you're evaluating is indeed valid, you are cleared to move on to the next evaluative task.

## Clarity

This issue is about the meanings of the terms (words) used in the premises. Sometimes the same term can have several different senses (meanings). Or sometimes it may be unclear just what is meant at all by a particular word. If we are unsure of what a certain term means within an argument, we must suspend judgment on its overall effectiveness until that term has been rendered clear to everyone's satisfaction.

For example, suppose someone offered the following as a premise: "All persons have souls." We first have to find out precisely what is meant both by the word "person" and by the word "soul" before we can go on to evaluate the truth of the premise. Indeed, many people actually have very different understandings of these terms. Consider "soul," for instance. For some, this is a nonphysical object that contains our essence and can survive our deaths. For others, this is a *physical* object—our heart, for instance, or the collection of energy surrounding us or contained within us. For still others, "soul" is just another word for our emotions, or our personality, or even our ability to get funky. So in order to assert a premise about *everyone* having a soul, the arguer here must specify which sense of the term she has in mind. Otherwise, the arguer and her audience may well be talking past one another, in which case nothing is accomplished.

The same will be true of other controversial terms, especially if they carry a lot of weight in an argument. And it may actually be surprising just what some of those terms will be. One commonly offered argument against abortion is the following:

1.   It's wrong to kill a human being.
2.   A fetus is a human being.
3.   Thus, it's wrong to kill a fetus.

Now it may seem as if all the terms in this argument are fairly clear. But what of the phrase "human being"? What *is* a human being, exactly? It's actually extraordinarily difficult to come up with an understanding of that phrase that will render the second premise true in a way that won't also include all sorts of entities one doesn't want to include and exclude entities one wants to include. For instance, many people have thought that one can say that a human being is simply defined biologically, as anything with a standard human genetic code (a certain number of chromosomes, say). But this won't work, because *every cell in the human body* has a standard human genetic code, but we surely don't want to say that when we shave, or scratch ourselves, that we're mass murderers, killing off all those innocent human beings. This would also mean that trying to kill off cancer cells—which are human and alive as well—would be immoral, which would be crazy. So this definition of "human being" captures too much. On the other hand, it captures too little, for there are some clear-cut human beings—those with Downs syndrome—that have *one extra* chromosome, and so would fail to meet the conditions of the definition. But then if this definition won't work, what kind of definition can we agree on that will render premise 2 true? This is actually quite a vexed question, and we leave you to ponder it. But the main point is that clarity is key: if the crucial terms in the argument are not clear, there's no point in evaluating the argument further. If, however, you get a "yes" answer to the clarity question, then you're ready to move on to the third evaluative question.

## Soundness

A **sound** argument is one that is valid and has all true premises. The conclusion of a sound argument, therefore, must necessarily be true as well. Here's an example:

1.   All of the casinos in Las Vegas, Nevada, have slot machines.
2.   Caesar's Palace is a casino in Las Vegas, Nevada.
3.   Thus, Caesar's Palace has slot machines.

Of course, presenting a sound argument isn't as easy as it looks. Even if one's argument is both valid and clear, it will often contain premises whose truth can be questioned. For instance, while the anti-abortion argument certainly has a clarity problem in the second premise, the first premise is problematic as well for a different reason. After all, is it *always* wrong to kill a human being? Many of us actually think there are instances when it's perfectly morally permissible to do so. The least controversial example is self-defense (although others might say cases of war and the death penalty constitute plausible examples as well), and this is just the sort of case that some writers have used to defend the moral permissibility of abortion: if it's permissible to kill someone in defense of one's own life or life prospects, then it may be permissible to kill a fetus when it constitutes a threat to the mother's life or life prospects.

As you work your way through the readings in the text, then, try to evaluate the deductive arguments given via these three questions about validity, clarity, and soundness. In so doing, you will likely want to make use of some standard tools of the philosophical trade, which we will detail in a moment.

Let us now turn to the evaluation of *inductive* arguments. In assessing whether such an argument is any good, one begins with this question:

■ Is the argument **inductively strong**, that is, do the premises provide strong support for the conclusion?

As before, if the answer is "yes," we then proceed to ask whether the argument's premises are clear and, if so, we proceed to determine whether its premises are true. A good inductive argument, then, will be inductively strong, its premises will be clear, and its premises will be true. Let us say a bit more about inductive strength.

## Inductive Strength

What does it mean to say that the premises of an argument provide "strong support" for its conclusion? Earlier, in explaining inductive arguments, it was noted that in giving this sort of argument, one is trying to give reasons relative to which the conclusion is probably true. So, to say that an argument is inductively strong is to say that *if the premises are true, then it is probable that the conclusion is also true.* An inductive argument whose premises do not provide strong support for its conclusion is called **inductively weak**. Notice that probability comes in degrees: an inductive argument may be more or less strong, or more or less weak, depending on *how* probable the premises make the conclusion. Suppose I have a jar with 100 marbles in it, and I don't let you look into the jar. Rather, I have you reach in and take out one marble at a time so you can see what color it is. The first one you take out is red. Now consider this argument:

1. There are 100 marbles in the jar.
2. The first marble to be inspected for color is red.
   _____
3. Therefore, all marbles in the jar are red.

This is obviously a very weak argument. But now suppose you keep on taking out marble after marble until you have examined 89 of them. And suppose all 89 are red. Then pretty clearly you've got enough evidence for giving a fairly strong argument for the conclusion that all 100 marbles are red. Of course, if I'm a wise guy, I might have put a lone blue marble at the bottom of the jar, so your evidence, while strong, does not guarantee the truth of the conclusion: your argument based on the 89 marbles is not valid. But it is inductively fairly strong. By examining more marbles and finding them to be red, your evidence will be even stronger. So although inductive arguments can be more or less inductively strong, validity is all or nothing: Either an argument is valid (period) or it is invalid (period)—either the conclusion follows necessarily from the premises or it doesn't.

How does one judge whether an inductive argument is strong or weak? This depends on the kind of inductive argument in question. Let us consider the two kinds described previously.

## Inductive Generalizations

Briefly, there are two aspects of an inductive generalization to which you need to pay attention: the size of the sample, and the representativeness of the sample. First consider sample size. It should be obvious that, if you're trying to draw a generalization from a set of observations, the more observations you've got in the sample set, the more plausible that generalization will be. Suppose, for instance, that you have people living on both sides of you who have nothing better to do than to keep track of your comings and goings. One neighbor, Michael, sees you water your roses on three Saturdays in a row, and concludes from those observations that you water your roses every Saturday. Your other neighbor, Powell, sees the same three Saturday waterings that Michael does, but then continues to watch for the next three weeks, and only then concludes that you water your roses every Saturday. Powell's argument has greater inductive strength than Michael's, simply because he has more samples to draw from. It's worth keeping in mind, of course, that Powell could well be mistaken; it might be that you watered on only those Saturdays he observed, and that you'll never water the roses again. Nevertheless, Powell's argument remains more plausible than Michael's: relative strength is a value in inductive arguments.

The second important aspect of an inductive argument is the representativeness of the sample set. What you want, ideally, is a random population of samples to draw from, one that hasn't been biased in favor of one conclusion or another, and one that contains an adequate variety of samples. The more representative the sample set, the greater the inductive strength of the argument. Suppose you were trying to determine if global warming has occurred, and you had the funding to get only 100 sample average temperatures. Surely you would try to get average temperatures from 100 different climates around the world, rather than 100 samples from different towns in New Jersey.

How are sample size and representativeness related? The larger the sample size, the more likely one's sample will not be biased and hence the more likely the sample will be representative of the population. So, representativeness is the more important of the two features one uses to evaluate inductive generalizations; size is often a good indicator of representativeness.

In evaluating inductive arguments, then, ask these questions about sample size and representativeness. Very weak inductive arguments are often easy to spot, and they commit a particular sort of common fallacy we discuss in the next section.

## Arguments by Analogy

Whenever one draws an analogy between two or more things, one is calling attention to similarities between the things being compared, as in the example about taking Philosophy of Religion from Professor Smith. But there are bound to be dissimilarities between the things being compared. Perhaps in the Professor

Smith example, the Philosophy of Science and Ethics courses the speaker is referring to were taught at 2 pm, and the upcoming course in Philosophy of Religion is being taught at 8 am. This difference might be important. After all, if Smith is not an early riser and so is resentful about having to teach at 8 in the morning, this might affect his demeanor; he might not be entertaining at that hour. If this is the case, then the argument by analogy is at least somewhat weakened. On the other hand, time of day may make no difference to how Smith teaches his courses. The point here is that from the fact that there are differences between the items featured in an analogical argument, it does not automatically follow that the argument lacks inductive strength. What matters are differences between the things being compared that would block the inference to the conclusion. So, in evaluating an argument from analogy, one is looking to see whether the things being compared are indeed similar enough to support the conclusion and whether there are any dissimilarities that would weaken the support between premises and conclusion. Arguments by analogy that fail to measure up to these requirements commit a fallacy that will be presented in the next section, in which we go over some common mistakes in philosophical reasoning. But, first, let us summarize the key points in this section:

- In evaluating an argument, there are three general questions one must ask: (1) Do the premises provide logical support for the conclusion? For deductive arguments, is the argument valid? For inductive arguments, is the argument inductively strong? (2) Are the premises clear? (3) Are the premises true? A good argument requires a "yes" answer to each of these questions.
- An argument is valid just in case the following is true: if the premises are true, then the conclusion must be true. Arguments that are not valid are invalid.
- An argument is inductively strong just in case the following is true: if the premises are true, then it is probable that the conclusion is true. Arguments that are not inductively strong are inductively weak.
- To determine the strength of an inductive generalization (in which one infers a general claim about a population based on a sample), consider the size and representativeness of the sample in relation to the population.
- To determine the strength of an analogical argument (in which one draws a conclusion about some item based on its similarity to items with which it is being compared), consider whether there are any undermining dissimilarities between the target item mentioned in the conclusion and the items mentioned in the premises to which the target is being compared.

## WHAT ARE SOME COMMON MISTAKES
## IN PHILOSOPHICAL REASONING?

When an argument goes wrong, it typically does so in one of six ways. This is by no means to suggest that these are the only ways an argument can go wrong; instead, these are just some very common failures of validity, clarity, soundness, or inductive strength.

## A. It Has Counterexamples

**Counterexamples** are exceptions to so-called "universal" principles, and point-ing these out is likely something you already commonly do. When someone makes a claim like "All X's are Y's," pointing out a counterexample just involves pointing out an example of an X that isn't a Y. It is a way of questioning the *soundness* of an argument. So were I to conclude my five-year study by saying "All swans are white," you could undermine my conclusion by finding a non-white swan. Or if someone were to claim, "It's wrong to kill a human being," you could point out what we have already noted, that it's not wrong in cases of self-defense. Or if someone were to assert that it's always wrong to lie, you could simply point out that this is false in the case where you're planning a sur-prise birthday party for your friend and you need to keep her in the dark, or in a case in which a notorious child-killer comes to your door and asks if your children are home (and they are).

> **Tip:** *When evaluating an argument that involves a universal principle of the form,* All Xs are Ys, *test the truth of the principle by trying to think of an X that is not a Y.*

## B. It Begs the Question

An argument that **begs the question** is one that is valid but utterly empty, devoid of any real content, so it ends up not establishing anything at all. This is bad, because it defeats the very point of an argument, which is to give some evidence (the premises) for some additional further claim (the conclusion). When you beg the question, however, you simply provide no support at all for your conclusion, and thus you give your audience no reason whatsoever to accept what you've said.

Specifically, one may beg the question in one of two ways: (a) by assuming without argument the very thing one is trying to prove, or (b) by answering a ques-tion with a variation of the very question asked. Consider a few examples of (a). Suppose you were to present the following argument: "Capital punishment is mur-der; therefore it is wrong." If that's the whole of your argument, then you've assumed precisely what you were supposed to prove. What you're trying to prove is that capital punishment is morally wrong. But in "arguing" for that conclusion, you've assumed that capital punishment is wrong because the definition of "murder" just is "wrongful killing." So your argument really amounts to the following: "Capital punishment is wrongful killing; therefore capital punishment is wrong."

Consider another example: "The world wasn't created by God, because matter has always existed, and because the world is made of matter, the world has always existed." Your conclusion is allegedly that the world wasn't created by God, but in arguing for that conclusion, you've simply asserted that the world wasn't created by God ("matter/the world has always existed"). When it comes right down to it, arguments that beg the question are essentially of the following form: X, therefore X.

Now consider some examples of (b). Suppose two dudes are sitting around talk-ing. "Dude," says one, "why does acid make you see things that aren't there?" "Dude," says the other, "it's because it has a hallucinogenic effect, dude." No new information has passed between these gentlemen. Instead, to have a hallucinogenic effect *just is* to make you see things that aren't there.

Finally, consider the following exchange:
"God exists."
"Why?"
"Because it says so in the Bible."
"But why should I believe the Bible?"
"Because it's the inspired word of God."

So this person is appealing to the Bible to support belief in God, and then appealing to the existence of God to support belief in the Bible. This exchange reveals why begging the question is also known as **circular reasoning**.

*Tip: When evaluating an argument, be on the lookout for any premises that assume true what the argument is supposed to establish.*

### C. It Leads to a Contradiction or Absurdity

Showing how an argument is susceptible to this worry is called **running a reductio** on it, because it has yielded a **reductio ad absurdum** (it has been "reduced to absurdity"). How does one run a reductio on an argument? The first task is to assume a premise or conclusion in the argument to be true. Next, one may try to show that either (a) a *contradiction,* or (b) a patently *absurd* situation must follow. If this is the case, then the original premise or conclusion must be either (a) *false* (if a contradiction was yielded), or (b) *implausible* (if an absurdity was yielded).

Consider first a few reductios of type (a). These are fairly rare, but they can be quite powerful. Suppose you were to say, in a conspiratorial fashion, "You know, I *always* lie." To run a reductio on this assertion, we will assume it is true. If the statement is true, that you always lie, then it's false, for here is precisely a statement in which you *haven't* lied. But any statement that embodies a contradiction—it's both true and not true—has to be false.

One might also use a reductio of this type for a constructive purpose. Suppose, for instance, that you've got a conclusion you want to establish. One technique (rare but very effective) is to assume the *opposite* of what you want to establish, and then show how that assumption leads to a contradiction. If that occurs, the original assumption has to be false, and so the conclusion you wanted has to be true. Both Anselm and Thomas Aquinas, in our readings on the existence of God, run precisely this sort of argument. Anselm offers the assumption that God doesn't exist (the opposite of what he believes), and then he shows that, if we fully understand the concept of God, that assumption leads to a contradiction, which means the original assumption is false, and God must necessarily exist. Similarly, Aquinas considers the chain of causation that exists in the world—everything we know of that exists was caused to exist by something else—and so offers as an assumption that the chain of causation goes back infinitely, with no first cause (again, the opposite of what he believes). If that were true, he argues, nothing now could exist. But of course things now *do* exist, which is the contradiction that forces us to deny that there could be an infinite chain of causes and embrace the conclusion that Aquinas wants, namely, that there was a first cause itself uncaused, called God.

Now turn to the much more widely used reductio of type (b). Here you're simply trying to show that someone's statement leads to something patently absurd, in which case that statement is implausible (but not necessarily false). So suppose you offer the following anti-abortion argument:

1. It's wrong to prevent a potential person from coming into existence.
2. A fetus is a potential person.

---

3. Thus, it's wrong to prevent a fetus from coming into existence.

Now focus just on the first premise. Suppose it were indeed wrong to prevent a potential person from coming into existence. That would mean that contraception would of course be wrong. But it would also have a much more absurd consequence. If it were true, then when you and your date were grappling in the backseat of the car on a Saturday night, you could honestly say, "But, honey, if you don't, it's *murder!*" Yes, if this principle were true, *failing to have sex constantly* would be immoral, given that you'd be preventing the existence of potential people. Simply reading this book would be grounds for moral blame. But that's utterly absurd, so the initial principle is quite implausible.

**Socrates**, a famous ancient Greek philosopher, was the king of the reductio. He was constantly walking the streets of Athens, showing anyone who'd give it a try why their arguments and definitions were subject to withering reductios. In the dialogue *Gorgias,* for example, Socrates is talking with Callicles about the best sort of life one might lead. Callicles believes that it's the life wherein one gets as much pleasure as possible, so one should try to make one's appetites as large as possible and then constantly try to fill them. Socrates, however, replies by running a reductio that we may modify a bit. When you get a mosquito bite, it can actually feel intensely pleasurable to scratch that itch. But now suppose you were to get bit by a magical mosquito, whose itch never goes away. If Callicles were right, then the best life would be one spent scratching that intensely pleasurable itch. But that can't be true. And then Socrates hints at something much darker. Suppose some man were to get extreme, maximal pleasure from raping young boys. If Callicles were right, a life spent raping young boys would be the best life possible for that man. But that's utterly absurd, which makes the original principle implausible. As Socrates later makes clear, there are good pleasures and bad pleasures, and some should be altogether avoided, regardless of the nice feelings they may bring.

> *Tip: When evaluating an argument, ask whether any of its statements, were they taken as true, would lead to a further claim that is either obviously false or patently absurd.*

## D. It Equivocates

An argument **equivocates** when a key word in the argument shifts its meaning in the course of the argument. Many words and phrases have multiple meanings. So the word "bank" may refer either to the building on the corner or to the side of the river. But if one trades on the multiple senses of a word or phrase within the argument itself, one has equivocated *on* that term and one has actually rendered one's argument invalid. To illustrate, consider the following argument:

1. Only man is rational.
2. No woman is a man.

---

3. Thus, no woman is rational.

This argument equivocates on the term "man." In the first premise, it means "humans." In the second, it means "male." And once we substitute these actual meanings into the argument, it obviously fails to establish its conclusion (that is, it's actually invalid).

See if you can spot the (3!) equivocations in the following argument:

1. God is love.
2. Love is blind.
3. Stevie Wonder is blind.

---

4. Thus, Stevie Wonder is God.

*Tip: When evaluating an argument, especially arguments that depend on terms (words) that have multiple meanings, make sure that those terms are being used with the same meaning throughout the argument.*

## E. Its Generalizations Are Too Hasty

A **hasty generalization** is an inductive argument with either a severely small sample size—a sample size far too small to warrant anything like the conclusion drawn—or an unrepresentative sample set. As an example of the former, consider an argument from John Perry's *Dialogue on Personal Identity and Immortality*. In this dialogue, Sam Miller is trying to persuade Gretchen Weirob, a dying philosophy professor, that her soul is the source of her identity, and it can survive the death of her body. In responding to Weirob's worry that Miller can't know that she, Weirob, even has a soul, Miller suggests that he at least knows that *he* has a soul, and so he can infer that everyone else, including Weirob, has a soul as well. It should be obvious how weak this inductive argument is, though: even if Miller could establish that he has a soul (no easy task!), it's very dangerous to infer that everyone else is just like him in this regard. After all, if he had a wart on his left pinky toe, should he infer that everyone else had such a wart in that location as well? He is trying to draw a very general principle about billions of people on the basis of just one sample, and this is a very hasty generalization.

As an example of a hasty generalization with regard to an unrepresentative sample set, consider the global warming example given previously. Inferring that the average temperature of the earth has been rising based solely on 100 sample temperatures from different towns in New Jersey is far too hasty a generalization, for it is drawing a conclusion about the warming of the entire globe on the basis of samples taken from a tiny fraction of it.

*Tip: When evaluating an inductive generalization, look to see if the sample is truly representative of the population. Sample size is often useful for this purpose.*

## F. It Involves a False Analogy

To commit the fallacy of **false analogy** is to offer an argument based on an analogy where there are important dissimilarities between the things or items that are the basis of the analogy (the comparison base) and the thing or item that the conclusion is about (the target item). John Searle (in a reading included in Chapter 3 on the mind-body problem) argues that the attempt by some philosophers to compare the mind to a digital computer in order to draw conclusions about how the mind works is a bad analogy. The philosophers he is criticizing have proposed that the relation between the mind and brain (body) is analogous to the relation between the software and hardware of a computer. On the basis of this analogy, the conclusion of the analogical argument in question is that the mind is much like computer software—a program that manipulates symbols governed by rules. Searle's criticism of this argument involves pointing out what he takes to be a crucial dissimilarity between the mind and the workings of a computer that undermines the analogy and therefore blocks the inference to the conclusion that the mind operates like the software of a computer. (We won't spoil your fun by revealing Searle's objection here.) If Searle's objection works, then the mind-computer argument from analogy commits the false analogy fallacy.

> *Tip: When evaluating an analogical argument, look for any dissimilarities between the item mentioned in the conclusion (the target item) and the other items (comparison base) to which the target is being compared that would tend to undermine the analogy and weaken the argument.*

## CONCLUSION

With this brief introduction to the methods of philosophy in hand, we may turn now to some of the most important subjects of philosophy in the readings that follow. In particular, we will be looking at three broad areas: nature, knowledge, and norms. In other words, what is the nature of certain important aspects of reality, such as mind, free will, personal identity, and God? Furthermore, what is knowledge and is there anything we can know? And what are the norms, or principles, for the living of our lives, both with respect to ourselves and to our dealings with one another? As you read through these selections, keep in mind the evaluative tools discussed. What is the precise argument being presented? What type of argument—inductive or deductive—is it? Is it valid (if deductive) or inductively strong (if inductive)? Are the premises clear; is the argument sound? Is it subject to the various common problems we have encountered?

Earlier in this introduction, we distinguished between constructive philosophy and critical philosophy. As we noted, philosophy isn't just a critical, destructive enterprise, simply in the business of tearing down arguments. There is a constructive, positive point to all of this as well, for we are ultimately looking for the *right* answers to these vexing questions. We want to find answers, to understand the nature of ourselves and the world around us. To that end, we want to find arguments that *aren't* susceptible to these critical worries, and one of your tasks will be to examine whether any of the many positions presented here can actually succeed at that crucially important project.

# 2

# Personal Identity & Immortality

## MOTIVATION

Suppose you are at your parents' house one day when your mother hands you a photograph of a five-year-old child and says, "Look at this picture of you I found!" "I'd forgotten how cute I was!" you exclaim, and your father chimes in, "Yes, but you were such a handful back then." All of those present agree, then, that what's being examined is a picture of *you* from several years ago. But now think for a second about the relation between yourself and that five-year-old child. What *makes* that child you? You don't have any physical features in common (all the molecules constituting you at five have long since bounced off and been replaced by other molecules), you don't really even resemble that child physically, you are (hopefully!) quite different psychologically from that child, you may not remember much, if anything, about that child and his/her life, and so forth. So what could possibly make you the *same person* as that child?

This is the primary question of personal identity, more generally posed as follows: what makes someone in existence at one point in time identical with someone in existence at a different point in time? Beyond the intrinsically interesting nature of the question, there are three practical reasons philosophers are motivated to try and answer this question.

1.  **Responsibility**: We hold people responsible—eligible for praise and blame, punishment and reward—for a variety of deeds, for example, for the commission of crimes, or for the violation of moral rules. But in order for our assignments of responsibility to make any sense, it must be the case, it seems,

**17**

that the person we hold responsible for the act is actually *the same person as* the one who performed the act. Suppose you are caught cheating on an exam. The first question the dean will ask you after you've been hauled into his office will be, "Did you cheat on the exam?" In other words, "Are you (the person sitting before me now) identical to the person who cheated on the exam?" If you are identical to that person, then at least one necessary condition for holding you responsible has been met. So whatever it is that *makes* you identical to that person is going to be essential to justifying such attributions of responsibility.

2.  **Concern/Anticipation for the Future**: Suppose I have built a "replicator" machine, one that can produce an exact duplicate of someone based merely on a DNA sample. Suppose further that I tell you that I've taken a hair of yours and will produce a replica of you tonight, and then torture the heck out of that poor person tomorrow morning. What emotions might you experience in hearing this news? If you're a decent human being (which surely you are), you'll be concerned and have compassion for the plight of your replica, but it will only be the sort of concern and compassion you'd ordinarily have in response to the expected suffering of any other innocent human being.

    However, if I were to tell you instead that I'm going to torture *you* tomorrow morning, you would likely react very differently. Now it is, as they say, *personal*. Your concern level will go way up and will probably be of an entirely different *kind* than your concern in the first case.

    Now consider the flip side of future-related concern, namely, anticipation. Suppose I told you that I was going, as in the first case, to produce a replica of you, but instead of torture I was going to give that replica a million dollars tomorrow. Again, think about what your reaction would be. While you might be happy for that replica, and perhaps a little hopeful that because the replica will be just like you, he or she might toss a little cash your way, you won't be nearly as excited as you would be if I were to say that I was going to award *you* a million dollars tomorrow. You only *anticipate* the awarding of the cash, in other words, when you will be the awardee.

    In every instance, your reactions seem perfectly rational. But how do we account for the rationality of anticipation or special concern only in the non-replica versions of each case? As suggested, it seems as if the rationality of anticipation/special concern depends on personal identity—you are justified in caring about someone's future in this special way only when it's *your* future. But what, then, makes someone's future *your* future (and not that of someone else)?

3.  **Immortality**: Finally, most everyone wants to know whether or not they can survive the deaths of their bodies and live forever. But we have to have a theory of personal identity in place *first* in order to determine whether or not that's even possible. Suppose, for instance, that what makes me identical to that child in the photograph is some sort of physical continuity: the body I now have is a physical continuer of the body that child had. If this is the right criterion of personal identity generally, though, then it will be *impossible* for me to survive the death of my body. A criterion of personal identity, therefore, by providing us with a criterion of survival generally, will also imply certain things about the possibility of surviving into some sort of afterlife.

# CRUCIAL DISTINCTIONS

There are two terms crucial to the issue of personal identity that are, unfortunately, ambiguous, and failing to pay attention to their different senses can disrupt the whole enterprise. It is important, then, that we deal with them immediately.

The first is the term "same person." Suppose that, when handed the photograph by your mother, you sigh and say, "I'm afraid, Mom, that I am no longer the same person as that little child you loved so much." What are you saying, exactly? Well, there's a sense in which you *aren't* the same person insofar as you are different (likely psychologically) from that child. But there is clearly another sense in which you *are* the same person as that child, given your clear implication that *you yourself* have changed, where change is compatible with identity.

The ambiguity in the phrase "same person" stems from an ambiguity in the more general term "identity," so it's with reference to that term that we need to make our first essential distinction.

> X and Y are **qualitatively identical** if and only if they have exactly similar qualities.

> X and Y are **quantitatively identical** if and only if whatever is true of X is true of Y and vice versa.

The best way to explain this distinction is by considering examples. If you bought two brand-new copies of this book, they would likely be qualitatively identical. They would have exactly similar qualities: they would both have exactly similar shape, size, pages, words, cost, and so on. But they nevertheless could not be quantitatively identical. Why not? For one thing, they occupy different points in space-time, so whatever is true of one (namely, its particular location in space-time) is not true of the other. To make this point even more explicit, you could hold one book right side up and the other upside down.

Each copy of the book, then, will be quantitatively identical *only with itself.* Quantitative identity is also known as **numerical identity**, and in both cases the relevant quantity, or number, is *one, as in one and the same thing.* So if X refers to the copy of the book held steady in your right hand, say, at *this* precise moment in time, and Y refers to the copy of the book still in your right hand at *this later* precise moment in time, then X is quantitatively identical to Y insofar as it is one and the same thing as Y. Notice further that quantitative identity, unlike qualitative identity, is compatible with qualitative changes. So if you were to take your copy of the book and then fold up the corner of the title page, it would still be the same book—quantitatively—as the book you bought, even though one of its original qualities (an unfolded title page) has changed.

To get a better feel for quantitative identity, consider some cases where X and Y are different names for one and the same person. Start with Marshall Mathers, also known as Eminem. Marshall Mathers is quantitatively identical with Eminem, so for the phrase "Marshall Mathers appeared in court today," you can simply substitute the phrase "Eminem appeared in court today," because whatever is true of the one will always be true of the other. Similarly for other iconic artists throughout our history. See if you can fill in the following blanks (answers below): Calvin Broadus is quantitatively identical with _____, Robert Zimmerman is quantitatively identical with _____, and Samuel Langhorn Clemens is quantitatively identical with _____.[1]

Regarding the preceding three motivating issues, the question we are concerned with is one of *quantitative* identity. What makes me the same person as the child in the photo, then, even though we're not qualitatively identical to one another (we in fact share very few, if any, qualities)?

This leads to the second distinction we need to make. What we're looking for is a criterion of personal identity, but "criterion" has two senses as well. To draw the appropriate distinction, we will use some standard philosophical terminology that is, unfortunately, rather unwieldy.

> X is a **metaphysical criterion** of Y just in case X provides an explication of what Y consists in, an explication of Y's nature.

> X is an **epistemological criterion** of Y just in case X provides an explication of *how we can know* what Y's nature consists in.

To understand this distinction, suppose I tell you that what makes you the same person as that child in the photo is that you both have the same *soul*. You then respond, "Well maybe, but how could we ever *know* that? After all, the soul is supposedly nonphysical, but because we can have evidence only for the existence of physical objects, we could never have any evidence whatsoever for the existence of souls." While this would be an important claim to consider, it would not be directly responsive to my initial assertion, and that's because we have each offered a criterion for personal identity in the different senses just delineated. On the one hand, I have offered a metaphysical criterion: the nature of personal identity consists in persistence of the same soul. On the other hand, you have offered an epistemological criterion: we can know about what personal identity consists in only if it consists in something for which we could have some empirical evidence. But these two senses of "criterion" are actually quite independent of one another. For instance, even if we could never know whether or not your soul now is the same as the soul had by that child in the photograph (if you even actually *have* a soul at all), it could still be true that personal identity consists in sameness of soul, that what makes you identical to that child is the identity of your (shared) soul. And alternatively, what provides the means for our knowledge of identity is going to hold regardless of what actual metaphysical criterion of identity is true.

So what sense of "criterion" are we interested in here? Clearly it's the metaphysical sense of the term: we want to know what the nature of identity consists in, regardless of whether or not we could ever know if that nature obtains in any individual case. As Gretchen Weirob, the star of John Perry's *A Dialogue on Personal Identity and Immortality,* puts it, "Simply persuade me that my survival, after the death of this body, is *possible,* and I promise to be comforted." This is a request for demonstration that the nature of personal identity is consistent with postmortem survival—a metaphysical issue—and not a request for demonstration for how she can *know* if the means to her postmortem survival obtain—an epistemological issue. (Although note that Weirob herself may conflate the two senses of

---

[1]The answers are, respectively, Snoop Dogg, Bob Dylan, and Mark Twain.

"criterion" in her response to Miller's Soul Criterion—examine for yourself whether or not this is the case.)

Given these two important distinctions, then, what we want may be put as follows: What makes person X at time t1 quantitatively identical to person Y at time t2? This is a question about the nature of the quantitative identity relation. But while we are going to ask this question about persons, I'd be willing to bet that, at this stage of the game, we can't even answer this question yet about *objects,* which lack the complicating features of psychology that persons have. To see why, consider the following puzzle.

## THE YACHT PUZZLE

Suppose I buy a nice new yacht that I like to show off to the neighbors, so I store it out on my front yard. Consider, then, three cases.

CASE 1: A year after buying the yacht and putting it in my front yard, I notice that one of the planks on the deck is going bad, so I go to The Home Depot and buy a new "deterioration-proof" plank exactly like the original. I then remove the bad plank, burn that piece of wood, and replace it with the new one. Surely the identity of my original yacht has been preserved—quantitative identity is compatible with qualitative change, remember. But if this is true, then the identity of my original yacht should be preserved through the next plank replacement a few weeks later, and the next plank replacement a few weeks after that, and so on through the years. After ten years, then, suppose that all of the original parts of the yacht have been gradually replaced, right down to the Bob Marley commemorative beer bottle opener by the mini-fridge. Is this yacht quantitatively identical to the original yacht? It seems that it is, despite all the qualitative changes that have taken place. Indeed, one way to think about it is this: when I bought the yacht, it came with a legal title referring to *that* yacht as mine. Does the title still refer to the ten-years-later yacht as mine (i.e., as identical to the original)? It seems so.

CASE 2: A year after buying the yacht and putting it in my front yard, I realize I shouldn't shove my good fortune into my neighbors' faces, so I decide to move the yacht to my barn out back. Unfortunately, I have no money left for movers after my big yacht purchase, and I have no friends who will volunteer to help me, so I realize I'll have to do it myself. I am, however, incredibly lazy. So I start by taking one plank off the yacht and carrying it to the barn. A few weeks later, I take another plank off the yacht and carry it to the barn. And so forth. After ten years, I've finally got all the pieces of the yacht in the barn, so I reassemble the yacht there (fortunately, I numbered all the original pieces so they all go in the same place they were in the yard yacht). Is the newly reassembled (but seriously deteriorated) yacht in the barn quantitatively identical to the original yard yacht? Surely it is: the barn yacht has all the original planks, assembled in the same order. My yacht title must refer to the barn yacht now.

So far, so good. But what about this?

> CASE 3: A year after buying the yacht and putting it in my front yard, I decide to go study Buddhism with the Dalai Lama for ten years. I want my yacht taken care of, though, so after some cajoling I get you to promise to do so while I'm gone. The first day you come by to check on the yacht, you discover one of the planks is going bad. So you take out the plank, toss it in the barn, and then replace it on the yard yacht with a new "deterioration-proof" plank from The Home Depot. A few weeks later, the same thing occurs: you toss the old plank into the barn, and you replace it on the yard yacht. And so on. After ten years, then, all the original pieces of the yard yacht have been tossed into the barn and replaced. And because you're bored one day, you go into the barn and assemble all the old planks and pieces back into place as a (seriously deteriorated) yacht. There are, then, two yachts: one deteriorated yacht in the barn and one deterioration-proof yacht in the yard.

I return. You ask me how my time with the Dalai Lama was, and I reply, "It was peaceful and enlightening. Now where the hell's my yacht?!" You quickly take me to the yacht in the yard. Seeing it, I yell, "That's not my yacht! Mine was nicely broken in, and you've got this brand new thing here. But not one atom of my yacht remains! Sure, this one's *better* than the one I left you, but I was sentimentally attached to the old boat and I want *that* one back!"

Trying to cover things over, you hustle me to the barn and say, "Ta da!" Now I look at the barn yacht and say, "But this yacht's a complete wreck! You promised to keep my yacht repaired!"

You (and we) now have a real conundrum on our hands: Which of these yachts is the same yacht (quantitatively) as the one I left you to take care of? There are four options—the yard yacht, the barn yacht, neither, or both—each of which has serious problems.

1. *Both?* Perhaps both yachts are now quantitatively identical with the original? But this can't be true, simply because there are clearly *two* yachts in existence now, but I left you only one, and $2 \neq 1$.

2. *Neither?* Has my original yacht been *destroyed,* and now there are two yachts in its place, neither of which is identical with the original? This may seem tempting given our response to #1, but it can't be right either, simply because of our response in Cases 1 and 2. In both cases, my yacht survived. How, then, could a double success in Case 3 somehow *eliminate the existence* of my yacht? This seems terribly implausible—surely my title refers to *one* of these yachts, doesn't it?

3. *The Barn Yacht?* This may now seem to be the best answer: The one yacht that has the best chance of being mine must be the one with all the original pieces, right? But now we can run a similar worry in miniature, namely, what *makes* each of the planks in the barn yacht identical to the ones in the original yacht? In the intervening ten years, all of the molecules constituting the original planks have themselves bounced off and been replaced by exact duplicates. So why think the barn planks are any more identical to the original planks than those now in the yard yacht? If you think they are because the various

replacement molecules have preserved the general *form* of the planks, then why not say the same about the yard yacht, namely, it has preserved the identity of the original in virtue of its various replacement planks preserving the general *form* of the yacht?

4.  *The Yard Yacht?* So now we've been driven to this option, but there are problems with it as well. For one thing, I (the owner) don't seem to think it's mine. Should it *matter* what I think, though? Won't identity obtain regardless of my thoughts on the matter (imagine if I simply declared myself to have a new identity one day)? In addition, it's not so clear that quantitative identity can be preserved through *all* sorts of changes. For example, suppose you let the yard yacht deteriorate until you hear I'm coming home, at which point you quickly replace the whole thing with an entirely new yacht in one fell swoop. Surely that new yard yacht would not be identical to the original! But isn't that just what you've done in the original Case 3, only gradually? But then why should the rate of change matter to the identity of the object?

What we've seen here are various attempts to figure out the nature of identity for physical bodies, and we've been left with a complete mess. But persons have bodies *and* minds—an internal, psychological life—and that addition would seem to make things even messier.

## THE CRITERIA

Very briefly, there are four general criteria presented in our readings for explicating the nature of personal identity. Each criterion fills in the following blank: *X at t1 is the same person as Y at t2 if and only if*

1.  *Y has the same soul as X* (the **Soul Criterion**).
2.  *Y has the same body as X* (the **Body Criterion**).
3.  *Y has the same brain as X* (the **Brain Criterion**).
4.  *Y remembers the thoughts and experiences of X* (the **Memory Criterion**).[2]

Obviously, each one needs more detailed explanation and defense, but at first glance it should be clear what each general proposal involves. In particular, it should be clear what each criterion would imply about the possibility of immortality, for example: it would seem to be possible on 1 and 4, and impossible on 2 and 3. Similarly for the questions of responsibility and anticipation/concern: if 1 is true, say, then some future person will be responsible for my actions, and I'll be justified in anticipating his experiences, if and only if he has my soul. And so forth, down the list.

---

[2]This list should not be taken to be exhaustive, however. There are several other possible criteria, some of which have gained real traction in the philosophical community in recent years. These are just the four most popular historical options.

In "The Meeting," a science fiction story about a possible future way in which to "repair" cognitively damaged children, we are pulled between two possible criteria, the Brain (or Memory) Criterion and the Body Criterion. When reading it, ask yourself where your sympathies lie.

In Plato's dialogue *Phaedo,* Socrates gives an argument for why we should not fear death: it is the moment when the soul separates from the body, and thus when it finally becomes free to pursue true knowledge, without the hindrances that come with having a body.

In "The Myth of the Soul," Clarence Darrow argues that belief in immortality is a delusion. Not only is there no evidence of immortality, he claims, but the various reasons people give for believing in it are pretty bad. He considers and rejects several possibilities: that our souls survive our deaths, that our streams of consciousness (in the form of memories) can extend beyond our deaths, or that our bodies may be resurrected in the afterlife.

In "The Prince and the Cobbler," John Locke argues in favor of the Memory Criterion by making use of a very famous thought experiment: What if the stream of consciousness of a prince were somehow exchanged with that of a cobbler? Who would be who? Would the person in the prince's body be the prince, or would identity go where consciousness flows?

In John Perry's "A Dialogue on Personal Identity and Immortality," we see all four criteria fight it out. Gretchen Weirob, a dying philosophy professor, wants to know whether or not it's possible to survive the death of her body, and her clergyman friend (Sam Miller) and former graduate student (Dave Cohen) both try to defend the criteria rendering immortality possible against the powerful *reductios* of Weirob. Weirob herself holds the Body Criterion, and by the end of the dialogue, it's difficult to see how she could be wrong, in which case it looks as if immortality is impossible.

In Derek Parfit's "The Unimportance of Identity," we see a radically different approach to the issue. Parfit applies a version of the Yacht Puzzle to persons in order to show that the practical concerns (e.g., anticipation/concern) we thought were attached to personal identity really aren't; instead, the question of identity is actually unimportant with respect to what matters in our lives. This is a view to which Dave Cohen obliquely refers in the final lines of Perry's dialogue, and it is an alternative to the search for identity that may well be worth exploring. Indeed, you might ask yourself what Parfit's view would actually imply about issues such as moral responsibility and the possibility of immortality.

## PUZZLE CASES

Finally, a word (warning?) about puzzle cases. There will be a lot of far-out, science-fictiony cases mentioned in what follows: talk of brain transplants, mind transplants, body swaps, cloning, split brains, and so forth. The reason our authors do this is that they're trying to isolate certain elements of our existence to see whether our theories about personal identity will hold up in every possible instance. This is actually similar to the strategy taken by some scientists. Einstein, for example, famously tried to imagine what it would be like to travel at the speed of light. Such a thing is deeply impossible, of course, but he was able to learn important things about the nature of space-time from such thought experiments.

So it will be here. We can learn very important things about our concepts and criteria of personal identity by imagining such far-out cases. What we're trying to do is bring out conflicts in various theories by imagining these cases and seeing how the theory deals with them. After all, if a theory of personal identity is to be adequate, it should give us the right answer in every case. But if we imagine a new case in which we have strong intuitions about what the answer ought to be, yet our theory doesn't give it, something has likely gone wrong, then, with the theory. In other words, our intuitions in these puzzle cases count as data, so the better our various criteria do in accounting for them, the more plausible they are likely to be.

# 1

# The Meeting

FREDERIK POHL AND C. M. KORNBLUTH

*Frederik Pohl (born 1919) and C. M. Kornbluth (1923–1958) are noted American science fiction authors and were frequent collaborators. The following is their Hugo Award–winning short story. In it, the parents of nine-year-old Tommy Vladek have a very difficult decision to make. Tommy is severely mentally handicapped, incapable of anything even remotely approximating a normal life, but it is possible for him to receive a certain sort of transplant that will likely result in the mentally and physically healthy boy his parents have always hoped for. Will the survivor of the transplant be Tommy, though? And if not, should that matter to his parents' decision? As you read, ask yourself what you would do in their position.*

Harry Vladek was too large a man for his Volkswagen, but he was too poor a man to trade it in, and as things were going he was going to stay that way a long time. He applied the brakes carefully ("master cylinder's leaking like a sieve, Mr. Vladek; what's the use of just fixing up the linings?"—but the estimate was a hundred and twenty-eight dollars, and where was it going to come from?) and parked in the neatly graveled lot. He squeezed out of the door, the upsetting telephone call from Dr. Nicholson on his mind, locked the car up, and went into the school building.

The Parent-Teachers Association of the Bingham County School for Exceptional Children was holding its first meeting of the term. Of the twenty people already there, Vladek knew only Mrs. Adler, the principal, or headmistress, or owner of the school. She was the one he needed to talk to most, he thought. Would there be any chance to see her privately? Right now she sat across the room at her scuffed golden oak desk in a posture chair, talking in low, rapid tones with a grayhaired woman in a tan suit. A teacher? She seemed too old to be a parent, although his wife had told him some of the kids seemed to be twenty or more.

It was 8:30 and the parents were still driving up to the school, a converted building that had once been a big country house—almost a mansion. The living room was full of elegant reminders of that. Two chandeliers. Intricate vineleaf

SOURCE: Originally published in *The Magazine of Fantasy and Science Fiction* (November 1972). Permission by the authors' agent, Robert P. Mills, Ltd. Copyright © 1972 by Mercury Press, Inc.

molding on the plaster above the dropped ceiling. The pink-veined white marble fireplace, unfortunately prominent because of the unsuitable andirons, too cheap and too small, that now stood in it. Golden oak sliding double doors to the hall. And visible through them a grim, fireproof staircase of concrete and steel. They must, Vladek thought, have had to rip out a beautiful wooden thing to install the fireproof stairs for compliance with the state school laws.

People kept coming in, single men, single women, and occasionally a couple. He wondered how the couples managed their baby-sitting problem. The subtitle on the school's letterhead was "an institution for emotionally disturbed and cerebrally damaged children capable of education." Harry's nine-year-old, Thomas, was one of the emotionally disturbed ones. With a taste of envy he wondered if cerebrally damaged children could be baby-sat by any reasonably competent grownup. Thomas could not. The Vladeks had not had an evening out together since he was two, so that tonight Margaret was holding the fort at home, no doubt worrying herself sick about the call from Dr. Nicholson, while Harry was representing the family at the P.T.A.

As the room filled up, chairs were getting scarce. A young couple was standing at the end of the row near him, looking around for a pair of empty seats. "Here," he said to them. "I'll move over." The woman smiled politely and the man said thanks. Emboldened by an ashtray on the empty seat in front of him, Harry pulled out his pack of cigarettes and offered it to them, but it turned out they were nonsmokers. Harry lit up anyway, listening to what was going on around him.

Everybody was talking. One woman asked another, "How's the gall bladder? Are they going to take it out after all?" A heavy man said to a short man with bushy sideburns, "Well, my accountant says the tuition's medically deductible if the school is for *psychosomatic,* not just for psycho. That we've got to clear up." The short man told him positively, "Right, but all you need is a doctor's letter; he recommends the school, refers the child to the school." And a very young woman said intensely, "Dr. Shields was very optimistic, Mrs. Clerman. He says without a doubt the thyroid will make Georgie accessible. And then—" A light-coffee-colored black man in an aloha shirt told a plump woman, "He really pulled a wing-ding over the weekend, two stitches in his face, busted my fishing pole in three places." And the woman said, "They get so bored. My little girl has this thing about crayons so that rules out coloring books altogether. You wonder what you can do."

Harry finally said to the young man next to him, "My name's Vladek. I'm Tommy's father; he's in the beginners group."

"That's where ours is," said the young man. "He's Vern. Six years old. Blonde like me. Maybe you've seen him."

Harry did not try very hard to remember. The two or three times he had picked Tommy up after class he had not been able to tell one child from another in the great bustle of departure. Coats, handkerchiefs, hats, one little boy who always hid in the supply closet and a little boy who never wanted to go home and hung onto the teacher. "Oh, yes," he said politely.

The young man introduced himself and his wife; they were named Murray and Celia Logan. Harry leaned over the man to shake the wife's hand, and she said, "Aren't you new here?"

"Yes. Tommy's been in the school a month. We moved in from Elmira to be near it." He hesitated, then added, "Tommy's nine, but the reason he's in the beginner's group is that Mrs. Adler thought it would make the adjustment easier."

Logan pointed to a suntanned man in the first row. "See that fellow with the glasses? He moved here from *Texas*. Of course, he's got money."

"It must be a good place," Harry said questioningly.

Logan grinned, his expression a little nervous.

"How's your son?" Harry asked.

"That little rascal," said Logan. "Last week I got him another copy of the *My Fair Lady* album, I guess he's used up four or five of them, and he goes around singing 'luv-er-ly, luv-er-ly.' But *look* at you? No."

"Mine doesn't talk," said Harry.

Mrs. Logan said judiciously, "Ours talks. Not *to* anybody, though. It's like a wall."

"I know," said Harry, and pressed. "Has, ah, has Vern shown much improvement with the school?"

Murray Logan pursed his lips. "I would say, yes. The bedwetting's not too good, but life's a great deal smoother in some ways. You know, you don't hope for a dramatic breakthrough. But in little things, day by day, it goes smoother. Mostly smoother. Of course there are setbacks."

Harry nodded, thinking of seven years of setbacks, and two years of growing worry and puzzlement before that. He said, "Mrs. Adler told me that, for instance, a special outbreak of destructiveness might mean something like a plateau in speech therapy. So the child fights it and breaks out in some other direction."

"That too," said Logan, "but what I meant—Oh, they're starting."

Vladek nodded, stubbing out his cigarette and absent-mindedly lighting another. His stomach was knotting up again. He wondered at these other parents, who seemed so safe and, well, untouched. Wasn't it the same with them as with Margaret and himself? And it had been a long time since either of them had felt the world comfortable around them, even without Dr. Nicholson pressing for a decision. He forced himself to lean back and look as tranquil as the others.

Mrs. Adler was tapping her desk with a ruler, "I think everybody who is coming is here," she said. She leaned against the desk and waited for the room to quiet down. She was short, dark, plump and surprisingly pretty. She did not look at all like a competent professional. She looked so unlike her role that, in fact, Harry's heart had sunk three months ago when their correspondence about admitting Tommy had been climaxed by the long trip from Elmira for the interview. He had expected a steel-gray lady with rimless glasses, a Valkyrie in a white smock like the nurse who had held wriggling, screaming Tommy while waiting for the suppository to quiet him down for his first EEG, a disheveled old fraud, he didn't know what. Anything except this pretty young woman. Another blind alley, he had thought in despair. Another, after a hundred too many already. First, "Wait for him to outgrow it." He doesn't. Then, "We must reconcile ourselves to God's will." But you don't want to. Then give him the prescription three times a day for three months. And it doesn't work. Then chase around for six months with the Child Guidance Clinic to find out it's only letterheads and one circuit-riding doctor who doesn't have time for anything. Then, after four dreary, weepy weeks of soul-searching, the State Training

School, and find out it has an eight-year waiting list. Then the private custodial school, and find they're fifty-five hundred dollars a year—without medical treatment!—and where do you get fifty-five hundred dollars a year? And all the time everybody warns you, as if you didn't know it; "Hurry! Do something! Catch it early! This is the critical stage! Delay is fatal!" And then this soft-looking little woman; how could she do anything?

She had rapidly shown him how. She had questioned Margaret and Harry incisively, turned to Tommy, rampaging through that same room like a rogue bull, and turned his rampage into a game. In three minutes he was happily experimenting with an indestructible old windup cabinet Victrola, and Mrs. Adler was saying to the Vladeks, "Don't count on a miracle cure. There isn't any. But improvements, yes, and I think we can help Tommy."

Perhaps she had, thought Vladek bleakly. Perhaps she was helping as much as anyone ever could.

Meanwhile Mrs. Adler had quickly and pleasantly welcomed the parents, suggested they remain for coffee and get to know each other, and introduced the PTA president, a Mrs. Rose, tall, prematurely gray and very executive. "This being the first meeting of the term," she said, "there are no minutes to be read; so we'll get to the committee work reports. What about the transportation problem, Mr. Baer?"

The man who got up was old. More than sixty; Harry wondered what it was like to have your life crowned with a late retarded child. He wore all the trappings of success—a four hundred dollar suit, an electronic wrist watch, a large gold fraternal ring. In a slight German accent he said, "I was to the district school board and they are not cooperating. My lawyer looked it up and the trouble is all one word. What the law says, the school board may, that is the word, may, reimburse parents of handicapped children for transportation to private schools. Not shall, you understand, but may. They were very frank with me. They said they just didn't want to spend the money. They have the impression we're all rich people here."

Slight sour laughter around the room.

"So my lawyer made an appointment, and we appeared before the full board and presented the case—we don't care, reimbursement, a school bus, anything so we can relieve the transportation burden a little. The answer was no." He shrugged and remained standing, looking at Mrs. Rose, who said:

"Thank you, Mr. Baer. Does anybody have any suggestions?"

A woman said angrily, "Put some heat on them. We're all voters!"

A man said, "Publicity, that's right. The principle is perfectly clear in the law, one taxpayer's child is supposed to get the same service as another taxpayer's child. We should write letters to the papers."

Mr. Baer said, "Wait a minute. Letters I don't think mean anything, but I've got a public relations firm; I'll tell them to take a little time off my food specialities and use it for the school. They can use their own know-how, how to do it; they're the experts."

This was moved, seconded and passed, while Murray Logan whispered to Vladek, "He's Marijane Garlic Mayonnaise. He had a twelve-year-old girl in very bad shape that Mrs. Adler helped in her old private classes. He bought this building for her, along with a couple of other parents."

Harry Vladek was musing over how it felt to be a parent who could buy a building for a school that would help your child, while the committee reports continued. Some time later, to Harry's dismay, the business turned to financing, and there was a vote to hold a fundraising theater party for which each couple with a child in the school would have to sell "at least" five pairs of orchestra seats at sixty dollars a pair. Let's get this straightened out now, he thought, and put up his hand.

"My name is Harry Vladek," he said when he was recognized, "and I'm brand new here. In the school and in the county. I work for a big insurance company, and I was lucky enough to get a transfer here so my boy can go to the school. But I just don't know anybody yet that I can sell tickets to for sixty dollars. That's an awful lot of money for my kind of people."

Mrs. Rose said, "It's an awful lot of money for most of us. You can get rid of your tickets, though. We've got to. It doesn't matter if you try a hundred people and ninety-five say no just as long as the others say yes."

He sat down, already calculating. Well, Mr. Crine at the office. He was a bachelor and he did go to the theater. Maybe work up an office raffle for another pair. Or two pairs. Then there was, let's see, the real estate dealer who had sold them the house, the lawyer they'd used for the closing—

Well. It had been explained to him that the tuition, while decidedly not nominal, eighteen hundred dollars a year in fact, did not cover the cost per child. Somebody had to pay for the speech therapist, the dance therapist, the full-time psychologist and the part-time psychiatrist, and all the others, and it might as well be Mr. Crine at the office. And the lawyer.

And half an hour later Mrs. Rose looked at the agenda, checked off an item and said, "That seems to be all for tonight. Mr. and Mrs. Perry brought us some very nice cookies, and we all know that Mrs. Howe's coffee is out of this world. They're in the beginners room, and we hope you'll all stay to get acquainted. The meeting is adjourned."

Harry and the Logans joined the polite surge to the beginners room, where Tommy spent his mornings. "There's Miss Hackett," said Celia Logan. That was the beginners' teacher. She saw them and came over, smiling. Harry had seen her only in a tentlike smock, her armor against chocolate milk, finger paints and sudden jets from the "water play" corner of the room. Without it she was handsomely middle-aged in a green pants suit.

"I'm glad you parents have met," she said. "I wanted to tell you that your little boys are getting along nicely. They're forming a sort of conspiracy against the others in the class. Vern swipes their toys and gives them to Tommy."

"He *does?*" cried Logan.

"Yes indeed. I think he's beginning to relate. And, Mr. Vladek, Tommy's taken his thumb out of his month for minutes at a time. At least half a dozen times this morning, without my saying a word."

Harry said excitedly, "You know, I thought I noticed he was tapering off. I couldn't be sure. You're positive about that?"

"Absolutely," she said. "And I bluffed him into drawing a face. He gave me that glare of his when the others were drawing; so I started to take the paper away. He grabbed it back and scribbled a kind of Picassoish face in one second flat. I wanted to save it for Mrs. Vladek and you, but Tommy got it and shredded it in the methodical way he has."

"I wish I could have seen it," said Vladek.

"There'll be others. I can see the prospect of real improvement in your boys," she said, including the Logans in her smile. "I have a private case afternoons that's really tricky. A nine-year-old boy, like Tommy. He's not bad except for one thing. He thinks Donald Duck is out to get him. His parents somehow managed to convince themselves for two years that he was kidding them, in spite of three broken TV picture tubes. Then they went to a psychiatrist and learned the score. Excuse me, I want to talk to Mrs. Adler."

Logan shook his head and said, "I guess we could be worse off, Vladek. Vern giving something to another boy! How do you like that?"

"I like it," his wife said radiantly.

"And did you hear about that other boy? Poor kid. When I hear about something like that—And then there was the Baer girl. I always think it's worse when it's a little girl because, you know, you worry with little girls that somebody will take advantage; but our boys'll make out, Vladek. You hear what Miss Hackett said."

Harry was suddenly impatient to get home to his wife. "I don't think I'll stay for coffee, or do they expect you to?"

"No, no, leave when you like."

"I have a half-hour drive," he said apologetically and went through the golden oak doors, past the ugly but fireproof staircase, out onto the graveled parking lot. His real reason was that he wanted very much to get home before Margaret fell asleep so he could tell her about the thumbsucking. Things were happening, definite things, after only a month. And Tommy drew a face. And Miss Hackett said—

He stopped in the middle of the lot. He had remembered about Dr. Nicholson, and besides, what was it, exactly, that Miss Hackett had said? Anything about a normal life? Not anything about a cure? "Real improvement," she said, but improvement how far?

He lit a cigarette, turned and plowed his way back through the parents to Mrs. Adler. "Mrs. Adler," he said, "may I see you just for a moment?"

She came with him immediately out of earshot of the others. "Did you enjoy the meeting, Mr. Vladek?"

"Oh, sure. What I wanted to see you about is that I have to make a decision. I don't know what to do. I don't know who to go to. It would help a lot if you could tell me, well, what are Tommy's chances?"

She waited a moment before she responded. "Are you considering committing him, Mr. Vladek?" she demanded.

"No, it's not exactly that. It's—well, what can you tell me, Mrs. Adler? I know a month isn't much. But is he ever going to be like everybody else?"

He could see from her face that she had done this before and had hated it. She said patiently, " 'Everybody else,' Mr. Vladek, includes some terrible people who just don't happen, technically, to be handicapped. Our objective isn't to make Tommy like 'everybody else.' It's just to help him to become the best and most rewarding Tommy Vladek he can."

"Yes, but what's going to happen later on? I mean, if Margaret and I—if anything happens to us?"

She was suffering. "There is simply no way to know, Mr. Vladek," she said gently. "I wouldn't give up hope. But I can't tell you to expect miracles."

Margaret wasn't asleep; she was waiting up for him, in the small living room of the small new house. "How was he?" Vladek asked, as each of them had asked the other on returning home for seven years.

She looked as though she had been crying, but she was calm enough. "Not too bad. I had to lie down with him to get him to go to bed. He took his gland-gunk well, though. He licked the spoon."

"That's good," he said and told her about the drawing of the face, about the conspiracy with little Vern Logan, about the thumb-sucking. He could see how pleased she was, but she only said: "Dr. Nicholson called again."

"I told him not to bother you!"

"He didn't bother me, Harry, He was very nice. I promised him you'd call back."

"It's eleven o'clock, Margaret. I'll call him in the morning."

"No, I said tonight, no matter what time. He's waiting, and he said to be sure and reverse the charges."

"I wish I'd never answered the son of a bitch's letter," he burst out and then, apologetically: "Is there any coffee? I didn't stay for it at the school."

She had put the water on to boil when she heard the car whine into the driveway, and the instant coffee was ready in the cup. She poured it and said, "You have to talk to him, Harry. He has to know tonight."

" 'Know tonight! Know tonight'," he mimicked savagely. He scalded his lips on the coffee cup and said, "What do you want me to do, Margaret? How do I make a decision like this? Today I picked up the phone and called the company psychologist, and when his secretary answered, I said I had the wrong number. I didn't know what to say to him."

"I'm not trying to pressure you, Harry. But he has to know."

Vladek put down the cup and lit his fiftieth cigarette of the day. The little dining room—it wasn't that, it was a breakfast alcove off the tiny kitchen, but they called it a dining room even to each other—was full of Tommy. The new paint on the wall where Tommy had peeled off the cups-and-spoons wallpaper. The Tommy-proof latch on the stove. The one odd aqua seat that didn't match the others on the kitchen chairs, where Tommy had methodically gouged it with the handle of his spoon. He said, "I know what my mother would tell me, talk to the priest. Maybe I should. But we've never even been to Mass here."

Margaret sat down and helped herself to one of his cigarettes. She was still a good-looking woman. She hadn't gained a pound since Tommy was born, although she usually looked tired. She said carefully and straightforwardly, "We agreed, Harry. You said you would talk to Mrs. Adler, and you've done that. We said if she didn't think Tommy would ever straighten out we'd talk to Dr. Nicholson. I know it's hard on you, and I know I'm not much help. But I don't know what to do, and I have to let you decide."

Harry looked at his wife, lovingly and hopelessly, and at that moment the phone rang. It was, of course. Dr. Nicholson.

"I haven't made a decision," said Harry Vladek at once. "You're rushing me, Dr. Nicholson."

The distant voice was calm and assured. "No, Mr. Vladek, it's not me that's rushing you. The other boy's heart gave out an hour ago. That's what's rushing you."

"You mean he's dead?" cried Vladek.

"He's on the heart-lung machine, Mr. Vladek. We can hold him for at least eighteen hours, maybe twenty-four. The brain is all right. We're getting very good waves on the oscilloscope. The tissue match with your boy is satisfactory. Better than satisfactory. There's a flight out of JFK at six-fifteen in the morning, and I've reserved space for yourself, your wife and Tommy. You'll be met at the airport. You can be here by noon; so we have time. Only just time, Mr. Vladek. It's up to you now."

Vladek said furiously, "I can't decide that! Don't you understand? I don't know how."

"I do understand, Mr. Vladek," said the distant voice and, strangely Vladek thought, it seemed he did. "I have a suggestion. Would you like to come down anyhow? I think it might help you to see the other boy, and you can talk to his parents. They feel they owe you something even for going this far. And they want to thank you."

"Oh, no!" cried Vladek.

The doctor went on: "All they want is for their boy to have a life. They don't expect anything but that. They'll give you custody of the child—your child, yours and theirs. He's a very fine little boy, Mr. Vladek. Eight years old. Reads beautifully. Makes model airplanes. They let him ride his bike because he was so sensible and reliable, and the accident wasn't his fault. The truck came right up on the sidewalk and hit him."

Harry was trembling. "That's like giving me a bribe," he said harshly. "That's telling me I can trade Tommy in for somebody smarter and nicer."

"I didn't mean it that way, Mr. Vladek. I only wanted you to know the kind of boy you can save."

"You don't even know the operation's going to work?"

"No," agreed the doctor. "Not positively. I can tell you that we've transplanted animals, including primates, and human cadavers, and one pair of terminal cases; but you're right, we've never had a transplant into a well body. I've shown you all the records, Mr. Vladek. We went over them with your own doctor when we first talked about this possibility, five months ago. This is the first case since then when the match was close and there was a real hope for success, but you're right, it's still unproved. Unless you help us prove it. For what it's worth, I think it will work. But no one can be sure."

Margaret had left the kitchen, but Vladek knew where she was from the scratchy click in the earpiece: in the bedroom, listening on the extension phone. He said at last, "I can't say now. Dr. Nicholson, I'll call you back in— in half an hour. I can't do any more than that right now."

"That's a great deal, Mr. Vladek. I'll be waiting right here for your call."

Harry sat down and drank the rest of his coffee. You had to be an expert in a lot of things to get along, he was thinking. What did he know about brain transplants? In one way, a lot. He knew that the surgery part was supposed to be straightforward, but the tissue rejection was the problem, and Dr. Nicholson thought he had that licked. He knew that every doctor he had talked to, and he had now talked to seven of them, had agreed that medically it was probably sound enough, and that every one of them had carefully clammed up when he got the conversation around to whether it was right. It was his decision, not theirs, they all said, sometimes just by their silence. But who was he to decide?

Margaret appeared in the doorway. "Harry. Let's go upstairs and look at Tommy."

He said harshly, "Is that supposed to make it easier for me to murder my son?"

She said, "We talked that out, Harry, and we agreed it isn't murder. Whatever it is. I only think that Tommy ought to be with us when we decide, even if he doesn't know what we're deciding."

The two of them stood next to the outsize crib that held their son, looking in the night light at the long fair lashes against the chubby cheeks and the pouted lips around the thumb. Reading. Model airplanes. Riding a bike. Against a quick sketch of a face and the occasional, cherished tempestuous bruising flurry of kisses.

Vladek stayed there the full half hour and then, as he had promised, went back to the kitchen, picked up the phone and began to dial.

## READING COMPREHENSION QUESTIONS

1.  Suppose the Vladeks decide to go through with the operation described for Tommy. If your child were in Tommy's condition, would you want him to undergo such an operation (if all the other technological conditions were in place as well)? Why or why not?

2.  In order to fully appreciate the difficulty of the Vladek's decision, explain the case for *both* sides of the issue here. In other words, one could argue that Tommy will be the survivor of the operation, or one could argue that the brain donor will be the survivor. Put forward the best case for each side, then.

3.  Is there a *third* option in this case, namely, that neither Tommy *nor* the brain donor will be the survivor, but rather it will be someone else? Provide an argument for this possibility.

# 2

# Phaedo

PLATO

*Plato (ca. 427–347 B.C.E.) was one of the greatest philosophers in history. He was born, and lived much of his life, in Athens, Greece, and was a student of Socrates—himself famous for wandering the streets of Athens instigating philosophical discussions with anyone who was willing (which perhaps contributed to his untimely death at the hands of the state). Later in life, Plato founded the Academy, essentially a university of higher learning, where he taught philosophy. In his philosophical writings, Plato wrote mostly in dialogue form, with Socrates as his lead character. In this selection, taken from the dialogue* Phaedo, *Socrates is in a prison cell, awaiting execution by poison. In his discussion with Simmias, Socrates argues for why true philosophers shouldn't fear death, and his answer has to do with the immortality of the soul. As you read, try to figure out just what his argument for this conclusion is, as well as whether or not you agree with it.*

What again shall we say of the actual acquirement of knowledge?—is the body, if invited to share in the inquiry, a hinderer or a helper? I mean to say, have sight and hearing any truth in them? Are they not, as the poets are always telling us, inaccurate witnesses? and yet, if even they are inaccurate and indistinct, what is to be said of the other senses?—for you will allow that they are the best of them?

Certainly, he [Simmias] replied.

Then when does the soul attain truth?—for in attempting to consider anything in company with the body she is obviously deceived.

Yes, that is true.

Then must not existence be revealed to her in thought, if at all?

Yes.

And thought is best when the mind is gathered into herself and none of these things trouble her—neither sounds nor sights nor pain nor any pleasure—when she has as little as possible to do with the body, and has no bodily sense or feeling, but is aspiring after being?

That is true.

And in this the philosopher dishonors the body; his soul runs away from the body and desires to be alone and by herself?

That is true.

SOURCE: Taken from the Internet Classics Archive. Translated by Benjamin Jowett. This edition is in the public domain.

Well, but there is another thing, Simmias: Is there or is there not an absolute justice?

Assuredly there is.

And an absolute beauty and absolute good?

Of course.

But did you ever behold any of them with your eyes?

Certainly not.

Or did you ever reach them with any other bodily sense? (and I speak not of these alone, but of absolute greatness, and health, and strength, and of the essence or true nature of everything). Has the reality of them ever been perceived by you through the bodily organs? or rather, is not the nearest approach to the knowledge of their several natures made by him who so orders his intellectual vision as to have the most exact conception of the essence of that which he considers?

Certainly.

And he attains to the knowledge of them in their highest purity who goes to each of them with the mind alone, not allowing when in the act of thought the intrusion or introduction of sight or any other sense in the company of reason, but with the very light of the mind in her clearness penetrates into the very fight of truth in each; he has got rid, as far as he can, of eyes and ears and of the whole body, which he conceives of only as a disturbing element, hindering the soul from the acquisition of knowledge when in company with her—is not this the sort of man who, if ever man did, is likely to attain the knowledge of existence?

There is admirable truth in that, Socrates, replied Simmias.

And when they consider all this, must not true philosophers make a reflection, of which they will speak to one another in such words as these: We have found, they will say, a path of speculation which seems to bring us and the argument to the conclusion that while we are in the body, and while the soul is mingled with this mass of evil, our desire will not be satisfied, and our desire is of the truth. For the body is a source of endless trouble to us by reason of the mere requirement of food; and also is liable to diseases which overtake and impede us in the search after truth: and by filling us so full of loves, and lusts, and fears, and fancies, and idols, and every sort of folly, prevents our ever having, as people say, so much as a thought. For whence come wars, and fightings, and factions? Whence but from the body and the lusts of the body? For wars are occasioned by the love of money, and money has to be acquired for the sake and in the service of the body; and in consequence of all these things the time which ought to be given to philosophy is lost. Moreover, if there is time and an inclination toward philosophy, yet the body introduces a turmoil and confusion and fear into the course of speculation, and hinders us from seeing the truth: and all experience shows that if we would have pure knowledge of anything we must be quit of the body, and the soul in herself must behold all things in themselves: then I suppose that we shall attain that which we desire, and of which we say that we are lovers, and that is wisdom, not while we live, but after death, as the argument shows; for if while in company with the body the soul cannot have pure knowledge, one of two things seems to follow—either knowledge is not to be attained at all, or, if at all, after death. For then, and not till then, the soul will be in herself alone and without the body. In this present life, I reckon that we make the nearest approach to knowledge when we have the least possible concern or interest in the body, and are not saturated with the bodily nature, but remain pure until the hour when God himself is pleased to release us. And then the foolishness of the body will be cleared away and we shall be pure and hold converse with other pure souls, and know of ourselves the clear light everywhere; and this is surely the light of truth. For no impure thing is allowed to approach the pure. These are the sort of words, Simmias, which the true lovers of wisdom cannot help saying to one another, and thinking. You will agree with me in that?

Certainly, Socrates.

But if this is true, O my friend, then there is great hope that, going whither I go, I shall there be satisfied with that which has been the chief concern of you and me in our past lives. And now that the hour of departure is appointed to me, this is the hope with which I depart, and not I only, but every man who believes that he has his mind purified.

Certainly, replied Simmias.

And what is purification but the separation of the soul from the body, as I was saying before; the habit of the soul gathering and collecting herself into herself, out of all the courses of the body; the dwelling in her own place alone, as in another life, so also in this, as far as she can; the release of the soul from the chains of the body?

Very true, he said.

And what is that which is termed death, but this very separation and release of the soul from the body?

To be sure, he said.

And the true philosophers, and they only, study and are eager to release the soul. Is not the separation and release of the soul from the body their especial study?

That is true.

And as I was saying at first, there would be a ridiculous contradiction in men studying to live as nearly as they can in a state of death, and yet repining when death comes.

Certainly.

Then, Simmias, as the true philosophers are ever studying death, to them, of all men, death is the least terrible. Look at the matter in this way: how inconsistent of them to have been always enemies of the body, and wanting to have the soul alone, and when this is granted to them, to be trembling and repining; instead of rejoicing at their departing to that place where, when they arrive, they hope to gain that which in life they loved (and this was wisdom), and at the same time to be rid of the company of their enemy. Many a man has been willing to go to the world below in the hope of seeing there an earthly love, or wife, or son, and conversing with them. And will he who is a true lover of wisdom, and is persuaded in like manner that only in the world below he can worthily enjoy her, still repine at death? Will he not depart with joy? Surely he will, my friend, if he be a true philosopher. For he will have a firm conviction that there only, and nowhere else, he can find wisdom in her purity. And if this be true, he would be very absurd, as I was saying, if he were to fear death.

## READING COMPREHENSION QUESTIONS

1.  Socrates argues early on in this selection that one can attain knowledge of things like absolute beauty and absolute good only with one's mind or soul (terms Socrates uses interchangeably). What exactly does he *mean* by this claim?

2.  Socrates contrasts the mind with the body, which he thinks actually hinders the soul's acquisition of pure knowledge. How so?

3.  According to Socrates, it would be "very absurd" for a true philosopher to fear death. What precisely is his argument for this claim? Does this conclusion hold for everyone (even if they're not true philosophers)? Why or why not?

# 3

# The Myth of the Soul

### CLARENCE DARROW

*Clarence Darrow (1857–1938) was an American lawyer who took on some of the most famous cases and causes of his time. He defended Leopold and Loeb, teenagers who killed solely for thrills (see part of Darrow's concluding argument in the selection "Leopold and Loeb" in Chapter 4), as well as John Scopes in the famous "Monkey Trial" of 1925. In this essay, Darrow, an agnostic, discusses the conditions that make it rational to believe something in general, and then he tries to show that we have no good reason to believe that we can survive the deaths of our bodies. To achieve this latter task, Darrow attacks the three methods that people suggest might get them from here to the afterlife, namely, the survival of their souls, the survival of their consciousnesses, or the resurrection of their bodies.*

There is, perhaps, no more striking example of the credulity of man than the widespread belief in immortality. This idea includes not only the belief that death is not the end of what we call life, but that personal identity involving memory persists beyond the grave. So determined is the ordinary individual to hold fast to this belief that, as a rule, he refuses to read or to think upon the subject lest it cast

SOURCE: Taken from http://www.positiveatheism.org/hist/darrow0.htm. This selection is in the public domain.

doubt upon his cherished dream. Of those who may chance to look at this contribution, many will do so with the determination not to be convinced; and will refuse even to consider the manifold reasons that might weaken their faith. I know that this is true, for I know the reluctance with which I long approached the subject and my firm determination not to give up my hope. Thus the myth will stand in the way of a sensible adjustment to facts.

Even many of those who claim to believe in immortality still tell themselves and others that neither side of the question is susceptible of proof. Just what can these hopeful ones believe that the word "proof" involves? The evidence against the persistence of personal consciousness is as strong as the evidence of gravitation, and much more obvious. It is as convincing and unassailable as the proof of the destruction of wood or coal by fire. If it is not certain that death ends personal identity and memory, then almost nothing that man accepts as true is susceptible of proof.

The beliefs of the race and its individuals are relics of the past. Without careful examination, no one can begin to understand how many of man's cherished opinions have no foundation in fact. The common experience of all men should teach them how easy it is to believe what they wish to accept. Experienced psychologists know perfectly well that if they desire to convince a man of some idea, they must first make him *want* to believe it. There are so many hopes, so many strong yearnings and desires attached to the doctrine of immortality that it is practically impossible to create in any mind the wish to be mortal. Still, in spite of strong desires, millions of people are filled with doubts and fears that will not down. After all, is it not better to look the question squarely in the face and find out whether we are harboring a delusion?

It is customary to speak of a "belief in immortality." First, then, let us see what is meant by the word "belief." If I take a train in Chicago at noon, bound for New York, I believe I will reach that city the next morning. I believe it because I have been to New York. I have read about the city, I have known many other people who have been there, and their stories are not inconsistent with any known facts in my own experience. I have even examined the time tables and I know just how I will go and how long the trip will take. In other words, when I board the train for New York, I believe I will reach that city because I have *reason* to believe it.

But if I am told that next week I shall start on a trip to Goofville; that I shall not take my body with me; that I shall stay for all eternity: can I find a single fact connected with my journey—the way I shall go, the part of me that is to go, the time of the journey, the country I shall reach, its location in space, the way I shall live there—or anything that would lead to a rational belief that I shall really make the trip? Have I ever known anyone who has made the journey and returned? If I am really to believe, I must try to get some information about all these important facts.

But people hesitate to ask questions about life after death. They do not ask, for they know that only silence comes out of the eternal darkness of endless space. If people really believed in a beautiful, happy, glorious land waiting to receive them when they died; if they believed that their friends would be waiting to meet them; if they believed that all pain and suffering would be left behind: why should they live through weeks, months, and even years of pain and torture while a cancer eats its way to the vital parts of the body? Why should one fight off death? Because he does *not* believe in any real sense: he only hopes. Everyone knows that there is no real evidence of any such state of bliss; so we are told not to search for proof. We are to accept through faith alone. But every thinking person knows that faith can only come through belief. Belief implies a condition of mind that accepts a certain idea. This condition can be brought about only by evidence. True, the evidence may be simply the unsupported statement of your grand-mother; it may be wholly insufficient for reasoning men; but, good or bad, it must be enough for the believer or he could not believe.

Upon what evidence, then, are we asked to believe in immortality? There is no evidence. One is told to rely on faith, and no doubt this serves the purpose so long as one can believe blindly whatever he is told. But if there is no evidence upon which to build a positive belief in immortality, let us examine the other side of the question. Perhaps evidence can be found to support a positive convic-tion that immortality is a delusion.

The belief in immortality expresses itself in two different forms. On the one hand, there is a belief in the immortality of the "soul." This is sometimes inter-preted to mean simply that the identity, the consciousness, the memory of the individual persists after death. On the other hand, many religious creeds have for-mulated a belief in "the resurrection of the body"—which is something else again. It will be necessary to examine both forms of this belief in turn.

The idea of continued life after death is very old. It doubtless had its roots back in the childhood of the race. In view of the limited knowledge of primitive man, it was not unreasonable. His dead friends and relatives visited him in dreams and visions and were present in his feeling and imagination until they were for-gotten. Therefore the lifeless body did not raise the question of dissolution, but rather of duality. It was thought that man was a dual being possessing a body and a soul as separate entities, and that when a man died, his soul was released from his body to continue its life apart. Consequently, food and drink were placed upon the graves of the dead to be used in the long journey into the unknown. In modified forms, this belief in the duality of man persists to the present day. But primitive man had no conception of life as having a beginning and an end. In this he was like the rest of the animals. To-day, everyone of ordinary intelligence knows how life begins, and to examine the beginnings of life leads to inevitable conclusions about the way life ends. If man has a soul, it must creep in somewhere during the period of gestation and growth.

All the higher forms of animal life grow from a single cell. Before the individual life can begin its development, it must be fertilized by union with another cell; then the cell divides and multiplies until it takes the form and pattern of its kind. At a certain regular time the being emerges into the world. During its term of life mil-lions of cells in its body are born, die, and are replaced until, through age, disease, or some catastrophe, the cells fall apart and the individual life is ended.

It is obvious that but for the fertilization of the cell under right conditions, the being would not have lived. It is idle to say that the initial cell has a soul. In one sense it has life; but even that is precarious and depends for its continued life upon union with another cell of the proper kind. The human mother is the bearer of probably ten thousand of one kind of cell, and the human father of countless bil-lions of the other kind. Only a very small fraction of these result in human life. If the unfertilized cells of the female and the unused cells of the male are human beings possessed of souls, then the population of the world is infinitely greater than has ever been dreamed. Of course no such idea as belief in the immortality of the germ cells could satisfy the yearnings of the individual for a survival of life after death.

If that which is called a "soul" is a separate entity apart from the body, when, then, and where and how was this soul placed in the human structure? The individual began with the union of two cells, neither of which had a soul. How could these two soulless cells produce a soul? I must leave this search to the metaphysicians. When they have found the answer, I hope they will tell me, for I should really like to know.

We know that a baby may live and fully develop in its mother's womb and then, through some shock at birth, may be born without life. In the past, these babies were promptly buried. But now we know that in many such cases, where the bodily structure is complete, the machine may be set to work by artificial respiration or electricity. Then it will run like any other human body through its allotted term of years. We also know that in many cases of drowning, or when some mishap virtually destroys life without hopelessly impairing the body, artificial means may set it in motion once more, so that it will complete its term of existence until the final catastrophe comes. Are we to believe that somewhere around the stillborn child and somewhere in the vicinity of the drowned man there hovers a detached soul waiting to be summoned back into the body by a pulmotor? This, too, must be left to the metaphysicians.

The beginnings of life yield no evidence of the beginnings of a soul. It is idle to say that the something in the human being which we call "life" is the soul itself, for the soul is generally taken to distinguish human beings from other forms of life. There is life in all animals and plants, and at least potential life in inorganic matter. This potential life is simply unreleased force and matter—the great storehouse from which all forms of life emerge and are constantly replenished. It is impossible to draw the line between inorganic matter and the simpler forms of plant life, and equally impossible to draw the line between plant life and animal life, or between other forms of animal life and what we human beings are pleased to call the highest form. If the thing which we call "life" is itself the soul, then cows have souls; and, in the very nature of things, we must allow souls to all forms of life and to inorganic matter as well.

Life itself is something very real, as distinguished from the soul. Every man knows that his life had a beginning. Can one imagine an organism that has a beginning and no end? If I did not exist in the infinite past, why should I, or could I, exist in the infinite future? "But," say some, "your consciousness, your memory may exist even after you are dead. This is what we mean by the soul." Let us examine this point a little.

I have no remembrance of the months that I lay in my mother's womb. I cannot recall the day of my birth nor the time when I first opened my eyes to the light of the sun. I cannot remember when I was an infant, or when I began to creep on the floor, or when I was taught to walk, or anything before I was five or six years old. Still, all of these events were important, wonderful, and strange in a new life. What I call my "consciousness," for lack of a better word and a better understanding, developed with my growth and the crowding experiences I met at every turn. I have a hazy recollection of the burial of a boy soldier who was shot toward the end of the Civil War. He was buried near the schoolhouse when I was seven years old. But I have no remembrance of the assassination of Abraham Lincoln, although I must then have been eight years old. I must have known about it at the time, for my family and my community idolized Lincoln, and all America was in mourning at his death. Why do I remember the dead boy soldier who was buried a year before? Perhaps because I knew him well. Perhaps because his family was close to my childish life. Possibly because it came to me as my first knowledge of death. At all events, it made so deep an impression that I recall it now.

"Ah, yes," say the believers in the soul, "what you say confirms our own belief. You certainly existed when these early experiences took place. You were conscious of them at the time, even though you are not aware of it now. In the same way, may not your consciousness persist after you die, even though you are not now aware of the fact?"

On the contrary, my fading memory of the events that filled the early years of my life leads me to the opposite conclusion. So far as these incidents are concerned, the mind and consciousness of the boy are already dead. Even now, am I fully alive? I am seventy-one years old. I often fail to recollect the names of some of those I knew full well. Many events do not make the lasting impression that they once did. I know that it will be only a few years, even if my body still survives decay, when few important matters will even register in my mind. I know how it is with the old. I know that physical life can persist beyond the time when the mind can fully function. I know that if I live to an extreme old age, my mind will fail. I shall eat and drink and go to my bed in an automatic way. Memory—which is all that binds me to the past—will already be dead. All that will remain will be a vegetative existence; I shall sit and doze in the chimney corner, and my body will function in a measure even though the ego will already be practically dead. I am sure that if I die of what is called "old age," my consciousness will gradually slip away with my failing emotions; I shall no more be aware of the near approach of final dissolution than is the dying tree.

In primitive times, before men knew anything about the human body or the universe of which it is a part, it was not unreasonable to believe in spirits, ghosts, and the duality of man. For one thing, celestial geography was much simpler then. Just above the earth was a firmament in which the stars were set, and above the firmament was heaven. The place was easy of access and in dreams the angels were seen going up and coming down on a ladder. But now we have a slightly more adequate conception of space and the infinite universe of which we are so small a part. Our great telescopes reveal countless worlds and planetary systems which make our own sink into utter insignificance in comparison. We have every reason to think that beyond our sight there is endless space filled with still more planets, so infinite in size and number that no brain has the smallest conception of their extent. Is there any reason to think that in this universe, with its myriads of worlds, there is no other life so important as our own? Is it possible that the inhabitants of the earth have been singled out for special favor and endowed with souls and immortal life? Is it at all reasonable to suppose that any special account is taken of the human atoms that forever come and go upon this planet?

If man has a soul that persists after death, that goes to a heaven of the blessed or to a hell of the damned, where are these places? It is not so easily imagined as it once was. How does the soul make its journey? What does immortal man find when he gets there, and how will he live after he reaches the end of endless space? We know that the atmosphere will be absent; that there will be no light, no heat—only the infinite reaches of darkness and frigidity. In view of modern knowledge, can anyone *really believe* in the persistence of individual life and memory?

There are those who base their hope of a future life upon the resurrection of the body. This is a purely religious doctrine. It is safe to say that few intelligent men who are willing to look obvious facts in the face hold any such belief. Yet we are seriously told that Elijah was carried bodily to heaven in a chariot of fire, and that Jesus arose from the dead and ascended into heaven. The New Testament abounds in passages that support this doctrine. St. Paul states the tenet over and over again. In the fifteenth chapter of first Corinthians he says: "If Christ be preached that he rose from the dead, how say some among you that there is no resurrection of the dead? . . . And if Christ be not risen, then is our preaching vain. . . . For if the dead rise not, then is not Christ raised." The Apostles' Creed says: "I believe in the resurrection of the body." This has been carried into substantially all the orthodox creeds; and while it is more or less minimized by neglect and omission, it is still a cardinal doctrine of the orthodox churches.

Two thousand years ago, in Palestine, little was known of man, of the earth, or of the universe. It was then currently believed that the earth was only four thousand years old, that life had begun anew after the deluge about two thousand years before, and that the entire earth was soon to be destroyed. To-day it is fairly well established that man has been upon the earth for a million years. During that long stretch of time the world has changed many times; it is changing every moment. At least three or four ice ages have swept across continents, driving death before them, carrying human beings into the sea or burying them deep in the earth. Animals have fed on man and on each other. Every dead body, no matter whether consumed by fire or buried in the earth, has been resolved into its elements, so that the matter and energy that once formed human beings has fed animals and plants and other men. As the great naturalist, Fabre, has said: "At the banquet of life each is in turn a guest and a dish." Thus the body of every man now living is in part made from the bodies of those who have been dead for ages.

Yet we are still asked to believe in the resurrection of the body. By what alchemy, then, are the individual bodies that have successively fed the generations of men to be separated and restored to their former identities? And if I am to be resurrected, what particular *I* shall be called from the grave, from the animals and plants and the bodies of other men who shall inherit this body I now call my own? My body has been made over and over, piece by piece, as the days went by, and will continue to be so made until the end. It has changed so slowly that each new cell is fitted into the living part, and will go on changing until the final crisis comes. Is it the child in the mother's womb or the tottering frame of the old man that shall be brought back? The mere thought of such a resurrection beggars reason, ignores facts, and enthrones blind faith, wild dreams, hopeless hopes, and cowardly fears as sovereigns of the human mind. . . .

The thing we call "life" is nothing other than a state of equilibrium which endures for a short span of years between the two opposing tendencies of nature—the one that builds up, and the one that tears down. In old age, the

tearing-down process has already gained the ascendency, and when death inter-
venes, the equilibrium is finally upset by the complete stoppage of the building-
up process, so that nothing remains but complete disintegration. The energy thus
released may be converted into grass or trees or animal life; or it may lie dormant
until caught up again in the crucible of nature's laboratory. But whatever happens,
the man—the *You* and the *I*—like the lump of coal that has been burned, is
gone—irrevocably dispersed. All the King's horses and all the King's men cannot
restore it to its former unity.

 The idea that man is a being set apart, distinct from all the rest of nature, is
born of man's emotions, of his loves and hates, of his hopes and fears, and of
the primitive conceptions of undeveloped minds. The *You* or the *I* which is
known to our friends does not consist of an immaterial something called a
"soul" which cannot be conceived. We know perfectly well what we mean
when we talk about this *You* and this *Me:* and it is equally plain that the whole
fabric that makes up our separate personalities is destroyed, dispersed, disintegrated
beyond repair by what we call "death.". . .

 And after all, is the belief in immortality necessary or even desirable for man?
Millions of men and women have no such faith; they go on with their daily tasks
and feel joy and sorrow without the lure of immortal life. The things that really
affect the happiness of the individual are the matters of daily living. They are the
companionship of friends, the games and contemplations. They are misunderstandings and cruel judgments, false friends and debts, poverty and disease.
They are our joys in our living companions and our sorrows over those who
die. Whatever our faith, we mainly live in the present—in the here and now.
Those who hold the view that man is mortal are never troubled by metaphysical
problems. At the end of the day's labor we are glad to lose our consciousness in
sleep; and intellectually, at least, we look forward to the long rest from the stresses
and storms that are always incidental to existence.

 When we fully understand the brevity of life, its fleeting joys and unavoidable
pains; when we accept the fact that all men and women are approaching an inevitable doom: the consciousness of it should make us more kindly and considerate of
each other. This feeling should make men and women use their best efforts to help
their fellow travelers on the road, to make the path brighter and easier as we journey on. It should bring a closer kinship, a better understanding, and a deeper sympathy for the wayfarers who must live a common life and die a common death.


## READING COMPREHENSION QUESTIONS

1.  In this article, Darrow offers two very general arguments about immortality.
    The first has to do with the conditions under which it is rational to believe
    something. What sort of conditions does Darrow think are necessary for
    belief in general, and what does he say about whether or not belief in
    immortality meets these conditions?

2.  The second very general argument Darrow offers has to do with finding
    evidence "to support a positive conviction that immortality is a delusion." To

find such evidence, he explores three possible avenues for achieving immortality: (a) one's soul survives, (b) one's consciousness (memory) survives, or (c) one's body is resurrected. Are these the only possibilities for immortality? What if Darrow's arguments against these possibilities succeed? Would that in fact make belief in immortality a "delusion"?

3.  Explain and critically evaluate Darrow's argument against (a), the belief that one's soul survives the death of one's body.

4.  Explain and critically evaluate Darrow's argument against (b), the belief that one's consciousness or memory survives the death of one's body.

5.  Explain and critically evaluate Darrow's argument against (c), the belief that one's body can be resurrected after its death.

6.  At the end of the article, Darrow mentions that losing the belief in immortality would not be so bad, and in fact it could have some good consequences. What is his argument for this view, and do you accept it? Why or why not?

# 4

# The Prince and the Cobbler

JOHN LOCKE

*John Locke (1632–1704), a famous English philosopher and political theorist, wrote influential essays and books on numerous topics in epistemology, metaphysics, and ethics. In this selection from his* Essay Concerning Human Understanding *(1690), Locke provides a famous thought experiment: suppose the soul of a prince, carrying with it his stream of consciousness, were switched with that of a cobbler. The person with the prince's body would now seem to remember the thoughts and experiences of the cobbler, and vice versa. Would the person in the prince's body now be* the cobbler? *If so, what does that tell us about the nature of personal identity? If not, what does* that *tell us about the nature of personal identity?*

9. . . .To find wherein personal identity consists, we must consider what *person* stands for;—which, I think, is a thinking intelligent being, that has reason and reflection, and can consider itself as itself, the same thinking thing, in different

SOURCE: From John Locke, *An Essay Concerning Human Understanding* (Oxford: Oxford at the Clarendon Press, 1894). This selection is in the public domain.

times and places; which it does only by that consciousness which is inseparable from thinking, and, as it seems to me, essential to it: it being impossible for any one to perceive without *perceiving* that he does perceive. When we see, hear, smell, taste, feel, meditate, or will anything, we know that we do so. Thus it is always as to our present sensations and perceptions: and by this every one is to himself that which he calls *self:* it not being considered, in this case, whether the same self be continued in the same or diverse substances. For, since consciousness always accompanies thinking, and it is that which makes every one to be what he calls self, and thereby distinguishes himself from all other thinking things, in this alone consists personal identity, i.e., the sameness of a rational being: and as far as this consciousness can be extended backwards to any past action or thought, so far reaches the identity of that person; it is the same self now it was then; and it is by the same self with this present one that now reflects on it, that that action was done.

10. But it is further inquired, whether it be the same identical substance. This few would think they had reason to doubt of, if these perceptions, with their consciousness, always remained present in the mind, whereby the same thinking thing would be always consciously present, and, as would be thought, evidently the same to itself. But that which seems to make the difficulty is this, that this consciousness being interrupted always by forgetfulness, there being no moment of our lives wherein we have the whole train of all our past actions before our eyes in one view, but even the best memories losing the sight of one part whilst they are viewing another; and we sometimes, and that the greatest part of our lives, not reflecting on our past selves, being intent on our present thoughts, and in sound sleep having no thoughts at all, or at least none with that consciousness which remarks our waking thoughts; I say, in all these cases, our consciousness being interrupted, and we losing the sight of our past selves, doubts are raised whether we are the same thinking thing, i.e. the same *substance* or no. Which, however reasonable or unreasonable, concerns not *personal* identity at all. The question being what makes the same person; and not whether it be the same identical substance, which always thinks in the same person, which, in this case, matters not at all: different substances, by the same consciousness (where they do partake in it) being united into one person, as well as different bodies by the same life are united into one animal, whose identity is preserved in that change of substances by the unity of one continued life. For, it being the same consciousness that makes a man be himself to himself, personal identity depends on that only, whether it be annexed solely to one individual substance, or can be continued in a succession of several substances. For as far as any intelligent being *can* repeat the idea of any past action with the same consciousness it had of it at first, and with the same consciousness it has of any present action; so far it is the same personal self. For it is by the consciousness it has of its present thoughts and actions, that it is *self to itself* now, and so will be the same self, as far as the same consciousness can extend to actions past or to come; and would be by distance of time, or change of substance, no more two persons, than a man be two men by wearing other clothes to-day than he did yesterday, with a long or a short sleep between: the same consciousness uniting those distant actions into the same person, whatever substances contributed to their production.

11. That this is so, we have some kind of evidence in our very bodies, all whose particles, whilst vitally united to this same thinking conscious self, so that *we feel*

when they are touched, and are affected by, and conscious of good or harm that happens to them, are a part of ourselves; i.e. of our thinking conscious self. Thus, the limbs of his body are to every one a part of himself; he sympathizes and is concerned for them. Cut off a hand, and thereby separate it from that consciousness he had of its heat, cold, and other affections, and it is then no longer a part of that which is himself, any more than the remotest part of matter. Thus, we see the *substance* whereof personal self consisted at one time may be varied at another, without the change of personal identity; there being no question about the same person, though the limbs which but now were a part of it, be cut off. . . .

15. And thus may we be able, without any difficulty, to conceive the same person at the resurrection, though in a body not exactly in make or parts the same which he had here,—the same consciousness going along with the soul that inhabits it. But yet the soul alone, in the change of bodies, would scarce to any one but to him that makes the soul the man, be enough to make the same man. For should the soul of a prince, carrying with it the consciousness of the prince's past life, enter and inform the body of a cobbler, as soon as deserted by his own soul, every one sees he would be the same *person* with the prince, accountable only for the prince's actions: but who would say it was the same *man*? The body too goes to the making the man, and would, I guess, to everybody determine the man in this case, wherein the soul, with all its princely thoughts about it, would not make another man: but he would be the same cobbler to every one besides himself. I know that, in the ordinary way of speaking, the same person, and the same man, stand for one and the same thing. And indeed every one will always have a liberty to speak as he pleases, and to apply what articulate sounds to what ideas he thinks fit, and change them as often as he pleases. But yet, when we will inquire what makes the same *spirit, man,* or *person,* we must fix the ideas of spirit, man, or person in our minds; and having resolved with ourselves what we mean by them, it will not be hard to determine, in either of them, or the like, when it is the same, and when not.

16. But though the same immaterial substance or soul does not alone, wherever it be, and in whatsoever state, make the same *man;* yet it is plain, consciousness, as far as ever it can be extended—should it be to ages past—unites existences and actions very remote in time into the same *person,* as well as it does the existences and actions of the immediately preceding moment: so that whatever has the consciousness of present and past actions, is the same person, to whom they both belong. Had I the same consciousness that I saw the ark and Noah's flood, as that I saw an overflowing of the Thames last winter, or as that I write now, I could no more doubt that I who write this now, that saw the Thames overflowed last winter, and that viewed the flood at the general deluge, was the same *self,*—place that self in what *substance* you please—than that I who write this am the same *myself* now whilst I write (whether I consist of all the same substance, material or immaterial, or no) that I was yesterday. For as to this point of being the same self, it matters not whether this present self be made up of the same or other substances—I being as much concerned, and as justly accountable for any action that was done a thousand years, since, appropriated to me now by this self-consciousness, as I am for what I did the last moment.

17. *Self* is that conscious thinking thing,—whatever substance made up of, (whether spiritual or material, simple or compounded, it matters not)—which

is sensible or conscious of pleasure and pain, capable of happiness or misery, and so is concerned for itself, as far as that consciousness extends. Thus every one finds that, whilst comprehended under that consciousness, the little finger is as much a part of himself as what is most so. Upon separation of this little finger, should this consciousness go along with the little finger, and leave the rest of the body, it is evident the little finger would be the person, the same person; and self then would have nothing to do with the rest of the body. As in this case it is the consciousness that goes along with the substance, when one part is separate from another, which makes the same person, and constitutes this inseparable self: so it is in reference to substances remote in time. That with which the consciousness of this present thinking thing *can* join itself, makes the same person, and is one self with it, and with nothing else; and so attributes to itself, and owns all the actions of that thing, as its own, as far as that consciousness reaches, and no further; as every one who reflects will perceive.

18. In this personal identity is founded all the right and justice of reward and punishment; happiness and misery being that for which every one is concerned for *himself,* and not mattering what becomes of any *substance,* not joined to or affected with that consciousness. For, as it is evident in the instance I gave but now, if the consciousness went along with the little finger when it was cut off, that would be the same self which was concerned for the whole body yesterday, as making part of itself, whose actions then it cannot but admit as its own now. Though, if the same body should still live, and immediately from the separation of the little finger have its own peculiar consciousness, whereof the little finger knew nothing, it would not at all be concerned for it, as a part of itself, or could own any of its actions, or have any of them imputed to him. . . .

26. *Person,* as I take it, is the name for this self. Wherever a man finds what he calls himself, there, I think, another may say is the same person. It is a forensic term, appropriating actions and their merit; and so belongs only to intelligent agents, capable of a law, and happiness; and misery. This personality extends itself beyond present existence to what is past, only by consciousness,—whereby it becomes concerned and accountable, owns and imputes to itself past actions, just upon the same ground and for the same reason as it does the present. All which is founded in a concern for happiness, the unavoidable concomitant of consciousness; that which is conscious of pleasure and pain, desiring that that self that is conscious should be happy. And therefore whatever past actions it cannot reconcile or *appropriate* to that present self by consciousness, it can be no more concerned in than if they had never been done: and to receive pleasure or pain, i.e. reward or punishment, on the account of any such action, is all one as to be made happy or miserable in its first being, without any demerit at all. For, supposing a *man* punished now for what he had done in another life, whereof he could be made to have no consciousness at all, what difference is there between that punishment and being *created* miserable? And therefore, conformable to this, the apostle tells us, that, at the great day, when every one shall "receive according to his doings, the secrets of all hearts shall be laid open." The sentence shall be justified by the consciousness all persons shall have, that *they themselves,* in what bodies soever they appear, or what substances soever that consciousness adheres to, are the *same* that committed those actions, and deserve that punishment for them.)

## READING COMPREHENSION QUESTIONS

1.  Try to put Locke's definition of a "person" entirely in your own words. Does this strike you as the right definition? Why or why not? What's the difference, according to Locke, between a *person* and a *man*?

2.  What is Locke's criterion of quantitative personal identity across time (a phrase discussed in the introduction to this segment)? Suppose I think that what makes me the same person across time is some identical *substance* that has persisted across time. How does Locke argue against such a view? (One way to think about the answer is to think about how Locke's own favored view differs from the substance view, as well as what his view can *explain* that the substance view can't.)

3.  What exactly is the point of the prince/cobbler case? (The first sentence of that paragraph is quite crucial here.)

4.  Consider the motivations for inquiring into the nature of personal identity we discussed in the introduction to this segment: responsibility, self-concern, and immortality. What does Locke's view imply about each of these?

# 5

---

# A Dialogue on Personal Identity
# and Immortality

JOHN PERRY

*John Perry (born 1943) is the Henry Waldgrave Stuart Professor of Philosophy at Stanford University. He has written many important articles in the fields of personal identity, philosophy of mind, philosophy of language, and metaphysics.*

*In this selection, Perry sets up a fictional dialogue between three characters: Gretchen Weirob, a philosophy professor; Sam Miller, her friend and a clergyman; and Dave Cohen, her former student. Weirob has been in a terrible motorcycle accident and is in the hospital dying of massive internal wounds. Although she has been an atheist to this point, she still hopes for the comfort of being able to*

anticipate surviving the death of her body. The question she asks that motivates the
dialogue, then, is whether or not it's at all possible for there to be someone in an
afterlife who is her, someone she could reasonably anticipate being. The answer to
this question depends on what the right criterion of personal identity is—what it is
that could possibly make her the same person as someone in the afterlife—so the
dialogue participants spend their time discussing this matter. Weirob believes that
she is essentially her body, and given the fact that her body will die, she can see no
reason to believe that she won't die as well; hence she believes that immortality is
impossible. So her challenge is this: Give me an alternative theory of personal
identity that (a) provides a mechanism to get me to the afterlife, and (b) is possible
to conceive without contradiction or deep absurdity.

There are three nights in which discussion takes place. In the first night of the
dialogue, Miller tries to provide a popular argument for why Weirob could survive
the death of her body, namely, that her soul could survive. Miller (along with
many other people) believes the soul is a person's essence and that it is an
immaterial (nonphysical) substance that could survive the death of the physical
substance (the body) in which it resides. The soul theory thus responds to the first
part of Weirob's challenge: It provides a mechanism to get Weirob to the afterlife.

Unfortunately, Weirob believes it fails the second part of her challenge because
of the soul's immaterial nature. She points out that, if the soul theory were true, we
could never have the grounds to reidentify anyone because we have no grounds for
reidentifying someone's soul. After all, we can't see a soul, or touch a soul, or taste
a soul, etc., so we just have no way to determine sameness of soul across time. But
obviously we do have the grounds to reidentify people—we do this all the time—
so the soul theory must be false (it leads to this contradiction). Miller tries various
strategies to respond to this argument. First, he claims, we typically reidentify
people by their bodies, and there's a one-to-one correlation between bodies and
souls, so we can actually reidentify people's souls indirectly this way. Weirob
points out, though, that Miller simply has no grounds to establish such a correlation in the first place: How could he possibly know there's such a relation between
bodies and souls? Miller then tries to suggest that we reidentify one another's
psychologies, or minds, and that there's a one-to-one correlation between minds and
souls, but Weirob responds in the same way: There's no reason to think this.
Indeed, it's possible that we each get a new, exactly similar replacement soul every
ten years, or every five years, or every year, or every moment (there could be a river
of souls running through us). If we were truly our souls, then our identity could
conceivably be changing from moment to moment (with the arrival of each new
soul). But then we simply don't—and couldn't—judge identity in terms of souls
at all; indeed, souls are irrelevant to our identity, and so couldn't provide the
relevant mechanism to give Weirob a reason to anticipate the afterlife.

In the second night of the dialogue, excerpted here, Miller and Cohen try to
convince Weirob of a different theory of identity, one fashioned on John Locke's
memory theory, articulated in the previous reading selection. Miller begins by
admitting the failure of the soul theory with respect to reidentification, but he goes on
to identify a similar problem with Weirob's own body theory. He then proposes a new
theory that avoids these problems and allows for the possibility of immortality: It's
possible that God could create someone in the afterlife who remembers Weirob's
thoughts and experiences, and if that were the case, this person would be her. Weirob

*offers several objections as well to this theory and the various refinements of it Miller and Cohen attempt. As you read, try to figure out whether her objections succeed in undermining this theory as a possible mechanism to the afterlife.*

*Finally, in the Third Night, after having given up on the possibility of immortality, the dialogue participants discuss the nature of ordinary identity across time: Does it consist in bodies or brains? After much vigorous discussion, but before they resolve the issues, Weirob dies.*

# THE SECOND NIGHT

WEIROB: Well, Sam, have you figured out a way to make sense of the identity of immaterial souls?

MILLER: No, I have decided it was a mistake to build my argument on such a dubious notion.

WEIROB: Have you then given up on survival? I think such a position would be a hard one for a clergyman to live with, and would feel bad about having pushed you so far.

MILLER: Don't worry. I'm more convinced than ever. I stayed up late last night thinking and reading, and I'm sure I can convince you now.

WEIROB: Get with it, time is running out.

MILLER: First, let me explain why, independently of my desire to defend survival after death, I am dissatisfied with your view that personal identity is just bodily identity. My argument will be very similar to the one you used to convince me that personal identity could not be identified with identity of an immaterial soul.

Consider a person waking up tomorrow morning, conscious, but not yet ready to open her eyes and look around and, so to speak, let the new day officially begin.

WEIROB: Such a state is familiar enough, I admit.

MILLER: Now couldn't such a person tell who she was? That is, even before opening her eyes and looking around, and in particular before looking at her body or making any judgments about it, wouldn't she be able to say who she was? Surely most of us, in the morning, know who we are before opening our eyes and recognizing our own bodies, do we not?

WEIROB: You seem to be right about that.

MILLER: But such a judgment as this person makes—we shall suppose she judges "I am Gretchen Weirob"—is a judgment of personal identity. Suppose she says to herself, "I am the very person who was arguing with Sam Miller last night." This is clearly a statement about her identity with someone who was alive the night before. And she could make this judgment without examining her body at all. You could have made just this judgment this morning, before opening your eyes.

WEIROB: Well, in fact I did so. I remembered our conversation of last night and said to myself, "Could I be the rude person who was so hard on Sam Miller's attempts to comfort me?" And, of course, my answer was that I not only could be but was that very rude person.

MILLER: But then by the same principle you used last night personal identity cannot be bodily identity. For you said that it could not be identity of immaterial soul because we were not judging as to identity of immaterial soul when we judge as to personal identity. But by the same token, as my example shows, we are not judging as to bodily identity when we judge as to personal identity. For we can judge who we are, and that we are the very person who did such and such and so and so, without having to make any judgments at all about the body. So, personal identity, while it may not consist of identity of an immaterial soul, does not consist in identity of material body either.

WEIROB: I did argue as you remember. But I also said that the notion of the identity of an immaterial unobservable unextended soul seemed to make no sense at all. This is one reason that cannot be what we are judging about, when we judge as to personal identity. Bodily identity at least makes sense. Perhaps we are assuming sameness of body, without looking.

MILLER: Granted. But you do admit that we do not in our own cases actually need to make a judgment of bodily identity in order to make a judgment of personal identity?

WEIROB: I don't think I will admit it. I will let it pass, so that we may proceed.

MILLER: Okay. Now it seems to me we are even able to imagine awakening and finding ourselves to have a *different* body than the one we had before. Suppose yourself just as I have described you. And now suppose you finally open your eyes and see, not the body you have grown so familiar with over the years, but one of a fundamentally different shape and size.

WEIROB: Well, I should suppose I had been asleep for a very long time and lost a lot of weight—perhaps I was in a coma for a year or so.

MILLER: But isn't it at least conceivable that it should not be your old body at all? I seem to be able to imagine awakening with a totally new body.

WEIROB: And how would you suppose that this came about?

MILLER: That's beside the point. I'm not saying I can imagine a procedure that would bring this about. I'm saying I can imagine it happening to me. In Kafka's *Metamorphosis,* someone awakens as a cockroach. I can't imagine what would make this happen to me or anyone else, but I can imagine awakening with the body of a cockroach. It is incredible that it should happen—that I do not deny. I simply mean I can imagine experiencing it. It doesn't seem contradictory or incoherent, simply unlikely and inexplicable.

WEIROB: So, if I admit this can be imagined, what follows then?

MILLER: Well, I think it follows that personal identity does not just amount to bodily identity. For I would not, finding that I had a new body, conclude that I was not the very same person I was before. I would be the same *person*, though I did not have the same *body*. So we would have identity of person but not identity of body. So personal identity cannot just amount to bodily identity.

WEIROB: Well suppose—and I emphasize *suppose*—I grant you all of this. Where does it leave you? What do you claim I have recognized as the same, if not my body and not my immaterial soul?

MILLER: I don't claim that you have recognized anything as the same, except the person involved, that is, you yourself.

WEIROB: I'm not sure what you mean.

MILLER: . . . Suppose I take a visitor to the stretch of river by the old Mill, and then drive him toward Manhattan. After an hour-or-so drive we see another stretch of river, and I say, "That's the same river we saw this morning." . . . I don't thereby imply that the very same molecules of water are seen both times. And the places are different, perhaps a hundred miles apart. And the shape and color and level of pollution might all be different. What do I see later in the day that is identical with what I saw earlier in the day?

WEIROB: Nothing except the river itself.

MILLER: Exactly. But now notice that what I see, strictly speaking, is not the whole river but only a part of it. I see different parts of the same river at the two different times. So really, if we restrict ourselves to what I literally see, I do not judge identity at all, but something else.

WEIROB: And what might that be?

MILLER: In saying that the river seen earlier, and the river seen later, are one and the same river, do I mean any more than that the stretch of water seen later and that stretch of water seen earlier are connected by other stretches of water?

WEIROB: That's about right. If the stretches of water are so connected there is but one river of which they are both parts.

MILLER: Yes, that's what I mean. The statement of identity, "This river is the same one we saw this morning," is in a sense about rivers. But in a way it is also about stretches of water or river parts.

WEIROB: So is all of this something special about rivers?

MILLER: Not at all. It is a recurring pattern. After all, we constantly deal with objects extended in space and time. But we are seldom aware of the objects as a whole, but only of their parts or stretches of their histories. When a statement of identity is not just something trivial, like "This bed is this bed," it is usually because we are really judging that different parts fit together, in some appropriate pattern, into a certain kind of whole.

WEIROB: I'm not sure I see just what you mean yet.

MILLER: Let me give you another example. Suppose we are sitting together watching the first game of a double-header. You ask me, "Is this game identical with this game?" This is a perfectly stupid question, though, of course, strictly speaking it makes sense and the answer is "yes."

But now suppose you leave in the sixth inning to go for hot dogs. You are delayed, and return after about forty-five minutes or so. You ask, "Is this the same game I was watching?" Now your question is not stupid, but perfectly appropriate.

WEIROB: Because the first game might still be going on or it might have ended, and the second game begun, by the time I return.

MILLER: Exactly. Which is to say somehow different parts of the game—different innings, or at least different plays—were somehow involved in your question. That's why it wasn't stupid or trivial but significant.

WEIROB: So, you think that judgments as to the identity of an object of a certain kind—rivers or baseball games or whatever—involve judgments as to the *parts* of those things being connected in a certain way, and are significant only when different parts are involved. Is that your point?

MILLER: Yes, and I think it is an important one. How foolish it would be, when we ask a question about the identity of baseball games, to look for something *else,* other than the game as a whole, which had to be the same. It could be the same game, even if different players were involved. It could be the same game, even if it had been moved to a different field. These other things, the innings, the plays, the players, the field, don't have to be the same at the different times for the game to be the same, they just have to be related in certain ways so as to make that complex whole we call a single game.

WEIROB: You think we were going off on a kind of a wild-goose chase when we asked whether it was the identity of soul or body that was involved in the identity of persons?

MILLER: Yes. The answer I should now give is neither. We are wondering about the identity of the person. Of course, if by "soul" we just mean "person," there is no problem. But if we mean, as I did yesterday, some other thing whose identity is already understood, which has to be the same when persons are the same, we are just fooling ourselves with words.

WEIROB: With rivers and baseball games, I can see that they are made up of parts connected in a certain way. The connection is, of course, different in the two cases, as is the sort of "part" involved. River parts must be connected physically with other river parts to form a continuous whole. Baseball innings must be connected so that the score, batting order, and the like are carried over from the earlier inning to the later one according to the rules. Is there something analagous we are to say about persons?

MILLER: Writers who concern themselves with this speak of "person-stages." That is just a stretch of consciousness, such as you and I are aware of now. I am aware of a flow of thoughts and feelings that are mine, you are aware of yours. A person is just a whole composed of such stretches as parts, not some substance that underlies them, as I thought yesterday, and not the body in which they occur, as you seem to think. That is the conception of a person I wish to defend today.

WEIROB:  So when I awoke and said to myself, "I am the one who was so rude to Sam Miller last night," I was judging that a certain stretch of consciousness I was then aware of, and an earlier one I remembered having been aware of, form a single whole of the appropriate sort—a single stream of consciousness, we might say.

MILLER:  Yes, that's it exactly. You need not worry about whether the same immaterial soul is involved, or even whether that makes sense. Nor need you worry about whether the same body is involved, as indeed you do not since you don't even have to open your eyes and look. Identity is not, so to speak, something under the person-stages, nor in something they are attached to, but something you build from them.

    Now survival, you can plainly see, is no problem at all once we have this conception of personal identity. All you need suppose is that there is, in Heaven, a conscious being, and that the person-stages that make her up are in the appropriate relation to those that now make you up, so that they are parts of the same whole—namely, you. If so, you have survived. So will you admit now that survival is at least possible?

WEIROB:  Hold on, hold on. Comforting me is not that easy. You will have to show that it is possible that these person-stages or stretches of consciousness be related in the appropriate way. And to do that, won't you have to tell me what that way is?

MILLER:  Yes, of course. I was getting ahead of myself. It is right at this point that my reading was particularly helpful. In a chapter of his *Essay On Human Understanding* Locke discusses this very question. He suggests that the relation between two person-stages or stretches of consciousness that makes them stages of a single person is just that the later one contains memories of the earlier one. He doesn't say this in so many words—he talks of "extending our consciousness back in time." But he seems to be thinking of memory.

WEIROB:  So, any past thought or feeling or intention or desire that I can remember having is mine?

MILLER:  That's right. I can remember only my own past thoughts and feelings, and you only yours. Of course, everyone would readily admit that. Locke's insight is to take this relation as the source of identity and not just its consequence. To remember—or more plausibly, to be able to remember—the thoughts and feelings of a person who was conscious in the past is just what it is to be that person.

    Now you can easily see that this solves the problem of the possibility of survival. As I was saying, all you need to do is imagine someone at some future time, not on this earth and not with your present thoughts and feelings, remembering the very conversation we are having now. This does not require sameness of anything else, but it amounts to sameness of person. So, now will you admit it?

WEIROB:  No, I don't.

MILLER:  Well, what's the problem now?

WEIROB: I admit that if I remember having a certain thought or feeling had by some person in the past, then I must indeed be that person. Though I can remember watching others think, I cannot remember their thinking, any more than I can experience it at the time it occurs if it is theirs and not mine. This is the kernel of Locke's idea, and I don't see that I could deny it.

But we must distinguish—as I'm sure you will agree—between *actually* remembering and merely *seeming* to remember. Many men who think that they are Napoleon claim to remember losing the battle of Waterloo. We may suppose them to be sincere, and to really seem to remember it. But they do not actually remember because they were not at the battle and are not Napoleon.

MILLER: Of course I admit that we must distinguish between actually remembering and only seeming to.

WEIROB: And you will admit too, I trust, that the thought of some person at some far place and some distant time seeming to remember this conversation I am having with you would not give me the sort of comfort that the prospect of survival is supposed to provide. I would have no reason to anticipate future experiences of this person, simply because she is to *seem* to remember my experiences. The experiences of such a deluded imposter are not ones I can look forward to having.

MILLER: I agree.

WEIROB: So the mere possibility of someone in the future seeming to remember this conversation does not show the possibility of my surviving. Only the possibility of someone actually remembering this conversation—or, to be precise, the experiences I am having—would show that.

MILLER: Of course. But what are you driving at? Where is the problem? I can imagine someone being deluded, but also someone actually being you and remembering your present thoughts.

WEIROB: But, what's the difference? How do you know *which* of the two you are imagining, and *what* you have shown possible?

MILLER: Well, I just imagine the one and not the other. I don't see the force of your argument.

WEIROB: Let me try to make it clear with another example. Imagine two persons. One is talking to you, saying certain words, having certain thoughts, and so forth. The other is not talking to you at all, but is in the next room being hypnotized. The hypnotist gives to this person a post-hypnotic suggestion that upon awakening he will remember having had certain thoughts and having uttered certain words to you. The thoughts and words he mentions happen to be just the thoughts and words which the first person actually thinks and says. Do you understand the situation?

MILLER: Yes, continue.

WEIROB: Now, in a while, both of the people are saying sentences which begin, "I remember saying to Sam Miller . . ." and "I remember thinking as I talked to Sam Miller . . ." And they both report remembering just the same thoughts and utterances. One of these will be remembering and the other only seeming to remember, right?

MILLER: Of course.

WEIROB: Now which one is *actually* remembering?

MILLER: Why, the very one who was in the room talking to me, of course. The other one is just under the influence of the suggestion made by the hypnotist and not remembering talking to me at all.

WEIROB: Now you agree that the difference between them does not consist in the content of what they are now thinking or saying.

MILLER: Agreed. The difference is in the relation to the past thinking and speaking. In the one case the relation of memory obtains. In the other, it does not.

WEIROB: But they both satisfy part of the conditions of remembering, for they both *seem to remember.* So there must be some further condition that the one satisfies and the other does not. I am trying to get you to say what that further condition is.

MILLER: Well, I said that the one who had been in this room talking would be remembering.

WEIROB: In other words, given two putative rememberers of some past thought or action, the real rememberer is the one who, in addition to seeming to remember the past thought or action, actually thought it or did it.

MILLER: Yes.

WEIROB: That is to say, the one who is identical with the person who did the past thinking and uttering.

MILLER: Yes, I admit it.

WEIROB: So, your argument just amounts to this. Survival is possible, because imaginable. It is imaginable, because my identity with some Heavenly person is imaginable. To imagine it, we imagine a person in Heaven who, first, seems to remember my thoughts and actions, and second, is me.

Surely, there could hardly be a tighter circle. If I have doubts that the Heavenly person is me, I will have doubts as to whether she is really remembering or only seeming to. No one could doubt the possibility of some future person who, after death, seemed to remember the things he thought and did. But that possibility does not resolve the issue about the possibility of survival. Only the possibility of someone *actually* remembering could do that—for that, as we agree, is sufficient for identity. But doubts about survival and identity simply go over without remainder into doubts about whether the memories would be actual or merely apparent. You guarantee me no more than the possibility of a deluded Heavenly imposter.

COHEN: But wait, Gretchen. I think Sam was less than fair to his own idea just now.

WEIROB: You think you can break out of the circle of using real memory to explain identity, and identity to mark the difference between real and apparent memory? Feel free to try.

COHEN: Let us return to your case of the hypnotist. You point out that we have two putative rememberers. You ask what marks the difference, and claim the answer must be the circular one that the real rememberer is the person who actually had the experiences both seem to remember.

But that is not the only possible answer. The experiences themselves cause the later apparent memories in the one case, while the hypnotist causes them in the other. We can say that the rememberer is the one of the two whose memories were *caused in the right* way by the earlier experiences. We thus distinguish between the rememberer and the hypnotic subject, without appeal to identity. . . .

WEIROB: You analyze personal identity into memory, and memory into apparent memory which is caused in the right way. A person is a certain sort of causal process.

COHEN: Right.

WEIROB: Suppose now for the sake of argument I accept this. How does it help Sam in his defense of the possibility of survival? In ordinary memory, the causal chain from remembered event to memory of it never leads us outside the confines of a single body. Indeed, the normal process of which you speak surely involves storage of information somehow in the brain. How can the states of my brain, when I die, influence in the appropriate way the apparent memories of the Heavenly person Sam takes to be me?

COHEN: Well, I didn't intend to be defending the possibility of survival. That is Sam's problem. I just like the idea that personal identity can be explained in terms of memory, and not just in terms of identity of the body.

MILLER: But surely, this does provide me with the basis for further defense. Your challenge, Gretchen, was to explain the difference between two persons in Heaven, one who actually remembers your experience—and so is you—and one who simply seems to remember it. But can I not just say that the one who is you is the one whose states were caused in the appropriate way? I do not mean the way they would be in a normal case of earthly memory. But in the case of the Heavenly being who is you, God would have created her with the brain states (or whatever) she has *because* you had the ones you had at death. Surely it is not the exact form of the dependence of my later memories on my earlier perceptions that makes them really memories, but the fact that the process involved has preserved information.

WEIROB: So if God creates a Heavenly person, designing her brain to duplicate the brain I have upon death, that person is me. If, on the other hand, a Heavenly being should come to be with those very same memory-like states by accident (if there are accidents in Heaven) it would not be me.

MILLER: Exactly. Are you satisfied now that survival makes perfectly good sense?

WEIROB: No, I'm still quite unconvinced.

The problem I see is this. If God could create one person in Heaven, and by designing her after me, make her me, why could he not make two such bodies, and cause this transfer of information into both of them? Would both of these Heavenly persons then be me? It seems as clear as anything in philosophy that from

A is B

and

C is B

where by "is" we mean identity, we can infer,

A is C.

So, if each of these Heavenly persons is me, they must be each other. But then they are not two but one. But my assumption was that God creates two, not one. He could create them physically distinct, capable of independent movement, perhaps in widely separated Heavenly locations, each with her own duties to perform, her own circle of Heavenly friends, and the like.

So either God, by creating a Heavenly person with a brain modeled after mine, does not really create someone identical with me but merely someone similar to me, or God is somehow limited to making only one such being. I can see no reason why, if there were a God, He should be so limited. So I take the first option. He could create someone similar to me, but not someone who would *be* me. Either your analysis of memory is wrong, and such a being does not, after all, remember what I am doing or saying, or memory is not sufficient for personal identity. Your theory has gone wrong somewhere, for it leads to absurdity.

COHEN: But wait. Why can't Sam simply say that if God makes one such creature, she is you, while if he makes more, none of them is you? It's possible that he makes only one. So it's possible that you survive. Sam always meant to allow that it's *possible* that you won't survive. He had in mind the case in which there is no God to make the appropriate Heavenly persons, or God exists, but doesn't make even one. You have simply shown that there is another way of not surviving. Instead of making too few Heavenly rememberers, He makes too many. So what? He might make the right number, and then you would survive.

WEIROB: Your remarks really amount to a change in your position. Now you are not claiming that memory alone is enough for personal identity. Now, it is memory *plus* lack of competition, the absence of other rememberers, that is needed for personal identity.

COHEN: It does amount to a change of position. But what of it? Is there anything untenable about the position as changed?

WEIROB: Let's look at this from the point of view of the Heavenly person. She says to herself, "Oh, I must be Gretchen Weirob, for I remember doing what she did and saying what she said." But now that's a pretty tenuous conclusion, isn't it? She is really only entitled to say, "Oh, either I'm Gretchen Weirob, or God has created more than one being like me, and none of us is." Identity has become something dependent on things wholly extrinsic to her. Who she is now turns on not just her states of mind and their relation to my states of mind, but on the existence or nonexistence of other people. Is this really what you want to maintain?

Or look at it from my point of view. God creates one of me in Heaven. Surely I should be glad if convinced this was to happen. Now he creates another, and I should despair again, for this means I won't survive after all. How can doubling a good deed make it worthless?

COHEN: Are you saying that there is some contradiction in my suggestion that only creation of a unique Heavenly Gretchen counts as your survival?

WEIROB: No, it's not contradictory, as far as I can see. But it seems odd in a way that shows that something somewhere is wrong with your theory. Here is a certain relationship I have with a Heavenly person. There being such a person, to whom I am related in this way, is something that is of great importance to me, a source of comfort. It makes it appropriate for me to anticipate having her experiences, since she is just me. Why should my having that relation to another being destroy my relation to this one? You say because then I will not be identical with either of them. But since you have provided a theory about what that identity consists in, we can look and see what it amounts to for me to be or not to be identical. If she is to remember my experience, I can rightly anticipate hers. But then it seems the doubling makes no difference. And yet it must, for one cannot be identical with two. So you add, in a purely *ad hoc* manner, that her memory of me isn't enough to make my anticipation of her experiences appropriate, if there are two rather than one so linked. Isn't it more reasonable to conclude, since memory does not secure identity when there are two Heavenly Gretchens, it also doesn't when there is only one?

COHEN: There is something *ad hoc* about it, I admit. But perhaps that's just the way our concept works. You have not elicited a contradiction. . .

WEIROB: An infinite pile of absurdities has the same weight as a contradiction. And absurdities can be generated without limit from your account. Suppose God created this Heavenly person before I died. Then He in effect kills me; if He has already created her, then you really are not talking to whom you think, but someone new, created by Gretchen Weirob's strange death moments ago. Or suppose He first creates one being in Heaven, who is me. Then He creates another. Does the first cease to be me? If God can create such beings in Heaven, surely He can do so in Albuquerque. And there is nothing on your theory to favor this body before you as Gretchen Weirob's, over the one belonging to the person created in Albuquerque. So I am to suppose that if God were to do this, I would suddenly cease to be. I'm tempted to say I would cease to be Gretchen Weirob. But that would be a confused way of putting it. There would be here, in my place, a new person with false memories of having been Gretchen Weirob, who has just died of competition—a strange death if ever there was one. She would have no right to my name, my bank account, or the services of my doctor, who is paid from insurance premiums paid for by deductions from Gretchen Weirob's past salary. Surely this is nonsense; however carefully God should choose to duplicate me, in Heaven or in Albuquerque, I would not cease to be, or cease to be who I am. You may reply that God, being benevolent, would never create an extra Gretchen Weirob. But I do not say that he would, but only that if he did this would not, as your theory implies, mean that I cease to exist. Your theory gives the wrong answer in this possible circumstance, so it must be wrong. I think I have been given no motivation to abandon the most obvious and straightforward view on these matters. I am a live body, and when that body dies, my existence will be at an end.

## FOOTNOTES

The arguments against the view that personal identity consists in bodily identity are also suggested by Locke, as is the theory that memory is crucial. The argument that the memory theory is circular was made by Joseph Butler in "Of Personal Identity," an Appendix to his *Analogy of Religion,* first published in 1736. Locke's memory theory has been developed by a number of modern authors, including H.P. Grice, A.M. Quinton and, in a different direction, Sydney Shoemaker. The possibility of circumventing Butler's charge of circularity by an appeal to causation is noted by Shoemaker in his article "Persons and Their Pasts" *(American Philosophical Quarterly,* 1970) and by David Wiggins in *Identity and Spatial Temporal Continuity.* The "duplication argument" was apparently first used by the eighteenth-century freethinker, Antony Collins. Collins assumed that something like Locke's theory of personal identity was correct, and used the duplication argument to raise problems for the doctrine of immortality.

## READING COMPREHENSION QUESTIONS

1. A baseball doubleheader is two baseball games, played back to back (with just a short break in between). Describe Miller's doubleheader example, and explain in detail the point of the case.

2. How does Miller's talk of Kafka's *The Metamorphosis* support the claim that no souls or bodies are involved in personal identity? What *is* the Lockean criterion of identity he offers toward the beginning of the "Second Night"?

3. In answering Weirob's question of how one might distinguish between actually remembering and only seeming to, Miller suggests that the one who actually remembers some past experience is just the person who actually *experienced* the thing he now remembers. Weirob complains that this answer "could hardly be a tighter circle." Explain why she thinks this answer begs the question (is circular).

4. Cohen tries to save Miller's view by talking about actual memories being "caused in the right way." How does this save Miller's view from circularity, and what is Weirob's "duplication" worry in response?

5.  As a last ditch effort to save the memory criterion toward the end of the "Second Night," Cohen suggests that, as long as God just makes one person in heaven who remembers Weirob's life (and her memories were caused in the right way), then that would be sufficient for her to survive. Weirob ridicules this idea. How so? Do you think her response is a good one? Why or why not?

# 6

# The Unimportance of Identity

### DEREK PARFIT

*Derek Parfit (born 1942) is a Senior Research Fellow at All Souls College in Oxford. He has written many influential works on personal identity and ethics, including the 1984 book* Reasons and Persons. *In this selection, Parfit argues that, when it comes to caring about my future, say, it matters far less that it's* my *future—that that future person will be me—than it does that that future person will be related to me in the right way psychologically. He argues for this point by means of a famous case, fission, wherein each half of my brain is transplanted into a different body that is just like mine. What would happen to me? Parfit argues that I would not survive fission, but that everything that* matters *would survive, in which case personal identity just isn't important to the things that matter in our lives.*

Personal identity is widely thought to have great rational and moral significance. Thus it is the fact of identity which is thought to give us our reason for concern about our own future. And several moral principles, such as those of desert or distributive justice, presuppose claims about identity. The separateness of persons, or the non-identity of different people, has been called "the basic fact for morals."

I can comment here on only one of these questions: what matters in our survival. I mean by that, not what makes our survival good, but what makes our survival matter, whether it will be good or bad. What is it, in our survival, that gives us a reason for special anticipatory or prudential concern? . . .

Most of us believe that we should care about our future because it will be *our* future. I believe that what matters is not identity but certain other relations. To help us to decide between these views, we should consider cases where identity and those relations do not coincide.

SOURCE: From *Identity*, edited by Henry Harris. Copyright © 1995 by the Board of Management of the Herbert Spencer Lectureship. Used by permission.

Which these cases are depends on which criterion of identity we accept. I shall start with the simplest form of the Physical Criterion, according to which a person continues to exist if and only if that person's body continues to exist. That must be the view of those who believe that persons just are bodies. And it is the view of several of the people who identify persons with human beings. Let's call this the *Bodily Criterion.*

Suppose that, because of damage to my spine, I have become partly paralysed. I have a brother, who is dying of a brain disease. With the aid of new techniques, when my brother's brain ceases to function, my head could be grafted onto the rest of my brother's body. Since we are identical twins, my brain would then control a body that is just like mine, except that it would not be paralysed.

Should I accept this operation? Of those who assume that identity is what matters, three groups would answer No. Some accept the Bodily Criterion. These people believe that, if this operation were performed, I would die. The person with my head tomorrow would be my brother, who would mistakenly think that he was me. Other people are uncertain what would happen. They believe that it would be risky to accept this operation, since the resulting person might not be me. Others give a different reason why I should reject this operation: that it would be indeterminate whether that person would be me. On all these views, it matters who that person would be.

On my view, that question is unimportant. If this operation were performed, the person with my head tomorrow would not only believe that he was me, seem to remember living my life, and be in every other way psychologically like me. These facts would also have their normal cause, the continued existence of my brain. And this person's body would be just like mine. For all these reasons, his life would be just like the life that I would have lived, if my paralysis had been cured. I believe that, given these facts, I should accept this operation. It is irrelevant whether this person would be me.

That may seem all important. After all, if he would not be me, I shall have ceased to exist. But, if that person would not be me, this fact would just consist in another fact. It would just consist in the fact that my body will have been replaced below the neck. When considered on its own, is that second fact important? Can it matter in itself that the blood that will keep my brain alive will circulate, not through my own heart and lungs, but through my brother's heart and lungs? Can it matter in itself that my brain will control, not the rest of my body, but the rest of another body that is exactly similar?. . .

According to my argument, we should now conclulde that neither of these facts could matter greatly. Since it would not be in itself important that my head would be grafted onto this body, and that would be all there was to the fact that the resulting person would not be me, it would not be in itself important that this person would not be me. Perhaps it would not be irrational to regret these facts a little. But, I believe, they would be heavily outweighed by the fact that, unlike me, the resulting person would not be paralysed. . . .

On my view, what matters is what is going to happen. If I knew that my head could be grafted onto the rest of a body that is just like mine, and that the resulting person would be just like me, I need not ask whether the resulting person could be correctly called me. That is not a further difference in what is going to happen. . . .

It may now be objected: "By choosing this example, you are cheating. Of course you should accept this operation. But that is because the resulting person *would* be you. We should reject the Bodily Criterion. So this case cannot show that identity is not what matters."

Since there are people who accept this criterion, I am not cheating. It is worth trying to show these people that identity is not what matters. But I accept part of this objection. I agree that we should reject the Bodily Criterion. . . .

I am now assuming that we accept the Brain-Based Psychological Criterion. We believe that, if there will be one future person who will have enough of my brain to be psychologically continuous with me, that person would be me. On this view, there is another way to argue that identity is not what matters.

We can first note that, just as I could survive with less than my whole body, I could survive with less than my whole brain. People have survived, and with little psychological change, even when, through a stroke or injury, they have lost the use of half their brain.

Let us next suppose that the two halves of my brain could each fully support ordinary psychological functioning. That may in fact be true of certain people. If it is not, we can suppose that, through some technological advance, it has been made true of me. Since our aim is to test our beliefs about what matters, there is no harm in making such assumptions.

We can now compare two more possible operations. In the first, after half my brain is destroyed, the other half would be successfully transplanted into the empty skull of a body that is just like mine. Given our assumptions, we should conclude that, here too, I would survive. Since I would survive if my brain were transplanted, and I would survive with only half my brain, it would be unreasonable to deny that I would survive if that remaining half were transplanted. So, in this *Single Case,* the resulting person would be me.

Consider next the *Double Case,* or *My Division.* Both halves of my brain would be successfully transplanted, into different bodies that are just like mine. Two people would wake up, each of whom has half my brain, and is, both physically and psychologically, just like me.

Since these would be two different people, it cannot be true that each of them is me. That would be a contradiction. If each of them was me, each would be one and the same person: me. So they could not be two different people.

Could it be true that only one of them is me? That is not a contradiction. But, since I have the same relation to each of these people, there is nothing that could make me one of them rather than the other. It cannot be true, of either of these people, that he is the one who could be correctly called me.

How should I regard these two operations? Would they preserve what matters in survival? In the Single Case, the one resulting person would be me. The relation between me now and that future person is just an instance of the relation between me now and myself tomorrow. So that relation would contain what matters. In the Double Case, my relation to that person would be just the same. So this relation must still contain what matters. Nothing is missing. But that person cannot here be claimed to be me. So identity cannot be what matters.

We may object that, if that person isn't me, something *is* missing. *I'm* missing. That may seem to make all the difference. How can everything still be there if *I'm* not there?

Everything is still there. The fact that I'm not there is not a real absence. The relation between me now and that future person is in itself the same. As in the Single Case, he has half my brain, and he is just like me. The difference is only that, in this Double Case, I also have the same relation to the other resulting person. Why am I not there? The explanation is only this. When this relation holds between me now and a single person in the future, we can be called one and the same person. When this relation holds between me now and *two* future people, I cannot be called one and the same as each of these people. But that is not a difference in the nature or the content of this relation. In the Single Case, where half my brain will be successfully transplanted, my prospect is survival. That prospect contains what matters. In the Double Case, where both halves will be successfully transplanted, nothing would be lost.

It can be hard to believe that identity is not what matters. But that is easier to accept when we see why, in this example, it is true. It may help to consider this analogy. Imagine a community of persons who are like us, but with two exceptions. First, because of facts about their reproductive system, each couple has only two children, who are always twins. Second, because of special features of their psychology, it is of great importance for the development of each child that it should not, through the death of its sibling, become an only child. Such children suffer psychological damage. It is thus believed, in this community, that it matters greatly that each child should have a twin.

Now suppose that, because of some biological change, some of the children in this community start to be born as triplets. Should their parents think this a disaster, because these children don't have twins? Clearly not. These children don't have twins only because they each have *two* siblings. Since each child has two siblings, the trio must be called, not twins, but triplets. But none of them will suffer damage as an only child. These people should revise their view. What matters isn't having a twin: it is having at least one sibling.

In the same way, we should revise our view about identity over time. What matters isn't that there will be someone alive who will be me. It is rather that there will be at least one living person who will be psychologically continuous with me as I am now, and/or who has enough of my brain. When there will be only one such person, he can be described as me. When there will be two such people, we cannot claim that each will be me. But that is as trivial as the fact that, if I had two identical siblings, they could not be called my twins.

If, as I have argued, personal identity is not what matters, we must ask what does matter. There are several possible answers. And, depending on our answer, there are several further implications. Thus there are several moral questions which I have no time even to mention. I shall end with another remark about our concern for our own future.

That concern is of several kinds. We may want to survive partly so that our hopes and ambitions will be achieved. We may also care about our future in the kind of way in which we care about the well-being of certain other people, such as our relatives or friends. But most of us have, in addition, a distinctive kind of egoistic concern. If I know that my child will be in pain, I may care about his pain more than I would about my own future pain. But I cannot fearfully anticipate my child's pain. And if I knew that my Replica would take up my life where I leave off, I would not look forward to that life.

This kind of concern may, I believe, be weakened, and be seen to have no ground, if we come to accept [my] view. In our thoughts about our own identity, we are prone to illusions. That is why the so-called "problem cases" seem to raise problems: why we find it hard to believe that, when we know the other facts, it is an empty or a merely verbal question whether we shall still exist. Even after we accept [my] view, we may continue, at some level, to think and feel as if that view were not true. Our own continued existence may still seem an independent fact, of a peculiarly deep and simple kind. And that belief may underlie our anticipatory concern about our own future. . . .

Even the use of the word "I" can lead us astray. Consider the fact that, in a few years, I shall be dead. This fact can seem depressing. But the reality is only this. After a certain time, none of the thoughts and experiences that occur will be directly causally related to this brain, or be connected in certain ways to these present experiences. That is all this fact involves. And, in that redescription, my death seems to disappear.

## READING COMPREHENSION QUESTIONS

1.  Parfit's article is about the reasons we have for caring about our own futures. What reasons do you take yourself to have for caring about, say, your retirement-age self? For example, should you put money into a retirement account for him/her? Why (especially given that he or she is likely to be very different from you-now by then)?

2.  Consider the first case Parfit gives, in which my head is transplanted onto the body of my twin brother. Normally we would think that, whether or not I should accept the operation depends on whether or not the resulting person would be me. Explain Parfit's argument against this view. Do you agree? Why or why not?

3.  In your own words, explain Parfit's reasoning in the *My Division* case for why neither resulting person would be me. Do you agree with this reasoning? Why or why not? Are there any other possible options on the identity of the survivors?

4.  Explain how Parfit uses the *My Division* case to argue for the unimportance of identity. Do you agree with this argument? Why or why not?

5.  Does Parfit's position have any implication for the question of whether or not we can survive the deaths of our bodies? In other words, suppose Parfit is right that identity is unimportant for anticipation and self-concern: would it be possible for what *does* matter to survive our deaths? If so, would this be a satisfactory form of immortality?

# 3

# The Mind-Body Problem

## MOTIVATION

Suppose, as you are reading this chapter, that you are eating a banana. The banana has a certain taste—there is something it is like to taste a banana—it's got that distinctive banana flavor. Perhaps as you arc eating, you also have a craving for peanut butter to go with the banana. Suppose you believe that there is some in the kitchen, so you put down this book, walk from your bedroom to the kitchen, and look for the jar of peanut butter. You find the jar, spread some peanut butter on the banana, and take a bite. You see by the clock in the kitchen that it is almost time to leave for class, so you begin to look for your books, remembering that you left one of them in the car. You grab your books and a coat, and off you go.

The taste and smell of the banana, the craving for peanut butter, the belief that there is a jar of peanut butter in a certain place, the visual experiences you have as you look at the clock, the memory of having left the book in the car—all of these experiences and thoughts are part of one's conscious mental life. Some of these mental goings-on—like craving peanut butter and believing that there is some in the kitchen—lead you to engage in certain sorts of outward behavior, such as going to the kitchen. If asked to explain why you went to the kitchen, you would refer to the relevant parts of your mental life—in this case, your craving and your belief. Mental states and events seemingly cause the outward physical behavior that we can see. When you lift your head so that you can see the clock, the light waves bouncing off the clock impinge on the retinas of your eyes, setting up a complex physical process in the brain. The result is that you undergo or have a visual experience. Physical events in one's environment as well as physical events in the brain and central nervous system seem to cause mental events—for example, the visual experience of the clock.

All of this is familiar, a part of commonsense thinking. But it is also very puzzling when one stops to think about it. Consider for a moment the experience of tasting a banana. When you bite down on the banana and part of it comes into contact with your tongue, a certain series of physical events is triggered that lead to a particular sensation—something that is yours that you alone experience. But how in the world can some physical chain of events lead to a conscious experience? Indeed, how can consciousness result from the activity of a physical organ that is itself composed of billions of mindless cells? This is one way of posing the central philosophical puzzle about the mind that is known as the *mind-body problem.*

As we shall see, philosophers and other thinkers have proposed a variety of solutions to this problem. According to one proposal, one's mind is a kind of spiritual substance that is utterly different from, but still interacts with, one's physical body. Other proposals claim that the mind just is the brain. How to think about mind and body is central to how we understand ourselves. But this issue is not only theoretically interesting; it has great practical significance too. After all, if the mind is not a spiritual substance, then presumably one cannot survive one's physical death. So the issues of personal identity and immortality, featured in Chapter 2, are deeply intertwined with the mind-body issue.

But before getting into the various theories that address the mind-body problem, let's dwell on the problem a bit more to get a deeper feel for it.

## THE MIND-BODY PROBLEM

The mind-body problem addresses the following sets of questions:

- What is the nature of the mind? Or, if what we call the mind is just a collection of mental states and processes, what is the nature of such states and processes?

- How is the mind—or how are mental states and processes—related to the physical body and its states and processes? In particular, how is the mind, or how are mental states and processes, related to the brain and its states and processes?

The reason for calling the mind-body problem a *problem* and the reason these questions have proven very difficult to answer is that there are facts about our mental lives that make it hard to understand how the mind is or even can be related to the brain—a physical organ. To appreciate the depth of this problem, consider some fundamental aspects of mentality.[1]

First, there is the spectacular fact that one is conscious for much of one's life, having all sorts of experiences associated with one's five senses as well as experiencing pleasure on some occasions and pain on others, remembering things, thinking about things, making plans, and so on. The point about being conscious is often brought out by observing that many if not all experiences have qualitative what-it-is-likeness to them, sometimes referred to as **qualia**. There is something

---

[1]The following discussion follows the discussion of the mind-body problem in the article by John R. Searle included in our readings.

it is like to see red that is different from what it is like to see blue. We've already mentioned the taste and smell of a banana. The same may be said about experiences associated with the other three sense modalities. And, of course, bodily sensations such as pain have a what-it-is-likeness; more precisely, there is something that it is like to experience a certain sort of pain. The pain one experiences from touching a hot stove is different from a pain in one's tooth. How could consciousness in general, and the qualitative character of particular mental states in particular, possibly be *just* a matter of brain matter and its activity—a bunch of neurons firing? Indeed, how could a bunch of neurons firing even *give rise* to conscious experience? Call this the problem of consciousness.

Second, human beings have beliefs, desires, hopes, fears, and other mental states that have what philosophers call **intentionality**—such states point to or refer to all sorts of things; they have *aboutness*. You probably believe that Boston is in Massachusetts. Your belief is a psychological attitude that has a certain *content*: it is about a particular city, a particular state, and a particular relation between them (the former being located within the latter). Such contents are referred to as *propositions*. Belief is one among many psychological attitudes that one can have in relation to some proposition. For instance, I might not believe *that a Democrat will be elected the next U.S. president*. But, suppose I hope so. Then my psychological attitude is one of hoping that is directed toward a proposition. Believing, desiring, hoping, fearing, considering, supposing—all of these are among the sorts of mental states whose contents have aboutness or intentionality. (Note that the term "intentionality," as used in this context, does not just refer to intentions, as when one intends to get up early in the morning. Rather, as noted, the term refers more broadly to such states as beliefs, hopes, fears, and so forth.)

But how could a bunch of neurons firing in one's brain be *about* anything? Those neurons aren't about anything; they don't refer to or represent anything. So how can a state of the brain have intentionality, or even give rise to something that does? The fact that mental states have intentionality makes it hard to suppose that they are brain states or any kind of physical state. And if they aren't, how can we understand their relation to brain states? Call this the problem of intentionality.

Third, conscious mental states are *subjective* in the sense that the ones you have cannot be experienced by anyone else; those experiences are yours and yours alone. Granted, other people can have experiences that are *like* yours: when I look at a red object, the subjective experience I have may be qualitatively like the one you have when you look at that same object from the same angle, under the same lighting conditions, and so forth. But neither of us can, as it were, get inside the other person's head and have *that person's* experiences. By contrast, events in the brain are open to public observation; a surgeon performing brain surgery can observe your brain, but in doing so, she will not be observing your experiences as you do from the inside. The upshot of these reflections is nicely summed up by Thomas Nagel: "If what happens in your experience is inside your mind in a way in which what happens in your brain is not, it looks as though your experiences and other mental states can't just be physical states of your brain."[2] Call this the problem of subjectivity.

_____

[2]Thomas Nagel, *What Does It All Mean?* Oxford: Oxford University Press, 1986, p. 30.

Fourth, as noted earlier, one ordinarily gives causal explanations of human behavior by appealing to such mental states as beliefs and desires. (Try explaining why it is that you are now reading this introduction.) But how can beliefs and desires—mental phenomena—cause anything? Presumably, one's belief that there is peanut butter in the kitchen, and one's desire to eat some right now, somehow conspire to cause certain brain activity that sets up a causal chain of physical events resulting in the bodily motion of walking to the kitchen. But now consider the initial pattern of physical brain events at the beginning of the series of physical events. There is a looming puzzle about mental causation that John Searle (one of our authors) nicely raises by asking: "Are we supposed to think that thoughts can wrap themselves around the axons or shake the dendrites or sneak inside the cell wall and attack the cell nucleus?" Call this the problem of mental causation.

What emerges from these reflections are the following points, each the source of a problem.

### The Problems of Mentality

- Human beings are conscious; they have all sorts of experiences that have a rich qualitative what-it-is-likeness to them. But how can brain states either be or result in conscious experience? The problem of consciousness.

- Human beings also have mental states with intentionality. But how can brain states either be or result in states that are about anything? The problem of intentionality.

- One's conscious mental states are marked by subjectivity. But how could it be that brain states, which are not marked by subjectivity, either are or give rise to states that are? The problem of subjectivity,

- Human behavior can be causally explained by appealing to mental states. But how can mental states have any causal effect on brain activity? The problem of mental causation.

The first three problems have to do with how brain activity can cause or give rise to mental activity. The fourth problem has to do with how mental activity can cause or give rise to brain activity. The source of both problems has to do with the apparent nature of physical, material bodies (brains) and the mental: *brain states and mental states appear to be very different in nature.*

The challenge posed by the mind-body problem, then, is to answer the two main questions about mentality mentioned at the outset of this section, and do so in a way that plausibly addresses the four problems just mentioned. Ideally, one would like a theory that addresses all problems in a way that accommodates the phenomena (consciousness, intentionality, subjectivity, and mental causation) that give rise to them. But doing so has proved hard to do. Let us see why, by taking a brief tour of some of the major theories of mind.

## SOME THEORIES OF MIND AND BODY

Most theories about mind and body can be usefully divided into two main camps: dualism and materialism. Within each camp, we find a variety of specific theories. In what follows, we consider some representative theories from both camps, as well as a theory that arguably belongs in neither.

## Dualism

According to **dualism**, the nature of the mind is something nonphysical, and so the mind is not a topic that is properly addressed by sciences such as physics or chemistry. Hence, the label "dualism"—human beings are composites of two very different sorts of things or states: mental states and physical states (also referred to as material states). Why be a dualist? Here are two reasons (there are others). First, according to many of the world's religions, human beings have an immortal soul that is understood to be a kind of spiritual substance. If believing in souls is required by one's religious outlook, then consistency demands belief in the mind as a spiritual substance. A second reason, available to anyone, is based on introspection. Just turn your thoughts inward and focus on the contents of your conscious experience. What is your visual experience like as you read these words? How about that humming sound coming from the person sitting next to you that sounds like "Whole Lot of Love"? Doesn't introspection reveal to us that such conscious mental states are *utterly* different in nature compared to physical bodies and their states? If you say "yes," then you are a mind-body dualist. But being a dualist leaves one with many options about the exact nature of the mind and its relation to the body. Here are some of the options.

**Substance dualism** is, as lately noted, deeply entrenched in many of the world's religions and is probably the view held by most people. The term *substance* here refers to the idea that there is an "object" or "thing"—the mind—and mental states and activities such as beliefs, desires, feelings, and thinking, are states and activities *of* the mind. So, on this picture of reality, there are two radically different kinds of things: on the one hand, there are physical objects composed of matter that are located in space and have such properties as weight and mass. On the other hand, there is "mind stuff" that is the home, as it were, of mental states and events—mental properties.

How are these two radically different sorts of substances related? According to the sixteenth-century French philosopher René Descartes, they causally interact: one's brain is capable of having causal effects on one's mind (or mental states occurring within it), and vice versa. This two-way interactionist dualist view, strongly associated with Descartes, is known as **Cartesian dualism**.

Descartes' view takes very seriously the source of the mind-body problem— the apparent very large difference between the mental and the physical. However, this view has particular trouble in addressing the problem of mental causation, because it seems utterly mysterious that something that is nonspatial can be in any sort of causal contact with something that is spatial. This mystery is perhaps somewhat overcome by **popular dualism**.[3] This species of substance dualism—a "ghost in a machine" view—locates the mind in space; your mind, on this view, is right there in your head, and (according to one speculation) it perhaps works by exchanging some sort of energy with parts of the brain and central nervous system. Of course, the sort of energy in question has not yet been discovered, so the mystery surrounding substance dualism awaits a solution.

---

[3]This is the label Paul Churchland gives to the view. See his *Matter and Consciousness*, 2nd ed., Cambridge, Mass: MIT Press, 1988, p. 9.

But postulating a substance—mind stuff—is not the only way to be a dualist, and perhaps being a substance dualist only adds to the mystery of how the mental is related to the physical. Instead of substance dualism, one might embrace **property dualism**. In this view humans are composed of one kind of stuff—physical stuff. However, this physical stuff—the brain in particular—possesses both physical properties and mental properties. One substance, two kinds of properties. As with substance dualism, one can distinguish varieties of property dualism.

**Interactionistic property dualism**, like its substance counterpart, is the view that events in the brain can cause mental events and states, and that mental events can cause states in the brain. Chemical activity in the brain caused by stubbing your toe in turn causes the pain you experience. The painful experience—the property of being in pain—causally initiates a chemical reaction in your brain that leads to your hopping around on one foot. Thus, two-way interaction between physical and mental properties. This view is defended by Curt Ducasse in Reading 8 in this chapter. By contrast, **epiphenomenalism** is a version of property dualism according to which physical brain events cause mental events; however, mental events are causally impotent—mere epiphenomena (from the Greek word "epi," meaning "above"). Think of a steam engine train giving off steam as it accelerates along the tracks. The position of the train at any one place and time can be completely causally explained by appealing to the workings of the engine and its physical environment. The steam is caused by the operation of the train, but it plays no causal role in the movement of the train; it is merely given off by the activity of the train's engine. According to the epiphenomenalist, mental events are like the steam: they are caused by physical events in the brain, but they are causally inefficacious. In short, on this view, your mind is just along for the ride.

Of course, these versions of property dualism have their share of problems, particularly concerning the problem of mental causation. Interactionistic property dualism, despite not postulating two kinds of substance, must still make sense of the causal connection between two sorts of very different kinds of properties. And, of course, the epiphenomenalist must claim that our commonsense belief in mental causation is just a massive illusion—a hard pill to swallow. When you have a craving for peanut butter and you believe that there is some nearby in the kitchen, isn't your walking to the kitchen caused by your craving and your belief?

## Materialism

The problems with dualism, together with increasing scientific knowledge of the brain and central nervous system, have led many philosophers and scientists to embrace some form of materialism. **Materialism** in this context (also called physicalism) is the view that human beings, as well as nonhuman animals with a mental life, are thoroughly material or physical beings. They are, in short, complicated physical beings, all of whose properties are physical: no special mental mind stuff, no special mental properties. As with dualism, there are many species of materialism. The two species that have had the most impact on philosophical thought about the mind-body problem are behaviorism and the identity theory. Because there are different versions of both species, we shall present particular versions of each type of view, mentioning some of the other versions as we proceed.

What is known as **philosophical** (or **logical**) **behaviorism** is primarily a view about the meaning (semantics) of mental terms (and the sentences in which they occur). According to this view, mental terms can be *defined* by terms that refer to behavior and dispositions to behave.[4] For instance, the sentence "Mary wants a Coke" is taken by the logical behaviorist to be equivalent in meaning to a set of "If,...then..." sentences such as: "If Mary is near a Coke machine with correct change, she will put money in the machine"; "If Mary has a Coke, she will drink it"; and so on. The important thing to notice is that the initial sentence about what Mary *wants* is being analyzed as equivalent in meaning to sentences that do not include any mental terms. Rather, all that the "If,...then..." sentences mention are stimuli (Mary's being near a Coke machine, Mary's having a Coke) and responses (Mary's putting money in the machine, Mary's drinking). This way of understanding mental talk is supposed to have implications for understanding what we are really talking about when we use mental terms or talk about the mind. According to the logical behaviorist, when we make statements using mental terms, we are referring not to some inner mental states or processes, but rather to complex dispositions to behave. Because behavior is taken to be a physical event that we can observe, this view is one way of defending a materialist picture of human beings.

Why be a philosophical behaviorist? One big motivator is that this view avoids the mysteries associated with all forms of dualism. At one time (in the 1950s), it seemed like the only way to not be a dualist. But two problems confront the logical behaviorist. One problem concerns the very possibility of being able to adequately define mental terms solely in terms of behavioral dispositions that make no mention of mental phenomena. This technical problem is discussed in our reading by Jerry Fodor. The other problem is more obvious: the philosophical behaviorist, rather than accommodating the various features of our mental lives described earlier, denies that there are any internal mental states having the various features in question. But this seems incredible! Try sticking yourself with a needle and see if you aren't convinced that you experience a pain—something that is an inner state of yourself. It seems, then, that instead of addressing the various problems associated with conscious experience, intentionality, subjectivity, and mental causation, the logical behaviorist claims that they are really pseudo-problems that can be set aside.

A less radical materialist view is the **central-state identity theory** (identity theory, for short), which claims that there are indeed internal mental states. But as the label suggests, in this view, mental states and events are identical to brain states and events. So, for instance (to take one of the favorite examples of identity theorists), not only is the property of being in pain *correlated* in human beings with the property of there being C-fiber firings in the brain, the mental property, pain, is **numerically** or, what is the same thing, **quantitatively identical**[5] with the

---

[4]Another kind of behaviorism, "radical behaviorism," associated with psychologist John B. Watson, is discussed by Jerry Fodor in the selection included in our readings.

[5]You may recall the distinction between quantitative or numerical identity and qualitative identity from the introduction to Chapter 2.

physical property of C fiber firing.[6] Thus, human beings are thoroughly physical, material beings, living in a material world. Sometimes this view is called **reductive materialism** for obvious reasons: the proposal is that mental states can be reduced to brain states.

Why be an identity theorist? Well, here are two reasons. First, if mind and body are really identical, then the problem of mental causation is apparently solved because the mental just is something physical. Another reason is the progress that has been made in neuroscience in coming to understand how certain brain processes associated with mental processes work. Of course, a property dualist grants that mental states and processes depend on brain states and processes, but the identity theorist has a simpler theory: physical stuff with physical properties. Why not go with the simpler of two theories unless there is some good reason to prefer the more complex one?

One objection often raised against the central-state identity theory is that in *identifying* mental properties with properties of the human brain, it fails to correctly characterize the nature of the mental. The point is perhaps best understood by considering functionalism—a theory of mind that many philosophers believe is an advance over the identity theory in how it understands the nature of the mental.

**Functionalism** is a view about the nature of the mind according to which the nature or essence of a mental state is its causal role in relation to (a) *environmental inputs to the body*, (b) *other mental states,* and (c) *behavioral outputs.* The standard example used to illustrate this view is pain (which makes a nice contrast to the pain C-fibers example mentioned by defenders of the identity theory). According to functionalism, pain is a state that (a) is typically caused by certain stimuli to the body such as stepping on a sharp object, (b) typically causes the person in pain to be in further mental states such as anguish and thinking that the foot must be attended to immediately, and (c) typically causes such outward behavior as crying out and wincing. The idea is that the essential nature of pain is its functional role in the system—something that is properly specified in terms of its various causal relations. The same is true for all mental states, according to the functionalist.

Notice that this account of the mental is somewhat like the account offered by the behaviorist in that there is reference to environmental stimuli and behavioral outputs in characterizing mental states. However, and crucially, the functionalist (unlike the behaviorist) also appeals to other *internal* mental states as part of the causal profile of any one mental state, and this makes it somewhat like the identity theory. However, while the identity theory *identifies* each type of mental state with some type of physical state, functionalism does not.

In order to get a better feel for the difference between the identity theory and functionalism, let's consider something whose nature has to do with its function rather than what it is made of. Consider a human heart, made up of various natural bodily tissues just like other bodily organs. What makes something a heart is

---

[6]The identity theory can be developed either as a theory about mental property types—called *type physicalism*, which is the view being described here—or as a theory about particular mental events—called *token physicalism*. The difference between the two and their comparative plausibility is described in the selection by Jerry Fodor.

not the stuff it's made of; otherwise, artificial hearts made of synthetic material would not be hearts. Bad news for so-called artificial heart patients! Clearly, the essential nature of a heart—what makes something a heart—is the function it performs in a body, not the type of material it's composed of. It would be a mistake, therefore, to *identify* the property of being a heart with the property of being made of natural bodily tissue. This idea of functional role as *essence* is what functionalism is all about.

Let's now return from this short digression about hearts and consider the difference between the identity theory and functionalism, and why many philosophers have rejected the former in favor of the latter.

Let's suppose that pain in humans is correlated with the firing of C-fibers. As explained a moment ago, the identity theorist claims that pain *just is* C-fiber firing—that these properties are numerically identical. But if so, then that means that without C-fibers firing in an organism, there is no pain. After all, how could there be pain without C-fiber firing if the two kinds of states are *identical*? But now consider a species of intelligent beings—let's make them Martians. Martians, we are supposing, have nearly the same mental lives as do we humans: they think, reason, feel pain, and all the rest. However, suppose also that Martians turn out to be made of very different physical stuff compared to humans—their physical makeup is silicon based, unlike humans, whose physical makeup is carbon based. So, we suppose Martians don't have C-fibers as part of their physical constitution. Now there's a problem. No C-fibers firing, no pain, according to the identity theory. But it seems clear that there very well could be (even if in fact there isn't) a species with a different physical constitution compared to humans but who nevertheless have experiences of pain.

Functionalism neatly avoids this problem because it does not identify mental properties with physical properties. Rather, as noted, it understands the essence of mental states and properties functionally—in terms of their causal roles. This means that if the silicon-based stuff in Martians can be organized into states that have the right causal roles, then Martians can be said to experience pain (and other sorts of mental states). In short, on this view, the essence of the mental is not the *matter* that makes up the creature, as the identity theory would have it; rather it is the functional (causal) role played by certain states that are "realized" in that matter. Mental states are thus "multiply realizable." What this means is simply that such states can come to be, as it were, in very different types of physical stuff. Indeed, if the functionalist is right about the nature of the mental, then a nonphysical spiritual being could enjoy mental states, so long as that being could be in nonphysical states that play the relevant causal roles that constitute the essence of mental states. This is why functionalism is not strictly speaking a materialist view of the mind. On the other hand, functionalism is compatible with a picture according to which mental states and processes that occur in humans are in fact realized by physical brain states.

Although functionalism, since its inception in the 1960s, has enjoyed a large following among philosophers, and perhaps remains the leading theory in philosophy of mind, it is not without its critics. The basic worry is that because functionalism construes the nature of mental states in purely relational terms—entirely in terms of causal role—the view fails to capture the inner, qualitative features of conscious experiences that seem to be an essential feature of the mental. This particular worry is often illustrated by the case of the inverted spectrum discussed in the readings by both Fodor and David Chalmers. A similar problem arises in connection with the problem of intentionality, which Searle illustrates with his Chinese room argument. (We will let the reader learn the details of these two imaginative objections by reading the relevant selections.) If functionalism is not able to overcome these problems, then it will not have answered the main questions posed by the mind-body problem; it will not have specified the nature of the mental and explained how mental states are related to brain states. But then *if* functionalism is not the solution to the mind-body problem, what is?

In our readings, both Searle and Chalmers attempt to address this question, though in very different ways. Searle proposes a solution to the mind-body problem, according to which mental states are both caused by and realized in brain states. Furthermore, according to Searle, "the way, in short, to dispel the mystery [of conscious experience] is to understand the [neurophysiological] processes" that are associated with mental states. In opposition to Searle, Chalmers argues that understanding how such neurophysiological processes work may address the "easy" problems of consciousness—problems that concern how the brain carries out certain tasks. But such understanding, he claims, does not address what he calls the "hard" problem—the problem of understanding how such processes can give rise to conscious experiences that have the various features that underlie the problems of mentality with which we began. Chalmers proposes that nothing short of recognizing consciousness as a fundamental property of reality, governed by (as yet undiscovered) fundamental laws relating the mental to the physical, will be adequate in coming to grips with the mind-body problem. Chalmers is thus advocating a form of property dualism as well as a basic reconception of the fundamental elements of reality.

The proposals of both Searle and Chalmers have met with objections, but here is a place to conclude our introduction to the mind-body problem and invite our readers to ponder it for themselves as they study the following selections.

The mind-body problem is alive and well. It continues to baffle.

# 7

# They're Made Out of Meat

TERRY BISSON

*Terry Bisson's (very) short story is a dialogue between two nonhuman aliens, who are astounded at the fact that human beings, given their physical makeup (they're made of "meat"), have any sort of mental life.*

"They're made out of meat."

"Meat?"

"Meat. They're made out of meat."

"Meat?"

"There's no doubt about it. We picked up several from different parts of the planet, took them aboard our recon vessels, and probed them all the way through. They're completely meat."

"That's impossible. What about the radio signals? The messages to the stars?"

"They use the radio waves to talk, but the signals don't come from them. The signals come from machines."

"So who made the machines? That's who we want to contact."

"*They* made the machines. That's what I'm trying to tell you. Meat made the machines."

"That's ridiculous. How can meat make a machine? You're asking me to believe in sentient meat."

"I'm not asking you, I'm telling you. These creatures are the only sentient race in that sector and they're made out of meat."

"Maybe they're like the orfolei. You know, a carbon-based intelligence that goes through a meat stage."

"Nope. They're born meat and they die meat. We studied them for several of their life spans, which didn't take long. Do you have any idea what's the life span of meat?"

"Spare me. Okay, maybe they're only part meat. You know, like the weddilei. A meat head with an electron plasma brain inside."

"Nope. We thought of that, since they do have meat heads, like the weddilei. But I told you, we probed them. They're meat all the way through."

"No brain?"

SOURCE: © 1990 by Omni Publications International, Ltd. First published in *Omni*, April 1991. Reprinted in Terry Bisson, *Bears Discover Fire and Other Stories* (New York: Tom Doherty Associates, Inc., 1993).

"Oh, there's a brain all right. It's just that the brain is made out of meat! That's what I've been trying to tell you."

"So . . . what does the thinking?"

"You're not understanding, are you? You're refusing to deal with what I'm telling you. The brain does the thinking. The meat."

"Thinking meat! You're asking me to believe in thinking meat!"

"Yes, thinking meat! Conscious meat! Loving meat. Dreaming meat. The meat is the whole deal! Are you beginning to get the picture or do I have to start all over?"

"Omigod. You're serious then. They're made out of meat."

"Thank you. Finally. Yes. They are indeed made out of meat. And they've been trying to get in touch with us for almost a hundred of their years."

"Omigod. So what does this meat have in mind?"

"First it wants to talk to us. Then I imagine it wants to explore the Universe, contact other sentiences, swap ideas and information. The usual."

"We're supposed to talk to meat."

"That's the idea. That's the message they're sending out by radio. 'Hello. Anyone out there? Anybody home?' That sort of thing."

"They actually do talk, then. They use words, ideas, concepts?"

"Oh, yes. Except they do it with meat."

"I thought you just told me they used radio."

"They do, but what do you think is on the radio? Meat sounds. You know how when you slap or flap meat, it makes a noise? They talk by flapping their meat at each other. They can even sing by squirting air through their meat."

"Omigod. Singing meat. This is altogether too much. So what do you advise?"

"Officially or unofficially?"

"Both."

"Officially, we are required to contact, welcome, and log in any and all sentient races or multibeings in this quadrant of the Universe, without prejudice, fear, or favor. Unofficially, I advise that we erase the records and forget the whole thing."

"I was hoping you would say that."

"It seems harsh, but there is a limit. Do we really want to make contact with meat?"

"I agree one hundred percent. What's there to say? 'Hello, meat. How's it going?' But will this work? How many planets are we dealing with here?"

"Just one. They can travel to other planets in special meat containers, but they can't live on them. And being meat, they can only travel through C space. Which limits them to the speed of light and makes the possibility of their ever making contact pretty slim. Infinitesimal, in fact."

"So we just pretend there's no one home in the Universe."

"That's it."

"Cruel. But you said it yourself, who wants to meet meat? And the ones who have been aboard our vessels, the ones you probed? You're sure they won't remember?"

"They'll be considered crackpots if they do. We went into their heads and smoothed out their meat so that we're just a dream to them."

"A dream to meat! How strangely appropriate, that we should be meat's dream."

"And we marked the entire sector *unoccupied*."

"Good. Agreed, officially and unofficially. Case closed. Any others? Anyone interesting on that side of the galaxy?"

"Yes, a rather shy but sweet hydrogen-core cluster intelligence in a class–nine star in G445 zone was in contact two galactic rotations ago, wants to be friendly again."

"They always come around."

"And why not? Imagine how unbearably, how unutterably cold the Universe would be if one were all alone . . ."

## READING COMPREHENSION QUESTION

1.  What questions regarding the philosophical mind-body problem are raised by Bisson's story?

# 8

# In Defense of Dualism

CURT DUCASSE

*Curt Ducasse (1881–1969) was professor of philosophy at Brown University from 1926 until his retirement in 1951. He was author of* The Philosophy of Art *(1930),* Nature, Mind and Death *(1951), and* A Critical Examination of the Belief in a Life after Death *(1961). In the following article (which was originally presented at a symposium in 1959), Ducasse defends a version of interactionistic property dualism—the view according to which human beings undergo both physical events and mental (or "psychical") events, and events of one type can cause and be caused by events of the other type.*

N either in the section of this symposium on "The Mind-Body Problem" nor in that on "The Brain and the Machine" is much, if any, attention given to the dualist-interactionist conception of the relation between mind and brain. A

SOURCE: From: Curt Ducasse, "A Defense of Dualism," in Sidney Hook, ed., *Dimensions of Mind,* New York: Collier Press, 1960.

summary presentation of the case for it and against its rivals may therefore be appropriate here.

The first point to which attention must be called is that, beyond question, there are things—events, substances, processes, relations, etc.—denominated "material," or "physical," that there are also certain others denominated instead "mental," or "psychical," and that no thing is denominated both "physical" and "psychical," or both "material" and "mental." Rocks, trees, water, air, animal and human bodies, and the processes occurring among them or within them, are examples of the things called "material" or "physical"; emotions, desires, moods, sensations, cravings, images, thoughts, etc., are examples of the things called "mental" or "psychical."

To question whether the first *really* are physical or the second *really* are psychical would be absurd, as it would be absurd to question whether a certain boy whom his parents named "George" really was George. For just as "George" is a name, so "physical" or "material," and "psychical" or "mental," are names, and a name is essentially a *pointer,* which does point at—designates, indicates, denotes, directs attention to—whatever it actually is employed to point at.

It is necessary, however, to ask what characteristic shared by all the things called "physical" or "material" determined their being all designated by one and the same name; and the same question arises with regard to those denominated instead "psychical" or "mental." Evidently the characteristic concerned had to be an obvious, not a recondite one, since investigation of the recondite characteristics respectively of physical and of psychical things could begin only *after* one knew which things were the physical and which the psychical ones.

In the case of the things called "physical," the patent characteristic common to and peculiar to them, which determined their being all denoted by one and the same name, was simply that all of them were, or were capable of being, *perceptually public*—the same tree, the same thunderclap, the same wind, the same dog, the same man, etc., can be perceived by every member of a human public suitably located in space and in time. To be material or physical, then, *basically* means to be, or to be capable of being, perceptually public. And the unperceivable, recondite things physicists discover—electrons, protons, etc., and the processes that occur among them—only have title at all to be also called physical *derivatively*—in virtue, namely, (and *only* in virtue) of their being *constituents* of the things that are perceptually public.

On the other hand, the patent characteristic which functioned as a basis for the application of one identical name to all the things called "psychical" or "mental" was their *inherently private* character, attention to them, as distinguished from attention to what they may signify, being accordingly termed "introspection," not "perception."

The events called "psychical," it must be emphasized, are private in a sense radically different from that in which the events occurring inside the body are private. The latter are private only in the sense that visual, tactual, or other exteroceptive perception of them is *difficult*—indeed, even more difficult for the person whose body is concerned than for other persons—such perception of those events being possible, perhaps, only by means of special instruments, or perhaps only by anatomical "introspection"(!), i.e., by opening up the body surgically and looking at the processes going on inside it. The "privacy" of intra-somatic stimuli, including so-called "covert behavior," is thus purely adventitious. The privacy of psychical events, on the other hand, is *inherent and ultimate*.

It is sometimes alleged, of course, that their privacy too is only adventitious. But this allegation rests only on failure to distinguish between being *public* and being *published*. Psychical events can be more or less adequately published. That is, perceptually public forms of behavior correlated with occurrence of them can function as *signs* that they are occurring—but *only* as signs, for correlation is not identity. Indeed, correlation presupposes non-identity.

Psychical events *themselves* are never *public* and never can be made so. That, for example, I *now remember* having dreamed of a Siamese cat last night is something which I can *publish* by means of perceptually public words, spoken or written. Other persons are then *informed of it*. But to be informed *that I remember* having so dreamed is one thing, and to *remember* having so dreamed is altogether another thing, and one *inherently private*. The dreaming itself was not, and the remembering itself is not, a *public* event at all and cannot possibly be made so in the way in which my *statement* that I remember that I so dreamed is or can be made public.

How then does it happen that we have names understood by all for events of inherently private kinds? The answer is, of course, that we heard those names— e.g., "anger," "desire," "remembering," etc.,—uttered by other persons when they perceived us behaving in certain more or less stereotyped manners. But the point crucial here is that although each of us acquires his vocabulary for mental events in this way, the words of it, at the times when they are applied by others to *his* behavior, denote *from him* not primarily or perhaps at all his behavior, but the particular kind of inherently private event, i.e., of physical state, which *he* is experiencing at the time. It is only in "behaviorese," i.e., in the language of dogmatic behaviorism, that for example the word "anger," and the words "anger-behavior," both denote the same event, to wit, the event which ordinary language terms "behaving angrily."

There are several varieties of behaviorism, but they agree in that they attempt to account for the behavior of organisms wholly without invoking a psychical cause for any behavior—that is, wholly by reference to physical, perceptually public causes, present and/or past.

Dogmatic behaviorism is the pious belief that the causes of the behavior of organisms, including human organisms, *are never other than physical*. Nothing but this dogma dictates that even when no physical occurrences are actually found that would account for a given behavior, physical occurrences nevertheless *must* be assumed to have taken place.

Empirical or methodological behaviorism, on the other hand, is not thus fideistic. It is simply *a research program,* perfectly legitimate and often fruitful—the program, namely, of *seeking,* for all behavior, causes consisting of physical, i.e., of perceptually public stimulus events, present and past. Evidently, the fact that one undertakes to search for causes of this kind for all behavior leaves entirely open the possibility that, in many of the innumerable cases where no physical causes adequate to account for the given behavior can in fact be observed, the behavior had a psychical not a physical cause.

For, contrary to what is sometimes alleged, causation of a physical by a psychical event, or of a psychical event by stimulation of a physical sense organ, is not in the least paradoxical. The causality relation—whether defined in terms of regularity of succession, or (preferably) in terms of single antecedent difference—does not presuppose at all that its cause-term and its effect-term both belong to the same ontological category, but only that both of them be *events*.

Moreover, the objection that we cannot understand how a psychical event could cause a physical one (or vice versa) has no basis other than blindness to the fact that the "how" of causation is capable at all of being either mysterious or understood only in cases of *remote* causation, never in cases of *proximate* causation. For the question as to the "how" of causation of a given event by a given other event never has any other sense than *through what intermediary causal steps* does the one cause the other. Hence, to ask it in a case of proximate causation is to be guilty of what Professor Ryle has called a "category mistake"—a mistake, incidentally, of which he is himself guilty when he alleges that the "how" of psycho-physical causation would be mysterious.

Again, the objection to interactionism that causation, in either direction, as between psychical and physical events is precluded by the principle of the conservation of energy (or of energy-matter) is invalid for several reasons.

(A) One reason is that the conservation which that principle asserts is not something known to be true without exception, but is, as M. T. Keeton has pointed out, only a defining-postulate of the notion of a *wholly closed* physical world, so that the question whether psycho-physical or physico-psychical causation ever occurs is (but in different words) the question whether the physical world *is* wholly closed. And that question is not answered by dignifying as a "principle" the assumption that the physical world is wholly closed.

(B) Anyway, as C. D. Broad has pointed out, it might be the case that whenever a given amount of energy vanishes from, or emerges in, the physical world at one place, then an equal amount of energy respectively emerges in, or vanishes from, that world at another place.

(C) And thirdly, if "energy" is meant to designate something experimentally measurable, then "energy" is defined in terms of causality, *not* "causality" in terms of transfer of energy. That is, it is not known that *all* causation, or, in particular, causation as between psychical and physical events, involves transfer of energy.

These various objections to interactionism—which, let it be noted, would automatically be objections also to epiphenomenalism—are thus wholly without force.

Epiphenomenalism, however, is open to the charge of being *arbitrary* in asserting that psychical events are always effects of physical events but never themselves cause other psychical events nor cause any physical events. For the experimental evidence we have—that, for instance, the decision to raise one's arm causes it to rise under normal circumstances—is of exactly the same form as the experimental evidence we have that, under normal circumstances, burning one's skin causes occurrence of pain.

Psychophysical "parallelism" has widely been adopted as supposedly an alternative escaping the difficulties which—mistakenly, as we have now seen—are alleged to stand in the way of interactionism. "Parallelism," however, is really the name not of a solution but of a problem. For the parallelism itself remains to be accounted for. And the "double-aspect" explanation, or would-be explanation, of it is but an empty figure of speech unless and until the "substance," of which mind and brain are alleged to be two "aspects," has first been shown to exist. And this never yet has been done.

Interactionism, then, as presented in what precedes, though not as presented by Descartes, is a perfectly tenable conception of the relation between some mental events and some brain events, allowing as it does also that some brain events have bodily causes, and that some mental events directly cause some other mental events. It conceives minds as consisting, like material substances, of sets of systematically interrelated dispositions, i.e., of capacities, abilities, powers, and susceptibilities, each of which can be analyzed as a causal connection, more or less enduring, between any event of some particular kind—C, occurring in a state of affairs of some particular kind—S, and a sequent event in it, of some particular kind—E. The series *of exercises* of the different dispositions (which together define the *nature* of a given mind) constitutes the *history* of that particular mind, i.e., its *existence* as distinguished from only its *description*.


## READING COMPREHENSION QUESTIONS

1. According to Ducasse, what common characteristic do physical (material) things (including events and states) share?

2. According to Ducasse, what is the common characteristic of mental (psychical) states?

3. Ducasse distinguishes between a mental state's being *public* from its being *published*. How does he distinguish them? And why does he think this distinction is important?

4. Ducasse objects to what he calls "dogmatic behaviorism," but he does not object to "methodological behaviorism." How does Ducasse distinguish these two kinds of behaviorism? Why does he object to the former, but not to the latter?

5. One standard objection to versions of interactionistic dualism is that they end up having to posit some mysterious kind of causation between mind and body or between mental events and physical events. How does Ducasse respond to this objection? Do you find what he says plausible? Why or why not?

6. Another objection to dualistic interaction Ducasse considers is based on the principle of the conservation of energy. State the objection and Ducasse's reply to it. Explain why you do or do not find his reply convincing.

# 9

# Dualism: For and Against

PAUL M. CHURCHLAND

*Paul M. Churchland is professor at the University of California, San Diego,
where he currently holds the Valtz Chair of Philosophy. He is also a member of the
Cognitive Science Faculty, the Institute for Neural Computation, and the Science
Studies Faculty. He is author of* A Neurocomputational Perspective: The
Nature of Mind and the Structure of Science *(1989),* Matter and Consciousness *(1984), from which our selection is taken, and* Neurophilosophy at
Work *(2007). After describing some major forms of dualism, Churchland proceeds to examine a variety of arguments that have been used in defense of dualism,
but argues that none of them is convincing. He then offers a number of arguments
against dualism, including arguments that appeal to recent work in neuroscience.*

The dualistic approach to mind encompasses several quite different theories, but
they are all agreed that the essential nature of conscious intelligence resides in
something *nonphysical,* in something forever beyond the scope of sciences like physics, neurophysiology, and computer science. Dualism is not the most widely held
view in the current philosophical and scientific community, but it is the most common theory of mind in the public at large, it is deeply entrenched in most of the
world's popular religions, and it has been the dominant theory of mind for most
of Western history. It is thus an appropriate place to begin our discussion.

## SUBSTANCE DUALISM

The distinguishing claim of this view is that each mind is a distinct nonphysical
thing, an individual "package" of nonphysical substance, a thing whose identity
is independent of any physical body to which it may be temporarily "attached."
Mental states and activities derive their special character, on this view, from their
being states and activities of this unique, nonphysical substance.

This leaves us wanting to ask for more in the way of a *positive* characterization
of the proposed mind-stuff. It is a frequent complaint with the substance dualist's
approach that his characterization of it is so far almost entirely negative. This need
not be a fatal flaw, however, since we no doubt have much to learn about the

SOURCE: From Paul M. Churchland, *Matter and Consciousness* (Cambridge: MIT Press,
1984); 2nd ed., 1988.

underlying nature of mind, and perhaps the deficit here can eventually be made good. On this score, the philosopher René Descartes (1596–1650) has done as much as anyone to provide a positive account of the nature of the proposed mind-stuff, and his views are worthy of examination.

Descartes theorized that reality divides into two basic kinds of substance. The first is ordinary matter, and the essential feature of this kind of substance is that it is extended in space: any instance of it has length, breadth, height, and occupies a determinate position in space. Descartes did not attempt to play down the importance of this type of matter. On the contrary, he was one of the most imaginative physicists of his time, and he was an enthusiastic advocate of what was then called "the mechanical philosophy." But there was one isolated corner of reality he thought could not be accounted for in terms of the mechanics of matter: the conscious reason of Man. This was his motive for proposing a second and radically different kind of substance, a substance that has no spatial extension or spatial position whatever, a substance whose essential feature is the activity of *thinking*. This view is known as *Cartesian dualism*.

As Descartes saw it, the real *you* is not your material body, but rather a nonspatial thinking substance, an individual unit of mind-stuff quite distinct from your material body. This nonphysical mind is in systematic causal interaction with your body. The physical state of your body's sense organs, for example, causes visual/auditory/tactile experiences in your mind. And the desires and decisions of your nonphysical mind cause your body to behave in purposeful ways. Its causal connections to your mind are what make your body yours, and not someone else's.

The main reasons offered in support of this view were straightforward enough. First, Descartes thought that he could determine, by direct introspection alone, that he was essentially a thinking substance and nothing else. And second, he could not imagine how a purely physical system could ever use *language* in a relevant way, or engage in mathematical *reasoning,* as any normal human can. Whether these are good reasons, we shall discuss presently. Let us first notice a difficulty that even Descartes regarded as a problem.

If "mind-stuff" is so utterly different from "matter-stuff" in its nature— different to the point that it has no mass whatever, no shape whatever, and no position anywhere in space—then how is it possible for my mind to have any causal influence on my body at all? As Descartes himself was aware (he was one of the first to formulate the law of the conservation of momentum), ordinary matter in space behaves according to rigid laws, and one cannot get bodily movement (= momentum) from nothing. How is this utterly insubstantial "thinking substance" to have any influence on ponderous matter? How can two such different things be in any sort of causal contact? Descartes proposed a very subtle material substance—"animal spirits"—to convey the mind's influence to the body in general. But this does not provide us with a solution, since it leaves us with the same problem with which we started: how something ponderous and spatial (even 'animal spirits') can interact with something entirely nonspatial.

In any case, the basic principle of division used by Descartes is no longer as plausible as it was in his day. It is now neither useful nor accurate to characterize ordinary matter as that-which-has-extension-in-space. Electrons, for example, are bits of matter, but our best current theories describe the electron as a point-particle with no extension whatever (it even lacks a determinate spatial position). And according to Einstein's theory of gravity, an entire star can achieve this same status, if it undergoes a complete gravitational collapse. If there truly is a division between mind and body, it appears that Descartes did not put his finger on the dividing line.

Such difficulties with Cartesian dualism provide a motive for considering a less radical form of substance dualism, and that is what we find in a view I shall call *popular dualism*. This is the theory that a person is literally a "ghost in a machine," where the machine is the human body, and the ghost is a spiritual substance, quite unlike physical matter in its internal constitution, but fully possessed of spatial properties even so. In particular, minds are commonly held to be *inside* the bodies they control; inside the head, on most views, in intimate contact with the brain.

This view need not have the difficulties of Descartes'. The mind is right there in contact with the brain, and their interaction can perhaps be understood in terms of their exchanging energy of a form that our science has not yet recognized or understood. Ordinary matter, you may recall, is just a form or manifestation of energy. (You may think of a grain of sand as a great deal of energy condensed or frozen into a small package, according to Einstein's relation, $E = mc^2$.) Perhaps mind-stuff is a well-behaved form or manifestation of energy also, but a different form of it. It is thus *possible* that a dualism of this alternative sort be consistent with familiar laws concerning the conservation of momentum and energy. This is fortunate for dualism, since those particular laws are very well established indeed.

This view will appeal to many for the further reason that it at least holds out the possibility (though it certainly does not guarantee) that the mind might survive the death of the body. It does not guarantee the mind's survival because it remains possible that the peculiar form of energy here supposed to constitute a mind can be produced and sustained only in conjunction with the highly intricate form of matter we call the brain, and must disintegrate when the brain disintegrates. So the prospects for surviving death are quite unclear even on the assumption that popular dualism is true. But even if survival were a clear consequence of the theory, there is a pitfall to be avoided here. Its promise of survival might be a reason for *wishing* dualism to be true, but it does not constitute a reason for *believing* that it *is* true. For that, we would need independent empirical evidence that minds do indeed survive the permanent death of the body. Regrettably, and despite the exploitative blatherings of the supermarket tabloids (TOP DOCS PROVE LIFE AFTER DEATH!!!), we possess no such evidence.

As we shall see later in this section, when we turn to evaluation, positive evidence for the existence of this novel, nonmaterial, thinking *substance* is in general on the slim side. This has moved many dualists to articulate still less extreme forms of dualism, in hopes of narrowing further the gap between theory and available evidence.

## PROPERTY DUALISM

The basic idea of the theories under this heading is that while there is no *substance* to be dealt with here beyond the physical brain, the brain has a special set of *properties* possessed by no other kind of physical object. It is these special properties that are nonphysical: hence the term *property dualism*. The properties in question

THE MIND-BODY PROBLEM          87

are the ones you would expect: the property of having a pain, of having a sensation of red, of thinking that *P,* of desiring that *Q,* and so forth. These are the
properties that are characteristic of conscious intelligence. They are held to be
nonphysical in the sense that they cannot ever be reduced to or explained solely
in terms of the concepts of the familiar physical sciences. They will require a
wholly new and autonomous science—the "science of mental phenomena"—if
they are ever to be adequately understood.

From here, important differences among the positions emerge. Let us begin
with what is perhaps the oldest version of property dualism: *epiphenomenalism.*
This term is rather a mouthful, but its meaning is simple. The Greek prefix
"epi-" means "above," and the position at issue holds that mental phenomena
are not a part of the physical phenomena in the brain that ultimately determine
our actions and behavior, but rather ride "above the fray." Mental phenomena
are thus *epi*phenomena. They are held to just appear or emerge when the growing
brain passes a certain level of complexity.

But there is more. The epiphenomenalist holds that while mental phenomena
are caused to occur by the various activities of the brain, *they do not have any causal
effects in turn.* They are entirely impotent with respect to causal effects on the physical world. They are *mere* epiphenomena. (To fix our ideas, a vague metaphor may
be helpful here. Think of our conscious mental states as little sparkles of shimmer-
ing light that occur on the wrinkled surface of the brain, sparkles which are caused
to occur by physical activity in the brain, but which have no causal effects on the
brain in return.) This means that the universal conviction that one's actions are
determined by one's desires, decisions, and volitions is false! One's actions are
exhaustively determined by physical events in the brain, which events *also*
cause the epiphenomena we call desires, decisions, and volitions. There is therefore a constant conjunction between volitions and actions. But according to the
epiphenomenalist, it is mere illusion that the former cause the latter.

What could motivate such a strange view? In fact, it is not too difficult to
understand why someone might take it seriously. Put yourself in the shoes of a
neuroscientist who is concerned to trace the origins of behavior back up the
motor nerves to the active cells in the motor cortex of the cerebrum, and to
trace in turn their activity into inputs from other parts of the brain, and from
the various sensory nerves. She finds a thoroughly physical system of awesome
structure and delicacy, and much intricate activity, all of it unambiguously chemical or electrical in nature, and she finds no hint at all of any nonphysical inputs of
the kind that substance dualism proposes. What is she to think? From the standpoint of her researches, human behavior is exhaustively a function of the activity
of the physical brain. And this opinion is further supported by her confidence that
the brain has the behavior-controlling features it does exactly because those features have been ruthlessly selected for during the brain's long evolutionary history.
In sum, the seat of human behavior appears entirely physical in its constitution, in
its origins, and in its internal activities.

On the other hand, our neuroscientist has the testimony of her own introspection to account for as well. She can hardly deny that she has experiences,
beliefs, and desires, nor that they are connected in some way with her behavior.
One bargain that can be struck here is to admit the *reality* of mental properties, as
nonphysical properties, but demote them to the status of impotent epiphenomena

that have nothing to do with the scientific explanation of human and animal behavior. This is the position the epiphenomenalist takes, and the reader can now perceive the rationale behind it. It is a bargain struck between the desire to respect a rigorously scientific approach to the explanation of behavior, and the desire to respect the testimony of introspection.

The epiphenomenalist's "demotion" of mental properties—to causally impotent by-products of brain activity—has seemed too extreme for most property dualists, and a theory closer to the convictions of common sense has enjoyed somewhat greater popularity. This view, which we may call *interactionist property dualism,* differs from the previous view in only one essential respect: the interactionist asserts that mental properties do indeed have causal effects on the brain, and thereby, on behavior. The mental properties of the brain are an integrated part of the general causal fray, in systematic interaction with the brain's physical properties. One's actions, therefore, are held to be caused by one's desires and volitions after all.

As before, mental properties are here said to be *emergent* properties, properties that do not appear at all until ordinary physical matter has managed to organize itself, through the evolutionary process, into a system of sufficient complexity. Examples of properties that are emergent in this sense would be the property of being *solid,* the property of being *colored,* and the property of being *alive.* All of these require matter to be suitably organized before they can be displayed. With this much, any materialist will agree. But any property dualist makes the further claim that mental states and properties are *irreducible,* in the sense that they are not just organizational features of physical matter, as are the examples cited. They are said to be novel properties beyond prediction or explanation by physical science.

This last condition—the irreducibility of mental properties—is an important one, since this is what makes the position a dualist position. But it sits poorly with the joint claim that mental properties emerge from nothing more than the organizational achievements of physical matter. If that is how mental properties are produced, then one would expect a physical account of them to be possible. The simultaneous claim of evolutionary emergence *and* physical irreducibility is prima facie puzzling.

A property dualist is not absolutely bound to insist on both claims. He could let go the thesis of evolutionary emergence, and claim that mental properties are *fundamental* properties of reality, properties that have been here from the universe's inception, properties on a par with length, mass, electric charge, and other fundamental properties. There is even an historical precedent for a position of this kind. At the turn of this century it was still widely believed that electromagnetic phenomena (such as electric charge and magnetic attraction) were just an unusually subtle manifestation of purely *mechanical* phenomena. Some scientists thought that a reduction of electromagnetics to mechanics was more or less in the bag. They thought that radio waves, for example, would turn out to be just travelling oscillations in a very subtle but jellylike aether that fills space everywhere. But the aether turned out not to exist. So electromagnetic properties turned out to be fundamental properties in their own right, and we were forced to add electric charge to the existing list of fundamental properties (mass, length, and duration).

Perhaps mental properties enjoy a status like that of electromagnetic properties: irreducible, but not emergent. Such a view may be called *elemental-property dualism,* and it has the advantage of clarity over the previous view. Unfortunately, the parallel with electromagnetic phenomena has one very obvious failure. Unlike electromagnetic properties, which are displayed at all levels of reality from the subatomic level on up, mental properties are displayed only in large physical systems that have evolved a very complex internal organization. The case for the evolutionary emergence of mental properties through the organization of matter is extremely strong. They do not appear to be basic or elemental at all. This returns us, therefore, to the issue of their irreducibility. Why should we accept this most basic of the dualist's claims? Why be a dualist?

## ARGUMENTS FOR DUALISM

Here we shall examine some of the main considerations commonly offered in support of dualism. Criticism will be postponed for a moment so that we may appreciate the collective force of these supporting considerations.

A major source of dualistic convictions is the religious belief many of us bring to these issues. Each of the major religions is in its way a theory about the cause or purpose of the universe, and Man's place within it, and many of them are committed to the notion of an immortal soul—that is, to some form of substance dualism. Supposing that one is consistent, to consider disbelieving dualism is to consider disbelieving one's religious heritage, and some of us find that difficult to do. Call this the *argument from religion.*

A more universal consideration is the *argument from introspection.* The fact is, when you center your attention on the contents of your consciousness, you do not clearly apprehend a neural network pulsing with electrochemical activity: you apprehend a flux of thoughts, sensations, desires, and emotions. It seems that mental states and properties, as revealed in introspection, could hardly be more different from physical states and properties if they tried. The verdict of introspection, therefore, seems strongly on the side of some form of dualism— on the side of property dualism, at a minimum.

A cluster of important considerations can be collected under the *argument from irreducibility.* Here one points to a variety of mental phenomena where it seems clear that no purely physical explanation could possibly account for what is going on. Descartes has already cited our ability to use language in a way that is relevant to our changing circumstances, and he was impressed also with our faculty of Reason, particularly as it is displayed in our capacity for mathematical reasoning. These abilities, he thought, must surely be beyond the capacity of any physical system. More recently, the introspectible qualities of our sensations (sensory "qualia"), and the meaningful content of our thoughts and beliefs, have also been cited as phenomena that will forever resist reduction to the physical. Consider, for example, seeing the color or smelling the fragrance of a rose. A physicist or chemist might know everything about the molecular structure of the rose, and of the human brain, argues the dualist, but that knowledge would not enable him to predict or anticipate the quality of these inexpressible experiences.

Finally, parapsychological phenomena are occasionally cited in favor of dualism. Telepathy (mind reading), precognition (seeing the future), telekinesis (thought control of material objects), and clairvoyance (knowledge of distant objects) are all awkward to explain within the normal confines of psychology and physics. If these phenomena are real, they might well be reflecting the superphysical nature that the dualist ascribes to the mind. Trivially they are *mental* phenomena, and if they are also forever beyond physical explanation, then at least some mental phenomena must be irreducibly nonphysical.

Collectively, these considerations may seem compelling. But there are serious criticisms of each, and we must examine them as well. Consider first the argument from religion. There is certainly nothing wrong in principle with appealing to a more general theory that bears on the case at issue, which is what the appeal to religion amounts to. But the appeal can only be as good as the scientific credentials of the religion(s) being appealed to, and here the appeals tend to fall down rather badly. In general, attempts to decide scientific questions by appeal to religious orthodoxy have a very sorry history. That the stars are other suns, that the earth is not the center of the universe, that diseases are caused by microorganisms, that the earth is billions of years old, that life is a physicochemical phenomenon; all of these crucial insights were strongly and sometimes viciously resisted, because the dominant religion of the time happened to think otherwise. Giordano Bruno was burned at the stake for urging the first view; Galileo was forced by threat of torture in the Vatican's basement to recant the second view; the firm belief that disease was a punishment visited by the Devil allowed public health practices that brought chronic plagues to most of the cities of Europe; and the age of the earth and the evolution of life were forced to fight an uphill battle against religious prejudice even in an age of supposed enlightenment.

History aside, the almost universal opinion that one's own religious convictions are the reasoned outcome of a dispassionate evaluation of all of the major alternatives is almost demonstrably false for humanity in general. If that really were the genesis of most people's convictions, then one would expect the major faiths to be distributed more or less randomly or evenly over the globe. But in fact they show a very strong tendency to cluster: Christianity is centered in Europe and the Americas, Islam in Africa and the Middle East, Hinduism in India, and Buddhism in the Orient. Which illustrates what we all suspected anyway: that *social forces* are the primary determinants of religious belief for people in general. To decide scientific questions by appeal to religious orthodoxy would therefore be to put social forces in place of empirical evidence. For all of these reasons, professional scientists and philosophers concerned with the nature of mind generally do their best to keep religious appeals out of the discussion entirely.

The argument from introspection is a much more interesting argument, since it tries to appeal to the direct experience of everyman. But the argument is deeply suspect, in that it assumes that our faculty of inner observation or introspection reveals things as they really are in their innermost nature. This assumption is suspect because we already know that our other forms of observation—sight, hearing, touch, and so on—do no such thing. The red surface of an apple does not *look* like a matrix of molecules reflecting photons at certain critical wavelengths, but that is what it is. The sound of a flute does not *sound* like a sinusoidal compression wave train in the atmosphere, but that is what it is. The warmth of the summer air does not *feel* like the mean kinetic energy of millions of tiny molecules, but that is what it is. If one's pains and hopes and beliefs do not *introspectively* seem like electrochemical states in a neural network, that may be only because our faculty of introspection, like our other senses, is not sufficiently penetrating to reveal such hidden details. Which is just what one would expect anyway. The argument from introspection is therefore entirely without force, unless we can somehow argue that the faculty of introspection is quite different from all other forms of observation.

The argument from irreducibility presents a more serious challenge, but here also its force is less than first impression suggests. Consider first our capacity for mathematical reasoning which so impressed Descartes. The last ten years have made available, to anyone with fifty dollars to spend, electronic calculators whose capacity for mathematical reasoning—the calculational part, at least—far surpasses that of any normal human. The fact is, in the centuries since Descartes' writings, philosophers, logicians, mathematicians, and computer scientists have managed to isolate the general principles of mathematical reasoning, and electronics engineers have created machines that compute in accord with those principles. The result is a hand-held object that would have astonished Descartes. This outcome is impressive not just because machines have proved capable of some of the capacities boasted by human reason, but because some of those achievements invade areas of human reason that past dualistic philosophers have held up as forever closed to mere physical devices.

Although debate on the matter remains open, Descartes' argument from language use is equally dubious. The notion of a *computer language* is by now a commonplace: consider BASIC, PASCAL, FORTRAN, APL, LISP, and so on. Granted, these artificial "languages" are much simpler in structure and content than human natural language, but the differences may be differences only of degree, and not of kind. As well, the theoretical work of Noam Chomsky and the generative grammar approach to linguistics have done a great deal to explain the human capacity for language use in terms that invite simulation by computers. I do not mean to suggest that truly conversational computers are just around the corner. We have a great deal yet to learn, and fundamental problems yet to solve (mostly having to do with our capacity for inductive or theoretical reasoning). But recent progress here does nothing to support the claim that language use must be forever impossible for a purely physical system. On the contrary, such a claim now appears rather arbitrary and dogmatic.

The next issue is also a live problem: How can we possibly hope to explain or to predict the intrinsic qualities of our sensations, or the meaningful content of our beliefs and desires, in purely physical terms? This is a major challenge to the materialist. But as we shall see in later sections, active research programs are already under way on both problems, and positive suggestions are being explored. It is in fact not impossible to imagine how such explanations might go, though the materialist cannot yet pretend to have solved either problem. Until he does, the dualist will retain a bargaining chip here, but that is about all. What the dualists need in order to establish their case is the conclusion that a physical reduction is outright impossible, and that is a conclusion they have failed to establish.

Rhetorical questions, like the one that opens this paragraph, do not constitute arguments. And it is equally difficult, note, to imagine how the relevant phenomena could be explained or predicted solely in terms of the substance dualist's non-physical mind-stuff. The explanatory problem here is a major challenge to everybody, not just to the materialist. On this issue then, we have a rough standoff.

The final argument in support of dualism urged the existence of parapsychological phenomena such as telepathy and telekinesis, the point being that such mental phenomena are (a) real, and (b) beyond purely physical explanation. This argument is really another instance of the argument from irreducibility discussed above, and as before, it is not entirely clear that such phenomena, even if real, must forever escape a purely physical explanation. The materialist can already suggest a possible mechanism for telepathy, for example. On his view, thinking is an electrical activity within the brain. But according to electromagnetic theory, such changing motions of electric charges must produce electromagnetic waves radiating at the speed of light in all directions, waves that will contain information about the electrical activity that produced them. Such waves can subsequently have effects on the electrical activity of other brains, that is, on their thinking. Call this the "radio transmitter/receiver" theory of telepathy.

I do not for a moment suggest that this theory is true; the electromagnetic waves emitted by the brain are fantastically weak (billions of times weaker than the ever present background electromagnetic flux produced by commercial radio stations), and they are almost certain to be hopelessly jumbled together as well. This is one reason why, in the absence of systematic, compelling, and repeatable evidence for the existence of telepathy, one must doubt its possibility. But it is significant that the materialist has the theoretical resources to suggest a detailed possible explanation of telepathy, if it were real, which is more than any dualist has so far done. It is not at all clear, then, that the materialist *must* be at an explanatory disadvantage in these matters. Quite the reverse.

Put the preceding aside, if you wish, for the main difficulty with the argument from parapsychological phenomena is much, much simpler. Despite the endless pronouncements and anecdotes in the popular press, and despite a steady trickle of serious research on such things, there is no significant or trustworthy evidence that such phenomena even exist. The wide gap between popular conviction on this matter, and the actual evidence, is something that itself calls for research. For there is not a single parapsychological effect that can be repeatedly or reliably produced in any laboratory suitably equipped to perform and control the experiment. Not one. Honest researchers have been repeatedly hoodwinked by "psychic" charlatans with skills derived from the magician's trade, and the history of the subject is largely a history of gullibility, selection of evidence, poor experimental controls, and outright fraud by the occasional researcher as well. If someone really does discover a repeatable parapsychological effect, then we shall have to reevaluate the situation, but as things stand, there is nothing here to support a dualist theory of mind.

Upon critical examination, the arguments in support of dualism lose much of their force. But we are not yet done: there are arguments against dualism, and these also require examination.

## ARGUMENTS AGAINST DUALISM

The first argument against dualism urged by the materialists appeals to the greater *simplicity* of their view. It is a principle of rational methodology that, if all else is equal, the simpler of two competing hypotheses should be preferred. This principle is sometimes called "Ockham's Razor"—after William of Ockham, the medieval philosopher who first enunciated it—and it can also be expressed as follows: "Do not multiply entities beyond what is strictly necessary to explain the phenomena." The materialist postulates only one kind of substance (physical matter), and one class of properties (physical properties), whereas the dualist postulates two kinds of matter and/or two classes of properties. And to no explanatory advantage, charges the materialist.

This is not yet a decisive point against dualism, since neither dualism nor materialism can yet explain all of the phenomena to be explained. But the objection does have some force, especially since there is no doubt at all that physical matter exists, while spiritual matter remains a tenuous hypothesis.

If this latter hypothesis brought us some definite explanatory advantage obtainable in no other way, then we would happily violate the demand for simplicity, and we would be right to do so. But it does not, claims the materialist. In fact, the advantage is just the other way around, he argues, and this brings us to the second objection to dualism: the relative *explanatory impotence* of dualism as compared to materialism.

Consider, very briefly, the explanatory resources already available to the neurosciences. We know that the brain exists and what it is made of. We know much of its microstructure: how the neurons are organized into systems and how distinct systems are connected to one another, to the motor nerves going out to the muscles, and to the sensory nerves coming in from the sense organs. We know much of their microchemistry: how the nerve cells fire tiny electrochemical pulses along their various fibers, and how they make other cells fire also, or cease firing. We know some of how such activity processes sensory information, selecting salient or subtle bits to be sent on to higher systems. And we know some of how such activity initiates and coordinates bodily behavior. Thanks mainly to neurology (the branch of medicine concerned with brain pathology), we know a great deal about the correlations between damage to various parts of the human brain, and various behavioral and cognitive deficits from which the victims suffer. There are a great many isolated deficits—some gross, some subtle—that are familiar to neurologists (inability to speak, or to read, or to understand speech, or to recognize faces, or to add/subtract, or to move a certain limb, or to put information into long-term memory, and so on), and their appearance is closely tied to the occurrence of damage to very specific parts of the brain.

Nor are we limited to cataloguing traumas. The growth and development of the brain's microstructure is also something that neuroscience has explored, and such development appears to be the basis of various kinds of learning by the organism. Learning, that is, involves lasting chemical and physical changes in the brain. In sum, the neuroscientist can tell us a great deal about the brain, about its constitution and the physical laws that govern it; he can already explain much of our behavior in terms of the physical, chemical, and electrical properties of the brain; and he has the theoretical resources available to explain a good deal more as our explorations continue.

Compare now what the neuroscientist can tell us about the brain, and what he can do with that knowledge, with what the dualist can tell us about spiritual substance, and what he can do with those assumptions. Can the dualist tell us anything about the internal constitution of mind-stuff? Of the nonmaterial elements that make it up? Of the laws that govern their behavior? Of the mind's structural connections with the body? Of the manner of its operations? Can he explain human capacities and pathologies in terms of its structures and its defects? The fact is, the dualist can do none of these things, because no detailed theory of mind-stuff has ever been formulated. Compared to the rich resources and explanatory successes of current materialism, dualism is less a theory of mind than it is an empty space waiting for a genuine theory of mind to be put in it.

Thus argues the materialist. But again, this is not a completely decisive point against dualism. The dualist can admit that the brain plays a major role in the administration of both perception and behavior—on his view the brain is the *mediator* between the mind and the body—but he may attempt to argue that the materialist's current successes and future explanatory prospects concern only the mediative functions of the brain, not the *central* capacities of the nonphysical mind, capacities such as reason, emotion, and consciousness itself. On these latter topics, he may argue, both dualism *and* materialism currently draw a blank.

But this reply is not a very good one. So far as the capacity for reasoning is concerned, machines already exist that execute in minutes sophisticated deductive and mathematical calculations that would take a human a lifetime to execute. And so far as the other two mental capacities are concerned, studies of such things as depression, motivation, attention, and sleep have revealed many interesting and puzzling facts about the neurochemical and neurodynamical basis of both emotion and consciousness. The *central* capacities, no less than the peripheral, have been addressed with profit by various materialist research programs.

In any case, the (substance) dualist's attempt to draw a sharp distinction between the unique "mental" capacities proper to the nonmaterial mind, and the merely mediative capacities of the brain, prompts an argument that comes close to being an outright refutation of (substance) dualism. If there really is a distinct entity in which reasoning, emotion, and consciousness take place, and if that entity is dependent on the brain for nothing more than sensory experiences as input and volitional executions as output, *then one would expect reason, emotion, and consciousness to be relatively invulnerable to direct control or pathology by manipulation or damage to the brain.* But in fact the exact opposite is true. Alcohol, narcotics, or senile degeneration of nerve tissue will impair, cripple, or even destroy one's capacity for rational thought. Psychiatry knows of hundreds of emotion-controlling chemicals (lithium, chlorpromazine, amphetamine, cocaine, and so on) that do their work when vectored into the brain. And the vulnerability of consciousness to the anesthetics, to caffeine, and to something as simple as a sharp blow to the head, shows its very close dependence on neural activity in the brain. All of this makes perfect sense if reason, emotion, and consciousness are activities of the brain itself. But it makes very little sense if they are activities of something else entirely.

We may call this the argument from the *neural dependence* of all known mental phenomena. Property dualism, note, is not threatened by this argument, since, like materialism, property dualism reckons the brain as the seat of all mental activity. We shall conclude this section, however, with an argument that cuts against both varieties of dualism: the argument from *evolutionary history*.

What is the origin of a complex and sophisticated species such as ours? What, for that matter, is the origin of the dolphin, the mouse, or the housefly? Thanks to the fossil record, comparative anatomy, and the biochemistry of proteins and nucleic acids, there is no longer any significant doubt on this matter. Each existing species is a surviving type from a number of variations on an earlier type of organism; each earlier type is in turn a surviving type from a number of variations on a still earlier type of organism; and so on down the branches of the evolutionary tree until, some three billion years ago, we find a trunk of just one or a handful of very simple organisms. These organisms, like their more complex offspring, are just self-repairing, self-replicating, energy-driven molecular structures. (That evolutionary trunk has its own roots in an earlier era of purely chemical evolution, in which the molecular elements of life were themselves pieced together.) The mechanism of development that has structured this tree has two main elements: (1) the occasional blind variation in types of reproducing creature, and (2) the selective survival of some of these types due to the relative reproductive advantage enjoyed by individuals of those types. Over periods of geological time, such a process can produce an enormous variety of organisms, some of them very complex indeed.

For purposes of our discussion, the important point about the standard evolutionary story is that the human species and all of its features are the wholly physical outcome of a purely physical process. Like all but the simplest of organisms, we have a nervous system. And for the same reason: a nervous system permits the discriminative guidance of behavior. But a nervous system is just an active matrix of cells, and a cell is just an active matrix of molecules. We are notable only in that our nervous system is more complex and powerful than those of our fellow creatures. Our inner nature differs from that of simpler creatures in degree, but not in kind.

If this is the correct account of our origins, then there seems neither need, nor room, to fit any nonphysical substances or properties into our theoretical account of ourselves. We are creatures of matter. And we should learn to live with that fact.

Arguments like these have moved most (but not all) of the professional community to embrace some form of materialism. This has not produced much unanimity, however, since the differences between the several materialist positions are even wider than the differences that divide dualism.

## READING COMPREHENSION QUESTIONS

1.  State the four arguments for dualism that Churchland discusses. State his objections to each. Do you find his objections convincing? Explain.

2.  According to Churchland, dualism (as compared to materialism) suffers from the problem of "explanatory impotence." What is this problem? How does Churchland attempt to show that it is a problem for dualism? Do you think

Churchland is correct in thinking that mind-body materialism has an explanatory advantage over dualism? Explain.

3.  Churchland claims that what he calls the "argument from neural dependence" is "close to being an outright refutation of (substance) dualism." Present the steps of this argument. Why does Churchland think that property dualism is not threatened by this argument?

4.  Churchland claims that what he calls the "argument from evolutionary history" threatens *both* substance and property dualism. Present the steps of this argument. Do you think the argument is convincing? Why or why not?

# 10

---

# The Mind-Body Problem

JERRY A. FODOR

*Jerry A. Fodor is State of New Jersey Professor of Philosophy at Rutgers University. His many publications include* The Modularity of Mind *(1983),* Concepts: Where Cognitive Science Went Wrong *(1998), and* The Mind Doesn't Work That Way *(2001). In the early part of his essay, Fodor provides an overview of the major problems for both dualist and materialist theories of mind that eventually led many philosophers, beginning in the 1960s, to embrace functionalism. After explaining the elements of functionalism, Fodor proceeds to examine how well the theory does at accounting for both the qualitative and intentional contents of mental states.*

Modern philosophy of science has been devoted largely to the formal and systematic description of the successful practices of working scientists. The philosopher does not try to dictate how scientific inquiry and argument ought to be conducted. Instead he tries to enumerate the principles and practices that have contributed to good science. The philosopher has devoted the most attention to analyzing the methodological peculiarities of the physical sciences. The analysis has helped to clarify the nature of confirmation, the logical structure of scientific theories, the formal properties of statements that express laws and the question of whether theoretical entities actually exist.

SOURCE: From Jerry A. Fodor, "The Mind-Body Problem," *Scientific American*; January 1981.

It is only rather recently that philosophers have become seriously interested in the methodological tenets of psychology. Psychological explanations of behavior refer liberally to the mind and to states, operations and processes of the mind. The philosophical difficulty comes in stating in unambiguous language what such references imply.

Traditional philosophies of mind can be divided into two broad categories: dualist theories and materialist theories. In the dualist approach the mind is a nonphysical substance. In materialist theories the mental is not distinct from the physical; indeed, all mental states, properties, processes and operations are in principle identical with physical states, properties, processes and operations. Some materialists, known as behaviorists, maintain that all talk of mental causes can be eliminated from the language of psychology in favor of talk of environmental stimuli and behavioral responses. Other materialists, the identity theorists, contend that there are mental causes and that they are identical with neurophysiological events in the brain.

In the past 15 years a philosophy of mind called functionalism that is neither dualist nor materialist has emerged from philosophical reflection on developments in artificial intelligence, computational theory, linguistics, cybernetics and psychology. All these fields, which are collectively known as the cognitive sciences, have in common a certain level of abstraction and a concern with systems that process information. Functionalism, which seeks to provide a philosophical account of this level of abstraction, recognizes the possibility that systems as diverse as human beings, calculating machines and disembodied spirits could all have mental states. In the functionalist view the psychology of a system depends not on the stuff it is made of (living cells, mental or spiritual energy) but on how the stuff is put together. Functionalism is a difficult concept, and one way of coming to grips with it is to review the deficiencies of the dualist and materialist philosophies of mind it aims to displace.

## [DUALISM]

The chief drawback of dualism is its failure to account adequately for mental causation. If the mind is nonphysical, it has no position in physical space. How, then, can a mental cause give rise to a behavioral effect that has a position in space? To put it another way, how can the nonphysical give rise to the physical without violating the laws of the conservation of mass, of energy and of momentum?

The dualist might respond that the problem of how an immaterial substance can cause physical events is not much obscurer than the problem of how one physical event can cause another. Yet there is an important difference: there are many clear cases of physical causation but not one clear case of nonphysical causation. Physical interaction is something philosophers, like all other people, have to live with. Nonphysical interaction, however, may be no more than an artifact of the immaterialist construal of the mental. Most philosophers now agree that no argument has successfully demonstrated why mind-body causation should not be regarded as a species of physical causation.

Dualism is also incompatible with the practices of working psychologists. The psychologist frequently applies the experimental methods of the physical sciences to the study of the mind. If mental processes were different in kind from physical processes, there would be no reason to expect these methods to work in the realm of the mental. In order to justify their experimental methods many psychologists urgently sought an alternative to dualism.

## [RADICAL BEHAVIORISM]

In the 1920's John B. Watson of Johns Hopkins University made the radical suggestion that behavior does not have mental causes. He regarded the behavior of an organism as its observable responses to stimuli, which he took to be the causes of its behavior. Over the next 30 years psychologists such as B. F. Skinner of Harvard University developed Watson's ideas into an elaborate world view in which the role of psychology was to catalogue the laws that determine causal relations between stimuli and responses. In this "radical behaviorist" view the problem of explaining the nature of the mind-body interaction vanishes; there is no such interaction.

Radical behaviorism has always worn an air of paradox. For better or worse, the idea of mental causation is deeply ingrained in our everyday language and in our ways of understanding our fellow men and ourselves. For example, people commonly attribute behavior to beliefs, to knowledge and to expectations. Brown puts gas in his tank because he believes the car will not run without it. *Jones writes not "acheive"* but "achieve" because he knows the rule about putting *i* before *e*. Even when a behavioral response is closely tied to an environmental stimulus, mental processes often intervene. Smith carries an umbrella because the sky is cloudy, but the weather is only part of the story. There are apparently also mental links in the causal chain: observation and expectation. The clouds affect Smith's behavior only because he observes them and because they induce in him an expectation of rain.

The radical behaviorist is unmoved by appeals to such cases. He is prepared to dismiss references to mental causes, however plausible they may seem, as the residue of outworn creeds. The radical behaviorist predicts that as psychologists come to understand more about the relations between stimuli and responses they will find it increasingly possible to explain behavior without postulating mental causes.

The strongest argument against behaviorism is that psychology has not turned out this way; the opposite has happened. As psychology has matured, the framework of mental states and processes that is apparently needed to account for experimental observations has grown all the more elaborate. Particularly in the case of human behavior psychological theories satisfying the methodological tenets of radical behaviorism have proved largely sterile, as would be expected if the postulated mental processes are real and causally effective.

Nevertheless, many philosophers were initially drawn to radical behaviorism because, paradoxes and all, it seemed better than dualism. Since a psychology committed to immaterial substances was unacceptable, philosophers turned to radical behaviorism because it seemed to be the only alternative materialist philosophy of mind. The choice, as they saw it, was between radical behaviorism and ghosts.

By the early 1960's philosophers began to have doubts that dualism and radical behaviorism exhausted the possible approaches to the philosophy of mind. Since the two theories seemed unattractive, the right strategy might be to develop a materialist philosophy of mind that nonetheless allowed for mental causes. Two such philosophies emerged, one called logical behaviorism and the other called the central-state identity theory.

# [LOGICAL BEHAVIORISM]

Logical behaviorism is a semantic theory about what mental terms mean. The basic idea is that attributing a mental state (say thirst) to an organism is the same as saying that the organism is disposed to behave in a particular way (for example to drink if there is water available). On this view every mental ascription is equivalent in meaning to an if-then statement (called a behavioral hypothetical) that expresses a behavioral disposition. For example, "Smith is thirsty" might be taken to be equivalent to the dispositional statement "If there were water available, then Smith would drink some." By definition a behavioral hypothetical includes no mental terms. The if-clause of the hypothetical speaks only of stimuli and the then-clause speaks only of behavioral responses. Since stimuli and responses are physical events, logical behaviorism is a species of materialism.

The strength of logical behaviorism is that by translating mental language into the language of stimuli and responses it provides an interpretation of psychological explanations in which behavioral effects are attributed to mental causes. Mental causation is simply the manifestation of a behavioral disposition. More precisely, mental causation is what happens when an organism has a behavioral disposition and the if-clause of the behavioral hypothetical expressing the disposition happens to be true. For example, the causal statement "Smith drank some water because he was thirsty" might be taken to mean "If there were water available, then Smith would drink some, and there was water available."

I have somewhat oversimplified logical behaviorism by assuming that each mental ascription can be translated by a unique behavioral hypothetical. Actually the logical behaviorist often maintains that it takes an open-ended set (perhaps an infinite set) of behavioral hypotheticals to spell out the behavioral disposition expressed by a mental term. The mental ascription "Smith is thirsty" might also be satisfied by the hypothetical "If there were orange juice available, then Smith would drink some" and by a host of other hypotheticals. In any event the logical behaviorist does not usually maintain he can actually enumerate all the hypotheticals that correspond to a behavioral disposition expressing a given mental term. He only insists that in principle the meaning of any mental term can be conveyed by behavioral hypotheticals.

The way the logical behaviorist has interpreted a mental term such as thirsty is modeled after the way many philosophers have interpreted a physical disposition such as fragility. The physical disposition "The glass is fragile" is often taken to mean something like "If the glass were struck, then it would break." By the same token the logical behaviorist's analysis of mental causation is similar to the received analysis of one kind of physical causation. The causal statement "The glass broke because it was fragile" is taken to mean something like "If the glass were struck, then it would break, and the glass was struck."

By equating mental terms with behavioral dispositions the logical behaviorist has put mental terms on a par with the nonbehavioral dispositions of the physical sciences. That is a promising move, because the analysis of nonbehavioral dispositions is on relatively solid philosophical ground. An explanation attributing the breaking of a glass to its fragility is surely something even the staunchest materialist can accept. By arguing that mental terms are synonymous with dispositional terms, the logical behaviorist has provided something the radical behaviorist could not: a materialist account of mental causation.

Nevertheless, the analogy between mental causation as construed by the logical behaviorist and physical causation goes only so far. The logical behaviorist treats the manifestation of a disposition as the sole form of mental causation, whereas the physical sciences recognize additional kinds of causation. There is the kind of causation where one physical event causes another, as when the breaking of a glass is attributed to its having been struck. In fact, explanations that involve event-event causation are presumably more basic than dispositional explanations, because the manifestation of a disposition (the breaking of a fragile glass) always involves event-event causation and not vice versa. In the realm of the mental many examples of event-event causation involve one mental state's causing another, and for this kind of causation logical behaviorism provides no analysis. As a result the logical behaviorist is committed to the tacit and implausible assumption that psychology requires a less robust notion of causation than the physical sciences require.

Event-event causation actually seems to be quite common in the realm of the mental. Mental causes typically give rise to behavioral effects by virtue of their interaction with other mental causes. For example, having a headache causes a disposition to take aspirin only if one also has the desire to get rid of the headache, the belief that aspirin exists, the belief that taking aspirin reduces headaches and so on. Since mental states interact in generating behavior, it will be necessary to find a construal of psychological explanations that posits mental processes: causal sequences of mental events. It is this construal that logical behaviorism fails to provide.

Such considerations bring out a fundamental way in which logical behaviorism is quite similar to radical behaviorism. It is true that the logical behaviorist, unlike the radical behaviorist, acknowledges the existence of mental states. Yet since the underlying tenet of logical behaviorism is that references to mental states can be translated out of psychological explanations by employing behavioral hypotheticals, all talk of mental states and processes is in a sense heuristic. The only facts to which the behaviorist is actually committed are facts about relations between stimuli and responses. In this respect logical behaviorism is just radical behaviorism in a semantic form. Although the former theory offers a construal of mental causation, the construal is Pickwickian.* What does not really exist cannot cause anything, and the logical behaviorist, like the radical behaviorist, believes deep down that mental causes do not exist.

---

*[Special or esoteric.—Eds.]

# [CENTRAL-STATE IDENTITY THEORY]

An alternative materialist theory of the mind to logical behaviorism is the central-state identity theory. According to this theory, mental events, states and processes are identical with neurophysiological events in the brain, and the property of being in a certain mental state (such as having a headache or believing it will rain) is identical with the property of being in a certain neurophysiological state. On this basis it is easy to make sense of the idea that a behavioral effect might sometimes have a chain of mental causes; that will be the case whenever a behavioral effect is contingent on the appropriate sequence of neurophysiological events.

The central-state identity theory acknowledges that it is possible for mental causes to interact causally without ever giving rise to any behavioral effect, as when a person thinks for a while about what he ought to do and then decides to do nothing. If mental processes are neurophysiological, they must have the causal properties of neurophysiological processes. Since neurophysiological processes are presumably physical processes, the central-state identity theory ensures that the concept of mental causation is as rich as the concept of physical causation.

The central-state identity theory provides a satisfactory account of what the mental terms in psychological explanations refer to, and so it is favored by psychologists who are dissatisfied with behaviorism. The behaviorist maintains that mental terms refer to nothing or that they refer to the parameters of stimulus-response relations. Either way the existence of mental entities is only illusory. The identity theorist, on the other hand, argues that mental terms refer to neurophysiological states. Thus he can take seriously the project of explaining behavior by appealing to its mental causes.

The chief advantage of the identity theory is that it takes the explanatory constructs of psychology at face value, which is surely something a philosophy of mind ought to do if it can. The identity theory shows how the mentalistic explanations of psychology could be not mere heuristics but literal accounts of the causal history of behavior. Moreover, since the identity theory is not a semantic thesis, it is immune to many arguments that cast in doubt logical behaviorism. A drawback of logical behaviorism is that the observation "John has a headache" does not seem to mean the same thing as a statement of the form "John is disposed to behave in such and such a way." The identity theorist, however, can live with the fact that "John has a headache" and "John is in such and such a brain state" are not synonymous. The assertion of the identity theorist is not that these sentences mean the same thing but only that they are rendered true (or false) by the same neurophysiological phenomena.

The identity theory can be held either as a doctrine about mental particulars (John's current pain or Bill's fear of animals) or as a doctrine about mental universals, or properties (having a pain or being afraid of animals). The two doctrines, called respectively token physicalism and type physicalism, differ in strength and plausibility. Token physicalisim maintains only that all the mental particulars that happen to exist are neurophysiological, whereas type physicalism makes the more sweeping assertion that all the mental particulars there could possibly be are neurophysiological. Token physicalism does not rule out the logical possibility of machines and disembodied spirits having mental properties. Type physicalism dismisses this possibility because neither machines nor disembodied spirits have neurons.

Type physicalism is not a plausible doctrine about mental properties even if token physicalism is right about mental particulars. The problem with type physicalism is that the psychological constitution of a system seems to depend not on its hardware, or physical composition, but on its software, or program. Why should the philosopher dismiss the possibility that silicon-based Martians have pains, assuming that the silicon is properly organized? And why should the philosopher rule out the possibility of machines having beliefs, assuming that the machines are correctly programmed? If it is logically possible that Martians and machines could have mental properties, then mental properties and neurophysiological processes cannot be identical, however much they may prove to be coextensive.

What it all comes down to is that there seems to be a level of abstraction at which the generalizations of psychology are most naturally pitched. This level of abstraction cuts across differences in the physical composition of the systems to which psychological generalizations apply. In the cognitive sciences, at least, the natural domain for psychological theorizing seems to be all systems that process information. The problem with type physicalism is that there are possible information-processing systems with the same psychological constitution as human beings but not the same physical organization. In principle all kinds of physically different things could have human software.

This situation calls for a relational account of mental properties that abstracts them from the physical structure of their bearers. In spite of the objections to logical behaviorism that I presented above, logical behaviorism was at least on the right track in offering a relational interpretation of mental properties: to have a headache is to be disposed to exhibit a certain pattern of relations between the stimuli one encounters and the responses one exhibits. If that is what having a headache is, however, there is no reason in principle why only heads that are physically similar to ours can ache. Indeed, according to logical behaviorism, it is a necessary truth that any system that has our stimulus-response contingencies also has our headaches.

## [THE RISE OF FUNCTIONALISM]

All of this emerged 10 or 15 years ago as a nasty dilemma for the materialist program in the philosophy of mind. On the one hand the identity theorist (and not the logical behaviorist) had got right the causal character of the interactions of mind and body. On the other the logical behaviorist (and not the identity theorist) had got right the relational character of mental properties. Functionalism has apparently been able to resolve the dilemma. By stressing the distinction computer science draws between hardware and software the functionalist can make sense of both the causal and the relational character of the mental.

The intuition underlying functionalism is that what determines the psychological type to which a mental particular belongs is the causal role of the particular in the mental life of the organism. Functional individuation is differentiation with respect to causal role. A headache, for example, is identified with the type of mental state that among other things causes a disposition for taking aspirin in people who believe aspirin relieves a headache, causes a desire to rid oneself of the pain one is feeling, often causes someone who speaks English to say such things as "I have a headache" and is brought on by overwork, eyestrain and tension. This list is presumably not complete. More will be known about the nature of a headache as psychological and physiological research discovers more about its causal role.

Functionalism construes the concept of causal role in such a way that a mental state can be defined by its causal relations to other mental states. In this respect functionalism is completely different from logical behaviorism. Another major difference is that functionalism is not a reductionist thesis. It does not foresee, even in principle, the elimination of mentalistic concepts from the explanatory apparatus of psychological theories.

The difference between functionalism and logical behaviorism is brought out by the fact that functionalism is fully compatible with token physicalism. The functionalist would not be disturbed if brain events turn out to be the only things with the functional properties that define mental states. Indeed, most functionalists fully expect it will turn out that way.

Since functionalism recognizes that mental particulars may be physical, it is compatible with the idea that mental causation is a species of physical causation. In other words, functionalism tolerates the materialist solution to the mind-body problem provided by the central-state identity theory. It is possible for the functionalist to assert both that mental properties are typically defined in terms of their relations and that interactions of mind and body are typically causal in however robust a notion of causality is required by psychological explanations. The logical behaviorist can endorse only the first assertion and the type physicalist only the second. As a result functionalism seems to capture the best features of the materialist alternatives to dualism. It is no wonder that functionalism has become increasingly popular. . . .

## [FUNCTIONALISM AND TURING MACHINES]

Some philosophers are suspicious of functionalism because it seems too easy. Since functionalism licenses the individuation of states by reference to their causal role, it appears to allow a trivial explanation of any observed event E, that is, it appears to postulate an E-causer. for example, what makes the valves in a machine open? Why, the operation of a valve opener. And what is a valve opener? Why, anything that has the functionally defined property of causing valves to open.

In psychology this kind of question-begging often takes the form of theories that in effect postulate homunculi* with the selfsame intellectual capacities the theorist set out to explain. Such is the case when visual perception is explained by simply postulating psychological mechanisms that process visual information. The behaviorist has often charged the mentalist, sometimes justifiably, of mongering this kind of question-begging pseudo explanation. The charge will have to be met if functionally defined mental states are to have a serious role in psychological theories.

---

*[Internal little men.—Eds.]

The burden of the accusation is not untruth but triviality. There can be no doubt that it is a valve opener that opens valves, and it is likely that visual perception is mediated by the processing of visual information. The charge is that such putative functional explanations are mere platitudes. The functionalist can meet this objection by allowing functionally defined theoretical constructs only where mechanisms exist that can carry out the function and only where he has some notion of what such mechanisms might be like. One way of imposing this requirement is to identify the mental processes that psychology postulates with the operations of the restricted class of possible computers called Turing machines.

A Turing machine can be informally characterized as a mechanism with a finite number of program states. The inputs and outputs of the machine are written on a tape that is divided into squares each of which includes a symbol from a finite alphabet. The machine scans the tape one square at a time. It can erase the symbol on a scanned square and print a new one in its place. The machine can execute only the elementary mechanical operations of scanning, erasing, printing, moving the tape and changing state.

The program states of the Turing machine are defined solely in terms of the input symbols on the tape, the output symbols on the tape, the elementary operations and the other states of the program. Each program state is therefore functionally defined by the part it plays in the overall operation of the machine. Since the functional role of a state depends on the relation of the state to other states as well as to inputs and outputs, the relational character of the mental state is captured by the Turing-machine version of functionalism. Since the definition of a program state never refers to the physical structure of the system running the program, the Turing-machine version of functionalism also captures the idea that the character of a mental state is independent of its physical realization. A human being, a roomful of people, a computer and a disembodied spirit would all be a Turing machine if they operated according to a Turing-machine program.

The proposal is to restrict the functional definition of psychological states to those that can be expressed in terms of the program states of Turing machines. If this restriction can be enforced, it provides a guarantee that psychological theories will be compatible with the demands of mechanisms. Since Turing machines are very simple devices, they are in principle quite easy to build. Consequently by formulating a psychological explanation as a Turing-machine program the psychologist ensures that the explanation is mechanistic, even though the hardware realizing the mechanism is left open.

There are many kinds of computational mechanisms other than Turing machines, and so the formulation of a functionalist psychological theory in Turing-machine notation provides only a sufficient condition for the theory's being mechanically realizable. What makes the condition interesting, however, is that the simple Turing machine can perform many complex tasks. Although the elementary operations of the Turing-machine are restricted, iterations of the operations enable the machine to carry out any well-defined computation on discrete symbols.

An important tendency in the cognitive sciences is to treat the mind chiefly as a device that manipulates symbols. If a mental process can be functionally defined as an operation on symbols, there is a Turing machine capable of carrying out the computation and a variety of mechanisms for realizing the Turing machine. Where the manipulation of symbols is important the Turing machine provides a connection between functional explanation and mechanistic explanation.

The reduction of a psychological theory to a program for a Turing machine is a way of exorcising the homunculi. The reduction ensures that no operations have been postulated except those that could be performed by a familiar mechanism. Of course, the working psychologist usually cannot specify the reduction for each functionally individuated process in every theory he is prepared to take seriously. In practice the argument usually goes in the opposite direction; if the postulation of a mental operation is essential to some cherished psychological explanation, the theorist tends to assume that there must be a program for a Turing machine that will carry out that operation.

The "black boxes" that are common in flow charts drawn by psychologists often serve to indicate postulated mental processes for which Turing reductions are wanting. Even so, the possibility in principle of such reductions serves as a methodological constraint on psychological theorizing by determining what functional definitions are to be allowed and what it would be like to know that everything has been explained that could possibly need explanation.

## [FUNCTIONALISM AND QUALITATIVE CONTENT]

Such is the origin, the provenance and the promise of contemporary functionalism. How much has it actually paid off? This question is not easy to answer because much of what is now happening in the philosophy of mind and the cognitive sciences is directed at exploring the scope and limits of the functionalist explanations of behavior. I shall, however, give a brief overview.

An obvious objection to functionalism as a theory of the mind is that the functionalist definition is not limited to mental states and processes. Catalysts, Coke machines, valve openers, pencil sharpeners, mousetraps and ministers of finance are all in one way or another concepts that are functionally defined, but none is a mental concept such as pain, belief and desire. What, then, characterizes the mental? And can it be captured in a functionalist framework?

The traditional view in the philosophy of mind has it that mental states are distinguished by their having what are called either qualitative content or intentional content. I shall discuss qualitative content first.

It is not easy to say what qualitative content is; indeed, according to some theories, it is not even possible to say what it is because it can be known not by description but only by direct experience. I shall nonetheless attempt to describe it. Try to imagine looking at a blank wall through a red filter. Now change the filter to a green one and leave everything else exactly the way it was. Something about the character of your experience changes when the filter does, and it is this kind of thing that philosophers call qualitative content. I am not entirely comfortable about introducing qualitative content in this way, but it is a subject with which many philosophers are not comfortable.

The reason qualitative content is a problem for functionalism is straightforward. Functionalism is committed to defining mental states in terms of their causes and effects. It seems, however, as if two mental states could have all the same causal relations and yet could differ in their qualitative content. Let me illustrate this with the classic puzzle of the inverted spectrum.

It seems possible to imagine two observers who are alike in all relevant psychological respects except that experiences having the qualitative content of red for one observer would have the qualitative content of green for the other. Nothing about their behavior need reveal the difference because both of them see ripe tomatoes and flaming sunsets as being similar in color and both of them call that color "red." Moreover, the causal connection between their (qualitatively distinct) experiences and their other mental states could also be identical. Perhaps they both think of Little Red Riding Hood when they see ripe tomatoes, feel depressed when they see the color green and so on. It seems as if anything that could be packed into the notion of the causal role of their experiences could be shared by them, and yet the qualitative content of the experiences could be as different as you like. If this is possible, then the functionalist account does not work for mental states that have qualitative content. If one person is having a green experience while another person is having a red one, then surely they must be in different mental states.

The example of the inverted spectrum is more than a verbal puzzle. Having qualitative content is supposed to be a chief factor in what makes a mental state conscious. Many psychologists who are inclined to accept the functionalist framework are nonetheless worried about the failure of functionalism to reveal much about the nature of consciousness. Functionalists have made a few ingenious attempts to talk themselves and their colleagues out of this worry, but they have not, in my view, done so with much success. (For example, perhaps one is wrong in thinking one can imagine what an inverted spectrum would be like.) As matters stand, the problem of qualitative content poses a serious threat to the assertion that functionalism can provide a general theory of the mental.

## [FUNCTIONALISM AND INTENTIONAL CONTENT]

Functionalism has fared much better with the intentional content of mental states. Indeed, it is here that the major achievements of recent cognitive science are found. To say that a mental state has intentional content is to say that it has certain semantic properties. For example, for Enrico to believe Galileo was Italian apparently involves a three-way relation between Enrico, a belief and a proposition that is the content of the belief (namely the proposition that Galileo was Italian). In particular it is an essential property of Enrico's belief that it is about Galileo (and not about, say, Newton) and that it is true if, and only if, Galileo was indeed Italian. Philosophers are divided on how these considerations fit together, but it is widely agreed that beliefs involve semantic properties such as expressing a proposition, being true or false and being about one thing rather than another.

It is important to understand the semantic properties of beliefs because theories in the cognitive sciences are largely about the beliefs organisms have. Theories of learning and perception, for example, are chiefly accounts of how the host of beliefs an organism has are determined by the character of its experiences and its genetic endowment. The functionalist account of mental states does not by itself provide the required insights. Mousetraps are functionally defined, yet mousetraps do not express propositions, and they are not true or false.

There is at least one kind of thing other than a mental state that has intentional content: a symbol. Like thoughts, symbols seem to be about things. If someone says "Galileo was Italian," his utterance, like Enrico's belief, expresses a proposition about Galileo that is true or false depending on Galileo's homeland. This parallel between the symbolic and the mental underlies the traditional quest for a unified treatment of language and mind. Cognitive science is now trying to provide such a treatment.

The basic concept is simple but striking. Assume that there are such things as mental symbols (mental representations) and that mental symbols have semantic properties. On this view having a belief involves being related to a mental symbol, and the belief inherits its semantic properties from the mental symbol that figures in the relation. Mental processes (thinking, perceiving, learning and so on) involve causal interactions among relational states such as having a belief. The semantic properties of the words and sentences we utter are in turn inherited from the semantic properties of the mental states that language expresses.

Associating the semantic properties of mental states with those of mental symbols is fully compatible with the computer metaphor, because it is natural to think of the computer as a mechanism that manipulates symbols. A computation is a causal chain of computer states, and the links in the chain are operations on semantically interpreted formulas in a machine code. To think of a system (such as the nervous system) as a computer is to raise questions about the nature of the code in which it computes and the semantic properties of the symbols in the code. In fact, the analogy between minds and computers actually implies the postulation of mental symbols. There is no computation without representation.

The representational account of the mind, however, predates considerably the invention of the computing machine. It is a throwback to classical epistemology, which is a tradition that includes philosophers as diverse as John Locke, David Hume, George Berkeley, René Descartes, Immanuel Kant, John Stuart Mill and William James.

Hume, for one, developed a representational theory of the mind that included five points. First, there exist "Ideas," which are a species of mental symbol. Second, having a belief involves entertaining an Idea. Third, mental processes are causal associations of Ideas. Fourth, Ideas are like pictures. And fifth, Ideas have their semantic properties by virtue of what they resemble: the Idea of John is about John because it looks like him.

Contemporary cognitive psychologists do not accept the details of Hume's theory, although they endorse much of its spirit. Theories of computation provide a far richer account of mental processes than the mere association of Ideas. And only a few psychologists still think that imagery is the chief vehicle of mental representation. Nevertheless, the most significant break with Hume's theory lies in the abandoning of resemblance as an explanation of the semantic properties of mental representations.

Many philosophers, starting with Berkeley, have argued that there is something seriously wrong with the suggestion that the semantic relation between a thought and what the thought is about could be one of resemblance. Consider the thought that John is tall. Clearly the thought is true only of the state of affairs consisting of John's being tall. A theory of the semantic properties of a thought should therefore explain how this particular thought is related to this particular state of affairs. According to the resemblance theory, entertaining the thought involves having a mental image that shows John to be tall. To put it another way, the relation between the thought that John is tall and his being tall is like the relation between a tall man and his portrait.

The difficulty with the resemblance theory is that any portrait showing John to be tall must also show him to be many other things: clothed or naked, lying, standing or sitting, having a head or not having one, and so on. A portrait of a tall man who is sitting down resembles a man's being seated as much as it resembles a man's being tall. On the resemblance theory it is not clear what distinguishes thoughts about John's height from thoughts about his posture.

The resemblance theory turns out to encounter paradoxes at every turn. The possibility of construing beliefs as involving relations to semantically interpreted mental representations clearly depends on having an acceptable account of where the semantic properties of the mental representations come from. If resemblance will not provide this account, what will?

The current idea is that the semantic properties of a mental representation are determined by aspects of its functional role. In other words, a sufficient condition for having semantic properties can be specified in causal terms. This is the connection between functionalism and the representational theory of the mind. Modern cognitive psychology rests largely on the hope that these two doctrines can be made to support each other.

No philosopher is now prepared to say exactly how the functional role of a mental representation determines its semantic properties. Nevertheless, the functionalist recognizes three types of causal relations among psychological states involving mental representations, and they might serve to fix the semantic properties of mental representations. The three types are causal relations among mental states and stimuli, mental states and responses and some mental states and other ones.

Consider the belief that John is tall. Presumably the following facts, which correspond respectively to the three types of causal relations, are relevant to determining the semantic properties of the mental representation involved in the belief. First, the belief is a normal effect of certain stimulations, such as seeing John in circumstances that reveal his height. Second, the belief is the normal cause of certain behavioral effects, such as uttering "John is tall." Third, the belief is a normal cause of certain other beliefs and a normal effect of certain other beliefs. For example, anyone who believes John is tall is very likely also to believe someone is tall. Having the first belief is normally causally sufficient for having the second belief. And anyone who believes everyone in the room is tall and also believes John is in the room will very likely believe John is tall. The third belief is a normal effect of the first two. In short, the functionalist maintains that the proposition expressed by a given mental representation depends on the causal properties of the mental states in which that mental representation figures.

The concept that the semantic properties of mental representations are determined by aspects of their functional role is at the center of current work in the cognitive sciences. Nevertheless, the concept may not be true. Many philosophers who are unsympathetic to the cognitive turn in modern psychology doubt its truth, and many psychologists would probably reject it in the bald and unelaborated way that I have sketched it. Yet even in its skeletal form, there is this much to be said in its favor: It legitimizes the notion of mental representation, which has become increasingly important to theorizing in every branch of the cognitive sciences. Recent advances in formulating and testing hypotheses about the character of mental representations in fields ranging from phonetics to computer vision suggest that the concept of mental representation is fundamental to empirical theories of the mind.

The behaviorist has rejected the appeal to mental representation because it runs counter to his view of the explanatory mechanisms that can figure in psychological theories. Nevertheless, the science of mental representation is now flourishing. The history of science reveals that when a successful theory comes into conflict with a methodological scruple, it is generally the scruple that gives way. Accordingly the functionalist has relaxed the behaviorist constraints on psychological explanations. There is probably no better way to decide what is methodologically permissible in science than by investigating what successful science requires.

## READING COMPREHENSION QUESTIONS

1. What is "radical behaviorism"? According to Fodor, what is the strongest argument against this view?

2. What is "logical behaviorism"? According to Fodor, what advantage does this view seem to have over radical behaviorism? What is the main objection to this theory, according to Fodor?

3. State the central-state identity theory. What advantages does it have over behaviorism? What is the main problem for the identity theory? (Note: To answer this question, you will need to review the distinction between *token* versions of the identity theory and *type* versions.)

4. Just before Fodor introduces functionalism, he explains a "nasty dilemma" for materialist accounts of the mind. State the dilemma.

5. How is functionalism supposed to avoid the dilemma mentioned in the previous question?

6. What is the "triviality worry" that some philosophers raise against functionalism?

7. Fodor claims that one way of meeting the worry mentioned in the previous questions is for the functionalist to identify mental states with a class of computers called *Turing machines*. What is a Turing machine? How is the use of such machines supposed to help the functionalist overcome the triviality worry?

*The next two questions concern an objection to functionalism that has to do with what Fodor calls the "qualitative content" of mental states.*

8. Explain (using examples) what qualitative content is. Why is such content so important for theories of mind?

9. The objection to functionalist theories of mind, based on the qualitative content of mental states, involves the puzzle of the inverted spectrum. What is this puzzle? How does it figure into an objection to functionalism?

10. What is intentional content? How, according to Fodor, does the functionalist theory fare in accounting for such content?

# 11

# Minds, Brains, and Machines

JOHN SEARLE

*John Searle is the Mills Professor of Philosophy and Mind and Language at the University of California, Berkeley. He is author of numerous books and articles, including* The Rediscovery of the Mind *(1994);* Mind, Language and Society *(2000); and* Freedom and Neurobiology: Reflections on Free Will, Language, and Political Power *(2006). In Part I of the following selection, Searle defends a solution to the mind-body problem according to which mental states are both caused by and realized in the brain. Then, in Part II, he criticizes what is called "strong AI" (artificial intelligence)—a version of functionalism according to which (roughly) the mind is a computer program. In criticizing this view, he appeals to his well-known Chinese room argument.*

## I. THE MIND–BODY PROBLEM

For thousands of years, people have been trying to understand their relationship to the rest of the universe. For a variety of reasons many philosophers today are reluctant to tackle such big problems. Nonetheless, the problems remain, and in this [article] I am going to attack some of them.

At the moment, the biggest problem is this: We have a certain commonsense picture of ourselves as human beings which is very hard to square with our overall

SOURCE: From John Searle, *Minds, Brains and Science* (Cambridge: Harvard University Press), 1984.

"scientific" conception of the physical world. We think of ourselves as *conscious, free, mindful, rational* agents in a world that science tells us consists entirely of mindless, meaningless physical particles. Now, how can we square these two conceptions? How, for example, can it be the case that the world contains nothing but unconscious physical particles, and yet that it also contains consciousness? How can a mechanical universe contain intentionalistic human beings—that is, human beings that can represent the world to themselves? How, in short, can an essentially meaningless world contain meanings?

Such problems spill over into other more contemporary-sounding issues: How should we interpret recent work in computer science and artificial intelligence—work aimed at making intelligent machines? Specifically, does the digital computer give us the right picture of the human mind? And why is it that the social sciences in general have not given us insights into ourselves comparable to the insights that the natural sciences have given us into the rest of nature? What is the relation between the ordinary, commonsense explanations we accept of the way people behave and scientific modes of explanation?

In this first [part], I want to plunge right into what many philosophers think of as the hardest problem of all: What is the relation of our minds to the rest of the universe? This, I am sure you will recognise, is the traditional mind-body or mind-brain problem. In its contemporary version it usually takes the form: how does the mind relate to the brain?

I believe that the mind-body problem has a rather simple solution, one that is consistent both with what we know about neurophysiology and with our commonsense conception of the nature of mental states—pains, beliefs, desires and so on. But before presenting that solution, I want to ask why the mind-body problem seems so intractable. Why do we still have in philosophy and psychology after all these centuries a "mind-body problem" in a way that we do not have, say, a "digestion-stomach problem?" Why does the mind seem more mysterious than other biological phenomena?

I am convinced that part of the difficulty is that we persist in talking about a twentieth-century problem in an outmoded seventeenth-century vocabulary. When I was an undergraduate, I remember being dissatisfied with the choices that were apparently available in the philosophy of mind: you could be either a monist or a dualist. If you were a monist, you could be either a materialist or an idealist. If you were a materialist, you could be either a behaviourist or a physicalist. And so on. One of my aims in what follows is to try to break out of these tired old categories. Notice that nobody feels he has to choose between monism and dualism where the "digestion-stomach problem" is concerned. Why should it be any different with the "mind-body problem?"

But, vocabulary apart, there is still a problem or family of problems. Since Descartes, the mind-body problem has taken the following form: how can we account for the relationships between two apparently completely different kinds of things? On the one hand, there are mental things, such as our thoughts and feelings; we think of them as subjective, conscious, and immaterial, On the other hand, there are physical things; we think of them as having mass, as extended in space, and as causally interacting with other physical things. Most attempted solutions to the mind-body problem wind up by denying the existence of, or in some way downgrading the status of, one or the other of these types of things. Given the successes of the physical sciences, it is not surprising that in our stage of intellectual development the temptation is to downgrade the status of mental entities. So, most of the recently fashionable materialist conceptions of the mind—such as behaviourism, functionalism, and physicalism—end up by denying, implicitly or explicitly, that there are any such things as minds as we ordinarily think of them. That is, they deny that we do really intrinsically have subjective, conscious, mental states and that they are as real and as irreducible as anything else in the universe.

Now, why do they do that? Why is it that so many theorists end up denying the intrinsically mental character of mental phenomena? If we can answer that question, I believe that we will understand why the mind-body problem has seemed so intractable for so long.

There are four features of mental phenomena which have made them seem impossible to fit into our "scientific" conception of the world as made up of material things. And it is these four features that have made the mind-body problem really difficult. They are so embarrassing that they have led many thinkers in philosophy, psychology, and artificial intelligence to say strange and implausible things about the mind.

The most important of these features is consciousness. I, at the moment of writing this, and you, at the moment of reading it, are both conscious. It is just a plain fact about the world that it contains such conscious mental states and events, but it is hard to see how mere physical systems could have consciousness. How could such a thing occur? How, for example, could this grey and white gook inside my skull be conscious?

I think the existence of consciousness ought to seem amazing to us. It is easy enough to imagine a universe without it, but if you do, you will see that you have imagined a universe that is truly meaningless. Consciousness is the central fact of specifically human existence because without it all of the other specifically human aspects of our existence—language, love, humour, and so on—would be impossible. I believe it is, by the way, something of a scandal that contemporary discussions in philosophy and psychology have so little of interest to tell us about consciousness.

The second intractable feature of the mind is what philosophers and psychologists call "intentionality," the feature by which our mental states are directed at, or are about, or refer to, or are of objects and states of affairs in the world other than themselves. "Intentionality," by the way, doesn't just refer to intentions, but also to beliefs, desires, hopes, fears, love, hate, lust, disgust, shame, pride, irritation, amusement, and all of those mental states (whether conscious or unconscious) that refer to, or are about, the world apart from the mind. Now the question about intentionality is much like the question about consciousness. How can this stuff inside my head be *about* anything? How can it *refer* to anything? After all, this stuff in the skull consists of "atoms in the void," just as all of the rest of material reality consists of atoms in the void. Now how, to put it crudely, can atoms in the void represent anything?

The third feature of the mind that seems difficult to accommodate within a scientific conception of reality is the subjectivity of mental states. This subjectivity is marked by such facts as that I can feel my pains, and you can't. I see the world from my point of view; you see it from your point of view. I am aware of myself and my internal mental states, as quite distinct from the selves and mental states of other people. Since the seventeenth century we have come to think of reality as something which must be equally accessible to all competent observers—that is, we think it must be objective. Now, how are we to accommodate the reality of *subjective* mental phenomena with the scientific conception of reality as totally *objective?*

Finally, there is a fourth problem, the problem of mental causation. We all suppose, as part of common sense, that our thoughts and feelings make a real difference to the way we behave, that they actually have some *causal* effect on the physical world. I decide, for example, to raise my arm and—lo and behold—my arm goes up. But if our thoughts and feelings are truly mental, how can they affect anything physical? How could something mental make a physical difference? Are we supposed to think that our thoughts and feelings can somehow produce chemical effects on our brains and the rest of our nervous system? How could such a thing occur? Are we supposed to think that thoughts can wrap themselves around the axons or shake the dendrites or sneak inside the cell wall and attack the cell nucleus?

But unless some such connection takes place between the mind and the brain, aren't we just left with the view that the mind doesn't matter, that it is as unimportant causally as the froth on the wave is to the movement of the wave? I suppose if the froth were conscious, it might think to itself: "What a tough job it is pulling these waves up on the beach and then pulling them out again, all day long!" But we know the froth doesn't make any important difference. Why do we suppose our mental life is any more important than a froth on the wave of physical reality?

These four features, consciousness, intentionality, subjectivity, and mental causation are what make the mind-body problem seem so difficult. Yet, I want to say, they are all real features of our mental lives. Not every mental state has all of them. But any satisfactory account of the mind and of mind-body relations must take account of all four features. If your theory ends up by denying any one of them, you know you must have made a mistake somewhere.

The first thesis I want to advance toward 'solving the mind-body problem' is this:

> Mental phenomena, all mental phenomena whether conscious or
> unconscious, visual or auditory, pains, tickles, itches, thoughts, indeed,
> all of our mental life, are caused by processes going on in the brain.

To get a feel for how this works, let's try to describe the causal processes in some detail for at least one kind of mental state. For example, let's consider pains. Of course, anything we say now may seem wonderfully quaint in a generation, as our knowledge of how the brain works increases. Still, the *form* of the explanation can remain valid even though the *details* are altered. On current views, pain signals are transmitted from sensory nerve endings to the spinal cord by at least two types of fibres—there are Delta A fibres, which are specialised for prickling sensations, and C fibres, which are specialised for burning and aching sensations. In the spinal cord, they pass through a region called the tract of Lissauer and terminate on the neurons of the cord. As the signals go up the spine, they enter the brain by two separate pathways: the prickling pain pathway and the burning pain pathway. Both pathways go through the thalamus, but the prickling pain is more localised afterwards in the somato-sensory cortex, whereas the burning pain pathway transmits signals, not only upwards into the cortex, but also laterally into the hypothalamus and other regions at the base of the brain. Because of these differences, it is much easier for us to localise a prickling sensation—we can tell fairly accurately where someone is sticking a pin into our skin, for example—whereas burning and aching pains can be more distressing because they activate more of the nervous system. The actual sensation of pain appears to be caused both by the stimulation of the basal regions of the brain, especially the thalamus, and the stimulation of the somato-sensory cortex.

Now for the purposes of this discussion, the point we need to hammer home is this: our sensations of pains are caused by a series of events that begin at free nerve endings and end in the thalamus and in other regions of the brain. Indeed, as far as the actual sensations are concerned, the events inside the central nervous system are quite sufficient to cause pains—we know this both from the phantom-limb pains felt by amputees and the pains caused by artificially stimulating relevant portions of the brain. I want to suggest that what is true of pain is true of mental phenomena generally. To put it crudely, and counting all of the central nervous system as part of the brain for our present discussion, everything that matters for our mental life, all of our thoughts and feelings, are caused by processes inside the brain. As far as causing mental states is concerned, the crucial step is the one that goes on inside the head, not the external or peripheral stimulus. And the argument for this is simple. If the events outside the central nervous system occurred, but nothing happened in the brain, there would be no mental events. But if the right things happened in the brain, the mental events would occur even if there was no outside stimulus. (And that, by the way, is the principle on which surgical anaesthesia works: the outside stimulus is prevented from having the relevant effects on the central nervous system.)

But if pains and other mental phenomena are caused by processes in the brain, one wants to know: what are pains? What are they really? Well, in the case of pains, the obvious answer is that they are unpleasant sorts of sensations. But that answer leaves us unsatisfied because it doesn't tell us how pains fit into our overall conception of the world.

Once again, I think the answer to the question is obvious, but it will take some spelling out. To our first claim—that pains and other mental phenomena are caused by brain processes, we need to add a second claim:

> Pains and other mental phenomena just are features of the brain (and perhaps the rest of the central nervous system).

One of the primary aims of this [part of the chapter] is to show how *both* of these propositions can be true together. How can it be both the case that brains cause minds and yet minds just are features of brains? I believe it is the failure to see how both these propositions can be true together that has blocked a solution to the mind-body problem for so long. There are different levels of confusion that such a pair of ideas can generate. If mental and physical phenomena have cause and effect relationships, how can one be a feature of the other? Wouldn't that imply that the mind caused itself—the dreaded doctrine *of causa sui*? But at the bottom of our puzzlement is a misunderstanding of causation. It is tempting to think that whenever A causes B there must be two discrete events, one identified as the cause, the other identified as the effect; that all causation functions in the same way as billiard balls hitting each other. This crude mode of the causal relationships between the brain and the mind inclines us to accept some kind of dualism; we are inclined to think that events in one material realm, the "physical," cause events in another insubstantial realm, the "mental." But that seems to me a mistake. And the way to remove the mistake is to get a more sophisticated concept of causation. To do this, I will turn away from the relations between mind and brain for a moment to observe some other sorts of causal relationships in nature.

A common distinction in physics is between micro- and macro-properties of systems—the small and large scales. Consider, for example, the desk at which I am now sitting, or the glass of water in front of me. Each object is composed of micro-particles. The micro-particles have features at the level of molecules and atoms as well as at the deeper level of subatomic particles. But each object also has certain properties such as the solidity of the table, the liquidity of the water, and the transparency of the glass, which are surface or global features of the physical systems. Many such surface or global properties can be causally explained by the behaviour of elements at the micro-level. For example, the solidity of the table in front of me is explained by the lattice structure occupied by the molecules of which the table is composed. Similarly, the liquidity of the water is explained by the nature of the interactions between the $H_2O$ molecules. Those macro-features are causally explained by the behaviour of elements at the micro-level.

I want to suggest that this provides a perfectly ordinary model for explaining the puzzling relationships between the mind and the brain. In the case of liquidity, solidity, and transparency, we have no difficulty at all in supposing that the surface features are *caused by* the behaviour of elements at the micro-level, and at the same time we accept that the surface phenomena *just are* features of the very systems in question. I think the clearest way of stating this point is to say that the surface feature is both *caused by* the behaviour of micro-elements, and at the same time is *realised in* the system that is made up of the micro-elements. There is a cause and effect relationship, but at the same time the surface features are just higher level features of the very system whose behaviour at the micro-level causes those features.

In objecting to this someone might say that liquidity, solidity, and so on are identical with features of the micro-structure. So, for example, we might just define solidity as the lattice structure of the molecular arrangement, just as heat often is identified with the mean kinetic energy of molecule movements. This point seems to me correct but not really an objection to the analysis that I am proposing. It is a characteristic of the progress of science that an expression that is originally defined in terms of surface features, features accessible to the senses, is subsequently defined in terms of the micro-structure that causes the surface features. Thus, to take the example of solidity, the table in front of me is solid in the ordinary sense that it is rigid, it resists pressure, it supports books, it is not easily penetrable by most other objects such as other tables, and so on. Such is the commonsense notion of solidity. And in a scientific vein one can define solidity as whatever micro-structure causes these gross observable features. So one can then say either that solidity just is the lattice structure of the system of molecules and that solidity so defined causes, for example, resistance to touch and pressure. Or one can say that solidity consists of such high level features as rigidity and resistance to touch and pressure and that it is caused by the behaviour of elements at the micro-level.

If we apply these lessons to the study of the mind, it seems to me that there is no difficulty in accounting for the relations of the mind to the brain in terms of the brain's functioning to cause mental states. Just as the liquidity of the water is caused by the behaviour of elements at the micro-level, and yet at the same time it is a feature realised in the system of micro-elements, so in exactly that sense of "caused by" and "realised in" mental phenomena are caused by processes going on in the brain at the neuronal or modular level, and at the same time they are realised in the very system that consists of neurons. And just as we need the micro/macro distinction for any physical system, so for the same reasons we need the micro/macro distinction for the brain. And though we can say of a system of particles that it is 10°C or it is solid or it is liquid, we cannot say of any given particle that this particle is solid, this particle is liquid, this particle is 10°C. I can't for example reach into this glass of water, pull out a molecule and say: "This one's wet."

In exactly the same way, as far as we know anything at all about it, though we can say of a particular brain: "This brain is conscious," or: "This brain is experiencing thirst or pain," we can't say of any particular neuron in the brain: "This neuron is in pain, this neuron is experiencing thirst." To repeat this point, though there are enormous empirical mysteries about how the brain works in detail, there are no logical or philosophical or metaphysical obstacles to accounting for the relation between the mind and the brain in terms that are quite familiar to us from the rest of nature. Nothing is more common in nature than for surface features of a phenomenon to be both caused by and realised in a micro-structure, and those are exactly the relationships that are exhibited by the relation of mind to brain.

Let us now return to the four problems that I said faced any attempt to solve the mind-brain problem.

First, how is consciousness possible?

The best way to show how something is possible is to show how it actually exists. We have already given a sketch of how pains are actually caused by neurophysiological processes going on in the thalamus and the sensory cortex. Why is it then that many people feel dissatisfied with this sort of answer? I think that by pursuing an analogy with an earlier problem in the history of science we can dispel this sense of puzzlement. For a long time many biologists and philosophers thought it was impossible, in principle, to account for the existence of *life* on purely biological grounds. They thought that in addition to the biological processes some other element must be necessary, some *élan vital* must be postulated in order to lend life to what was otherwise dead and inert matter. It is hard today to realise how intense the dispute was between vitalism and mechanism even a generation ago, but today these issues are no longer taken seriously. Why not? I think it is not so much because mechanism won and vitalism lost, but because we have come to understand better the biological character of the processes that are characteristic of living organisms. Once we understand how the features that are characteristic of living beings have a biological explanation, it no longer seems mysterious to us that matter should be alive. I think that exactly similar considerations should apply to our discussions of consciousness. It should seem no more mysterious, in principle, that this hunk of matter, this grey and white oatmeal-textured substance of the brain, should be conscious than it seems mysterious that this other hunk of matter, this collection of nucleo-protein molecules stuck onto a calcium frame, should be alive. The way, in short, to dispel the mystery is to understand the processes. We do not yet fully understand the processes, but we understand their general *character,* we understand that there are certain specific electrochemical activities going on among neurons or neuron-modules and perhaps other features of the brain and these processes cause consciousness.

Our second problem was, how can atoms in the void have intentionality? How can they be about something?

As with our first question, the best way to show how something is possible is to show how it actually exists. So let's consider *thirst.* As far as we know anything about it, at least certain kinds of thirst are caused in the hypothalamus by sequences of nerve firings. These firings are in turn caused by the action of angiotensin in the hypothalamus, and angiotensin, in turn, is synthesised by renin, which is secreted by the kidneys. Thirst, at least of these kinds, is caused by a series of events in the central nervous system, principally the hypothalamus, and it is realised in the hypothalamus. To be thirsty is to have, among other things, the desire to drink. Thirst is therefore an intentional state: it has content; its content determines under what conditions it is satisfied, and it has all the rest of the features that are common to intentional states.

As with the "mysteries" of life and consciousness, the way to master the mystery of intentionality is to describe in as much detail as we can how the phenomena are caused by biological processes while being at the same time realised in biological systems. Visual and auditory experiences, tactile sensations, hunger, thirst, and sexual desire, are all caused by brain processes and they are realised in the structure of the brain, and they are all intentional phenomena.

I am not saying we should lose our sense of the mysteries of nature. On the contrary, the examples I have cited are all in a sense astounding. But I am saying that they are neither more nor less mysterious than other astounding features of the world, such as the existence of gravitational attraction, the process of photosynthesis, or the size of the Milky Way.

Our third problem: how do we accommodate the subjectivity of mental states within an objective conception of the real world?

It seems to me a mistake to suppose that the definition of reality should exclude subjectivity. If "science" is the name of the collection of objective and systematic truths we can state about the world, then the existence of subjectivity is an objective scientific fact like any other. If a scientific account of the world attempts to describe how things are, then one of the features of the account will be the subjectivity of mental states, since it is just a plain fact about biological evolution that it has produced certain sorts of biological systems, namely human and certain animal brains, that have subjective features. My present state of consciousness is a feature of my brain, but its conscious aspects are accessible to me in a way that they are not accessible to you. And your present state of consciousness is a feature of your brain and its conscious aspects are accessible to you in a way that they are not accessible to me. Thus the existence of subjectivity is an objective fact of biology. It is a persistent mistake to try to define "science" in terms of certain features of existing scientific theories. But once this provincialism is perceived to be the prejudice it is, then any domain of facts whatever is a subject of systematic investigation. So, for example, if God existed, then that fact would be a fact like any other. I do not know whether God exists, but I have no doubt at all that subjective mental states exist, because I am now in one and so are you. If the fact of subjectivity runs counter to a certain definition of "science," then it is the definition and not the fact which we will have to abandon.

Fourth, the problem of mental causation for our present purpose is to explain how mental events can cause physical events. How, for example, could anything as "weightless" and "ethereal" as a thought give rise to an action?

The answer is that thoughts are not weightless and ethereal. When you have a thought, brain activity is actually going on. Brain activity causes bodily movements by physiological processes. Now, because mental states are features of the brain, they have two levels of description—a higher level in mental terms, and a lower level in physiological terms. The very same causal powers of the system can be described at either level.

Once again, we can use an analogy from physics to illustrate these relationships. Consider hammering a nail with a hammer. Both hammer and nail have a certain kind of solidity. Hammers made of cottonwool or butter will be quite useless, and hammers made of water or steam are not hammers at all. Solidity is a real causal property of the hammer. But the solidity itself is caused by the behaviour of particles at the micro-level and it is realised in the system which consists of micro-elements. The existence of two causally real levels of description in the brain, one a macro-level of mental processes and the other a micro-level of neuronal processes is exactly analogous to the existence of two causally real levels of description of the hammer. Consciousness, for example, is a real property of the brain that can cause things to happen. My conscious attempt to perform an action such as raising my arm causes the movement of the arm. At the higher level of description, the intention to raise my arm causes the movement of the arm. But at the lower level of description, a series of neuron firings starts a chain of events that results in the contraction of the muscles. As with the case of hammering a nail, the same sequence of events has two levels of description. Both of them are causally real, and the higher level causal features are both caused by and realised in the structure of the lower level elements.

To summarise: on my view, the mind and the body interact, but they are not two different things, since mental phenomena just are features of the brain. One way to characterise this position is to see it as an assertion of both physicalism and mentalism. Suppose we define "naive physicalism" to be the view that all that exists in the world are physical particles with their properties and relations. The power of the physical model of reality is so great that it is hard to see how we can seriously challenge naive physicalism. And let us define "naive mentalism" to be the view that mental phenomena really exist. There really are mental states; some of them are conscious; many have intentionality; they all have subjectivity; and many of them function causally in determining physical events in the world. The thesis of this first [part] can now be stated quite simply. Naive mentalism and naive physicalism are perfectly consistent with each other. Indeed, as far as we know anything about how the world works, they are not only consistent, they are both true.

## II. CAN COMPUTERS THINK?

In the previous [part], I provided at least the outlines of a solution to the so-called "mind-body problem." Though we do not know in detail how the brain functions, we do know enough to have an idea of the general relationships between brain processes and mental processes. Mental processes are caused by the behaviour of elements of the brain. At the same time, they are realised in the structure that is made up of those elements. I think this answer is consistent with the standard biological approaches to biological phenomena. Indeed, it is a kind of commonsense answer to the question, given what we know about how the world works. However, it is very much a minority point of view. The prevailing view in philosophy, psychology, and artificial intelligence is one which emphasises the analogies between the functioning of the human brain and the functioning of digital computers. According to the most extreme version of this view, the brain is just a digital computer and the mind is just a computer program. One could summarise this view—call it "strong artificial intelligence," or "strong AI"—by saying that the mind is to the brain, as the program is to the computer hardware.

This view has the consequence that there is nothing essentially biological about the human mind. The brain just happens to be one of an indefinitely large number of different kinds of hardware computers that could sustain the programs which make up human intelligence. On this view, any physical system whatever that had the right program with the right inputs and outputs would have a mind in exactly the same sense that you and I have minds. So, for example, if you made a computer out of old beer cans powered by windmills; if it had the right program, it would have to have a mind. And the point is not that for all we know it might have thoughts and feelings, but rather that it must have thoughts and feelings, because that is all there is to having thoughts and feelings: implementing the right program.

Most people who hold this view think we have not yet designed programs which are minds. But there is pretty much general agreement among them that it's only a matter of time until computer scientists and workers in artificial intelligence design the appropriate hardware and programs which will be the equivalent of human brains and minds. These will be artificial brains and minds which are in every way the equivalent of human brains and minds.

Many people outside of the field of artificial intelligence are quite amazed to discover that anybody could believe such a view as this. So, before criticising it, let me give you a few examples of the things that people in this field have actually said. Herbert Simon of Carnegie-Mellon University says that we already have machines that can literally think. There is no question of waiting for some future machine, because existing digital computers already have thoughts in exactly the same sense that you and I do. Well, fancy that! Philosophers have been worried for centuries about whether or not a machine could think, and now we discover that they already have such machines at Carnegie-Mellon. Simon's colleague Alan Newell claims that we have now discovered (and notice that Newell says "discovered" and not "hypothesised" or "considered the possibility," but we have *discovered*) that intelligence is just a matter of physical symbol manipulation; it has no essential connection with any specific kind of biological or physical wetware or hardware. Rather, any system whatever that is capable of manipulating physical symbols in the right way is capable of intelligence in the same literal sense as human intelligence of human beings. Both Simon and Newell, to their credit, emphasise that there is nothing metaphorical about these claims; they mean them quite literally. Freeman Dyson is quoted as having said that computers have an advantage over the rest of us when it comes to evolution. Since consciousness is just a matter of formal processes, in computers these formal processes can go on in substances that are much better able to survive in a universe that is cooling off than beings like ourselves made of our wet and messy materials. Marvin Minsky of MIT says that the next generation of computers will be so intelligent that we will "be lucky if they are willing to keep us around the house as household pets." My all-time favourite in the literature of exaggerated claims on behalf of the digital computer is from John McCarthy, the inventor of the term "artificial intelligence." McCarthy says even "machines as simple as thermostats can be said to have beliefs." And indeed, according to him, almost any machine capable of problem-solving can be said to have beliefs. I admire McCarthy's courage. I once asked him: "What beliefs does your thermostat have?" And he said: "My thermostat has three beliefs—it's too hot in here, it's too cold in here, and it's just right in here." As a philosopher, I like all these claims for a simple reason. Unlike most philosophical theses, they are reasonably clear, and they admit of a simple and decisive refutation. It is this refutation that I am going to undertake in this [part of the] chapter.

The nature of the refutation has nothing whatever to do with any particular stage of computer technology. It is important to emphasise this point because the temptation is always to think that the solution to our problems must wait on some as yet uncreated technological wonder. But in fact, the nature of the refutation is completely independent of any state of technology. It has to do with the very definition of a digital computer, with what a digital computer is.

It is essential to our conception of a digital computer that its operations can be specified purely formally; that is, we specify the steps in the operation of the computer in terms of abstract symbols—sequences of zeroes and ones printed on a tape, for example. A typical computer "rule" will determine that when a machine is in a certain state and it has a certain symbol on its tape, then it will perform a certain operation such as erasing the symbol or printing another symbol and then enter another state such as moving the tape one square to the left. But the symbols have no meaning; they have no semantic content; they are not about anything. They have to be specified purely in terms of their formal or syntactical structure. The zeroes and ones, for example, are just numerals; they don't even stand for numbers. Indeed, it is this feature of digital computers that makes them so powerful. One and the same type of hardware, if it is appropriately designed, can be used to run an indefinite range of different programs. And one and the same program can be run on an indefinite range of different types of hardwares.

But this feature of programs, that they are defined purely formally or syntactically, is fatal to the view that mental processes and program processes are identical. And the reason can be stated quite simply. There is more to having a mind than having formal or syntactical processes. Our internal mental states, by definition, have certain sorts of contents. If I am thinking about Kansas City or wishing that I had a cold beer to drink or wondering if there will be a fall in interest rates, in each case my mental state has a certain mental content in addition to whatever formal features it might have. That is, even if my thoughts occur to me in strings of symbols, there must be more to the thought than the abstract strings, because strings by themselves can't have any meaning. If my thoughts are to be *about* anything, then the strings must have a *meaning* which makes the thoughts about those things. In a word, the mind has more than a syntax, it has a semantics. The reason that no computer program can ever be a mind is simply that a computer program is only syntactical, and minds are more than syntactical. Minds are semantical, in the sense that they have more than a formal structure, they have a content.

To illustrate this point I have designed a certain thought-experiment. Imagine that a bunch of computer programmers have written a program that will enable a computer to simulate the understanding of Chinese. So, for example, if the computer is given a question in Chinese, it will match the question against its memory, or data base, and produce appropriate answers to the questions in Chinese. Suppose for the sake of argument that the computer's answers are as good as those of a native Chinese speaker. Now then, does the computer, on the basis of this, understand Chinese, does it literally understand Chinese, in the way that Chinese speakers understand Chinese? Well, imagine that you are locked in a room, and in this room are several baskets full of Chinese symbols. Imagine that you (like me) do not understand a word of Chinese, but that you are given a rule book in English for manipulating these Chinese symbols. The rules specify the manipulations of the symbols purely formally, in terms of their syntax, not their semantics. So the rule might say: "Take a squiggle-squiggle sign out of basket number one and put it next to a squoggle-squoggle sign from basket number two." Now suppose that some other Chinese symbols are passed into the room, and that you are given further rules for passing back Chinese symbols out of the room. Suppose that unknown to you the symbols passed into the room are called "questions" by the people outside the room, and the symbols you pass back out of the room are called "answers to the questions." Suppose, furthermore, that the programmers are so good at designing the programs and that you are so good at manipulating the symbols, that very soon your answers are indistinguishable from those of a native Chinese speaker. There you are locked in your room shuffling your Chinese symbols and passing out Chinese symbols in response to incoming Chinese symbols. On the basis of the situation as I have described it, there is no way you could learn any Chinese simply by manipulating these formal symbols.

Now the point of the story is simply this: by virtue of implementing a formal computer program from the point of view of an outside observer, you behave exactly as if you understood Chinese, but all the same you don't understand a word of Chinese. But if going through the appropriate computer program for understanding Chinese is not enough to give *you* an understanding of Chinese, then it is not enough to give *any other digital computer* an understanding of Chinese. And again, the reason for this can be stated quite simply. If you don't understand Chinese, then no other computer could understand Chinese because no digital computer, just by virtue of running a program, has anything that you don't have. All that the computer has, as you have, is a formal program for manipulating uninterpreted Chinese symbols. To repeat, a computer has a syntax, but no semantics. The whole point of the parable of the Chinese room is to remind us of a fact that we knew all along. Understanding a language, or indeed, having mental states at all, involves more than just having a bunch of formal symbols. It involves having an interpretation, or a meaning attached to those symbols. And a digital computer, as defined, cannot have more than just formal symbols because the operation of the computer, as I said earlier, is defined in terms of its ability to implement programs. And these programs are purely formally specifiable—that is, they have no semantic content.

We can see the force of this argument if we contrast what it is like to be asked and to answer questions in English, and to be asked and to answer questions in some language where we have no knowledge of any of the meanings of the words. Imagine that in the Chinese room you are also given questions in English about such things as your age or your life history, and that you answer these questions. What is the difference between the Chinese case and the English case? Well again, if like me you understand no Chinese and you do understand English, then the difference is obvious. You understand the questions in English because they are expressed in symbols whose meanings are known to you. Similarly, when you give the answers in English you are producing symbols which are meaningful to you. But in the case of the Chinese, you have none of that. In the case of the Chinese, you simply manipulate formal symbols according to a computer program, and you attach no meaning to any of the elements.

Various replies have been suggested to this argument by workers in artificial intelligence and in psychology, as well as philosophy. They all have something in common; they are all inadequate. And there is an obvious reason why they have to be inadequate, since the argument rests on a very simple logical truth, namely, syntax alone is not sufficient for semantics, and digital computers insofar as they are computers have, by definition, a syntax alone.

I want to make this clear by considering a couple of the arguments that are often presented against me.

Some people attempt to answer the Chinese room example by saying that the whole system understands Chinese. The idea here is that though I, the person in the room manipulating the symbols do not understand Chinese, I am just the central processing unit of the computer system. They argue that it is the whole system, including the room, the baskets full of symbols and the ledgers containing the programs and perhaps other items as well, taken as a totality, that understands Chinese. But this is subject to exactly the same objection I made before. There is no way that the system can get from the syntax to the semantics. I, as the central processing unit have no way of figuring out what any of these symbols means; but then neither does the whole system.

Another common response is to imagine that we put the Chinese understanding program inside a robot. If the robot moved around and interacted causally with the world, wouldn't that be enough to guarantee that it understood Chinese? Once again the inexorability of the semantics-syntax distinction overcomes this manoeuvre. As long as we suppose that the robot has only a computer for a brain then, even though it might behave exactly as if it understood Chinese, it would still have no way of getting from the syntax to the semantics of Chinese. You can see this if you imagine that I am the computer. Inside a room in the robot's skull I shuffle symbols without knowing that some of them come in to me from television cameras attached to the robot's head and others go out to move the robot's arms and legs. As long as all I have is a formal computer program, I have no way of attaching any meaning to any of the symbols. And the fact that the robot is engaged in causal interactions with the outside world won't help me to attach any meaning to the symbols unless I have some way of finding out about that fact. Suppose the robot picks up a hamburger and this triggers the symbol for hamburger to come into the room. As long as all I have is the symbol with no knowledge of its causes or how it got there, I have no way of knowing what it means. The causal interactions between the robot and the rest of the world are irrelevant unless those causal interactions are represented in some mind or other. But there is no way they can be if all that the so-called mind consists of is a set of purely formal, syntactical operations.

It is important to see exactly what is claimed and what is not claimed by my argument. Suppose we ask the question that I mentioned at the beginning: "Could a machine think?" Well, in one sense, of course, we are all machines. We can construe the stuff inside our heads as a meat machine. And of course, we can all think. So, in one sense of "machine," namely that sense in which a machine is just a physical system which is capable of performing certain kinds of operations, in that sense, we are all machines, and we can think. So, trivially, there are machines that can think. But that wasn't the question that bothered us. So let's try a different formulation of it. Could an artefact think? Could a man-made machine think? Well, once again, it depends on the kind of artefact. Suppose we designed a machine that was molecule-for-molecule indistinguishable from a human being. Well then, if you can duplicate the causes, you can presumably duplicate the effects. So once again, the answer to that question is, in principle at least, trivially yes. If you could build a machine that had the same structure as a human being, then presumably that machine would be able to think. Indeed, it would be a surrogate human being. Well, let's try again.

The question isn't: "Can a machine think?" or: "Can an artefact think?" The question is: "Can a digital computer think?" But once again we have to be very careful in how we interpret the question. From a mathematical point of view, anything whatever can be described as if it were a digital computer. And that's because it can be described as instantiating or implementing a computer program. In an utterly trivial sense, the pen that is on the desk in front of me can be described as a digital computer. It just happens to have a very boring computer program. The program says: "Stay there." Now since in this sense, anything whatever is a digital computer, because anything whatever can be described as implementing a computer program, then once again, our question gets a trivial answer. Of course our brains are digital computers, since they implement any number of computer programs. And of course our brains can think. So once again, there is a trivial answer to the question. But that wasn't really the question we were trying to ask. The question we wanted to ask is this: "Can a digital computer as defined, think?" That is to say: "Is instantiating or implementing the right computer program with the right inputs and outputs, sufficient for, or constitutive of, thinking?" And to this question, unlike its predecessors, the answer is clearly "no." And it is "no" for the reason that we have spelled out, namely, the computer program is defined purely syntactically. But thinking is more than just a matter of manipulating meaningless symbols, it involves meaningful semantic contents. These semantic contents are what we mean by "meaning."

It is important to emphasise again that we are not talking about a particular stage of computer technology. The argument has nothing to do with the forthcoming, amazing advances in computer science. It has nothing to do with the distinction between serial and parallel processes, or with the size of programs, or the speed of computer operations, or with computers that can interact causally with their environment, or even with the invention of robots. Technological progress is always grossly exaggerated, but even subtracting the exaggeration, the development of computers has been quite remarkable, and we can reasonably expect that even more remarkable progress will be made in the future. No doubt we will be much better able to simulate human behaviour on computers than we can at present, and certainly much better than we have been able to in the past. The point I am making is that if we are talking about having mental states, having a mind, all of these simulations are simply irrelevant. It doesn't matter how good the technology is, or how rapid the calculations made by the computer are. If it really is a computer, its operations have to be defined syntactically, whereas consciousness, thoughts, feelings, emotions, and all the rest of it involve more than a syntax. Those features, by definition, the computer is unable to *duplicate* however powerful may be its ability to *simulate*. The key distinction here is between duplication and simulation. And no simulation by itself ever constitutes duplication.

What I have done so far is give a basis to the sense that those citations I began this talk with are really as preposterous as they seem. There is a puzzling question in this discussion though, and that is: "Why would anybody ever have thought that computers could think or have feelings and emotions and all the rest of it?" After all, we can do computer simulations of any process whatever that can be given a formal description. So, we can do a computer simulation of the flow of money in the British economy, or the pattern of power distribution in the Labour party. We can do computer simulation of rain storms in the home counties, or warehouse fires in East London. Now, in each of these cases, nobody supposes that the computer simulation is actually the real thing; no one supposes that a computer simulation of a storm will leave us all wet, or a computer simulation of a fire is likely to burn the house down. Why on earth would anyone in his right mind suppose a computer simulation of mental processes actually had mental processes? I don't really know the answer to that, since the idea seems to me, to put it frankly, quite crazy from the start. But I can make a couple of speculations.

First of all, where the mind is concerned, a lot of people are still tempted to some sort of behaviourism. They think if a system behaves as if it understood Chinese, then it really must understand Chinese. But we have already refuted this form of behaviourism with the Chinese room argument. Another assumption made by many people is that the mind is not a part of the biological world, it is not a part of the world of nature. The strong artificial intelligence view relies on that in its conception that the mind is purely formal; that somehow or other, it cannot be treated as a concrete product of biological processes like any other biological product. There is in these discussions, in short, a kind of residual dualism. AI partisans believe that the mind is more than a part of the natural biological world; they believe that the mind is purely formally specifiable. The paradox of this is that the AI literature is filled with fulminations against some view called "dualism," but in fact, the whole thesis of strong AI rests on a kind of dualism. It rests on a rejection of the idea that the mind is just a natural biological phenomenon in the world like any other.

I want to conclude this [discussion] by putting together the thesis of the [first part] and the thesis of this one. Both of these theses can be stated very simply. And indeed, I am going to state them with perhaps excessive crudeness. But if we put them together I think we get a quite powerful conception of the relations of minds, brains and computers. And the argument has a very simple logical structure, so you can see whether it is valid or invalid. The first premise is:

1.  *Brains cause minds.*

    Now, of course, that is really too crude. What we mean by that is that mental processes that we consider to constitute a mind are caused, entirely caused, by processes going on inside the brain. But let's be crude, let's just abbreviate that as three words—brains cause minds. And that is just a fact about how the world works. Now let's write proposition number two:

2.  *Syntax is not sufficient for semantics.*

    That proposition is a conceptual truth. It just articulates our distinction between the notion of what is purely formal and what has content. Now, to these two propositions—that brains cause minds and that syntax is not sufficient for semantics—let's add a third and a fourth:

3.  *Computer programs are entirely defined by their formal, or syntactical, structure.*

    That proposition, I take it, is true by definition; it is part of what we mean by the notion of a computer program.

4.  *Minds have mental contents; specifically, they have semantic contents.*

    And that, I take it, is just an obvious fact about how our minds work. My thoughts, and beliefs, and desires are about something, or they refer to something, or they concern states of affairs in the world; and they do that because their content directs them at these states of affairs in the world. Now, from these four premises, we can draw our first conclusion; and it follows obviously from premises 2, 3 and 4:

**Conclusion 1.**    *No computer program by itself is sufficient to give a system a mind. Programs, in short, are not minds, and they are not by themselves sufficient for having minds.*

Now, that is a very powerful conclusion, because it means that the project of trying to create minds solely by designing programs is doomed from the start. And it is important to re-emphasise that this has nothing to do with any particular state of technology or any particular state of the complexity of the program. This is a purely formal, or logical, result from a set of axioms which are agreed to by all (or nearly all) of the disputants concerned. That is, even most of the hardcore enthusiasts for artificial intelligence agree that in fact, as a matter of biology, brain processes cause mental states, and they agree that programs are defined purely formally. But if you put these conclusions together with certain other things that we know, then it follows immediately that the project of strong AI is incapable of fulfilment.

However, once we have got these axioms, let's see what else we can derive. Here is a second conclusion:

**Conclusion 2.**    *The way that brain functions cause minds cannot be solely in virtue of running a computer program.*

And this second conclusion follows from conjoining the first premise together with our first conclusion. That is, from the fact that brains cause minds and that programs are not enough to do the job, it follows that the way that brains cause minds can't be solely by running a computer program. Now that also I think is an important result, because it has the consequence that the brain is not, or at least is not just, a digital computer. We saw earlier that anything can trivially be described as if it were a digital computer, and brains are no exception. But the importance of this conclusion is that the computational properties of the brain are simply not enough to explain its functioning to produce mental states. And indeed, that ought to seem a commonsense scientific conclusion to us anyway because all it does is remind us of the fact that brains are biological engines; their biology matters. It is not, as several people in artificial intelligence have claimed, just an irrelevant fact about the mind that it happens to be realised in human brains.

Now, from our first premise, we can also derive a third conclusion:

**Conclusion 3.**    *Anything else that caused minds would have to have causal powers at least equivalent to those of the brain.*

And this third conclusion is a trivial consequence of our first premise. It is a bit like saying that if my petrol engine drives my car at seventy-five miles an hour, then any diesel engine that was capable of doing that would have to have a power output at least equivalent to that of my petrol engine. Of course, some other system might cause mental processes using entirely different chemical or biochemical features from those the brain in fact uses. It might turn out that there are beings on other planets, or in other solar systems, that have mental states and use an entirely different biochemistry from ours. Suppose that Martians arrived on earth and we concluded that they had mental states. But suppose that when their heads were opened up, it was discovered that all they had inside was green slime. Well still, the green slime, if it functioned to produce consciousness and all the rest of their mental life, would have to have causal powers equal to those of the human brain. But now, from our first conclusion, that programs are not enough, and our third conclusion, that any other system would have to have causal powers equal to the brain, conclusion four follows immediately:

**Conclusion 4.**    *For any artefact that we might build which had mental states equivalent to human mental states, the implementation of a computer program would not by itself be sufficient. Rather the artefact would have to have powers equivalent to the powers of the human brain.*

The upshot of this discussion I believe is to remind us of something that we have known all along: namely, mental states are biological phenomena. Consciousness, intentionality, subjectivity and mental causation are all a part of our biological life history, along with growth, reproduction, the secretion of bile, and digestion.

# READING COMPREHENSION QUESTIONS

1. Describe in your own words the four features of the mind (each of which is associated with a problem) which, according to Searle, makes the mind-body problem seem especially difficult. *Why* do these features seem to make the problem difficult?

2. State Searle's argument for the claim that what is crucial in causing mental states is what goes on inside the head, and not external stimuli.

3. What does Searle identify as the "crude model" of causal relationships? Why does he think that this model should be rejected?

4. Searle's solution to the mind-body problem is to argue that mental events are both *caused by* and are *realized in* the brain. What reasons does he offer for this solution? Do you think Searle has solved the mind-body problem? (Readers may want to revisit this question after reading the next article by David J. Chalmers.)

5. Briefly state how Searle's solution to the mind-body problem addresses the four problems of the mind that he describes early in the essay? Do you find what he says convincing? Why or why not?

6. Early in part II, Searle describes a view of the mind (and mental states) that he calls "strong artificial intelligence." State the view in question.

7. In his discussion of strong AI, Searle distinguishes syntax from semantics. Explain this distinction using examples.

8. In arguing against strong AI, Searle claims that because minds are semantical but a computer program is only syntactical, the mind can't be understood as a computer program. He illustrates this point with a thought experiment involving a Chinese room. Explain the thought experiment and how it is supposed to illustrate the claim in question.

9. Why does Searle claim that it is in principle impossible for a computer to think?

# 12

# The Puzzle of Conscious Experience

DAVID J. CHALMERS

*David J. Chalmers is professor of philosophy and ARC Federation Fellow, Research School of Social Sciences, Australian National University. He is author of* The Conscious Mind *(1996). Chalmers distinguishes between what he calls the "easy" and "hard" problems of conscious experience. The easy problems concern how the brain carries out various tasks—problems that neuroscience can eventually solve. By contrast, the hard problem concerns the link between brain activity and conscious experiences, which Chalmers thinks cannot be solved by neuroscience or any of the other sciences. He suggests that in order to account for the relation between the brain and consciousness, science will have to recognize consciousness as a fundamental feature of reality governed by a unique set of fundamental laws. Chalmers concludes with speculations about what such laws might be like.*

Conscious experience is at once the most familiar thing in the world and the most mysterious. There is nothing we know about more directly than consciousness, but it is extraordinarily hard to reconcile it with everything else we know. Why does it exist? What does it do? How could it possibly arise from neural processes in the brain? These questions are among the most intriguing in all of science.

From an objective viewpoint, the brain is relatively comprehensible. When you look at this page, there is a whir of processing: photons strike your retina, electrical signals are passed up your optic nerve and between different areas of your brain, and eventually you might respond with a smile, a perplexed frown or a remark. But there is also a subjective aspect. When you look at the page, you are conscious of it, directly experiencing the images and words as part of your private, mental life. You have vivid impressions of colored flowers and vibrant sky. At the same time, you may be feeling some emotions and forming some thoughts. Together such experiences make up consciousness: the subjective, inner life of the mind.

For many years, consciousness was shunned by researchers studying the brain and the mind. The prevailing view was that science, which depends on objectivity, could not accommodate something as subjective as consciousness. The behaviorist

SOURCE: From David J. Chalmers, "The Puzzle of Conscious Experience," *Scientific American,* December 1995.

movement in psychology, dominant earlier in this century, concentrated on external behavior and disallowed any talk of internal mental processes. Later, the rise of cognitive science focused attention on processes inside the head. Still, consciousness remained off-limits, fit only for late-night discussion over drinks.

Over the past several years, however, an increasing number of neuroscientists, psychologists and philosophers have been rejecting the idea that consciousness cannot be studied and are attempting to delve into its secrets. As might be expected of a field so new, there is a tangle of diverse and conflicting theories, often using basic concepts in incompatible ways. To help unsnarl the tangle, philosophical reasoning is vital.

The myriad views within the field range from reductionist theories, according to which consciousness can be explained by the standard methods of neuroscience and psychology, to the position of the so-called mysterians, who say we will never understand consciousness at all. I believe that on close analysis both of these views can be seen to be mistaken and that the truth lies somewhere in the middle.

Against reductionism I will argue that the tools of neuroscience cannot provide a full account of conscious experience, although they have much to offer. Against mysterianism I will hold that consciousness might be explained by a new kind of theory. The full details of such a theory are still out of reach, but careful reasoning and some educated inferences can reveal something of its general nature. For example, it will probably involve new fundamental laws, and the concept of information may play a central role. These faint glimmerings suggest that a theory of consciousness may have startling consequences for our view of the universe and of ourselves.

## THE HARD PROBLEM

Researchers use the word "consciousness" in many different ways. To clarify the issues, we first have to separate the problems that are often clustered together under the name. For this purpose, I find it useful to distinguish between the "easy problems" and the "hard problem" of consciousness. The easy problems are by no means trival—they are actually as challenging as most in psychology and biology—but it is with the hard problem that the central mystery lies.

The easy problems of consciousness include the following: How can a human subject discriminate sensory stimuli and react to them appropriately? How does the brain integrate information from many different sources and use this information to control behavior? How is it that subjects can verbalize their internal states? Although all these questions are associated with consciousness, they all concern the objective mechanisms of the cognitive system. Consequently, we have every reason to expect that continued work in cognitive psychology and neuroscience will answer them.

The hard problem, in contrast, is the question of how physical processes in the brain give rise to subjective experience. This puzzle involves the inner aspect of thought and perception: the way things feel for the subject. When we see, for example, we experience visual sensations, such as that of vivid blue. Or think of the ineffable sound of a distant oboe, the agony of an intense pain, the sparkle of happiness or the meditative quality of a moment lost in thought. All are part of what I am calling consciousness. It is these phenomena that pose the real mystery of the mind.

To illustrate the distinction, consider a thought experiment devised by the Australian philosopher Frank Jackson. Suppose that Mary, a neuroscientist in the 23rd century, is the world's leading expert on the brain processes responsible for color vision. But Mary has lived her whole life in a black-and-white room and has never seen any other colors. She knows everything there is to know about physical processes in the brain—its biology, structure and function. This understanding enables her to grasp everything there is to know about the easy problems: how the brain discriminates stimuli, integrates information and produces verbal reports. From her knowledge of color vision, she knows the way color names correspond with wavelengths on the light spectrum. But there is still something crucial about color vision that Mary does not know: what it is like to experience a color such as red. It follows that there are facts about conscious experience that cannot be deduced from physical facts about the functioning of the brain.

Indeed, nobody knows why these physical processes are accompanied by conscious experience at all. Why is it that when our brains process light of a certain wavelength, we have an experience of deep purple? Why do we have any experience at all? Could not an unconscious automaton have performed the same tasks just as well? These are questions that we would like a theory of consciousness to answer.

I am not denying that consciousness arises from the brain. We know, for example, that the subjective experience of vision is closely linked to processes in the visual cortex. It is the link itself that perplexes, however. Remarkably, subjective experience seems to emerge from a physical process. But we have no idea how or why this is.

## IS NEUROSCIENCE ENOUGH?

Given the flurry of recent work on consciousness in neuroscience and psychology, one might think this mystery is starting to be cleared up. On closer examination, however, it turns out that almost all the current work addresses only the easy problems of consciousness. The confidence of the reductionist view comes from the progress on the easy problems, but none of this makes any difference where the hard problem is concerned.

Consider the hypothesis put forward by neurobiologists Francis Crick of the Salk Institute for Biological Studies in San Diego and Christof Koch of the California Institute of Technology. They suggest that consciousness may arise from certain oscillations in the cerebral cortex, which become synchronized as neurons fire 40 times per second. Crick and Koch believe the phenomenon might explain how different attributes of a single perceived object (its color and shape, for example), which are processed in different parts of the brain, are merged into a coherent whole. In this theory, two pieces of information become bound together precisely when they are represented by synchronized neural firings.

The hypothesis could conceivably elucidate one of the easy problems about how information is integrated in the brain. But why should synchronized oscillations give rise to a visual experience, no matter how much integration is taking place? This question involves the hard problem, about which the theory has nothing to offer. Indeed, Crick and Koch are agnostic about whether the hard problem can be solved by science at all.

The same kind of critique could be applied to almost all the recent work on consciousness. In his 1991 book *Consciousness Explained,* philosopher Daniel C. Dennett laid out a sophisticated theory of how numerous independent processes in the brain combine to produce a coherent response to a perceived event. The theory might do much to explain how we produce verbal reports on our internal states, but it tells us very little about why there should be a subjective experience behind these reports. Like other reductionist theories, Dennett's is a theory of the easy problems.

The critical common trait among these easy problems is that they all concern how a cognitive or behavioral function is performed. All are ultimately questions about how the brain carries out some task—how it discriminates stimuli, integrates information, produces reports and so on. Once neurobiology specifies appropriate neural mechanisms, showing how the functions are performed, the easy problems are solved. The hard problem of consciousness, in contrast, goes beyond problems about how functions are performed. Even if every behavioral and cognitive function related to consciousness were explained, there would still remain a further mystery: Why is the performance of these functions accompanied by conscious experience? It is this additional conundrum that makes the hard problem hard.

## THE EXPLANATORY GAP

Some have suggested that to solve the hard problem, we need to bring in new tools of physical explanation: nonlinear dynamics, say, or new discoveries in neuroscience, or quantum mechanics. But these ideas suffer from exactly the same difficulty. Consider a proposal from Stuart R. Hameroff of the University of Arizona and Roger Penrose of the University of Oxford. They hold that consciousness arises from quantum-physical processes taking place in microtubules, which are protein structures inside neurons. It is possible (if not likely) that such a hypothesis will lead to an explanation of how the brain makes decisions or even how it proves mathematical theorems, as Hameroff and Penrose suggest. But even if it does, the theory is silent about how these processes might give rise to conscious experience. Indeed, the same problem arises with any theory of consciousness based only on physical processing.

The trouble is that physical theories are best suited to explaining why systems have a certain physical structure and how they perform various functions. Most problems in science have this form; to explain life, for example, we need to describe how a physical system can reproduce, adapt and metabolize. But consciousness is a different sort of problem entirely, as it goes beyond the explanation of structure and function.

Of course, neuroscience is not irrelevant to the study of consciousness. For one, it may be able to reveal the nature of the neural correlate of consciousness—the brain processes most directly associated with conscious experience. It may even give a detailed correspondence between specific processes in the brain and related components of experience. But until we know why these processes give rise to conscious experience at all, we will not have crossed what philosopher Joseph Levine has called the explanatory gap between physical processes and consciousness. Making that leap will demand a new kind of theory.

## A TRUE THEORY OF EVERYTHING

In searching for an alternative, a key observation is that not all entities in science are explained in terms of more basic entities. In physics, for example, space-time, mass and charge (among other things) are regarded as fundamental features of the world, as they are not reducible to anything simpler. Despite this irreducibility, detailed and useful theories relate these entities to one another in terms of fundamental laws. Together these features and laws explain a great variety of complex and subtle phenomena.

It is widely believed that physics provides a complete catalogue of the universe's fundamental features and laws. As physicist Steven Weinberg puts it in his 1992 book *Dreams of a Final Theory,* the goal of physics is a "theory of everything" from which all there is to know about the universe can be derived. But Weinberg concedes that there is a problem with consciousness. Despite the power of physical theory, the existence of consciousness does not seem to be derivable from physical laws. He defends physics by arguing that it might eventually explain what he calls the objective correlates of consciousness (that is, the neural correlates), but of course to do this is not to explain consciousness itself. If the existence of consciousness cannot be derived from physical laws, a theory of physics is not a true theory of everything. So a final theory must contain an additional fundamental component.

Toward this end, I propose that conscious experience be considered a fundamental feature, irreducible to anything more basic. The idea may seem strange at first, but consistency seems to demand it. In the 19th century it turned out that electromagnetic phenomena could not be explained in terms of previously known principles. As a consequence, scientists introduced electromagnetic charge as a new fundamental entity and studied the associated fundamental laws. Similar reasoning should apply to consciousness. If existing fundamental theories cannot encompass it, then something new is required.

Where there is a fundamental property, there are fundamental laws. In this case, the laws must relate experience to elements of physical theory. These laws will almost certainly not interfere with those of the physical world; it seems that the latter form a closed system in their own right. Rather the laws will serve as a bridge, specifying how experience depends on underlying physical processes. It is this bridge that will cross the explanatory gap.

Thus, a complete theory will have two components: physical laws, telling us about the behavior of physical systems, from the infinitesimal to the cosmological, and what we might call psychophysical laws, telling us how some of those systems are associated with conscious experience. These two components will constitute a true theory of everything.

## SEARCHING FOR A THEORY

Supposing for the moment that they exist, how might we uncover such psychophysical laws? The greatest hindrance in this pursuit will be a lack of data. As I have described it, consciousness is subjective, so there is no direct way to monitor it in others. But this difficulty is an obstacle, not a dead end. For a start, each one of us has access to our own experiences, a rich trove that can be used to formulate theories. We can also plausibly rely on indirect information, such as subjects' descriptions of their experiences. Philosophical arguments and thought experiments also have a role to play. Such methods have limitations, but they give us more than enough to get started.

These theories will not be conclusively testable, so they will inevitably be more speculative than those of more conventional scientific disciplines. Nevertheless, there is no reason they should not be strongly constrained to account accurately for our own first-person experiences, as well as the evidence from subjects' reports. If we find a theory that fits the data better than any other theory of equal simplicity, we will have good reason to accept it. Right now we do not have even a single theory that fits the data, so worries about testability are premature.

We might start by looking for high-level bridging laws, connecting physical processes to experience at an everyday level. The basic contour of such a law might be gleaned from the observation that when we are conscious of something, we are generally able to act on it and speak about it—which are objective, physical functions. Conversely, when some information is directly available for action and speech, it is generally conscious. Thus, consciousness correlates well with what we might call "awareness": the process by which information in the brain is made globally available to motor processes such as speech and bodily action.

The notion may seem trivial. But as defined here, awareness is objective and physical, whereas consciousness is not. Some refinements to the definition of awareness are needed, in order to extend the concept to animals and infants, which cannot speak. But at least in familiar cases, it is possible to see the rough outlines of a psychophysical law: where there is awareness, there is consciousness, and vice versa.

To take this line of reasoning a step further, consider the structure present in the conscious experience. The experience of a field of vision, for example, is a constantly changing mosaic of colors, shapes and patterns and as such has a detailed geometric structure. The fact that we can describe this structure, reach out in the direction of many of its components and perform other actions that depend on it suggests that the structure corresponds directly to that of the information made available in the brain through the neural processes of awareness.

Similarly, our experiences of color have an intrinsic three-dimensional structure that is mirrored in the structure of information processes in the brain's visual cortex. This structure is illustrated in the color wheels and charts used by artists. Colors are arranged in a systematic pattern—red to green on one axis, blue to yellow on another, and black to white on a third. Colors that are close to one another on a color wheel are experienced as similar. It is extremely likely that they also correspond to similar perceptual representations in the brain, as part of a system of complex three-dimensional coding among neurons that is not yet fully understood. We can recast the underlying concept as a principle of structural coherence: the structure of conscious experience is mirrored by the structure of information in awareness, and vice versa.

Another candidate for a psychophysical law is a principle of organizational invariance. It holds that physical systems with the same abstract organization will give rise to the same kind of conscious experience, no matter what they are made of. For example, if the precise interactions between our neurons could be duplicated with silicon chips, the same conscious experience would arise. The idea is somewhat controversial, but I believe it is strongly supported by thought experiments describing the gradual replacement of neurons by silicon chips. The remarkable implication is that consciousness might someday be achieved in machines.

## DANCING QUALIA IN A SYNTHETIC BRAIN

Whether consciousness could arise in a complex, synsthetic system is a question many people find intrinsically fascinating. Although it may be decades or even centuries before such a system is built, a simple thought experiment offers strong evidence that an artificial brain, if organized appropriately, would indeed have precisely the same kind of conscious experiences as a human being.

Consider a silicon-based system in which the chips are organized and function in the same way as the neurons in your brain. That is, each chip in the silicon system does exactly what its natural analogue does and is interconnected to surrounding elements in precisely the same way. Thus, the behavior exhibited by the artificial system will be exactly the same as yours. The crucial question is: Will it be conscious in the same way that you are?

Let us assume, for the purpose of argument, that it would *not* be. (Here we use a reasoning technique known as reductio ad absurdum, in which the opposite hypothesis is assumed and then shown to lead to an untenable conclusion.) That is, it either has different experiences—an experience of blue, say, when you are seeing red—or no experience at all. We will consider the first case; the reasoning proceeds similarly in both cases.

Because chips and neurons have the same function, they are interchangeable, with the proper interfacing. Chips therefore can replace neurons, producing a continuum of cases in which a successively larger proportion of neurons are replaced by chips. Along this continuum, the conscious experience of the system will also change. For example, we might replace all the neurons in your visual cortex with an identically organized version made of silicon. The resulting brain, with an artificial visual cortex, will have a different conscious experience from the original: where you had previously seen red, you may now experience purple (or perhaps a faded pink, in the case where the wholly silicon system has no experience at all).

Both visual cortices are then attached to your brain, through a two-position switch. With the switch in one mode, you use the natural visual cortex; in the other, the artificial cortex is activated. When the switch is flipped, your experience changes from red to purple, or vice versa. When the switch is flipped repeatedly, your experiences "dance" between the two different conscious states (red and purple), known as qualia.

Because your brain's organization has not changed, however, there can be no behavioral change when the switch is thrown. Therefore, when asked about what you are seeing, you will say that nothing has changed. You will hold that you are seeing red and have seen nothing but red—even though the two colors are dancing before your eyes. This conclusion is so unreasonable that it is best taken as a reduction ad absurdum of the original assumption—that an artificial system with identical organization and functioning has a different conscious experience from that of a neural brain. Retraction of the assumption establishes the opposite: that systems with the same organization have the same conscious experience.

## INFORMATION: PHYSICAL AND EXPERIENTIAL

The ultimate goal of a theory of consciousness is a simple and elegant set of fundamental laws, analogous to the fundamental laws of physics. The principles described [previously] are unlikely to be fundamental, however. Rather they seem to be high-level psychophysical laws, analogous to macroscopic principles in physics such as those of thermodynamics or kinematics. What might the underlying fundamental laws be? No one knows, but I don't mind speculating.

I suggest that the primary psychophysical laws may centrally involve the concept of information. The abstract notion of information, as put forward in the 1940s by Claude E. Shannon of the Massachusetts Institute of Technology, is that of a set of separate states with a basic structure of similarities and differences between them. We can think of a 10-bit binary code as an information state, for example. Such information states can be embodied in the physical world. This happens whenever they correspond to physical states (voltages, say); the differences between them can be transmitted along some pathway, such as a telephone line.

We can also find information embodied in conscious experience. The pattern of color patches in a visual field, for example, can be seen as analogous to that of the pixels covering a display screen. Intriguingly, it turns out that we find the same information states embedded in conscious experience and in underlying physical processes in the brain. The three-dimensional encoding of color spaces, for example, suggests that the information state in a color experience corresponds directly to an information state in the brain. We might even regard the two states as distinct aspects of a single information state, which is simultaneously embodied in both physical processing and conscious experience.

A natural hypothesis ensues. Perhaps information, or at least some information, has two basic aspects: a physical one and an experiential one. This hypothesis has the status of a fundamental principle that might underlie the relation between physical processes and experience. Wherever we find conscious experience, it exists as one aspect of an information state, the other aspect of which is embedded in a physical process in the brain. This proposal needs to be fleshed out to make a satisfying theory. But it fits nicely with the principles mentioned earlier—systems with the same organization will embody the same information, for example—and it could explain numerous features of our conscious experience.

The idea is at least compatible with several others, such as physicist John A. Wheeler's suggestion that information is fundamental to the physics of the universe. The laws of physics might ultimately be cast in informational terms, in which case we would have a satisfying congruence between the constructs in both physical and psychophysical laws. It may even be that a theory of physics and a theory of consciousness could eventually be consolidated into a single grander theory of information.

A potential problem is posed by the ubiquity of information. Even a thermostat embodies some information, for example, but is it conscious? There are at least two possible responses. First, we could constrain the fundamental laws so that only some information has an experiential aspect, perhaps depending on how it is physically processed. Second, we might bite the bullet and allow that all information has an experiential aspect—where there is complex information processing, there is complex experience, and where there is simple information processing, there is simple experience. If this is so, then even a thermostat might have experiences, although they would be much simpler than even a basic color experience, and there would certainly be no accompanying emotions or thoughts. This seems odd at first, but if experience is truly fundamental, we might expect it to be widespread. In any case, the choice between these alternatives should depend on which can be integrated into the most powerful theory.

Of course, such ideas may be all wrong. On the other hand, they might evolve into a more powerful proposal that predicts the precise structure of our conscious experience from physical processes in our brains. If this project succeeds, we will have good reason to accept the theory. If it fails, other avenues will be pursued, and alternative fundamental theories may be developed. In this way, we may one day resolve the greatest mystery of the mind.

## READING COMPREHENSION QUESTIONS

1. According to Chalmers, what is the hard problem of consciousness? What makes it hard?

2. Recount the thought experiment (attributed to Frank Jackson) of Mary in her black-and-white room. What point does Chalmers make with this example? Do you find what he says convincing? (Readers may want to consult the issue of *Scientific American* in which this article appeared, which also includes a short reply by Francis Crick and Christof Koch, whose view of consciousness is mentioned by Chalmers. Crick and Koch have a different explanation of what Mary doesn't know.)

3. Present Chalmers's reductio ad absurdum argument that he uses in connection with what he calls "dancing qualia." Begin by formulating the conclusion of the argument and then proceed to isolate the argument's premises. (Readers may wish to review what is said about reductio arguments in the introductory chapter.) Do you think this is a good argument? Why or why not?

4. What does Chalmers mean by the term "psychophysical law," which he mentions in the section entitled, "A True Theory of Everything"? What sorts of psychophysical laws does Chalmers think a true theory of everything might include?

5. How do you think Searle (the author of the previous article) would respond to Chalmers's hard problem?

# 4

# Free Will, Determinism, and Responsibility

## MOTIVATION

The problem of free will is centuries, perhaps millennia, old, but for many it remains a problem we aren't even close to solving. One of the confounding reasons is that *the* problem of free will isn't a single problem at all; instead, it is a nest of related but independent problems. Often, those who tackle the problem fail to recognize either the distinctness of the issues or the interesting and subtle ways in which they are related to one another. For our purposes, it will be enough to distinguish and articulate three of the primary questions at issue.

1. Do humans ever *act freely?*
2. Do humans have *free will?*
3. Are humans ever *morally responsible?*

To answer any of these three questions, we must embark on genuine metaphysical investigation, given that all three questions presuppose an understanding of the *nature* of the possible phenomena in question. In other words, in order to know whether or not humans ever act freely, we first need to understand what the nature of free action *is* (or would be, if there were such a thing), and the same goes for the questions of free will and moral responsibility. One important way of coming to such understanding is simply to ask ourselves what the terms in question *mean*. Of our various authors, C. A. Campbell and Walter T. Stace do this quite explicitly, but we can get a rough feel for both the questions and why they are important by considering some ordinary cases designed to get our intuitions pumping. The following scenarios will likely seem to become increasingly difficult to answer as you go, and that might give you some indication of where the more difficult problems here lie, but each scenario will also bring out some issues discussed by our various authors.

>   CASE 1: Nicole is looking through the paper one Saturday afternoon for a movie. She wants to see a movie she hasn't seen before, and there are only two such movies out there: an animated kid's movie about peace, love, and tolerance (called *Big Barney's Lovin' Playhouse*) and a new Jet Li martial arts movie. Nicole hates kid's movies (especially animated ones with "Lovin'" in the title) and loves Jet Li martial arts movies. She thus decides to go to the action movie. Does Nicole act freely in doing so?
>
>   *Issues to consider:* We're trying to get some clue into the nature of free action here (or what's also known as **free agency**). It will likely seem to most of you that Nicole acts freely, but why? Haven't her loves and hates determined what she'll do? Or does her being able to do what she wants to do ensure her freedom? What would it take for her action, then, to be unfree?
>
>   CASE 2: Lynda and her husband Alfonso are trying to decide what movie to see together one evening. She really wants to see the new love story with Robert Redford (*The Goat Whisperer*), and he really wants to see the director's cut of *Showgirls*. After some discussion, Alfonso agrees to go with Lynda to the Redford movie, *even though he really doesn't want to.* Does he act freely?
>
>   *Issues to consider:* Again, we're focused on free agency here. Notice now, though, that our actor *didn't* do what he wanted to do (unlike in Case 1). Does that undermine his freedom in any way? What if there was an unspoken "threat" that if he went to *Showgirls* on his own, he'd be in some trouble when they got home? Does that serve to change the order and strength of his wants? Has he thus been coerced?
>
>   CASE 3A: Shakira is out driving her new Honda Accord when she stops at a light. A young man comes up to her window with a gun and says he'll blow her head off if she doesn't get out and give him the car. She gets out and gives him the car. Does she act freely?
>
>   *Issues to consider:* This is clearly a case of coercion. Does it undermine Shakira's free agency, though? If not, what would it take to do so? If so, how is the case any different (if it is) from Case 2?
>
>   CASE 3B: Shakira has asked to borrow *your* new Honda Accord, and while she's stopped at a light, a young man comes up to her window with a gun and says he'll blow her head off if she doesn't get out and give him the car. She gets out and gives him the car. Does she act freely? *Is she morally responsible for what she's done?*
>
>   *Issues to consider:* Presumably, your answer here about Shakira's agency will be the same as in Case 3a. But because now her actions have entered into the arena of moral assessment (she's giving away your property, after all), we can ask about her **moral responsibility,** which for our purposes simply means "appropriately subject to praise or blame." So has

Shakira, in giving away your car, done something that's worthy of praise or blame? If so, which one, and why? What if the young man who'd come up to her had simply said, "Nice car!" and she had then gotten out and given it to him? Would she be blameworthy then? What's the relevant difference (if any) between the two cases? Notice also that it could be possible to hold that Shakira does act freely but that she's nevertheless *not* morally responsible, which should indicate to you one way in which Questions 1 and 3 might be distinct.

CASE 4: Winona is a kleptomaniac who, whenever she's in a store, has an overwhelming and irresistible impulse to steal something, regardless of how she feels about the object she steals. She's in a store now and stuffs a pack of pencils into her pocket, even though she doesn't want any pencils, doesn't need any pencils, and wishes like crazy that she could resist her impulse to steal the pencils. Does she act freely? Is she morally responsible for her action?

*Issues to consider:* Here we're assuming that kleptomania is a genuine psychological disorder and that Winona really has it (set aside, then, questions about how we could know she's really a kleptomaniac and isn't just faking it). Also, it's important to focus just on the action in question here; after all, you might be tempted to say, "Well, she shouldn't have gone into the store!" But that's a different action than the stealing itself. So given that she's there already (maybe she was dragged there by some evil or clueless person), is she responsible for the specific action of *stealing?* Why or why not? Once again, you might think she acts freely but isn't responsible (or vice versa). If you think she's responsible, what would it take to *not* be responsible? If you think she isn't responsible, what's the difference between her and an ordinary thief (assuming that an ordinary thief *would be* responsible for stealing)?

CASE 5: Alvin is a heroin addict, and he currently feels an overwhelming craving for the drug, which he happens to have on him. He hates being an addict, and he wishes he weren't addicted. Nevertheless, he shoots up. Does he act freely? Is he morally responsible?

*Issues to consider:* Is Alvin's case relevantly different from Winona's case? Why or why not? What role does his not wanting to be an addict play in your assessment of his freedom and/or responsibility?

CASE 6: Little Janey is a two-year-old who takes out her crayons one day and writes all over the walls of the house, incurring the wrath of her parents. Does Janey act freely? Is she morally responsible?

*Issues to consider:* Obviously, the main issue here is about the moral responsibility of young children. Are they moral agents, appropriately subject to (moral) praise and blame? Just because her parents may yell at her, that doesn't necessarily amount to the kind of moral responsibility at issue here. People also yell at their dogs, but surely dogs can't be morally responsible for their actions. ("Spot, can't you see that what you've done is immoral, insofar as your relieving yourself on our neighbor's cat harmed her both physically and emotionally?") So what *is* the kind of moral responsibility at issue? Do young children have it? If so, why? If not, how are they relevantly different from the rest of us (assuming the rest of us *are* morally responsible).

CASE 7: Once upon a time there was a boy named Kody who was raised in a poor, urban environment. His mom did drugs while she was pregnant with him, and then she died of an overdose shortly after his birth. He went to live with his grandma, who had seven other kids to deal with. While there, he was beaten by the other kids and sexually abused by an uncle. He hardly ever attended school, and the social services people either never caught on to his situation or were too burdened by other cases to do anything about it. As he grew up, he saw the local gangbangers and drug dealers hanging out with each other laughing and talking, driving BMWs, wearing cool clothes and jewelry, etc., and because he didn't get any real supervision at home, he started hanging out with those older kids, who took him in and treated him like family. Soon he became initiated into a gang. At the age of 16, in an act of loyalty to his fellow gang members, he killed a rival gang member in a drive-by shooting. Did Kody act freely? Should we hold Kody morally responsible for his actions? What do we do with him? Could he have done otherwise?[1]

*Issues to consider:* Imagine yourself in Kody's shoes, having gone through the events of his life yourself. Would you have turned out any differently? Does that matter? What of all those people who come from similar circumstances who *don't* join gangs and kill people? Indeed, what's the difference between them and people like Kody? Is it a difference that's relevant to free agency and moral responsibility?

You may well have noticed that in none of these scenarios did we broach the question of *free will*; instead, we focused either on free action or moral responsibility. There are a couple of reasons for this. First, the phrase "free will" is actually quite obscure; specifically, the term "will" is quite obscure. What is a "will," after all? Thus, to ask whether or not Nicole has free will when she goes to the action movie, say, is really just to invite a kind of puzzlement: what do you *mean*, after all? So it's difficult to elicit your intuitions about some concept unless you first have at least a rough and ready understanding of it (as we seem to with the concepts of free action and moral responsibility).

Second, there are actually powerful reasons to think that we have *perfect* freedom of the will. Think for a moment about what seems to be the opposite of free will, namely, doing something *against* your will. So suppose you have been dragged off to prison for some crime you didn't commit. We will surely

---

[1]This case is loosely based on the actual young life of "Monster" Kody Scott. See his autobiography under the name Sanyika Shakur, called *Monster: The Autobiography of an L.A. Gang Member* (New York: Grove Press, 1993).

be tempted to say that when you are literally dragged away from the courtroom, you lack free will. But this wouldn't be entirely accurate, for while it's certainly true that you are "moving toward the prison" against your will, all that this implies is that there is an *impediment* to your will, that is, you're being prevented from doing *what you will*. But that doesn't mean your will *itself* is unfree; it just means you can't carry out your will in action. On this conception of willing, then, it looks like the will simply consists in a kind of wanting, intending, or trying, and because we're always capable of that, our wills are always free. There may indeed be impediments to actually doing what we want, intend, or try, but that doesn't undermine our freedom to want, intend, or try in the first place.[2] It would seem, then, that talk of free will is just a kind of red herring, a misnomer for the real target of our worries, which would seem to be those impediments to willing, what we typically think of as roadblocks to our freedom of *action*.

Nevertheless, three of our authors explicitly discuss freedom of the will (Holbach, Campbell, and Stace). But as you should notice, they do so simply as a way of talking about freedom of action, so we will restrict our discussion in what follows to just that sort of freedom.

## DETERMINISM VS. INDETERMINISM

The fundamental worry about free action comes with the possible truth of a theory about the nature of the universe, known as

> **determinism**—the theory that the state of the universe at any point in time is entirely fixed by the state of the universe at a prior time, in combination with the laws of nature.

Another way to put this is that the universe is precisely as it is right now entirely because the universe was the way it was a minute ago, say, as well as because the laws of nature are as they are. We can think of the universe at any point in time as a big collection of events, or happenings. On this theory, everything that happens, *including human actions and choices*, is completely fixed in all of its details by *preceding* events (operating according to physical laws). This means, then, that there is no way for anything other than what has actually happened to happen: every event that occurs *has* to occur precisely as it does, and there's no way for any other event to occur instead.

---

[2]There may be some complications here, especially with respect to cases in which one is pushed toward embarking down one path or another, via hypnosis or brainwashing, say, but it is not clear that even these sorts of events would undermine that most basic freedom of *willing*. For discussion, see Rogers Allbriton, "Freedom of Will and Freedom of Action," *The Proceedings and Addresses of the American Philosophical Association* 59:2 (1985): 239–251 (reprinted in Gary Watson, ed., *Free Will,* 2nd ed. (Oxford: Oxford University Press, 2002), pp. 408–423), and Gary Watson, "Free Action and Free Will," in *Agency and Answerability* (Oxford: Oxford University Press, 2004), pp.161–196, esp. pp.184–189.

To illustrate, flip a coin. The coin will land as it does because of several factors: the position it was in on your thumb, the force with which you flipped it, the climate conditions present, and so forth. On determinism, given all of these factors, it was impossible for the coin not to land as it did. Furthermore, if we could figure out and recreate *all* of those conditions precisely (which is likely impossible), the precise events that occurred the first time you flipped the coin would occur again, in exactly the same way. It was the only event that could have occurred, given the previous state of the world.

Now this theory says that all human actions are determined in this way as well. Every single action you perform is totally determined by certain causes and conditions in place prior to your performing it. Indeed, everything you do is completely determined by the way the world was *even before you were born*. And if there were someone with perfect knowledge of every detail of the state of the world, along with all the laws of nature, she could predict with perfect accuracy every single action you would ever perform.

Suppose that you don't believe this, though; that is, you believe instead that some human actions, at least, are not determined, that not every action you perform is one you *had* to perform, in the sense implied by determinism. You are, then, someone who affirms

> **indeterminism**—the theory that the state of the universe at any point in time is *not* entirely fixed by the state of the universe at a prior time in combination with the laws of nature.

In other words, the indeterminist just denies determinism, maintaining instead that *some* events aren't determined by preceding events, and the paradigm cases of these undetermined events are some human actions. It's important to keep in mind here that what the indeterminist is claiming is that some human actions are entirely *uncaused* by preceding events, that there are no conditions or physical causes in the natural world that determine their occurrence. So what this advocate seems to be saying is that some human actions are outside the chain of natural event causation.

One way to see the attractiveness of this theory is to consider your own experience. Suppose you've got a choice between clicking your heels and flapping your arms. Nobody knows which one you'll choose; indeed, at this point, *you* may not even know what you're going to choose. Suppose, then, that you opt to click your heels. It sure seems as if *you* chose to do that, rather than flap your arms, which you also could have done. Isn't that, then, an undetermined action? After all, you surely could've done other than what you did, so it seems your action here wasn't determined, an idea we need to explore now.

## DOING OTHERWISE

Determinism suggests that every event that occurs is the only one that could have occurred in the circumstances. But this implies that no matter what it is I've just done, I could not have done otherwise. That seems to mean that I *had* to do what I just did and so did not act freely.

Suppose a mad scientist has secretly wired my brain such that I do his bidding at the press of a button; for example, he has me fix liver and eat it (even though I detest liver), and he has me go around pinching people on the buttocks. Surely I don't act freely when he presses that button: there are causes in place that determine that I do what I do. Determinism seems to imply that the same is true of *all* our actions, that we can never do otherwise than what we do, given the circumstances. And this in turn would seem to undermine our freedom. At first consideration, then, being able to do otherwise looks to be a necessary condition for free action.

But of course we think people act freely all the time. Are we wrong to do so, or does that just mean that determinism can't be true? Because the latter seems more likely, perhaps we should embrace indeterminism. Unfortunately, we run into a similar problem. If you're an indeterminist, for instance, how would you explain why I suddenly start flapping my arms like a deranged bird? If you start your answer with, "Because . . . ," it looks like you're going to fall into the determinist's trap, given that you're offering a possible *cause* of the action. Instead, if you want to be an indeterminist about this particular action, you need to say that it just happened by chance.

But if that's the case, then where is freedom? How is undetermined, random action free? How is an action without an explanation a free action? Suppose that, contrary to all known biological possibility, my right arm occasionally shoots out perpendicular to my body, and there's just no physical or causal story at all for why it happens. This is truly an undetermined action. But again, how could this possibly be *free?* I certainly don't decide to flip my arm out. It just happens. But if it happens without any cause whatsoever, then it's not something over which I have any control, and it's certainly not something I could have *refrained* from doing. In other words, if my action is undetermined, I *also* could not have done otherwise.

So it looks like both determinism and indeterminism would imply that it's impossible for me ever to do otherwise than what I do, and this leads to a very powerful dilemma.

## THE DETERMINISM/INDETERMINISM DILEMMA

1. If determinism is true, then we can never do other than what we do, because our determined actions are all completely caused.

2. If indeterminism is true, then we can never do other than what we do, because our undetermined/uncaused actions would be random.

3. Being able to do other than what we do is a necessary condition of acting freely.

4. Either determinism is true or else indeterminism is true.

5. Thus, we lack a necessary condition of acting freely, that is, we never act freely.

How might you respond? One way not open to us is denying the fourth premise, for that's simply a logical truth, given the definitions of "determinism" and "indeterminism." It says simply that either everything is determined or not everything is determined, and that has to be true.

There are, then, just four ways remaining to react to this dilemma: either accept the conclusion by affirming premise 1 or 2, or deny premise 1, 2, or 3. Let us then consider each possibility in turn.

1a.  The first possible response is simply to accept the conclusion of the dilemma by embracing premise 1, and then adding a premise affirming that determinism is indeed true. This view is called **hard determinism**, and it is explicitly laid out and defended in our readings by Holbach and Clarence Darrow. Holbach's emphasis is on our lack of free agency (including a diagnosis of why it is that people persist in thinking they're free agents when they're clearly not), whereas Darrow's emphasis is on the lack of moral responsibility implied by our lack of free agency.

1b.  A corresponding route to the same place consists in accepting the conclusion of the dilemma by embracing premise 2, and then adding a premise affirming that indeterminism is indeed true. Very few, if any, philosophers have advanced such a view, but it is certainly a possible position, one we can call **hard indeterminism.** In fact, this might very well seem a plausible move in light of the findings of quantum mechanics indicating randomness at the microphysical level. Nevertheless, such randomness, while revealing the falsity of determinism, would not seem to establish any more freedom in the course of events than would determinism.

2.  The second general way philosophers respond to the dilemma is to deny premise 1 and then affirm (or at least allow for) the truth of determinism. This is to take the position known as **soft determinism,** or **compatibilism,** the view that (1) determinism is (or could be) true, and (2) determinism is compatible with free agency. This is the view held by Stace. The general soft determinist view is that, while determinism is true, we can nevertheless act freely. How so? There are typically two steps here. First, soft determinists most often define "free action" simply as "action unimpeded by obstacles," so that one acts freely whenever one is able to do what one chooses, even if one's choices have themselves been determined by preceding events. How, though, could one do otherwise if one's choices were themselves determined? Answering this question is the task of the second step, which is to assert that it all depends on how you interpret the phrase "could have done otherwise." What soft determinists often say, then, is that the phrase "I could have done otherwise" simply means "If I had *chosen* differently, I *would* have done otherwise." Thus, if one's actions are caused by one's choices—that is, if one's actions are *determined* by one's choices—it could still be the case that, even if determinism is true, if one had chosen differently, one indeed would have done differently. So if all that's required for freedom is that one have the ability to do otherwise, and the ability to do otherwise is simply the ability to act according to one's choices, then it seems freedom is compatible with

all actions being determined. We shall see, however, how Campbell runs a fairly powerful argument against this idea in his essay.

3.  The third general way philosophers respond to the dilemma (and the second general way of denying its conclusion) is to deny premise 2 and then affirm the truth of indeterminism. The resulting view is called **libertarianism**, according to which (1) determinism is *incompatible* with free agency, and (2) determinism is false. This is the view defended by Campbell. Again, there are two steps to the conclusion. First, libertarians must show why determinism is incompatible with free agency, and they typically do so (as Campbell does) by insisting on a robust conception of being able to do otherwise as necessary for freedom: one must genuinely be able to refrain from doing what one does in order to be free, and this seems to require being able to act against, or outside of, the ordinary chain of natural event causation. But if indeterminism has to be true in order for us to act freely, doesn't that make our actions random, and thus no freer than determined actions? Here's where the second step comes in. According to libertarians, our actions, in order to be free, must be neither determined by preceding events *nor* random. In other words, the libertarian has to hold that there's a kind of middle road, a road that denies that all human actions are determined *in the way all natural events are caused*. Libertarians typically claim that, in order to be free, human actions must have a cause (so they're not just random, uncaused events), but the cause cannot be the same type of cause that produces all other types of events (in which case we couldn't do otherwise). So if I perform some free action, it must be the case that my action was caused, not by some preceding event (like a desire or a belief), but by *me*, the agent. After all, say libertarians, I am not an event; I am a *human!* There must then be a special kind of causation that only humans and God possess, a power that can't really be explained in natural, deterministic terms. But while this view may seem initially plausible, it is also quite obscure. How is it, for instance, that I can be a prime mover unmoved, a first cause itself uncaused? What is the nature of my relation to the natural world of ordinary event causation? That is, how precisely can I interact with this world of physical, natural causes, if I myself am not a cause *of that sort*? Indeed, what *am* I, essentially? And when, precisely, am I truly free? (Notice, for instance, the very limited range of free actions that occur according to Campbell's account.)

4.  The fourth general way of responding to the dilemma (and the third way of denying it) is to deny premise 3, that a necessary condition of free action is the ability to do otherwise. Call such a view **structuralism** (for reasons given here). While this may strike you as a weird or surprising move to make, it becomes quite plausible once we consider an example or two. Suppose first that an evil genius knows everything you're going to choose to do, and he also has the power to literally change your mind whenever you're about to choose to do something he doesn't want you to do. Suppose, further, that he wants you to kill your neighbor, something you've been pondering for a while anyway. In fact, you've already begun to draw up a plan to kill the neighbor, and so the demon waits at the ready, just in case you're about

to decide to do otherwise. If he knows you're about to decide otherwise, he'll just implant an irresistible impulse in you to decide to kill your neighbor. As it turns out, though, the demon doesn't have to do a thing: you decide all on your own to kill your neighbor, and you carry through the plan without a hitch. Here, then, is the question: in killing the neighbor, did you act freely? The answer must be yes. Could you have done otherwise? No: if you were about to decide to do otherwise, the demon would have intervened and made you decide to kill the neighbor anyway. This case strongly suggests, then, that one can act freely without being able to do otherwise, and that premise 3 is false.[3] What seems to matter for free action instead is the general *structure* of one's will—that is, that one's actions depend on one's choices, and that one's choices are "one's own," in some important sense. But if premise 3 is false, then perhaps compatibilism's problematic reinterpretation of "being able to do otherwise" isn't necessary, which might make it a more plausible response to the dilemma. What you should think about, of course, is whether this sort of case really undermines the necessity for free action of being able to do otherwise.

Thus, there are several interesting and important ways to reply to the determinism/indeterminism dilemma. Their success is another matter, however.

## MORAL RESPONSIBILITY

We have to this point simply been talking about free agency. But the question of moral responsibility is closely related here, as our initial cases revealed. What is the nature of the relation? There are two popular ways to connect up the issue of moral responsibility to that of free agency.

The first way is simply to ride on the coattails of the determinism/indeterminism dilemma, specifically on the alleged necessary condition of being able to do otherwise. Thus, one might revise the initial premise 3 to read as follows: "Being able to do other than what we do is a necessary condition for acting freely *and being morally responsible for our actions*." Alternatively, one might revise premise 3 differently to read, "Being able to do other than what we do is a necessary condition for acting freely, and acting freely is a necessary condition for being morally responsible for those free actions one performs." The difference between the two revisions is subtle but important, for though both would require the ability to do otherwise as necessary for both free action and moral responsibility, only the first version would allow that there might be quite distinct *additional* conditions for each.

At any rate, the conclusion of the argument would now have to read that we never act freely *nor* are we morally responsible for our actions. The various

---

[3]This is a variation on a case first articulated in print by Harry Frankfurt in "Alternate Possibilities and Moral Responsibility," *Journal of Philosophy* 66:23 (1969): 829–839; reprinted in Watson, *Free Will*, pp.167–176. Frankfurt's original case was meant to show that the ability to do otherwise was not a necessary condition of moral *responsibility*, but it works equally well, it seems, with respect to acting freely.

responses to the argument would remain the same. One might accept the conclusion or deny one of the first three premises (thereby affirming the possibility of
moral responsibility), and the names of the various views that take one of those
options would correspond to the labels already given.

A second way to construct an argument against the possibility of moral
responsibility would be to focus not on being able to *do* otherwise, but instead
on being able to *determine oneself* otherwise. The argument goes as follows:

1.  An agent A is morally responsible for her actions at any particular point
    in time only if A is able to determine her *self* at that point in time.

2.  A is *not* able to determine herself at that (or any particular) point in time.

3.  Thus, A is not morally responsible for her actions.

This is essentially the argument presented by Galen Strawson, and the idea
behind it is simple and familiar (it's what he calls the Basic Argument). In order
to be truly responsible for your actions, you have to be the ultimate cause of yourself—of your character, likes/dislikes, desires, etc. But it's a logical impossibility for
*anything* to be the cause of itself (it would have to exist prior to itself, which is
absurd—see Aquinas's the Cosmological Argument to prove God's existence,
later in this volume). Thus no one is ever truly responsible for his or her actions.
So if, for example, you're moved to try and change yourself, you're only moved to
do so by your current character and desires. But those are things for which you
cannot be held responsible: you didn't make yourself that way. Or if you did,
then it was in virtue of another set of psychological dispositions for which
you're not responsible. And this chain will go back until you're definitely at a psychological stage for which we'd all agree you're not responsible.

This is a view of moral responsibility according to which you're only *truly*
morally responsible for your actions now if there was some point in your past
at which you were somehow the *original* cause of yourself or your character.
But that's impossible. So Galen Strawson thinks of true responsibility as somehow
having to be passed down from that original point to bestow responsibility on our
present actions. But because we can never originate that chain of responsibility,
we're never responsible for what we do.

Of course, the plausibility of this account depends entirely on what we mean
by "true moral responsibility." Galen Strawson indicates what he thinks it means,
drawing on an analogy with our thoughts and beliefs about heaven and hell. But
Galen Strawson's father, Sir P. F. Strawson, presents a very different understanding
of responsibility, based on our actual practices and reactions to morally charged
actions. P. F. Strawson argues that our actual practices are simply immune to
any theoretical conclusions about determinism or indeterminism, for they are
deeply ingrained in our particularly human form of life. This is to explode the
determinism/indeterminism dilemma as irrelevant.

Notice, then, the different methods father and son deploy. On Galen
Strawson's method, we need to start with a *definition* of moral responsibility
(something for which the idea of heaven and hell "makes sense"), and then
go on to show that the conditions required by the definition are impossible
for humans to meet. We are thus never justified in attributing moral responsibility to one another. On P. F. Strawson's method, though, we start with our

ordinary attributions of moral responsibility, show that we simply could not give them up (so that the question of justification becomes practically moot), and then go on to construct a theory explaining the actual conditions of responsibility (and nonresponsibility) in our everyday lives. As in most areas of philosophy, the method with which one approaches an issue typically goes a long way toward determining the answers one will reach. As you read, then, you should think about which method might be preferable.

In addition, as you read, think about what the various authors would say about the cases with which we began and why, as well as about what you think is the best way to go with respect to this tangled web of issues. This is definitely one of the most difficult and puzzling arenas remaining in philosophy, and any help in resolving these issues would be greatly appreciated.

# 13

# Leopold and Loeb

CLARENCE DARROW

*See the Clarence Darrow biography prior to his article "The Myth of the Soul" in Chapter 2. This next selection is a brief excerpt from Darrow's astonishing twelve-hour summation in the trial of Richard Loeb and Nathan Leopold in 1924. These intelligent young men from privileged backgrounds kidnapped and murdered a fourteen-year-old acquaintance, Bobby Franks, and did so just for the thrill of it, as an attempt to commit "the perfect crime." A zealous prosecutor asked for the death penalty for both boys, but Darrow, after getting the boys to plead guilty, argued strenuously (and at length!) for them to receive life in prison. He based his argument, as you will see, on determinism, according to which all our actions are entirely determined by a variety of preceding causes, from our genetic inheritance to our environment and upbringing. As a result, the responsibility for our actions is really traceable to these formative causes. So because Loeb, for instance, was overwhelmed by the advantageous situation into which he'd been born (his parents were millionaires), and he'd been pushed too deeply into his studies, and he'd been heavily influenced by the many detective stories he read, he was led quite "naturally," according to Darrow, to commit the crime. By the end of his summation, both the presiding judge and several spectators were in tears. Two weeks later, the judge announced his decision. Although he insisted his judgment was not affected by consideration of the causes of the crime, he gave the boys life in prison.*

I have tried to study the lives of these two most unfortunate boys. Three months ago, if their friends and the friends of the family had been asked to pick out the most promising lads of their acquaintance, they probably would have picked these two boys. With every opportunity, with plenty of wealth, they would have said that those two would succeed. In a day, by an act of madness, all this is destroyed, until the best they can hope for now is a life of silence and pain, continuing to the end of their years. How did it happen?

Let us take Dickie Loeb first. I do not claim to know how it happened; I have sought to find out. I know that something, or some combination of things, is responsible for his mad act. I know that there are no accidents in nature. I know that effect follows cause.

SOURCE: From Alvin V. Sellers, *The Loeb-Leopold Case*. This selection is in the public domain.

Can I find what was wrong? I think I can. Here was a boy at a tender age, placed in the hands of a governess, intellectual, vigorous, devoted, with a strong ambition for the welfare of this boy. He was pushed in his studies, as plants are forced in hothouses. He had no pleasures, such as a boy should have, except as they were gained by lying and cheating. Now, I am not criticising the nurse. I suggest that some day your Honor look at her picture. It explains her fully. Forceful, brooking no interference, she loved the boy, and her ambition was that he should reach the highest perfection. No time to pause, no time to stop from one book to another, no time to have those pleasures which a boy ought to have to create a normal life.

And what happened? Your Honor, what would happen? Nothing strange or unusual. This nurse was with him all the time, except when he stole out at night, from two to fourteen years of age, and it is instructive to read her letter to show her attitude. It speaks volumes; tells exactly the relation between these two people. He, scheming and planning as healthy boys would do, to get out from under her restraint. She, putting before him the best books, which children generally do not want; and he, when she was not looking, reading detective stories, which he devoured, story after story, in his young life. Of all this there can be no question. What is the result? Every story he read was a story of crime. We have a statute in this state, passed only last year, if I recall it, which forbids minors reading stories of crime. The legislature in its wisdom felt that it would produce criminal tendencies in the boys who read them. The legislature of this State has given its opinion, and forbidden boys to read these books. He read them day after day. He never stopped. While he was passing through college at Ann Arbor he was still reading them. When he was a senior he read them, and almost nothing else.

Now, these facts are beyond dispute. He early developed the tendency to mix with crime, to be a detective; as a little boy shadowing people on the street; as a little child going out with his phantasy of being the head of a band of criminals. How did this grow and develop in him? Let us see. It seems to me as natural as the day following the night. Every detective story is a story of a sleuth getting the best of it; trailing some unfortunate individual through devious ways until his victim is finally landed in jail or stands on the gallows. They all show how smart the detective is, and where the criminal himself falls down.

This boy early in his life conceived the idea that there could be a crime that nobody could ever detect; that there could be one where the detective did not land his game.

He wanted to commit a perfect crime. There had been growing in his brain, dwarfed and twisted—as every act in this case shows it to have been dwarfed and twisted—there had been growing this scheme, not due to any wickedness of Dickie Loeb, for he is a child. It grew as he grew; it grew from those around him; it grew from the lack of the proper training until it possessed him. He believed he could plan the perfect crime. He had thought of it and talked of it for years—and then came this sorry act of his, utterly irrational and motiveless, a plan to commit a perfect crime which must contain kidnapping, and there must be ransom, or else it could not be perfect, and they must get the money. . . .

The law knows and has recognized childhood for many and many a long year. The brain of the child is the home of dreams, of castles, of visions, of illusions and of delusions. In fact, there could be no childhood without delusions, for delusions are always more alluring than facts. Delusions, dreams and hallucinations are a part of the warp and woof of childhood. You know it and I know it. I remember, when I was a child, the men seemed as tall as the trees, the trees as tall as the mountains. I can remember very well when, as a little boy, I swam the deepest spot in the river for the first time. I swam breathlessly and landed with as much sense of glory and triumph as Julius Caesar felt when he led his army across the Rubicon. I have been back since, and I can almost step across the same place, but it seemed an ocean then. And those men who I thought were so wonderful were dead and left nothing behind. I had lived in a dream. I had never known the real world which I met, to my discomfort and despair, and that dispelled the illusions of my youth.

The whole life of childhood is a dream and an illusion, and whether they take one shape or another shape depends not upon the dreamy boy but on what surrounds him. As well might I have dreamed of burglars and wished to be one as to dream of policemen and wished to be one. Perhaps I was lucky, too, that I had no money. We have grown to think that the misfortune is in not having it. The great misfortune in this case is the money. That has destroyed these lives. That has fostered these illusions. That has promoted this mad act. And, if Your Honor shall doom them to die, it will be because they are the sons of the rich. . . .

The books he read by day were not the books he read by night. We are all of us moulded somewhat by the influences around us and, on people who read, perhaps books are the greatest and the strongest of these influences. We all know where our lives have been influenced by books. The nurse, strict and jealous and watchful, gave him one kind of book; by night he would steal off and read the other.

Which, think you, shaped the life of Dickie Loeb? Is there any kind of question about it? A child: was it pure maliciousness? Was a boy of five or six or seven to blame for it? Where did he get it? He got it where we all get our ideas, and these books became a part of his dreams and a part of his life, and as he grew up his visions grew to hallucinations. He went out on the street and fantastically directed his companions, who were not there, in their various moves to complete the perfect crime.

Before I would tie a noose around the neck of a boy I would try to call back into my mind the emotions of youth. I would try to remember what the world looked like to me when I was a child. I would try to remember how strong were these instinctive, persistent emotions that moved my life. I would try to remember how weak and inefficient was youth in the presence of the surging, controlling feelings of the child. One that honestly remembers and asks himself the question and tries to unlock the door that he thinks is closed, and calls back the boy, can understand the boy.

But, Your Honor, that is not all there is to boyhood. Nature is strong and she is pitiless. She works in her own mysterious way, and we are her victims. We have not much to do with it ourselves. Nature takes this job in hand, and we play our parts. In the words of old Omar Khayyam, we are only:

> Impotent pieces in the game He plays
> Upon this checkerboard of nights and days,
> Hither and thither moves, and checks, and slays,
> And one by one back in the closet lays.

What had this boy to do with it? He was not his own father; he was not his own mother; he was not his own grandparents. All of this was handed to him. He did not surround himself with governesses and wealth. He did not make himself. And yet he is to be compelled to pay.

There was a time in England, running down as late as the beginning of the last century, when judges used to convene court and call juries to try a horse, a dog, a pig, for crime. I have in my library a story of a judge and jury and lawyers trying and convicting an old sow for lying down on her ten pigs and killing them.

Do you mean to tell me that Dickie Loeb had any more to do with his making than any other product of heredity that is born upon the earth? . . .

For God's sake, are we crazy? In the face of history, of every line of philosophy, against the teaching of every religionist and seer and prophet the world has ever given us, we are still doing what our barbaric ancestors did when they came out of the caves and the woods.

From the age of fifteen to the age of twenty or twenty-one, the child has the burden of adolescence, of puberty and sex thrust upon him. Girls are kept at home and carefully watched. Boys without instruction are left to work the period out for themselves. It may lead to excess. It may lead to disgrace. It may lead to perversion. Who is to blame?

Your Honor, it is the easiest thing in the world to be a parent. We talk of motherhood, and yet every woman can be a mother. We talk of fatherhood, and yet every man can be a father. Nature takes care of that. It is easy to be a parent. But to be wise and farseeing enough to understand the boy is another thing; only a very few are so wise and so farseeing as that. When I think of the light way Nature has of picking out parents and populating the earth, having them born and die, I cannot hold human beings to the same degree of responsibility that young lawyers hold them when they are enthusiastic in a prosecution. I know what it means.

I know there are no better citizens in Chicago than the fathers of these poor boys. I know there were no better women than their mothers. But I am going to be honest with this court, if it is at the expense of both. I know that one of two things happened to Richard Loeb; that this terrible crime was inherent in his organism, and came from some ancestor, or that it came through his education and his training after he was born. Do I need to prove it? Judge Crowe said at one point in this case, when some witness spoke about their wealth, that probably that was responsible.

To believe that any boy is responsible for himself or his early training is an absurdity that no lawyer or judge should be guilty of today. Somewhere this came to this boy. If his failing came from his heredity, I do not know where or how. None of us are bred perfect and pure, and the color of our hair, the color of our eyes, our stature, the weight and fineness of our brain, and everything about us could, with full knowledge, be traced with absolute certainty; if we had the pedigree it could be traced just the same in a boy as it could in a dog, a horse or cow.

I do not know what remote ancestors may have sent down the seed that corrupted him, and I do not know through how many ancestors it may have passed until it reached Dickie Loeb. All I know is that it is true, and there is not a biologist in the world who will not say that I am right. If it did not come that way, then I know that if he was normal, if he had been understood, if he had been trained as he should have been, it would not have happened. Not that anybody may not slip, but I know it and your Honor knows it, and every schoolhouse and every church in the land are evidences of it. Else why build them?

Every effort to protect society is an effort toward training the youth to keep the path. Every bit of training in the world proves it, and it likewise proves that it sometimes fails. I know that if this boy had been understood and properly trained—properly for him—and the training that he got might have been the very best for someone else—but if it had been the proper training for him he would not be in this court room today with the noose above his head. If there is responsibility anywhere, it is back of him; somewhere in the infinite number of his ancestors, or in his surroundings, or in both.

We may have all the dreams and visions and build all the castles we wish, but the castles of youth should be discarded with youth, and when they linger to the time when boys should think wiser things, then it indicates a diseased mind. "When I was young I thought as a child, I spoke as a child, I understood as a child; but now I have put off childish things," said the Psalmist twenty centuries ago. It is when these dreams of boyhood, these phantasies of youth still linger, and the growing boy is still a child—a child in emotion, a child in feeling, a child in hallucinations—that you can say that it is the dreams and the hallucinations of childhood that are responsible for his conduct. There is not an act in all this horrible tragedy that was not the act of a child, the act of a child wandering around in the morning of life, moved by the new feelings of a boy, moved by the uncontrolled impulses which his teaching was not strong enough to take care of, moved by the dreams and the hallucinations which haunt the brain of a child. I say, your Honor, that it would be the height of cruelty, of injustice, of wrong and barbarism to visit the penalty upon this boy.

## READING COMPREHENSION QUESTIONS

1.  Darrow's conclusion is obvious: it would be wrong to penalize Richard Loeb for the murder, even though he did it. What, though, is Darrow's argument for this conclusion? See if you can put it in premise–conclusion form, as discussed in the introduction to this book.

2.  Suppose Darrow is right that Loeb himself bears no responsibility for the crime. Is there any reason why the general form of Darrow's argument wouldn't also apply in every other criminal case, or is there something special about Loeb that makes Darrow's argument apply only to him?

3.  In the introduction, we pointed out that one of the key aspects of a successful argument is clarity, that is, all the terms in the argument should be clear,

with agreed-upon definitions. Is Darrow's argument clear in this way? In evaluating this aspect of the argument, focus on his understanding of the term "responsibility," and then answer the following questions. What does he mean by this term? Is this what we generally understand by "responsibility"? Is it an appropriate understanding of the term for a criminal trial?

4.  Darrow claims near the end, "To believe that any boy is responsible for himself or his early training is an absurdity that no lawyer or judge should be guilty of today." Explain why he thinks this. Do you agree? Why or why not?

# 14

# The Illusion of Free Will

### BARON D'HOLBACH

*Paul-Henri Thiry, Baron d'Holbach (1723–1789) was a radical French thinker,*
a philosophe. *He was one of the first declared atheists in Europe, arguing that the*
*universe was like a machine, operating in accordance with natural laws and without*
*any need of God as its designing hand or first cause. In this selection, from* The
System of Nature *(1770), Holbach makes the case for hard determinism, the*
*view that all events, including human actions, are entirely determined by preceding*
*events. What it would take for an action to be free, according to Holbach, is for it to*
*be entirely uncaused. But no human action is ever uncaused, so no human action is*
*free. Holbach sets forth his case quite eloquently, and then he defends the view from*
*several objections, including the compatibilist objection that freedom is just the*
*ability to do what one wants without external interference. Finally, Holbach*
*diagnoses why it is that people persist in believing in the illusion of free will,*
*despite the fact that they ought to be able to see quite easily the chain of causes that*
*determines their actions.*

**M**an is a being purely physical; in whatever manner he is considered, he is
connected to universal nature, and submitted to the necessary and immuta-
ble laws that she imposes on all the beings she contains, according to their peculiar
essences or to the respective properties with which, without consulting them, she
endows each particular species. Man's life is a line that nature commands him to
describe upon the surface of the earth, without his ever being able to swerve
from it, even for an instant. He is born without his own consent; his organization
does in nowise depend upon himself; his ideas come to him involuntarily; his habits
are in the power of those who cause him to contract them; he is unceasingly modified by causes, whether visible or concealed, over which he has no control, which
necessarily regulate his mode of existence, give the hue to his way of thinking, and
determine his manner of acting. He is good or bad, happy or miserable, wise or
foolish, reasonable or irrational, without his will being for any thing in these various
states. Nevertheless, in despite of the shackles by which he is bound, it is pretended
he is a free agent, or that independent of the causes by which he is moved, he determines his own will, and regulates his own condition. . . .

The will, as we have elsewhere said, is a modification of the brain, by which it
is disposed to action, or prepared to give play to the organs. This will is necessarily

SOURCE: From Baron d'Holbach, *The System of Nature,* trans. H. D. Robinson. This
selection is in the public domain.

determined by the qualities, good or bad, agreeable or painful, of the object or the motive that acts upon his senses, or of which the idea remains with him, and is resuscitated by his memory. In consequence, he acts necessarily, his action is the result of the impulse he receives either from the motive, from the object, or from the idea which has modified his brain, or disposed his will. When he does not act according to this impulse, it is because there comes some new cause, some new motive, some new idea, which modifies his brain in a different manner, gives him a new impulse, determines his will in another way, by which the action of the former impulse is suspended: thus, the sight of an agreeable object, or its idea, determines his will to set him in action to procure it; but if a new object or a new idea more powerfully attracts him, it gives a new direction to his will, annihilates the effect of the former, and prevents the action by which it was to be procured. This is the mode in which reflection, experience, reason, necessarily arrests or suspends the action of man's will: without this he would of necessity have followed the anterior impulse which carried him towards a then desirable object. In all this he always acts according to necessary laws, from which he has no means of emancipating himself.

If when tormented with violent thirst, he figures to himself in idea, or really perceives a fountain, whose limpid streams might cool his feverish want, is he sufficient master of himself to desire or not to desire the object competent to satisfy so lively a want? It will no doubt be conceded, that it is impossible he should not be desirous to satisfy it; but it will he said—if at this moment, it is announced to him that the water he so ardently desires is poisoned, he will, notwithstanding his vehement thirst, abstain from drinking it; and it has, therefore, been falsely concluded that he is a free agent. The fact, however, is, that the motive in either case is exactly the same: his own conservation. The same necessity that determined him to drink before he knew the water was deleterious, upon this new discovery equally determines him not to drink; the desire of conserving himself either annihilates or suspends the former impulse; the second motive becomes stronger than the preceding, that is, the fear of death, or the desire of preserving himself, necessarily prevails over the painful sensation caused by his eagerness to drink: but, it will be said, if the thirst is very parching, an inconsiderate man without regarding the danger will risk swallowing the water. Nothing is gained by this remark; in this case, the anterior impulse only regains the ascendency; he is persuaded that life may possibly be longer preserved, or that he shall derive a greater good by drinking the poisoned water than by enduring the torment, which, to his mind, threatens instant dissolution: thus the first becomes the strongest and necessarily urges him on to action. Nevertheless, in either case, whether he partakes of the water, or whether he does not, the two actions will be equally necessary; they will be the effect of that motive which finds itself most puissant; which consequently acts in the most coercive manner upon his will.

This example will serve to explain the whole phenomena of the human will. This will, or rather the brain, finds itself in the same situation as a bowl, which, although it has received an impulse that drives it forward in a straight line, is deranged in its course whenever a force superior to the first obliges it to change its direction. The man who drinks the poisoned water appears a madman; but the actions of fools are as necessary as those of the most prudent individuals. The motives that determine the voluptuary and the debauchee to risk their health,

are as powerful, and their actions are as necessary, as those which decide the wise
man to manage his. But, it will be insisted, the debauchee may be prevailed on to
change his conduct: this does not imply that he is a free agent; but that motives
may be found sufficiently powerful to annihilate the effect of those that previously
acted upon him; then these new motives determine his will to the new mode of
conduct he may adopt as necessarily as the former did to the old mode.

Man is said to *deliberate,* when the action of the will is suspended; this happens
when two opposite motives act alternately upon him. *To deliberate,* is to hate and
to love in succession; it is to be alternately attracted and repelled; it is to be
moved, sometimes by one motive, sometimes by another. Man only deliberates
when he does not distinctly understand the quality of the objects from which
he receives impulse, or when experience has not sufficiently apprised him of
the effects, more or less remote, which his actions will produce. He would
take the air, but the weather is uncertain; he deliberates in consequence; he
weighs the various motives that urge his will to go out or to stay at home; he
is at length determined by that motive which is most probable; this removes
his indecision, which necessarily settles his will, either to remain within or to
go abroad: this motive is always either the immediate or ultimate advantage he
finds, or thinks he finds, in the action to which he is persuaded. . . .

Choice by no means proves the free agency of man: he only deliberates when
he does not yet know which to choose of the many objects that move him, he is
then in an embarrassment, which does not terminate until his will is decided by the
greater advantage he believes he shall find in the object he chooses, or the action
he undertakes. From whence it may be seen, that choice is necessary, because he
would not determine for an object, or for an action, if he did not believe that he
should find in it some direct advantage. That man should have free agency it
were needful that he should be able to will or choose without motive, or that he
could prevent motives coercing his will. Action always being the effect of his
will once determined, and as his will cannot be determined but by a motive
which is not in his own power, it follows that he is never the master of the determination of his own peculiar will; that consequently he never acts as a free agent. It
has been believed that man was a free agent because he had a will with the power of
choosing; but attention has not been paid to the fact that even his will is moved by
causes independent of himself; is owing to that which is inherent in his own organization, or which belongs to the nature of the beings acting on him.[1] Is he the
master of willing not to withdraw his hand from the fire when he fears it will be
burnt? Or has he the power to take away from fire the property which makes
him fear it? Is he the master of not choosing a dish of meal, which he knows to
be agreeable, or analogous to his palate; of not preferring it to that which he
knows to be disagreeable or dangerous? It is always according to his sensations,

---

[1]Man passes a great portion of his life without even willing. His will depends on the motive
by which he is determined. If he were to render an exact account of every thing he does in
the course of each day—from rising in the morning to lying down at night—he would find
that not one of his actions have been in the least voluntary; that they have been mechanical,
habitual, determined by causes he was not able to foresee; to which he was either obliged to
yield, or with which he was allured to acquiesce: he would discover, that all the motives of
his labours, of his amusements, of his discourses of his thoughts, have been necessary; that
they have evidently either reduced him or drawn him along.

to his own peculiar experience, or to his suppositions, that he judges of things, either well or ill; but whatever may be his judgment, it depends neccessarily on his mode of feeling, whether habitual or accidental, and the qualities he finds in the causes that move him, which exist in despite of himself. . . .

In short, the actions of man are never free; they are always the necessary consequence of his temperament, of the received ideas, and of the notions, either true or false, which he has formed to himself of happiness; of his opinions, strengthened by example, by education, and by daily experience. So many crimes are witnessed on the earth only because every thing conspires to render man vicious and criminal; the religion he has adopted, his government, his education, the examples set before him, irresistibly drive him on to evil: under these circumstances, morality preaches virtue to him in vain. . . .

Man, then, is not a free agent in any one instant of his life; he is necessarily guided in each step by those advantages, whether real or fictitious, that he attaches to the objects by which his passions are roused: these passions themselves are necessary in a being who unceasingly tends towards his own happiness; their energy is necessary, since that depends on his temperament; his temperament is necessary, because it depends on the physical elements which enter into his composition; the modification of this temperament is necessary, as it is the infallible and inevitable consequence of the impulse he receives from the incessant action of moral and physical beings.

In despite of these proofs of the want of free agency in man, so clear to unprejudiced minds, it will, perhaps, be insisted upon with no small feeling of triumph, that if it be proposed to any one, to move or not to move his hand, an action in the number of those called *indifferent,* he evidently appears to be the master of choosing; from which it is concluded that evidence has been offered of his free agency. The reply is, this example is perfectly simple; man in performing some action which he is resolved on doing, does not by any means prove his free agency: the very desire of displaying this quality, excited by the dispute, becomes a necessary motive, which decides his will either for the one or the other of these actions: what deludes him in this instance, or that which persuades him he is a free agent at this moment, is, that he does not discern the true motive which sets him in action, namely, the desire of convincing his opponent: if in the heat of the dispute he insists and asks, "Am I not the master of throwing myself out of the window?" I shall answer him, no; that whilst he preserves his reason there is no probability that the desire of proving his free agency, will become a motive sufficiently powerful to make him sacrifice his life to the attempt: if, notwithstanding this, to prove he is a free agent, he should actually precipitate himself from the window, it would not be a sufficient warranty to conclude he acted freely, but rather that it was the violence of his temperament which spurred him on to this folly. Madness is a state, that depends upon the heat of the blood, not upon the will. A fanatic or a hero, braves death as necessarily as a more phlegmatic man or a coward flies from it.

It is said that free agency is the absence of those obstacles competent to oppose themselves to the actions of man, or to the exercise of his faculties: it is pretended that he is a free agent whenever, making use of these faculties, he produces the effect he has proposed to himself. In reply to this reasoning, it is sufficient to consider that it in nowise depends upon himself to place or remove the obstacles that either determine or resist him; the motive that causes his action is no more in his own power than the obstacle that impedes him, whether this obstacle or motive be within his own machine or exterior of his person: he is not master of the thought presented to his mind, which determines his will; this thought is excited by some cause independent of himself.

To be undeceived on the system of his free agency, man has simply to recur to the motive by which his will is determined; he will always find this motive is out of his own control. It is said: that in consequence of an idea to which the mind gives birth, man acts freely if he encounters no obstacle. But the question is, what gives birth to this idea in his brain? Was he the master either to prevent it from presenting itself, or from renewing itself in his brain? Does not this idea depend either upon objects that strike him exteriorly and in despite of himself, or upon causes, that without his knowledge, act within himself and modify his brain? Can he prevent his eyes, cast without design upon any object whatever, from giving him an idea of this object, and from moving his brain? He is not more master of the obstacles; they are the necessary effects of either interior or exterior causes, which always act according to their given properties. A man insults a coward, this necessarily irritates him against his insulter, but his will cannot vanquish the obstacle that cowardice places to the object of his desire, because his natural conformation, which does not depend upon himself, prevents his having courage. In this case, the coward is insulted in despite of himself; and against his will is obliged patiently to brook the insult he has received.

The partisans of the system of free agency appear ever to have confounded constraint with necessity. Man believes he acts as a free agent, every time he does not see any thing that places obstacles to his actions; he does not perceive that the motive which causes him to will, is always necessary and independent of himself. A prisoner loaded with chains is compelled to remain in prison; but he is not a free agent in the desire to emancipate himself; his chains prevent him from acting , but they do not prevent him from willing; he would save himself if they would loose his fetters; but he would not save himself as a free agent; fear or the idea of punishment would be sufficient motives for his action.

Man may, therefore, cease to be restrained, without, for that reason, becoming a free agent; in whatever manner he acts, he will act necessarily, according to motives by which he shall be determined. He may be compared to a heavy body that finds itself arrested in its descent by any obstacle whatever; take away this obstacle, it will gravitate or continue to fall; but who shall say this dense body is free to fall or not? Is not its descent the necessary effect of its own specific gravity? The virtuous Socrates submitted to the laws of his country, although they were unjust; and though the doors of his jail were left open to him, he would not save himself; but in this he did not act as a free agent: the invisible chains of opinion, the secret love of decorum, the inward respect for the laws, even when they were iniquitous, the fear of tarnishing his glory, kept him in his prison; they were motives sufficiently powerful with this enthusiast for virtue, to induce him to wait death with tranquillity; it was not in his power to save himself, because he could find no potential motive to bring him to depart, even for an instant, from those principles to which his mind was accustomed.

Man, it is said, frequently acts against his inclination, from whence it is falsely concluded he is a free agent; but when he appears to act contrary to his inclination, he is always determined to it by some motive sufficiently efficacious to vanquish this inclination. A sick man, with a view to his cure, arrives at conquering his repugnance to the most disgusting remedies: the fear of pain, or the dread of death, then becomes necessary motives; consequently this sick man cannot be said to act freely. . . .

It is the great complication of motion in man, it is the variety of his action, it is the multiplicity of causes that move him, whether simultaneously or in continual succession, that persuades him he is a free agent: if all his motions were simple, if the causes that move him did not confound themselves with each other, if they were distinct, if his machine were less complicated, he would perceive that all his actions were necessary, because he would be enabled to recur instantly to the cause that made him act. A man who should be always obliged to go towards the west, would always go on that side; but he would feel that, in so going, he was not a free agent: if he had another sense, as his actions or his motion, augmented by a sixth, would be still more varied and much more complicated, be would believe himself still more a free agent than he does with his live senses.

It is, then, for want of recurring to the causes that move him; for want of being able to analyze, from not being competent to decompose the complicated motion of his machine, that man believes himself a free agent: it is only upon his own ignorance that he founds the profound yet deceitful notion he has of his free agency; that he builds those opinions which he brings forward as a striking proof of his pretended freedom of action. If, for a short time, each man was willing to examine his own peculiar actions, search out their true motives to discover their concatenation, he would remain convinced that the sentiment he has of his natural free agency, is a chimera that must speedily be destroyed by experience.

Nevertheless it must be acknowledged that the multiplicity and diversity of the causes which continually act upon man, frequently without even his knowledge, render it impossible, or at least extremely difficult for him to recur to the true principles of his own peculiar actions, much less the actions of others: they frequently depend upon causes so fugitive, so remote from their effects, and which, superficially examined, appear to have so little analogy, so slender a relation with them, that it requires singular sagacity to bring them into light. This is what renders the study of the moral man a task of such difficulty; this is the reason why his heart is an abyss, of which it is frequently impossible for him to fathom the depth. . . .

From all that has been advanced in this chapter, it results, that in no one moment of his existence is man a free agent. He is not the architect of his own conformation, which he holds from nature; he has no control over his own ideas, or over the modification of his brain; these are due to causes, that in despite of him, and without his own knowledge, unceasingly act upon him; he is not the master of not loving or coveting that which he finds amiable or desirable; he is not capable of refusing to deliberate, when he is uncertain of the effects certain objects will produce upon him; he cannot avoid choosing that which he believes will be most advantageous to him; in the moment when his will is determined by his choice he is not competent to act otherwise than he does. In what instance, then, is he the master of his own actions? In what moment is he a free agent? . . .

## READING COMPREHENSION QUESTIONS

1. According to Holbach, what would it take to be a free agent, and why is no human a free agent?

2. In your own words, describe Holbach's example of the guy with "violent thirst" heading to the fountain. What is the point of this passage?

3. Many people think we truly demonstrate our freedom when we deliberate between two (or more) courses of action, and then we decide on one or the other after weighing the reasons for both sides. How does Holbach describe the process of deliberation? Does this seem accurate to your own experience? Why or why not?

4. A compatibilist (see introduction to this reading) would respond to Holbach that he misunderstands what freedom is, that it is really just the absence of external impediments to action. In other words, if you are able to do what you want to do, with nothing outside of you getting in your way, then you are a free agent. Holbach considers this objection explicitly and rejects it. In your own words, explain this response.

5. Holbach thinks that freedom is an illusion, that we suppose ourselves to be free agents when we really are not. But what is his diagnosis for this illusion? In other words, why does he think we persist in believing ourselves to be free?

# 15

# Has the Self 'Free Will'?

C. A. CAMPBELL

*C. A. Campbell (1897–1974) was a philosopher who taught at the University of Glasgow. He wrote several pieces on free will, including the book* On Selfhood and Godhood, *from which this selection is taken. In this essay, Campbell clearly lays out both the motivations for libertarianism as well as the main thesis of the view. To get an understanding of what free will actually is, he says, we must view it in the context of its being a necessary condition for moral responsibility. So what is moral responsibility? According to Campbell, it has to do with appropriate attributions of praise and blame, and he suggests we can understand what free will is ultimately by figuring out just what conditions must be in place for us to appropriately blame or praise people for their actions. Campbell thus lays out three necessary and sufficient conditions for moral responsibility (and thus free will). But because these conditions presuppose that determinism is false, free will must require indeterminism, the view that not all events are determined by preceding events. The next step in Campbell's argument is to consider whether or not people ever actually meet these conditions of freedom, and his answer is "yes" (which is what makes him a libertarian). His evidence for this positive view comes from consideration of what deliberation and action feels like from the inside for us, and in affirming that we do occasionally act freely, Campbell specifies just when that occurs and precisely what the capacity for such freedom consists in.*

It is something of a truism that in philosophic enquiry the exact formulation of a problem often takes one a long way on the road to its solution. In the case of the Free Will problem I think there is a rather special need of careful formulation. For there are many sorts of human freedom; and it can easily happen that one wastes a great deal of labour in proving or disproving a freedom which has almost nothing to do with the freedom which is at issue in the traditional problem of Free Will. The abortiveness of so much of the argument for and against Free Will in contemporary philosophical literature seems to me due in the main to insufficient pains being taken over the preliminary definition of the problem. There is, indeed, one outstanding exception, Professor Broad's brilliant inaugural lecture entitled, "Determinism, Indeterminism, and Libertarianism,"[1] in which forty three pages are devoted to setting out the problem, as against seven to its solution I confess that the solution does not seem to myself to follow upon the formulation quite as easily as all that:[2] but Professor Broad's eminent example fortifies me in my decision to give here what may seem at first sight a disproportionate amount of time to the business of determining the essential characteristics of the kind of freedom with which the traditional problem is concerned.

Fortunately we can at least make a beginning with a certain amount of confidence. It is not seriously disputable that the kind of freedom in question is the freedom which is commonly recognised to be in some sense a precondition of moral responsibility. Clearly, it is on account of this integral connection with moral responsibility that such exceptional importance has always been felt to attach to the Free Will problem. But in what precise sense is free will a precondition of moral responsibility, and thus a postulate of the moral life in general? This is an exceedingly troublesome question; but until we have satisfied ourselves about the answer to it, we are not in a position to state, let alone decide, the question whether "Free Will" in its traditional, ethical, significance is a reality.

Our first business, then, is to ask, exactly what kind of freedom is it which is required for moral responsibility? And as to method of procedure in this inquiry, there seems to me to be no real choice. I know of only one method that carries with it any hope of success; viz. the critical comparison of those acts for which, on

SOURCE: From C. A. Campbell, *On Selfhood and Godhood.* Copyright © 1957 George Allen & Unwin. Used by permission.

[1]Reprinted in *Ethics and the History of Philosophy, Selected Essays.*

[2]I have explained the grounds for my dissent from Broad's final conclusion on pp. 27 ff. of *In Defence of Free Will* (Jackson Son & Co., 1938).

due reflection, we deem it proper to attribute moral praise or blame to the agents, with those acts for which, on due reflection, we deem such judgments to be improper. The ultimate touchstone, as I see it, can only be our moral consciousness as it manifests itself in our more critical and considered moral judgments. The "linguistic" approach by way of the analysis of moral *sentences* seems to me, despite its present popularity, to be an almost infallible method for reaching wrong results in the moral field; but I must reserve what I have to say about this.

The first point to note is that the freedom at issue (as indeed the very name "Free *Will* Problem" indicates) pertains primarily not to overt acts but to inner acts. The nature of things has decreed that, save in the case of one's self, it is only overt acts which one can directly observe. But a very little reflection serves to show that in our moral judgments upon others their overt acts are regarded as significant only in so far as they are the expression of inner acts. We do not consider the acts of a robot to be morally responsible acts; nor do we consider the acts of a man to be so save in so far as they are distinguishable from those of a robot by reflecting an inner life of choice. Similarly, from the other side, if we are satisfied (as we may on occasion be, at least in the case of ourselves) that a person has definitely elected to follow a course which he believes to be wrong, but has been prevented by external circumstances from translating his inner choice into an overt act, we still regard him as morally blame worthy. Moral freedom, then, pertains to *inner* acts.

The next point seems at first sight equally obvious and uncontroversial; but, as we shall see, it has awkward implications if we are in real earnest with it (as almost nobody is). It is the simple point that the act must be one of which the person judged can be regarded as the *sole* author. It seems plain enough that if there are any *other* determinants of the act, external to the self, to that extent the act is not an act which the *self* determines and to that extent not an act for which the self can be held morally responsible. The self is only part-author of the act, and his moral responsibility can logically extend only to those elements within the act (assuming for the moment that these can be isolated) of which he is the *sole* author.

The awkward implications of this apparent truism will be readily appreciated. For, if we are mindful of the influences exerted by heredity and environment, we may well feel some doubt whether there is any act of will at all of which one can truly say that the self is sole author, sole determinant. No man has a voice in determining the raw material of impulses and capacities that constitute his hereditary endowment, and no man has more than a very partial control of the material and social environment in which he is destined to live his life. Yet it would be manifestly absurd to deny that these two factors do constantly and profoundly affect the nature of a man's choices. That this is so we all of us recognise in our moral judgments when we "make allowances," as we say, for a bad heredity or a vicious environment, and acknowledge in the victim of them a diminished moral responsibility for evil courses. Evidently we do *try*, in our moral judgments, however crudely, to praise or blame a man only in respect of that of which we can regard him as *wholly* the author. And evidently we do recognise that, for a man to be the author of an act in the full sense required for moral responsibility, it is not enough merely that he "wills" or "chooses" the act: since even the most unfortunate victim of heredity or environment does, as a rule, "will" what he does. It is significant, however, that the ordinary man, though well enough aware of the influence upon choices of heredity and environment, does not feel obliged thereby to give up his assumption that moral predicates *are* somehow applicable. Plainly he still believes that there is *something* for which a man is morally responsible, something of which we can fairly say that he is the sole author. *What is this something?* To that question common sense is not ready with an explicit answer though an answer is, I think, implicit in the line which its moral judgments take. I shall do what I can to give an explicit answer later in this lecture. Meantime it must suffice to observe that, if we are to be true to the deliverances of our moral consciousness, it is very difficult to deny that *sole* authorship is a necessary condition of the morally responsible act.

Thirdly we come to a point over which much recent controversy has raged. We may approach it by raising the following question. Granted an act of which the agent is sole author, does this 'sole authorship' suffice to make the act a morally free act? We may be inclined to think that it does, until we contemplate the possibility that an act of which the agent is sole author might conceivably occur as a necessary expression of the agent's nature; the way in which, e.g. some philosophers have supposed the Divine act of creation to occur. This consideration excites a legitimate doubt; for it is far from easy to see how a person can be regarded as a proper subject for moral praise or blame in respect of an act which he *cannot help* performing—even if it be his own "nature" which necessitates it. Must we not recognise it as a condition of the morally free act that the agent "could have acted otherwise" than he in fact did? It is true, indeed, that we sometimes praise or blame a man for an act about which we are prepared to say, in the light of our knowledge of his established character, that he "could do no other." But I think that a little reflection shows that in such cases we are not praising or blaming the man strictly for what he does *now* (or at any rate we ought not to be), but rather for those past acts of his which have generated the firm habit of mind from which his *present* act follows "necessarily." In other words, our praise and blame, so far as justified, are really retrospective, being directed not to the agent *qua* performing *this* act, but to the agent *qua* performing those past acts which have built up his present character, and in respect to which we presume that he *could* have acted otherwise, that there really *were* open possibilities before him. These cases, therefore, seem to me to constitute no valid exception to what I must take to be the rule, viz. that a man can be morally praised or blamed for an act only if he could have acted otherwise.

Now philosophers today are fairly well agreed that it is a postulate of the morally responsible act that the agent "could have acted otherwise" in *some* sense of that phrase. But sharp differences of opinion have arisen over the way in which the phrase ought to be interpreted. There is a strong disposition to water down its apparent meaning by insisting that it is not (as a postulate of moral responsibility) to be understood as a straightforward categorical proposition, but rather as a disguised hypothetical proposition. All that we really require to be assured of, in order to justify our holding X morally responsible for an act, is, we are told, that X could have acted otherwise *if* he had *chosen* otherwise (Moore, Stevenson); or perhaps that X could have acted otherwise *if* he had had a different character, or *if* he had been placed in different circumstances.

I think it is easy to understand, and even, in a measure, to sympathise with, the motives which induce philosophers to offer these counter-interpretations. It is not just the fact that "X could have acted otherwise," as a bald categorical state-ment, is incompatible with the universals way of causal law—though this is, to some philosophers, a serious stone of stumbling. The more widespread objection is that it at least looks as though it were incompatible with that causal continuity of an agent's character with his conduct which is implied when we believe (surely with justice) that we can often tell the sort of thing a man will do from our knowledge of the sort of man, he is.

We shall have to make our accounts with that particular difficulty later. At this stage I wish merely to show that neither of the hypothetical propositions suggested—and I think the same could be shown for *any* hypothetical alterna-tive—is an acceptable substitute for the categorical proposition "X could have acted otherwise" as the presupposition of moral responsibility.

Let us look first at the earlier suggestion—"X could have acted otherwise *if* he had chosen otherwise." Now clearly there are a great many acts with regard to which we are entirely satisfied that the agent is thus situated. We are often perfectly sure that—for this is all it amounts to—if X had chosen otherwise, the circumstances presented no external obstacle to the translation of that choice into action. For example, we often have no doubt at all that X, who in point of fact told a lie, could have told the truth *if* he had so chosen. But does our confidence on this score allay all legitimate doubts about whether X is really blameworthy? Does it entail that X is free in the sense required for moral respon-sibility? Surely not. The obvious question immediately arises: "But *could* X have *chosen* otherwise than he did?" It is doubt about the true answer to *that* question which leads most people to doubt the reality of moral responsibility. Yet on this crucial question the hypothetical proposition which is offered as a sufficient state-ment of the condition justifying the ascription of moral responsibility gives us no information whatsoever.

Indeed this hypothetical substitute for the categorical "X could have acted otherwise" seems to me to lack all plausibility unless one contrives to forget why it is, after all, that we ever come to feel fundamental doubts about man's moral responsibility. Such doubts are born, surely, when one becomes aware of certain reputable world-views in religion or philosophy, or of certain reputable scientific beliefs, which in their several ways imply that man's actions are neces-sitated, and thus could not be otherwise than they in fact are. But clearly a doubt so based is not even touched by the recognition that a man could very often act otherwise *if* he so chose. That proposition is entirely compatible with the neces-sitarian theories which generate our doubt: indeed it is this very compatibility that has recommended it to some philosophers, who are reluctant to give up either moral responsibility or Determinism. The proposition which we *must* be able to affirm if moral praise or blame of X is to be justified is the categorical propo-sition that X could have acted otherwise because—not if—he could have chosen otherwise; or, since it is essentially the inner side of the act that matters, the pro-positions imply that X could have chosen otherwise.

For the second of the alternative formulae suggested we cannot spare more than a few moments. But its inability to meet the demands it is required to meet is almost transparent. "X could have acted otherwise," as a statement of a precondition of X's moral responsibility, really means (we are told) "X could have acted otherwise *if* he were differently constituted, or *if* he had been placed in different circumstances." It seems a sufficient reply to this to point out that the person whose moral responsibility is at issue is X; a specific individual, in a specific set of circumstances. It is totally irrelevant to X's moral responsibility that we should be able to say that some person differently constituted from X, or X in a different set of circumstances, could have done something different from what X did.

Let me, then, briefly sum up the answer at which we have arrived to our question about the kind of freedom required to justify moral responsibility. It is that a man can be said to exercise free will in a morally significant sense only in so far as his chosen act is one of which he is the sole cause or author, and only if—in the straightforward, categorical sense of the phrase—he "could have chosen otherwise."

I confess that this answer is in some ways a disconcerting one; disconcerting, because most of us, however objective we are in the actual conduct of our thinking, would *like* to be able to believe that moral responsibility is real: whereas the freedom required for moral responsibility, on the analysis we have given, is certainly far more difficult to establish than the freedom required on the analyses we found ourselves obliged to reject. If, e.g., moral freedom entails only that I could have acted otherwise *if* I had chosen otherwise, there is no real "problem" about it at all. I am "free" in the normal case where there is no external obstacle to prevent my translating the alternative choice into action, and not free in other cases. Still less is there a problem if all that moral freedom entails is that I could have acted otherwise *if* I had been a differently constituted person, or been in different circumstances. Clearly I am *always* free in *this* sense of freedom. But, as I have argued, these so-called "freedoms" fail to give us the pre-conditions of moral responsibility, and hence leave the freedom of the traditional free-will problem, the freedom that people are really concerned about, precisely where it was. . . .

That brings me to the second, and more constructive, part of this lecture. From now on I shall be considering whether it is reasonable to believe that man does in fact possess a free will of the kind specified in the first part of the lecture. If so, just how and where within the complex fabric of volitional life are we to locate it?—for although free will must presumably belong (if anywhere) to the volitional side of human experience, it is pretty clear from the way in which we have been forced to define it that it does not pertain simply to volition as such; not even to all volitions that are commonly dignified with the name "choices." It has been, I think, one of the more serious impediments to profitable discussion of the Free Will problem that Libertarians and Determinists alike have so often failed to appreciate the comparatively narrow area within which the free will that is necessary to "save" morality is required to operate. It goes without saying that this failure has been gravely prejudicial to the case for Libertarianism. I attach a good deal of importance, therefore, to the problem of locating free will correctly within the volitional orbit. Its solution forestalls and annuls, I believe, some of the more tiresome clichés of Determinist criticism.

We saw earlier that Common Sense's practice of "making allowances" in its moral judgments for the Influence of heredity and environment indicates Common Sense's conviction, both that a just moral judgment must discount determinants of choice over which the agent has no control, and also (since it still accepts

moral judgments as legitimate) that something of moral relevance survives which
can be regarded as genuinely self-originated. We are now to try to discover
what this 'something' is. And I think we may still usefully take Common Sense
as our guide. Suppose one asks the ordinary intelligent citizen *why* he deems it
proper to make allowances for X, whose heredity and/or environment are unfortunate. He will tend to reply, I think, in some such terms as these: that X has more
and stronger temptations to deviate from what is right than Y or Z, who are normally circumstanced, so that he must put forth a *stronger moral effort* if he is to
achieve the same level of external conduct. The intended implication seems to
be that X is just as morally praiseworthy as Y or Z *if* he exerts an equivalent
moral effort, even though he may not thereby achieve an equal success in con-
forming his will to the "concrete" demands of duty. And this implies, again,
Common Sense's belief that *in moral effort* we have something for which a man
is responsible *without qualification,* something that is *not* affected by heredity and
environment but depends *solely* upon the self itself.

Now in my opinion Common Sense has here, in Principle, hit upon the one
and only defensible answer. Here, and here alone, so far as I can see, in the act of
deciding whether to put forth or withhold the moral effort required to resist
temptation and rise to duty, is to be found an act which is free in the sense
required for moral responsibility; an act of which the self is sole author, and of
which it is true to say that "it could be" (or, after the event, "could have
been") "otherwise." Such is the thesis which we shall now try to establish.

The species of argument appropriate to the establishment of a thesis of this sort
should fall, I think, into two phases. First, there should be a consideration of the
evidence of the moral agent's own inner experience. What *is* the act of moral decision, and what does it imply, from the standpoint of the actual participant? Since
there is no way of knowing the act of moral decision—or for that matter any
other form of activity—except by actual participation in it, the evidence of the subject, or agent, is on an issue of this kind of primary importance. It can hardly, however, be taken as in itself conclusive. For even if that evidence should be
overwhelmingly to the effect that moral decision does have the characteristics
required by moral freedom, the question is bound to be raised—and in view of
considerations from other quarters pointing in a contrary direction is *rightly*
raised—Can we *trust* the evidence of inner experience? That brings us to what
will be the second phase of the argument. We shall have to go on to show, if
we are to make good our case, that the extraneous considerations so often supposed
to be fatal to the belief in moral freedom are in fact innocuous to it. . . .

When we decide to exert moral effort to resist a temptation, we feel quite
certain that we *could* withhold the effort; just as, if we decide to withhold the
effort and yield to our desires, we feel quite certain that we *could* exert it—
otherwise we should not blame ourselves afterwards for having succumbed. It
may be, indeed, that this conviction is mere self-delusion. But that is not at the
moment our concern. It is enough at present to establish that the act of deciding
to exert or to withhold moral effort, as we know it from the inside in actual moral
living, belongs to the category of acts which "could have been otherwise."

*Mutatis mutandis,* the same reply is forthcoming if we ask, "Is it possible for the
moral agent in the taking of his decision to *dis*believe that he is the *sole* author of

that decision?" Clearly he cannot disbelieve that it is *he* who takes the decision. That, however, is not in itself sufficient to enable him, on reflection, to regard himself as *solely* responsible for the act. For his "character" as so far formed might conceivably be a factor in determining it, and no one can suppose that the constitution of his "character" is uninfluenced by circumstances of heredity and environment with which *he* has nothing to do. But as we pointed out in the last lecture, the very essence of the moral decision as it is experienced is that it is a decision whether or not to *combat* our strongest desire, and our strongest desire *is* the expression in the situation of our character as so far formed. Now clearly our character cannot be a factor in determining the decision whether or not to *oppose* our character. I think we are entitled to say, therefore, that the act of moral decision is one in which the self is for itself not merely "author" but "sole author."

We may pass on then to the second phase of our constructive argument; and this will demand more elaborate treatment. Even if a moral agent *qua* making a moral decision in the situation of "temptation" cannot help believing that he has free will in the sense at issue—a moral freedom between real alternatives, between genuinely open possibilities—are there, nevertheless, objections to a freedom of this kind so cogent that we are bound to distrust the evidence of "inner experience?"

I begin by drawing attention to a simple point whose significance tends, I think, to be underestimated. If the phenomenological analysis we have offered is substantially correct, no one while functioning as a moral agent can help believing that he enjoys free will. Theoretically he may be completely convinced by Determinist arguments, but when actually confronted with a personal situation of conflict between duty and desire he is quite certain that it lies with him here and now whether or not he will rise to duty. It follows that if Determinists could produce convincing theoretical arguments against a free will of this kind, the awkward predicament would ensue that man has to deny as a theoretical being what he has to assert as a practical being. Now I think the Determinist ought to be a good deal more worried about this than he usually is. He seems to imagine that a strong case on general theoretical grounds is enough to prove that the "practical" belief in free will, even if inescapable for us as practical beings, is mere illusion. But in fact it proves nothing of the sort. There is no reason whatever why a belief that we find ourselves obliged to hold *qua* practical beings should be required to give way before a belief which we find ourselves obliged to hold *qua* theoretical beings; or, for that matter, *vice versa*. All that the theoretical arguments of Determinism can prove, unless they are reinforced by a refutation of the phenomenological analysis that supports Libertarianism, is that there is a radical conflict between the theoretical and the practical sides of man's nature, an antinomy at the very heart of the self. And this is a state of affairs with which no one can easily rest satisfied. I think therefore that the Determinist ought to concern himself a great deal more than he does with phenomenological analysis, in order to show, if he can, that the assurance of free will is not really an inexpugnable element in man's practical consciousness. There is just as much obligation upon him, convinced though he may be of the soundness of his theoretical arguments, to expose the errors of the Libertarian's phenomenological analysis, as there is upon us, convinced though we may be of the soundness of the Libertarian's phenomenological analysis, to expose the errors of the Determinist's theoretical arguments.

However, we must at once begin the discharge of our own obligation. The rest of this lecture will be devoted to trying to show that the arguments which seem to carry the most weight with Determinists are, to say the least of it, very far from compulsive. . . .

These arguments can, I think, be reduced in principle to no more than two: first, the argument from "predictability;" second, the argument from the alleged meaninglessness of an act supposed to be the self's act and yet not an expression of the self's character. Contemporary criticism of free will seems to me to consist almost exclusively of variations on these two themes. I shall deal with each in turn.

On the first we touched in passing at an earlier stage. Surely it is beyond question (the critic urges) that when we know a person intimately we can foretell with a high degree of accuracy how he will respond to at least a large number of practical situations. One feels safe in predicting that one's dog-loving friend will not use his boot to repel the little mongrel that comes yapping at his heels; or again that one's wife will not pass with incurious eyes (or indeed pass at all) the new hat shop in the city. So to behave would not be (as we say) "in character." But, so the criticism runs, you with your doctrine of 'genuinely open possibilities,' of a free will by which the self can diverge from its own character, remove all rational basis from such prediction. You require us to make the absurd supposition that the success of countless predictions of the sort in the past has been mere matter of chance. If you *really* believed in your theory, you would not be surprised if tomorrow your friend with the notorious horror of strong drink should suddenly exhibit a passion for whisky and soda, or if your friend whose taste for reading has hitherto been satisfied with the sporting columns of the newspapers should be discovered on a fine Saturday afternoon poring over the works of Hegel. But of course you *would* be surprised. Social life would be sheer chaos if there were not well-grounded social expectations; and social life is not sheer chaos. Your theory is hopelessly wrecked upon obvious facts.

Now whether or not this criticism holds good against some versions of Libertarian theory I need not here discuss. It is sufficient if I can make it clear that against the version advanced in this lecture, according to which free will is localized in a relatively narrow field of operation, the criticism has no relevance whatsoever.

Let us remind ourselves briefly of the setting within which, on our view, free will functions. There is X, the course which we believe we ought to follow, and Y, the course towards which we feel our desire is strongest. The freedom which we ascribe to the agent is the freedom to put forth or refrain from putting forth the moral effort required to resist the pressure of desire and do what he thinks he ought to do.

But then there is surely an immense range of practical situations—covering by far the greater part of life—in which there is no question of a conflict within the self between what he most desires to do and what he thinks he ought to do.

Indeed such conflict is a comparatively rare phenomenon for the majority of men. Yet over that whole vast range there is nothing whatever in our version of Libertarianism to prevent our agreeing that character determines conduct. In the absence, real or supposed, of any "moral" issue, what a man chooses will be simply that course which, after such reflection as seems called for, he deems most likely to bring him what he most strongly desires; and that is the same as to say the course to which his present character inclines him.

Over by far the greater area of human choices, then, our theory offers no more barrier to successful prediction on the basis of character than any other theory. For where there is no clash of strongest desire with duty, the free will we are defending has no business. There is just nothing for it to do.

But what about the situations—rare enough though they may be—in which there *is* this clash and in which free will does therefore operate? Does our theory entail that there, at any rate, as the critic seems to suppose, "anything may happen?"

Not by any manner of means. In the first place, and by the very nature of the case, the range of the agent's possible choices is bounded by what he thinks he ought to do on the one hand, and what he most strongly desires on the other. The freedom claimed for him is a freedom of decision to make or withhold the effort required to do what he thinks he ought to do. There is no question of a freedom to act in some "wild" fashion, out of all relation to his characteristic beliefs and desires. This so-called "freedom of caprice," so often charged against the Libertarian, is, to put it bluntly, a sheer figment of the critic's imagination, with no *habitat* in serious Libertarian theory. Even in situations where free will does come into play it is perfectly possible, on a view like ours, given the appropriate knowledge of a man's character to predict within certain limits how he will respond.

But "probable" prediction in such situations can, I think, go further than this. It is obvious that where desire and duty are at odds, the felt "gap" (as it were) between the two may vary enormously in breadth in different cases. The moderate drinker and the chronic tippler may each want another glass, and each deem it his duty to abstain, but the felt gap between desire and duty in the case of the former is trivial beside the great gulf which is felt to separate them in the case of the latter. Hence it will take a far harder moral effort for the tippler than for the moderate drinker to achieve the same external result of abstention. So much is a matter of common agreement. And we are entitled, I think, to take it into account in prediction, on the simple principle that the harder the moral effort required to resist desire the less likely it is to occur. Thus in the example taken, most people would predict that the tippler will very probably succumb to his desires, whereas there is a reasonable likelihood that the moderate drinker will make the comparatively slight effort needed to resist them. So long as the prediction does not pretend to more than a measure of probability, there is nothing in our theory which would disallow it.

I claim, therefore, that the view of free will I have been putting forward is consistent with predictability of conduct on the basis of character over a very wide field indeed. And I make the further claim that that field will cover all the situations in life concerning which there is any empirical evidence that successful prediction is possible.

Let us pass on to consider the second main line of criticism. This is, I think, much the more illuminating of the two, if only because it compels the Libertarian to make explicit certain concepts which are indispensable to him, but which, being desperately hard to state clearly, are apt not to be stated at all. The critic's fundamental point might be stated somewhat as follows:

"Free will as you describe it is completely unintelligible. On your own showing no *reason* can be given, because there just *is* no reason, why a man decides to exert rather than to withhold moral effort, or *vice versa*. But such an act—or more properly, such an "occurrence"—it is nonsense to speak of as an act of a *self*. If there is nothing in the self's character to which it is, even in principle, in any way traceable, the self has nothing to do with it. Your so-called "freedom," therefore, so far from supporting the self's moral responsibility, destroys it as surely as the crudest Determinism could do."

If we are to discuss this criticism usefully, it is important, I think, to begin by getting clear about two different senses of the word "intelligible."

If, in the first place, we mean by an "intelligible" act one whose occurrence is in principle capable of being inferred, since it follows necessarily from something (though we may not know in fact from what), then it is certainly true that the Libertarian's free will is unintelligible. But that is only saying, is it not, that the Libertarian's "free" act is not an act which follows necessarily from something! This can hardly rank as a *criticism* of Libertarianism. It is just a description of it. That there can be nothing unintelligible in *this* sense is precisely what the Determinist has got to *prove*.

Yet it is surprising how often the critic of Libertarianism involves himself in this circular mode of argument. Repeatedly it is urged against the Libertarian, with a great air of triumph, that on his view he can't say *why* I now decide to rise to duty, or now decide to follow my strongest desire in defiance of duty. Of course he can't. If he could *he* wouldn't be a Libertarian. To "account for" a "free" act is a contradiction in terms. A free will is *ex hypothesi* the sort of thing of which the request for an *explanation* is absurd. The assumption that an explanation must be in principle possible for the act of moral decision deserves to rank as a classic example of the ancient fallacy of "begging the question."

But the critic usually has in mind another sense of the word "unintelligible." He is apt to take it for granted that an act which is unintelligible in the *above* sense (as the morally free act of the Libertarian undoubtedly is) is unintelligible in the *further* sense that we can attach no meaning to it. And this is an altogether more serious matter. If it could really be shown that the Libertarian's "free will" were unintelligible in this sense of being meaningless, that, for myself at any rate, would be the end of the affair. Libertarianism would have been conclusively refuted.

But it seems to me manifest that this can *not* be shown. The critic has allowed himself, I submit, to become the victim of a widely accepted but fundamentally vicious assumption. He has assumed that whatever is meaningful must exhibit its meaningfulness to those who view it from the standpoint of external observation. Now if one chooses thus to limit one's self to the role of external observer, it is, I think, perfectly true that one can attach no meaning to an act which is the act of something we call a "self" and yet follows from nothing in that self's character. But then *why should we* so limit ourselves, when what is under consideration is a subjective activity? For the apprehension of subjective acts there is *another* standpoint available, that of *inner experience,* of the practical consciousness in its actual functioning. If our free will should turn out to be something to which we can attach a meaning from *this* standpoint, no more is required. And no more ought to be expected. For I must repeat that only from the inner standpoint of living experience *could* anything of the nature of "activity" be directly grasped. Observation from without is in the nature of the case impotent to apprehend the active *qua* active. We can from without observe sequences of states. If into these we read activity (as we sometimes do), this can only be on the basis of what we discern in ourselves from the inner standpoint. It follows that if anyone insists upon taking his criterion of the meaningful simply from the standpoint of external observation, he is really deciding in advance of the evidence that the notion of activity, and *a fortiori* the notion of a free will, is "meaningless." He looks for the free act through a medium which is in the nature of the case incapable of revealing it, and then, because inevitably he doesn't find it, he declares that it doesn't exist!

But if, as we surely ought in this context, we adopt the inner standpoint, then (I am suggesting) things appear in a totally different light. From the inner standpoint, it seems to me plain, there is no difficulty whatever in attaching meaning to an act which is the self's act and which nevertheless does not follow from the self's character. . . . It is thrown into particularly clear relief where the moral decision is to make the moral effort required to rise to duty. For the very function of moral effort, as it appears to the agent engaged in the act, is to enable the self to act against the line of least resistance, against the line to which his character as so far formed most strongly inclines him. But if the self is thus conscious here of *combating* his formed character, he surely cannot possibly suppose that the act, although his own act, *issues from* his formed character? I submit, therefore, that the self knows very well indeed from the inner standpoint what is meant by an act which is the *self's* act and which nevertheless does not follow from the self's *character.*

What this implies—and it seems to me to be an implication of cardinal importance for any theory of the self that aims at being more than superficial—is that the nature of the self is for itself something more than just its character as so far formed. The "nature" of the self and what we commonly call the "character" of the self are by no means the same thing, and it is utterly vital that they should not be confused. The "nature" of the self comprehends, but is not without remainder reducible to, its "character;" it must, if we are to be true to the testimony of our experience of it, be taken as including *also* the authentic creative power of fashioning and re-fashioning "character.". . .

There we must leave the matter. But as this lecture has been, I know, somewhat densely packed, it may be helpful if I conclude by reminding you, in bald summary, of the main things I have been trying to say. Let me set them out in so many successive theses.

1. The freedom which is at issue in the traditional Free Will problem is the freedom which is presupposed in moral responsibility.

2. Critical reflection upon carefully considered attributions of moral responsibility reveals that the only freedom that will do is a freedom which pertains to inner acts of choice, and that these acts must be acts (a) of which the self is *sole* author, and (b) which the self could have performed otherwise.

3. From phenomenological analysis of the situation of moral temptation we find that the self as engaged in this situation is inescapably convinced that it possesses a freedom of precisely the specified kind, located in the decision to exert or withhold the moral effort needed to rise to duty where the pressure of its desiring nature is felt to pull it in a contrary direction.

Passing to the question of the reality of this moral freedom which the moral agent believes himself to possess, we argued:

4. Of the two types of Determinist criticism which seem to have most influence today, that based on the predictability of much human behaviour fails to touch a Libertarianism which confines the area of free will as above indicated. Libertarianism so understood is compatible with all the predictability that the empirical facts warrant. And:

5. The second main type of criticism, which alleges the "meaninglessness" of an act which is the self's act and which is yet not determined by the self's character, is based on a failure to appreciate that the standpoint of inner experience is not only legitimate but indispensable where what is at issue is the reality and nature of a subjective activity. The creative act of moral decision is inevitably meaningless to the mere external observer; but from the inner standpoint it is as real, and as significant, as anything in human experience.

## READING COMPREHENSION QUESTIONS

1. In your own words, explain Campbell's three conditions of the freedom required for moral responsibility.

2. In discussing the ability to do otherwise, Campbell directly addresses the compatibilist interpretation of that phrase—that one would have acted otherwise if one had chosen otherwise (see also the discussion of this interpretation in the introduction to this chapter). In your own words, explain why Campbell rejects this interpretation.

3. In discussing the second condition of freedom and moral responsibility, Campbell notes that we're looking for that *something* of which agents are sole authors, that something that is genuinely self-originated. What does that *something* turn out to be? In other words, explain what it is about free and responsible agents that Campbell thinks isn't affected by heredity or environment, the thing that is the true expression of the self's authorship of its actions.

4. In your own words, explain what Campbell sees as the difference between the self and the self's character. What role does this distinction play in his overall argument?

5. Campbell talks in this article about "phenomenological analysis," which is just another way of saying he's relying on evidence "from the inside" about what happens when one acts. In other words, Campbell thinks that reflection on one's internal psychological goings-on at the time of deliberation and action provides some evidence in favor of libertarianism, simply because from that internal perspective it seems his three conditions for the freedom required by

moral responsibility are indeed fulfilled. Describe, then, what he thinks goes
on from the internal perspective when one is free and responsible. Do you
agree with this "phenomenological analysis," or do things seem to work
differently for you?

# 16

# The Problem of Free Will

WALTER T. STACE

*Walter T. Stace (1886–1967) taught at Princeton University and wrote many
books and articles on the philosophy of religion, ancient Greek philosophy,
metaphysics, ethics, and social and political thought. In this article, he appeals to
common usage to determine the correct definition of free will, which he thinks turns
out to be quite different from the definition maintained by hard determinists like
Holbach and libertarians like Campbell. Stace considers several uses of the phrase
"doing it of one's own free will" and concludes that sometimes we do indeed act of
our own free will, despite the fact that our action was caused. What this must
mean, then, is that causation alone doesn't undermine free will. Instead, only
certain* types *of causes undermine our free will. Stace articulates just what these
special types of causes are, and then he considers some implications and possible
objections to his account.*

A great problem which the rise of scientific naturalism has created for the modern mind concerns the foundations of morality. The old religious foundations
have largely crumbled away, and it may well be thought that the edifice built upon
them by generations of men is in danger of collapse. A total collapse of moral
behavior is . . . very unlikely. For a society in which this occurred could not survive. Nevertheless the danger to moral standards inherent in the virtual disappear-
ance of their old religious foundations is not illusory.

I shall first discuss the problem of free will, for it is certain that if there is no free
will there can be no morality. Morality is concerned with what men ought and
ought not to do. But if a man has no freedom to choose what he will do, if whatever he does is done under compulsion, then it does not make sense to tell him that

SOURCE: From W. T. Stace, "Is Determinism Inconsistent with Free Will," in *Religion and
the Modern Mind*, pp. 248–258. Copyright © 1952 by W. T. Stace, renewed © 1980 by
Blanche Stace. Reprinted by permission of HarperCollins Publishers.

he ought not to have done what he did and that he ought to do something different. All moral precepts would in such a case be meaningless. Also if he acts always
under compulsion, how can he be held morally responsible for his actions? How
can he, for example, be punished for what he could not help doing?

It is to be observed that those learned professors of philosophy or psychology
who deny the existence of free will do so only in their professional moments and
in their studies and lecture rooms. For when it comes to doing anything practical,
even of the most trivial kind, they invariably behave as if they and others were
free. They inquire from you at dinner whether you will choose this dish or
that dish. They will ask a child why he told a lie, and will punish him for not having chosen the way of truthfulness. All of which is inconsistent with a disbelief in
free will. This should cause us to suspect that the problem is not a real one; and
this, I believe, is the case. The dispute is merely verbal, and is due to nothing but a
confusion about the meanings of words. It is what is now fashionably called a
semantic problem.

How does a verbal dispute arise? Let us consider a case which, although it is
absurd in the sense that no one would ever make the mistake which is involved in
it, yet illustrates the principle which we shall have to use in the solution of the
problem. Suppose that someone believed that the word "man" means a certain
sort of five-legged animal; in short that "five-legged animal" is the correct *definition* of man. He might then look around the world, and rightly observing that
there are no five-legged animals in it, he might proceed to deny the existence
of men. This preposterous conclusion would have been reached because he
was using an incorrect definition of "man." All you would have to do to show
him his mistake would be to give him the correct definition; or at least to
show him that his definition was wrong. Both the problem and its solution
would, of course, be entirely verbal. The problem of free will, and its solution,
I shall maintain, is verbal in exactly the same way. The problem has been created
by the fact that learned men, especially philosophers, have assumed an incorrect
definition of free will, and then finding that there is nothing in the world
which answers to their definition, have denied its existence. As far as logic is concerned, their conclusion is just as absurd as that of the man who denies the existence of men. The only difference is that the mistake in the latter case is obvious
and crude, while the mistake which the deniers of free will have made is rather
subtle and difficult to detect.

Throughout the modern period, until quite recently, it was assumed, both by
the philosophers who denied free will and by those who defended it, that *determinism is inconsistent with free will*. If a man's actions were wholly determined by
chains of causes stretching back into the remote past, so that they could be predicted beforehand by a mind which knew all the causes, it was assumed that they
could not in that case be free. This implies that a certain definition of actions done
from free will was assumed, namely that they are actions *not* wholly determined by
causes or predictable beforehand. Let us shorten this by saying that free will was
defined as meaning indeterminism. This is the incorrect definition which has led
to the denial of free will. As soon as we see what the true definition is we shall find
that the question whether the world is deterministic, as Newtonian science
implied, or in a measure indeterministic, as current physics teaches, is wholly irrelevant to the problem.

Of course there is a sense in which one can define a word arbitrarily in any way one pleases. But a definition may nevertheless be called correct or incorrect. It is correct if it accords with a *common usage* of the word defined. It is incorrect if it does not. And if you give an incorrect definition, absurd and untrue results are likely to follow. For instance, there is nothing to prevent you from arbitrarily defining a man as a five-legged animal, but this is incorrect in the sense that it does not accord with the ordinary meaning of the word. Also it has the absurd result of leading to a denial of the existence of men. This shows that *common usage is the criterion for deciding whether a definition is correct or not.* And this is the principle which I shall apply to free will. I shall show that indeterminism is not what is meant by the phrase "free will" *as it is commonly used.* And I shall attempt to discover the correct definition by inquiring how the phrase is used in ordinary conversation.

Here are a few samples of how the phrase might be used in ordinary conversation. It will be noticed that they include cases in which the question whether a man acted with free will is asked in order to determine whether he was morally and legally responsible for his acts.

JONES: I once went without food for a week.

SMITH: Did you do that of your own free will?

JONES: No. I did it because I was lost in a desert and could find no food.

But suppose that the man who had fasted was Mahatma Gandhi. The conversation might then have gone:

GANDHI: I once fasted for a week.

  SMITH: Did you do that of your own free will?

GANDHI: Yes. I did it because I wanted to compel the British Government to give India its independence.

Take another case. Suppose that I had stolen some bread, but that I was as truthful as George Washington. Then, if I were charged with the crime in court, some exchange of the following sort might take place:

JUDGE: Did you steal the bread of your own free will?

STACE: Yes. I stole it because I was hungry.

Or in different circumstances the conversation might run:

JUDGE: Did you steal of your own free will?

STACE: No. I stole because my employer threatened to beat me if I did not.

At a recent murder trial in Trenton some of the accused had signed confessions, but afterwards asserted that they had done so under police duress. The following exchange might have occurred:

JUDGE: Did you sign this confession of your own free will?

PRISONER: No. I signed it because the police beat me up.

Now suppose that a philosopher had been a member of the jury. We could imagine this conversation taking place in the jury room.

FOREMAN OF THE JURY: The prisoner says he signed the confession because he was beaten, and not of his own free will.

PHILOSOPHER: This is quite irrelevant to the case. There is no such thing as free will.

FOREMAN: Do you mean to say that it makes no difference whether he signed because his conscience made him want to tell the truth or because he was beaten?

PHILOSOPHER: None at all. Whether he was caused to sign by a beating or by some desire of his own—the desire to tell the truth, for example—in either case his signing was causally determined, and therefore in neither case did he act of his own free will. Since there is no such thing as free will, the question whether he signed of his own free will ought not to be discussed by us.

The foreman and the rest of the jury would rightly conclude that the philosopher must be making some mistake. What sort of a mistake could it be? There is only one possible answer. The philosopher must be using the phrase "free will" in some peculiar way of his own which is not the way in which men usually use it when they wish to determine a question of moral responsibility. That is, he must be using an incorrect definition of it as implying action not determined by causes.

Suppose a man left his office at noon, and were questioned about it. Then we might hear this:

JONES: Did you go out of your own free will?

SMITH: Yes. I went out to get my lunch.

But we might hear:

JONES: Did you leave your office of your own free will?

SMITH: No. I was forcibly removed by the police.

We have now collected a number of cases of actions which, in the ordinary usage of the English language, would be called cases in which people have acted of their own free will. We should also say in all these cases that they *chose* to act as they did. We should also say that they could have acted otherwise, if they had chosen. For instance, Mahatma Gandhi was not compelled to fast; he chose to do so. He could have eaten if he had wanted to. When Smith went out to get his lunch, he chose to do so. He could have stayed and done some more work, if he had wanted to. We have also collected a number of cases of the opposite kind. They are cases in which men were not able to exercise their free will. They had no choice. They were compelled to do as they did. The man in the desert did not fast of his own free will. He had no choice in the matter. He was compelled to fast because there was nothing for him to eat. And so with the other cases. It ought to be quite easy, by an inspection of these cases, to tell what we ordinarily mean when we say that a man did or did not exercise free will. We ought therefore to be able to extract from them the proper definition of the term. Let us put the cases in a table:

| *Free Acts* | *Unfree Acts* |
|---|---|
| Gandhi fasting because he wanted to free India. | The man fasting in the desert because there was no food. |
| Stealing bread because one is hungry. | Stealing because one's employer threatened to beat one. |
| Signing a confession because one wanted to tell the truth. | Signing because the police beat one. |
| Leaving the office because one wanted one's lunch. | Leaving because forcibly removed. |

It is obvious that to find the correct definition of free acts we must discover what characteristic is common to all the acts in the left-hand column, and is, at the same time, absent from all the acts in the right-hand column. This characteristic which all free acts have, and which no unfree acts have, will be the defining characteristic of free will.

Is being uncaused, or not being determined by causes, the characteristic of which we are in search? It cannot be, because although it is true that all the acts in the right-hand column have causes, such as the beating by the police or the absence of food in the desert, so also do the acts in the left-hand column. Mr. Gandhi's fasting was caused by his desire to free India, the man leaving his office by his hunger, and so on. Moreover there is no reason to doubt that these causes of the free acts were in turn caused by prior conditions, and that these were again the results of causes, and so on back indefinitely into the past. Any physiologist can tell us the causes of hunger. What caused Mr. Gandhi's tremendously powerful desire to free India is no doubt more difficult to discover. But it must have had causes. Some of them may have lain in peculiarities of his glands or brain, others in his past experiences, others in his heredity, others in his education. Defenders of free will have usually tended to deny such facts. But to do so is plainly a case of special pleading, which is unsupported by any scrap of evidence. The only reasonable view is that all human actions, both those which are freely done and those which are not, are either wholly determined by causes, or at least as much determined as other events in nature. It may be true, as the physicists tell us, that nature is not as deterministic as was once thought. But whatever degree of determinism prevails in the world, human actions appear to be as much determined as anything else. And if this is so, it cannot be the case that what distinguishes actions freely chosen from those which are not free is that the latter are determined by causes while the former are not. Therefore, being uncaused or being undetermined by causes, must be an incorrect definition of free will.

What, then, is the difference between acts which are freely done and those which are not? What is the characteristic which is present to all the acts in the left-hand column and absent from all those in the right-hand column? Is it not obvious that, although both sets of actions have causes, the causes of those in the left-hand column are *of a different kind* from the causes of those in the right-hand column? The free acts are all caused by desires, or motives, or by some sort of internal psychological states of the agent's mind. The unfree acts, on the other hand, are all caused by physical forces or physical conditions, outside the agent. Police arrest means physical force exerted from the outside; the absence of food in the desert is a physical condition of the outside world. We may therefore frame the following rough definitions. *Acts freely done are those whose immediate causes are psychological states in the agent. Acts not freely done are those whose immediate causes are states of affairs external to the agent.*

It is plain that if we define free will in this way, then free will certainly exists, and the philosopher's denial of its existence is seen to be what it is—nonsense. For it is obvious that all those actions of men which we should ordinarily attribute to the exercise of their free will, or of which we should say that they freely chose to do them, are in fact actions which have been caused by their own desires, wishes, thoughts, emotions, impulses, or other psychological states.

In applying our definition we shall find that it usually works well, but that there are some puzzling cases which it does not seem exactly to fit. These puzzles can always be solved by paying careful attention to the ways in which words are used, and remembering that they are not always used consistently. I have space for only one example. Suppose that a thug threatens to shoot you unless you give him your wallet, and suppose that you do so. Do you, in giving him your wallet, do so of your own free will or not? If we apply our definition, we find that you acted freely, since the immediate cause of the action was not an actual outside force but the fear of death, which is a psychological cause. Most people, however, would say that you did not act of your own free will but under compulsion. Does this show that our definition is wrong? I do not think so. Aristotle, who gave a solution of the problem of free will substantially the same as ours (though he did not use the term "free will") admitted that there are what he called "mixed" or borderline cases in which it is difficult to know whether we ought to call the acts free or compelled. In the case under discussion, though no actual force was used, the gun at your forehead so nearly approximated to actual force that we tend to say the case was one of compulsion. It is a borderline case.

Here is what may seem like another kind of puzzle. According to our view an action may be free though it could have been predicted beforehand with certainty. But suppose you told a lie, and it was certain beforehand that you would tell it. How could one then say, "You could have told the truth"? The answer is that it is perfectly true that you could have told the truth *if* you had wanted to. In fact you would have done so, for in that case the causes producing your action, namely your desires, would have been different, and would therefore have produced different effects. It is a delusion that predictability and free will are incompatible. This agrees with common sense. For if, knowing your character, I predict that you will act honorably, no one would say when you do act honorably, that this shows you did not do so of your own free will.

Since free will is a condition of moral responsibility, we must be sure that our theory of free will gives a sufficient basis for it. To be held morally responsible for one's actions means that one may be justly punished or rewarded, blamed or praised, for them. But it is not just to punish a man for what he cannot help doing. How can it be just to punish him for an action which it was certain beforehand that he would do? We have not attempted to decide whether, as a matter of fact, all events, including human actions, are completely determined. For that question is irrelevant to the problem of free will. But if we assume for the purposes of argument that complete determinism is true, but that we are nevertheless free, it may then be asked whether such a deterministic free will is compatible with moral responsibility. For it may seem unjust to punish a man for an action which it could have been predicted with certainty beforehand that he would do.

But that determinism is incompatible with moral responsibility is as much a delusion as that it is incompatible with free will. You do not excuse a man for doing a wrong act because, knowing his character, you felt certain beforehand that he would do it. Nor do you deprive a man of a reward or prize because, knowing his goodness or his capabilities, you felt certain beforehand that he would win it.

Volumes have been written on the justification of punishment. But so far as it affects the question of free will, the essential principles involved are quite simple. The punishment of a man for doing a wrong act is justified, either on the ground that it will correct his own character, or that it will deter other people from doing similar acts. The instrument of punishment has been in the past, and no doubt still is, often unwisely used; so that it may often have done more harm than good. But that is not relevant to our present problem. Punishment, if and when it is justified, is justified only on one or both of the grounds just mentioned. The question then is how, if we assume determinism, punishment can correct character or deter people from evil actions.

Suppose that your child develops a habit of telling lies. You give him a mild beating. Why? Because you believe that his personality is such that the usual motives for telling the truth do not cause him to do so. You therefore supply the missing cause, or motive, in the shape of pain and the fear of future pain if he repeats his untruthful behavior. And you hope that a few treatments of this kind will condition him to the habit of truth-telling, so that he will come to tell the truth without the infliction of pain. You assume that his actions are determined by causes, but that the usual causes of truth-telling do not in him produce their usual effects. You therefore supply him with an artificially injected motive, pain and fear, which you think will in the future cause him to speak truthfully.

The principle is exactly the same where you hope, by punishing one man, to deter others from wrong actions. You believe that the fear of punishment will cause those who might otherwise do evil to do well.

We act on the same principle with non-human, and even with inanimate, things, if they do not behave in the way we think they ought to behave. The rose bushes in the garden produce only small and poor blooms, whereas we want large and rich ones. We supply a cause which will produce large blooms, namely fertilizer. Our automobile does not go properly. We supply a cause which will make it go better, namely oil in the works. The punishment for the man, the fertilizer for the plant, and the oil for the car, are all justified by the same principle and in the same way. The only difference is that different kinds of things require different kinds of causes to make them do what they should. Pain may be the appropriate remedy to apply, in certain cases, to human beings, and oil to the machine. It is, of course, of no use to inject motor oil into the boy or to beat the machine.

Thus we see that moral responsibility is not only consistent with determinism, but requires it. The assumption on which punishment is based is that human behavior is causally determined. If pain could not be a cause of truth-telling there would be no justification at all for punishing lies. If human actions and volitions were uncaused, it would be useless either to punish or reward, or indeed to do anything else to correct people's bad behavior. For nothing that you could do would in any way influence them. Thus moral responsibility would entirely disappear. If there were no determinism of human beings at all, their actions would be completely unpredictable and capricious, and therefore irresponsible. And this is in itself a strong argument against the common view of philosophers that free will means being undetermined by causes.

## READING COMPREHENSION QUESTIONS

1. According to Stace, morality would be meaningless without free will. Explain his reasoning for this claim.

2. Stace objects that both hard determinists and libertarians define "free will" as "indeterminism." Explain (a) what this *means*, exactly, (b) what Stace thinks the proper definition of "free will" is, and (c) why he thinks this.

3. What is the *method* by which Stace tries to figure out the proper definition of "free will"? Why does he choose this method? Can you think of any other words or phrases where Stace's method might not yield *any* determinate definition?

4. Consider Stace's definition of free and unfree acts. He is making a sweeping statement here, essentially claiming that all free acts have the condition he cites in common, and all unfree acts share the opposite condition. In evaluating such a sweeping claim, you should look immediately for counterexamples (see the introduction to this volume). Can you think of any counterexamples here? That is, can you find examples of actions with immediate internal psychological causes that are nevertheless *unfree*, or examples of actions with immediate external causes that are nevertheless *free*?

5. In your own words, explain why Stace thinks determinism is actually *necessary* for moral responsibility.

6. Stace offers two (and only two) justifications for punishment, if compatibilism is true. What are these two justifications? Do you think these are the *only* two correct justifications for punishment? If so, say why, and if not, say why not.

# 17

# The Impossibility of Moral Responsibility

GALEN STRAWSON

*Galen Strawson (born 1952) has written essays on various topics in philosophy of mind and metaphysics, as well as on historical figures like Locke, Hume, and Kant. He is currently a professor of philosophy at the University of Reading and at the City University of New York's Graduate Center. In this selection, he offers a powerful argument (which he calls the Basic Argument) for precisely the position of the title, namely, why it's impossible for anyone to be morally responsible for his or her actions. Of course, crucial to this enterprise is a careful and precise account of the nature of moral responsibility, and Strawson gives such an account, drawing from longstanding religious views about the kind of responsibility that would be necessary to justify heaven and hell. Strawson's essential idea is that, in order for us to be genuinely morally responsible for our actions, we would have to be ultimately responsible for originating the very characters from which those actions flow. But none of us could ever bear such ultimate responsibility, so none of could be responsible for any of our eventual actions.*

## I

There is an argument, which I will call the Basic Argument, which appears to prove that we cannot be truly or ultimately morally responsible for our actions. According to the Basic Argument, it makes no difference whether determinism is true or false. We cannot be truly or ultimately morally responsible for our actions in either case.

The Basic Argument has various expressions in the literature of free will, and its central idea can be quickly conveyed. (1) Nothing can be *causa sui*—nothing can be the cause of itself. (2) In order to be truly morally responsible for one's actions one would have to be *causa sui*, at least in certain crucial mental respects. (3) Therefore nothing can be truly morally responsible

In this paper I want to reconsider the Basic Argument, in the hope that anyone who thinks that we can be truly or ultimately morally responsible for our actions will be prepared to say exactly what is wrong with it. I think that the point that it has to make is obvious, and that it has been underrated in recent discussion of free will—perhaps because it admits of no answer. I suspect that it is obvious in such a way that insisting on it too much is likely to make it seem less obvious than it is, given the innate contrasuggestibility of human beings in general and philosophers in particular. But I am not worried about making it seem less obvious than it is so long as it gets adequate attention. As far as its validity is concerned, it can look after itself.

A more cumbersome statement of the Basic Argument goes as follows.

1. Interested in free action, we are particularly interested in actions that are performed for a reason (as opposed to "reflex" actions or mindlessly habitual actions).

2. When one acts for a reason, what one does is a function of how one is, mentally speaking. (It is also a function of one's height, one's strength, one's place and time, and so on. But the mental factors are crucial when moral responsibility is in question.)

3. So if one is to be truly responsible for how one acts, one must be truly responsible for how one is, mentally speaking—at least in certain respects.

4. But to be truly responsible for how one is, mentally speaking, in certain respects, one must have brought it about that one is the way one is, mentally speaking, in certain respects. And it is not merely that one must have caused oneself to be the way one is, mentally speaking. One must have consciously and explicitly chosen to be the way one is, mentally speaking, in certain respects, and one must have succeeded in bringing it about that one is that way.

5. But one cannot really be said to choose, in a conscious, reasoned, fashion, to be the way one is mentally speaking, in any respect at all, unless one already exists, mentally speaking, already equipped with some principles of choice, "P1"—preferences, values, pro-attitudes, ideals—in the light of which one chooses how to be.

6. But then to be truly responsible, on account of having chosen to be the way one is, mentally speaking, in certain respects, one must be truly responsible for one's having the principles of choice P1 in the light of which one chose how to be.

7. But for this to be so one must have chosen P1, in a reasoned, conscious, intentional fashion.

8. But for this, i.e. (7), to be so one must already have had some principles of choice P2, in the light of which one chose P1.

9. And so on. Here we are setting out on a regress that we cannot stop. True self-determination is impossible because it requires the actual completion of an infinite series of choices of principles of choice.

10. So true moral responsibility is impossible, because it requires true self-determination, as noted in (3).

This may seem contrived, but essentially the same argument can be given in a more natural form. (1) It is undeniable that one is the way one is, initially, as a result of heredity and early experience, and it is undeniable that these are things for which one cannot be held to be in any way responsible (morally or otherwise).

(2) One cannot at any later stage of life hope to accede to true moral responsibility for the way one is by trying to change the way one already is as a result of heredity and previous experience. For (3) both the particular way in which one is moved to try to change oneself, and the degree of one's success in one's attempt at change, will be determined by how one already is as a result of heredity and previous experience. And (4) any further changes that one can bring about only after one has brought about certain initial changes will in turn be determined, via the initial changes, by heredity and previous experience. (5) This may not be the whole story, for it may be that some changes in the way one is are traceable not to heredity and experience but to the influence of indeterministic or random factors. But it is absurd to suppose that indeterministic or random factors, for which one is ex hypothesi in no way responsible, can in themselves contribute in any way to one's being truly morally responsible for how one is.

The claim, then, is not that people cannot change the way they are. They can, in certain respects (which tend to be exaggerated by North Americans and underestimated, perhaps, by Europeans). The claim is only that people cannot be supposed to change themselves in such a way as to be or become truly or ultimately morally responsible for the way they are, and hence for their actions.

## II

I have encountered two main reactions to the Basic Argument. On the one hand it convinces almost all the students with whom I have discussed the topic of free will and moral responsibility. On the other hand it often tends to be dismissed, in contemporary discussion of free will and moral responsibility, as wrong, or irrelevant, or fatuous, or too rapid, or an expression of metaphysical megalomania.

I think that the Basic Argument is certainly valid in showing that we cannot be morally responsible in the way that many suppose. And I think that it is the natural light, not fear, that has convinced the students I have taught that this is so. That is why it seems worthwhile to restate the argument in a slightly different—simpler and looser—version, and to ask again what is wrong with it.

Some may say that there is nothing wrong with it, but that it is not very interesting, and not very central to the free will debate. I doubt whether any non-philosopher or beginner in philosophy would agree with this view. If one wants to think about free will and moral responsibility, consideration of some version of the Basic Argument is an overwhelmingly natural place to start. It certainly has to be considered at some point in a full discussion of free will and moral responsibility, even if the point it has to make is obvious. Belief in the kind of absolute moral responsibility that it shows to be impossible has for a long time been central to the Western religious, moral, and cultural tradition, even if it is now slightly on the wane (a disputable view). It is a matter of historical fact that concern about moral responsibility has been the main motor . . . of discussion of the issue of free will. The only way in which one might hope to show (1) that the Basic Argument was not central to the free will debate would be to show (2) that the issue of moral responsibility was not central to the free will debate. There are, obviously, ways of taking the word "free" in which (2) can be maintained. But (2) is clearly false none the less. . . .

## III

[I]t is important to try to be precise about what sort of responsibility is under discussion. What sort of "true" moral responsibility is being said to be both impossible and widely believed in?

An old story is very helpful in clarifying this question. This is the story of heaven and hell. As I understand it, true moral responsibility is responsibility of such a kind that, if we have it, then it *makes sense,* at least, to suppose that it could be just to punish some of us with (eternal) torment in hell and reward others with (eternal) bliss in heaven. The stress on the words "makes sense" is important, for one certainly does not have to believe in any version of the story of heaven and hell in order to understand the notion of true moral responsibility that it is being used to illustrate. Nor does one have to believe in any version of the story of heaven and hell in order to believe in the existence of true moral responsibility. On the contrary: many atheists have believed in the existence of true moral responsibility. The story of heaven and hell is useful simply because it illustrates, in a peculiarly vivid way, the *kind* of absolute or ultimate accountability or responsibility that many have supposed themselves to have, and that many do still suppose themselves to have. It very clearly expresses its scope and force.

But one does not have to refer to religious faith in order to describe the sorts of everyday situation that are perhaps primarily influential in giving rise to our belief in true responsibility. Suppose you set off for a shop on the evening of a national holiday, intending to buy a cake with your last ten pound note. On the steps of the shop someone is shaking an Oxfam tin. You stop, and it seems completely clear to you that it is entirely up to you what you do next. That is, it seems to you that you are truly, radically free to choose, in such a way that you will be ultimately morally responsible for whatever you do choose. Even if you believe that determinism is true, and that you will in five minutes time be able to look back and say that what you did was determined, this does not seem to undermine your sense of the absoluteness and inescapability of your freedom, and of your moral responsibility for your choice. The same seems to be true even if you accept the validity of the Basic Argument stated in section I, which concludes that one cannot be in any way ultimately responsible for the way one is and decides. In both cases, it remains true that as one stands there, one's freedom and true moral responsibility seem obvious and absolute to one.

Large and small, morally significant or morally neutral, such situations of choice occur regularly in human life. I think they lie at the heart of the experience of freedom and moral responsibility. They are the fundamental source of our inability to give up belief in true or ultimate moral responsibility. There are further questions to be asked about why human beings experience these situations of choice as they do. It is an interesting question whether any cognitively sophisticated, rational, self-conscious agent must experience situations of choice in this way. But they are the experiential rock on which the belief in true moral responsibility is founded. . . .

## V

Let me now restate the Basic Argument in very loose—as it were conversational—terms. New forms of words allow for new forms of objection, but they may be helpful none the less.

1. You do what you do, in any situation in which you find yourself, because of the way you are.

So

2. To be truly morally responsible for what you do you must be truly responsible for the way you are—at least in certain crucial mental respects.

Or:

1. What you intentionally do, given the circumstances in which you (believe you) find yourself, flows necessarily from how you are.

Hence

2. You have to get to have some responsibility for how you are in order to get to have some responsibility for what you intentionally do, given the circumstances in which you (believe you) find yourself.

Comment. Once again the qualification about "certain mental respects" is one I will take for granted. Obviously one is not responsible for one's sex, one's basic body pattern, one's height, and so on. But if one were not responsible for anything about oneself, how could one be responsible for what one did, given the truth of (1)? This is the fundamental question, and it seems clear that if one is going to be responsible for any aspect of oneself, it had better be some aspect of one's mental nature.

I take it that (1) is incontrovertible, and that it is (2) that must be resisted. For if (1) and (2) are conceded the case seems lost, because the full argument runs as follows.

1. You do what you do because of the way you are.

So

2. To be truly morally responsible for what you do you must be truly responsible for the way you are—at least in certain crucial mental respects.

But

3. You cannot be truly responsible for the way you are, so you cannot be truly responsible for what you do.

Why can't you be truly responsible for the way you are? Because

4. To be truly responsible for the way you are, you must have intentionally brought it about that you are the way you are, and this is impossible.

Why is it impossible? Well, suppose it is not. Suppose that

5. You have somehow intentionally brought it about that you are the way you now are, and that you have brought this about in such a way that you can now be said to be truly responsible for being the way you are now.

For this to be true

6.  You must already have had a certain nature N in the light of which you intentionally brought it about that you are as you now are.

But then

7.  For it to be true that you and you alone are truly responsible for how you now are, you must be truly responsible for having had the nature N in the light of which you intentionally brought it about that you are the way you now are.

So

8.  You must have intentionally brought it about that you had that nature N, in which case you must have existed already with a prior nature in the light of which you intentionally brought it about that you had the nature N in the light of which you intentionally brought it about that you are the way you now are . . .

Here one is setting off on the regress. Nothing can be *causa sui* in the required way. Even if such causal "aseity" is allowed to belong unintelligibly to God, it cannot plausibly be supposed to be possessed by ordinary finite human beings. . . .

The rephrased argument is essentially exactly the same as before, although the first two steps are now more simply stated. It may seem pointless to repeat it, but the questions remain. Can the Basic Argument simply be dismissed? Is it really of no importance in the discussion of free will and moral responsibility? (No and No) Shouldn't any serious defense of free will and moral responsibility thoroughly acknowledge the respect in which the Basic Argument is valid before going on to try to give its own positive account of the nature of free will and moral responsibility? Doesn't the argument go to the heart of things if the heart of the free will debate is a concern about whether we can be truly morally responsible in the absolute way that we ordinarily suppose? (Yes and Yes)

We are what we are, and we cannot be thought to have made ourselves *in such a way* that we can be held to be free in our actions *in such a way* that we can be held to be morally responsible for our actions *in such a way* that any punishment or reward for our actions is ultimately just or fair. Punishments and rewards may seem deeply appropriate or intrinsically "fitting" to us in spite of this argument, and many of the various institutions of punishment and reward in human society appear to be practically indispensable in both their legal and non-legal forms. But if one takes the notion of justice that is central to our intellectual and cultural tradition seriously, then the evident consequence of the Basic Argument is that there is a fundamental sense in which no punishment or reward is ever ultimately just. It is exactly as just to punish or reward people for their actions as it is to punish or reward them for the (natural) colour of their hair or the (natural) shape of their faces. The point seems obvious, and yet it contradicts a fundamental part of our natural self-conception, and there are elements in human thought that move very deeply against it. When it comes to questions of responsibility, we tend to feel that we are somehow responsible for the way we are. Even more importantly, perhaps, we tend to feel that our explicit self-conscious awareness of ourselves as agents who are able to deliberate about what to do, in situations of choice, suffices to constitute us as morally responsible free agents in the strongest sense whatever the conclusion of the Basic Argument.

## VI

I have suggested that it is step (2) of the restated Basic Argument that must be rejected, and of course it can be rejected, because the phrases "truly responsible" and "truly morally responsible" can be defined in many ways. I will briefly consider three sorts of response to the Basic Argument, and I will concentrate on their more simple expressions, in the belief that truth in philosophy, especially in areas of philosophy like the present one, is almost never very complicated.

(I) The first is *compatibilist*. Compatibilists believe that one can be a free and morally responsible agent even if determinism is true. Roughly, they claim, with many variations of detail, that one may correctly be said to be truly responsible for what one does, when one acts, just so long as one is not caused to act by any of a certain set of constraints (kleptomaniac impulses, obsessional neuroses, desires that are experienced as alien, post-hypnotic commands, threats, instances of *force majeure,* and so on). Clearly, this sort of compatibilist responsibility does not require that one should be truly responsible for how one is in any way at all, and so step (2) of the Basic Argument comes out as false. One can have compatibilist responsibility even if the way one is is totally determined by factors entirely outside one's control.

It is for this reason, however, that compatibilist responsibility famously fails to amount to any sort of true *moral* responsibility, given the natural, strong understanding of the notion of true moral responsibility (characterized above by reference to the story of heaven and hell). One does what one does entirely because of the way one is, and one is in no way ultimately responsible for the way one is. So how can one be justly punished for anything one does? Compatibilists have given increasingly refined accounts of the circumstances in which punishment may be said to be appropriate or intrinsically fitting. But they can do nothing against this basic objection.

Many compatibilists have never supposed otherwise. They are happy to admit the point. They observe that the notions of true moral responsibility and justice that are employed in the objection cannot possibly have application to anything real, and suggest that the objection is therefore not worth considering. In response, proponents of the Basic Argument agree that the notions of true moral responsibility and justice in question cannot have application to anything real; but they make no apologies for considering them. They consider them because they are central to ordinary thought about moral responsibility and justice. So far as most people are concerned, they are the subject, if the subject is moral responsibility and justice.

(II) The second response is *libertarian*. Incompatibilists believe that freedom and moral responsibility are incompatible with determinism, and some of them are libertarians, who believe that we are free and morally responsible agents, and that determinism is therefore false. In an ingenious statement of the incompatibilist-libertarian case, Robert Kane argues that agents in an undetermined world can have free will, for they can "have the power to make choices for which they have ultimate responsibility." That is, they can "have the power to make choices which can only and finally be explained in terms of their own wills (i.e. character, motives, and efforts of will)."[1] Roughly, Kane sees this power as grounded in the possible occurrence, in agents, of efforts of will that have two main features: first, they are partly indeterministic in their nature, and hence indeterminate in their outcome; second, they occur in cases in which agents are trying to make a difficult choice between the options that their characters dispose them to consider. (The paradigm cases will be cases in which they face a conflict between moral duty and non-moral desire.)

But the old objection to libertarianism recurs. How can this indeterminism help with *moral* responsibility? Granted that the truth of determinism rules out true moral responsibility, how can the falsity of determinism help? How can the occurrence of partly random or indeterministic events contribute in any way to one's being truly morally responsible either for one's actions or for one's character? If my efforts of will shape my character in an admirable way, and in so doing are partly indeterministic in nature, while also being shaped (as Kane grants) by my already existing character, why am I not merely lucky?

The general objection applies equally whether determinism is true or false, and can be restated as follows. We are born with a great many genetically determined predispositions for which we are not responsible. We are subject to many early influences for which we are not responsible. These decisively shape our characters, our motives, the general bent and strength of our capacity to make efforts of will. We may later engage in conscious and intentional shaping procedures—call them S-procedures—designed to affect and change our characters, motivational structure, and wills. Suppose we do. The question is then why we engage in the particular S-procedures that we do engage in, and why we engage in them in the particular way that we do. The general answer is that we engage in the particular S-procedures that we do engage in, given the circumstances in which we find ourselves, because of certain features of the way we already are. (Indeterministic factors may also play a part in what happens, but these will not help to make us responsible for what we do.) And these features of the way we already are—call them character features, or C-features—are either wholly the products of genetic or environmental influences, deterministic or random, for which we are not responsible, or are at least partly the result of earlier S-procedures, which are in turn either wholly the product of C-features for which we are not responsible, or are at least partly the product of still earlier S-procedures, which are in turn either the products of C-features for which we are not responsible, or the product of such C-features together with still earlier S-procedures—and so on. In the end, we reach the first S-procedure, and this will have been engaged in, and engaged in the particular way in which it was engaged in, as a result of genetic or environmental factors, deterministic or random, for which we were not responsible.

Moving away from the possible role of indeterministic factors in character or personality formation, we can consider their possible role in particular instances of deliberation and decision. Here too it seems clear that indeterministic factors cannot, in influencing what happens, contribute to true moral responsibility in any way. In

[1]Kane p. 254. I have omitted some italics. R. Kane, "Two Kinds of Incompatibilism," *Philosophy and Phenomenological Research* 50 (1989): 219–254.

the end, whatever we do, we do it either as a result of random influences for which we are not responsible, or as a result of non-random influences for which we are not responsible, or as a result of influences for which we are proximally responsible but not ultimately responsible. The point seems obvious. Nothing can be ultimately *causa sui* in any respect at all. Even if God can be, we can't be. . . .

There is a further, familiar problem with the view that moral responsibility depends on indeterminism. If one accepts the view, one will have to grant that it is impossible to know whether any human being is ever morally responsible. For moral responsibility now depends on the falsity of determinism, and determinism is unfalsifiable. There is no more reason to think that determinism is false than that it is true, in spite of the impression sometimes given by scientists and popularizers of science.

(III) The third option begins by accepting that one cannot be held to be ultimately responsible for one's character or personality or motivational structure. It accepts that this is so whether determinism is true or false. It then directly challenges step (2) of the Basic Argument. It appeals to a certain picture of the self in order to argue that one can be truly free and morally responsible in spite of the fact that one cannot be held to be ultimately responsible for one's character or personality or motivational structure. This picture has some support in the "phenomenology" of human choice—we sometimes experience our choices and decisions as if the picture were an accurate one. But it is easy to show that it cannot be accurate in such a way that we can be said to be truly or ultimately morally responsible for our choices or actions.

It can be set out as follows. One is free and truly morally responsible because one's self is, in a crucial sense, independent of one's character or personality or motivational structure—one's CPM, for short. Suppose one is in a situation which one experiences as a difficult choice between A, doing one's duty, and B, following one's non-moral desires. Given one's CPM, one responds in a certain way. One's desires and beliefs develop and interact and constitute reasons for both A and B. One's CPM makes one tend towards A or B. So far the problem is the same as ever: whatever one does, one will do what one does because of the way one's CPM is, and since one neither is nor can be ultimately responsible for the way one's CPM is, one cannot be ultimately responsible for what one does.

Enter one's self, S. S is imagined to be in some way independent of one's CPM. S (i.e. one) considers the deliverances of one's CPM and decides in the light of them, but it—S—incorporates a power of decision that is independent of one's CPM in such a way that one can after all count as truly and ultimately morally responsible in one's decisions and actions, even though one is not ultimately responsible for one's CPM. Step (2) of the Basic Argument is false because of the existence of S.

The trouble with the picture is obvious. S (i.e. one) decides on the basis of the deliverances of one's CPM. But whatever S decides, it decides as it does because of the way it is (or else partly or wholly because of the occurrence in the decision process of indeterministic factors for which it—i.e. one—cannot be responsible, and which cannot plausibly be thought to contribute to one's true moral responsibility). And this returns us to where we started. To be a source of true or ultimate responsibility, S must be responsible for being the way it is. But this is impossible, for the reasons given in the Basic Argument.

The story of S and CPM adds another layer to the description of the human decision process, but it cannot change the fact that human beings cannot be ultimately self-determining in such a way as to be ultimately morally responsible for how they are, and thus for how they decide and act. The story is crudely presented, but it should suffice to make clear that no move of this sort can solve the problem.

"Character is destiny," as Novalis is often reported as saying. The remark is inaccurate, because external circumstances are part of destiny, but the point is well taken when it comes to the question of moral responsibility. Nothing can be *causa sui,* and in order to be truly morally responsible for one's actions one would have to be *causa sui,* at least in certain crucial mental respects. One cannot institute oneself in such a way that one can take over true or assume moral responsibility for how one is in such a way that one can indeed be truly morally responsible for what one does. This fact is not changed by the fact that we may be unable not to think of ourselves as truly morally responsible in ordinary circumstances. Nor is it changed by the fact that it may be a very good thing that we have this inability—so that we might wish to take steps to preserve it, if it looked to be in danger of fading. As already remarked, many human beings are unable to resist the idea that it is their capacity for fully explicit self-conscious deliberation, in a situation of choice, that suffices to constitute them as truly morally responsible agents in the strongest possible sense. The Basic Argument shows that this is a mistake. However self-consciously aware we are, as we deliberate and reason, every act and operation of our mind happens as it does as a result of features for which we are ultimately in no way responsible. But the conviction that self-conscious awareness of one's situation can be a sufficient foundation of strong free will is very powerful. It runs deeper than rational argument, and it survives untouched, in the everyday conduct of life, even after the validity of the Basic Argument has been admitted.

## READING COMPREHENSION QUESTIONS

1. At the beginning of the article, Strawson is so kind as to lay out the Basic Argument in stepwise form, offering the premises (1)–(9), followed by the conclusion in (10) that true moral responsibility is impossible. Pick one of the premises, explain the reasoning behind it, and then critically evaluate it, i.e., explain whether it's plausible or implausible, and why.

2. Strawson makes clear that the kind of moral responsibility he's talking about is the kind that "makes sense" of the notions of heaven and hell. Explain what he means by this, and then discuss whether or not this is the right understanding of "moral responsibility." (In other words, what do *you* think is the way we should understand the phrase "moral responsibility," and is Strawson talking about that understanding or some other?)

3. Explain the compatibilist response to the Basic Argument (represented by Walter T. Stace in this volume), and explain why Strawson rejects it.

4. Explain the libertarian response to the Basic Argument, and explain why Strawson rejects it.

5. Explain the "phenomenological" response to the Basic Argument (represented by C. A. Campbell in this volume), and explain why Strawson rejects it.

# 18

# Freedom and Resentment

P. F. STRAWSON

*P. F. Strawson (1919–2006), father of the preceding author, Galen Strawson, wrote several influential articles and books on a variety of topics in philosophy, including metaphysics, philosophy of language, logic, Kant, and free will. This selection, edited from one of his most influential essays, attempts to dissolve the conflict between determinists (represented by Darrow, Holbach, and Stace in our readings) and libertarians (represented by Campbell) on the nature of freedom and moral responsibility.*

*While it is in some respects a difficult article, Strawson is really just trying to remind us of a fairly basic and familiar point about the way in which we deal with one another all the time as human beings. Determinists (whom Strawson calls "optimists") typically give an account that is entirely* future *oriented when they apply their view to punishment and moral responsibility: what we're doing in punishing someone, or holding them responsible generally, is simply trying to correct his or her character or deter others from doing what he or she did. (Stace makes this argument explicitly). But libertarians (whom Strawson calls "pessimists") balk at such an account, for they say punishment presupposes guilt, which presupposes freedom, which presupposes that determinism is false. In resolving this dispute, Strawson tries to sketch an account in which the optimist offers something substantially more to ameliorate the concerns of the pessimist, in exchange for the pessimist's concession that determinism could be true. What Strawson urges the optimist to add is an admission of the ways in which we actually engage with one another on a personal level when we make our attributions of moral responsibility—when, for instance, we react with resentment when someone violates the basic moral demand for goodwill. We react in these ways all the time, and expression of these reactions is just what attributions of responsibility consist in, according to Strawson. Now if the pessimist were right, we ought to suspend such reactions whenever we found out that someone's action was in fact* determined—*after all, if responsibility presupposes freedom, and freedom presupposes indeterminism, then any instance of determined action would have to be unfree and non-responsible action. But as Strawson points out, the reasons we* actually *suspend these reactions*

SOURCE: © The British Academy 1963. Reproduced by permission from *Proceedings of the British Academy*, 1962.

*have nothing to do with determinism; instead, they have to do with our finding out the action was an accident, or that the agent was a child, or wasn't himself, or was insane. But if determinism is actually irrelevant to our practices of holding people responsible, and yet this reaction is precisely a deeply human response to what the agent has done (and so isn't just an attempt to correct the agent's character or deter others in the future), we might have a story here that could be adopted by the optimist in a way that ameliorates the pessimist's major concern.*

## I

Some philosophers say they do not know what the thesis of determinism is. Others say, or imply, that they do know what it is. Of these, some—the pessimists perhaps—hold that if the thesis is true, then the concepts of moral obligation and responsibility really have no application, and the practices of punishing and blaming, of expressing moral condemnation and approval, are really unjustified. Others—the optimists perhaps—hold that these concepts and practices in no way lose their *raison d'être* if the thesis of determinism is true. Some hold even that the justification of these concepts and practices requires the truth of the thesis. There is another opinion which is less frequently voiced: the opinion, it might be said, of the genuine moral sceptic. This is that the notions of moral guilt, of blame, of moral responsibility are inherently confused and that we can see this to be so if we consider the consequences either of the truth of determinism or of its falsity. The holders of this opinion agree with the pessimists that these notions lack application if determinism is true, and add simply that they also lack it if determinism is false. If I am asked which of these parties I belong to, I must say it is the first of all, the party of those who do not know what the thesis of determinism is. But this does not stop me from having some sympathy with the others, and a wish to reconcile them. . . . This lecture is intended as a move towards reconciliation; so is likely to seem wrongheaded to everyone.

But can there be any possibility of reconciliation between such clearly opposed positions as those of pessimists and optimists about determinism? Well, there might be a formal withdrawal on one side in return for a substantial concession on the other. Thus, suppose the optimist's position were put like this: (1) the facts as we know them do not show determinism to be false; (2) the facts as we know them supply an adequate basis for the concepts and practices which the pessimist feels to be imperilled by the possibility of determinism's truth. Now it might be that the optimist is right in this, but is apt to give an inadequate account of the facts as we know them, and of how they constitute an adequate basis for the problematic concepts and practices; that the reasons he gives for the adequacy of the basis are themselves inadequate and leave out something vital. It might be that the pessimist is rightly anxious to get this vital thing back and, in the grip of his anxiety, feels he has to go beyond the facts as we know them; feels that the vital thing can be secure only if, beyond the facts as we know them, there is the further fact that determinism is false. Might *he* not be brought to make a formal withdrawal in return for a vital concession?

## II

Let me enlarge very briefly on this, by way of preliminary only. Some optimists about determinism point to the efficacy of the practices of punishment, and of moral condemnation and approval, in regulating behaviour in socially desirable ways.[1] In the fact of their efficacy, they suggest, is an adequate basis for these practices; and this fact certainly does not show determinism to be false. To this the pessimists reply, all in a rush, that *just* punishment and *moral* condemnation imply moral guilt and guilt implies moral responsibility and moral responsibility implies freedom and freedom implies the falsity of determinism. And to this the optimists are wont to reply in turn that it is true that these practices require freedom in a sense, and the existence of freedom in this sense is one of the facts as we know them. But what "freedom" means here is nothing but the absence of certain conditions the presence of which would make moral condemnation or punishment inappropriate. They have in mind conditions like compulsion by another, or innate incapacity, or insanity, or other less extreme forms of psychological disorder, or the existence of circumstances in which the making of any other choice would be morally inadmissible or would be too much to expect of any man. To this list they are constrained to add other factors which, without exactly being limitations of freedom, may also make moral condemnation or punishment inappropriate or mitigate their force: as some forms of ignorance, mistake, or accident. And the general reason why moral condemnation or punishment are inappropriate when these factors or conditions are present is held to be that the practices in question will be generally efficacious means of regulating behaviour in desirable ways only in cases where these factors are *not* present. Now the pessimist admits that the facts as we know them include the existence of freedom, the occurrence of cases of free action, in the negative sense which the optimist concedes; and admits, or rather insists, that the existence of freedom in this sense is compatible with the truth of determinism. Then what does the pessimist find missing? When he tries to answer this question, his language is apt to alternate between the very familiar and the very unfamiliar. Thus he may say, familiarly enough, that the man who is the subject of justified punishment, blame or moral condemnation must really *deserve* it; and then add, perhaps, that, in the case at least where he is blamed for a positive act rather than an omission, the condition of his really deserving blame is something that goes beyond the negative freedoms that the optimist concedes. It is, say, a genuinely free identification of the will with the act. And this is the condition that is incompatible with the truth of determinism.

The conventional, but conciliatory, optimist need not give up yet. He may say: Well, people often decide to do things, really intend to do what they do, know just what they're doing in doing it: the reasons they think they have for doing what they do, often really are their reasons and not their rationalizations. These facts, too, are included in the facts as we know them. If this is what you mean by freedom—by the identification of the will with the act—then freedom may again be conceded. But again the concession is compatible with the truth of the determinist thesis. For it would not follow from that thesis that nobody decides

---

[1]Cf. P. H. Nowell-Smith, 'Freewill and Moral Responsibility', *Mind* (1948).

to do anything; that nobody ever does anything intentionally; that it is false that people sometimes know perfectly well what they are doing. I tried to define freedom negatively. You want to give it a more positive look. But it comes to the same thing. Nobody denies freedom in this sense, or these senses, and nobody claims that the existence of freedom in these senses shows determinism to be false.

But it is here that the lacuna in the optimistic story can be made to show. For the pessimist may be supposed to ask: But *why* does freedom in this sense justify blame, etc.? You turn towards me first the negative, and then the positive, faces of a freedom which nobody challenges. But the only reason you have given for the practices of moral condemnation and punishment in cases where this freedom is present is the efficacy of these practices in regulating behaviour in socially desirable ways. But this is not a sufficient basis, it is not even the right *sort* of basis, for these practices as we understand them.

Now my optimist, being the sort of man he is, is not likely to invoke an intuition of fittingness at this point. So he really has no more to say. And my pessimist, being the sort of man he is, has only one more thing to say; and that is that the admissibility of these practices, as we understand them, demands another kind of freedom, the kind that in turn demands the falsity of the thesis of determinism. But might we not induce the pessimist to give up saying this by giving the optimist something more to say?

## III

I have mentioned punishing and moral condemnation and approval; and it is in connection with these practices or attitudes that the issue between optimists and pessimists—or, if one is a pessimist, the issue between determinists and libertarians—is felt to be particularly important. But it is not of these practices and attitudes that I propose, at first, to speak. These practices or attitudes permit, where they do not imply, a certain detachment from the actions or agents which are their objects. I want to speak, at least at first, of something else: of the non-detached attitudes and reactions of people directly involved in transactions with each other; of the attitudes and reactions of offended parties and beneficiaries; of such things as gratitude, resentment, forgiveness, love, and hurt feelings. Perhaps something like the issue between optimists and pessimists arises in this neighbouring field too; and since this field is less crowded with disputants, the issue might here be easier to settle; and if it is settled here, then it might become easier to settle it in the disputant-crowded field.

What I have to say consists largely of commonplaces. So my language, like that of commonplace generally, will be quite unscientific and imprecise. The central commonplace that I want to insist on is the very great importance that we attach to the attitudes and intentions towards us of other human beings, and the great extent to which our personal feelings and reactions depend upon, or involve, our beliefs about these attitudes and intentions. I can give no simple description of the field of phenomena at the centre of which stands this commonplace truth: for the field is too complex. Much imaginative literature is devoted to exploring its complexities; and we have a large vocabulary for the purpose. There are simplifying styles of handling it in a general way. . . . These simplifications are of use to me only if they help to emphasize how much we actually mind, how much it matters to us, whether the actions of other people—and particularly of *some* other people—reflect attitudes towards us of goodwill, affection, or esteem on the one hand or contempt, indifference, or malevolence on the other. If someone treads on my hand accidentally, while trying to help me, the pain may be no less acute than if he treads on it in contemptuous disregard of my existence or with a malevolent wish to injure me But I shall generally feel in the second case a kind and degree of resentment that I shall not feel in the first. If someone's actions help me to some benefit I desire, then I am benefited in any case; but if he intended them so to benefit me because of his general goodwill towards me, I shall reasonably feel a gratitude which I should not feel at all if the benefit was an incidental consequence, unintended or even regretted by him, of some plan of action with a different aim.

These examples are of actions which confer benefits or inflict injuries over and above any conferred or inflicted by the mere manifestation of attitude and intention themselves. We should consider also in how much of our behaviour the benefit or injury resides mainly or entirely in the manifestation of attitude itself. So it is with good manners, and much of what we call kindness, on the one hand; with deliberate rudeness, studied indifference, or insult on the other.

Besides resentment and gratitude, I mentioned just now forgiveness. This is a rather unfashionable subject in moral philosophy at present, but to be forgiven is something we sometimes ask, and forgiving is something we sometimes say we do. To ask to be forgiven is in part to acknowledge that the attitude displayed in our actions was such as might properly be resented and in part to repudiate that attitude for the future (or at least for the immediate future), and to forgive is to accept the repudiation and to forswear the resentment.

We should think of the many different kinds of relationship which we can have with other people—as sharers of a common interest, as members of the same family, as colleagues, as friends, as lovers, as chance parties to an enormous range of transactions and encounters. Then we should think, in each of these connections in turn, and in others, of the kind of importance we attach to the attitudes and intentions towards us of those who stand in these relationships to us, and of the kinds of *reactive* attitudes and feelings to which we ourselves are prone. In general, we demand some degree of goodwill or regard on the part of those who stand in these relationships to us, though the forms we require it to take vary widely in different connections. The range and intensity of our *reactive* attitudes towards goodwill, its absence or its opposite vary no less widely. I have mentioned, specifically, resentment and gratitude; and they are a usefully opposed pair. But, of course, there is a whole continuum of reactive attitude and feeling stretching on both sides of these and—the most comfortable area—in between them.

The object of these commonplaces is to try to keep before our minds something it is easy to forget when we are engaged in philosophy, especially in our cool, contemporary style, viz. what it is actually like to be involved in ordinary inter-personal relationships, ranging from the most intimate to the most casual.

## IV

It is one thing to ask about the general causes of these reactive attitudes I have alluded to: it is another to ask about the variations to which they are subject, the particular conditions in which they do or do not seem natural or reasonable or appropriate, and it is a third thing to ask what it would be like, what it *is* like, not to suffer them. I am not much concerned with the first question: but I am with the second, and perhaps even more with the third.

Let us consider, then, occasions for resentment: situations in which one person is offended or injured by the action of another and in which—in the absence of special considerations—the offended person might naturally or normally be expected to feel resentment. Then let us consider what sorts of special considerations might be expected to modify or mollify this feeling or remove it altogether. It needs no saying now how multifarious these considerations are. But, for my purpose, I think they can be roughly divided into two kinds. To the first group belong all those which might give occasion for the employment of such expressions as "He didn't mean to," "He hadn't realized," "He didn't know," and also all those which might give occasion for the use of the phrase "He couldn't help it," when this is supported by such phrases as "He was pushed," "He had to do it," "It was the only way," "They left him no alternative," etc. Obviously these various pleas, and the kinds of situations in which they would be appropriate, differ from each other in striking and important ways. But for my present purpose they have something still more important in common. None of them invites us to suspend towards the agent, either at the time of his action or in general, our ordinary reactive attitudes. They do not invite us to view the *agent* as one in respect of whom these attitudes are in any way inappropriate. They invite us to view the *injury* as one in respect of which a particular one of these attitudes is inappropriate. They do not invite us to see the *agent* as other than a fully responsible agent. They invite us to see the *injury* as one for which he was not fully, or at all, responsible. They do not suggest that the agent is in any way an inappropriate object of that kind of demand for goodwill or regard which is reflected in our ordinary reactive attitudes. They suggest instead that the fact of injury was not in this case incompatible with that demand's being fulfilled, that the fact of injury was quite consistent with the agent's attitude and intentions being just what we demand they should be.[2] The agent was just ignorant of the injury he was causing, or had lost his balance through being pushed or had reluctantly to cause the injury for reasons which acceptably override his reluctance. The offering of such pleas by the agent and their acceptance by the sufferer is something in no way opposed to, or outside the context of, ordinary inter-personal relationships and the manifestation of ordinary reactive attitudes. Since things go wrong and situations are complicated, it is an essential and integral element in the transactions which are the life of these relationships.

The second group of considerations is very different. I shall take them in two sub-groups of which the first is far less important than the second. In connection with the first sub-group we may think of such statements as "He wasn't himself"

---

[2]Perhaps not in every case *just* what we demand they should be, but in any case *not* just what we demand they should not be. For my present purpose these differences do not matter.

"He has been under very great strain recently," "He was acting under post-hypnotic suggestion;" in connection with the second, we may think of "He's only a child," "He's a hopeless schizophrenic," "His mind has been systematically perverted," "That's purely compulsive behaviour on his part." Such pleas as these do, as pleas of my first general group do not, invite us to suspend our ordinary reactive attitudes towards the agent, either at the time of his action or all the time. They do not invite us to see the agent's action in a way consistent with the full retention of ordinary interpersonal attitudes and merely inconsistent with one particular attitude. They invite us to view the agent himself in a different light from the light in which we should normally view one who has acted as he has acted. I shall not linger over the first subgroup of cases. Though they perhaps raise, in the short term, questions akin to those raised, in the long term, by the second subgroup, we may dismiss them without considering those questions by taking that admirably suggestive phrase, "He wasn't himself," with the seriousness that—for all its being logically comic—it deserves. We shall not feel resentment against the man he is for the action done by the man he is not; or at least we shall feel less. We normally have to deal with him under normal stresses; so we shall not feel towards him, when he acts as he does under abnormal stresses, as we should have felt towards him had he acted as he did under normal stresses.

The second and more important subgroup of cases allows that the circumstances were normal, but presents the agent as psychologically abnormal—or as morally undeveloped. The agent was himself; but he is warped or deranged, neurotic or just a child. When we see someone in such a light as this, all our reactive attitudes tend to be profoundly modified. I must deal here in crude dichotomies and ignore the ever-interesting and ever illuminating varieties of case. What I want to contrast is the attitude (or range of attitudes) of involvement or participation in a human relationship, on the one hand, and what might be called the objective attitude (or range of attitudes) to another human being, on the other. Even in the same situation, I must add, they are not altogether *exclusive* of each other; but they are, profoundly, *opposed* to each other. To adopt the objective attitude to another human being to see him, perhaps, as an object of social policy; as a subject for what, in a wide range of sense, might be called treatment; as something certainly to be taken account, perhaps precautionary account, of; to be managed or handled or cured or trained; perhaps simply to be avoided, though *this* gerundive is not peculiar to cases of objectivity of attitude. The objective attitude may be emotionally toned in many ways, but not in all ways: it may include repulsion or fear, it may include pity or even love, though not all kinds of love. But it cannot include the range of reactive feelings and attitudes which belong to involvement or participation with others in inter-personal human relationships; it cannot include resentment, gratitude, forgiveness, anger, or the sort of love which two adults can sometimes be said to feel reciprocally, for each other. If your attitude towards someone is wholly objective, then though you may fight him, you cannot quarrel with him, and though you may talk to him, even negotiate with him, you cannot reason with him. You can at most pretend to quarrel, or to reason, with him.

Seeing someone, then, as warped or deranged or compulsive in behaviour or peculiarly unfortunate in his formative circumstances—seeing someone so tends, at least to some extent, to set him apart from normal participant reactive attitudes on the part of one who sees him, tends to promote, at least in the civilized, objective attitudes. But there is something curious to add to this. The objective attitude is not only something we naturally tend to fall into in cases like these, where participant attitudes are partially or wholly inhibited by abnormalities or by immaturity. It is also something which is available as a resource in other cases too. We look with an objective eye on the compulsive behaviour of the neurotic or the tiresome behaviour of a very young child, thinking in terms of treatment or training. But we *can* sometimes look with something like the same eye on the behaviour of the normal and the mature. We *have* this resource and can sometimes use it: as a refuge, say, from the strains of involvement; or as an aid to policy; or simply out of intellectual curiosity. Being human, we cannot, in the normal case, do this for long, or altogether. If the strains of involvement, say, continue to be too great, then we have to do something else—like severing a relationship. But what is above all interesting is the tension there is, in us, between the participant attitude and the objective attitude. One is tempted to say: between our humanity and our intelligence. But to say this would be to distort both notions.

What I have called the participant reactive attitudes are essentially natural human reactions to the good or ill will or indifference of others towards us, as displayed in *their* attitudes and actions. The question we have to ask is: What effect would, or should, the acceptance of the truth of a general thesis of determinism have upon these reactive attitudes? More specifically, would, or should, the acceptance of the truth of the thesis lead to the decay or the repudiation of all such attitudes? Would, or should, it mean the end of gratitude, resentment, and forgiveness; of all reciprocated adult loves; of all the essentially *personal* antagonisms?

But how can I answer, or even pose, this question without knowing *exactly* what the thesis of determinism is? Well, there is one thing we do know: that if there is a coherent thesis of determinism, then there must be a sense of "determined" such that, if that thesis is true, then all behaviour whatever is determined in that sense. Remembering this, we can consider at least what possibilities lie formally open; and then perhaps we shall see that the question can be answered *without* knowing exactly what the thesis of determinism is. We can consider what possibilities lie open because we have already before us an account of the ways in which particular reactive attitudes, or reactive attitudes in general, may be, and, sometimes, we judge, should be, inhibited. Thus I considered earlier a group of considerations which tend to inhibit, and, we judge, should inhibit, resentment, in particular cases of an agent causing an injury, without inhibiting reactive attitudes in general towards that agent. Obviously this group of considerations cannot strictly bear upon our question; for that question concerns reactive attitudes in general. But resentment has a particular interest; so it is worth adding that it has never been claimed as a consequence of the truth of determinism that one or another of *these* considerations was operative in every case of an injury being caused by an agent; that it would follow from the truth of determinism that anyone who caused an injury *either* was quite simply ignorant of causing it *or* had acceptably overriding reasons for acquiescing reluctantly in causing it *or* . . . , etc. The prevalence of this happy state of affairs would not be a consequence of the reign of universal determinism, but of the reign of universal goodwill. We cannot, then, find here the possibility of an affirmative answer to our question, even for the particular case of resentment.

Next, I remarked that the participant attitude, and the personal reactive attitudes in general, tend to give place, and, it is judged by the civilized, should give place, to objective attitudes, just in so far as the agent is seen as excluded from ordinary adult human relationships by deep-rooted psychological abnormality—or simply by being a child. But it cannot be a consequence of any thesis which is not itself self-contradictory that abnormality is the universal condition.

Now this dismissal might seem altogether too facile; and so, in a sense, it is. But whatever is too quickly dismissed in this dismissal is allowed for in the only possible form of affirmative answer that remains. We can sometimes, and in part, I have remarked, look on the normal (those we rate as "normal") in the objective way in which we have learned to look on certain classified cases of abnormality. And our question reduces to this: could, or should, the acceptance of the determinist thesis lead us always to look on everyone exclusively in this way? For this is the only condition worth considering under which the acceptance of determinism could lead to the decay or repudiation of participant reactive attitudes.

It does not seem to be self-contradictory to suppose that this might happen. So I suppose we must say that it is not absolutely inconceivable that it should happen. But I am strongly inclined to think that it is, for us as we are, practically inconceivable. The human commitment to participation in ordinary inter-personal relationships is, I think, too thoroughgoing and deeply rooted for us to take seriously the thought that a general theoretical conviction might so change our world that, in it, there were no longer any such things as inter-personal relationships as we normally understand them; and being involved in inter-personal relationships as we normally understand them precisely is being exposed to the range of reactive attitudes and feelings that is in question.

This, then, is a part of the reply to our question. A sustained objectivity of inter-personal attitude, and the human isolation which that would entail, does not seem to be something of which human beings would be capable even if some general truth were a theoretical ground for it. But this is not all. There is a further point, implicit in the foregoing, which must be made explicit. Exceptionally, I have said, we can have direct dealings with human beings without any degree of personal involvement, treating them simply as creatures to be handled in our own interests, or our side's, or society's—or even theirs. In the extreme case of the mentally deranged, it is easy to see the connection between the possibility of a wholly objective attitude and the impossibility of what we understand by ordinary inter-personal relationships. Given this latter impossibility, no other civilized attitude is available than that of viewing the deranged person simply as something to be understood and controlled in the most desirable fashion. To view him as outside the reach of personal relationships is already, for the civilized, to view him in this way. For reasons of policy or self-protection we may have occasion, perhaps temporary, to adopt a fundamentally similar attitude to a "normal" human being; to concentrate, that is, on understanding "how he works," with a view to determining our policy accordingly or to finding in that very understanding a relief from the strains of involvement. Now it is certainly true that in the case of the abnormal, though not in the case of the normal, our adoption of the objective attitude is a consequence of our viewing the agent as *incapacitated* in some or all respects for ordinary inter-personal relationships. He is thus incapacitated, perhaps, by the fact that his picture of reality is pure fantasy, that he does not, in a sense, live in the real world at all, or by the fact that his behaviour is, in part, an unrealistic acting out of unconscious purposes; or by the fact that he is an idiot, or a moral idiot. But there is something else which, *because* this is true, is equally certainly *not* true. And that is that there is a sense of "determined" such that (1) if determinism is true, all behaviour is determined in this sense, and (2) determinism might be true, i.e. it is not inconsistent with the facts as we know them to suppose that all behaviour might be determined in this sense, and (3) our adoption of the objective attitude towards the abnormal is the result of prior embracing of the belief that the behaviour, or the relevant stretch of behaviour, of the human being in question *is* determined in this sense. Neither in the case of the normal, then, nor in the case of the abnormal is it true that, when we adopt an objective attitude, we do so *because* we hold such a belief. So my answer has two parts. The first is that we cannot, as we are, seriously envisage ourselves adopting a thoroughgoing objectivity of attitude to others as a result of theoretical conviction of the truth of determinism; and the second is that when we do in fact adopt such an attitude in a particular case, our doing so is not the consequence of a theoretical conviction which might be expressed as "Determinism in this case," but is a consequence of our abandoning, for different reasons in different cases the ordinary inter-personal attitudes.

It might be said that all this leaves the real question unanswered, and that we cannot hope to answer it without knowing exactly what the thesis of determinism is. For the real question is not a question about what we actually do, or why we do it. It is not even a question about what we would *in fact* do if a certain theoretical conviction gained general acceptance. It is a question about what it would be *rational* to do if determinism were true, a question about the rational justification of ordinary inter-personal attitudes in general. To this I shall reply, first, that such a question could seem real only to one who had utterly failed to grasp the purport of the preceding answer, the fact of our natural human commitment to ordinary interpersonal attitudes. This commitment is part of the general framework of human life, not something that can come up for review as particular cases can come up for review within this general framework. And I shall reply, second, that if we could imagine what we cannot have, viz. a choice in this matter, then we could choose rationally only in the light of an assessment of the gains and losses to human life, its enrichment or impoverishment; and the truth or falsity of a general thesis of determinism would not bear on the rationality of *this* choice. . . .

# VI

And now we can try to fill in the lacuna which the pessimist finds in the optimist's account of the concept of moral responsibility, and of the bases of moral condemnation and punishment; and to fill it in from the facts as we know them. For, as I have already remarked, when the pessimist himself seeks to fill it in, he rushes beyond the facts as we know them and proclaims that it cannot be filled in at all unless determinism is false.

Yet a partial sense of the facts as we know them is certainly present to the pessimist's mind. When his opponent, the optimist, undertakes to show that the truth of determinism would not shake the foundations of the concept of moral responsibility and of the practices of moral condemnation and punishment, he typically refers, in a more or less elaborated way, to the efficacy of these practices in regulating behaviour in socially desirable ways. These practices are represented solely as instruments of policy, as methods of individual treatment and social control. The pessimist recoils from this picture; and in his recoil there is, typically, an element of emotional shock. He is apt to say, among much else, that the humanity of the offender himself is offended by *this* picture of his condemnation and punishment.

The reasons for this recoil—the explanation of the sense of an emotional, as well as a conceptual, shock—we have already before us. The picture painted by the optimists is painted in a style appropriate to a situation envisaged as wholly dominated by objectivity of attitude. The only operative notions invoked in this picture are such as those of policy, treatment, control. But a thoroughgoing objectivity of attitude, excluding as it does the moral reactive attitudes, excludes at the same time essential elements in the concepts of *moral* condemnation and *moral* responsibility. This is the reason for the conceptual shock. The deeper emotional shock is a reaction, not simply to an inadequate conceptual analysis, but to the suggestion of a change in our world. I have remarked that it is possible to cultivate an exclusive objectivity of attitude in some cases, and for some reasons, where; the object of the attitude is not set aside from developed inter-personal and moral attitudes by immaturity or abnormality. And the suggestion which seems to be contained in the optimist's account is that such an attitude should be universally adopted to all offenders. This is shocking enough in the pessimist's eyes. But, sharpened by shock, his eyes see further. It would be hard to make *this* division in our natures. If to all offenders, then to all mankind. Moreover, to whom could this recommendation be, in any real sense, addressed? Only to the powerful, the authorities. So abysses seem to open.[3]

But we will confine our attention to the case of the offenders. The concepts we are concerned with are those of responsibility and guilt, qualified as "moral," on the one hand—together with that of membership of a moral community; of demand, indignation, disapprobation and condemnation, qualified as "moral," on the other hand—together with that of punishment. Indignation, disapprobation, like resentment, tend to inhibit or at least to limit our goodwill towards the object of these attitudes, tend to promote an at least partial and temporary withdrawal of goodwill: they do so in proportion as they are strong; and their strength is in general proportioned to what is felt to be the magnitude of the injury and to the degree to which the agent's will is identified with, or indifferent to, it. (These, of course, are not contingent connections.) But these attitudes of disapprobation and indignation are precisely the correlates of the moral demand in the case where the demand is felt to be disregarded. The making of the demand *is* the proneness to such attitudes. The holding of them does not, as the holding of objective attitudes does, involve as a part of itself viewing their object other than as a member of the moral community. The partial withdrawal of goodwill which *these* attitudes entail, the modification *they* entail of the general demand that another should, if possible, be spared suffering, is, rather, the consequence

---

[3]See J. D. Mabbott's 'Freewill and Punishment', in *Contemporary British Philosophy*, 3rd ser. (London: Allen & Unwin, 1956).

of *continuing* to view him as a member of the moral community; only as one who has offended against its demands. . . .

[S]avage or civilized, we have some belief in the utility of practices of condemnation and punishment. But the social utility of these practices, on which the optimist lays such exclusive stress, is not what is now in question. What is in question is the pessimist's justified sense that to speak in terms of social utility alone is to leave out something vital in our conception of these practices. The vital thing can be restored by attending to that complicated web of attitudes and feelings which form an essential part of the moral life as we know it, and which are quite opposed to objectivity of attitude. Only by attending to this range of attitudes can we recover from the facts as we know them a sense of what we mean, i.e. of *all* we mean, when, speaking the language of morals, we speak of desert, responsibility, guilt, condemnation, and justice. But we *do* recover it from the facts as we know them. We do not have to go beyond them. Because the optimist neglects or misconstrues these attitudes, the pessimist rightly claims to find a lacuna in his account. We can fill the lacuna for him. But in return we must demand of the pessimist a surrender of his metaphysics.

Optimist and pessimist misconstrue the facts in very different styles. But in a profound sense there is something in common to their misunderstandings. Both seek, in different ways, to overintellectualize the facts. Inside the general structure or web of human attitudes and feelings of which I have been speaking, there is endless room for modification, redirection, criticism, and justification. But questions of justification are internal to the structure or relate to modifications internal to it. The existence of the general framework of attitudes itself is something we are given with the fact of human society. As a whole, it neither calls for, nor permits, an external "rational" justification. Pessimist and optimist alike show themselves, in different ways, unable to accept this. The optimist's style of overintellectualizing the facts is that of a characteristically incomplete empiricism, a one-eyed utilitarianism. He seeks to find an adequate basis for certain social practices in calculated consequences, and loses sight (perhaps wishes to lose sight) of the human attitudes of which these practices are, in part, the expression. The pessimist does not lose sight of these attitudes, but is unable to accept the fact that it is just these attitudes themselves which fill the gap in the optimist's account. Because of this, he thinks the gap can be filled only if some general metaphysical proposition is repeatedly verified, verified in all cases where it is appropriate to attribute moral responsibility. This proposition he finds it as difficult to state coherently and with intelligible relevance as its determinist contradictory. Even when a formula has been found ("contra-causal freedom" or something of the kind) there still seems to remain a gap between its applicability in particular cases and its supposed moral consequences. . . .

If we sufficiently, that is *radically,* modify the view of the optimist, his view is the right one. It is far from wrong to emphasize the efficacy of all those practices which express or manifest our moral attitudes, in regulating behaviour in ways considered desirable; or to add that when certain of our beliefs about the efficacy of some of these practices turns out to be false, then we may have good reason for dropping or modifying those practices. What *is* wrong is to forget that these practices, and their reception, the reactions to them, really *are* expressions of our moral attitudes and not merely devices we calculatingly employ for regulative purposes.

Our practices do not merely exploit our natures, they express them. Indeed the very understanding of the kind of efficacy these expressions of our attitudes have turns on our remembering this. When we do remember this, and modify the optimist's position accordingly, we simultaneously correct its conceptual deficiencies and ward off the dangers it seems to entail, without recourse to the obscure and panicky metaphysics of libertarianism.

## READING COMPREHENSION QUESTIONS

1. In your own words, explain the position held by Strawson's "optimist" and that held by his "pessimist."

2. Explain the disagreement between the optimist and the pessimist regarding the practice of punishment in section II of Strawson's article.

3. Explain in detail what Strawson means by the term "reactive attitude."

4. Strawson says there are, in general, two kinds of considerations that get us to modify, mollify, or eliminate our feelings of resentment after we first perceive that someone has wronged us. Call the first kind "excusing conditions," and the second kind "exempting conditions." Explain what each kind consists in, and articulate, as best you can, some of the differences between them.

5. The key argument Strawson makes in this selection is an answer to his own question, "What effect would, or should, the acceptance of the truth of a general thesis of determinism have upon these reactive attitudes?" Explain how he answers this question.

6. The overall goal of the article is to get the pessimist (the indeterminist or libertarian) to withdraw his appeal to a "panicky metaphysics" in return for a vital concession from the optimist (the compatibilist). What exactly is this concession demanded of the optimist and how does Strawson think it can be made? (Warning: this is a hard question!)

# 5

# The Existence of God

## MOTIVATION

Suppose one of your classmates came up to you after class one day and said the following:

> Do you have a moment? I'd like to share my testimony with you. Over the weekend, I had a powerful mystical experience (and yes, I was completely sober and awake at the time). I had a vision in which I was "told" that the only supernatural forces in the universe are Invisible Green Goblins. There are millions of them, and we are to start worshipping them and giving them the respect that they deserve. They're tired of people talking about this non-existent "God" fellow, so they came to me and told me to spread the word to the uninitiated. That's you. So I guess I'm now their prophet. I'm telling you, though, they definitely exist. I have faith that they do. They are responsible for the creation of the universe and they are the ones who provide for us when it is most needed. Beyond my testimony, I can't give you any *direct* proof of their existence, but I can give you some indirect proof. When you lose a sock in the dryer, they are the ones responsible. They take them as a sacrifice. Indeed, what other explanation could there be? What's that? "If they're invisible how can they be green?" Well, their ways are a mystery to us. All hail the Invisible Green Goblins![1]

---

[1] A scenario inspired by Brad Art, in *What is the Best Life? An Introduction to Ethics* (Belmont, CA: Wadsworth Publishing Company, 1993), pp. 77–78.

If you heard such testimony, would you believe it? If not, why not? Furthermore, is belief in God any different from belief in the IGGs? In other words, think about the kind of belief that belief in God is. It's definitely different from other types of beliefs, such as the belief that there are marks on this page, or that grass is green. So what are the features of belief in God that make it different in kind from these latter beliefs, and what, if any, are the features of belief in God that make it different from belief in the IGGs?

## TYPES OF REASONS FOR BELIEF

The authors of the readings in this chapter address issues such as this by thinking philosophically about the nature of, and concepts involved in, belief in God. Such a project involves the attempt to answer the following two very general questions:

1.   What reasons are there (if any) for belief in God(s)?

2.   Are these reasons *good* reasons?

Consider question 1 for a moment. Here's a possible answer: people believe in God because they've been raised that way. Now while this may be true, it doesn't provide the particular *kind* of reason we're looking for here, and to see why, we need to introduce a distinction between two kinds of reasons.

> An **explanatory reason** for X's belief B provides an explanation, typically a causal story, for why X has come to believe B.

> A **justifying reason** for X's belief B provides a justification for X's believing B, that is, a consideration in favor of X's *continued belief* in B.

So an explanation of why X believes B simply provides a story for why X *in fact* believes B; a justification for X to believe B provides a story for why X *ought to* believe B. With this distinction in mind, then, we can see that the story about upbringing provides merely an explanatory reason for why many people believe in God. But what we're obviously looking for are possible reasons for why people *ought* to believe in God, so we need to revise question 1 to explicitly reflect that fact: what *justifying* reasons are there (if any) for belief in God(s)?

## REASONS FOR BELIEF IN GOD

What answers might be given to this question? Think about it this way: suppose you were a believer who wanted to convert a nonbeliever. How would you do so? What reasons could you give this person? There are several kinds of general reasons people have offered to justify religious belief over the years. Here are just a few, put very informally.

1.   *The universe had to come from somewhere!* The idea here is that the universe couldn't have just popped into existence all on its own; it had to have been caused to exist by something that existed independently from it, and God fills that explanatory gap quite nicely.

This is known as the **Cosmological Argument**, and its most famous advocate is Thomas Aquinas, a medieval theologian and philosopher, and his more precise argument for this conclusion is found in our readings.

2. *You can't get things like eyes and brains by accident!* The idea here is that there are certain features of the world that reveal to us a kind of complexity that can only be the product of, yes, intelligent design, and who else but God could have been that designer?

   This is what's known as the **Teleological Argument**, or the **Argument from Design**, and it is currently perhaps the most popular argument for the existence of God. We have included the version given by its most famous proponent, William Paley, in our readings. In that selection, Paley runs an argument by analogy, comparing the universe to a watch. If we ran across a watch, with its complex arrangement of parts together serving a particular purpose, we would surely infer that it had a watchmaker. But there are many aspects of the natural world that exhibit such complexity and purpose, and so we should infer that the natural world itself had an intelligent designer, called God.

3. *What other explanation could there be for the miracles that have occurred throughout history?* The big assumption, of course, is that certain miracles have occurred—including, for example, the resurrection of Jesus—but granting that assumption, it looks like God would have to be behind them and would thus have to exist.

   In our readings, this **Argument from Miracles** is debated by William Lane Craig and Walter Sinnott-Armstrong. Craig maintains both that we have good reason to believe that Jesus rose from the dead and thus that God exists as the best explanation of that miracle. Sinnott-Armstrong, on the other hand, denies both arguments, insisting that we don't have good reason to believe that Jesus rose from the dead, and so no reason (based on this alleged miracle) to believe God exists as the cause.

   In addition to these three arguments included in our readings, there are several others people have offered, including the following:

4. *You can't get morality without God!* There are certain actions that are objectively immoral, wrong no matter what you think about them. For example, it's wrong to torture innocent babies for fun. But how could this be possible? There's an analogue here to laws: there are certain actions that are illegal, regardless of what you think about them, and what makes them wrong is simply that they were determined to be so by some legislative body. But then morality must work in the same way: if there is an objective moral "law," then there must be a divine legislative "body," called God.

5. *One can experience the presence of God directly in certain circumstances.* Not much commentary is needed here: many people throughout history have offered this as their sole reason for belief in God.

6. *God answers prayers.* This could be a kind of empirical test to determine God's existence: if you pray for something to happen and it in fact happens, perhaps this is evidence for God's causing it to happen (and thus obviously for God's existence).

What all these putative justifying reasons have in common is that they are attempts to point to some empirical phenomena that, in order to be fully explained, (most likely) require God's existence. So in order to explain the phenomena of miracles, answered prayers, certain experiential states, objective morality, design in nature, or the universe itself, God either must or probably must exist.

These have been the most popular kinds of justifying reasons for the existence of God, and they are all what's known as **a posteriori justifications**, which are justifications with reference to experience. A way to remember this term is that they are justifications that are *posterior to,* or after, experience.

So why are you justified in believing that there are marks on this page? You can *see* them. Your belief is justified with reference to your own particular experience. Similarly, why are you justified in believing that the earth is round? Again, your justification will be a posteriori: either you've read about it, or heard it from a trustworthy source, or sailed around it yourself, or (in very rare cases) actually seen it from outer space. At any rate, virtually all of our justified beliefs are justified a posteriori, and most arguments for the existence of God take this form.

There is, though, another sort of justification, namely, **a priori justification**, which is a justification *without* reference to experience. This may seem rather odd, but the idea is that there could be certain propositions one is justified in believing without any reference to one's senses or one's general experience. What might these be?

Why are you justified in believing that all triangles have three sides? Have you done some scientific investigation, trying to gather all the triangles in the world together and then noting whether or not each one has three sides? Of course not. Your justification here comes directly from your understanding of the *concept* of a triangle. Once you understand the concept (which will of course require some experience in the world), you will then be justified in believing all sorts of propositions about triangles, including several, perhaps, that are the product of geometrical or logical inference.

Similarly, why are you justified in believing that all bachelors are unmarried males? Have you done a poll? "Excuse me, are you a bachelor? Excellent. Are you then also an unmarried male? Fantastic. Thanks for your time." Of course not. You are justified in believing this proposition entirely from consideration of the concept of bachelorhood.

Now as we've said, most arguments for the existence of God are a posteriori justifications: they start with some phenomenon we have experienced, and then infer on the basis of that phenomenon that God probably or definitely exists. But there was one significant exception to this pattern, namely, St. Anselm's **Ontological Argument**, which attempted to prove the existence of God in an entirely a priori fashion. What Anselm attempted to do was prove that God must exist *solely by consideration of the concept of "God."* Very briefly (and roughly), Anselm argued that thinking about the concept of God, as the greatest possible being, should reveal to us that God, *in order* to be the greatest possible being, would have to have as one of his perfections the property of existence in reality. For without that property, God wouldn't actually be the greatest possible being, the thing to which our concept of God commits us. It's an ingenious argument, although it has its difficulties. One such difficulty was articulated by Gaunilo, a contemporary of Anselm's, who tried to construct a parody of Anselm's argument in order to show that the same sort of argument could "prove" the existence of *anything.* You will have to assess for yourself whether or not Gaunilo's challenge succeeds.

In all the preceding instances, the argument in question tries to justify believing in God on the basis of the likely truth of the proposition "God exists." In other words, every one of these arguments tries to prove that God exists, with the assumed premise that you ought, *as a result,* believe that God exists—after all, if something is true, you ought to believe it. But there's actually a more direct route to justifying belief in God, namely, showing why it's in your best interest to do so, *regardless* of whether or not God actually exists. This is the move made famous in Blaise **Pascal's Wager**. He argues that, given the expected pay-offs (eternal happiness for believers, eternal damnation for unbelievers), it's utterly obvious that you should be a believer, even though, as Pascal argues, there could simply be no rational grounds for belief, that is, no way to demonstrate that God either exists or doesn't exist. The risks of believing and being wrong are nothing; the risks of not believing and being wrong are genuinely nasty. So you ought to believe for purely prudential reasons.

## REASONS AGAINST BELIEF IN GOD

Most arguments casting doubt on religious belief take aim at one or more of the properties alleged to be attached to God, in particular the "omnis," the properties of omnipotence (being all-powerful), omniscience (being all-knowing), omnibenevolence (being all-good), omnipresence (being everywhere at once), and so forth. One example, taking aim at God's alleged omnipotence, might be familiar to you: could God create a stone too heavy for him to lift? If he could create such a stone, then he couldn't lift it, which is a limit on his power. And if he couldn't create such a stone, then that's a limit on his power. Either way, if omnipotence consists in the ability to do *anything*, God could not be omnipotent. Indeed, this is actually an attack on the logical possibility of omnipotence, so *no* possible being could have such a property. Can you think of any replies to this problem?

Another classic problem has to do with God's alleged omniscience. If God truly knows everything, then he knew fifty years ago that I was going to sin today by coveting my neighbor's wife (say). But if he knew I would covet today, and he can't be wrong, then I couldn't have done anything *but* covet today, which seems to be a limit on my free will. In other words, it seems that a crucial necessary condition for having free will is the ability to refrain from the actions one performs. But if God knows I'm going to do X, I can't refrain from X without making God wrong (which God could never be), so I can't refrain from X, and thus seem to lack free will. (See the introduction to Chapter 4, "Free Will, Determinism, and Responsibility," for more on the ability to do otherwise.) So it looks like we either have to abandon God's omniscience or abandon free will, neither of which is a very attractive option for religious believers. Can you think of a reply?

Far and away the most troublesome problem for belief in God, however, has been the problem of evil, articulated in our readings by David Hume's character Philo (himself echoing a challenge laid down in ancient times by Epicurus), and depicted powerfully by Fyodor Dostoevsky, in the selection from *The Brothers Karamazov*: if God wants to prevent the evil in the world but can't, then he's not omnipotent; if God can prevent the evil in the world, but doesn't want to, he's not omnibenevolent; either way, God must lack a property crucial to religious belief.

This argument is intended to undermine the compatibility of two of God's alleged properties (omnipotence and omnibenevolence), but many people have taken it to undermine the point of religious belief altogether. After all, if God isn't all-good or powerful enough to stop evil, then even if he exists, he's not really worth worshipping or paying much attention to, it might seem. More strongly, if the very concept of God requires both properties, then the absence of one or the other simply implies that God could not exist.

There have been numerous replies to the problem of evil given over the years, and they break down into two types: "cheap" solutions and theodicies. Cheap solutions are those that don't really grapple seriously with the problem itself, and they include (a) denying God's omnipotence in a way that supposedly retains reason to worship him (as a theologian put it to one of us, "God sees the Nazis killing all those poor Jews, and it breaks his heart, but he can't do anything about it"); (b) denying the existence of evil, or at least insisting that the good far outweighs the evil (a response Hume's character Cleanthes gives); or (c) abandoning faith altogether (while perhaps a legitimate response to the argument, it's a "cheap" solution nonetheless because no further intellectual costs are spent on the argument).

**Theodicies**, on the other hand, are attempts to justify the presence of evil in the world, while also maintaining God's power and goodness. Theodicies provide, in other words, possible justifying reasons for why God allows all this evil to take place. In our readings, Eleonore Stump provides one very thoughtful theodicy, according to which the horrors we see in the world turn a mirror on ourselves. Although this mirror reveals that we're part of a species that commits all sorts of atrocities, it can also be a means to discover the great *goodness* in the world as well as in—to a much higher degree—God. Beyond Stump's response, though, you might consider what other responses could be given on behalf of the theist to this very difficult problem.

## BASIC CONCEPTS AND VOCABULARY

There are a number of terms that regularly come up in discussion of these issues, so it's important that we begin with a common understanding of them.

A. **Atheism**—the belief that there is/are no god(s) of any kind. The atheist contends that, *whatever* your concept of god or gods is, such entities don't exist. The form of assertion presented by the atheist, then, is "I believe that God does not exist." This attitude toward God would be similar to the attitude most of us now have about Santa Claus.

B. **Agnosticism**—the belief that we don't have sufficient reason either to affirm or to deny any god's existence. Notice the distinction between atheism and agnosticism. The atheist offers the positive contention that there are no gods, while the agnostic simply contends that we have no way of knowing whether there are gods or not. The form of assertion presented by the agnostic is "I do not believe that God exists," and also "I do not believe that God does not exist."

We can distinguish agnosticism into two different types.

1. **Superficial agnosticism**—the belief that, while the concept of God is perfectly coherent, we nevertheless don't have sufficient reason either to affirm or to deny God's existence *because there's insufficient evidence either way.*

2. **Deep agnosticism**—the belief that we don't have sufficient reason either to affirm or to deny God's existence *because the very concept of God is incoherent.*

   On deep agnosticism, the concept "God" is like the concept of a round idea. The concept itself simply makes no intelligible sense. For example, one way to think about the problem of evil might be in these terms: if part of the concept of God is that he's all-good, then this just makes no sense if there's evil in the world. Or think about omnipotence and goodness: there's supposedly an entity that can do anything but he can't sin? That seems incoherent. Or God somehow transcends space and time? That just makes no sense, one might think.

   You might say, well, if the concept of God is incoherent, then one should be an *atheist*, not an agnostic, with respect to it. But suppose I were to ask you, "Do you believe in round ideas?" Your utter confusion in reply would be appropriate: "How can I believe or not believe in something that just makes no sense?!" That's a kind of deep agnosticism about the existence of round ideas, which is akin to the kind of utter confusion expressed by the deep agnostic about the existence of God.

C. **Naturalism**—the theory that everything can be wholly explained in terms of natural phenomena (i.e., no supernatural explanations needed). This is the basic viewpoint of the practice of science.

D. **Theism**—belief in the existence of god(s). You are a theist if you believe in the existence of any kind of god whatsoever.

E. **Deism**—the belief in an "absentee" god, that is, one who long ago set things in motion but thereafter left it alone. This was the belief of certain eighteenth-century English philosophers, as well as many of the Founding Fathers of the United States. There is no "personal" god on this view.

F. **Polytheism**—the belief in a multitude of personal gods, each responsible for a different department of life. This was, of course, the belief of the Greeks, Romans, Norwegians, and countless other groups throughout history.

G. **Henotheism**—the belief that there are many gods, but only one to which I owe my allegiance. This was the case in the ancient Middle East, when many tribes roamed the area, each willing to believe in other tribes' gods, but sacrificing to and worshipping only their own.

H. **Monotheism**—the belief that there is only one Supreme Being, who is both personal and moral. Most people who are theists in the Western world are monotheists.

With these concepts and the other background issues laid out, it's time to begin your task of answering the second general question of the overall project: are the justifying reasons given by our authors for or against belief in God *good* reasons?

# 19

# Rebellion

FYODOR DOSTOEVSKY

*The Russian novelist Fyodor Dostoevsky (1821–1881) produced some of the greatest works in world literature, including* Crime and Punishment, Notes from the Underground, *and* The Idiot. *In this selection, from Dostoevsky's last and perhaps greatest novel,* The Brothers Karamazov, *we come in at the tail end of a long conversation between two of the brothers, Ivan and Alyosha, that has turned into a blistering monologue by Ivan. The younger brother, Alyosha, is a novice, studying to become a monk. His older brother, Ivan, while not an atheist, is nevertheless no fan of God, and here he tries to explain why with his particular version of the problem of evil. Ivan talks about atrocities done to children, and he focuses on two particularly heinous cases, examples Dostoevsky culled from actual newspaper accounts from the early nineteenth century. Ivan asks the question many have asked: how could a loving God allow these sorts of things to happen? He then considers various possible answers—that evil will be avenged in hell, that the evil of the world produces a higher harmony, that evil is necessary for the production of eventually greater happiness—and finds them not only implausible but downright offensive. As you read, think about whether or not there are ways to respond to Ivan's challenge on behalf of the theist.*

"I've collected a great, great deal about Russian children, Alyosha. There was a little girl of five who was hated by her father and mother, 'most worthy and respectable people, of good education and breeding'. . . .

"This poor child of five was subjected to every possible torture by those cultivated parents. They beat her, thrashed her, kicked her for no reason till her body was one bruise. Then they went to greater refinements of cruelty—shut her up all night in the cold and frost in a privy, and because she didn't ask to be taken up at night (as though a child of five sleeping its angelic, sound sleep could be trained to wake and ask), they smeared her face and filled her mouth with excrement, and it was her mother, her mother, did this! And that mother could sleep, hearing the poor child's groans! Can you understand why a little creature, who can't even understand what's done to her, should beat her little aching heart with her tiny fist in the dark and the cold, and weep her meek unresentful tears to dear, kind God to protect her? Do you understand that, friend and brother, you pious and humble novice? Do you understand why this infamy must be and is permitted?

SOURCE: From *The Brothers Karamazov*, trans. Constance Garnett. This edition is in the public domain.

Without it, I am told, man could not have existed on earth, for he could not have known good and evil. Why should he know that diabolical good and evil when it costs so much? Why, the whole world of knowledge is not worth that child's prayer to 'dear, kind God'! I say nothing of the sufferings of grown-up people, they have eaten the apple, damn them, and the devil take them all! But these little ones! I am making you suffer, Alyosha, you are not yourself. I'll leave off if you like."

"Never mind. I want to suffer too," muttered Alyosha.

"One picture, even one more, because it's so curious, so characteristic, and I have only just read it in some collection of Russian antiquities. I've forgotten the name. I must look it up. It was in the darkest days of serfdom at the beginning of the century, and long live the Liberator of the People! There was in those days a general of aristocratic connections, the owner of great estates, one of those men—somewhat exceptional, I believe, even then—who, retiring from the service into a life of leisure, are convinced that they've earned absolute power over the lives of their subjects. There were such men then. So our general, settled on his property of two thousand souls, lives in pomp, and domineers over his poor neighbours as though they were dependants and buffoons. He has kennels of hundreds of hounds and nearly a hundred dog-boys—all mounted, and in uniform. One day a serf boy, a little child of eight, threw a stone in play and hurt the paw of the general's favourite hound. 'Why is my favourite dog lame?' He is told that the boy threw a stone that hurt the dog's paw. 'So you did it.' The general looked the child up and down. 'Take him.' He was taken—taken from his mother and kept shut up all night. Early that morning the general comes out on horse-back, with the hounds, his dependants, dog-boys, and hunts-men, all mounted around him in full hunting parade. The servants are summoned for their edification, and in front of them all stands the mother of the child. The child is brought from the lock-up. It's a gloomy, cold, foggy autumn day, a capital day for hunting. The general orders the child to be undressed; the child is stripped naked. He shivers, numb with terror, not daring to cry. . . . 'Make him run,' commands the general, 'Run! run!' shout the dog-boys. The boy runs. . . . 'At him!' yells the general, and he sets the whole pack of hounds on the child. The hounds catch him, and tear him to pieces before his mother's eyes! . . . I believe the general was afterwards declared incapable of administering his estates. Well—what did he deserve? To be shot? To be shot for the satisfaction of our moral feelings? . . .

Ivan for a minute was silent, his face became all at once very sad.

"Listen! I took the case of children only to make my case clearer. Of the other tears of humanity with which the earth is soaked from its crust to its centre, I will say nothing. I have narrowed my subject on purpose. I am a bug, and I recognise in all humility that I cannot understand why the world is arranged as it is. Men are themselves to blame, I suppose; they were given paradise, they wanted freedom, and stole fire from heaven, though they knew they would become unhappy, so there is no need to pity them. With my pitiful, earthly, Euclidian understanding, all I know is that there is suffering and that there are none guilty; that cause follows effect, simply and directly; that everything flows and finds its level—but that's only Euclidian nonsense. I know that, and I can't consent to live by it! What comfort is it to me that there are none guilty and that cause follows effect simply and directly, and that I know it? I must have justice, or I will destroy myself. And not justice in some remote infinite time and space, but here on earth, and that I could see myself. I have believed in it. I want to see it, and if I am dead by then, let me rise again, for if it all happens without me, it will be too unfair. Surely I haven't suffered simply that I, my crimes and my sufferings may manure the soil of the future harmony for somebody else. I want to see with my own eyes the hind lie down with the lion and the victim rise up and embrace his murderer. I want to be there when everyone suddenly understands what it has all been for. All the religions of the world are built on this longing, and I am a believer. But then there are the children, and what am I to do about them? That's a question I can't answer. For the hundredth time, I repeat, there are numbers of questions, but I've only taken the children, because in their case what I mean is so unanswerably clear. Listen! If all must suffer to pay for the eternal harmony, what have children to do with it? Tell me, please? It's beyond all comprehension why they should suffer, and why they should pay for the harmony. Why should they, too, furnish material to enrich the soil for the harmony of the future? I understand solidarity in sin among men. I understand solidarity in retribution, too; but there can be no such solidarity with children. And if it is really true that they must share responsibility for all their fathers' crimes, such a truth is not of this world and is beyond my comprehension. Some jester will say, perhaps, that the child would have grown up and have sinned, but you see he didn't grow up, he was torn to pieces by the dogs at eight years old. Oh, Alyosha, I am not blaspheming! I understand, of course, what an upheaval of the universe it will be, when everything in heaven and earth blends in one hymn of praise and everything that lives and has lived cries aloud: 'Thou art just, O Lord, for Thy ways are revealed.' When the mother embraces the fiend who threw her child to the dogs, and all three cry aloud with tears: 'Thou art just, O Lord!' then, of course, the crown of knowledge will be reached and all will be made clear. But what pulls me up here is that I can't accept that harmony. And while I am on earth I make haste to take my own measures. You see, Alyosha, perhaps it really may happen that if I live to that moment, or rise again to see it, I, too, perhaps, may cry aloud with the rest, looking at the mother embracing the child's torturer: 'Thou art just, O Lord!' but I don't want to cry aloud then. While there is still time I hasten to protect myself and so I renounce the higher harmony altogether. It's not worth the tears of that one tortured child who beat itself on the breast with its little fist and prayed in its stinking outhouse, with its unexpiated tears to 'dear, kind God'! It's not worth it, because those tears are unatoned for. They must be atoned for, or there can be no harmony. But how? How are you going to atone for them? Is it possible? By their being avenged? But what do I care for avenging them? What do I care for a hell for oppressors? What good can hell do, since those children have already been tortured? And what becomes of harmony, if there is hell? I want to forgive. I want to embrace. I don't want more suffering. And if the sufferings of children go to swell the sum of sufferings which was necessary to pay for truth, then I protest that the truth is not worth such a price. I don't want the mother to embrace the oppressor who threw her son to the dogs! She dare not forgive him! Let her forgive him for herself, if she will, let her forgive the torturer for the immeasurable suffering of her mother's heart. But the sufferings of her tortured child she has no right to forgive; she dare not forgive the torturer, even if the child were to forgive him! And if that is so, if they dare not forgive, what becomes of harmony? Is there in the whole world a being who would have the right to forgive and could forgive? I don't want harmony. From love for humanity I don't want it. I would rather be left with the unavenged suffering. I would rather remain with my unavenged suffering and unsatisfied indignation, even *if I were wrong*. Besides, too high a price is asked for harmony; it's beyond our means to pay so much to enter on it. And so I hasten to give back my entrance ticket, and if I am an honest man I am bound to give it back as soon as possible. And that I am doing. It's not God that I don't accept, Alyosha, only I most respectfully return Him the ticket."

"That's rebellion," murmured Alyosha, looking down.

"Rebellion? I am sorry you call it that," said Ivan earnestly. "One can hardly live in rebellion, and I want to live. Tell me yourself, I challenge you—answer. Imagine, that you are creating a fabric of human destiny with the object of making men happy in the end, giving them peace and rest at last, but that it was essential and inevitable to torture to death only one tiny creature—that baby beating its breast with its fist, for instance—and to found that edifice on its unavenged tears, would you consent to be the architect on those conditions? Tell me and tell the truth."

"No, I wouldn't consent," said Alyosha softly.

## READING COMPREHENSION QUESTIONS

1.  Ivan focuses on the case of children in his discussion of the evils of the world. Why?

2.  What precisely is Ivan's point in this passage? Does he use these cases to deny the existence of God? Why think that? If not, then what is he trying to show?

# 20

# The Ontological Argument

### ST. ANSELM

# The Lost Island Objection

### GAUNILO

*St. Anselm (1033–1109) was one of the most influential philosophers and theologians of medieval Europe. He wrote several important books providing rational proofs for the existence of God, and he eventually became archbishop of Canterbury in 1093. In this selection from his book* Proslogium, *Anselm lays out his most famous (and favorite) argument for the existence of God, the Ontological Argument. In it, he tries to show that God must exist, simply given the nature of the* concept *of God. Anselm refers to God as "a being than which nothing greater can be conceived," by which he simply means that for anything to deserve the name God, it would have to be the greatest conceivable being, possessing every property that could make a being great (i.e., a great-making property). He then challenges you to conceive of this being, a being with all the great-making properties a being could have. Now suppose this being didn't also exist in reality (outside of your head). Then it wouldn't be the greatest conceivable being. Why not? Because you could imagine a greater being than it, namely, one that also existed in reality! Therefore, if you're truly imagining the greatest conceivable being, you should realize that that being—God—must also exist in reality.*

*In the short reading that immediately follows, Gaunilo of Marmoutiers, a monk who was a contemporary of Anselm's, offers a parody of Anselm's argument in which he "proves" the existence of a magical lost island with the help of Anselm's own reasoning. If Gaunilo is right, something has gone terribly wrong in Anselm's argument, because it could be used to establish the existence of virtually anything. Anselm's response to Gaunilo was short and sweet: if you can actually run through my* exact *reasoning and come to the conclusion that the lost island exists, I'll give it to you. In other words, Anselm thought his reasoning was very precise and special, establishing* only *the existence of God and nothing more. One thing to consider as you read is why that would be the case.*

SOURCE: From *Proslogium; Monologium; An Appendix in Behalf of the Fool by Gaunilon; and Cur Deus Homo,* trans. Sidney Norton Deane. This edition is in the public domain.

## ANSELM: THE ONTOLOGICAL ARGUMENT

### Chapter II

Truly there is a God, although the fool hath said in his heart, There is no God.

And so, Lord, do thou, who dost give understanding to faith, give me, so far as thou knowest it to be profitable, to understand that thou art as we believe; and that thou art that which we believe. And, indeed, we believe that thou art a being than which nothing greater can be conceived. Or is there no such nature, since the fool hath said in his heart, there is no God? (Psalms xiv. 1). But, at any rate, this very fool, when he hears of this being of which I speak—a being than which nothing greater can be conceived—understands what he hears, and what he understands is in his understanding; although he does not understand it to exist.

For, it is one thing for an object to be in the understanding, and another to understand that the object exists. When a painter first conceives of what he will after-wards perform, he has it in his understanding, but he does not yet understand it to be, because he has not yet performed it. But after he has made the painting, he both has it in his understanding, and he understands that it exists, because he has made it.

Hence, even the fool is convinced that something exists in the understanding, at least, than which nothing greater can be conceived. For, when he hears of this, he understands it. And whatever is understood, exists in the understanding. And assuredly that, than which nothing greater can be conceived, cannot exist in the understanding alone. For, suppose it exists in the understanding alone: then it can be conceived to exist in reality; which is greater.

Therefore, if that, than which nothing greater can be conceived, exists in the understanding alone, the very being, than which nothing greater can be conceived, is one, than which a greater can be conceived. But obviously this is impossible. Hence, there is no doubt that there exists a being, than which nothing greater can be conceived, and it exists both in the understanding and in reality.

### Chapter III

God cannot be conceived not to exist.—God is that, than which nothing greater can be conceived.—That which can be conceived not to exist is not God.

And it assuredly exists so truly, that it cannot be conceived not to exist. For, it is possible to conceive of a being which cannot be conceived not to exist; and this is greater than one which can be conceived not to exist. Hence, if that, than which nothing greater can be conceived, can be conceived not to exist, it is not that, than which nothing greater can be conceived. But this is an irreconcilable contradiction. There is, then, so truly a being than which nothing greater can be conceived to exist, that it cannot even be conceived not to exist; and this being thou art, O Lord, our God.

So truly, therefore, dost thou exist, O Lord, my God, that thou canst not be conceived not to exist; and rightly. For, if a mind could conceive of a being better than thee, the creature would rise above the Creator; and this is most absurd. And, indeed, whatever else there is, except thee alone, can be conceived not to exist. To thee alone, therefore, it belongs to exist more truly than all other beings, and hence in a higher degree than all others. For, whatever else exists does not exist so truly, and hence in a less degree it belongs to it to exist. Why, then, has the fool said in his heart, there is no God (Psalms xiv. 1), since it is so evident, to a rational mind, that thou dost exist in the highest degree of all? Why, except that he is dull and a fool?

## GUANILO: THE LOST ISLAND OBJECTION

6. For example: it is said that somewhere in the ocean is an island, which, because of the difficulty, or rather the impossibility, of discovering what does not exist, is called the lost island. And they say that this island has an inestimable wealth of all manner of riches and delicacies in greater abundance than is told of the Islands of the Blest; and that having no owner or inhabitant, it is more excellent than all other countries, which are inhabited by mankind, in the abundance with which it is stored.

Now if some one should tell me that there is such an island, I should easily understand his words, in which there is no difficulty. But suppose that he went on to say, as if by a logical inference: "You can no longer doubt that this island which is more excellent than all lands exists somewhere, since you have no doubt that it is in your understanding. And since it is more excellent not to be in the understanding alone, but to exist both in the understanding and in reality, for this reason it must exist. For if it does not exist, any land which really exists will be more excellent than it; and so the island already understood by you to be more excellent will not be more excellent."

If a man should try to prove to me by such reasoning that this island truly exists, and that its existence should no longer be doubted, either I should believe that he was jesting, or I know not which I ought to regard as the greater fool: myself, supposing that I should allow this proof; or him, if he should suppose that he had established with any certainty the existence of this island. For he ought to show first that the hypothetical excellence of this island exists as a real and indubitable fact, and in no wise as any unreal object, or one whose existence is uncertain, in my understanding.

## READING COMPREHENSION QUESTIONS

1.   In this article, "that than which nothing greater can be conceived" is Anselm's long and unwieldy way of referring to God. In the final line of Chapter II, he is saying that God exists "both in the understanding and in reality," that is, God really and truly exists. Can you piece together his argument for this claim in Chapter II? (It's very difficult, but focus on the use Anselm makes of that long and unwieldy term for God.)

2.   What is the point of Anselm's painter example in Chapter II? How does this point play a role in the larger argument for the existence of God?

3.   In Chapter III, Anselm argues for a subtly different point, namely, that one can't even *conceive* of God's not existing. Can you piece together his argument for this claim?

4.   Gaunilo offers the example of the Lost Island as an objection to Anselm. What exactly is the objection? Can you think of any way for Anselm to reply?

# 21

# The Cosmological Argument

ST. THOMAS AQUINAS

*Thomas Aquinas (1224–1274) is perhaps the greatest philosopher and theologian of the Catholic Church. He wrote on a variety of important philosophical and theological topics. He was canonized by Pope John XXII only forty-nine years after his death. In this selection from his magnum opus,* Summa Theologica, *Aquinas is presenting his famous Five Ways to prove God's existence. The most popular of these is Aquinas's second way, known as the Cosmological Argument. In general, a cosmological argument points to some phenomenon in nature, lists various possible explanations for that phenomenon, and then eliminates all but one, which remains as the only possible explanation. The phenomenon Aquinas points to here is the chain of causation, or what he calls the "order of efficient causes." Things that exist were caused to exist, and this chain of causation goes back a long ways. Does it go back* infinitely, *though? Either it does or it doesn't, says Aquinas. Aquinas supposes that it does, but this leads to a contradiction, which means the chain can't go back infinitely; instead, there must have been a first cause, what we call God. As you read, try to figure out the details of Aquinas's reasoning for why the chain of causation couldn't be infinite. In addition, see if you can figure out just what Aquinas's other four arguments for God's existence are all about.*

## WHETHER GOD EXISTS?

### Objection 1

It seems that God does not exist; because if one of two contraries be infinite, the other would be altogether destroyed. But the word "God" means that He is infinite goodness. If, therefore, God existed, there would be no evil discoverable; but there is evil in the world. Therefore God does not exist.

## Objection 2

Further, it is superfluous to suppose that what can be accounted for by a few principles has been produced by many. But it seems that everything we see in the world can be accounted for by other principles, supposing God did not exist. For all natural things can be reduced to one principle which is nature; and all voluntary things can be reduced to one principle which is human reason, or will. Therefore there is no need to suppose God's existence.

*On the contrary,* It is said in the person of God: *"I am Who am."* (Ex. 3:14)

*I answer that,* The existence of God can be proved in five ways.

The first and more manifest way is the argument from motion. It is certain, and evident to our senses, that in the world some things are in motion. Now whatever is in motion is put in motion by another, for nothing can be in motion except it is in potentiality to that towards which it is in motion; whereas a thing moves inasmuch as it is in act. For motion is nothing else than the reduction of something from potentiality to actuality. But nothing can be reduced from potentiality to actuality, except by something in a state of actuality. Thus that which is actually hot, as fire, makes wood, which is potentially hot, to be actually hot, and thereby moves and changes it. Now it is not possible that the same thing should be at once in actuality and potentiality in the same respect, but only in different respects. For what is actually hot cannot simultaneously be potentially hot; but it is simultaneously potentially cold. It is therefore impossible that in the same respect and in the same way a thing should be both mover and moved, i.e. that it should move itself. Therefore, whatever is in motion must be put in motion by another. If that by which it is put in motion be itself put in motion, then this also must needs be put in motion by another, and that by another again. But this cannot go on to infinity, because then there would be no first mover, and, consequently, no other mover; seeing that subsequent movers move only inasmuch as they are put in motion by the first mover; as the staff moves only because it is put in motion by the hand. Therefore it is necessary to arrive at a first mover, put in motion by no other; and this everyone understands to be God.

The second way is from the nature of the efficient cause. In the world of sense we find there is an order of efficient causes. There is no case known (neither is it, indeed, possible) in which a thing is found to be the efficient cause of itself; for so it would be prior to itself, which is impossible. Now in efficient causes it is not possible to go on to infinity, because in all efficient causes following in order, the first is the cause of the intermediate cause, and the intermediate is the cause of the ultimate cause, whether the intermediate cause be several, or only one. Now to take away the cause is to take away the effect. Therefore, if there be no first cause among efficient causes, there will be no ultimate, nor any intermediate cause. But if in efficient causes it is possible to go on to infinity, there will be no first efficient cause, neither will there be an ultimate effect, nor any intermediate efficient causes; all of which is plainly false. Therefore it is necessary to admit a first efficient cause, to which everyone gives the name of God.

The third way is taken from possibility and necessity, and runs thus. We find in nature things that are possible to be and not to be, since they are found to be generated, and to corrupt, and consequently, they are possible to be and not to be. But it is impossible for these always to exist, for that which is possible not to be at some time is not. Therefore, if everything is possible not to be, then at one time there could have been nothing in existence. Now if this were true, even now there would be nothing in existence, because that which does not exist only begins to exist by something already existing. Therefore, if at one time nothing was in existence, it would have been impossible for anything to have begun to exist; and thus even now nothing would be in existence—which is absurd. Therefore, not all beings are merely possible, but there must exist something the existence of which is necessary. But every necessary thing either has its necessity caused by another, or not. Now it is impossible to go on to infinity in necessary things which have their necessity caused by another, as has been already proved in regard to efficient causes. Therefore we cannot but postulate the existence of some being having of itself its own necessity, and not receiving it from another, but rather causing in others their necessity. This all men speak of as God.

The fourth way is taken from the gradation to be found in things. Among beings there are some more and some less good, true, noble and the like. But "more" and "less" are predicated of different things, according as they resemble in their different ways something which is the maximum, as a thing is said to be hotter according as it more nearly resembles that which is hottest; so that there is something which is truest, something best, something noblest and, consequently, something which is uttermost being; for those things that are greatest in truth are greatest in being, as it is written in Metaph. ii. Now the maximum in any genus is the cause of all in that genus; as fire, which is the maximum heat, is the cause of all hot things. Therefore there must also be something which is to all beings the cause of their being, goodness, and every other perfection; and this we call God.

The fifth way is taken from the governance of the world. We see that things which lack intelligence, such as natural bodies, act for an end, and this is evident from their acting always, or nearly always, in the same way, so as to obtain the best result. Hence it is plain that not fortuitously, but designedly, do they achieve their end. Now whatever lacks intelligence cannot move towards an end, unless it be directed by some being endowed with knowledge and intelligence; as the arrow is shot to its mark by the archer. Therefore some intelligent being exists by whom all natural things are directed to their end; and this being we call God.

Reply to Objection 1: As Augustine says (Enchiridion xi): "Since God is the highest good, He would not allow any evil to exist in His works, unless His omnipotence and goodness were such as to bring good even out of evil." This is part of the infinite goodness of God, that He should allow evil to exist, and out of it produce good.

Reply to Objection 2: Since nature works for a determinate end under the direction of a higher agent, whatever is done by nature must needs be traced back to God, as to its first cause. So also whatever is done voluntarily must also be traced back to some higher cause other than human reason or will, since these can change or fail; for all things that are changeable and capable of defect must be traced back to an immovable and self-necessary first principle, as was shown in the body of the Article.

## READING COMPREHENSION QUESTIONS

1. According to Aquinas, why exactly can't something cause itself to exist?
2. The key to Aquinas's argument in the Second Way is showing that there couldn't have been a series of causes going back infinitely in time—that the chain of intermediate causes had to have started somewhere (and we call that first cause "God"). But what exactly is his argument for this claim?

# 22

# The Teleological Argument

WILLIAM PALEY

*William Paley (1743–1805) was a theologian and fellow at Christ College, Cambridge. In his most famous work, Natural Theology—a book that was deeply influential on the young Charles Darwin, and which is the source of this reading—Paley presents a common-sense argument for the existence of God, based on a fascinating analogy: the universe is like a watch. If one were to find a watch on the ground, one couldn't help but infer that it was designed, even if one had never seen a watch designed before, or even if one had never even seen a watch before. There are certain properties the watch itself exhibits that enable us to infer it was designed. Similarly, Paley suggests (although he doesn't quite say it explicitly), there are parts of the universe that have the same sorts of properties, and so enable us to infer that the universe was designed as well. As you read, try to figure out precisely what those properties are, and then think about whether or not parts of the universe really do exhibit those properties as well.*

## CHAPTER I

### State of the Argument

In crossing a heath, suppose I pitched my foot against a *stone,* and were asked how the stone came to be there, I might possibly answer that, for anything I knew to the contrary, it had lain there for ever; nor would it, perhaps, be very easy to show the absurdity of this answer. But suppose I had found a *watch* upon the ground, and

SOURCE: From William Paley, *Natural Theology.* This edition is in the public domain.

it should be inquired how the watch happened to be in that place, I should hardly think of the answer which I had before given—that for anything I knew, the watch might have always been there. Yet why should not this answer serve for the watch as well as for the stone? Why is it not as admissible in the second case as in the first? For this reason, and for no other—namely, that when we come to inspect the watch, we perceive (what we could not discover in the stone) that its several parts are framed and put together for a purpose that is to say, that they are so formed and adjusted as to produce motion, and that motion so regulated as to point out the hour of the day; that, if the different parts had been differently shaped from what they are, of a different size from what they are, or placed after any other manner, or in any other order, than that in which they are placed, either no motion at all would have been carried on in the machine, or none which would have answered the use that is now served by it. To reckon up a few of the plainest of these parts, and of their offices, all tending to one result:—We see a cylindrical box containing a coiled elastic spring, which, by its endeavour to relax itself, turns round the box. We next observe a flexible chain (artificially wrought for the sake of flexure) communicating the action of the spring from the box to the fusee. We then find a series of wheels, the teeth of which catch in and apply to each other, conducting the motion from the fusee to the balance, and from the balance to the pointer; and at the same time, by the size and shape of those wheels, so regulating that motion, as to terminate in causing an index, by an equable and measured progression, to pass over a given space in a given time. We take notice that the wheels are made of brass, in order to keep them from rust; the springs of steel, no other metal being so elastic; that over the face of the watch there is placed a glass, a material employed in no other part of the work, but in the room of which, if there had been any other than a transparent substance, the hour could not be seen without opening the case. This mechanism being observed (it requires, indeed, an examination of the instrument, and perhaps some previous knowledge of the subject, to perceive and understand it; but being once, as we have said, observed and understood), the inference, we think, is inevitable, that the watch must have had a maker; that there must have existed, at some time, and at some place or other, an artificer or artificers, who formed it for the purpose which we find it actually to answer—who comprehended its construction, and designed its use.

I. Nor would it, I apprehend, weaken the conclusion, that we had never seen a watch made; that we had never known an artist capable of making one; that we were altogether incapable of executing such a piece of workmanship ourselves, or of understanding in what manner it was performed; all this being no more than what is true of some exquisite remains of ancient art, of some lost arts, and, to the generality of mankind, of the more curious productions of modern manufacture. Does one man in a million know how oval frames are turned? Ignorance of this kind exalts our opinion of the unseen and unknown artist's skill, if he be unseen and unknown, but raises no doubt in our minds of the existence and agency of such an artist, at some former time, and in some place or other. Nor can I perceive that it varies at all the inference, whether the question arise concerning a human agent, or concerning an agent of a different species, or an agent possessing, in some respects, a different nature.

II. Neither, secondly, would it invalidate our conclusion, that the watch sometimes went wrong, or that it seldom went exactly right. The purpose of the machinery, the design, and the designer might be evident, and in the case supposed would be evident, in whatever way we accounted for the irregularity of the movement, or whether we could account for it or not. It is not necessary that a machine be perfect, in order to show with what design it was made; still less necessary, where the only question is—whether it were made with any design at all.

III. Nor, thirdly, would it bring any uncertainty into the argument if there were a few parts of the watch concerning which we could not discover, or had not yet discovered, in what manner they conduced to the general effect; or even some parts concerning which we could not ascertain whether they conduced to that effect in any manner whatever. For, as to the first branch of the case, if by the loss, or disorder, or decay of the parts in question, the movement of the watch were found, in fact, to be stopped, or disturbed, or retarded, no doubt would remain in our minds as to the utility or intention of these parts, although we should be unable to investigate the manner according to which, or the connection by which, the ultimate effect depended upon their action or assistance; and the more complex the machine is, the more likely is this obscurity to arise. Then, as to the second thing supposed—namely, that there were parts which might be spared, without prejudice to the movement of the watch, and that we had proved this by experiment—these superfluous parts, even if we were completely assured that they were such, would not vacate the reasoning which we had instituted concerning other parts. The indication of contrivance remained, with respect to them, nearly as it was before.

IV. Nor, fourthly, would any man in his senses think the existence of the watch, with its various machinery, accounted for, by being told that it was one out of possible combinations of material forms; that whatever he had found in the place where he found the watch, must have contained some internal configuration or other; and that this configuration might be the structure now exhibited—namely, of the works of a watch, as well as a different structure.

V. Nor, fifthly, would it yield his inquiry more satisfaction to be answered that there existed in things a principle of order, which had disposed the parts of the watch into their present form and situation. He never knew a watch made by the principle of order; nor can he even form to himself an idea of what is meant by a principle of order, distinct from the intelligence of the watchmaker. . . .

## CHAPTER II

### State of the Argument Continued

Suppose, in the next place, that the person who found the watch should, after some time, discover that, in addition to all the properties which he had hitherto observed in it, it possessed the unexpected property of producing, in the course of its movement, another watch like itself (the thing is conceivable); that it contained within it a mechanism, a system of parts, a mould, for instance, or a complex adjustment of lathes, files, and other tools, evidently and separately calculated for this purpose; let us inquire what effect ought such a discovery to have upon his former conclusion.

I. The first effect would be to increase his admiration of the contrivance, and his conviction of the consummate skill of the contriver. Whether he regarded the object of the contrivance, the distinct apparatus, the intricate, yet in many parts intelligible, mechanism by which it was carried on, he would perceive in this new observation nothing but an additional reason for doing what he had already done—for referring the construction of the watch to design, and to supreme art. If that construction *without* this property, or, which is the same thing, before this property had been noticed, proved intention and art to have been employed about it; still more strong would the proof appear when he came to the knowledge of this further property, the crown and perfection of all the rest.

II. He would reflect that though the watch before him were, *in some sense,* the maker of the watch which was fabricated in the course of its movements, yet it was in a very different sense from that in which a carpenter, for instance, is the maker of a chair—the author of its contrivance, the cause of the relation of its parts to their use. With respect to these, the first watch was no cause at all to the second; in no such sense as this was it the author of the constitution and order either of the parts which the new watch contained, or of the parts by the aid and instrumentality of which it was produced. We might possibly say, but with great latitude of expression, that a stream of water ground corn; but no latitude of expression would allow us to say, no stretch of conjecture could lead us to think, that the stream of water built the mill, though it were too ancient for us to know who the builder was. What the stream of water does in the affair is neither more nor less than this: by the application of an unintelligent impulse to a mechanism previously arranged, arranged independently of it, and arranged by intelligence, an effect is produced—namely, the corn is ground. But the effect results from the arrangement. The force of the stream cannot be said to be the cause or author of the effect, still less of the arrangement. Understanding and plan in the formation of the mill were not the less necessary, for any share which the water has in grinding the corn; yet is this share the same as that which the watch would have contributed to the production of the new watch, upon the supposition assumed in the last section. Therefore,

III. Though it be now no longer probable that the individual watch which our observer had found was made immediately by the hand of an artificer, yet doth not this alteration in anywise affect the inference, that an artificer had been originally employed and concerned in the production. The argument from design remains as it was. Marks of design and contrivance are no more accounted for now than they were before. In the same thing, we may ask for the cause of different properties. We may ask for the cause of the colour of a body, of its hardness, of its heat; and these causes may be all different. We are now asking for the cause of that subserviency to a use, that relation to an end, which we have remarked in the watch before us. No answer is given to this question by telling us that a preceding watch produced it. There cannot be design, without a designer; contrivance, without a contriver; order, without choice; arrangement, without anything capable of arranging; subserviency and relation to a purpose, without that which could intend a purpose; means suitable to an end, and executing their office, in accomplishing that end, without the end ever having been contemplated, or the means accommodated to it. Arrangement, disposition of parts, subserviency of means to an end, relation of instruments to a

use, imply the presence of intelligence and mind. No one, therefore, can rationally believe that the insensible, inanimate watch, from which the watch before
us issued, was the proper cause of the mechanism we so much admire in it—
could be truly said to have constructed the instrument, disposed its parts, assigned
their office, determined their order, action, and mutual dependency, combined
their several motions into one result, and that also a result connected with the util-
ities of other beings. All these properties, therefore, are as much unaccounted for
as they were before. . . .

The conclusion which the *first* examination of the watch—of its works, construction, and movement—suggested, was, that it must have had, for the cause and author
of that construction, an artificer who understood its mechanism and designed its use.
This conclusion is invincible. A *second* examination presents us with a new discovery.
The watch is found, in the course of its movement, to produce another watch similar
to itself; and not only so, but we perceive in it a system or organization separately
calculated for that purpose. What effect would this discovery have, or ought it to
have, upon our former inference? What, as hath already been said, but to increase
beyond measure our admiration of the skill which had been employed in the formation of such a machine? Or shall it, instead of this, all at once turn us round to an
opposite conclusion—namely, that no art or skill whatever has been concerned in
the business, although all other evidences of art and skill remain as they were, and
this last and supreme piece of art be now added to the rest? Can this be maintained
without absurdity? Yet this is atheism. . . .


## CHAPTER V

### Application of the Argument Continued

Every observation which was made in our first chapter concerning the watch,
may be repeated with strict propriety concerning the eye, concerning animals,
concerning plants, concerning, indeed, all the organized parts of the works of
nature. As,

I. When we are inquiring simply after the *existence* of an intelligent Creator,
imperfection, inaccuracy, liability to disorder, occasional irregularities, may subsist
in a considerable degree, without inducing any doubt into the question; just as a
watch may frequently go wrong, seldom perhaps exactly right, may be faulty in
some parts, defective in some, without the smallest ground of suspicion from thence
arising that it was not a watch, not made, or not made for the purpose ascribed to it.
When faults are pointed out, and when a question is started concerning the skill of
the artist, or dexterity with which the work is executed, then, indeed, in order to
defend these qualities from accusation, we must be able either to expose some
intractableness and imperfection in the materials, or point out some invincible difficulty in the execution, into which imperfection and difficulty the matter of complaint may be resolved; or, if we cannot do this, we must adduce such specimens of
consummate art and contrivance, proceeding from the same hand, as may convince
the inquirer of the existence in the case before him, of impediments like those
which we have mentioned, although, what from the nature of the case is very likely

to happen, they be unknown and unperceived by him. This we must do in order to vindicate the artist's skill, or at least the perfection of it; as we must also judge of his intention, and of the provisions employed in fulfilling that intention, not from an instance in which they fail, but from the great plurality of instances in which they succeed. But, after all, these are different questions from the question of the artist's existence; or, which is the same, whether the thing before us be a work of art or not; and the questions ought always to be kept separate in the mind. So likewise it is in the works of nature. Irregularities and imperfections are of little or no weight in the consideration, when that consideration relates simply to the existence of a Creator. When the argument respects his attributes, they are of weight; but are then to be taken in conjunction (the attention is not to rest upon them, but they are to be taken in conjunction) with the unexceptionable evidences which we possess of skill, power, and benevolence, displayed in other instances; which evidences may, in strength, number, and variety, be such, and may so overpower apparent blemishes, as to induce us, upon the most reasonable ground, to believe that these last ought to be referred to some cause, though we be ignorant of it, other than defect of knowledge or of benevolence in the Author.

## READING COMPREHENSION QUESTIONS

1.  Why would Paley think that the watch he found on the ground had a maker? In other words, what are the *general features* of the watch that enable one to infer that it was designed?

2.  Paley considers and rejects six possible objections to his inference about the watch, each mirroring some standard objections given to belief in a designer God. The first is that, because we've never seen a watch being designed, we can't infer that it had a designer. This is supposed to mirror the standard objection that, because we weren't around to see the world designed, we can't infer that it had a designer. But Paley rightly points out that we don't need to see a watch being designed to know it had a designer; features of the watch *itself* provide that knowledge. Presumably, then, features of the world itself provide the knowledge about its having a designer, even though we weren't around to see it being designed. Pick three other objections Paley considers, and then answer the following questions: what exactly is the objection with respect to the watch that Paley considers, what is the standard objection with respect to God that it mirrors, and how does Paley respond to the objection? (In each case, your answer should be similar in form to the one just given regarding the first objection Paley discusses.)

3.  For Paley, there are two sorts of inferences one might draw from the story about the watchmaker, namely, inferences about the watchmaker's existence, and inferences about the watchmaker's nature (i.e., about the watchmaker's skill). In Chapter V of the article, Paley considers the second sort of inference, and he's specifically worried about the case in which we find a watch that makes mistakes. What does Paley say regarding a possible inference that the watchmaker isn't perfect, and how is this discussion relevant for the analogy of the watchmaker and God?

# 23

# The Evidence of Miracles: An Exchange Between a Christian and an Atheist

WILLIAM LANE CRAIG AND WALTER SINNOTT-ARMSTRONG

*William Lane Craig is Research Professor of Philosophy at Talbot School of Theology, and Walter Sinnott-Armstrong is a Professor in the Department of Philosophy and Hardy Professor of Legal Studies at Dartmouth College. In this exchange, from a full-length book wherein they debate a variety of theological and philosophical matters, Craig and Sinnott-Armstrong debate the role of miracles in establishing the existence of God, focusing in particular on the alleged resurrection of Jesus. Craig begins by noting several facts he thinks we can ascertain regarding events surrounding Jesus's death (from a variety of sources), and then argues that the best explanation of those facts is that God raised Jesus from the dead and thus that God exists. Sinnott-Armstrong, on the other hand, is skeptical about the facts Craig identifies, but then argues that, even if Craig is right about the facts, he is wrong about what the best explanation of them would be.*

## 4. GOD MAKES SENSE OF THE LIFE, DEATH, AND RESURRECTION OF JESUS

### William Lane Craig

The historical person Jesus of Nazareth was a remarkable individual. New Testament critics have reached something of a consensus that the historical Jesus came on the scene with an unprecedented sense of divine authority, the authority to stand and speak in God's place. That's why the Jewish leadership instigated his crucifixion for the charge of blasphemy—in effect, for slandering God. He claimed that in himself the Kingdom of God had come, and as visible demonstrations of this fact he carried out a ministry of miracle-working and exorcisms. But the supreme confirmation of his claim was his resurrection from the dead. If Jesus did rise from the dead, then it would seem that we have a divine miracle on our hands and, thus, evidence for the existence of God.

Now in discussing this issue, I'm not going to treat the New Testament as an inspired and therefore inerrant book, but simply as a collection of ordinary Greek documents coming down to us from the first century. I'm not interested, therefore, in defending the infallibility of the gospels. Rather I'm interested in determining, first, what facts concerning the fate of Jesus of Nazareth can be credibly established on the basis of the evidence and, second, what is the best explanation of those facts.

So let's look at that first question. There are at least four facts about the fate of the historical Jesus that are widely accepted by New Testament historians today. It's worth emphasizing that I'm not talking just about conservative scholars, but about the broad mainstream of New Testament scholarship.

FACT #1: *After his crucifixion Jesus was buried by Joseph of Arimathea in a tomb.*

This fact is highly significant because it means that the location of Jesus' tomb was known to Jew and Christian alike in Jerusalem. New Testament researchers have established the fact of Jesus' honorable burial on the basis of evidence such as the following:

1. Jesus' burial is attested in the very old information (ca. < AD 36), which was handed on by Paul in his first letter to the church in Corinth, Greece.

2. The burial story is independently attested in the very old source material used by Mark in writing his gospel.

3. Given the understandable hostility in the early Christian movement toward the Jewish leaders, Joseph of Arimathea, as a member of the Jewish high court that condemned Jesus, is unlikely to be a Christian invention.

4. The burial story is simple and lacks any signs of legendary development.

5. No other competing burial story exists.

For these and other reasons, the majority of New Testament critics concur that Jesus was in fact buried by Joseph of Arimathea in a tomb. According to the late John A. T. Robinson of Cambridge University, the burial of Jesus in the tomb is "one of the earliest and best-attested facts about Jesus."

FACT #2: *On the Sunday after the crucifixion, Jesus' tomb was found empty by a group of his women followers.*

Among the reasons that have led most scholars to this conclusion are the following:

1. In stating that Jesus "was buried and he was raised on the third day," the old information transmitted by Paul in I Cor. 15.3–5 implies the empty tomb.

2. The empty tomb story is also multiply and independently attested in Mark, Matthew, and John's source material, some of which is very early.

3. The empty tomb story as related in Mark, our earliest account, is simple and lacks signs of legendary embellishment.

4. Given that the testimony of women was regarded as so unreliable that they were not even permitted to serve as witnesses in a Jewish court of law, the fact

that it is women, rather than men, who are the chief witnesses to the empty tomb is best explained by the historical facticity of the narrative in this regard.

5. The earliest known Jewish response to the proclamation of Jesus' resurrection, namely, "The disciples came and stole away his body" (Matt. 28:13–15), was itself an attempt to explain why the body was missing and thus presupposes the empty tomb.

One could go on, but I think enough has been said to indicate why, in the words of Jacob Kremer, an Austrian specialist on the resurrection, "By far most exegetes hold firmly to the reliability of the biblical statements concerning the empty tomb."

FACT #3: *On multiple occasions and under various circumstances, different individuals and groups of people experienced appearances of Jesus alive from the dead.*

This is a fact that is virtually universally acknowledged among New Testament scholars, for the following reasons:

1. Given its early date, as well as Paul's personal acquaintance with the people involved, the list of eyewitnesses to Jesus' resurrection appearances, quoted by Paul in I Cor. 15.5–8, guarantees that such appearances occurred.

2. The appearance narratives in the gospels provide multiple, independent attestation of the appearances.

Even the skeptical German New Testament critic Gerd Lüdemann therefore concludes, "It may be taken as historically certain that Peter and the disciples had experiences after Jesus' death in which Jesus appeared to them as the risen Christ."

Finally, FACT #4: *The original disciples suddenly and sincerely came to believe that Jesus was risen from the dead despite their having every predisposition to the contrary.*

Think of the situation the disciples faced following Jesus' crucifixion:

1. Their leader was dead, and Jewish Messianic expectations included no idea of a Messiah who, instead of triumphing over Israel's enemies, would be shamefully executed by them as a criminal.

2. According to Old Testament law, Jesus' execution exposed him as a heretic, a man literally accursed by God.

3. Jewish beliefs about the afterlife precluded anyone's rising from the dead to glory and immortality before the general resurrection of the dead at the end of the world.

Nevertheless, the original disciples suddenly came to believe so strongly that God had raised Jesus from the dead that they were willing to die for the truth of that belief. Luke Johnson, a New Testament scholar at Emory University, states, "Some sort of powerful, transformative experience is required to generate the sort of movement earliest Christianity was." N. T. Wright, an eminent British scholar, concludes, "That is why, as a historian, I cannot explain the rise of early Christianity unless Jesus rose again, leaving an empty tomb behind him."

In summary, then, there are four facts concerning the fate of Jesus of Nazareth that are agreed upon by the majority of scholars who have written on this subject: Jesus' honorable burial by Joseph of Arimathea, the discovery of his empty tomb, his post-mortem appearances, and the origin of the disciples' belief in his resurrection.

But that leads to our second concern: what is the best explanation of these facts? I think that the best explanation in this case is the one that was given by the eyewitnesses: God raised Jesus from the dead. In his book *Justifying Historical Descriptions,* historian C. B. McCullagh lists six tests that historians use in determining which is the best explanation for a given body of historical facts. The hypothesis "God raised Jesus from the dead" passes all these tests.

1. It has great *explanatory scope.* It explains why the tomb was found empty, why the disciples saw post-mortem appearances of Jesus, and why the Christian faith came into being.

2. It has great *explanatory power.* It explains why the body of Jesus was gone, why people repeatedly saw Jesus alive despite his earlier public execution, and so forth.

3. It is *plausible.* Given the historical context of Jesus' own unparalleled life and claims, the resurrection makes sense as the divine confirmation of those radical claims.

4. It is *not ad hoc* or *contrived.* It requires only one additional hypothesis: that God exists.

5. It is *in accord with accepted beliefs.* The hypothesis "God raised Jesus from the dead" does not in any way conflict with the accepted belief that people don't rise *naturally* from the dead. The Christian accepts *that* belief as wholeheartedly as he accepts the hypothesis that God raised Jesus from the dead.

6. It *far outstrips any of its rival theories* in meeting conditions 1–5. Down through history, various alternative explanations of the facts have been offered; for example, the conspiracy theory, the apparent death theory, the hallucination theory, and so forth. Such hypotheses have been almost universally rejected by contemporary scholarship. No naturalistic hypothesis has, in fact, attracted a great number of scholars. Thus, the best explanation of the established facts seems to be that God raised Jesus from the dead.

Thus, it seems to me that we have a good inductive argument for the existence of God based on the evidence for the resurrection of Jesus. It may be summarized as follows:

1. There are four established facts concerning the fate of Jesus of Nazareth: his honorable burial by Joseph of Arimathea, the discovery of his empty tomb, his post-mortem appearances, and the origin of his disciples' belief in his resurrection.

2. The hypothesis "God raised Jesus from the dead" is the best explanation of these facts.

3. The hypothesis "God raised Jesus from the dead" entails that God exists.

4. Therefore God exists. . . .

## 2. MIRACLES

### Walter Sinnott-Armstrong

Craig's other arguments do not refer to morality. The next one refers to the resurrection of Jesus. If that resurrection occurred, it would be a miracle.

Some atheists try to prove the impossibility of miracles. One attempt defines a miracle as a violation of a law of nature and defines a law of nature as a generalization without any exception. Then, if Jesus walked on water, this act would be an exception to generalizations about buoyancy that we took to be laws of nature, so those generalizations would not really be laws of nature, and Jesus' walk on water would not really be a miracle. This is a cheap verbal trick. If anyone walks on water without any natural explanation, that is a miracle in my book. Such miracles are *logically possible*. I agree with Craig about this.

It is still a big step to the claim that we have *adequate evidence* to believe in any miracle. When people declare that a miracle occurred, we need to look at the evidence for and against their claims. The evidence *against* the miracle includes all of the evidence for the generalization that the miracle violates. Our common generalizations about buoyancy are supported by copious observations, plentiful testimony, numerous experiments, abundant explanations, and ample theories. To outweigh so much evidence, one would need a very strong reason to believe in any miracle.

I doubt that this burden is carried for any alleged miracle, but here I will focus on Craig's claims about the resurrection of Jesus. What is Craig's evidence for this miracle? First, "Jesus' tomb was found empty by a group of his women followers." Unfortunately, our records come from years later. Craig describes the Gospels as "very early" and cites a date "ca. < AD 36." The scholars whom I consulted suggested that dates > AD 50 are more likely. In any case, Craig's own dates imply years after Jesus' death, which is plenty of time for distortions to spread. The supposed witnesses were surely prompted often in the intervening years. They were likely subjected to tremendous social pressures. Their emotions undoubtedly ran high. They probably had neither the training nor the opportunity nor the inclination to do a careful, impartial investigation. Most people at that time were gullible, as shown by the plethora of cults. These are exactly the kinds of factors that psychologists have found to distort memory and eyewitness testimony in many cases. We would and should heavily discount witnesses like these in legal trials.

To defend his sources, Craig suggests that Jesus' followers had no expectation that Jesus would rise from the dead. Witnesses *with* expectations are less reliable, but this does not show that witnesses *without* expectations *are* reliable. Moreover, we can't know that Craig's supposed witnesses had no expectations. Narratives like the story of Jesus' resurrection were common in that area around that time. One similar tale was about Mithras, a Persian warrior-god whose cults flourished just before the time of Jesus. Early Christians associated the two, and Roman soldiers referred to Mithras as "the Soldier's Christ." In addition, Jesus was supposed to have raised Lazarus from the dead, so it would have been natural to ask, "If Jesus could raise Lazarus, why couldn't God raise Jesus?" Finally, even if the story of resurrection was new, "new" does not imply "true." So it is hardly clear that the tomb was empty.

Suppose it was empty. There are still (at least!) two possibilities: (1) Jesus' body disappeared and rose into heaven, or (2) someone took the body without being caught. Which is more likely? The answer is obvious, because lots of items are taken without the thief being caught. In this case, the women were supposed to have found the door open and a person inside. (Mark 16:4–5) If so, many people had motive and opportunity to move the body. On the other hand, we have tons of evidence that bodies do not disappear and rise into heaven. Craig claims that Jesus' resurrection is *"plausible," "in accord with accepted beliefs,"* and *"not ad hoc."* To the contrary, nothing could be more *ad hoc* than a unique exception to otherwise accepted physical principles. Just imagine that I return from a hard day at the office to find that my favorite ice cream, which I had saved for tonight, is gone from my refrigerator. My wife and kids all deny that they took it. They are honest. Still, I wouldn't seriously consider the possibility that my ice cream ascended into heaven and sits at the right hand of Ben and Jerry. Analogously, nobody would think that about Jesus' body if they did not already believe in God. Any reasonable person who looks at the evidence without prejudice would conclude that either the tomb was not empty or someone took the body, even if we don't know which.

Similar considerations apply to Craig's claim, "On multiple occasions and under various circumstances, different individuals and groups of people experienced appearances of Jesus alive from the dead." Craig describes these reports as "independent," but how can he possibly know that some of his supposed witnesses did not hear stories about the others? There were years for these stories to spread. Once one person claimed to see Jesus, it would naturally have become a badge of honor for anyone to make similar claims. In these circumstances, the multiplication of proclamations hardly "guarantees" anything. I cannot explain every one of these reports, because there is so little evidence and so much uncertainty about the circumstances. Nonetheless, these gaps in our knowledge are no reason to give up well-established physics on the basis of decades-old reports by self-interested parties who faced social pressures and promptings with predispositions to believe. Craig's burden of proof cannot be carried by such feeble testimony.

## READING COMPREHENSION QUESTIONS

1.  Craig undertakes two tasks in his part of the exchange: to present facts about what happened to Jesus of Nazareth, and then to present an inductive argument[1] for the existence of God, based on those facts. Consider first the four "facts" Craig cites. Explain (a) why Craig thinks these count as facts, and (b) why Sinnott-Armstrong is skeptical about them. (Make sure to stick to a discussion of the so-called facts themselves, not the *use* Craig makes of them).

2.  The second task Craig undertakes is to present his inductive argument. Very briefly, it is that the best explanation for the four facts is that God raised Jesus

---

[1]See the Introduction to this volume for a discussion of this term.

from the dead and thus God exists. In your own words, explain how Sinnott-Armstrong responds to this specific argument.

3.  Craig argues that God's existing is the best explanation for the four facts, while Sinnott-Armstrong argues that it's not the best explanation. Explain whose position *you* believe is more plausible, and why.

# 24

# The Wager

BLAISE PASCAL

*Blaise Pascal (1623–1662) was a famous French mathematician and contemporary of René Descartes. In 1650 he suddenly abandoned all of his mathematical research to focus on religious studies, and to "contemplate the greatness and the misery of man," as he put it. In this selection from* Pensées, *his only real philosophical work, Pascal offers his famous wager: either God exists or He doesn't, and I may believe He exists or not believe. Pascal then works out the expected payoffs if I believe that God exists, and he comes to what he thinks is the obvious conclusion: that it would crazy not to believe, given the prospect of an infinite reward in heaven.*

We know that there is an infinite, and are ignorant, of its nature. As we know it to be false that numbers are finite, it is therefore true that there is an infinity in number. But we do not know what it is. It is false that it is even, it is false that it is odd; for the addition of a unit can make no change in its nature. But it is a number, and every number is odd or even (this is certainly true of every finite number). So we may well know that there is a God without knowing what He is. Is there not one substantial truth, seeing there are so many things which are not the truth itself?

We know then the existence and nature of the finite, because we also are finite and have extension. We know the existence of the infinite, and are ignorant of its nature, because it has extension like us, but not limits like us. But we know neither the existence nor the nature of God, because He has neither extension nor limits.

But by faith we know His existence; in glory we shall know His nature. Now, I have already shown that we may well know the existence of a thing, without knowing its nature.

SOURCE: From Blaise Pascal *Pensées*, trans. W. F. Trotter. This edition is in the public domain.

Let us now speak according to natural lights.

If there is a God, He is infinitely incomprehensible, since, having neither parts nor limits, He has no affinity to us. We are then incapable of knowing either what He is or if He is. This being so, who will dare to undertake the decision of the question? Not we, who have no affinity to Him.

Who then will blame Christians for not being able to give a reason for their belief, since they profess a religion for which they cannot give a reason? They declare, in expounding it to the world, that it is a foolishness, *stultitiam;* and then you complain that they do not prove it! If they proved it, they would not keep their word; it is in lacking proofs, that they are not lacking in sense. "Yes, but although this excuses those who offer it as such, and takes away from them the blame of putting it forward without reason, it does not excuse those who receive it." Let us then examine this point, and say, "God is, or He is not." But to which side shall we incline? Reason can decide nothing here. There is an infinite chaos which separated us. A game is being played at the extremity of this infinite distance where heads or tails will turn up. What will you wager? According to reason, you can do neither the one thing nor the other; according to reason, you can defend neither of the propositions.

Do not then reprove for error those who have made a choice; for you know nothing about it. "No, but I blame them for having made, not this choice, but a choice; for again both he who chooses heads and he who chooses tails are equally at fault, they are both in the wrong. The true course is not to wager at all."

Yes; but you must wager. It is not optional. You are embarked. Which will you choose then? Let us see. Since you must choose, let us see which interests you least. You have two things to lose, the true and the good; and two things to stake, your reason and your will, your knowledge and your happiness; and your nature has two things to shun, error and misery. Your reason is no more shocked in choosing one rather than the other, since you must of necessity choose. This is one point settled. But your happiness? Let us weigh the gain and the loss in wagering that God is. Let us estimate these two chances. If you gain, you gain all; if you lose, you lose nothing. Wager, then, without hesitation that He is— "That is very fine. Yes, I must wager; but I may perhaps wager too much."— Let us see. Since there is an equal risk of gain and of loss, if you had only to gain two lives, instead of one, you might still wager. But if there were three lives to gain, you would have to play (since you are under the necessity of playing), and you would be imprudent, when you are forced to play, not to chance your life to gain three at a game where there is an equal risk of loss and gain. But there is an eternity of life and happiness. And this being so, if there were an infinity of chances, of which one only would be for you, you would still be right in wagering one to win two, and you would not stupidly, being obliged to play, by refusing to stake one life against three at a game in which out of an infinity of chances there is one for you, if there were an infinity of an infinitely happy life to gain. But there is here an infinity of an infinitely happy life to gain, a chance of gain against a finite number of chances of loss, and what you stake is finite. It is all divided; wherever the infinite is and there is not an infinity of chances of loss against that of gain, there is no time to hesitate, you must give all. And thus, when one is forced to play, he must renounce reason to preserve his life, rather than risk it for infinite gain, as likely to happen as the loss of nothingness.

For it is no use to say it is uncertain if we will gain, and it is certain that we risk, and that the infinite distance between the *certainty* of what is staked and the *uncertainty* of what will be gained, equals the finite good which is certainly staked against the uncertain infinite. It is not so, as every player stakes a certainty to gain an uncertainty, and yet he stakes a finite certainty to gain a finite uncertainty, without transgressing against reason. There is not an infinite distance between the certainty staked and the uncertainty of the gain; that is untrue. In truth, there is an infinity between the certainty of gain and the certainty of loss. But the uncertainty of the gain is proportioned to the certainty of the stake according to the proportion of the chances of gain and loss. Hence it comes that, if there are as many risks on one side as on the other, the course is to play even; and then the certainty of the stake is equal to the uncertainty of the gain, so far is it from fact that there is an infinite distance between them. And so our proposition is of infinite force, when there is the finite to stake in a game where there are equal risks of gain and of loss, and the infinite to gain. This is demonstrable; and if men are capable of any truths, this is one.

"I confess it, I admit it. But, still, is there no means of seeing the faces of the cards?"—Yes, Scripture and the rest, etc. "Yes, but I have my hands tied and my mouth closed; I am forced to wager, and am not free. I am not released, and am so made that I cannot believe. What, then, would you have me do?"

True. But at least learn your inability to believe, since reason brings you to this, and yet you cannot believe. Endeavour then to convince yourself, not by increase of proofs of God, but by the abatement of your passions. You would like to attain faith, and do not know the way; you would like to cure yourself of unbelief, and ask the remedy for it. Learn of those who have been bound like you, and who now stake all their possessions. These are people who know the way which you would follow, and who are cured of an ill of which you would be cured. Follow the way by which they began; by acting as if they believed, taking the holy water, having masses said, etc. Even this will naturally make you believe, and deaden your acuteness.—"But this is what I am afraid of."—And why? What have you to lose?

But to show you that this leads you there, it is this which will lessen the passions, which are your stumbling-blocks.

*The end of this discourse.*—Now, what harm will befall you in taking this side? You will be faithful, honest, humble, grateful, generous, a sincere friend, truthful. Certainly you will not have those poisonous pleasures, glory and luxury; but will you not have others? I will tell you that you will thereby gain in this life, and that, at each step you take on this road, you will see so great certainty of gain, so much nothingness in what you risk, that you will at last recognise that you have wagered for something certain and infinite, for which you have given nothing.

"Ah! This discourse transports me, charms me," etc.

If this discourse pleases you and seems impressive, know that it is made by a man who has knelt, both before and after it, in prayer to that Being, infinite and without parts, before whom he lays all he has, for you also to lay before Him all you have for your own good and for His glory, that so strength may be given to lowliness.

## READING COMPREHENSION QUESTIONS

1.  Pascal begins his discussion with an important background argument for why we are "incapable of knowing either what [God] is or if He is." That is, we're incapable of knowing either what God would be like or whether or not God exists. In fact, this is the motivation for the wager itself: if we can't be sure of anything either way, then it's a safer bet to believe that God exists. But what exactly is Pascal's argument for this background motivational claim? Do you agree? Why or why not?

2.  Suppose one bets on a prize fight. There are several factors one needs to figure out: (a) the amount that one will bet; (b) what exactly one will be betting on; (c) the payoff if one wins or loses the bet; and (d) what the odds are of one's winning or losing the bet. Identify what Pascal says about each of these factors in his own wager regarding belief in God.

3.  In the later part of the article, Pascal seems to be having a conversation with a kind of skeptic, whose remarks are presented in quotation marks. One worry about the wager that this skeptic raises is the possibility that he (the skeptic) is made so that he cannot believe. That is, even if the wager provides him strong reason to abandon his atheism and start believing that God exists, he can't just start believing *at will*. Indeed, suppose you'd be given $1 million to start believing—really believing—in Santa Claus again. This might seem to be an impossible task. Nevertheless, Pascal has a reply to this worry. What exactly is his reply, and how might he similarly counsel you to start believing in Santa Claus again (if you were to get a big payoff for doing so)?

# 25

# God

SIMON BLACKBURN

*Simon Blackburn (born 1944) is a professor of philosophy at Cambridge University. In this selection from* Think, *his highly accessible introduction to philosophy, Blackburn discusses the arguments for belief in God, presented here from Anselm, Aquinas, Paley, and Pascal, and finds them all wanting. As you read, ask yourself whether or not Blackburn is being fair to these authors' arguments, and whether or not his objections to them succeed.*

SOURCE: From Simon Blackburn, *Think*. Copyright © 1999 by Simon Blackburn. Used by permission from Oxford University Press.

## ANSELM'S ARGUMENT: DREAMBOATS AND TURKEYS

There is a story of a guru who attracted a large audience to a stadium with the promise of a definitive proof of the existence of God. When all were assembled, he dramatically revealed the *Oxford English Dictionary,* and showed that it contained the word "God." Since the word was there, with a definition, there had to be something answering to it. I do not know how the audience felt, or whether any of them managed to reflect that the dictionary also mentions Santa Claus and fairies, although admittedly qualifying them as mythical or imaginary. But it is interesting to think how there can be meaningful words with nothing answering to them.

The reason is that you can define a concept, but it is quite another question whether anything answers to the concept you define. You can define what you want from a partner, if you are minded to advertise in the dating columns:

> Thoughtful person in search of fun-loving, vegetarian, banjo-playing soccer fan, must be non-smoker.

This defines your dream partner—let us call him or her Dream-boat. But there may unfortunately not be any fun-loving, vegetarian, non-smoking, banjo-playing soccer fans. You can decide what you want to put into the description, but the world decides whether anybody meets it. Dreamboat may not exist.

The description is perfectly intelligible. It defines a condition that in principle someone could meet. It is just that as it happens, nobody does meet it. One way of putting this is to say that the terms have a *sense,* but no *reference.* You know what you mean, but you don't know whether there is anything that answers to it. You cannot argue from the sense to the reference, because whether there is a reference is a question of how the world is, not to be settled in the study, or by consulting a dictionary.

It might irk you to realize that there might be nobody to answer to your description. But you might hit on a plan to get round the problem. Why not add a postscript, specifying that the dream person should exist? So now you advertise:

> Thoughtful person in search of fun-loving, vegetarian, etc. *who exists.*

And now, you might think to yourself, I have solved my problem by definition.

Well, it is certainly true that nobody is going to call you to explain that they meet all the conditions except the last one. But then, anybody who called you after the original advertisement also existed: 'I call, therefore I am' is just as good an inference as "I think, therefore I am." And your adding the clause cannot have altered one jot the chance of someone meeting the other conditions—the ones you started with. So you have wasted your money on the last two words. Putting "who exists" is not further specifying the dream partner, and nor is it improving your chances that he or she in fact exists. Philosophers sometimes express this by saying that "existence is not a predicate," meaning that adding "and exists" is not like adding "and likes Guinness." You are in charge of sense: you can add what you like to the job description. But the world is in charge of reference: it says if anything exists meeting your conditions.

With this properly understood, we can now turn to the arguments. . . . Anselm defines God as a being "than which nothing greater can be conceived."

And he addresses himself to "the fool" (from Psalm 14) who has said in his heart that there is no God:

> *But when this same fool hears me say "something than which nothing greater can be thought," he surely understands what he hears, and what he understands exists in his understanding; even if he does not understand that it exists (in reality). . . . So even the fool must admit that something than which nothing greater can be thought exists at least in his understanding, since he understands this when he hears it, and whatever is understood, exists in the understanding. And surely that than which a greater cannot be thought cannot exist only in the understanding. For if it exists only in the understanding, it can be thought to exist in reality as well, which is greater. . . . [T]herefore, there is no doubt that something than which a greater cannot be thought exists both in the understanding and in reality.*

The notable thing about this argument is that it is purely a priori. It purports to prove God's existence simply from considering the concept or definition of God. It is like the specimen proof in mathematics, that deduces from the concept of a circle that chords dropped from a point to opposite ends of a diameter meet at right angles. The argument requires no empirical premises—no measuring, or results from experience.

Anselm's argument could be presented in two stages:

> The concept of God is understood. Whatever is understood, exists in the understanding. *So* God exists in the understanding.

And then:

> *Suppose* God only exists in the understanding, and not in reality. Then a greater being than God can be conceived: one that exists in reality. *But* God is defined as that than which nothing greater can be conceived. *So* no greater being can be conceived, by definition. But now we have a contradiction. *So* our original supposition was false.

This is an argument form . . . called *reductio ad absurdum*. Anselm has us make the original atheistic assumption, but only en route to showing that it is false, for it implies a contradiction. . . .

A monk named Gaunilo attacked the argument in Anselm's own time. Gaunilo pointed out that if the argument were good, it could be used to prove all sorts of conclusions that are too good to be true: for instance, that there exists a perfect island than which none greater can be conceived. Staying with Dreamboat, we can work it through like this. Suppose you carefully added to Dreamboat's specifications that he or she must be not only a great lover, but also as great a lover as can be imagined. Then you can argue in a parallel fashion:

> The concept of Dreamboat is understood. Whatever is understood, exists in the understanding. *So* Dreamboat exists in the understanding.

And then:

> *Suppose* Dreamboat only exists in the understanding, and not in reality. Then a greater lover than Dreamboat can be conceived: one that exists in reality. *But* Dreamboat is defined as that lover than which no greater

can be conceived. *So no greater lover than* Dreamboat can be conceived, by definition. But now we have a contradiction. *So* our original supposition was false.

Dreamboat exists in reality. Wonderful! But do not rejoice too quickly. You might also unfortunately prove by the same means that you have as dangerous a rival as can be imagined, for Dreamboat's affections. The crucial premise will be that real rivals are more dangerous than merely imagined ones—which they surely are. And the ontological argument looks set to prove the existence of the Devil—defined as that than which nothing worse can be conceived. For if something is to be that than which nothing worse can be conceived, it had better not exist only in the imagination, for then something worse can be conceived, namely a being that is that bad but also really exists (notice that existence in a devil is an *imperfection*: it makes him worse).

Most philosophers have recognized there is something fishy about the ontological argument—as fishy as trying to make sure that Dreamboat exists by writing the right job description. But they have not always agreed on just what the mistake must be. Part of the problem is the move of treating "existence as a predicate." . . . But it is hard to be sure that this move introduces the fatal flaw.

In my own view, the crucial problem lies in an ambiguity lurking in the comparison of "reality" and "conception." In the argument, things "in reality" are compared with things "in conception" (i.e. according to a definition, or in imagination or dreams), for such properties as greatness, or perfection. This sounds simple, as if we are comparing things in two different geographical regions, and we know that those in one region are greater or lesser than those in the other. It would be like asking whether chickens in Germany are heavier than chickens in France. But in fact it is not at all like that. Consider this sentence:

Real turkeys are heavier than imagined turkeys.

There seems to be a sense in which it is true. In that sense, imagined turkeys weigh nothing (after all, you cannot make even a small meal from one). But there is also a sense in which it is false, because you can imagine a turkey heavier than any real one—a five-hundred-pound turkey the size of a small barn, for example. In the ontological argument, "God" in imagination is compared with God in reality, like the imagined turkey compared to the real turkey, and found to weigh less. In the argument above, Dreamboat in reality is compared to imagined Dreamboat, and thought to be better: for surely even quite mediocre real lovers are greater lovers than imaginary ones! And this is supposed to contradict the definition. But that kind of comparison does not in fact show *anything* contradicting the definition.

It is as if a schoolteacher required you to imagine a turkey heavier than any actual turkey. You do so: you imagine a five-hundred-pound turkey. But the teacher then complains that since imagined turkeys always weigh less than real turkeys, you have failed to imagine what she asked for. Your imagined turkey weighs nothing (you can't eat it) and so you have "contradicted the definition" and you get no marks. Here you would be right to feel aggrieved. It is not you who went wrong, but the teacher.

This suggests that we must not think of "imagined turkeys" or "turkeys in the understanding" as kinds of turkey that can, in principle, be weighed against real ones but are always found to weigh less. Yet the ontological argument requires just this kind of comparison. It is here that it fails. For even if God only exists in imagination, like Dreamboat or the five-hundred-pound turkey, it does not follow that a greater being can be described or imagined. After all, the description had the superlatives put into it. But unhappily for Anselm's proof, that does not settle the question whether anything answers to it.


## ELEPHANTS AND TORTOISES

The ontological argument has always seemed fishy. St Thomas Aquinas (c. 1225–74), the greatest medieval theologian and philosopher, did not accept it. He preferred to argue that God is needed in order to *explain* the world or cosmos as we apprehend it. This argument, the *cosmological* argument, has a much stronger appeal to the imagination. There are various versions of it. They all require identifying a way in which things in the physical universe, things as we know them by touch and sight and the other senses, are *dependent* beings. And it is then argued that dependent beings eventually presuppose a being that is *not* itself dependent upon anything, as their explanation. One version of this, and perhaps the easiest to understand, is the *first cause* argument. Here is the character Demea, from Hume's *Dialogues Concerning Natural Religion* (these *Dialogues,* first published a year after Hume's death in 1776, are the classic philosophical analysis of traditional theological arguments, and I shall quote from them extensively in what follows):

> *Whatever exists must have a cause or reason of its existence, it being absolutely impossible for any thing to produce itself or be the cause of its own existence. In mounting up, therefore, from effects to causes, we must either go on in tracing an infinite succession, without any ultimate cause at all, or must at last have recourse to some ultimate cause, that is* necessarily *existent: Now, that the first supposition is absurd, may be thus proved. In the infinite chain or succession of causes and effects, each single effect is determined to exist by the power and efficacy of that cause which immediately preceded; but the whole eternal chain or succession, taken together, is not determined or caused by any thing: And yet it is evident that it requires a cause or reason, as much as any particular object which begins to exist in time. The question is still reasonable why this particular succession of causes existed from eternity, and not any other succession, or no succession at all. If there be no necessarily existent being, any supposition which can be formed is equally possible; nor is there any more absurdity in nothing's having existed from eternity, than there is in that succession of causes which constitutes the universe. What was it, then, which determined something to exist rather than nothing, and bestowed being on a particular possibility, exclusive of the rest?* External causes, *there are supposed to be* none. Chance *is a word without a meaning. Was it nothing? But that can never produce anything. We must, therefore, have recourse to a necessarily existent Being, who carries the reason of his existence in himself; and who cannot be supposed not to exist, without an express contradiction. There is, consequently, such a Being— that is, there is a Deity.*

The argument is powerfully presented, but is it valid?

Russell is supposed to have remarked that the first cause argument was bad, but uniquely, awfully bad, in that the conclusion not only failed to follow from the premises, but also actually contradicted them. His idea was that the argument starts off from the premise "everything has a [distinct, previous] cause," but ends with the conclusion that there must be something that has *no* distinct, previous cause, but "carries the *reason* of his existence in himself." Then the conclusion denies what the premise asserts.

Russell's dismissal is a little glib. For the point of the argument, from the theological perspective, is that although everything material or physical has a distinct previous cause, this very fact drives us to postulate something else, that has none. In the theological jargon, this would be a thing that is "necessary" or "causa sui;" a thing that is its own cause. And since this is not true of the ordinary things that surround us, we need to postulate something extraordinary, a Deity, as the bearer of this extraordinary self-sufficiency.

In Hume's *Dialogues* the problem with this is quickly exposed.

*It is pretended that the Deity is a necessarily existent being; and this necessity of his existence is attempted to be explained by asserting, that if we knew his whole essence or nature, we should perceive it to be as impossible for him not to exist, as for twice two not to be four. But it is evident that this can never happen, while our faculties remain the same as at present. It will still be possible for us, at any time, to conceive the nonexistence of what we formerly conceived to exist; nor can the mind ever lie under a necessity of supposing any object to remain always in being; in the same manner as we lie under a necessity of always conceiving twice two to be four. The words, therefore, "necessary existence," have no meaning; or, which is the same thing, none that is consistent.*

Hume's spokesman at this point, the character called Cleanthes, goes on to say that for all we know, the material world or universe as a whole itself might be the necessarily existent being, in spite of the way in which parts of it depend upon other parts. For it must be "unknown, inconceivable qualities" that make anything a "necessary existent." And for all we know, such unknown inconceivable qualities may attach to the ordinary physical universe, rather [than] to any immaterial thing or person or deity lying behind it.

It is important to remember here that as far as everyday experience goes, minds are just as much in need of explanation, just as much dependent beings, as physical objects. Postulating a mind that is somehow immune from dependency on anything else whatsoever is jumping away from experience just as violently as postulating a physical thing that is so.

The first cause argument speaks to worries that are natural and indeed according to some philosophers, notably Kant, inevitable. When we think back to the "big bang" our next question is why that event, then? We are not happy with the answer "no reason," because we are not happy with events "just happening:" the drive to explanation grips us. So we postulate something else, another cause lying behind this one. But the drive now threatens to go on forever. If we have cited God at this point, we either have to ask what caused God, or cut off the regress by arbitrary fiat. But if we exercise an arbitrary right to stop the regress at that point, we might as well have stopped it with the physical cosmos. In other words, we are in the position of the Indian philosopher, who asked what the world rested on replied an elephant, and asked what the elephant rested on, replied "a tortoise," and asked what the tortoise rested on, begged to change the subject.

There are versions of the cosmological argument that are not concerned with the first cause, in time. Rather, they consider the ongoing order of the universe: the uniformity of nature. It can seem an amazing fact that laws of nature keep on holding, that the frame of nature does not fall apart. One can think that these facts must be "dependent" and require a necessary sustaining cause (like Atlas propping up the world). But once more, there is either a regress, or a simple fiat that something has "unknown inconceivable properties" that make it self-sufficient. This would be something whose ongoing uniformity requires no explanation outside itself. And that might as well be the world as a whole as anything else. . . .

## THE WISE ARCHITECT

The same Cleanthes who is given the job of refuting the cosmological argument is the spokesman for a different attempt to prove the existence of a deity: the argument to *design*—the view that heaven and earth declare the glory of the creator. This argument was the showpiece of eighteenth-century theology, and still exerts a powerful influence. I shall follow the classic discussion given in Hume's *Dialogues*. Cleanthes presents the argument:

> Look round the world: Contemplate the whole and every part of it: You will find it to be nothing but one great machine, subdivided into an infinite number of lesser machines, which again admit of subdivisions to a degree beyond what human senses and faculties can trace and explain. All these various machines, and even their most minute parts, are adjusted to each other with an accuracy which ravishes into admiration all men who have ever contemplated them. The curious adapting of means to ends, throughout all nature, resembles exactly, though it much exceeds, the productions of human contrivance; of human design, thought, wisdom, and intelligence. Since, therefore, the effects resemble each other, we are led to infer, by all the rules of analogy, that the causes also resemble; and that the Author of Nature is somewhat similar to the mind of man, though possessed of much larger faculties, proportioned to the grandeur of the work which he has executed. By this argument a posteriori, and by this argument alone, do we prove at once the existence of a Deity, and his similarity to human mind and intelligence.

There are two important points about this argument. First, it is an argument by *analogy*. The world resembles the objects of human design. Therefore, just as it would be reasonable, coming across a watch, to postulate a human designer, so it is reasonable, coming across the entire frame of nature, to postulate a godly designer. Second, the argument is "a posteriori." That is, it argues from experience, or from what we know of the world as we find it. It is here that the evidence for design shines out.

After Darwinism had begun to offer a natural explanation of the way in which complex biological systems become adjusted to one another, the argument began to lose some of its lustre. But in fact Hume (and Kant) makes the right points without relying on any alternative explanation of such things as biological adaptation. And that is just as well, for the argument is not essentially about biology, which give us just one kind of instance of the adjustments of nature. Cosmology affords others. (For instance, on one current authoritative estimate, the chances of the various cosmological constants being adjusted so that organized life became possible anywhere in the universe, are 1 in 10 to the $10^{125}$—an unimaginable number—against. So perhaps it took a wise architect to adjust them.)

So how does Hume, in the persona of Philo, his spokesman in the *Dialogues,* attempt to rebut the argument to a designer? Philo points out that the argument takes one of the operations we encounter in nature, the operation of thought, as a "rule for the whole."

> *But, allowing that we were to take the* operations *of one part of nature upon another for the foundation of our judgment concerning the* origin *of the whole (which never can be admitted), yet why select so minute, so weak, so bounded a principle as the reason and design of animals is found to be upon this planet? What peculiar privilege has this little agitation of the brain which we call "thought," that we must thus make it the model of the whole universe? Our partiality in our own favour does indeed present it on all occasions; but sound philosophy ought carefully to guard against so natural an illusion.*

Argument by analogy requires certain condition in order to be reliable. First, the bases for the analogy should be extremely similar. Second, we should have experience covering the likely explanations. That is, we should know as much as possible about the kind of cause that produces this kind of effect. For example, a hole in a tree is quite similar to a hole in a human body. But to suppose "by analogy" that since the human is apt to die from the one, the tree is apt to die from the other, is to stretch our reasonings too far. We need more observation, more refined understanding of the way things fall out before we would be wise to make any such inference. It is this second kind of experience that is sadly lacking in theology, for we have no inkling of the kinds of "thing" that cause entire physical universes to come into existence.

Furthermore, resemblances are quite easy to come by, and Philo has a great deal of fun inventing them. First, even if the universe resembles a clock, still more it resembles a vegetable:

> *The world plainly resembles more an animal or a vegetable, than it does a watch or a knitting-loom. Its cause, therefore, it is more probable, resembles the cause of the former. The cause of the former is generation or vegetation. The cause, therefore, of the world, we may infer to be something similar or analogous to generation or vegetation.*

Of course, a theist is going to urge that this gets us nowhere, for it would only take us back to another vegetable-like cause, whose origin we would then ask about. But the same is true if we are taken back to something resembling a mind. If Cleanthes, defending the argument, stops the regress there, he cannot blame Philo, opposing the argument, for stopping the regress with a vegetable. As Philo says:

> *If I rest my system of cosmogony on the former, preferably to the latter, it is at my choice. The matter seems entirely arbitrary. And when Cleanthes asks me what is the cause of my great vegetative or generative faculty, I am equally entitled to ask him the cause of his great reasoning principle. These questions we have agreed to*

*forbear on both sides; and it is chiefly his interest on the present occasion to stick to this agreement. Judging by our limited and imperfect experience, generation has some privileges above reason: for we see every day the latter arise from the former, never the former from the latter.*

This final point is quite devastating. Cleanthes prides himself on the "scientific" nature of his reasoning: an argument by analogy, from experience. But then experience shows us how fragile, and dependent upon other things, the existence of intelligence is. In our experience minds require brains which are fragile, dependent, late, and unusual arrivals in nature. "Generation," that is, animal or vegetable growth from previous animal or vegetable life, is by contrast common, and as far as we ever observe, necessary for the existence of intelligence. So, arguing from experience, it is much less likely that there is a self-sustaining mind than some other physical cause responsible for the whole show. . . .

## INFINI—RIEN

None of the metaphysical arguments we have considered do much to confirm the hypothesis that the universe is the creation of a traditional God. . . . Faced with these blanks, religious faith may try to find other arguments.

An interesting and ingenious one is due to the French mathematician and theologian, Blaise Pascal (1632–62), and is known as Pascal's wager. Unlike the arguments we have been considering, it is not presented as an argument for the *truth* of religious belief, but for the *utility* of believing in some version of a monotheistic, Judaic, Christian, or Islamic, God.

The argument is this. First, Pascal confesses to metaphysical ignorance:

*Let us now speak according to natural lights.*

*If there is a God, he is infinitely incomprehensible, since, having neither parts, nor limits, He has no affinity to us. We are therefore incapable of knowing either what He is, or if He is . . . Who then will blame the Christians for not being able to give a reason for their belief, since they profess a religion for which they cannot give a reason?*

It is not too clear why this excuse is offered for the Christians, as opposed to those of other faiths, as well as believers in fairies, ghosts, the living Elvis, and L. Ron Hubbard. Still, suppose the choice is between religious belief and a life of religious doubt or denial:

*You must wager. It is not optional. Which will you choose then? . . . Let us weigh the gain and the loss in wagering that God is. Let us estimate these two chances. If you gain, you gain all; if you lose, you lose nothing. Wager, then, without hesitation that He is.*

With great clarity Pascal realizes that this is rather an odd reason for choosing a belief. But he also says, perceptively, that

*your inability to believe is the result of your passions, since reason brings you to this, and yet you cannot believe . . . Learn of those who have been bound like you, and who now stake all their possessions . . . Follow the way by which they*

*began; by acting as if they believe, taking the holy water, having masses said, etc.*
*Even this will naturally make you believe, and deaden your acuteness.*

After you have "stupefied" yourself, you have become a believer. And then you will reap the rewards of belief: infinite rewards, if the kind of God you believe in exists. And if it does not? Well, you have lost very little, in comparison with infinity: only what Pascal calls the "poisonous pleasures" of things like playing golf on Sundays instead of going to mass.

The standard way to present this argument is in terms of a two-by-two box of the options:

|                          | God exists | God does not |
| ------------------------ | ---------- | ------------ |
| I believe in him         | +infinity! | 0            |
| I do not believe in him  | −infinity! | 0            |

The zeros on the right correspond to the thought that not much goes better or worse in this life, whether or not we believe. This life is of vanishingly little account compared to what is promised to believers. The plus-infinity figure corresponds to infinite bliss. The minus-infinity figure in the bottom left corresponds to the traditional jealous God, who sends to Hell those who do not believe in him, and of course encourages his followers to give them a hard time here, as well. But the minus-infinity figure can be soft-pedalled. Even if we put 0 in the bottom left-hand box, the wager looks good. It would be good even if God does not punish disbelief, because there is still that terrific payoff of "+infinity" cranking up the choice. In decision-theory terms, the option of belief "dominates," because it can win, and cannot lose. So—go for it!

Unfortunately the lethal problem with this argument is simple, once it is pointed out.

Pascal starts from a position of metaphysical ignorance. We just know nothing about the realm beyond experience. But the set-up of the wager presumes that we *do* know something. We are supposed to know the rewards and penalties attached to belief in a Christian God. This is a God who will be pleasured and reward us for our attendance at mass, and will either be indifferent or, in the minus-infinity option, seriously discombobulated by our non-attendance. But this is a case of false options. For consider that if we are really ignorant metaphysically, then it is at least as likely that the options pan out like this:

There is indeed a very powerful, very benevolent deity. He (or she or they or it) has determined as follows. The good human beings are those who follow the natural light of reason, which is given to them to control their beliefs. These good humans follow the arguments, and hence avoid religious convictions. These ones with the strength of mind not to believe in such things go to Heaven. The rest go to Hell.

This is not such a familiar deity as the traditional jealous God, who cares above all that people believe in him. (Why is God so jealous? Alas, might his jealousy be a projection of human sectarian ambitions and emotions? Either you are with us or against us! The French sceptic Voltaire said that God created mankind in his image, and mankind returned the compliment.) But the problem for Pascal is that if we really know nothing, then we do not know whether the scenario just described is any less likely than the Christian one he presented. In fact, for my money, a God that punishes belief is just as likely, and a lot more reasonable, than one that punishes disbelief.

And of course, we could add the Humean point that whilst for Pascal it was a simple two-way question of mass versus disbelief, in the wider world it is also a question of the Koran versus mass, or L. Ron Hubbard versus the Swami Maharishi, or the Aquarian Concepts Community Divine New Order Government versus the First Internet Church of All. The wager has to be silent about those choices.

## EMOTION AND THE WILL TO BELIEVE

We can now briefly consider the "fideistic" line, that although the arguments are negligible, nevertheless people at least have a right to believe what they wish, and there may be some merit in blind faith, like the merit attaching to the mother who refuses to acknowledge her son's guilt in spite of damning evidence.

Philosophers professionally wedded to truth and reason are not apt to commend this attitude. The faith that defies reason might be called a blessing by others who share it, but credulity and superstition by those who don't, and distressingly apt to bring in its wake fanaticism and zealotry. Chapter 2 of the famous essay *On Liberty* by John Stuart Mill (1806–73) talks memorably of the atmosphere of "mental slavery" that sets in with the absence of the questing critical intellect. Even the truth, Mill says, when held as a prejudice independent of and proof against argument, "is but one superstition the more, accidentally clinging to the words which enunciate a truth." One classic discussion (by the late-nineteenth century English writer W. K. Clifford) compares beliefs held on insufficient evidence to stolen pleasures. An apt quotation is from Samuel Taylor Coleridge:

> He who begins by loving Christianity better than truth, will proceed by loving his own sect or Church better than Christianity, and end in loving himself better than all.

But although these views are attractive, it is actually quite hard to show that the habit of blind faith is necessarily so very bad. If, having got to Hume's inert proposition, we then invest it with hopes, fears, resolutions, and the embellishments of our own particular creeds, where is the harm in that? Is not simple piety a Good Thing?

Some people certainly think random belief is a good thing. I have in front of me the advertisement for a company calling itself "your metaphysical superstore." It specializes in New Age books and music, flower essence, essential oils and aromatherapy, magnetic therapy, light balance therapy, astrology and numerology, tarot and rune cards readings, crystals and gemstones, and at the end, like a rueful note of something approaching sanity, healing herbs. Why should thinkers mock the simple pieties of the people?

Of course, there are simple pieties that do not get this general protection. If I check into the Mysterious Mist and come back convinced that God's message to me is to kill young women, or people with the wrong-coloured skins, or people who go to the wrong church, or people who have sex the wrong way, that is not so good. So we have to use our human values, our own sense of good or bad, or right or wrong, to distinguish an admirable return from the mountain from a lunatic one.

We seem to be irretrievably in the domain of ethics here. And it would be impossible in a brief compass to assess the harms and benefits of religious belief, just as it is hard (although not impossible) to estimate the benefit or damage done by belief in magnetic therapy or Feng Shui or whatever. It clearly fills some function, answering to some human desires and needs. Some of the needs may be a common part of the human lot: . . . the need for ceremonies at crucial parts of life, or the need for poetry, symbol, myth, and music to express emotions and social relationships that we need to express. This is good. Unfortunately some of the desires may be a little less admirable: the desire to separatism, to schism, to imposing our way of life on others, to finding moral justifications for colonialism, or tribal or cultural imperialism, and all made guilt-free because done in the name of the Lord. For every peaceful benevolent mystic, there is an army chaplain, convincing the troops that God is on their side. Myself, I have never seen a bumper sticker saying "Hate if you Love Jesus," but I sometimes wonder why not. It would be a good slogan for the religious Right. . . .

Obviously the attitude one takes to the "fideism" that simply lets particular religious beliefs walk free from reason may depend heavily on what has recently been happening when they do so. Hume was born less than twenty years after the last legal religious executions in Britain, and himself suffered from the enthusiastic hostility of believers. If in our time and place all we see are church picnics and charities, we will not be so worried. But enough people come down the mountain carrying their own practical certainties to suggest that we ought to be.

Maybe some day something will be found that answers to the needs without pandering to the bad desires, but human history suggests that it would be unwise to bank on it.

## READING COMPREHENSION QUESTIONS

1. Briefly articulate what you think is Blackburn's best argument against Anselm's Ontological Argument.

2. Briefly articulate what you think is Blackburn's best argument against the Cosmological Argument.

3. Briefly articulate what you think is Blackburn's best argument against the Argument from Design.

4. Briefly articulate what you think is Blackburn's best argument against Pascal's Wager.

5. Explain what fideism is and briefly articulate Blackburn's *ethical* worries about it.

# 26

# The Problem of Evil

DAVID HUME

*David Hume (1711–1776), who was born and spent much of his life in Edinburgh, Scotland, was a leading philosopher in the Enlightenment. He wrote several important books on metaphysics, epistemology, ethics, political philosophy, and philosophy of religion. In this selection, Part X from his book* The Dialogues Concerning Natural Religion, *Hume presents a conversation between three characters. Cleanthes is an empiricist anthropomorphite[1] theist, someone who believes we can come to knowledge of God only through experience, through investigation of the natural world, and that the properties of God are just like ours, only greater; in other words, terms such as "good" and "powerful," mean exactly what they do when applied to God as when applied to us. Demea, on the other hand, is a mystic theist, someone who believes that true knowledge of God could only come through a divine vision, and that the properties of God are completely foreign to us; in other words, the terms "good" and "powerful" mean something totally different when applied to God than they do when applied to us. Finally, Philo is a skeptic, someone who has genuine doubts about religious belief. Philo was likely Hume's mouthpiece. Prior to this point in the dialogue, the characters have been discussing various arguments for the existence of God, and they have made an important distinction between natural properties and moral properties. Moral properties are those properties that make their bearer morally good or bad, such as kindness, cruelty, generosity, or stinginess. Natural properties, on the other hand, are all other properties, those which make their bearer neither morally good nor morally bad—for example, strength, power, intelligence, frailty, and so forth. The natural properties one has imply nothing about the moral properties one has, and vice versa, so one could be powerful and either cruel or kind, for example. Up to now, the characters have been investigating what nature implies about God's natural properties, much as both Aquinas and Paley have done in our earlier readings. Aquinas points to the chain of causation and concludes that God exists as the first cause, and so must be powerful. Paley points to the design in nature, infers that God designed it, and concludes that God must be intelligent. But now Hume's characters change their investigation to seeing what nature implies about*

---

[1]In general, anthropomorphism involves attributing human characteristics to objects ("the clever computer"), animals ("the friendly fawn"), natural phenomena ("the angry river"), and God.

SOURCE: From David Hume, *Dialogues Concerning Natural Religion*, reprinted with an introduction by Bruce M'Ewen. This edition is in the public domain.

*God's* moral *properties, and it's not a pretty picture. There are all sorts of evils in the world, which Philo and Demea document at length, and what this seems to imply is that God, if He exists, must be either not good or not powerful. Either way the theist has a powerful challenge on her hands.*

# PART X

IT is my opinion, I own, replied DEMEA, that each man feels, in a manner, the truth of religion within his own breast; and from a consciousness of his imbecility and misery, rather than from any reasoning, is led to seek protection from that Being, on whom he and all nature is dependent. So anxious or so tedious are even the best scenes of life, that futurity is still the object of all our hopes and fears. We incessantly look forward, and endeavour, by prayers, adoration, and sacrifice, to appease those unknown powers, whom we find, by experience, so able to afflict and oppress us. Wretched creatures that we are! what resource for us amidst the innumerable ills of life, did not Religion suggest some methods of atonement, and appease those terrors, with which we are incessantly agitated and tormented?

I am indeed persuaded, said PHILO, that the best and indeed the only method of bringing every one to a due sense of religion, is by just representations of the misery and wickedness of men. And for that purpose a talent of eloquence and strong imagery is more requisite than that of reasoning and argument. For is it necessary to prove, what every one feels within himself? 'Tis only necessary to make us feel it, if possible, more intimately and sensibly.

The people, indeed, replied DEMEA, are sufficiently convinced of this great and melancholy truth. The miseries of life, the unhappiness of man, the general corruptions of our nature, the unsatisfactory enjoyment of pleasures, riches, honours; these phrases have become almost proverbial in all languages. And who can doubt of what all men declare from their own immediate feeling and experience?

In this point, said PHILO, the learned are perfectly agreed with the vulgar; and in all letters, *sacred* and *profane,* the topic of human misery has been insisted on with the most pathetic eloquence that sorrow and melancholy could inspire. The poets, who speak from sentiment, without a system, and whose testimony has therefore the more authority, abound in images of this nature. From HOMER down to Dr YOUNG, the whole inspired tribe have ever been sensible, that no other representation of things would suit the feeling and observation of each individual.

As to authorities, replied DEMEA, you need not seek them. Look round this library of CLEANTHES. I shall venture to affirm, that, except authors of particular sciences, such as chemistry or botany, who have no occasion to treat of human life, there scarce is one of those innumerable writers, from whom the sense of human misery has not, in some passage or other, extorted a complaint and confession of it. At least, the chance is entirely on that side; and no one author has ever, so far as I can recollect, been so extravagant as to deny it.

There you must excuse me, said PHILO: LEIBNITZ has denied it; and is perhaps the first,[2] who ventured upon so bold and paradoxical an opinion; at least, the first, who made it essential to his philosophical system.

And by being the first, replied DEMEA, might he not have been sensible of his error? For is this a subject, in which philosophers can propose to make discoveries, especially in so late an age? And can any man hope by a simple denial (for the subject scarcely admits of reasoning) to bear down the united testimony of mankind, founded on sense and consciousness?

And why should man, added he, pretend to an exemption from the lot of all other animals? The whole earth, believe me, PHILO, is cursed and polluted. A perpetual war is kindled amongst all living creatures. Necessity, hunger, want, stimulate the strong and courageous: Fear, anxiety, terror, agitate the weak and infirm. The first entrance into life gives anguish to the new-born infant and to its wretched parent: Weakness, impotence distress, attend each stage of that life: and 'tis at last finished in agony and horror.

Observe too, says PHILO, the curious artifices of Nature, in order to embitter the life of every living being. The stronger prey upon the weaker, and keep them in perpetual terror and anxiety. The weaker too, in their turn, often prey upon the stronger, and vex and molest them without relaxation. Consider that innumerable race of insects, which either are bred on the body of each animal, or flying about infix their stings in him. These insects have others still less than themselves, which torment them. And thus on each hand, before and behind, above and below, every animal is surrounded with enemies, which incessantly seek his misery and destruction.

Man alone, said DEMEA, seems to be, in part, an exception to this rule. For by combination in society, he can easily master lions, tigers, and bears, whose greater strength and agility naturally enable them to prey upon him.

On the contrary, it is here chiefly, cried PHILO, that the uniform and equal maxims of Nature are most apparent. Man, it is true, can, by combination, surmount all his *real* enemies, and become master of the whole animal creation: but does he not immediately raise up to himself *imaginary* enemies, the daemons of his fancy, who haunt him with superstitious terrors, and blast every enjoyment of life? His pleasure, as he imagines, becomes, in their eyes, a crime: his food and repose give them umbrage and offence: his very sleep and dreams furnish new materials to anxious fear: and even death, his refuge from every other ill, presents only the dread of endless and innumerable woes. Nor does the wolf molest more the timid flock, than superstition does the anxious breast of wretched mortals.

Besides, consider, DEMEA; this very society, by which we surmount those wild beasts, our natural enemies; what new enemies does it not raise to us? What woe and misery does it not occasion? Man is the greatest enemy of man. Oppression, injustice, contempt, contumely, violence, sedition, war, calumny, treachery, fraud; by these they mutually torment each other: and they would soon dissolve that society which they had formed were it not for the dread of still greater ills which must attend their separation.

---

[2]That sentiment had been maintained by Dr. King and some few others, before LEIBNITZ, though by none of so great fame as that GERMAN philosopher.

But though these external insults, said DEMEA, from animals, from men, from all the elements, which assault us, form a frightful catalogue of woes, they are nothing in comparison of those, which arise within ourselves, from the distempered condition of our mind and body. How many lie under the lingering torment of diseases? Hear the pathetic enumeration of the great poet.

> Intestine stone and ulcer, colic-pangs,
> Demoniac frenzy, moping melancholy,
> And moon-struck madness, pining atrophy,
> Marasmus and wide-wasting pestilence.
> Dire was the tossing, deep the groans: DESPAIR
> Tended the sick, busiest from couch to couch.
> And over them triumphant DEATH his dart
> Shook, but delayed to strike, tho' oft invok'd
> With vows, as their chief good and final hope[3]

The disorders of the mind, continued DEMEA, though more secret, are not perhaps less dismal and vexatious. Remorse, shame, anguish, rage, disappointment, anxiety, fear, dejection, despair; who has ever passed through life without cruel inroads from these tormentors? How many have scarcely ever felt any better sensations? Labour and poverty, so abhorred by every one, are the certain lot of the far greater number; and those few privileged persons, who enjoy ease and opulence, never reach contentment or true felicity. All the goods of life united would not make a very happy man: but all the ills united would make a wretch indeed; and any one of them almost (and who can be free from every one), nay often the absence of one good (and who can possess all), is sufficient to render life ineligible.

Were a stranger to drop, on a sudden, into this world, I would show him, as a specimen of its ills, an hospital full of diseases, a prison crowded with malefactors and debtors, a field of battle strewed with carcases, a fleet floundering in the ocean, a nation languishing under tyranny, famine, or pestilence. To turn the gay side of life to him, and give him a notion of its pleasures; whither should I conduct him? to a ball, to an opera, to court? He might, justly think, that I was only showing him a diversity of distress and sorrow.

There is no evading such striking instances, said PHILO, but by apologies, which still farther aggravate the charge. Why have all men, I ask, in all ages, complained incessantly of the miseries of life? . . . . They have no just reason, says one: these complaints proceed only from their discontented, repining, anxious disposition. . . . And can there possibly, I reply, be a more certain foundation of misery, than such a wretched temper?

But if they were really as unhappy as they pretend, says my antagonist, why do they remain in life? . . . .

Not satisfied with life, afraid of death.

This is the secret chain, say I, that holds us. We are terrified, not bribed to the continuance of our existence.

---

[3]Milton: Paradise Lost, XI.

It is only a false delicacy, he may insist, which a few refined spirits indulge, and which has spread these complaints among the whole race of mankind. . . . And what is this delicacy, I ask, which you blame? Is it any thing but a greater sensibility to all the pleasures and pains of life? and if the man of a delicate, refined temper, by being so much more alive than the rest of the world, is only so much more unhappy; what judgment must we form in general of human life?

Let men remain at rest, says our adversary; and they will be easy. They are willing artificers of their own misery. . . . No! reply I; an anxious languor follows their repose: disappointment, vexation, trouble, their activity and ambition.

I can observe something like what you mention in some others, replied CLEANTHES: but I confess, I feel little or nothing of it in myself, and hope that it is not so common as you represent it.

If you feel not human misery yourself, cried DEMEA, I congratulate you on so happy singularity. Others, seemingly the most prosperous, have not been ashamed to vent their complaints in the most melancholy strains. Let us attend to the great, the fortunate Emperor, CHARLES V., when, tired with human grandeur, he resigned all his extensive dominions into the hands of his son. In the last harangue, which he made on that memorable occasion, he publicly avowed, *that the greatest prosperities which he had ever enjoyed, had been mixed with so many adversities, that he might truly say he had never enjoyed any satisfaction or contentment.* But did the retired life, in which he sought for shelter, afford him any greater happiness? If we may credit his son's account, his repentance commenced the very day of his resignation.

CICERO's fortune, from small beginnings, rose to the greatest lustre and renown; yet what pathetic complaints of the ills of life do his familiar letters, as well as philosophical discourses, contain? And suitably to his own experience, he introduces CATO, the great, the fortunate CATO, protesting in his old age, that, had he a new life in his offer, he would reject the present.

Ask yourself, ask any of your acquaintance, whether they would live over again the last ten or twenty years of their lives. No! but the next twenty, they say, will be better:

And from the dregs of life, hope to receive
What the first sprightly running could not give.[4]

Thus at last they find (such is the greatness of human misery; it reconciles even contradictions) that they complain, at once, of the shortness of life, and of its vanity and sorrow.

And is it possible, CLEANTHES, said PHILO, that after all these reflections, and infinitely more, which might be suggested, you can still persevere in your Anthropomorphism, and assert the moral attributes of the Deity, his justice, benevolence, mercy, and rectitude, to be of the same nature with these virtues in human creatures? His power we allow infinite: whatever he wills is executed: but neither man nor any other animal is happy: therefore he does not will their happiness. His wisdom is infinite: he is never mistaken in choosing the means to any end: but the course of nature tends not to human or animal felicity: therefore it is not established for that purpose. Through the whole compass of human knowledge,

---

[4]Dryden : Aurungzebe, Act IV., sc. i.

there are no inferences more certain and infallible than these. In what respect, then, do his benevolence and mercy resemble the benevolence and mercy of men?

EPICURUS's old questions are yet unanswered.

Is he willing to prevent evil, but not able? then is he impotent. Is he able, but not willing? then is he malevolent. Is he both able and willing? whence then is evil?

You ascribe, CLEANTHES, (and I believe justly) a purpose and intention to Nature. But what, I beseech you, is the object of that curious artifice and machinery, which she has displayed in all animals? The preservation alone of individuals and propagation of the species. It seems enough for her purpose, if such a rank he barely upheld in the universe, without any care or concern for the happiness of the members that compose it. No resource for this purpose: no machinery in order merely to give pleasure or ease: no fund of pure joy and contentment: no indulgence without some want or necessity accompanying it. At least, the few phenomena of this nature are overbalanced by opposite phenomena of still greater importance.

Our sense of music, harmony, and indeed beauty of all kinds, gives satisfaction, without being absolutely necessary to the preservation and propagation of the species. But what racking pains, on the other hand, arise from gouts, gravels, megrims, tooth-aches, rheumatisms; where the injury to the animal-machinery is either small or incurable? Mirth, laughter, play, frolic, seem gratuitous satisfactions, which have no farther tendency: spleen, melancholy, discontent, superstition, are pains of the same nature. How then does the divine benevolence display itself, in the sense of you Anthropomorphites? None but we Mystics, as you were pleased to call us, can account for this strange mixture of phenomena, by deriving it from attributes, infinitely perfect, but incomprehensible.

And have you at last, said CLEANTHES smiling, betrayed your intentions, PHILO? Your long agreement with DEMEA did indeed a little surprise me; but I find you were all the while erecting a concealed battery against me. And I must confess, that you have now fallen upon a subject, worthy of your noble spirit of opposition and controversy. If you can make out the present point, and prove mankind to be unhappy or corrupted, there is an end at once of all religion. For to what purpose establish the natural attributes of the Deity, while the moral are still doubtful and uncertain?

You take umbrage very easily, replied DEMEA, at opinions the most innocent, and the most generally received even amongst the religious and devout themselves: and nothing can be more surprising than to find a topic like this, concerning the wickedness and misery of man, charged with no less than Atheism and profaneness. Have not all pious divines and preachers, who have indulged their rhetoric on so fertile a subject; have they not easily, I say, given a solution of any difficulties, which may attend it? This world is but a point in comparison of the universe; this life but a moment in comparison of eternity. The present evil phenomena, therefore, are rectified in other regions, and in some future period of existence. And the eyes of men, being then opened to larger views of things, see the whole connection of general laws; and trace with adoration, the benevolence and rectitude of the Deity, through all the mazes and intricacies of his providence.

No! replied CLEANTHES, No! These arbitrary suppositions can never be admitted, contrary to matter of fact, visible and uncontroverted. Whence can any cause be known but from its known effects? Whence can any hypothesis be proved but from the apparent phenomena? To establish one hypothesis upon another, is building entirely in the air; and the utmost we ever attain, by these conjectures and fictions, is to ascertain the bare possibility of our opinion; but never can we, upon such terms, establish its reality.

The only method of supporting divine benevolence (and it is what I willingly embrace) is to deny absolutely the misery and wickedness of man. Your representations are exaggerated: Your melancholy views mostly fictitious: Your inferences contrary to fact and experience. Health is more common than sickness: Pleasure than pain: Happiness than misery. And for one vexation, which we meet with, we attain, upon computation, a hundred enjoyments.

Admitting your position, replied PHILO, which yet is extremely doubtful, you must, at the same time, allow, that, if pain be less frequent than pleasure, it is infinitely more violent and durable. One hour of it is often able to outweigh a day, a week, a month of our common insipid enjoyments: And how many days, weeks, and months are passed by several in the most acute torments? Pleasure, scarcely in one instance, is ever able to reach ecstacy and rapture: And in no one instance can it continue for any time at its highest pitch and altitude. The spirits evaporate; the nerves relax; the fabric is disordered; and the enjoyment quickly degenerates into fatigue and uneasiness. But pain often, good God, how often! rises to torture and agony; and the longer it continues, it becomes still more genuine agony and torture. Patience is exhausted; courage languishes; melancholy seizes us; and nothing terminates our misery but the removal of its cause, or another event, which is the sole cure of all evil, but which, from our natural folly, we regard with still greater horror and consternation.

But not to insist upon these topics, continued PHILO, though most obvious, certain and important; I must use the freedom to admonish you, CLEANTHES, that you have put this controversy upon a most dangerous issue and are unawares introducing a total Scepticism, into the most essential articles of natural and revealed theology. What! no method of fixing a just foundation for religion, unless we allow the happiness of human life, and maintain a continued existence even in this world, with all our present pains, infirmities, vexations, and follies, to be eligible and desirable! But this is contrary to every one's feeling and experience: It is contrary to an authority so established as nothing can subvert: No decisive proofs can ever be produced against this authority; nor is it possible for you to compute, estimate, and compare all the pains and all the pleasures in the lives of all men and of all animals: And thus by your resting the whole system of religion on a point, which, from its very nature, must for ever be uncertain, you tacitly confess, that that system is equally uncertain.

But allowing you, what never will be believed, at least, what you never possibly can prove, that animal, or at least, human happiness, in this life, exceeds its misery; you have yet done nothing: For this is not, by any means, what we expect from infinite power, infinite wisdom, and infinite goodness. Why is there any misery at all in the world? Not by chance surely. From some cause then. Is it from the intention of the Deity? But he is perfectly benevolent. Is it contrary to his intention? But he is almighty. Nothing can shake the solidity of this reasoning, so short, so clear, so decisive; except we assert, that these subjects exceed all human capacity and that our common measures of truth and falsehood are not applicable to them; a topic, which I have all along insisted on, but which you have, from the beginning, rejected with scorn and indignation.

But I will be contented to retire still from this intrenchment: For I deny that you can ever force me in it: I will allow, that pain or misery in man is *compatible* with infinite power and goodness in the Deity, even in your sense of these attributes: What are you advanced by all these concessions? A mere possible compatibility is not sufficient. You must *prove* these pure, unmixed, and uncontrollable attributes from the present mixed and confused phenomena, and from these alone. A hopeful undertaking! Were the phenomena ever so pure and unmixed, yet being finite, they would be insufficient for that purpose. How much more, where they are also so jarring and discordant!

Here, Cleanthes, I find myself at ease in my argument. Here I triumph. Formerly, when we argued concerning the natural attributes of intelligence and design, I needed all my sceptical and metaphysical subtilty to elude your grasp. In many views of the universe, and of its parts, particularly the latter, the beauty and fitness of final causes strike us with such irresistible force, that all objections appear (what I believe they really are) mere cavils and sophisms; nor can we then imagine how it was ever possible for us to repose any weight on them. But there is no view of human life or of the condition of mankind, from which, without the greatest violence, we can infer the moral attributes, or learn that infinite benevolence, conjoined with infinite power and infinite wisdom, which we must discover by the eyes of faith alone. It is your turn now to tug the labouring oar, and to support your philosophical subtilties against the dictates of plain reason and experience.

## READING COMPREHENSION QUESTIONS

1. Philo and Demea list several "miseries of life" in their discussion with Cleanthes. List what you believe are the five most serious such miseries. Are there any miseries and evils of our current life and times that deserve to be added to the list?

2. What, precisely, is the point of listing all these evils? In other words, Philo and Demea are presenting a version of the argument known as the problem of evil, so how exactly does their argument unfold?

3. What is Cleanthes' response to the problem of evil? Is it plausible?

4. What is Demea's response to the problem of evil? Is it plausible?

5. At the end of the reading, Philo grants to Cleanthes, for the sake of argument, a possibility that he in fact believes is false, namely, that human happiness "exceeds its misery." But Philo goes on to insist that, even if that's the case, it doesn't help Cleanthes avoid the Problem of Evil at all. Why not?

# 27

# The Mirror of Evil

ELEONORE STUMP

*Eleonore Stump (born 1947) is Robert J. Henle Professor of Philosophy at Saint Louis University. She has written numerous books and articles on medieval philosophy and philosophy of religion. In this selection, she suggests that seeing all the evil in the world, while horrifying, may also allow us to find our way into the goodness of God. Stump offers the metaphor of a child being weaned, initially overwhelmed by pain and loss, but who can eventually work through his suffering to genuinely see his mother—and in so doing feel her love for him, perhaps appreciating it fully for the first time. Just as a mother's love for her child is compatible with her allowing this sort of suffering for a higher purpose, so too may God's love for his children be compatible with His allowing evil in this world.*

There are different ways to tell the story of one's own coming to God. Straightforward autobiography has its merits, but, paradoxically, it can leave out the most important parts. I want to tell my story in a roundabout way that will, I hope, show directly what for me is and always has been the heart of the matter.

For reflective people, contemplation of human suffering tends to raise the problem of evil. If there is an omnipotent, omniscient, perfectly good God, how can it be that the world is full of evil? This response to evil is normal and healthy. I have discussed this problem myself in print and tried to find a solution to it. But there is another way to think about evil.

Consider just these examples of human suffering, which I take from my morning newspaper. Although the Marines are in Somalia, some armed Somalis are still stealing food from their starving neighbors, who are dying by the thousands. Muslim women and girls, some as young as ten years old, are being raped and tortured by Serb soldiers. In India, Hindus went on a rampage that razed a mosque and killed over 1,000 people. In Afghanistan gunmen fired into a crowded bazaar and shot ten people, including two children. Closer to home, the R. J. Reynolds company is trying to defend itself against charges that it is engaged in a campaign to entice adolescents to smoke. The recently defeated candidate for governor in my state, as well as lawyers and doctors employed by the state as advocates for disabled workers, are charged with stealing thousands of dollars from the fund designed for those workers. A high school principal is indicted on charges of molesting elementary and middle school boys over a period of twenty years. A man is being tried for murder in the death of a nine-year-old boy; he grabbed the boy to use as a shield in a gunfight. I could go on—racism, rape, assault, murder, greed and exploitation, war and genocide—but this is enough. By the time you read these examples, they will be dated, but you can find others just like them in your newspaper. There is no time, no part of the globe, free from evil. The crust of the earth is soaked with the tears of the suffering.

This evil is a mirror for us. It shows us our world; it also shows us ourselves. How could anyone steal at gunpoint food meant for starving children? How could anyone rape a ten-year-old girl? How could anyone bear to steal money from disabled workers or get rich by selling a product he knows will damage the health of thousands? But people do these things, and much worse things as well. We ourselves—you and I, that is—are members of the species that does such things, and we live in a world where the wrecked victims of this human evil float on the surface of all history, animate suffering flotsam and jetsam. The author of Ecclesiastes says, "I observed all the oppression that goes on under the sun: the tears of the oppressed with none to comfort them; and the power of their oppressors— with none to comfort them. Then I accounted those who died long since more fortunate than those who are still living" (4:1–2).[1]

Some people glance into the mirror of evil and quickly look away. They take note, shake their heads sadly, and go about their business. They work hard, they worry about their children, they help their friends and neighbors, and they look forward to Christmas dinner. I don't want to disparage them in any way. Tolkien's hobbits are people like this. There is health and strength in their ability to forget the evil they have seen. Their good cheer makes them robust.

But not everybody has a hobbit's temperament. Some people look into the mirror of evil and can't shut out the sight. You sit in your warm house with dinner on the table and your children around you, and you know that not far from you the homeless huddle around grates seeking warmth, children go hungry, and every other manner of suffering can be found. Is it human, is it decent, to enjoy your own good fortune and forget their misery? But it's morbid, you might say, to keep thinking about the evils of the world; it's depressive; it's sick. Even if that were true, how would you close your mind to what you'd seen once you'd looked into the mirror of evil?

Some people labor at obliviousness. They drown their minds in drinking, or they throw themselves into their work. At certain points in his life, Camus seems to have taken this tack. He was at Le Chambon writing feverishly, and obliviously, while the Chambonnais were risking their lives rescuing Jews.[2] Jonathan Swift, whose mordant grasp of evil is evident in his writings, was chronically

---

[1] I am quoting from the new Jewish Publications Society's translation. With the exception of quotations from Jeremiah 3 and Psalm 34, all quotations from the Hebrew Bible will be from this translation. The suffering of the Jews during the Holocaust reflects all the worst misery and all the deepest wickedness in the world, and so it seemed appropriate to use the Jewish translation of the Hebrew Bible in an essay on suffering.

[2] One of the first things Camus wrote in his diary on arriving in Le Panelier, the village on the outskirts of Le Chambon, was "This is oblivion" (quoted in Herbert R. Lottman, *Albert Camus* [Garden City, N.Y.: Doubleday, 1979], p. 276). During his stay in Le Chambon, he was writing *The Plague* and his play *Le Malentendu,* as well as making notes for *The Rebel.* Apparently, several of the names in *The Plague* are borrowed from the people of Le Chambon (Lottman, op. cit., p. 290).

afflicted with horror at the world around him; he favored violent exercise as an antidote.[3] The success of this sort of strategy, if it ever really does succeed, seems clearly limited.

Some people believe that evil can be eliminated, that Eden on earth is possible. Whatever it is in human behavior or human society that is responsible for the misery around us can be swept away, in their view. They are reformers on a global scale. The moral response to suffering, of course, is the Good Samaritan's: doing what we can to stop the suffering, to help those in need. Global reformers are different from Good Samaritans, though; global reformers mean to remove the human defects that produced the evil in the first place. The failure of the great communist social experiment is a sad example of the problems with this approach to evil. Every good family runs on the principle "from each according to his ability; to each according to his need." The extended human family in Eastern Europe intended to run on this principle and turned it instead into "from each according to his weakness; to each according to his greed." Ecclesiastes sums up the long-term prospects for global reform in this way: "I observed all the happenings beneath the sun, and I found that all is futile and pursuit of wind; a twisted thing that cannot be made straight, a lack that cannot be made good" (1:14–15).

And don't reason and experience suggest that Ecclesiastes has the right of it? The author of Ecclesiastes says, "I set my mind to study and to probe with wisdom all that happens under the sun . . . and I found that all is futile . . . as wisdom grows, vexation grows; to increase learning is to increase heartache" (1:13, 14, 18). This is a view that looks pathological to the hobbits of the world. But whether it *is* pathological depends on whose view of the world is right, doesn't it? A hobbit in a leper colony in a cheerful state of denial, oblivious to the disease in himself and others, wouldn't be mentally healthy either, would he? Ecclesiastes recognizes the goodness of hobbits. The author says over and over again, "eat your bread in gladness, and drink your wine in joy; . . . enjoy happiness with a woman you love all the fleeting days of life that have been granted to you under the sun" (9:7, 9). But the ability to eat, drink, and be merry in this way looks like a gift of God, a sort of blessed irrationality. For himself, Ecclesiastes says, "I loathed life. For I was distressed by all that goes on under the sun, because everything is futile and pursuit of wind" (2:17).

So, some people react with loathing to what they can't help seeing in the mirror of evil—loathing of the world, loathing of themselves. This malaise of spirit is more likely to afflict those living in some prosperity and ease, inhabitants of the court, say, or college students on scholarship. If you've just been fired or told you have six months to live or have some other large and urgent trouble, you're likely to think that you would be happy and life would be wonderful if only you didn't have *that* particular affliction. Given the attitude of Ecclesiastes, it's not surprising that the book was attributed to Solomon, who was as known for wealth and power as for wisdom.

The misery induced by the mirror of evil is vividly described by Philip Hallie in his book on Le Chambon.[4] Hallie had been studying cruelty for years and was working on a project on the Nazis. His focus was the medical experiments carried

---

[3]This included not only strenuous riding and walking but also "hedging and ditching"; See David Nokes, *Jonathan Swift. A Hypocrite Reversed* (Oxford: Oxford University Press, 1985), p. 341.

[4]Philip Hallie, *Lest Innocent Blood Be Shed* (Philadelphia: Harper and Row, 1979).

out on Jewish children in the death camps. Nazi doctors broke and rebroke "the bones of six- or seven- or eight-year-old Jewish children in order, the Nazis said, to study the processes of natural healing in young bodies" (p. 3). "Across all these studies," Hallie says, "the pattern of the strong crushing the weak kept repeating itself and repeating itself, so that when I was not bitterly angry, I was bored at the repetition of the patterns of persecution. . . . My study of evil incarnate had become a prison whose bars were my bitterness toward the violent, and whose walls were my horrified indifference to slow murder. Between the bars and the walls I revolved like a madman. . . . over the years I had dug myself into Hell" (p. 2).

Hallie shares with the author of Ecclesiastes an inability to look away from the loathsome horrors in the mirror of evil. The torment of this reaction to evil is evident, and it seems the opposite of what we expect from a religious spirit. It's no wonder that some people think Ecclesiastes has no place in the canonical Scriptures. To see why this view of Ecclesiastes is mistaken, we have to think not just about our reactive attitudes toward evil but also about our recognition of evil.

How does Hallie know—how do we know—that the torture of Jewish children by Nazi doctors is evil?

By reason, we might be inclined to answer. But that answer is not entirely right. It's true that our moral principles and our ethical theories rely on reason. But we build those principles and theories, at least in part, by beginning with strong intuitions about individual cases that exemplify wrongdoing, and we construct our ethical theories around those intuitions. We look for what the individual cases of wrongdoing have in common, and we try to codify their common characteristics into principles. Once the principles have been organized into a theory, we may also revise our original intuitions until we reach some point of reflective equilibrium, where our intuitions and theories are in harmony. But our original intuitions retain an essential primacy. If we found that our ethical theory countenanced those Nazi experiments on children, we'd throw away the theory as something evil itself.

But what exactly are these original intuitions? What cognitive faculty produces them? Not reason, apparently, since reason takes them as given and reflects on them. But equally clearly, not memory: We aren't remembering that it is evil to torture children. And not sense perception either. When we say that we just see the wrongness of certain actions, we certainly don't mean that it's visible.

At this stage in our understanding of our own minds and brains, we don't know enough to identify the cognitive faculty that recognizes evil intuitively. But it would be a mistake to infer that there is no such faculty.[5] It's clear that

---

[5]By talk of a faculty here, I don't mean to suggest that there is one neurobiological structure or even one neurobiological system that constitutes the faculty in question. There may be many subsystems that work together to produce the ability I am calling a cognitive faculty. Vision seems to be like this. It is entirely appropriate to speak of the faculty of vision, but many different neural subsystems have to work together properly in order for a person to be able to see. It may also be the case that some of the subsystems that constitute a faculty have multiple uses and function to constitute more than one faculty. This seems to be the case with vision, too. Our ability to see apparently requires the operation of some subsystem of associated memory, and this subsystem is also employed in other faculties, such as our ability to hear. The wild boy of Aveyronne, whose subsystem of associated memory was no use for dealing with urban sounds, was originally believed to be deaf and was brought to an institute for the deaf in Paris.

we have many other cognitive faculties that similarly can't be accounted for by the triad of reason, memory, and perception. We have the abilities to tell mood from facial expression, to discern affect from melody of speech. We have the ability to recognize people from seeing their faces. When I see my daughter's face, I know who she is, and not by reason, memory, or perception. There are people who suffer from prosopagnosia. In them, reason functions well, and so do memory and perception; they perform normally on standard tests for all those faculties. Furthermore, the links among reason, memory, and perception also seem intact. Prosopagnosics can remember what they've perceived and thought; they can reason about what they remember and what they're perceiving. Nonetheless, they can't recognize people they know on the basis of visual data acquired by seeing their faces. So it is plain that reason, memory, and perception no more exhaust the list of our cognitive faculties than animal, vegetable, and mineral exhaust the list of material objects in the world. That we have no idea *what* faculty has been damaged or destroyed in prosopagnosia obviously doesn't mean that there is no such faculty. Furthermore, there is no reason for being particularly skeptical about the reliability of such peculiar cognitive faculties. It seems to me that our cognitive faculties come as a set. If we accept some of them—such as reason—as reliable, on what basis would we hold skeptically aloof from any others? So I think it is clear that we have cognitive faculties that we don't understand much about but regularly and appropriately rely on, such as the ability to recognize people from their faces.

Our ability to recognize certain things as evil seems to me like this. We don't understand much about the faculty that produces moral intuitions in us, but we all regularly rely on it anyway.[6] The vaunted cultural relativity of morality doesn't seem to me an objection. The diversity of moral opinions in the world masks a great underlying similarity of view;[7] and perhaps a lot of the

---

[6]In claiming that we have a faculty that recognizes moral characteristics, I am not claiming that nurture and environment play no role in shaping our moral intuitions. It is difficult to make a principled distinction between what is innate and what has an environmental component, as philosophers of biology have helped us to see. And there are clear examples of characteristics that most of us strongly believe to be genetically determined but that nonetheless require the right environmental or cultural conditions to emerge. The human capacity for language is such a case. It seems clearly innate and genetically determined. And yet, as the few well-documented cases of feral children show, without human society and nurture at the right ages, a person will be permanently unable to acquire a language.

[7]Perhaps this isn't the best case to illustrate the point, but it is one of my favorites. In his public remarks during the period when he was rector, Heidegger tended to make statements of this sort: "Do not let principles and 'ideas' be the rules of your existence. The Fuehrer himself, and he alone, is the German reality of today, and of the future, and of its law." Cited in Victor Farias, *Heidegger and Nazism*, trans. Paul Burrell [Philadelphia: Temple University Press, 1989], p. 118. After Germany lost World War II, when the French moved into his town and confiscated his property because he was on their list as a known Nazi, he wrote an indignant letter to the commander of the French forces in his area. It begins this way: "What justice there is in treating me in this unheard of way is inconceivable to me" ("Mit welchem Rechtsgrund ich mit einem solchen unerhoerten Vorgehen betroffen werde, ist mir unerfindlich"). Cited in Hugo Ott, *Martin Heidegger. Unterwegs zu seiner Biographie* (Frankfurt: Campus Verlag, 1988), p. 296.

diversity is attributable not to moral differences but to differences in beliefs about empirical and metaphysical matters. I think, then, that we have some cognitive faculty for discerning evil in things, and that people in general treat it as they treat their other cognitive faculties: as basically reliable, even if fallible and subject to revision.

It also seems clear that this cognitive faculty can discern differences in kind and degree. For example, there is a great difference between ordinary wrongdoing and real wickedness. A young Muslim mother in Bosnia was repeatedly raped in front of her husband and father, with her baby screaming on the floor beside her. When her tormentors seemed finally tired of her, she begged permission to nurse the child. In response, one of the rapists swiftly decapitated the baby and threw the head in the mother's lap. This evil is different, and we feel it immediately. We don't have to reason about it or think it over. As we read the story, we are filled with grief and distress, shaken with revulsion and incomprehension. The taste of real wickedness is sharply different from the taste of garden-variety moral evil, and we discern it directly, with pain.

What is perhaps less easy to see is that this faculty also discerns goodness. We recognize acts of generosity, compassion, and kindness, for example, without needing to reflect much or reason it out. And when the goodness takes us by surprise, we are sometimes moved to tears by it. Hallie describes his first acquaintance with the acts of the Chambonnais in this way: "I came across a short article about a little village in the mountains of southern France. . . . I was reading the pages with an attempt at objectivity . . . trying to sort out the forms and elements of cruelty and of resistance to it. . . . About halfway down the third page of the account of this village, I was annoyed by a strange sensation on my cheeks. The story was so simple and so factual that I had found it easy to concentrate upon *it,* not upon my own feelings. And so, still following the story, and thinking about how neatly some of it fit into the old patterns of persecution, I reached up to my cheek to wipe away a bit of dust, and I felt tears upon my fingertips. Not one or two drops; my whole cheek was wet" (p. 3). Those tears, Hallie says, were "an expression of moral praise" (p. 4); and that seems right.

With regard to goodness, too, I think we readily recognize differences in kind and degree. We are deeply moved by the stories of the Chambonnais. People feel the unusual goodness of Mother Teresa and mark it by calling her a living saint. We sense something special in the volunteers who had been in Somalia well before the Marines came, trying to feed the starving. We don't have a single word for the contrary of wickedness, so 'true goodness' will have to do. True goodness tastes as different from ordinary instances of goodness as wickedness does from ordinary wrongdoing; and we discern true goodness, sometimes, with tears.

Why tears, do you suppose? A woman imprisoned for life without parole for killing her husband had her sentence unexpectedly commuted by the governor, and she wept when she heard the news. Why did she cry? Because the news was good, and she had been so used to hearing only bad. But why cry at good news? Perhaps because if most of your news is bad, you need to harden your heart to it. So you become accustomed to bad news, and to one extent or another, you learn to protect yourself against it, maybe by not minding so much. And then good news cracks your heart. It makes it feel keenly again all the evils to which it had become dull. It also opens it up to longing and hope, and hope is painful because what is hoped for is not yet here.[8]

For the same reasons, we sometimes weep when we are surprised by true goodness. The latest tales of horror in the newspaper distress us but don't surprise us. We have all heard so many stories of the same sort already. But true goodness is unexpected and lovely, and its loveliness can be heartbreaking. The stories of the Chambonnais rescuing Jews even on peril of their own imprisonment and death went through him like a spear, Hallie says. Perhaps if he had been less filled with the vision of the mirror of evil, he would have wept less over Le Chambon.

Some people glimpse true goodness by seeing it reflected in other people, as Hallie did. Others approach it more indirectly through beauty, the beauty of nature or mathematics or music. But I have come to believe that ultimately all true goodness of the heartbreaking kind is God's. And I think that it can be found first and most readily in the traces of God left in the Bible.

The biblical stories present God as the glorious creator of all the beauty of heaven and earth, the majestic ruler and judge of the world. But Rebecca feels able to turn to Him when she doesn't understand what's happening in her womb, Hannah brings Him her grief at her childlessness, and Deborah trusts Him for victory in a pitched battle with her people's oppressors. Ezekiel presents Him at his most uncompromisingly angry, filled with righteous fury at human evil. But when God commands the prophet to eat food baked in human excrement as a sign to the people of the coming disasters, the shocked prophet tells Him, "I can't!", and almighty God rescinds His command (Ez. 4:12–15). When His people are at their repellent moral worst, God addresses them in this way: "They say if a man put away his wife and she go from him and become another man's, shall he return to her again? . . . you have played the harlot with many lovers; yet return again to me, says the Lord" (Jer. 3:1). And when we won't come to Him, He comes to us, not to rule and command, but to be despised and rejected, to bear our griefs and sorrows, to be stricken for our sake, so that we might be healed by His suffering.

There is something feeble about attempting to describe in a few lines the moving goodness of God that the biblical stories show us; and the attempt itself isn't the sort of procedure the biblical narratives encourage, for the same reason, I think, that the Bible is conspicuously lacking in proofs for the existence of God.[9] Insofar as the Bible presents or embodies any method for comprehending the goodness of God or coming to God, it can be summed up in the Psalmist's invitation to individual listeners and readers: Taste and see that the Lord is good.

---

[8]Alvin Plantinga has suggested to me that not all tears have to do with suffering; there are also tears of joy, at the beauty of music or of nature, for example. But I am inclined to think that even tears of joy of that sort have to do with suffering. As C. S. Lewis maintained in *The Pilgrim's Regress,* and as Plantinga also recognizes, the vision of certain sorts of beauty fills us with an acute if inchoate longing for something—the source of the beauty perhaps— and a painful sense that we don't possess it, aren't part of it, now.

[9]Arguments for God's existence certainly have their place, but for most people that place is after, not before, coming to God. I have explained and defended this attitude toward arguments for God's existence in "Aquinas on Faith and Goodness," in *Being and Goodness,* ed. Scott MacDonald (Ithaca, N.Y.: Cornell University Press, 1991), pp. 179–207.

The Psalmist's mixed metaphor seems right. Whether we find it in the Chambonnais or in the melange of narrative, prayer, poetry, chronicle, and epistle that constitutes the Bible, the taste of true goodness calls to us, wakes us up, opens our hearts. If we respond with surprise, with tears, with gratitude, with determination not to lose the taste, with commitment not to betray it, that tasting leads eventually to seeing, to some sight of or insight into God.

Hallie left his college office and his family and went seeking the villagers of Le Chambon. He concluded his study of the Chambonnais years later this way:

> We are living in a time, perhaps like every other time, when there are many who, in the words of the prophet Amos, "turn judgment to wormwood." Many are not content to live with the simplicities of the prophet of the ethical plumbline, Amos, when he says in the fifth chapter of his Book: "Seek good, and not evil, that ye may live: and so the Lord, the God of Hosts, shall be with you." . . . We are afraid to be "taken in," afraid to be credulous, and we are not afraid of the darkness of unbelief about important matters. . . . But perplexity is a luxury in which I cannot indulge. . . . For me, as for my family, there is the same *kind* of urgency as far as making ethical judgments about Le Chambon is concerned as there was for the Chambonnais when they were making their ethical judgments upon the laws of Vichy and the Nazis. . . . For me [the] awareness [of the standards of goodness] is my awareness of God. I live with the same sentence in my mind that many of the victims of the concentration camps uttered as they walked to their deaths: *Shema Israel, Adonoi Elohenu, Adonoi Echod.* (pp. 291–293)

So, in an odd sort of way, the mirror of evil can also lead us to God. A loathing focus on the evils of our world and ourselves prepares us to be the more startled by the taste of true goodness when we find it and the more determined to follow that taste until we see where it leads. And where it leads is to the truest goodness of all—not to the boss of the universe whose word is moral law or to sovereignty that must not be dishonored, but to the sort of goodness of which the Chambonnais's goodness is only a tepid aftertaste. The mirror of evil becomes translucent, and we can see through it to the goodness of God. There are some people, then, and I count myself among them, for whom focus on evil constitutes a way to God. For people like this, Ecclesiastes is not depressing but deeply comforting.

If we taste and see the goodness of God, then the vision of our world that we see in the mirror of evil will look different, too. Start just with the fact of evil in the world, and the problem of evil presents itself forcefully to you. But start with a view of evil and a deep taste of the goodness of God, and you will know that there must be a morally sufficient reason for God to allow evil—not some legal and ultimately unsatisfying sort of reason, but the sort of reason that the Chambonnais would recognize and approve of, a reason in which true goodness is manifest. People are accustomed to say that Job got no answer to his anguished demand to know why God had afflicted him. But they forget that in the end Job says to God, "now I see you." If you could see the loving face of a truly good God, you would have an answer to the question why God had afflicted you. When you see the deep love in the face of a person you suppose has betrayed you, you know you were wrong. Whatever happened was done, out of love for you by a heart that would never betray you and a mind bent on your good.[10] To answer a mistaken charge of betrayal, someone who loves you can explain the misunderstanding or he can show his face. Sometimes showing his face heals the hurt much faster.

If a truly good God rules the world, then the world has a good mother, and life is under the mothering guidance of God. Even the most loathsome evils and the most horrendous suffering are in the hand of a God who is truly good. All these things have a season, as Ecclesiastes says, and all of them work together for good for those who love God—for those who are finding their way to the love of God, too, we might add.[11]

Nothing in this thought makes evil less evil. Suffering remains painful; violence and greed are still execrable. We still have an obligation to lessen the misery of others, and our own troubles retain their power to torment us. But it makes a

---

[10]Answers to the question of why God permits innocents to suffer admit of varying degrees of specificity. Theodicies typically provide fairly general answers. So, for example, Richard Swinburne's explanation of God's permitting natural evil is that the experience of natural evil gives people knowledge about how suffering is caused and so gives them the options necessary for the significant use of their free will. Although I don't share Swinburne's view, I think that his account does constitute an answer to the question of why God permits innocents to suffer from natural evil. It tells us that God will allow one person S to suffer in order to provide a benefit for a set of persons that may or may not include S, and that the benefit is the significant use of free will, brought about by knowledge of how to cause suffering. Nonetheless, Swinburne's account omits a great many details; it doesn't tell us, for instance, exactly what sort of knowledge is produced or precisely how the suffering conduces to the knowledge in question. And it obviously has nothing to say about the suffering of particular individuals; that is, it doesn't tell us what individuals were benefited and how they were benefited by the suffering of this or that individual innocent. Similarly, in seeing the face of a loving God, Job has an answer to his question about why God has afflicted him; but like the account of evil theodicies give, it is only a general answer. It lets Job see that God allows his suffering for his own spiritual or psychological good, out of love for him; but it doesn't tell him precisely what the nature of that spiritual good is or how it is connected to Job's suffering.

[11]In other work, I have argued that God uses suffering to further the redemption of the sufferer. Some people find this claim highly implausible. So, for example, in a recent article, "Victimization and the Problem of Evil: A Response to Ivan Karamazov" *(Faith and Philosophy* 9 '1992], pp. 301–319), Thomas Tracy notes "the stunning counterintuitiveness" of this claim (p. 308). His own preferred view is this: While God does want His creatures to be intimately related to Him, God sometimes lets an innocent person suffer not for some good accruing to her but rather just for the common good, or for the good of the system. I find it hard to understand in what sense the claim that suffering conduces to the redemption of the sufferer is supposed to be counterintuitive, since most of us have few if any intuitions about the redemption of other people and what conduces to it. On the other hand, if Tracy's line is meant just to suggest that this way of looking at suffering seems to stand our ordinary views on their head, then his line seems right but unworrisome; what would be surprising is if a Christian solution to the problem of evil didn't turn our ordinary views upside down. What seems to me truly counterintuitive is Tracy's suggestion that we could have a relationship of deep trust and love with a person who, we believed, had the power to alleviate our suffering but was nonetheless willing to let us suffer undeservedly and involuntarily in the interest of the common good. For a vivid illustration of the deep distress and resentment people feel toward those who respond to their trust in this way, see, for example, the description of communist marriage in China in Jung Chang, *Wild Sioans. Three Daughters of China* (New York: Simon and Schuster, 1991), esp. pp. 145–146, 176 298.

great difference to suppose that the sufferers of evil, maybe ourselves included, are in the arms of a mothering God.

Although, as Ecclesiastes is fond of saying, we often cannot understand the details of the reason why God does what He does in the world, when we see through the mirror of evil and taste the goodness of the Lord, we do understand the general reason, just as Job must have done when he said, "now I see you." Like a woman in childbirth, then, as Paul says, we feel our pains of the moment, but they are encircled by an understanding that brings peace and joy.

And so in an Alice-through-the-looking-glass way, the mirror of evil brings us around to the hobbit's way of seeing things at the end. "Go," says Ecclesiastes, "eat your bread in gladness and drink your wine in joy; for your action was long ago approved by God" (9:7). If God is mothering the earth and if its evils are in His hands, then you may be at peace with yourself and your world. You can be grateful for the good that comes your way without always contrasting it with the ghastliness elsewhere. This road to quiet cheerfulness is the long way to the goal, but perhaps for some people it is also the only way there.

Nothing in this view, of course, is incompatible with a robust program of social action. "Send your bread forth upon the waters; for after many days you will find it," Ecclesiastes says. "Distribute portions to seven or even to eight, for you cannot know what misfortune may occur on earth" (11:1–2.). If you are moved by goodness, then you will want to ally yourself with it, to diminish evils in the world, to alleviate suffering. Those who love God will hate evil, the Psalmist says (97:10). There is no love of God, I John says, in those without compassion for the world's needy (3:17). A good part of true religion, James says, is just visiting "the fatherless and the widows in their affliction" (1:27).

The spirit with which you respond to the evil around you will be different, though, if you see through it to the goodness of God on the other side. Someone asked Mother Teresa if she wasn't often frustrated because all the people she helped in Calcutta died. "Frustrated?" she said, "no—God has called me to be faithful, not successful." If God is the world's mother, then Mother Teresa doesn't have to be. Quiet cheer and enjoyment of the small pleasures of the world are compatible with succouring the dying in Calcutta in case the suffering ones are in the hands of a God who is truly good. Maybe that's why the Psalmist follows his line "Taste and see that the Lord is good" with "blessed is the man that trusts in him."

Even our own evils—our moral evils, our decay and death—lose their power to crush us if we see the goodness of God. The ultimate end of our lives is this, Ecclesiastes says: "the dust returns to the ground as it was, and the lifebreath returns to God who bestowed it" (12:7)—to God who loves us as a good mother loves her children. In the unending joy of that union, the suffering and sorrow of this short life will look smaller to us, as Paul says (Rom. 8:18). Nothing in this view of our relation to God makes *joie de vivre* seem any less crazy; sin and death are still real evils. But tasting the goodness of God makes seeing the world's evils and our own compatible with joy in the Lord.

I think the Psalmist is speaking for people who take this long way round to peace and cheer when he says, "I have taught myself to be contented like a weaned child with its mother; like a weaned child am I in my mind"

(131:2).[12] How can a child who is being weaned understand the evil of the weaning? What he wants is right there; there is nothing bad about his having it—it costs his mother nothing to satisfy him; the pain of doing without it is sharp and urgent. And so, for a while, the child will be overwhelmed by the evil of his situation. But sooner or later in his thrashing he will also see his mother, and that makes all the difference. His desire for what she will not give him is still urgent, and the pain of the deprivation remains sharp. But in seeing her, he feels her love of him. He senses her goodness, and he comes to trust her. As Isaiah puts it, he sucks consolation to the full in another way (66:11). That is how he can be both weaned and also resting peacefully by her side.

And doesn't it seem likely that he comes to see his mother as he does just because he finds the evil of weaning intolerable? How much did he see her when his focus was himself and what he wanted, the comfort of the breast and the taste of the milk? The evil of the weaning, which seems to separate him from her, in fact drives him toward recognizing her as a person, and a person who loves him.

For Hallie, for the author of Ecclesiastes, and for me, too, the ghastly vision in the mirror of evil becomes a means to finding the goodness of God, and with it peace and joy. I don't know any better way to sum it up than Habakkuk's. Habukkuk has the Ecclesiastes temperament. He begins his book this way: "How long, O lord, shall I cry out and You not listen, shall I shout to You, 'Violence!' and You not save? Why do You make me see iniquity, why do You look upon wrong? Raiding and violence are before me, Strife continues and contention goes on. That is why decision fails and justice never emerges" (1:1–4). But he ends his book this way. He presents the agricultural equivalent of nuclear holocaust: the worst sufferings imaginable to him, the greatest disaster for himself and his people. And he says this: "Though the fig tree does not bud, and no yield is on the vine, though the olive crop has failed, and the fields produce no grain, though sheep have vanished from the fold, and no cattle are in the pen, yet will I rejoice in the Lord, exult in the God who delivers me. My Lord God is my strength" (3:17–19).

This is the best I can do to tell my story.[13]

## READING COMPREHENSION QUESTIONS

1.  According to Stump, evil serves as a kind of mirror, so that when we see evil in the world, we also see ourselves. Briefly explain the several different ways in which people might react to this discovery, according to Stump. In which category does your own reaction to evil fall?

---

[12]The pastor of the South Bend, Indiana, Christian Reformed Church, Len vander Zee, whose sermons are so full of wit, wisdom, and learning that they are more worth publishing and reading than much that appears in the journals in the field, preached an insightful sermon on this passage and the problem of evil in 1992. If that sermon were published, it would be a foolish oversight not to cite it here; as it is, the closest I can come to citing it is to say that his sermons are available from his church office.

[13]I am grateful to my husband, Donald Stump, and to my friends William Alston, Alvin Plantinga, and Peter van Inwagen for helpful suggestions on an earlier draft of this essay. I am also deeply indebted to my two teachers: John Crossett, whose efforts on my behalf made this essay possible, and Norman Kretzmann, whose thoughtful collaboration has made all my work, this essay included, much better than it would have been otherwise.

2.  Stump argues that we have a cognitive faculty that enables us to recognize what is evil, as well as different degrees of evil. Based on what Stump says in the text, explain how she would respond to the following two objections to this view: (1) different cultures recognize different things as evil, so there could be no *human* (species-wide) faculty for recognizing evil; and (2) even if we can all recognize evil, we can't all distinguish between degrees of evils.

3.  At one point, Stump says, "So, in an odd sort of way, the mirror of evil can also lead us to God." As best you can, explain her argument for this assertion.

4.  Explain Stump's analogy between evil and weaning. Does this strike you as a good analogy? Why or why not?

5.  Consider Stump's overall account of evil here. Do you think what she says provides a suitable theodicy, that is, a justification of evil in the world that also maintains the possibility of God's goodness and power?

# 6

# Knowledge, Skepticism, and Belief

## MOTIVATION

Like most people, you probably take yourself to know many things. Consider, for instance, your immediate surroundings and what you are currently doing. As you are reading this sentence, ask yourself whether you know such things as that you are now awake reading this sentence, that this sentence is printed in a book of philosophy, that there are other sentences on this page and that the book is roughly of a certain size, shape, and weight. You will probably think the answer is obvious: "Of course I know these things!" In addition to what you think you know about your immediate surroundings, you also probably take yourself to have knowledge about your own past—that you grew up in such and such town or city, that you were in, say, Cancun last week, and so on. You also think there are other people—people with minds, who have thoughts and feelings—and you think you know these things. But in order to really know all this, it all must be real. But how do you know that right now you are *not* dreaming?

If you have seen the movie *The Matrix,* you may recall the scene in which Morpheus says to Neo:

> "Have you ever had a dream, Neo, that you were so sure was real?
> What if you were unable to wake from that dream, Neo? How would you
> know the difference between the dreamworld and the real world?"

Try pinching yourself. Does that convince you that you aren't dreaming? Should it? You might think that you just couldn't be dreaming what you now seem to be experiencing; your current experiences are so vivid and fit together so well.

Granted, your own imagination may not be up to the task of generating on its own the full, integrated range of visual, auditory, gustatory, olfactory, and tactile experiences that you are now having. But perhaps a sinister something of the sort featured in *The Matrix* is at work.

MORPHEUS: "What is the Matrix? Control."

MORPHEUS: "The Matrix is a computer-generated dreamworld built to keep us under control in order to change a human being into this" [he holds up a battery].

NEO: "No! I don't believe it! It's not possible!"

Long before the Wachowski brothers thought up *The Matrix*, sixteenth-century philosopher René Descartes raised the possibility of being systematically deceived by an evil genius in order to raise questions about his own knowledge. In the reading that is included in this chapter, Descartes considers the possibility that some powerful evil genius has caused him to have all of the ordinary beliefs he now has, but that all of his beliefs are false. *The Matrix* is a nonsupernatural version of Descartes' evil-genius scenario.

Contemporary philosophers writing about knowledge and skepticism like to talk about the possibility of your being a brain in a vat of nutrients hooked up to a computer (operated of course by a mad scientist or two), which sends signals to your brain that create a fully integrated dreamworld. (The short story by John Pollock included in our readings describes a brain-in-a-vat scenario.) Evil geniuses, *The Matrix*, and brains in vats are all versions of the same idea: that our experiences might be founded on a massive and systematic deception.

We bring up the possibility of dreaming and evil geniuses to make a philosophical point about knowledge regarding the external world. If, for all you can now tell, you could be in a Matrix dreamworld, then you can't really rule out the possibility that you are now having (or being made to have) a perfectly integrated dream. But if you can't rule out this hypothesis, then you don't really know all of the sorts of things that you think you do, including your current beliefs that you are awake, holding a book, and reading these sentences printed in the book. (Sorry.)

So, the possibility of being in a dreamworld seems to undermine your having any knowledge of the external world. Or does it? If it does, what *should* your attitude be toward the beliefs you currently have about the external world? *Should* you perhaps suspend belief—taking up an attitude of *non*belief—refusing to believe or disbelieve propositions about the external world? Could you even do this? These philosophical questions about knowledge, skepticism, and belief are addressed in the readings featured in this part of the book. Let us begin with the question of knowledge.

## EPISTEMOLOGY

The **theory of knowledge** or **epistemology** (derived from the Greek word for knowledge, "episteme") inquires into the nature, possibility, and scope of knowledge. And so, among the main questions it addresses are these:

What is knowledge?

Is knowledge possible?

If knowledge of some sort is possible, is it restricted to certain sorts of subject matter? For instance, if we can and do have knowledge of the external world, what about knowledge of right and wrong (moral knowledge) or of God and immortality (religious knowledge)?

There is a logical progression in the order of these questions. To be in a position to address the second question one must first inquire into the nature of knowledge in order to know what one is talking about when one raises questions about its possibility. And unless one can give an affirmative answer to the second question, there is no sense in raising the third. As we proceed in this introduction, we will say more about each of the topics raised by these three questions, particularly the first two.

But before moving on to the first question, regarding the nature of knowledge, let us make two further remarks about the field of epistemology.

First, in addition to raising various questions about knowledge, epistemologists also raise parallel questions about the justification of our beliefs, where to have a justified belief is a matter (roughly) of having evidence or reasons for the truth of that belief.[1] And one main reason that the theory of knowledge addresses questions of justification is that on a traditional conception of knowledge, knowing a proposition requires being justified in believing it. If this traditional conception is correct (a matter we take up next), then to understand knowledge, one must understand the nature of justification. So in addition to questions about knowledge, epistemologists also raise questions about the nature, possibility, and scope of justification.

Second, we have included two readings in this chapter that concern what is referred to as the "ethics of belief," even though this topic has received far less attention in epistemology than the topics of knowledge and justification. Perhaps this is because many epistemologists assume that the topic belongs to ethics rather than epistemology. In any case, it is a topic that involves questions of belief, justification, and knowledge and so it belongs at least partly within the field of epistemology.

With these preliminaries out of the way, let us now consider some basic concepts and positions regarding the nature, possibility, and scope of knowledge, after which we will turn to the ethics of belief.

## THREE KINDS OF KNOWLEDGE

"Do you know John? I do. He knows how to fix computers when they break. I told him about your computer problems and so he knows that you need help."

---

[1] If you have read the introduction to the chapter on the existence of God, you may recall the discussion of the difference between explanatory reasons for belief and justifying reasons for belief. Justifying reasons for a belief are the sorts of reasons that provide a justification for that belief—that provide reasons for thinking that the belief is true. Throughout this introduction, we use the term "evidence" very generally to refer to all kinds of grounds or reasons (including, for example, other beliefs, perceptual experience, and intuitive understanding) that have to do with truth.

The word "know" is used three times in this passage for three different types of knowledge. In the first sentence, its use has to do with being acquainted with someone. One can also be acquainted with things and events other than persons, including one's own pains, feelings, and perceptions. Call this *knowledge by acquaintance*. The word's second appearance has to do with knowing how to do something. You probably know how to ride a bike, drive a car, and how to look up a word in a dictionary. Call this *skill knowledge*. Finally, there is the use of "know" as when the speaker says, "He knows that you need help," in which knowledge has to do with propositions[2]—**propositional knowledge**. It is this third sort of knowledge that mainly concerns epistemologists because, traditionally, they have been particularly interested in what is involved in (nonaccidentally) having true beliefs. So let us concentrate exclusively on the philosophical controversy concerning propositional knowledge. (Because it is to be understood that we are concerned exclusively with propositional knowledge, we will henceforth drop the modifier "propositional.")

Let us now consider a basic division within epistemology regarding knowledge.

## SKEPTICISM VERSUS NONSKEPTICISM

The philosophical view according to which knowledge about a certain subject matter or domain is not only possible but is in fact something individuals typically possess is sometimes called "dogmatism." Unfortunately, this label suggests the unsavory idea that those who think they have knowledge about some domain are close-minded people who refuse to consider evidence that might contradict their beliefs about the domain in question. But someone who thinks that they have knowledge need not be close-minded at all; he or she might be ready to revise beliefs in light of new evidence. So, instead of using the word "dogmatism," let us simply refer to this view as **nonskepticism**, and those who hold it as nonskeptics.

Nonskepticism is opposed to skepticism. **Skepticism** about knowledge involves at a minimum the refusal to grant that there is knowledge. But in refusing to grant knowledge, there are two ways to be a skeptic. One kind of skeptic *denies* that there is knowledge, while another kind of skeptic is noncommittal and *withholds belief* about whether or not there is knowledge. The first kind of skepticism, call it **theoretical skepticism**, is to nonskepticism what atheism is to theism.[3] But like an agnostic regarding the existence of God, the second kind of skeptic we are considering is a kind of epistemological agnostic—neither affirming nor denying that there is knowledge. Let's call this kind of skeptical view **practical**

---

[2]A proposition is to be understood as the *content* of a belief that can be expressed by a declarative sentence. Notice that the same proposition can be expressed by different sentences. The sentence "Dallas is in Texas" expresses the same proposition in English as does the sentence "Dallas está en Tejas" in Spanish. So the content of the belief that Dallas is in Texas is the same as the content of the belief that Dallas está en Tejas.

[3]This view is also called **Cartesian skepticism** after Descartes, who, by the way, was not a skeptic but entertained certain sorts of skeptical arguments as part of a method for locating a firm foundation for knowledge. See the selection by Descartes included in our readings.

**skepticism**, because those who embrace it adopt a certain practical attitude of withholding both belief and disbelief regarding knowledge.[4] We mention practical skepticism because it is an important skeptical option that has found a number of supporters. However, the debate that is featured in our readings is between nonskeptics and theoretical skeptics and so the following discussion will focus mainly on these two positions.

In addition to the distinction between theoretical and practical skepticism about knowledge, we also need to be aware of the distinctions between local and global skepticism, and between mere ignorance and skepticism.[5] Let us take these distinctions in order.

**Local versus global skepticism**.     This distinction has to do with our third epistemological question, namely, the question of scope. There are different general types of subject matter or, as we are calling them, different domains about which one might have knowledge, including the external physical world, other minds, mathematics, religion, ethics, aesthetics, and politics. This list is not meant to be complete. A **local skeptic** is someone who is skeptical about knowledge of some domains but not about others. For instance, one might be a skeptic about the possibility of religious knowledge, but be a nonskeptic about knowledge of the external world. A **global skeptic** is someone who is skeptical about all subject matters, including, of course, philosophy. (This means that a consistent global skeptic will refuse to claim that she *knows* that global skepticism is true!)

**Ignorance versus theoretical skepticism**.     This distinction is important for understanding the central claim of the theoretical skeptic. There are many things about the external world that we currently don't know, but that future scientific investigation may reveal. About such matters, our current lack of knowledge is a matter of **ignorance**. Theoretical skepticism goes beyond claims of ignorance. A theoretical skeptic about, say, knowledge of the external world claims that not only do human beings happen to be ignorant of certain matters regarding the external world, they do not have *any* knowledge of the external world. The theoretical skeptic attempts to back up this sweeping claim by arguing that knowledge about such matters is not possible. At bottom, then, the theoretical skeptic is in the business of arguing that knowledge in a certain domain is not possible and that's why no one has any knowledge about that domain.

With all of these distinctions in mind we can clarify the main positions in the debate over knowledge as follows:

---

[4]This kind of epistemological skepticism is often called **Pyrrhonian skepticism** in honor of the ancient Greek philosopher Pyrrho of Elis (c. 365–c. 270 B.C.E.), who is regarded as one of the founders of skepticism.

[5]Another very important distinction in epistemology is between **a posteriori** and **a priori knowledge**. This distinction was introduced in the introduction to Chapter 4 in connection with justification. And it's the same distinction here, only applied to knowledge. A posteriori knowledge is knowledge that is gained on the basis of experience (it is knowledge that is acquired posterior to or after experience), while a priori knowledge is knowledge that can be acquired independently of sense experience. It is often claimed that mathematical knowledge is a priori. In this chapter we are mainly concerned with knowledge of the external world, which, of course, makes it a posteriori.

**Nonskepticism about knowledge** is the view that with regard to a certain domain or subject matter, knowledge is possible. For some domains, such as one's immediate external environment, the nonskeptic will claim that people typically do, in fact, have knowledge.

**Theoretical skepticism about knowledge** is the view that with respect to at least one domain regarding which many people claim to have knowledge, not only do they not have knowledge, but knowledge of that domain is not possible. Global skeptics include all domains; local skeptics are more selective.

**Practical skepticism about knowledge** involves taking a noncommittal position with respect to knowledge in some or all domains (regarding which people commonly claim to have knowledge) by refusing to affirm or deny knowledge about such domains.

Now that we have a basic understanding of the two main epistemological positions regarding the possibility of knowledge, let us proceed in the next section to consider the nature of knowledge, before turning to the debate between theoretical skeptics and nonskeptics.

## WHAT IS KNOWLEDGE?

As noted earlier, in order to inquire into the possibility of knowledge, one must first have a reasonably clear idea of what knowledge is supposed to be—its nature. When philosophers inquire into the nature of something, whether it is personal identity, free will, or knowledge, they are usually interested in providing a definition of whatever it is they are concerned with. Thus, epistemologists inquiring into the nature of knowledge typically aim to give a definition of knowledge, specifically, propositional knowledge—to define what it is for someone *S* to know some proposition *p*. The place to start in trying to define propositional knowledge is to think of conditions that must be met—**necessary conditions**—for knowing some proposition. But more is needed for such a definition: philosophers also aim to discover a list of necessary conditions that (taken together) jointly constitute a **sufficient condition** for knowledge, that is, that are *enough* for having knowledge. The idea is that by specifying a set of necessary and jointly sufficient conditions for propositional knowledge, one will have made progress toward illuminating the fundamental nature or essence of knowledge. Once we know what knowledge is—its nature—we can proceed to investigate the possibility and scope of knowledge.

So, let us see what progress can be made in defining knowledge.

In order to know some proposition *p*, one must believe that *p* is the case. One can't know that Springfield is the capital of Illinois unless one at least believes the proposition in question. Sometimes people will say things like, "I know that Matthew made the team, but I just can't believe it!" But here the speaker is not to be taken literally when he says he can't believe that Matthew made the team; rather, "I just can't believe it" is (in this context) just a way of expressing surprise at Matt's having made it. So here is one necessary condition for *S*'s knowing that *p*:

*S* believes *p* (the belief condition).

But clearly, believing a proposition is not sufficient (is not enough) to know that proposition. If someone honestly believes that Chicago is the capital of

Illinois, then no matter how fervently she believes it, her belief does not rise to the status of knowledge. One can't *know* what is, as a matter of fact, false (though one can *think* one knows some false proposition). Again, people will often say things like, "I just *knew* that Mary would join us for dinner," where it turns out that it is false that Mary joined them for dinner and the speaker knows it. Saying that she just *knew*, is a way of expressing one's *confidence* that Mary would show up; it need not be taken literally as a claim to know what is false. These observations suggest a further necessary condition for knowledge:

$p$ is true (the truth condition).[6]

If we put the belief and truth conditions together, do we have enough (are they jointly sufficient) for knowledge? If so, then we can define knowledge as true belief (TB) as follows (using "= def" as a way to indicate a proposed definition):

TB    S knows that $p$ = def:    S believes that $p$ and $p$ is true.

Most philosophers will not accept this as an adequate definition of knowledge because of cases such as the following.

One morning Stephen reads his horoscope in the local paper and on the sole basis of what it says, he comes to believe that by the end of the day he will have the $100 he needs (but which he does not now have) to buy a very fine metal detector. Later that day, he finds out that he's won a $100 lottery that he had entered weeks earlier and had since forgotten about.

As it happens, Stephen's belief that he will have the money by the end of that day turns out to be true. But that morning he has no real evidence for this belief (assuming that horoscopes are not reliable); instead, he lucks out in having a belief that is true. It would be different if he believed that he would have the $100 because his trustworthy loving mom had called him that morning and said she had sent a $100 check to him that would arrive later that day. In this latter case, the fact that he knows his mom to be trustworthy and the fact that she called him up and told him about the money would be very good evidence for his belief. To have good evidence for some proposition and to believe that proposition on the basis of that evidence is to be *justified* in holding that belief.[7] And justification is what seems to be missing in the horoscope example. So, let us add another condition for knowledge:

S is justified in believing $p$ (the justification condition).

(Notice that satisfying this condition without the truth condition being satisfied is not sufficient for knowledge. One can be justified in holding some belief,

---

[6]What is truth? This is another BIG philosophical issue whose pursuit would take us far too afield for present purposes. There are competing theories of truth: the correspondence theory, the coherence theory, the pragmatic theory, the redundancy theory, and others. Let us take for granted a very intuitive and commonly held view about the nature of truth, namely the **correspondence theory of truth**. According to this view, what makes a proposition true is that it corresponds to the facts it describes. A false proposition is one that fails to correspond to the facts it describes. So, for instance, the proposition *water is composed of H₂O molecules* is true just in case the liquid, water, is, as a matter of fact, composed of H₂O molecules. Again, the proposition *Springfield is (at this time) the capital of Illinois* is true just in case the city Springfield at this time really is the capital of Illinois.

[7]Some epistemologists would add that one's evidence must not be overridden by conflicting evidence or in some way undermined. But we may leave these subtleties aside.

but still be mistaken. I might be justified in believing that eating carrots is good for your eyes because there is scientific evidence that supports this claim, and that's why I believe it. But it may be false that carrots are good for your eyes, in which case I have a justified but false belief.)

The result of combining all three conditions gives us the following "justified true belief" (JTB) definition of knowledge—often called the "traditional" conception of knowledge:

> JTB   S knows that p = def:   S believes p, p is true, and S is justified in believing p.

JTB certainly seems to be an improvement over TB. But there is a further issue having to do with the justification condition. Notice that justification is a matter of degree—one can be more or less justified in believing some proposition, depending on the level and quality of one's evidence. But this raises an important question: *how* justified must one's belief be in order to have knowledge? This will depend on how strong one's evidence for the belief is. According to the epistemological tradition inspired by Descartes—the Cartesian tradition[8]—knowledge requires that one's evidence be enough to *guarantee* the truth of one's belief; that *given* one's evidence, one could not be mistaken in one's belief. After all, if we are interested in having reliable true beliefs, then the way of being sure is to have evidence that guarantees true belief. Furthermore, when someone claims to know something and they are challenged, they tend to back down from their knowledge claim if they realize that their evidence is not conclusive.

If we accept the **Cartesian conception of knowledge**, then knowledge is defined as justified *guaranteed* true belief (JGTB):

> JGTB   S knows that p = def:   S believes p, p is true, and one's justifying evidence for p guarantees the truth of p.[9]

Satisfaction of these conditions puts one in a position to *rule out* the possibility of being mistaken. An implication, then, of this Cartesian conception of knowledge is that if, for example, I know that the bird I'm looking at is a crow, then I must have evidence that is good enough to rule out the possibility that the bird in question is a cardinal, or a blue jay, or a goldfinch, or any species of bird, other than its being a crow. In short, if one really knows, then one is in a position to exclude alternative possibilities that are incompatible with one's belief. Because this idea of ruling out or excluding incompatible possibilities will play an important role in our discussion of debate between skeptics and nonskeptics, let us call it the **exclusion principle** (EP) and formulate it as follows:

> EP   In order to know some proposition p, one must be able, on the basis of one's evidence, to rule out or exclude (and thus know to be false) any proposition that one knows to be incompatible with p.[10]

---

[8]This term is widely used in philosophy to refer to ideas and themes from Descartes' work.

[9]Sometimes this conception of knowledge is called *infallibilism*.

[10]See Chapter 7 in Noah Lemos, *An Introduction to the Theory of Knowledge* (Cambridge, England: Cambridge University Press, 2007) for an excellent discussion of skepticism in general and the exclusion principle in particular.

Notice that EP is not being proposed as part of the definition of knowledge—to do so would make the resulting definition circular, because this principle refers to knowledge. Rather, as already noted, it should be understood as one implication of the JGTB definition under consideration.

## IS KNOWLEDGE POSSIBLE?

The version of skepticism that is raised by evil geniuses, brain in a vat, and the other skeptical scenarios with which we began concerns knowledge of the external world based on sense experience. Even though there are other species of skepticism—moral skepticism, religious skepticism, skepticism about the past, about other minds, and so on—let us stick to this version, which seems to pose one of the strongest challenges to common sense. This brings us back to a question raised at the outset of the chapter: don't you take yourself to know that you are now awake and that you are now, for instance, holding a book in your hands? Consider the proposition that you are now holding a book in your hands, which you would express by saying: *I am now holding a book in my hands.* If you are sitting in good light, eyes open, visual apparatus working, looking in the right direction, you have very good visual and perhaps tactile evidence for the truth of the proposition in question. But are you able to rule out all incompatible propositions? It would seem not. For consider what the skeptic has to say.

*Skeptic's Brain-in-a-Vat Argument*

S1. If you know that you are now holding a book in your hands, then you know that you are *not* a brain in a vat.
S2. You don't know that you are *not* a brain in a vat.
Therefore,
S3. You don't know that you are now holding a book in your hands.

To appreciate the force of this argument, let us consider each premise. Premise S1 is supposed to be based on the nature of knowledge. In particular, it is based on what we identified as an implication of the Cartesian conception of knowledge—the exclusion principle, EP. The proposition that you are a brain in a vat being caused to have dreamworld experiences—experiences that are indistinguishable from experiences that could otherwise be caused by an external world—is incompatible with the proposition that you are really holding a book in your hands—a real book. And this is something that has been called to your attention. So, EP implies that premise S1 is true. (Take a moment to think this through.) Furthermore (moving to premise S2), the evidence you currently have for your belief that you are now holding a book in your hands is not good enough to rule out the incompatible brain-in-a-vat proposition. So you don't know that you are *not* a brain in a vat. Putting S1 and S2 together we arrive at the conclusion that you don't know that you are now holding a book in your hands. This same form of argument can be run against any claim to know about the current state of the external world based on experience. The alarming result is theoretical skepticism regarding knowledge of the external world.

This argument is valid; so if the premises are true, then the conclusion must also be true. Therefore, in order to avoid skepticism, one must challenge at least one of the premises.

To deny premise S1 would require rejecting the exclusion principle. But if EP is an implication of the Cartesian conception of knowledge, then that conception must be wrong. We will return to this option momentarily.

The other option is to challenge premise S2 by arguing that you *do* know that you are not (at this moment) a brain in a vat. This is the option pursued by G. E. Moore (1873–1958), one of the most prominent philosophers in the first half of the twentieth century and a staunch defender of the commonsense, nonskeptical position. (A selection from Moore is included in our readings, though he does not work with the brain-in-a-vat scenario.) Moore's strategy was to turn the skeptic's argument on its head by denying the skeptic's conclusion and using the denial as a premise for concluding that one really does know that one is not a brain in a vat. Here, in outline, is how Moore argues:

*Moore's Reversal Argument*

M1. If you know that you now have a book in your hand, then you know that you are *not* a brain in a vat.
M2. You *do* know that you now have a book in your hand (denial of S3).
Therefore,
M3. You *do* know that you are *not* a brain in a vat (denial of S2).

Moore's argument might strike some readers as a case of begging the question— one of the common mistakes in argumentation that was discussed in the first chapter. Isn't Moore just *assuming* that the nonskeptic's position is true when, in the second premise, he denies the skeptic's conclusion? He clearly would be guilty of committing this fallacy if he did not offer non-question-begging reasons for accepting his second premise. But that is what he attempts to do in the selection included among our readings. Taking up the skeptic's position against Moore is Peter Unger in the reading that follows Moore's. Perhaps the skeptic about knowledge of the external world wins after all.

Of course, even if Unger comes out on top in this particular debate (and we aren't claiming he does), the nonskeptic has the option of revisiting the Cartesian conception of knowledge that both Moore and Unger seem to accept. And this brings us to our final point in this section.

Despite Moore's gallant attempt to rebut the skeptic's argument, many philosophers have concluded that *if* the Cartesian conception of knowledge really does correctly characterize the ordinary concept of knowledge, then our commonsense views about what we know (or can know) are just radically mistaken. But this has led many philosophers to question the Cartesian conception as well as the exclusion principle that leads to skepticism. One might consider just going back to the JTB definition and leave it at that.

But on the basis of two clever examples described by philosopher Edmund Gettier in his three-page (!) 1963 classic paper, "Is Justified True Belief Knowledge?" many epistemologists have come to believe that the three conditions mentioned in JTB are not jointly sufficient for knowledge.[11] It turns out that there are many so-called Gettier counterexamples to the JTB definition. Here is one of them.

---

[11] Gettier's paper was originally published in the journal *Analysis* (vol. 23, pp. 121–123), and has since been reprinted many times.

You are looking out your window at what you take to be a bird on your back fence about 30 feet away. It is a sunny day, you have your contacts in, and your view of that part of the fence is unobscured. You have very good visual evidence for the proposition *there is a bird on my back fence*, so you would seem to be justified in believing this proposition. However, some joker has glued a fake look-alike "bird" onto the part of the fence you happen to be looking at, while just a few feet away (but out of your line of vision) is a real bird sitting on your back fence. So your belief (notice the generality of the proposition you believe—it doesn't specify where on the fence the bird is sitting) is true. Hence, you have a justified true belief.

But intuitively, it seems that you don't *know* this. Given the setup, it's a matter of luck that your belief is true. After all, your evidence is not properly connected to the state of affairs that makes your belief true.

Reflection on Gettier counterexamples has prompted epistemologists to search for a fourth condition that, when added to the other three featured in the JTB conception, will yield a set of conditions that are jointly sufficient for knowledge.[12] And, of course, if one thinks that the more demanding Cartesian conception is too strong, the task will be to discover a fourth condition that strengthens the JTB conception without being too demanding. But this has proved *very* difficult and continues to be a source of controversy among epistemologists.

Although philosophers have not (yet) solved the problems of knowledge, the work they have done helps us to understand some of the complexities that must be confronted in trying to solve these problems.

Let us turn finally to the ethics of belief.

## THE ETHICS OF BELIEF

Suppose for a moment that you realize that you do not currently have knowledge about some subject matter. This may be due either to your lack of adequate evidence, or to the fact that knowledge about the matter in question is not possible. In such circumstances, what are your obligations (if any) with respect to what you believe about the subject matter in question? One answer to this question is what we may call the **sufficient evidence doctrine**:

> SED    One ought only to believe what one has sufficient evidence or justification for believing.

Of course, much will depend on what counts as "sufficient" justification. But perhaps it need not be evidence that is sufficient for knowledge. Perhaps one can have enough justification to satisfy the requirement even if one's justification is not also enough for knowledge.

SED implies that it would be wrong to hold some belief solely because it is convenient or because it makes one feel comfortable. We find a forceful defense of this doctrine, and a condemnation of holding beliefs for the sake of convenience or comfort, in the reading by William K. Clifford.

---

[12]However, some epistemologists have proposed accounts of knowledge that reject the justification condition. This option gets into complications that we cannot go into here.

This question about the ethics of belief may be raised in connection with any domain of inquiry, but it is very often raised in connection with religious belief. Presumably, having religious faith and, in particular, faith that God exists, involves having a belief for which one does not (or at least need not) have sufficient evidence of its truth. This would mean that according to SED, one would be violating an obligation in *believing* that God exists. Of course, one could, instead of believing that God exists, take up some other attitude such as *hoping*. To merely hope that God exists while not believing He does would be to give up a kind of conviction in God's existence that is important to many theists. So theists in particular have reason to examine the sufficient evidence doctrine.

One way of examining this doctrine is to do what Peter van Inwagen does in the reading that follows Clifford's. He asks what our lives would be like if we were to rigorously apply this epistemological requirement to all areas of life. In the course of examining this question, van Inwagen considers how one ought to respond in cases in which one's beliefs about a particular subject matter conflict with the beliefs of someone who one takes to be just as well informed as oneself about the subject in question. This is a question all of us are likely to face on some occasions.

Questions about knowledge—its nature, possibility, and scope—are important because people base their lives on what they think they know. Do we really know what we think we know? Skepticism challenges the common assumption that we do have knowledge. Global skeptics challenge all knowledge; local skeptics challenge knowledge about particular subject matters. This chapter invites readers to think about knowledge and the challenge of skepticism as well as what one ought to believe in cases in which one lacks sufficient evidence.

# 28

# A Brain in a Vat

### JOHN L. POLLOCK

*John Pollock is Regents Professor of Philosophy and Research Professor of Cognitive Science at the University of Arizona. He has published numerous articles and books, including* How to Build a Person *(1990),* Contemporary Theories of Knowledge *(1986), and* Thinking about Acting: Logical Foundations for Rational Decision Making *(2006). The following short story features a "brain-in-a-vat" scenario intended to challenge one's beliefs that one is aware of and has knowledge about the sort of external world of cities, people, trees, rocks, oceans, stars, and so on that are part of commonsense thinking.*

It all began that cold Wednesday night. I was sitting alone in my office watching the rain come down on the deserted streets outside, when the phone rang. It was Harry's wife, and she sounded terrified. They had been having a late supper alone in their apartment when suddenly the front door came crashing in and six hooded men burst into the room. The men were armed and they made Harry and Anne lay face down on the floor while they went through Harry's pockets. When they found his driver's license one of them carefully scrutinized Harry's face, comparing it with the official photograph and then muttered, "It's him all right." The leader of the intruders produced a hypodermic needle and injected Harry with something that made him lose consciousness almost immediately. For some reason they only tied and gagged Anne. Two of the men left the room and returned with a stretcher and white coats. They put Harry on the stretcher, donned the white coats, and trundled him out of the apartment, leaving Anne lying on the floor. She managed to squirm to the window in time to see them put Harry in an ambulance and drive away.

By the time she called me, Anne was coming apart at the seams. It had taken her several hours to get out of her bonds, and then she called the police. To her consternation, instead of uniformed officers, two plain clothed officials arrived and, without even looking over the scene, they proceeded to tell her that there was nothing they could do and if she knew what was good for her she would keep her mouth shut. If she raised a fuss they would put out the word that she was a psycho and she would never see her husband again.

Not knowing what else to do, Anne called me. She had had the presence of mind to note down the number of the ambulance, and I had no great difficulty

SOURCE: From John L. Pollock, *Contemporary Theories of Knowledge* (Lanham, MD: Rowman & Littlefield, 1986). Reprinted by permission of the author and Rowman and Littlefield Press.

tracing it to a private clinic at the outskirts of town. When I arrived at the clinic I was surprised to find it locked up like a fortress. There were guards at the gate and it was surrounded by a massive wall. My commando training stood me in good stead as I negotiated the 20 foot wall, avoided the barbed wire, and silenced the guard dogs on the other side. The ground floor windows were all barred, but I managed to wriggle up a drainpipe and get in through a secondstory window that someone had left ajar. I found myself in a laboratory. Hearing muffled sounds next door I peeked through the keyhole and saw what appeared to be a complete operating room and a surgical team laboring over Harry. He was covered with a sheet from the neck down and they seemed to be connecting tubes and wires to him. I stifled a gasp when I realized that they had removed the top of Harry's skull. To my considerable consternation, one of the surgeons reached into the open top of Harry's head and eased his brain out, placing it in a stainless steel bowl. The tubes and wires I had noted earlier were connected to the now disembodied brain. The surgeons carried the bloody mass carefully to some kind of tank and lowered it in. My first thought was that I had stumbled on a covey of futuristic Satanists who got their kicks from vivisection. My second thought was that Harry was an insurance agent. Maybe this was their way of getting even for the increases in their malpractice insurance rates. If they did this every Wednesday night, their rates were no higher than they should be!

My speculations were interrupted when the lights suddenly came on in my darkened hidey hole and I found myself looking up at the scariest group of medical men I had ever seen. They manhandled me into the next room and strapped me down on an operating table. I thought, "Oh, oh, I'm in for it now!" The doctors huddled at the other end of the room, but I couldn't turn my head far enough to see what they were doing. They were mumbling among themselves, probably deciding my fate. A door opened and I heard a woman's voice. The deferential manner assumed by the medical malpractitioners made it obvious who was boss. I strained to see this mysterious woman but she hovered just out of my view. Then, to my astonishment, she walked up and stood over me and I realized it was my secretary, Margot. I began to wish I had given her that Christmas bonus after all.

It was Margot, but it was a different Margot than I had ever seen. She was wallowing in the heady wine of authority as she bent over me. "Well Mike, you thought you were so smart, tracking Harry here to the clinic," she said. Even now she had the sexiest voice I have ever heard, but I wasn't really thinking about that. She went on, "It was all a trick just to get you here. You saw what happened to Harry. He's not really dead, you know. These gentlemen are the premier neuroscientists in the world today. They have developed a surgical procedure whereby they remove the brain from the body but keep it alive in a vat of nutrient. The Food and Drug Administration wouldn't approve the procedure, but we'll show them. You see all the wires going to Harry's brain? They connect him up with a powerful computer. The computer monitors the output of his motor cortex and provides input to the sensory cortex in such a way that everything appears perfectly normal to Harry. It produces a fictitious mental life that merges perfectly into his past life so that he is unaware that anything has happened to him. He thinks he is shaving right now and getting ready to go to the office and stick it to another neurosurgeon. But actually, he's just a brain in a vat."

"Once we have our procedure perfected we're going after the head of the Food and Drug Administration, but we needed some experimental subjects first.

Harry was easy. In order to really test our computer program we need someone who leads a more interesting and varied life—someone like you!" I was starting to squirm. The surgeons had drawn around me and were looking on with malevolent gleams in their eyes. The biggest brute, a man with a pockmarked face and one beady eye staring out from under his stringy black hair, was fondling a razor sharp scalpel in his still-bloody hands and looking like he could barely restrain his excitement. But Margot gazed down at me and murmured in that incredible voice, "I'll bet you think we're going to operate on you and remove your brain just like we removed Harry's, don't you? But you have nothing to worry about. We're not going to remove your brain. We already did—three months ago!"

With that they let me go. I found my way back to my office in a daze. For some reason, I haven't told anybody about this. I can't make up my mind. I am racked by the suspicion that I am really a brain in a vat and all this I see around me is just a figment of the computer. After all, how could I tell? If the computer program really works, no matter what I do, everything will seem normal. Maybe nothing I see is real. It's driving me crazy. I've even considered checking into that clinic voluntarily and asking them to remove my brain just so that I can be sure.

## READING COMPREHENSION QUESTIONS

1.   Would it help settle Mike's doubts were he to check into a clinic and have his brain removed? Why or why not?

2.   Can you think of any way of proving to yourself that you are not now a brain in a vat being caused to have the very experiences you are now having?

# 29

# Within the Sphere of the Doubtful

RENÉ DESCARTES

*French philosopher, scientist, and mathematician René Descartes (1598–1650) was one of the most influential figures in the rise of "modern philosophy." His most famous philosophical work is* Meditations on First Philosophy (1641), *and the selection below includes Meditation I and the opening paragraphs of Meditation II.*

SOURCE: From René Descartes, *Meditations on First Philosophy*, 2nd ed., 1642 (first published in 1641), in *The Philosophical Works of Descartes*, trans. E. S. Haldane and G. R. T. Ross, published by Cambridge University Press, Cambridge, 1931, and reprinted with their permission.

*In Meditation I, Descartes begins his search for a solid foundation for human knowledge by employing a "method of doubt" whereby one begins by examining the beliefs and convictions one currently holds about the external world and mathematics. Through a series of clever arguments involving the possibility of dreaming and of being deceived by an "evil genius," Descartes argues that none of his beliefs about the external world or mathematics is immune to doubt; none of them is certain. Because knowledge requires certainty, Descartes concludes that he lacks knowledge about the external world and mathematics. In Meditation II, Descartes begins his search for a solid foundation for knowledge that involves his famous "cogito" argument, which he elsewhere expresses as the argument* Cogito ergo sum, *"I am thinking, therefore I exist."*

## MEDITATION I

### Of the Things Which May be Brought within the Sphere of the Doubtful

It is now some years since I detected how many were the false beliefs that I had from my earliest youth admitted as true, and how doubtful was every-thing I had since constructed on this basis; and from that time I was convinced that I must once for all seriously undertake to rid myself of all the opinions which I had formerly accepted, and commence to build anew from the foundation, if I wanted to establish any firm and permanent structure in the sciences. But as this enterprise appeared to be a very great one, I waited until I had attained an age so mature that I could not hope that at any later date I should be better fitted to execute my design. This reason caused me to delay so long that I should feel that I was doing wrong were I to occupy in deliberation the time that yet remains to me for action. To-day, then, since very opportunely for the plan I have in view I have delivered my mind from every care [and am happily agitated by no passions] and since I have procured for myself an assured leisure in a peaceable retirement, I shall at last seriously and freely address myself to the general upheaval of all my former opinions.

Now for this object it is not necessary that I should show that all of these are false—I shall perhaps never arrive at this end. But inasmuch as reason already persuades me that I ought no less carefully to withhold my assent from matters which are not entirely certain and indubitable than from those which appear to me manifestly to be false, if I am able to find in each one some reason to doubt, this will suffice to justify my rejecting the whole. And for that end it will not be requisite that I should examine each in particular, which would be an endless undertaking; for owing to the fact that the destruction of the foundations of necessity brings with it the downfall of the rest of the edifice, I shall only in the first place attack those principles upon which all my former opinions rested.

All that up to the present time I have accepted as most true and certain I have learned either from the senses or through the senses; but it is sometimes proved to me that these senses are deceptive, and it is wiser not to trust entirely to anything by which we have once been deceived.

But it may be that although the senses sometimes deceive us concerning things which are hardly perceptible, or very far away, there are yet many others to be met with as to which we cannot reasonably have any doubt, although we recognise them by their means. For example, there is the fact that I am here, seated by the fire, attired in a dressing gown, having this paper in my hands and other similar matters. And how could I deny that these hands and this body are mine, were it not perhaps that I compare myself to certain persons, devoid of sense, whose cerebella are so troubled and clouded by the violent vapours of black bile, that they constantly assure us that they think they are kings when they are really quite poor, or that they are clothed in purple when they are really without covering, or who imagine that they have an earthenware head or are nothing but pumpkins or are made of glass. But they are mad, and I should not be any the less insane were I to follow examples so extravagant.

At the same time I must remember that I am a man, and that consequently I am in the habit of sleeping, and in my dreams representing to myself the same things or sometimes even less probable things, than do those who are insane in their waking moments. How often has it happened to me that in the night I dreamt that I found myself in this particular place, that I was dressed and seated near the fire, whilst in reality I was lying undressed in bed! At this moment it does indeed seem to me that it is with eyes awake that I am looking at this paper; that this head which I move is not asleep, that it is deliberately and of set purpose that I extend my hand and perceive it; what happens in sleep does not appear so clear nor so distinct as does all this. But in thinking over this I remind myself that on many occasions I have in sleep been deceived by similar illusions, and in dwelling carefully on this reflection I see so manifestly that there are no certain indications by which we may clearly distinguish wakefulness from sleep that I am lost in astonishment. And my astonishment is such that it is almost capable of persuading me that I now dream.

Now let us assume that we are asleep and that all these particulars, e.g. that we open our eyes, shake our head, extend our hands, and so on, are but false delusions; and let us reflect that possibly neither our hands nor our whole body are such as they appear to us to be. At the same time we must at least confess that the things which are represented to us in sleep are like painted representations which can only have been formed as the counterparts of something real and true, and that in this way those general things at least, i.e. eyes, a head, hands, and a whole body, are not imaginary things, but things really existent. For as a matter of fact, painters, even when they study with the greatest skill to represent sirens and satyrs by forms the most strange and extraordinary, cannot give them natures which are entirely new, but merely make a certain medley of the members of different animals; or if their imagination is extravagant enough to invent something so novel that nothing similar has ever before been seen, and that then their work represents a thing purely fictitious and absolutely false, it is certain all the same that the colours of which this is composed are necessarily real. And for the same reason, although these general things, to wit, [a body], eyes, a head, hands, and such like, may be imaginary, we are bound at the same time to confess that there are at least some other objects yet more simple and more universal, which are real and true; and of these just in the same way as with certain real colours, all these images of things which dwell in our thoughts, whether true and real or false and fantastic, are formed.

To such a class of things pertains corporeal nature in general, and its extension, the figure of extended things, their quantity or magnitude and number, as also the place in which they are, the time which measures their duration, and so on.

That is possibly why our reasoning is not unjust when we conclude from this that Physics, Astronomy, Medicine and all other sciences which have as their end the consideration of composite things, are very dubious and uncertain; but that Arithmetic, Geometry and other sciences of that kind which only treat of things that are very simple and very general, without taking great trouble to ascertain whether they are actually existent or not, contain some measure of certainty and an element of the indubitable. For whether I am awake or asleep, two and three together always form five, and the square can never have more than four sides, and it does not seem possible that truths so clear and apparent can be suspected of any falsity [or uncertainty].

Nevertheless I have long had fixed in my mind the belief that an all-powerful God existed by whom I have been created such as I am. But how do I know that He has not brought it to pass that there is no earth, no heaven, no extended body, no magnitude, no place, and that nevertheless [I possess the perceptions of all these things and that] they seem to me to exist just exactly as I now see them? And, besides, as I sometimes imagine that others deceive themselves in the things which they think they know best, how do I know that I am not deceived every time that I add two and three, or count the sides of a square, or judge of things yet simpler, if anything simpler can be imagined? But possibly God has not desired that I should be thus deceived, for He is said to be supremely good. If, however, it is contrary to His goodness to have made me such that I constantly deceive myself; it would also appear to be contrary to His goodness to permit me to be sometimes deceived, and nevertheless I cannot doubt that He does permit this.

There may indeed be those who would prefer to deny the existence of a God so powerful, rather than believe that all other things are uncertain. But let us not oppose them for the present, and grant that all that is here said of a God is a fable; nevertheless in whatever way they suppose that I have arrived at the state of being that I have reached—whether they attribute it to fate or to accident, or make out that it is by a continual succession of antecedents, or by some other method—since to err and deceive oneself is a defect, it is clear that the greater will be the probability of my being so imperfect as to deceive myself ever, as is the Author to whom they assign my origin the less powerful. To these reasons I have certainly nothing to reply, but at the end I feel constrained to confess that there is nothing in all that I formerly believed to be true, of which I cannot in some measure doubt, and that not merely through want of thought or through levity, but for reasons which are very powerful and maturely considered; so that henceforth I ought not the less carefully to refrain from giving credence to these opinions than to that which is manifestly false, if I desire to arrive at any certainty [in the sciences].

But it is not sufficient to have made these remarks, we must also be careful to keep them in mind. For these ancient and commonly held opinions still revert frequently to my mind, long and familiar custom having given them the right to occupy my mind against my inclination and rendered them almost masters of my belief; nor will I ever lose the habit of deferring to them or of placing my confidence in them, so long as I consider them as they really are, i.e. opinions in some measure doubtful, as I have just shown, and at the same time highly probable, so that there is much more reason to believe in than to deny them. That is why I consider that I shall not be acting amiss, if, taking of set purpose a contrary belief, I allow myself to be deceived, and for a certain time pretend that all these opinions are entirely false and imaginary, until at last, having thus balanced my former prejudices with my latter [so that they cannot divert my opinions more to one side than to the other], my judgment will no longer be dominated by bad usage or turned away from the right knowledge of the truth. For I am assured that there can be neither peril nor error in this course, and that I cannot at present yield too much to distrust, since I am not considering the question of action, but only of knowledge.

I shall then suppose, not that God who is supremely good and the fountain of truth, but some evil genius not less powerful than deceitful, has employed his whole energies in deceiving me; I shall consider that the heavens, the earth, colours, figures, sound, and all other external things are nought but the illusions and dreams of which this genius has availed himself in order to lay traps for my credulity; I shall consider myself as having no hands, no eyes, no flesh, no blood, nor any senses, yet falsely believing myself to possess all these things; I shall remain obstinately attached to this idea, and if by this means it is not in my power to arrive at the knowledge of any truth, I may at least do what is in my power [i.e. suspend my judgment], and with firm purpose avoid giving credence to any false thing, or being imposed upon by this arch deceiver, however powerful and deceptive he may be. But this task is a laborious one, and insensibly a certain lassitude leads me into the course of my ordinary life. And just as a captive who in sleep enjoys an imaginary liberty, when he begins to suspect that his liberty is but a dream, fears to awaken, and conspires with these agreeable illusions that the deception may be prolonged, so insensibly of my own accord I fall back into my former opinions, and I dread awakening from this slumber, lest the laborious wakefulness which would follow the tranquility of this repose should have to be spent not in daylight, but in the excessive darkness of the difficulties which have just been discussed.

## MEDITATION II

### Of the Nature of the Human Mind; and That
### It is More Easily Known than the Body

The Meditation of yesterday filled my mind with so many doubts that it is no longer in my power to forget them. And yet I do not see in what manner I can resolve them; and, just as if I had all of a sudden fallen into very deep water, I am so disconcerted that I can neither make certain of setting my feet on the bottom, nor can I swim and so support myself on the surface. I shall nevertheless make an effort and follow anew the same path as that on which I yesterday entered, i.e. I shall proceed by setting aside all that in which the least doubt could be supposed to exist, just as if I had discovered that it was absolutely false; and I shall ever follow in this road until I have met with something which is certain, or at least, if I can do nothing else, until I have learned for certain that there is nothing in the world that is certain. Archimedes, in order that he might draw the terrestrial globe out of its place, and transport it elsewhere, demanded only that one point should be fixed and immoveable; in the same way I shall have the right to conceive high hopes if I am happy enough to discover one thing only which is certain and indubitable.

I suppose, then, that all the things that I see are false, I persuade myself that nothing has ever existed of all that my fallacious memory represents to me. I consider that I possess no senses; I imagine that body, figure, extension, movement and place are but the fictions of my mind. What, then, can be esteemed as true? Perhaps nothing at all, unless that there is nothing in the world that is certain.

But how can I know there is not something different from those things that I have just considered, of which one cannot have the slightest doubt? Is there not some God, or some other being by whatever name we call it, who puts these reflections into my mind? That is not necessary, for is it not possible that I am capable of producing them myself? I myself, am I not at least something? But I have already denied that I had senses and body. Yet I hesitate, for what follows from that? Am I so dependent on body and senses that I cannot exist without these? But I was persuaded that there was nothing in all the world, that there was no heaven, no earth, that there were no minds, nor any bodies: was I not then likewise persuaded that I did not exist? Not at all; of a surety I myself did exist since I persuaded myself of something [or merely because I thought of something]. But there is some deceiver or other, very powerful and very cunning, who ever employs his ingenuity in deceiving me. Then without doubt I exist also if he deceives me, and let him deceive me as much as he will, he can never cause me to be nothing so long as I think that I am something. So that after having reflected well and carefully examined all things, we must come to the definite conclusion that this proposition: I am, I exist, is necessarily true each time that I pronounce it, or that I mentally conceive it. . . .

## READING COMPREHENSION QUESTIONS

1. In the opening two paragraphs, Descartes announces his plan for building a "firm and permanent structure in the sciences." Explain Descartes' so-called "method of doubt" for carrying out this project.

2. What is Descartes' point in bringing up the possibility of dreaming? Is there some test that one could use to distinguish waking experiences from dreams?

3. Exactly what sorts of beliefs does Descartes think he cannot doubt even if he is dreaming?

4. Why does Descartes dismiss the possibility that God is deceiving him? What reasons does he provide for this conclusion?

5. What are the steps in Descartes' "evil genius" argument? (You may want to begin by stating the conclusion, and then proceed to state each of the premises.)

6. At the end of the excerpt from Meditation II, Descartes writes, "I am, I exist, is necessarily true each time that I pronounce it, or that I mentally conceive it." Is Descartes giving an argument here? If so, what is its conclusion? What are its premises? If you don't think he is giving an argument, what is he doing?

# 30

# Certainty

G. E. MOORE

*British philosopher G. E. Moore (1873–1958) was one of the most influential philosophers of the twentieth century. He wrote* Principia Ethica *(1903), and many of his papers on knowledge are to be found in* Philosophical Papers *(1959). In this selection from his article "Certainty," Moore responds to skeptical arguments based on such claims as "You do not know for certain that you are not dreaming." Against such arguments, Moore employs a "reversal argument" and argues that because he does know such facts as that he is standing up (when he is delivering the lecture on which this article is based), he therefore knows that he is not (at that time) dreaming. He then proceeds to critically examine the case that might be made for the claim that he does not know for certain he is not dreaming.*

Suppose I say: "I know for certain that I am standing up; it is absolutely certain that I am; there is not the smallest chance that I am not." Many philosophers would say: "You are wrong: you do not know that you are standing up; it is *not* absolutely certain that you are; there is *some* chance, though perhaps only a very small one, that you are not." And one argument which has been used as an argument in favour of saying this, is an argument in the course of which the philosopher who used it would assert; "You do not know for certain that you are not dreaming; it is not absolutely certain that you are not; there is *some* chance, though perhaps only a very small one, that you are." And from this, that I do not know for certain that I am not dreaming, it is supposed to follow that I do not know for certain that I am standing up. It is argued: If it is not certain that you are not dreaming, then it is not certain that you are standing up. And that *if* I don't know that I'm not dreaming, I also don't know that I'm not sitting down, I don't feel at all inclined to dispute. From the hypothesis that I'am dreaming, it would, I think, certainly follow that I don't *know* that I am standing up; though I have never seen the matter argued, and though it is not at all clear to me how it is to be proved that it would follow. But, on the other hand, from the hypothesis that I am dreaming, it certainly would not follow that I am *not* standing up; for it is certainly logically possible that a man should be fast asleep and dreaming, while he is standing up and not lying down. It is therefore logically possible that I should both be standing up and also at the same time dreaming that I am; just as the story, about a well-known Duke of Devonshire, that he once dreamt that he was speaking in the House of Lords and, when he woke

SOURCE: From G. E. Moore, *Philosophical Papers* (New York: Collier Books), 1959.

up, found that he *was* speaking in the House of Lords, is certainly logically possible. And if, as is commonly assumed, when I am dreaming that I am standing up it may also be correct to say that I am *thinking* that I am standing up, then it follows that the hypothesis that I am now dreaming is quite consistent with the hypothesis that I am both thinking that I am standing up and also actually standing up. And hence, if as seems to me to be certainly the case and as this argument assumes, from the hypothesis that I am now dreaming it *would* follow that I don't know that I am standing up, there follows a point which is of great importance with regard to our use of the word "knowledge," and therefore also of the word "certainly"—a point which has been made quite conclusively more than once by Russell, namely that from the conjunction of the two facts that a man thinks that a given proposition *p* is true, and that *p* is in fact true, it does *not* follow that the man in question *knows* that *p* is true: in order that I may be justified in saying that I know that I am standing up, something more is required than the mere conjunction of the two facts that I both think I am and actually am—as Russell has expressed it, true belief is not identical with knowledge; and I think we may further add that even from the conjunction of the two facts that I feel certain that I am and that I actually am it would not follow that I know that I am, nor therefore that it *is* certain that I am. As regards the argument drawn from the fact that a man who dreams that he is standing up and happens at the moment actually to be standing up will nevertheless not *know* that he is standing up, it should indeed be noted that from the fact that a man is dreaming that he is standing up, it certainly does not *follow* that he *thinks* he is standing up; since it does sometimes happen in a dream that we *think* that it is a dream, and a man who thought this certainly might, although he was dreaming that he was standing up, yet *think* that he was not, although he could not *know* that he was not. It is not therefore the case, as might be hastily assumed, that, if I dream that I am standing up at a time when I am in fact lying down, I am necessarily *deceived:* I should be deceived only if I thought I was standing when I wasn't; and I may dream that I am, without thinking that I am. It certainly does, however, often happen that we do dream that so-and-so is the case, without at the time thinking that we are only dreaming; and in such cases, I think we may perhaps be said to *think* that what we dream is the case *is* the case, and to be deceived if it is not the case; and therefore also, in such cases, if what we dream to be the case happens also to *be* the case, we may be said to be thinking truly that it is the case, although we certainly do not *know* that it is.

I agree, therefore, with that part of this argument which asserts that if I don't know now that I'm not dreaming, it follows that I don't *know* that I am standing up, even if I both actually am and think that I am. But this first part of the argument is a consideration which cuts both ways. For, if it is true, it follows that it is also true that if I *do* know that I am standing up, then I do know that I am not dreaming. I can therefore just as well argue: since I do know that I'm standing up, it follows that I do know that I'm not dreaming; as my opponent can argue: since you don't know that you're not dreaming, it follows that you don't know that you're standing up. The one argument is just as good as the other, unless my opponent can give better reasons for asserting that I don't know that I'm not dreaming, than I can give for asserting that I do know that I am standing up.

What reasons can be given for saying that I don't know for certain that I'm not at this moment dreaming?

I do not think that I have ever seen clearly stated any argument which is supposed to show this. But I am going to try to state, as clearly as I can, the premisses and the reasonings from them, which I think have led so many philosophers to suppose that I really cannot now know for certain that I am not dreaming.

I said, you may remember, in talking of the seven assertions with which I opened this lecture, that I had "the evidence of my senses" for them, though I also said that I didn't think this was the only evidence I had for them, nor that this by itself was necessarily conclusive evidence. Now if I had *then* "the evidence of my senses" in favour of the proposition that I was standing up, I certainly have *now* the evidence of my senses in favour of the proposition that I *am* standing up, even though this may not be all the evidence that I have, and may not be conclusive. But have I, in fact, the evidence of my senses *at all* in favour of this proposition? One thing seems to me to be quite clear about our use of this phrase, namely, that, if a man at a given time is only dreaming that he is standing up, then it follows that he has *not* at that time the evidence of his senses in favour of that proposition: to say "Jones last night was *only* dreaming that he was standing up, and yet all the time he had the evidence of his senses that he was" is to say something self-contradictory. But those philosophers who say it is possible that I am now dreaming, certainly mean to say also that it is possible that I am *only dreaming* that I am standing up; and this view, we now see, entails that it is possible that I have *not* the evidence of my senses that I am. If, therefore, they are right, it follows that it is not certain even that I have the evidence of my senses that I am; it follows that it is not certain that I have *the evidence of my senses* for anything at all. If, therefore, I were to say now, that I certainly have the evidence of my senses in favour of the proposition that I am standing up, even if it's not certain that I am standing up, I should be begging the very question now at issue. For if it is not certain that I am not dreaming, it is not certain that I even have the evidence of my senses that I am standing up.

But, now, even if it is not certain that I have at this moment the evidence of my senses for anything at all, it is quite certain that I *either* have the evidence of my senses that I am standing up *or* have an experience which is *very like* having the evidence of my senses that I am standing up. *If* I am dreaming, this experience consists in having dream-images which are at least very like the sensations I should be having if I were awake and had the sensations, the having of which would constitute "having the evidence of my senses" that I am standing up. Let us use the expression "sensory experience," in such a way that this experience which I certainly am having will be a "sensory experience," whether or not it merely consists in the having of dream-images. If we use the expression "sensory experience" in this way, we can say, I think, that, if it is not certain that I am not dreaming now, then it is not certain that *all* the sensory experiences I am now having are not mere dream-images.

What then are the premisses and the reasonings which would lead so many philosophers to think that all the sensory experiences I am having now *may* be mere dream-images—that I do not know for certain that they are not?

So far as I can see, one premiss which they would certainly use would be this: "Some at least of the sensory experiences which you are having now are similar in important respects to dream-images which actually have occurred in dreams." This seems a very harmless premiss, and I am quite willing to admit that it is true. But I think there is a very serious objection to the procedure of using it as a premiss in favour of the derived conclusion. For a philosopher who does use it as a premiss, is, I think, in fact *implying,* though he does not expressly say, that he himself knows it to be true. He is *implying* therefore that he himself knows that dreams have occurred. And, of course, I think he would be right. All the philosophers I have ever met or heard of certainly did know that dreams have occurred: we all know that dreams *have* occurred. But can he consistently combine this proposition that he knows that dreams have occurred, with his conclusion that he does not know that he is not dreaming? Can anybody possibly know that dreams have occurred, if, at the time, he does not himself know that he is not dreaming? If he *is* dreaming, it may be that he is only dreaming that dreams have occurred; and if he does not know that he is not dreaming, can he possibly know that he is *not* only dreaming that dreams have occurred? Can he possibly know therefore that dreams *have* occurred? I do not think that he can; and therefore I think that anyone who uses this premiss and also asserts the conclusion that nobody ever knows that he is not dreaming, is guilty of an inconsistency. By using this premiss he implies that he himself knows that dreams have occurred; while, if his conclusion is true, it follows that he himself does not know that he is not dreaming, and therefore does not know that he is not only dreaming that dreams have occurred.

However, I admit that the premiss is true. Let us now try to see by what sort of reasoning it might be thought that we could get from it to the conclusion.

I do not see how we can get forward in that direction at all, unless we first take the following huge step, unless we say, namely: since there have been dream-images similar in important respects to some of the sensory experiences I am now having, it is logically possible that there should be dream-images *exactly like all* the sensory experiences I am now having, and logically possible, therefore, that all the sensory experiences I am now having *are* mere dream-images. And it might be thought that the validity of this step could be supported to some extent by appeal to matters of fact, though only, of course, at the cost of the same sort of inconsistency which I have just pointed out. It might be said, for instance, that some people have had dream-images which were *exactly like* sensory experiences which they had when they were awake, and that therefore it must be logically possible to have a dream-image exactly like a sensory experience which is *not* a dream-image. And then it may be said: If it is logically possible for some dream-images to be exactly like sensory experiences which are not dream-images, surely it must be logically possible for *all* the dream-images occurring in a dream at a given time to be exactly like sensory experiences which are not dream-images, and logically possible also for all the sensory experiences which a man has at a given time when he is awake to be exactly like all the dream-images which he himself or another man had in a dream at another time.

Now I cannot see my way to deny that it is logically possible that all the sensory experiences I am having now should be mere dream-images. And if this is logically possible, and if further the sensory experiences I am having now were the only experiences I am having, I do not see how I could possibly know for certain that I am not dreaming.

But the conjunction of my memories of the immediate past with these sensory experiences *may* be sufficient to enable me to know that I am not dreaming. I say it *may* be. But what if our sceptical philosopher says: It is *not* sufficient; and offers as an argument to prove that it is not, this. It is logically possible *both* that you should be having all the sensory experiences you are having, and also that you should be remembering what you do remember, and *yet* should be dreaming. If this *is* logically possible, then I don't see how to deny that I cannot possibly know for certain that I am not dreaming: I do not see that I possibly could. But can any reason be given for saying that it *is* logically possible? So far as I know nobody ever has, and I don't know how anybody ever could. And so long as this is not done my argument, "I know that I am standing up, and therefore I know that I am not dreaming," remains at least as good as his, "You don't know that you are not dreaming, and therefore don't know that you are standing up." And I don't think I've ever seen an argument expressly directed to show that it is not.

One final point should be made clear. It is certainly logically possible that I *should have* been dreaming now; I *might* have been dreaming now; and therefore the proposition that I *am* dreaming now is not self-contradictory. But what I am in doubt of is whether it is logically possible that I should *both* be having all the sensory experiences and the memories that I have and *yet* be dreaming. The conjunction of the proposition that I have these sense experiences and memories with the proposition that I am dreaming does seem to me to be very likely self-contradictory.

## READING COMPREHENSION QUESTIONS

1. In the opening paragraph of his article, Moore distinguishes between two claims: (1) "from the hypothesis that I am dreaming, . . . [it follows] that I don't *know* I am standing up" and (2) "from the hypothesis that I am dreaming, I am not standing up." He accepts the first claim but rejects the second. Why?

2. In the second paragraph of his article, Moore considers the skeptic's argument against knowledge and his own "reversal" argument in defense of knowledge. What does Moore say (at the end of this paragraph) about how a deadlock between these two arguments might be broken?

3. Moore claims (paragraph 5) that were he to assume that he had the "evidence of his senses" in favor of the belief that he is now standing, he would be begging the question against the skeptic. Why does he say this?

4. How does Moore propose to define the term "sensory experience"?

5. In examining how the skeptic might try to argue for the conclusion that one does not know that one is not dreaming, Moore considers a specific claim that a skeptic might try to use as a premise. The claim is as follows: *Some at least of the sensory experiences one is now having are similar in important respects to dream-images which actually have occurred in one's past.* Why does Moore argue that "there is a very serious objection to the *procedure* of using [this claim] as a premiss" in favor of the skeptic's conclusion?

6. After explaining the procedural problem with the skeptic's use of the italicized claim above (the one just mentioned in question 5), Moore then explains how the argument from this claim might proceed. State the steps in that argument as presented by Moore.

7. At the end of the selection, Moore claims that although it is logically possible that (despite his current sensory experiences) he could be dreaming, still "the conjunction of my memories of the immediate past with these sensory experiences *may* be sufficient to enable me to know that I am not dreaming." What might a skeptic say to this? (Support your answer with examples from the previous readings.)

# 31

# A Defense of Skepticism

PETER UNGER

*Peter Unger is professor of philosophy at New York University and author of* Living High and Letting Die *(1996) and* All the Power in the World *(2005). The following is an excerpt from Unger's 1975 book* Ignorance, *in which he replies to G. E. Moore's antiskeptical argument in defense of com-monsense knowledge about the external world. Skeptical arguments, such as Descartes' "evil genius" argument, appeal to "exotic" contrast cases (also often called "skeptical scenarios") in attempting to show that human beings cannot have knowledge of the external world. In the previous selection, Moore responds to such arguments with a "reversal" argument in which one argues from the claim that we do have some knowledge of the external world to the conclusion that in such cases we know that we are not in the position of someone featured in an exotic skeptical scenario. Unger has his readers dwell on the possibility that one really has been deceived by an evil genius and how "foolhardy and even dogmatic" one would then feel in having claimed to know about the external world. In the final section of the reading, Unger considers the question of whether the fact that the skeptic appeals to bizarre, exotic cases makes any difference to how we should feel about our ordinary knowledge claims.*

In these pages, I try to argue compellingly for skepticism. . . . The type of skepti-cism for which I first argue is perhaps the most traditional one: skepticism about knowledge. This is the thesis that no one ever knows anything about anything [about the external world]. . . .

SOURCE: From Peter Unger, *Ignorance* (Oxford: Oxford University Press, 1975).
Reprinted by permission of the author and Oxford University Press.

## I. A CLASSICAL FORM OF SKEPTICAL ARGUMENT

There are certain arguments for skepticism which conform to a familiar . . . pattern or form. These arguments rely, at least for their psychological power, on vivid descriptions of exotic contrast cases. The following is one such rough argument, this one in support of skepticism regarding any alleged knowledge of an external world. The exotic contrast case here concerns an evil scientist, and is described to be in line with the most up-to-date developments of science, or science fiction. We begin by arbitrarily choosing something concerning an external world which might conceivably, we suppose, be known, in one way or another, e.g., that there are rocks or, as we will understand it, that there is at least one rock.

Now, first, if someone, anyone knows that there are rocks, then the person can know the following quite exotic thing: There is no evil scientist deceiving him into falsely believing that there are rocks. This scientist uses electrodes to induce experiences and thus carries out his deceptions, concerning the existence of rocks or anything else. He first drills holes painlessly in the variously colored skulls or shells of his subjects and then implants his electrodes into the appropriate parts of their brains, or protoplasm, or systems. He sends patterns of electrical impulses into them through the electrodes, which are themselves connected by wires to a laboratory console on which he plays, punching various keys and buttons in accordance with his ideas of how the whole thing works and with his deceptive designs. The scientist's delight is intense, and it is caused not so much by his exercising his scientific and intellectual gifts as by the thought that he is deceiving various subjects about all sorts of things. Part of that delight is caused, on this supposition, by his thought that he is deceiving a certain person, perhaps yourself, into falsely believing that there are rocks. He is, then, an evil scientist, and he lives in a world which is entirely bereft of rocks.

Now, as we have agreed, if you know that there are rocks, then you can know that there is no such scientist doing this to you. But no one can ever know that this exotic situation does not obtain; no one can ever know that there is no evil scientist who is, by means of electrodes, deceiving him into falsely believing there to be rocks. That is our second premiss, and it is also very difficult to deny. So, thirdly, as a consequence of these two premises, we have our skeptical conclusion: You never know that there are rocks. But of course we have chosen our person, and the matter of there being rocks, quite arbitrarily, and this argument, it surely seems, may be generalized to cover any external matter at all. From this, we may conclude, finally, that nobody ever knows anything about the external world.

This argument is the same in form as the "evil demon" argument in Descartes' *Meditations;* it is but a more modern, scientific counterpart, with its domain of application confined to matters concerning the external world.[1] Taking the *Meditations* as our source of the most compelling skeptical argument the philosophical literature has to offer, we may call any argument of this form the classical argument for skepticism. . . .

---

[1]René Descartes, *Meditations on First Philosophy,* 2nd ed., 1642, in *The Philosophical Works of Descartes,* trans. E. S. Haldane and G. R. T. Ross (Cambridge, 1972), vol. I, Meditation I, pp. 144–149. The crux of what I take to be the main argument occurs near the end of Meditation I.

These arguments are exceedingly compelling. They tend to make skeptics of us all if only for a brief while. Anyone who would try to further skepticism, as I will try to do, will do well to link his own ideas to these arguments. For then, the very notable feelings and intuitions which they arouse may serve as support for the theses he would advance. . . .

## II. ON TRYING TO REVERSE THIS ARGUMENT: EXOTIC CASES AND FEELINGS OF IRRATIONALITY

Our skeptical conclusion would not be welcome to many philosophers. Indeed, most philosophers would be inclined to try to reverse the argument, perhaps in the manner made popular by G. E. Moore.[2] They would not, I think, wish to deny the first premiss, which in any case seems quite unobjectionable, at least in essential thrust. But even in its early formulation, they would be most happy to deny the second premiss, which is the more substantive one.

The Moorean attempt to reverse our argument will proceed like this: According to your argument, nobody ever knows that there are rocks. But I do know that there are rocks. This is something concerning the external world, and I do know it. Hence, somebody does know something about the external world. Mindful of our first premiss, the reversal continues: I can reason at least moderately well and thereby come to know things which I see to be entailed by things I already know. Before reflecting on classical arguments such as this, I may have never realized or even had the idea that from there being rocks it follows that there is no evil scientist who is deceiving me into falsely believing there to be rocks. But, having been presented with such arguments, I of course now know that this last follows from what I know. And so, while I might not have known before that there is no such scientist, at least I now do know that there is no evil scientist who is deceiving me into falsely believing that there are rocks. So far has the skeptical argument failed to challenge my knowledge successfully that it seems actually to have occasioned an increase in what I know about things.

While the robust character of this reply has a definite appeal, it also seems quite daring. Indeed, the more one thinks on it, the more it seems to be somewhat foolhardy and even dogmatic. One cannot help but think that for all this philosopher really can know, he might have all his experience artificially induced by electrodes, these being operated by a terribly evil scientist who, having an idea of what his "protégé" is saying to himself, chuckles accordingly. One thinks as well that for all one can know oneself, there really is no Moore or any other thinker with whose works one has actually had any contact. The belief that one has may, for all one really can know, be due to experiences induced by just such a chuckling operator. For all one can know, then, there may not really be any rocks. Positive assertions to the contrary, even on one's own part, seem quite out of place and even dogmatic.

---

[2]See several of Moore's most famous papers. But most especially, I suggest, see his "Four Forms of Scepticism" in his *Philosophical Papers* (New York, 1959), p. 226.

Suppose that you yourself have just positively made an attempt to reverse; you try to be a Moore. Now, we may suppose that electrodes are removed, that your experiences are now brought about through your perception of actual surroundings, and you are, so to speak, forced to encounter your deceptive tormentor. Wouldn't you be made to feel quite foolish, even embarrassed, by your claims to know? Indeed, you would seem to be exposed quite clearly as having been, not only wrong, but rather irrational and even dogmatic. And if there aren't ever any experiences of electrodes and so on, that happy fact can't mean that you are any less irrational and dogmatic in saying or thinking that you know. In thinking that you know, you will be equally and notably irrational and dogmatic. And, for at least that reason, in thinking yourself to know there is no such scientist, you will be wrong in either case. So it appears that one doesn't ever really know that there is no such scientist doing this thing.

Now, if you think or say to yourself that you are certain or sure that there is no scientist doing this, you may be doubly right, but even that does not seem to make matters much better for you. You may be right on one count because you may, I will suppose, be certain that there is no such scientist, and so be right in what you think. And in the second place, there may be no evil scientist deceiving you, so that you may be right in that of which you are certain. But, even if doubly right here, it seems just as dogmatic and irrational for you ever sincerely to profess this certainty. Thus it seems that, even if you are certain of the thing, and even if there is no scientist, you shouldn't be certain of it. It seems that you are wrong, then, and not right on a third count, namely, in being certain of the thing. It seems much better, perhaps perfectly all right, if you are instead only confident that there is no such scientist. It seems perfectly all right for you to believe there to be no evil scientist doing this. If you say not only that you believe it, but that you have some reason to believe this thing, what you say may seem somewhat suspect, at least on reasoned reflection, but it doesn't have any obvious tint of dogmatism or irrationality to it. Finally, you may simply assert, perhaps to yourself, that there is no evil scientist who is deceiving me into falsely believing that there are rocks. Perhaps strangely, this seems at least pretty nearly as foolhardy and dogmatic as asserting, or as thinking, that you know the thing. . . .

This idea, that claims to know about external things are at least somewhat foolhardy and dogmatic, applies in all possible situations, even the most exotic cases. Suppose, for example, that you actually do have a sequence of experience which seems to indicate that an evil scientist was deceiving you into falsely believing that there are rocks. You seem to be confronting an exotic scientist who shows you electrodes, points out places of insertion on your skull or shell, and explains in detail how the whole thing works. And you seem to see no rocks outside the window of this scientist's laboratory. The scientist assures you that there really are no such things as rocks, that he only created an impression of such things by stimulating certain groups of cells in your brain. After enough of this sort of thing dominates your experiences, you might suppose that you know that there is an evil scientist who deceived you in the past, but he now does not. And you may also come to suppose that you know that there were never any rocks at all. But should you think you know? These latter experiences might themselves find no basis in reality, for all you really might know. For all you can know, it may be that all the time your experiences are induced by electrodes which are operated by no scientist, and it may be that there are no scientists at all, and plenty of rocks. Whether or not this is the case, you may always have new experience to the effect that it is. Is the new experience part of an encounter with reality, or is it too only part of an induced stream, or perhaps even a random sequence of experience? No matter how involved the going gets, it may always get still more involved. And each new turn may make any previously developed claim to know seem quite irrational and dogmatic, if not downright embarrassing. No matter what turns one's experience takes, the statement that one knows there to be no scientist may be wrong for the reason that there is a scientist. But it will always be wrong, it seems, for the reason of dogmatism and irrationality, however this last is to be explained. . . .

## III. ORDINARY CASES

Largely because it is so exotic and bizarre, the case of a deceiving scientist lets one feel acutely the apparent irrationality in thinking oneself to know. But the exotic cases have no monopoly on generating feelings of irrationality.

If you are planning a philosophical book and trying to estimate the energy you will spend on each of the several chapters, you might think that you know that it will not take much to write the third chapter. For the argument there may seem already so clearly outlined in your head. But experience may later seem to show that this argument is far from clear. And much time and effort may become absorbed with no clear fruits to show for it. In that case, you will, I suggest, feel somewhat embarrassed and foolish, even if there is no other person to whom your idea that you knew was ever communicated. If you just believed, or even if you were quite confident that this chapter would not take much effort to write, then, I suggest, you would not feel nearly so foolish or embarrassed, oftentimes not at all.

Again, you may think you know that a certain city is the capital of a certain state, and you may feel quite content in this thought while watching another looking the matter up in the library. You will feel quite foolish, however, if the person announces the result to be another city, and if subsequent experience seems to show that announcement to be right. This will occur, I suggest, even if you are just an anonymous, disinterested bystander who happens to hear the question posed and the answer later announced. This is true even if the reference was a newspaper, *The Times,* and the capital was changed only yesterday. But these feelings will be very much less apparent, or will not occur at all, if you only feel very confident, at the outset, that the city is thus-and-such, which later is not announced. You might of course feel that you shouldn't be quite so confident of such things, or that you should watch out in the future. But you probably wouldn't feel, I suggest, that you were irrational to be confident of that thing at that time. Much less would you feel that you were dogmatic in so being.

Finally, if you positively asserted something to another in a conversation, as though reporting a known fact, later contrary experiences might well cause you to feel that you had overstepped the bounds of good sense and rationality. The feeling is that you have manifested a trait of a dogmatic personality. If you happen to be right, your extremely positive approach is not likely to be questioned. In case subsequent events seem to indicate you are wrong about the matter, then you come in for a severe judgement, whether or not this judgement is ever made out loud. This is a rather familiar social experience. (As I say this, even in trying to make my style a little less cautious, to be readable, I leave myself open to just such a judgement by putting the matter in such a positive, unqualified way.) I suggest that such feelings ought to be far more familiar, occurring even where you are right about the matter. They should not just occur where you are in fact wrong about things. Accordingly, we should avoid making these claims in any case, whether we be right or whether wrong in the matter, e.g., of which city is the capital of that state.

It is hard for us to think that there is any important similarity between such common cases as these and the case of someone thinking himself to know that there are rocks. Exotic contrast cases, like the case of the evil scientist, help one to appreciate that these cases are really essentially the same. By means of contrast cases, we encourage thinking of all sorts of new sequences of experience, sequences which people would never begin to imagine in the normal course of affairs. How would you react to such developments as these, no matter how exotic or unlikely? It appears that the proper reaction is to feel as irrational about claiming knowledge of rocks as you felt before, where, e.g., one was apparently caught in thought by the library reference to the state's capital. Who would have thought so, before thinking of contrast cases? Those cases help you see, I suggest, that in either case, no matter whether you are in fact right in the matter or whether wrong, thinking that you know manifests an attitude of dogmatism. Bizarre experiential sequences help show that there is no essential difference between any two external matters; the apparently most certain ones, like that of rocks, and the ones where thinking about knowing appears, even without the most exotic skeptical aids, not the way to think.

## READING COMPREHENSION QUESTIONS

1. In the third paragraph of section I, Unger presents the skeptic's argument in four steps—three premises and a conclusion. Identify the conclusion and each of the argument's premises.

2. In the second paragraph of section II, Unger presents Moore's so-called "reversal argument" in four steps. Identify the conclusion and each of the argument's premises.

3. What reasons does Unger give for claiming that the attempt to use Moore's reversal argument in reply to the skeptic is "foolhardy and even dogmatic"?

4. What does Unger say about cases in which one is *certain* and *sure* that one is not subject to some scientific experiment in which one's experiences are being induced by a computer, *and* it turns out that one is right—one's experiences are *not* being artificially induced?

5. According to Unger (in the final section of the essay), what is the function of exotic contrast cases in thinking about knowledge?

# 32

# The Ethics of Belief

WILLIAM K. CLIFFORD

*British philosopher and mathematician William K. Clifford (1845–1879) was*
*professor of mathematics at University College, London. He is author of* Seeing
and Thinking *(1879) and of the posthumously published* Mathematical
Papers *(1882). In the selection included here, Clifford explores questions about*
*the ethics of belief, stressing the social importance of the beliefs held by individuals.*
*He summarizes his inquiry by the famous dictum:* it is wrong, everywhere,
always, and for anyone, to believe anything upon insufficient evidence.

A shipowner was about to send to sea an emigrant-ship. He knew that she was
old, and not over-well built at the first; that she had seen many seas and climes,
and often had needed repairs. Doubts had been suggested to him that possibly she
was not seaworthy. These doubts preyed upon his mind, and made him unhappy;
he thought that perhaps he ought to have her thoroughly overhauled and refitted,
even though this should put him at great expense. Before the ship sailed, however,
he succeeded in overcoming these melancholy reflections. He said to himself that
she had gone safely through so many voyages and weathered so many storms
that it was idle to suppose she would not come safely home from this trip also.
He would put his trust in Providence, which could hardly fail to protect all these
unhappy families that were leaving their fatherland to seek for better times elsewhere. He would dismiss from his mind all ungenerous suspicions about the honesty of builders and contractors. In such ways he acquired a sincere and comfortable
conviction that his vessel was thoroughly safe and seaworthy; he watched her departure with a light heart, and benevolent wishes for the success of the exiles in their
strange new home that was to be; and he got his insurance-money when she went
down in mid-ocean and told no tales.

What shall we say of him? Surely this, that he was verily guilty of the death of
those men. It is admitted that he did sincerely believe in the soundness of his ship;
but the sincerity of his conviction can in no wise help him, because he had no
right to believe on such evidence as was before him. He had acquired his belief
not by honestly earning it in patient investigation, but by stifling his doubts.
And although in the end he may have felt so sure about it that he could not
think otherwise, yet inasmuch as he had knowingly and willingly worked himself
into that frame of mind, he must be held responsible for it.

SOURCE: Originally published in *Contemporary Review*, 1877.

Let us alter the case a little, and suppose that the ship was not unsound after all; that she made her voyage safely, and many others after it. Will that diminish the guilt of her owner? Not one jot. When an action is once done, it is right or wrong for ever; no accidental failure of its good or evil fruits can possibly alter that. The man would not have been innocent, he would only have been not found out. The question of right or wrong has to do with the origin of his belief, not the matter of it; not what it was, but how he got it; not whether it turned out to be true or false, but whether he had a right to believe on such evidence as was before him.

There was once an island in which some of the inhabitants professed a religion teaching neither the doctrine of original sin nor that of eternal punishment. A suspicion got abroad that the professors of this religion had made use of unfair means to get their doctrines taught to children. They were accused of wresting the laws of their country in such a way as to remove children from the care of their natural and legal guardians; and even of stealing them away and keeping them concealed from their friends and relations. A certain number of men formed themselves into a society for the purpose of agitating the public about this matter. They published grave accusations against individual citizens of the highest position and character, and did all in their power to injure these citizens in their exercise of their professions. So great was the noise they made, that a Commission was appointed to investigate the facts; but after the Commission had carefully inquired into all the evidence that could be got, it appeared that the accused were innocent. Not only had they been accused on insufficient evidence, but the evidence of their innocence was such as the agitators might easily have obtained, if they had attempted a fair inquiry. After these disclosures the inhabitants of that country looked upon the members of the agitating society, not only as persons whose judgment was to be distrusted, but also as no longer to be counted honourable men. For although they had sincerely and conscientiously believed in the charges they had made, yet they had no right to believe on such evidence as was before them. Their sincere convictions, instead of being honestly earned by patient inquiring, were stolen by listening to the voice of prejudice and passion.

Let us vary this case also, and suppose, other things remaining as before, that a still more accurate investigation proved the accused to have been really guilty. Would this make any difference in the guilt of the accusers? Clearly not; the question is not whether their belief was true or false, but whether they entertained it on wrong grounds. They would no doubt say, "Now you see that we were right after all; next time perhaps you will believe us." And they might be believed, but they would not thereby become honourable men. They would not be innocent, they would only be not found out. Every one of them, if he chose to examine himself *in foro conscientiae,* would know that he had acquired and nourished a belief, when he had no right to believe on such evidence as was before him; and therein he would know that he had done a wrong thing.

It may be said, however, that in both these supposed cases it is not the belief which is judged to be wrong, but the action following upon it. The shipowner might say, "I am perfectly certain that my ship is sound, but still I feel it my duty to have her examined, before trusting the lives of so many people to her." And it might be said to the agitator, "However convinced you were of the justice of your cause and the truth of your convictions, you ought not to have made a public attack upon any man's character until you had examined the evidence on both sides with the utmost patience and care."

In the first place, let us admit that, so far as it goes, this view of the case is right and necessary; right, because even when a man's belief is so fixed that he cannot think otherwise, he still has a choice in the action suggested by it, and so cannot escape the duty of investigating on the ground of the strength of his convictions; and necessary, because those who are not yet capable of controlling their feelings and thoughts must have a plain rule dealing with overt acts.

But this being premised as necessary, it becomes clear that it is not sufficient, and that our previous judgment is required to supplement it. For it is not possible so to sever the belief from the action it suggests as to condemn the one without condemning the other. No man holding a strong belief on one side of a question, or even wishing to hold a belief on one side, can investigate it with such fairness and completeness as if he were really in doubt and unbiased; so that the existence of a belief not founded on fair inquiry unfits a man for the performance of this necessary duty.

Nor is that truly a belief at all which has not some influence upon the actions of him who holds it. He who truly believes that which prompts him to an action has looked upon the action to lust after it, he has committed it already in his heart. If a belief is not realized immediately in open deeds, it is stored up for the guidance of the future. It goes to make a part of that aggregate of beliefs which is the link between sensation and action at every moment of all our lives, and which is so organized and compacted together that no part of it can be isolated from the rest, but every new addition modifies the structure of the whole. No real belief, however trifling and fragmentary it may seem, is ever truly insignificant; it prepares us to receive more of its like, confirms those which resembled it before, and weakens others; and so gradually it lays a stealthy train in our inmost thoughts, which may someday explode into overt action, and leave its stamp upon our character for ever.

And no one man's belief is in any case a private matter which concerns himself alone. Our lives are guided by that general conception of the course of things which has been created by society for social purposes. Our words, our phrases, our forms and processes and modes of thought, are common property, fashioned and perfected from age to age; an heirloom which every succeeding generation inherits as a precious deposit and a sacred trust to be handed on to the next one, not unchanged but enlarged and purified, with some clear marks of its proper handiwork. Into this, for good or ill, is woven every belief of every man who has speech of his fellows. An awful privilege, and an awful responsibility, that we should help to create the world in which posterity will live.

In the two supposed cases which have been considered, it has been judged wrong to believe on insufficient evidence, or to nourish belief by suppressing doubts and avoiding investigation. The reason of this judgment is not far to seek: it is that in both these cases the belief held by one man was of great importance to other men. But forasmuch as no belief held by one man, however seemingly trivial the belief, and however obscure the believer, is ever actually insignificant or without its effect on the fate of mankind, we have no choice but to extend our judgment to all cases of belief whatever. Belief, that sacred faculty which prompts the decisions of our will, and knits into harmonious working all the compacted energies of our being, is ours not for ourselves but for humanity. It is rightly used on truths which have been established by long experience and waiting toil, and which have stood in the fierce light of free and fearless questioning. Then it helps to bind men together, and to strengthen and direct their common action. It is desecrated when given to unproved and unquestioned statements, for the solace and private pleasure of the believer; to add a tinsel splendor to the plain straight road of our life and display a bright mirage beyond it; or even to drown the common sorrows of our kind by a self-deception which allows them not only to cast down, but also to degrade us. Whoso would deserve well of his fellows in this matter will guard the purity of his beliefs with a very fanaticism of jealous care, lest at any time it should rest on an unworthy object, and catch a stain which can never be wiped away.

It is not only the leader of men, statesmen, philosopher, or poet, that owes this bounden duty to mankind. Every rustic who delivers in the village alehouse his slow, infrequent sentences, may help to kill or keep alive the fatal superstitions which clog his race. Every hard-worked wife of an artisan may transmit to her children beliefs which shall knit society together, or rend it in pieces. No simplicity of mind, no obscurity of station, can escape the universal duty of questioning all that we believe.

It is true that this duty is a hard one, and the doubt which comes out of it is often a very bitter thing. It leaves us bare and powerless where we thought that we were safe and strong. To know all about anything is to know how to deal with it under all circumstances. We feel much happier and more secure when we think we know precisely what to do, no matter what happens, than when we have lost our way and do not know where to turn. And if we have supposed ourselves to know all about anything, and to be capable of doing what is fit in regard to it, we naturally do not like to find that we are really ignorant and powerless, that we have to begin again at the beginning, and try to learn what the thing is and how it is to be dealt with—if indeed anything can be learnt about it. It is the sense of power attached to a sense of knowledge that makes men desirous of believing, and afraid of doubting.

This sense of power is the highest and best of pleasures when the belief on which it is founded is a true belief, and has been fairly earned by investigation. For then we may justly feel that it is common property, and hold good for others as well as for ourselves. Then we may be glad, not that I have learned secrets by which I am safer and stronger, but that we men have got mastery over more of the world; and we shall be strong, not for ourselves but in the name of Man and his strength. But if the belief has been accepted on insufficient evidence, the pleasure is a stolen one. Not only does it deceive ourselves by giving us a sense of power which we do not really possess, but it is sinful, because it is stolen in defiance of our duty to mankind. That duty is to guard ourselves from such beliefs as from pestilence, which may shortly master our own body and then spread to the rest of the town. What would be thought of one who, for the sake of a sweet fruit, should deliberately run the risk of delivering a plague upon his family and his neighbors?

And, as in other such cases, it is not the risk only which has to be considered; for a bad action is always bad at the time when it is done, no matter what happens afterwards. Every time we let ourselves believe for unworthy reasons, we weaken our powers of self-control, of doubting, of judicially and fairly weighing evidence. We all suffer severely enough from the maintenance and support of false beliefs and the fatally wrong actions which they lead to, and the evil born when one such belief is entertained is great and wide. But a greater and wider evil arises when the credulous character is maintained and supported, when a habit of believing for unworthy reasons is fostered and made permanent. If I steal money from any person, there may be no harm done from the mere transfer of possession; he may not feel the loss, or it may prevent him from using the money badly. But I cannot help doing this great wrong towards Man, that I make myself dishonest. What hurts society is not that it should lose its property, but that it should become a den of thieves, for then it must cease to be society. This is why we ought not to do evil, that good may come; for at any rate this great evil has come, that we have done evil and are made wicked thereby. In like manner, if I let myself believe anything on insufficient evidence, there may be no great harm done by the mere belief; it may be true after all, or I may never have occasion to exhibit it in outward acts. But I cannot help doing this great wrong towards Man, that I make myself credulous. The danger to society is not merely that it should believe wrong things, though that is great enough; but that it should become credulous, and lose the habit of testing things and inquiring into them; for then it must sink back into savagery.

The harm which is done by credulity in a man is not confined to the fostering of a credulous character in others, and consequent support of false beliefs. Habitual want of care about what I believe leads to habitual want of care in others about the truth of what is told to me. Men speak the truth of one another when each reveres the truth in his own mind and in the other's mind; but how shall my friend revere the truth in my mind when I myself am careless about it, when I believe things because I want to believe them, and because they are comforting and pleasant? Will he not learn to cry, "Peace," to me, when there is no peace? By such a course I shall surround myself with a thick atmosphere of falsehood and fraud, and in that I must live. It may matter little to me, in my cloud-castle of sweet illusions and darling lies; but it matters much to Man that I have made my neighbors ready to deceive. The credulous man is father to the liar and the cheat, he lives in the bosom of this his family, and it is no marvel if he should become even as they are. So closely are our duties knit together, that whoso shall keep the whole law, and yet offend in one point, he is guilty of all.

To sum up: it is wrong always, everywhere, and for anyone, to believe anything upon insufficient evidence.

If a man, holding a belief which he was taught in childhood or persuaded of afterwards, keeps down and pushes away any doubts which arise about it in his mind, purposely avoids the reading of books and the company of men that call into question or discuss it, and regards as impious those questions which cannot easily be asked without disturbing it—the life of that man is one long sin against mankind. . . .

"But," says one, "I am a busy man; I have no time for the long course of study which would be necessary to make me in any degree a competent judge of certain questions, or even able to understand the nature of the arguments."

Then he should have no time to believe. . . .

## READING COMPREHENSION QUESTIONS

1. Clifford claims that even if the shipowner he describes had been correct in thinking that the ship in question was seaworthy, he still would have been just as guilty as he was in the actual story. What is Clifford's reason for this claim? Explain why you do or do not agree.

2. Clifford considers the objection that in the shipowner and agitator cases, it is not the *having* or *holding* of the beliefs in question that is wrong, but rather the actions based on those beliefs. What is Clifford's reply to this objection? Do you agree with him? Why or why not?

3. Why does Clifford think that human beings have a strong tendency to believe even when they lack sufficient evidence?

4. How does Clifford connect belief with pleasure and with self-control? Do you think he is correct about the connections? Explain.

5. Clifford claims that even if no harm results from believing something on insufficient evidence, doing so is "a great wrong towards Man." How does he argue for this claim? Do you agree with him?

6. What are the implications of Clifford's views on the ethics of belief for religious convictions? Do you agree with those implications? If not, why not?

# 33

# Is It Wrong Everywhere, Always, and for Anyone to Believe Anything on Insufficient Evidence?

PETER VAN INWAGEN

*Peter van Inwagen is John Cardinal O'Hara Professor of Philosophy at the University of Notre Dame. He is author of numerous articles and books, including* God, Knowledge and Mystery *(1995),* Ontology, Identity, and Modality *(2001), and* The Problem of Evil *(2006). As the title indicates, the selection from van Inwagen discusses William K. Clifford's famous dictum about the ethics*

SOURCE: From Peter van Inwagen, *Faith, Freedom, and Rationality*, ed. J. Jordan and D. Howard-Snyder. (Lanham, MA: Rowman and Littlefield, 1996), pp. 137–153. Reprinted by permission of the author and Rowman and Littlefield Press.

*of belief by considering what consequences it would have if we were to apply it to our everyday lives. To draw out what he thinks are the unacceptable consequences, van Inwagen considers disagreements over philosophical and political issues among individuals who are well-informed about those issues.*

My title is a famous sentence from W. K. Clifford's celebrated lecture, "The Ethics of Belief." What I want to do is not so much to challenge (or to vindicate) the principle this sentence expresses as to examine what the consequences of attempting consistently to apply it in our lives would be. Various philosophers have attempted something that might be described in these words, and have argued that a strict adherence to the terms of the principle would lead to a chain of requests for further evidence that would terminate only in such presumably unanswerable questions as What evidence have you for supposing that your sensory apparatus is reliable?, or Yes, but what considerations can you adduce in support of the hypothesis that the future will resemble the past?; and they have drawn the conclusion that anyone who accepts such propositions as that one's sensory apparatus is reliable or that the future will resemble the past must do so in defiance of the principle. You will be relieved to learn that an investigation along these lines is not on the program tonight. I am not going to raise the question whether a strict adherence to the principle would land us in the one of those very abstract sorts of epistemological predicament exemplified by uncertainty about the reliability of sense perception or induction. I shall be looking at consequences of accepting the principle that are much more concrete, much closer to our concerns as epistemically responsible citizens—citizens not only of the body politic but of the community of philosophers.

I shall, as I say, be concerned with Clifford's sentence and the lecture that it epitomizes. But I am going to make my way to this topic by a rather winding path. Please bear with me for a bit.

I begin my indirect approach to Clifford's sentence by stating a fact about philosophy. Philosophers do not agree about anything to speak of. That is, it is not very usual for agreement among philosophers on any important philosophical issue, to be describable as being, in a quite unambiguous sense, common. Oh, this philosopher may agree with that philosopher on many philosophical points; for that matter, if this philosopher is a former student of that philosopher, they may even agree on all philosophical points. But you don't find universal or near-universal agreement about very many important theses or arguments in philosophy. Indeed, it would be hard to find an important philosophical thesis that, say, ninety-five percent of, say, American analytical philosophers born between 1930 and 1950 agreed about in, say, 1987.

And why not? How can it be that equally intelligent and well-trained philosophers can disagree about the freedom of the will or nominalism or the covering-law model of scientific explanation when each is aware of all of the arguments and distinctions and other relevant considerations that the others are aware of? How—and now I will drop a broad hint about where I am going—how can we philosophers possibly regard ourselves as justified in believing much of anything of philosophical significance in this embarrassing circumstance? How can I believe (as I do) that free will is incompatible with determinism or that unrealized possibilities are not physical objects or that human beings are not four-dimensional things extended in time as well as in space, when David Lewis[1]—a philosopher of truly formidable intelligence and insight and ability—rejects these things I believe and is already aware of and understands perfectly every argument that I could produce in their defense?

Well, I do believe these things. And I believe that I am justified in believing them. And I am confident that I am right. But how can I take these positions? I don't know. That is itself a philosophical question, and I have no firm opinion about its correct answer. I suppose my best guess is that I enjoy some sort of philosophical insight (I mean in relation to these three particular theses) that, for all his merits, is somehow denied to Lewis. And this would have to be an insight that is incommunicable—at least I don't know how to communicate it—, for I have done all I can to communicate it to Lewis, and he has understood perfectly everything I have said, and he has not come to share my conclusions. But maybe my best guess is wrong. I'm confident about only one thing in this area: the question must have some good answer. For not only do my beliefs about these questions seem to me to be undeniably true, but (quite independently of any consideration of which theses it is that seem to me to be true), I don't want to be forced into a position in which I can't see my way clear to accepting any philosophical thesis of any consequence. Let us call this unattractive position philosophical skepticism. (Note that I am not using this phrase in its usual sense of "comprehensive and general skepticism based on philosophical argument." Note also that philosophical skepticism is not a thesis—if it were, it's hard to see how it could be accepted without pragmatic contradiction—but a state: philosophical skeptics are people who can't see their way clear to being nominalists or realists, dualists or monists, ordinary-language philosophers or phenomenologists; people, in short, who are aware of many philosophical options but take none of them, people who have listened to many philosophical debates but have never once declared a winner.) I think that any philosopher who does not wish to be a philosophical skeptic— I know of no philosopher who is a philosophical skeptic—must agree with me that this question has some good answer: whatever the reason, it must be possible for one to be justified in accepting a philosophical thesis when there are philosophers who, by all objective and external criteria, are at least equally well qualified to pronounce on that thesis and who reject it.

Will someone say that philosophical theses are theses of a very special sort, and that philosophy is therefore a special case? That adequacy of evidential support is much more easily achieved in respect of philosophical propositions than in respect of geological or medical or historical propositions? Perhaps because nothing really hangs on philosophical questions, and a false or unjustified philosophical opinion is therefore harmless? Or because philosophy is in some sense not about matters of empirical fact? As to the first of these two suggestions, I think it is false that nothing hangs on philosophical questions. What people have believed about the philosophical theses advanced by—for example—Plato, Locke, and Marx has had profound effects on history. I don't know what the world would be like if everyone who ever encountered philosophy immediately became, and thereafter

---

[1][Ed. note: David Lewis (1941–2001) was professor of philosophy at Princeton University and one of the most influential philosophers of his era.]

remained, a philosophical skeptic, but I'm willing to bet it would be a vastly different world. (In any case, I certainly hope this suggestion is false. I'd hate to have to defend my own field of study against a charge of adhering to loose epistemic standards by arguing that it's all right to adopt loose epistemic standards in philosophy because philosophy is detached from life to such a degree that philosophical mistakes can't do any harm.) In a more general, theoretical way, Clifford has argued, and with some plausibility, that it is *in principle* impossible to claim on behalf of any subject-matter whatever—on the ground that mistaken beliefs about the things of which that subject-matter treats are harmless—exemption from the strict epistemic standards to which, say, geological, medical, and historical beliefs are properly held. He argues,

> [That is not] truly a belief at all which has not some influence upon the actions of him who holds it. He who truly believes that which prompts him to an action has looked upon the action to lust after it, he has committed it already in his heart. If a belief is not realized immediately in open deeds, it is stored up for the guidance of the future. It goes to make a part of that aggregate of beliefs which is the link between sensation and action at every moment of all our lives, and which is so organized and compacted together that no part of it can be isolated from the rest, but every new addition modifies the structure of the whole. No real belief, however trifling and fragmentary it may seem, is ever truly insignificant; it prepares us to receive more of its like, confirms those which resembled it before, and weakens others; and so gradually it lays a stealthy train in our inmost thoughts, which may some day explode into overt action, and leave its stamp upon our character forever... And no one man's belief is in any case a private matter which concerns himself alone... no belief held by one man, however seemingly trivial the belief, and however obscure the believer, is actually insignificant or without its effect on the fate of mankind...

Whether or not you find this general, theoretical argument convincing, it does in any case seem quite impossible to maintain, given the actual history of the relation between philosophy and our social life, that it makes no real difference what people believe about philosophical questions.

The second suggestion—that philosophy is different (and that philosophers may therefore properly, in their professional work, observe looser epistemic standards than geologists or physicians observe in theirs) because it's not about matters of empirical fact—is trickier. Its premise is not that it doesn't make any difference what people believe about philosophical questions; it's rather that the world would look exactly the same whether any given philosophical thesis was true or false. I think that that's a dubious assertion. If the declarative sentences that philosophers characteristically write and speak in their professional capacity are meaningful at all, then many of them express propositions that are necessary truths or necessary falsehoods, and it's at least a very doubtful assertion that the world would look the same if some necessary truth were a falsehood or if some necessary falsehood were a truth. (Would anyone argue that mathematicians may properly hold themselves to looser epistemic standards than geologists because the world would look the same whether or not there was a greatest prime?) And even if it were true that philosophy was, in no sense of this versatile word, about matters of empirical fact, one might well raise the question why this should lend any support to the suggestion that philosophers were entitled to looser epistemic standards than geologists or physiologists, given that philosophical beliefs actually do have important effects on the behavior of those who hold them. Rather than address the issues that these speculations raise, however, I will simply change the subject.

Let us consider politics. Almost everyone will admit that it makes a difference what people believe about politics—I am using the word in its broadest possible sense—and it would be absurd to say that propositions like "Capital punishment is an ineffective deterrent" or "Nations that do not maintain a strong military capability actually increase the risk of war" are not about matters of empirical fact. And yet people disagree about these propositions (and scores of others of equal importance), and their disagreements about them bear a disquieting resemblance to the disagreements of philosophers about nominalism and free will and the covering-law model. That is, their disagreements are matters of interminable debate, and impressive authorities can be found on both sides of many of the interminable debates.

It is important to realize that this feature of philosophy and politics is not a universal feature of human discourse. It is clear, for example, that someone who believes in astrology believes in something that is simply indefensible. It would be hard to find a philosopher—I hope this is true—who believed that every philosopher who disagreed with his or her position on nominalism held a position that was indefensible in the same way that a belief in astrology was indefensible. It might be easier to find someone who held the corresponding position about disputed and important political questions. I suspect there really are people who think that those who disagree with them about the deterrent effect of capital punishment or the probable consequences of unilateral disarmament are not only mistaken but hold beliefs that are indefensible in the way that a belief in astrology is indefensible. I can only say that I regard this attitude as ludicrous. On each side of many interminably debated political questions—it is not necessary to my argument to say all—one can find well-informed (indeed, immensely learned) and highly intelligent men and women who adhere to the very highest intellectual standards. And this is simply not the case with debates about astrology. In fact, it is hardly possible to suppose that there could be a very interesting debate about the truth-values of the claims made by astrologers.

Everyone who is intellectually honest will admit this, will admit that there are interminable political debates with highly intelligent and well-informed people on both sides. And yet few will react to this state of affairs by becoming political skeptics, by declining to have any political beliefs that are disputed by highly intelligent and well-informed people. But how can this rejection of political skepticism be defended? How can responsible political thinkers believe that the Syndicalist Party is the last, best hope for Ruritania when they know full well that there are well-informed (even immensely learned) and highly intelligent people who argue vehemently—all the while adhering to the highest intellectual standards—that a Syndicalist government would be the ruin of Ruritania? Do the friends of Syndicalism claim to see gaps in the arguments of their opponents, "facts" that they have cited that are not really facts, real facts that they have chosen not to mention, a hidden agenda behind their opposition to Syndicalism? No doubt they do. Nevertheless, if they are intelligent and intellectually honest, they will be aware that if these claims were made in public debate, the opponents of Syndicalism would probably be able to muster a very respectable rebuttal. The friends of Syndicalism will perhaps be confident that they could effectively meet the points raised in this rebuttal, but, if they are intelligent and intellectually honest, they will be aware . . . and so, for all practical purposes, *ad infinitum*.

I ask again: what could it be that justifies us in rejecting political skepticism? How can I believe that my political beliefs are justified when these beliefs are rejected by people whose qualifications for engaging in political discourse are as impressive as David Lewis's qualifications for engaging in philosophical discourse? These people are aware of (at least) all the evidence and all the arguments that I am aware of, and they are (at least) as good at evaluating evidence and arguments as I. How, then, can I maintain that the evidence and arguments I can adduce in support of my beliefs actually justify these beliefs? If this evidence and these arguments are capable of that, then why aren't they capable of convincing these other people that these beliefs are correct? Well, as with philosophy, I am inclined to think that I must enjoy some sort of incommunicable insight that the others, for all their merits, lack. I am inclined to think that the evidence and arguments I can adduce in support of my beliefs do not constitute the totality of my justification for these beliefs. But all that I am willing to say for sure is that something justifies me in rejecting political skepticism, or at least that it is possible that something does: that it is not a necessary truth that one is not justified in holding a political belief that is controverted by intelligent and well-informed political thinkers. . . .

## READING COMPREHENSION QUESTIONS

1. Van Inwagen claims that he wants to avoid what he calls "philosophical skepticism." What is philosophical skepticism, and why does van Inwagen want to avoid it? Do you think it can be avoided? Explain why or why not.

2. Van Inwagen considers two suggestions as to why philosophical theses (over which philosophers disagree) might be exempt from the standards of evidence that apply to such disciplines as geology, medicine, and history. State the two suggestions. What does van Inwagen say about them? Explain why you either agree or disagree with him.

3. What is the contrast van Inwagen draws between political disagreement on the one hand and disagreement about astrology on the other? Explain why you agree or disagree with van Inwagen's contrast.

4. Toward the end of the selection, van Inwagen asks how it is that he can claim that the evidence and arguments that he uses in support of some of his philosophical beliefs can justify him in holding those beliefs, even though other equally well-informed philosophers are not convinced by the evidence

and his arguments. How does van Inwagen reply to this question? In light of his reply, do you think he is justified in his (controversial) philosophical beliefs? Why or why not?

5. How do the views of van Inwagen regarding philosophical and political beliefs apply to the ethics of religious belief? If you conclude that his views regarding the ethics of religious belief differ from those of Clifford, who do you think is right about the matter? Why?

# 7

# Ethics

## MOTIVATION

Suppose you are sitting in class taking an exam and you notice that the person next to you is cheating. Do you have an obligation to call it to the attention of the instructor—if not during the exam, then later?

Suppose one of your friends is pregnant as a result of having casual sex with someone she met at a party. She is thinking about having an abortion. She asks for your advice. What do you say to her?

Suppose a loved one who is now in his nineties is in constant pain, which the attending physicians can do little to relieve. He has been told that he only has a few weeks to live, and under these conditions he asks to be given a lethal drug that will end his life now. Should you support his request?

Each of these hypothetical cases involves having to make an ethical decision, give ethical advice, or decide whether to support an ethically important decision of someone else. Perhaps many of the ethically significant situations you confront in everyday life are ones in which the ethical thing to do strikes you as obvious. But in other cases, you may feel conflicted and perhaps stop to ask yourself what would be the right thing to do in that situation. If you take a further step back and ask the very general question, "What makes a right action right and a wrong action wrong?" you are asking the sort of philosophical question that is central to **ethics**—that branch of philosophy that inquires into the nature of right and wrong as well as into the nature of good and bad. In addressing questions of right and wrong, good and bad, philosophers engage in a process of ethical theorizing with the aim of producing an ethical theory. But this raises the following three questions:

- What is an ethical theory?

- What theories in ethics have philosophers proposed?
- How does one go about evaluating an ethical theory?

These are the questions that will occupy us in the rest of this chapter's introduction. To address them, we begin by explaining some of the basic concepts in ethics, as well as what an ethical theory is. We will then be in a position to preview the theories that are featured in our readings. We conclude with some remarks about how one goes about evaluating an ethical theory.

## BASIC CONCEPTS: THE RIGHT AND THE GOOD

In ethics, the terms "right" and "wrong" are used primarily to evaluate the morality of actions, and in this chapter the main concern will be with ethical theories that address the nature of right and wrong action (or right action, for short). As a start, it is helpful to notice that the term "right" has both a broad and a narrow sense. In the broad sense of the term, to say an action is right is to say that it is "alright" (not wrong) to perform, where it is left open whether the act, in addition to being alright, is an action that one ethically ought to perform—an obligation or duty. But sometimes "right" is used more narrowly to refer to actions that are ethically required or obligatory, as when someone says that a certain action is *the* right action to perform. Actions that are alright to perform (not wrong) and that are also alright *not* to perform (not obligatory) are ethically optional. So, we have three basic categories of ethical evaluation into which an action may fall. An action may be ethically *obligatory* (something one ethically ought to do, is ethically required to do, is one's duty), or ethically *optional*, or ethically *wrong*.

In ethics, the terms "good" and "bad" are used primarily in assessing the goodness or badness of persons (their character) as well as the goodness and badness of experiences, things, and states of affairs. It is perfectly fine to talk about actions being either good or bad, but philosophers prefer to reserve the terms "right" and "wrong" for evaluating actions.

When thinking about what does and does not have value, it is important to distinguish between something's having **intrinsic value** (that is, being intrinsically good or bad) and something's having **extrinsic value** (that is, being extrinsically good or bad). Something has intrinsic value when its value depends on features *inherent* to that thing. By contrast, something has extrinsic value when its goodness or badness depends on how it is related to something else that has intrinsic value. For instance, some philosophers maintain that happiness is intrinsically good—its goodness depends on the inherent nature of happiness itself—and that things such as money and power, while not intrinsically good, can nevertheless be extrinsically good (valuable) when they are used to bring about or contribute to happiness. Thus, the notion of intrinsic value is the more basic of the two notions and so philosophical accounts of value are primarily concerned with the nature of intrinsic value. As in the case of right and wrong action, there are three basic value categories: the *intrinsically good*, the *intrinsically bad* (also referred to as the intrinsically *evil*), and what we may call the *intrinsically value-neutral*—that is, the category of all those things that are neither intrinsically good nor bad (though they may sometimes have extrinsic value).

We mentioned at the outset of this section that most of the theories featured in this chapter primarily address questions about the nature of right and wrong action. So why bring up good and bad? One reason for doing so (as we shall see later) is that some of the theories of right conduct (for example, egoism, utilitarianism, and virtue ethics) base a theory of right action on a theory of the good.

In addition to the concepts of the right and the good (and related concepts), ethical theorists also are interested in the concepts of virtue and vice. This latter pair of concepts will come up later when we discuss virtue ethics.

Let us now turn to the issue of what an ethical theory is supposed to accomplish.

## THE CENTRAL AIM OF AN ETHICAL THEORY

An **ethical theory** addresses fundamental ethical questions about the nature of right and wrong, good and bad, by attempting to specify those underlying features of actions, persons, and other items of ethical evaluation that *make* them right or wrong, good or bad, and thus *explain why* such items have the ethical properties they have. This point can be put more simply by saying that an ethical theory aims to reveal the underlying *nature* or *essence* of the right and the good.

It is worth noting that in setting forth an ethical theory, philosophers often propose **ethical principles**—very general ethical statements that purport to specify what makes actions right or wrong and what makes something (including persons) good or bad. Principles that purport to explain what makes an action right or wrong are **principles of right conduct**. Two of the most widely discussed principles of right conduct are Mill's principle of utility and Kant's categorical imperative, both of which we will encounter in the next section. Such principles constitute the major part of a **theory of right conduct**—one main branch of an overall ethical theory. The other branch is **theory of value**, which features principles—**principles of value**—that purport to indicate what it is that makes something intrinsically good or intrinsically bad.

Of course, in addition to the search for ethical principles of right conduct and value, an ethical theory will also feature arguments offered in defense of those principles. We may sum this up by saying that the central aim of an ethical theory is to set forth and *defend* principles of right conduct and value that specify, respectively, what *makes* an action right or wrong and what *makes* something intrinsically good or bad. Principles that succeed in these tasks will thereby *explain* why right actions are right, wrong actions are wrong, and so forth.

Now that we have reviewed some basic concepts and the guiding aim of ethical theory, let us move on to a sampling of ethical theories.

## SEVEN ETHICAL THEORIES

The seven theories we are about to preview do not exhaust the field, but they represent some of the most prominent theories in the history of ethics, and they are the ones that readers will encounter in the selections included in this chapter.

Each theory will probably strike a familiar chord with readers because, as we shall see, they can be associated with familiar questions about ethics. The first six theories focus primarily on the nature of right and wrong. One should keep in mind that what follows are mere snapshots of each of the theories and are only meant to help readers get a sense for the various types of ethical theory.

### What's Wrong with Just Doing What Will Most Benefit You?

According to **ethical egoism**, what is right or wrong for *you* to do is really just a matter of what will be good *for you*—what will best promote your self-interest. Often, those who argue for ethical egoism appeal to a certain psychological thesis called **psychological egoism**, according to which all human actions are done solely for the sake of self-interest. Notice that ethical egoism is a normative theory about what one ought or ought not to do, while psychological egoism is a descriptive thesis about motivation. In the story of Gyges recounted in our selection from Plato, we find one of the story's characters, Glaucon, defending ethical egoism on the basis of psychological egoism.

### Isn't Ethics Just a Matter of the Norms and Practices of One's Group or Culture?

We learn from anthropology that different cultures often have different and conflicting beliefs about what is right and wrong. For instance, in some cultures it is believed that if an unwed woman becomes pregnant, it is the obligation of the family to put her to death to restore family honor. In other cultures this would be considered wrong. Impressed by such cultural differences, some philosophers have defended **ethical relativism** (sometimes called **cultural relativism**), according to which what's right or wrong for one to do depends on the ethical norms one's culture happens to accept. Thus, on this theory, if different cultures happen to accept different and conflicting ethical norms regarding some type of action, then an action that is right in one culture may be wrong in another. In our readings for this chapter, the relativist position is presented by anthropologist Ruth Benedict.

### Don't Right and Wrong Depend on the Will of God?

Whereas ethical relativism looks to cultural norms as the basis of right and wrong, the **divine command theory** attempts to base ethics on God's commands: what's right or wrong depends on God's will. This theory does *not* postulate moral principles independent of God, with God, because He is all knowing and wants us to do what's right, telling us what those principles are and commanding us to follow them. Rather, an act is right (in the narrow sense) *because* God commands it; God doesn't command it because it's antecedently right.

All three ethical theories described thus far—ethical egoism, relativism, and divine command—are briefly addressed and criticized in our selection by Thomas Nagel. Nagel's criticisms (which we won't describe here) are perhaps not decisive;

however they do raise some serious obstacles that defenders of any of these theories must overcome.

## Isn't Ethics a Matter of Doing the Most Good, Considering Everyone?

**Utilitarianism** was originally developed and defended by Jeremy Bentham (1748–1832) and later refined by John Stuart Mill (1806–1873). Their basic idea is that it is *human welfare* or *happiness* that alone is intrinsically good, and that the rightness or wrongness of actions depends entirely on how they affect human welfare or happiness. Like ethical egoism, this theory makes right and wrong depend on the *value* of the *consequences* of actions. But there is a huge difference between these theories in other respects. Whereas ethical egoism makes right and wrong depend entirely on how an action would affect the agent of that act, utilitarianism makes right and wrong depend on how one's action affects the welfare or happiness of all individuals affected by the act. In the selection included in this chapter, Mill refers to the utilitarian's fundamental principle of right conduct as the "Greatest Happiness Principle." It is often referred to as the **principle of utility**.

## Isn't Morality about What's Fair and What's Not Fair and Showing Respect for People Generally?

Most everyone has come across moral arguments that appeal to the **golden rule**: do unto others as you would have them do unto you. This rule encapsulates a kind of test for thinking about the morality of actions: it has the individual who is making a moral choice consider how he or she would like it were he or she on the receiving end of the action in question. Various objections have been made to the golden rule because, taken literally, it makes the rightness or wrongness of an action depend simply on what one does or would happen to *desire*. But people can have ethically abhorrent desires. A masochist who inflicts pain on others might cheerfully say that he would have others do unto him as he is doing to them. Do we want to conclude that his causing others pain is morally right?

Perhaps there is some interpretation of the golden rule that does not yield the wrong result in the case of the masochist and in other examples that have been used to criticize it.[1] Nevertheless there is something about the *spirit* of the golden rule that seems right. The idea suggested by this rule is that morality requires that we not treat people unfairly; that we respect other persons by taking them into account in our moral deliberations. Of course, utilitarianism tells us to take others into account by considering how one's actions will affect others' happiness. But there is another way to develop the idea suggested by the golden rule that does not have to do with maximizing happiness, and which we find in the ethical writings of German philosopher Immanuel Kant (1724–1804).

---

[1]For instance, Thomas Nagel, in the selection included in this chapter, argues that the question, "How would you like it if someone did that to you?"—the question associated with the golden rule—can be used to effectively argue that most people have a reason not to hurt others.

Central to **Kant's ethical theory** is the idea that ethical requirements can be expressed as commands or imperatives that categorically bid us to perform certain actions—requirements that apply to us regardless of what we might happen to want or desire or how such actions bear on the production of happiness. Kant thought that specific ethical requirements could be derived from a fundamental principle, which he called the **categorical imperative**. In explaining and illustrating his fundamental principle, Kant offered several formulations of it.

According to the **universal law formulation** of the categorical imperative, we can test for the difference between right and wrong action by performing a thought experiment in which one asks whether one can consistently will that one's policy of action ("maxim" in Kant-speak) be universally adopted. The idea behind this test seems to be that in acting on a policy that one could not consistently will that everyone act on, one is in effect exempting oneself from having to follow a rule that one thinks everyone else should follow. In short, one is being unfair. In the selection included in our readings, Kant illustrates how his test is supposed to work by considering the morality of suicide, making false promises, letting one's talents rust, and refusing to help those in need.

Kant also claims that his fundamental moral principle can be formulated in terms of the command to treat humanity (all individuals including oneself) as "ends in themselves" and never as mere means. This is called the **humanity formulation** of the categorical imperative. The central idea it expresses is that all human beings, in virtue of being rational and free, are deserving of certain kinds of treatment. Sometimes this idea is put in terms of people being owed respect. Respecting someone's humanity—treating that person as an end in herself— requires that one avoid treating her as a *mere* means to one's own personal ends. There is nothing wrong with asking someone for help and thus "using" that person as a means for getting or achieving something. We do this all the time. ("Hey, dude, what time is it?") What *is* morally objectionable, according to Kant, is to treat someone as a *mere* means—as though the person were some sort of instrument. Deception and coercion for personal gain are among the most obvious ways of treating someone as a *mere* means.

### Don't Right and Wrong Have to Do with Feelings and, in Particular, Feelings of Care for Others?

The ethical theories of Mill and Kant are often thought of as theories that concentrate on fairness and justice. In 1982, psychologist Carol Gilligan published an important and influential book, *In a Different Voice*, in which she argued that women often frame ethical issues in terms of care rather than in terms of justice. Gilligan's work as a psychologist concerns the descriptive issue of how people in general (and women in particular) do in fact think about moral issues. But this descriptive work has inspired what has come to be called the **ethics of care**, according to which considerations of care are central to considerations of right and wrong. In our readings, Nell Noddings develops an ethical theory of right and wrong that is rooted in what she calls a sentiment or feeling of natural caring that is typical of the spontaneous care that a mother has for her infant.

## In Deciding What's Right and What's Wrong, Shouldn't one Be Thinking about What Kind of Person One Should Aspire to Be and Try to Do What a Truly Virtuous Person Would Do?

Sometimes our moral thinking is dominated by thoughts about what sort of person one would be were one to perform some action. The thought of living up to certain ideals or standards of excellence is central to **virtue ethics**. Not being a selfish person, for example, is an ideal that one might use in evaluating some course of action: "Not helping her would be the kind of thing a selfish person would do, so I'm going to help." When our moral thinking takes this turn, we are evaluating actions in terms of virtue and vice. What are virtue and vice?

A **virtue** is a trait of character or mind that involves dispositions to act, feel, and think in certain ways and that is central in the *positive* evaluation of persons. The virtue of honesty, for instance, involves at a minimum being disposed to tell the truth and avoid lying, as well as the disposition to have certain feelings about truth telling (positive ones) and about lying (negative ones). Honesty, as a virtue, is a trait that has positive value and contributes to what makes someone a good person. A **vice**, then, is a trait of character or mind that involves dispositions to act, feel, and think in certain ways, and is central in the *negative* evaluation of persons. Dishonesty is a vice corresponding to the virtue of honesty. (Readers are invited to list other virtue/vice pairs.)

The readings in this chapter conclude with a selection from Aristotle, who is perhaps the single most important historical source for thinking about ethics in relation to virtue. In our selection, Aristotle is mainly interested in the question of the sort of person one ought to *be*, and hence in the question of what sort of life would be a good one for human beings to lead. He identifies the highest good for humans with happiness, and then proceeds to characterize a happy life as one that is lived in accordance with the virtues.

Although Aristotle's primary focus was on the question of what sort of person to *be* rather than on questions about the rightness and wrongness of actions, one might attempt (as some have) to explain the nature of right and wrong through considerations of virtue and vice. This possibility was hinted at previously in connection with not wanting to act in the manner of a selfish person.

This completes our brief tour of some main types of ethical theory. Let us conclude with some remarks about evaluating them.

## HOW TO EVALUATE AN ETHICAL THEORY

Recall that the central aim of a moral theory is to set forth and *defend* principles of right conduct and value that specify respectively what *makes* an action right or wrong and what *makes* something intrinsically good or bad. Such principles are thus intended to *explain* why an action is right or wrong or why something is (intrinsically) good or bad. Implicit in this aim are two demands that an ethical theory attempts to satisfy, and so there are two tasks (corresponding to these demands) that are involved in evaluating an ethical theory.

## Task 1: Evaluation of Arguments

When philosophers attempt to defend an ethical theory, they give arguments in favor of accepting the principles featured in the theory. Mill, for instance, attempts to give a "proof" of the principle of utility. One task, then, in evaluating an ethical theory is to evaluate the arguments that are offered in defense of the principles featured in that theory.

But, of course, even if one finds fault with the arguments offered in support of some ethical principle, one should not automatically conclude that the principle in question is false and that the associated ethical theory should be rejected. Perhaps the philosopher has not done a good job defending the principle in question. And this brings us to the second task.

## Task 2: Critical Examination of Ethical Principles

One way to critically evaluate an ethical principle or any generalization is to look for counterexamples—a topic covered in the introductory chapter. So, in evaluating ethical principles, one task is to look for counterexamples. A counterexample to an ethical principle of right conduct will be an example of an action that, for example, is clearly wrong (or clearly right), but that the principle (together with relevant information) classifies as right (or wrong).[2] For instance, according to the utilitarian principle of right conduct, the right act in any situation is the act that will maximize utility (that is, that will be better for society overall than any other alternative action open to the agent on the occasion in question). Now consider the following (rather simple) hypothetical case.

> A series of unsolved murders has been committed in a small community and the townspeople are up in arms threatening to riot unless the sheriff finds the guilty party and brings that person or persons to justice. The sheriff is completely stumped, but he has an idea. He knows of a homeless person with a criminal record who could easily be captured, framed, and punished for the murders—the sheriff alone happens to know that this person is not guilty of the murders. In thinking about what to do, the sheriff considers his options. He could keep on looking for the murderer(s), but there are no clues and the townspeople are getting increasingly angry by the day. But another option would be to capture, frame, and punish the innocent homeless individual for the murders in question. According to utilitarianism, what should the sheriff do?

If we stipulate that the consequences of framing the innocent person and thus warding off an otherwise inevitable riot are better overall than the consequences of continuing in vain to look for the real murderer(s), then the utilitarian theory implies that the sheriff morally ought to capture, frame, and punish the person he knows to be innocent of the crimes. But clearly it would be wrong for him to do

---

[2]Similar remarks apply to principles of value, but let us stay focused on principles of right conduct.

so! We thus have an apparent counterexample to the utilitarian principle of right conduct.

So in looking for counterexamples to a moral principle, one looks for cases in which the principle, together with the facts of the case, imply a mistaken verdict about the rightness or wrongness of the act featured in the example.

But of course, given the central aim of an ethical theory, we aren't just looking for principles that don't have counterexamples. We also want principles that tell us something about the *nature* of right and wrong—that properly provide an *explanation* of the rightness and wrongness of actions. When evaluating an ethical principle, one must consider the kind of explanation the ethical principle (and the associated theory) offers with regard to what makes an action right or wrong. To bring this point into sharper focus, suppose there were a perfectly reliable crystal ball which, for any ethical question anyone could ever ask, would give the correct moral verdict: it never fails. We could then formulate the following generalization:

> An action is right if and only if the crystal ball says it is; otherwise the action is wrong.

If the crystal ball is unfailingly reliable, then the generalization is true. But it doesn't tell us what we want to know as philosophers: What is it that *makes* and hence *explains* the difference between right and wrong? In evaluating an ethical principle, one must therefore ask whether the explanation being offered by the principle is correct. This can only be done by reflecting carefully on particular ethical issues and examining the sorts of considerations that the theory under scrutiny would have us consider in coming to a moral verdict about the particular issue. For instance, in studying utilitarianism, one might wonder whether its explanation of the wrongness of breaking a promise (in cases where promise breaking is or would be wrong) is a correct explanation in all such cases.

# 34

# The Myth of Gyges

## PLATO

*Plato (ca. 427–347 B.C.E), a student of Socrates and a teacher of Aristotle, was introduced in Chapter 2. In this famous passage from* The Republic, *Glaucon (one of the characters in the dialogue) argues to Socrates that, by nature, human beings are egoists strongly inclined to pursue their own self-interest. Thus "those who practice justice do so against their will because they lack the power to do wrong." To illustrate his point, Glaucon recounts the story of Gyges.*

So, if you agree, I will do the following: I will renew the argument of Thrasymachus; I will first state what people consider the nature and origin of justice; secondly, that all who practise it do so unwillingly as being something necessary but not good; thirdly, that they have good reason to do so, for, according to what people say, the life of the unjust man is much better than that of the just. . . .

Splendid, he said, then listen while I deal with the first subject I mentioned: the nature and origin of justice.

They say that to do wrong is naturally good, to be wronged is bad, but the suffering of injury so far exceeds in badness the good of inflicting it that when men have done wrong to each other and suffered it, and have had a taste of both, those who are unable to avoid the latter and practise the former decide that it is profitable to come to an agreement with each other neither to inflict injury nor to suffer it. As a result they begin to make laws and covenants, and the law's command they call lawful and just. This, they say, is the origin and essence of justice; it stands between the best and the worst, the best being to do wrong without paying the penalty and the worst to be wronged without the power of revenge. The just then is a mean between two extremes; it is welcomed and honoured because of men's lack of the power to do wrong. The man who has that power, the real man, would not make a compact with anyone not to inflict injury or suffer it. For him that would be madness. This then, Socrates, is, according to their argument, the nature and origin of justice.

Even those who practise justice do so against their will because they lack the power to do wrong. This we could realize very clearly if we imagined ourselves granting to both the just and the unjust the freedom to do whatever they liked.

SOURCE: From G. M. A. Grube, trans., *Plato's Republic*, copyright © 1974, revised 1992. Reprinted by permission of Hackett Publishing Co. Inc.

We could then follow both of them and observe where their desires led them, and we would catch the just man redhanded travelling the same road as the unjust. The reason is the desire for undue gain which every organism by nature pursues as a good, but the law forcibly sidetracks him to honour equality. The freedom I just mentioned would most easily occur if these men had the power which they say the ancestor of the Lydian Gyges possessed. The story is that he was a shepherd in the service of the ruler of Lydia. There was a violent rainstorm and an earthquake which broke open the ground and created a chasm at the place where he was tending sheep. Seeing this and marvelling, he went down into it. He saw, besides many other wonders of which we are told, a hollow bronze horse. There were window-like openings in it; he climbed through them and caught sight of a corpse which seemed of more than human stature, wearing nothing but a ring of gold on its finger. This ring the shepherd put on and came out. He arrived at the usual monthly meeting which reported to the king on the state of the flocks, wearing the ring. As he was sitting among the others he happened to twist the hoop of the ring towards himself, to the inside of his hand, and as he did this he became invisible to those sitting near him and they went on talking as if he had gone. He marvelled at this and, fingering the ring, he turned the hoop outward again and became visible. Perceiving this he tested whether the ring had this power and so it happened: if he turned the hoop inwards he became invisible, but was visible when he turned it outwards. When he realized this, he at once arranged to become one of the messengers to the king. He went, committed adultery with the king's wife, attacked the king with her help, killed him, and took over the kingdom.

Now if there were two such rings, one worn by the just man, the other by the unjust, no one, as these people think, would be so incorruptible that he would stay on the path of justice or bring himself to keep away from other people's property and not touch it, when he could with impunity take whatever he wanted from the market, go into houses and have sexual relations with anyone he wanted, kill anyone, free all those he wished from prison, and do the other things which would make him like a god among men. His actions would be in no way different from those of the other and they would both follow the same path. This, some would say, is a great proof that no one is just willingly but under compulsion, so that justice is not one's private good, since wherever either thought he could do wrong with impunity he would do so. Every man believes that injustice is much more profitable to himself than justice, and any exponent of this argument will say that he is right. The man who did not wish to do wrong with that opportunity and did not touch other people's property, would be thought by those who knew it to be very foolish and miserable. They would praise him in public, thus deceiving one another, for fear of being wronged. So much for my second topic.

As for the choice between the lives we are discussing, we shall be able to make a correct judgment about it only if we put the most just man and the most unjust man face to face; otherwise we cannot do so. By face to face I mean this: let us grant to the unjust the fullest degree of injustice and to the just the fullest justice, each being perfect in his own pursuit. First, the unjust man will act as clever craftsmen do—a top navigator for example or physician distinguishes what his craft can do and what it cannot; the former he will undertake, the latter he will pass by, and when he slips he can put things right. So the unjust man's correct attempts at wrongdoing must remain secret; the one who is caught must be considered a poor performer, for the extreme of injustice is to have a reputation for justice, and our perfectly unjust man must be granted perfection in injustice. We must not take this from him, but we must allow that, while committing the greatest crimes, he has provided himself with the greatest reputation for justice; if he makes a slip he must be able to put it right; he must be a sufficiently persuasive speaker if some wrongdoing of his is made public; he must be able to use force, where force is needed, with the help of his courage, his strength, and the friends and wealth with which he has provided himself.

Having described such a man, let us now in our argument put beside him the just man, simple as he is and noble, who, as Aeschylus put it, does not wish to appear just but to be so. We must take away his reputation, for a reputation for justice would bring him honour and rewards, and it would then not be clear whether he is what he is for justice's sake or for the sake of rewards and honour. We must strip him of everything except justice and make him the complete opposite of the other. Though he does no wrong, he must have the greatest reputation for wrongdoing so that he may be tested for justice by not weakening under ill repute and its consequences. Let him go his incorruptible way until death with a reputation for injustice throughout his life, just though he is, so that our two men reach the extremes, one of justice, the other of injustice, and let them be judged as to which of the two is the happier. . . .

## READING COMPREHENSION QUESTIONS

1.  In the beginning of the excerpt, Glaucon describes a certain view (that he claims is held by some people) about the nature and origin of justice. What is this view? Do you find it plausible? Keep in mind: Glaucon is reporting what some people claim is the *nature* of justice—what *makes* an action just or unjust.

2.  The story of Gyges and the ring is supposed to prove a claim about human beings. What is that claim? Do you find it plausible? Why or why not?

3.  In the final two paragraphs, Glaucon compares the life of a perfectly unjust man with the life of a perfectly just man. What point is Glaucon making with this comparison?

4.  In the editors' introduction to ethics, *psychological* egoism is distinguished from *ethical* egoism. How are these views presented and defended in Plato's story?

# 35

# A Defense of Ethical Relativism

RUTH BENEDICT

*Ruth Benedict (1887–1948) was a pioneering American anthropologist and wrote* Patterns of Culture *(1935), an important work in comparative anthropology. Benedict argues that careful study of the cultural practices of different peoples supports the idea that what is and is not behaviorally normal is culturally determined. She argues for a similar point in connection with such moral distinctions as good and bad, and right and wrong. She suggests that phrases like "it is morally good" should be understood as being synonymous with "it is habitual."*

Modern social anthropology has become more and more a study of the varieties and common elements of cultural environment and the consequences of these in human behavior. For such a study of diverse social orders primitive peoples fortunately provide a laboratory not yet entirely vitiated by the spread of a standardized worldwide civilization. Dyaks and Hopis, Fijians and Yakuts are significant for psychological and sociological study because only among these simpler peoples has there been sufficient isolation to give opportunity for the development of localized social forms. In the higher cultures the standardization of custom and belief over a couple of continents has given a false sense of the inevitability of the particular forms that have gained currency, and we need to turn to a wider survey in order to check the conclusions we hastily base upon this near-universality of familiar customs. Most of the simpler cultures did not gain the wide currency of the one which, out of our experience, we identify with human nature, but this was for various historical reasons, and certainly not for any that gives us as its carriers a monopoly of social good or of social sanity. Modern civilization, from this point of view, becomes not a necessary pinnacle of human achievement but one entry in a long series of possible adjustments.

These adjustments, whether they are in mannerisms like the ways of showing anger, or joy, or grief in any society, or in major human drives like those of sex, prove to be far more variable than experience in any one culture would suggest. In certain fields, such as that of religion or of formal marriage arrangements, these wide limits of variability are well known and can be fairly described. In others it is

SOURCE: From Ruth Benedict, "Anthropology and the Abnormal," *Journal of General Psychology* 10 (1934): 59–82. Reprinted by permission of Helen Dwight Reid Educational Foundation. Published by Heldref Publications, Washington, DC.

not yet possible to give a generalized account, but that does not absolve us of the task of indicating the significance of the work that has been done and of the problems that have arisen.

One of these problems relates to the customary modern normal–abnormal categories and our conclusions regarding them. In how far are such categories culturally determined, or in how far can we with assurance regard them as absolute? In how far can we regard inability to function socially as diagnostic of abnormality or in how far is it necessary to regard this as a function of the culture?

As a matter of fact, one of the most striking facts that emerges from a study of widely varying cultures is the ease with which our abnormals function in other cultures. It does not matter what kind of "abnormality" we choose for illustration, those which indicate extreme instability, or those which are more in the nature of character traits like sadism or delusions of grandeur or of persecution, there are well-described cultures in which these abnormals function at ease and with honor, and apparently without danger or difficulty to the society.

The most notorious of these is trance and catalepsy. Even a very mild mystic is aberrant in our culture. But most peoples have regarded even extreme psychic manifestations not only as normal and desirable, but even as characteristic of highly valued and gifted individuals. This was true even in our own cultural background in that period when Catholicism made the ecstatic experience the mark of sainthood. It is hard for us, born and brought up in a culture that makes no use of the experience, to realize how important a role it may play and how many individuals are capable of it, once it has been given an honorable place in any society. . . .

Cataleptic and trance phenomena are, of course, only one illustration of the fact that those whom we regard as abnormals may function adequately in other cultures. Many of our culturally discarded traits are selected for elaboration in different societies. Homosexuality is an excellent example, for in this case our attention is not constantly diverted, as in the consideration of trance, to the interruption of routine activity which it implies. Homosexuality poses the problem very simply. A tendency toward this trait in our culture exposes an individual to all the conflicts to which all aberrants are always exposed, and we tend to identify the consequences of this conflict with homosexuality. But these consequences are obviously local and cultural. Homosexuals in many societies are not incompetent, but they may be such if the culture asks adjustments of them that would strain any man's vitality. Wherever homosexuality has been given an honorable place in any society, those to whom it is congenial have filled adequately the honorable roles society assigns to them. Plato's *Republic* is, of course, the most convincing statement of such a reading of homosexuality. It is presented as one of the major means to the good life, and it was generally so regarded in Greece at that time.

The cultural attitude toward homosexuals has not always been on such a high ethical plane, but it has been very varied. Among many American Indian tribes there exists the institution of the berdache, as the French called them. These men-women were men who at puberty or thereafter took the dress and the occupations of women. Sometimes they married other men and lived with them. Sometimes they were men with no inversion, persons of weak sexual endowment who chose this role to avoid the jeers of the women. The berdaches were never regarded as of first-rate supernatural power, as similar men-women were in Siberia, but rather as leaders in women's occupations, good healers of certain diseases, or, among certain tribes, as the genial organizers of social affairs. In any case, they were socially placed. They were not left exposed to the conflicts that visit the deviant who is excluded from participation in the recognized pattern of his society.

The most spectacular illustrations of the extent to which normality may be culturally defined are those cultures where an abnormality of our culture is the cornerstone of their social structure. It is not possible to do justice to these possibilities in a short discussion. A recent study of an island of northwest Melanesia by Fortune describes a society built upon traits which we regard as beyond the border of paranoia. In this tribe the exogamic groups look upon each other as prime manipulators of black magic, so that one marries always into an enemy group which remains for life one's deadly and unappeasable foes. They look upon a good garden crop as a confession of theft, for everyone is engaged in making magic to induce into his garden the productiveness of his neighbors'; therefore no secrecy in the island is so rigidly insisted upon as the secrecy of a man's harvesting of his yams. Their polite phrase at the acceptance of a gift is, "And if you now poison me, how shall I repay you this present?" Their preoccupation with poisoning is constant; no woman ever leaves her cooking pot for a moment untended. Even the great affinal economic exchanges that are characteristic of this Melanesian culture area are quite altered in Dobu since they are incompatible with this fear and distrust that pervades the culture. They go farther and people the whole world outside their own quarters with such malignant spirits that all-night feasts and ceremonials simply do not occur here. They have even rigorous religiously enforced customs that forbid the sharing of seed even in one family group. Anyone else's food is deadly poison to you, so that communality of stores is out of the question. For some months before harvest the whole society is on the verge of starvation, but if one falls to the temptation and eats up one's seed yams, one is an outcast and a beachcomber for life. There is no coming back. It involves, as a matter of course, divorce and the breaking of all social ties.

Now in this society where no one may work with another and no one may share with another, Fortune describes the individual who was regarded by all his fellows as crazy. He was not one of those who periodically ran amok and, beside himself and frothing at the mouth, fell with a knife upon anyone he could reach. Such behavior they did not regard as putting anyone outside the pale. They did not even put the individuals who were known to be liable to these attacks under any kind of control. They merely fled when they saw the attack coming on and kept out of the way. "He would be all right tomorrow." But there was one man of sunny, kindly disposition who liked work and liked to be helpful. The compulsion was too strong for him to repress it in favor of the opposite tendencies of his culture. Men and women never spoke of him without laughing; he was silly and simple and definitely crazy. Nevertheless, to the ethnologist used to a culture that has, in Christianity, made his type the model of all virtue, he seemed a pleasant fellow. . . .

. . . Among the Kwakiutl it did not matter whether a relative had died in bed of disease, or by the hand of an enemy, in either case death was an affront to be wiped out by the death of another person. The fact that one had been caused to mourn was proof that one had been put upon. A chief's sister and her daughter had gone up to Victoria, and either because they drank bad whiskey or because their boat capsized they never came back. The chief called together his warriors, "Now I ask you, tribes, who shall wail? Shall I do it or shall another?" The spokesman answered, of course, "Not you, Chief. Let some other of the tribes." Immediately they set up the war pole to announce their intention of wiping out the injury, and gathered a war party. They set out, and found seven men and two children asleep and killed them. "Then they felt good when they arrived at Sebaa in the evening."

The point which is of interest to us is that in our society those who on that occasion would feel good when they arrived at Sebaa that evening would be the definitely abnormal. There would be some, even in our society, but it is not a recognized and approved mood under the circumstances. On the Northwest Coast those are favored and fortunate to whom that mood under those circumstances is congenial, and those to whom it is repugnant are unlucky. This latter minority can register in their own culture only by doing violence to their congenial responses and acquiring others that are difficult for them. The person, for instance, who, like a Plains Indian whose wife has been taken from him, is too proud to fight, can deal with the Northwest Coast civilization only by ignoring its strongest bents. If he cannot achieve it, he is the deviant in that culture, their instance of abnormality.

This head-hunting that takes place on the Northwest Coast after a death is no matter of blood revenge or of organized vengeance. There is no effort to tie up the subsequent killing with any responsibility on the part of the victim for the death of the person who is being mourned. A chief whose son has died goes visiting wherever his fancy dictates, and he says to his host, "My prince has died today, and you go with him." Then he kills him. In this, according to their interpretation, he acts nobly because he has not been downed. He has thrust back in return. The whole procedure is meaningless without the fundamental paranoid reading of bereavement. Death, like all the other untoward accidents of existence, confounds man's pride and can only be handled in the category of insults.

Behavior honored upon the Northwest Coast is one which is recognized as abnormal in our civilization, and yet it is sufficiently close to the attitudes of our own culture to be intelligible to us and to have a definite vocabulary with which we may discuss it. The megalomaniac paranoid trend is a definite danger in our society. It is encouraged by some of our major preoccupations, and it confronts us with a choice of two possible attitudes. One is to brand it as abnormal and reprehensible, and is the attitude we have chosen in our civilization. The other is to make it an essential attribute of ideal man, and this is the solution in the culture of the Northwest Coast.

These illustrations, which it has been possible to indicate only in the briefest manner, force upon us the fact that normality is culturally defined. An adult shaped to the drives and standards of either of these cultures, if he were transported into our civilization, would fall into our categories of abnormality. He would be faced with the psychic dilemmas of the socially unavailable. In his own culture, however, he is the pillar of society, the end result of socially inculcated mores, and the problem of personal instability in his case simply does not arise.

No one civilization can possibly utilize in its mores the whole potential range of human behavior. Just as there are great numbers of possible phonetic articulations, and the possibility of language depends on a selection and standardization of a few of these in order that speech communication may be possible at all, so the possibility of organized behavior of every sort, from the fashions of local dress and houses to the dicta of a people's ethics and religion, depends upon a similar selection among the possible behavior traits. In the field of recognized economic obligations or sex tabus this selection is as nonrational and subconscious a process as it is in the field of phonetics. It is a process which goes on in the group for long periods of time and is historically conditioned by innumerable accidents of isolation or of contact of peoples. In any comprehensive study of psychology, the selection that different cultures have made in the course of history within the great circumference of potential behavior is of great significance.

Every society, beginning with some slight inclination in one direction or another, carries its preference farther and farther, integrating itself more and more completely upon its chosen basis, and discarding those types of behavior that are uncongenial. Most of those organizations of personality that seem to us most incontrovertibly abnormal have been used by different civilizations in the very foundations of their institutional life. Conversely the most valued traits of our normal individuals have been looked on in differently organized cultures as aberrant. Normality, in short, within a very wide range, is culturally defined. It is primarily a term for the socially elaborated segment of human behavior in any culture; and abnormality, a term for the segment that that particular civilization does not use. The very eyes with which we see the problem are conditioned by the long traditional habits of our own society.

It is a point that has been made more often in relation to ethics than in relation to psychiatry. We do not any longer make the mistake of deriving the morality of our locality and decade directly from the inevitable constitution of human nature. We do not elevate it to the dignity of a first principle. We recognize that morality differs in every society, and is a convenient term for socially approved habits. Mankind has always preferred to say, "It is morally good," rather than "It is habitual," and the fact of this preference is matter enough for a critical science of ethics. But historically the two phrases are synonymous.

The concept of the normal is properly a variant of the concept of the good. It is that which society has approved. A normal action is one which falls well within the limits of expected behavior for a particular society. Its variability among different peoples is essentially a function of the variability of the behavior patterns that different societies have created for themselves, and can never be wholly divorced from a consideration of culturally institutionalized types of behavior.

Each culture is a more or less elaborate working-out of the potentialities of the segment it has chosen. In so far as a civilization is well integrated and consistent within itself, it will tend to carry farther and farther, according to its nature, its initial impulse toward a particular type of action, and from the point of view of any other culture those elaborations will include more and more extreme and aberrant traits.

Each of these traits, in proportion as it reinforces the chosen behavior patterns of that culture, is for that culture normal. Those individuals to whom it is congenial either congenitally, or as the result of childhood sets, are accorded prestige in that culture, and are not visited with the social contempt or disapproval which their traits would call down upon them in a society that was differently organized.

On the other hand, those individuals whose characteristics are not congenial to the selected type of human behavior in that community are the deviants, no matter how valued their personality traits may be in a contrasted civilization.

The Dobuan who is not easily susceptible to fear of treachery, who enjoys work and likes to be helpful, is their neurotic and regarded as silly. On the Northwest Coast the person who finds it difficult to read life in terms of an insult contest will be the person upon whom fall all the difficulties of the culturally unprovided for. The person who does not find it easy to humiliate a neighbor, nor to see humiliation in his own experience, who is genial and loving, may, of course, find some unstandardized way of achieving satisfactions in his society, but not in the major patterned responses that his culture requires of him. If he is born to play an important role in a family with many hereditary privileges, he can succeed only by doing violence to his whole personality. If he does not succeed, he has betrayed his culture; that is, he is abnormal.

I have spoken of individuals as having sets toward certain types of behavior, and of these sets as running sometimes counter to the types of behavior which are institutionalized in the culture to which they belong. From all that we know of contrasting cultures it seems clear that differences of temperament occur in every society. The matter has never been made the subject of investigation, but from the available material it would appear that these temperament types are very likely of universal recurrence. That is, there is an ascertainable range of human behavior that is found wherever a sufficiently large series of individuals is observed. But the proportion in which behavior types stand to one another in different societies is not universal. The vast majority of individuals in any group are shaped to the fashion of that culture. In other words, most individuals are plastic to the moulding force of the society into which they are born. In a society that values trance, as in India, they will have supernormal experience. In a society that institutionalizes homosexuality, they will be homosexual. In a society that sets the gathering of possessions as the chief human objective, they will amass property. The deviants, whatever the type of behavior the culture has institutionalized, will remain few in number, and there seems no more difficulty in moulding the vast malleable majority to the "normality" of what we consider an aberrant trait, such as delusions of reference, than to the normality of such accepted behavior patterns as acquisitiveness. The small proportion of the number of the deviants in any culture is not a function of the sure instinct with which the society has built itself upon the fundamental sanities, but of the universal fact that, happily, the majority of mankind quite readily take any shape that is presented to them. . . .

## READING COMPREHENSION QUESTIONS

1. In the fourth paragraph of her essay, Benedict claims that we learn from anthropology that "there are well-described cultures in which . . . abnormals function at ease and with honor, and apparently without danger or difficulty to society." What does she mean by "abnormals"? Which examples does she use to illustrate and defend her point about the functioning of abnormals in society?

2. What is the main conclusion that Benedict draws from her illustrations?

3. Some philosophers have held that it is possible to base a universal code of ethics on facts about our shared common human nature. How would Benedict respond to this idea? (The key to her response is to be found in the final paragraph of her article.)

4. According to Benedict what is the nature of the good—what makes something (including behavior) good or bad?

5. One point that Benedict stresses is that different cultures do in fact have different codes of ethical behavior. Suppose she is right about this. Does ethical relativism follow? (Readers may want to glance back at the chapter introduction to review this theory.)

6. If ethical relativism were true, what would it imply about the ethics of killing (or any other type of behavior?)

# 36

# Right and Wrong

## THOMAS NAGEL

*Thomas Nagel is professor of philosophy and law at New York University and author of many articles and books, including* Moral Questions *(1979) and* The View from Nowhere *(1986). In our reading, Nagel is concerned both with the foundation of morality—the basis of the distinction between right and wrong—as well as the content of morality—what moral requirements there are. Nagel is critical of attempts to provide a religious foundation for morality of the sort featured in divine command theories. Rather, he claims that the basis of morality rests with a direct concern for other people, including, of course, not hurting them. He also offers an argument based on the familiar question "How would you like it if someone did that to you?" that can be used to argue (based on an appeal to consistency) that most, if not all, people do have reason to conform to the moral demand not to hurt others. Nagel then turns to questions about the content of morality and, in particular, the question of how much one ought to consider the interests of others. His discussion of this question leads him to consider the threat to morality that is posed by ethical relativism and by psychological egoism.*

SOURCE: From Thomas Nagel, *What Does It All Mean?* (New York and Oxford: Oxford University Press), 1987.

S uppose you work in a library, checking people's books as they leave, and a friend asks you to let him smuggle out a hard-to-find reference work that he wants to own.

You might hesitate to agree for various reasons. You might be afraid that he'll be caught, and that both you and he will then get into trouble. You might want the book to stay in the library so that you can consult it yourself.

But you may also think that what he proposes is wrong—that he shouldn't do it and you shouldn't help him. If you think that, what does it mean, and what, if anything, makes it true?

To say it's wrong is not just to say it's against the rules. There can be bad rules which prohibit what isn't wrong—like a law against criticizing the government. A rule can also be bad because it requires something that *is* wrong—like a law that requires racial segregation in hotels and restaurants. The ideas of wrong and right are different from the ideas of what is and is not against the rules. Otherwise they couldn't be used in the evaluation of rules as well as of actions.

If you think it would be wrong to help your friend steal the book, then you will feel uncomfortable about doing it: in some way you won't want to do it, even if you are also reluctant to refuse help to a friend. Where does the desire not to do it come from; what is its motive, the reason behind it?

There are various ways in which something can be wrong, but in this case, if you had to explain it, you'd probably say that it would be unfair to other users of the library who may be just as interested in the book as your friend is, but who consult it in the reference room, where anyone who needs it can find it. You may also feel that to let him take it would betray your employers, who are paying you precisely to keep this sort of thing from happening.

These thoughts have to do with effects on others—not necessarily effects on their feelings, since they may never find out about it, but some kind of damage nevertheless. In general, the thought that something is wrong depends on its impact not just on the person who does it but on other people. They wouldn't like it, and they'd object if they found out.

But suppose you try to explain all this to your friend, and he says, "I know the head librarian wouldn't like it if he found out, and probably some of the other users of the library would be unhappy to find the book gone, but who cares? I want the book; why should I care about them?"

The argument that it would be wrong is supposed to give him a reason not to do it. But if someone just doesn't care about other people, what reason does he have to refrain from doing any of the things usually thought to be wrong, if he can get away with it: what reason does he have not to kill, steal, lie, or hurt others? If he can get what he wants by doing such things, why shouldn't he? And if there's no reason why he shouldn't, in what sense is it wrong?

Of course most people do care about others to some extent. But if someone doesn't care, most of us wouldn't conclude that he's exempt from morality. A person who kills someone just to steal his wallet, without caring about the victim, is not automatically excused. The fact that he doesn't care doesn't make it all right: He *should* care. But *why* should he care?

There have been many attempts to answer this question. One type of answer tries to identify something else that the person already cares about, and then connect morality to it.

For example, some people believe that even if you can get away with awful crimes on this earth, and are not punished by the law or your fellow men, such acts are forbidden by God, who will punish you after death (and reward you if you didn't do wrong when you were tempted to). So even when it seems to be in your interest to do such a thing, it really isn't. Some people have even believed that if there is no God to back up moral requirements with the threat of punishment and the promise of reward, morality is an illusion: "If God does not exist, everything is permitted."

This is a rather crude version of the religious foundation for morality. A more appealing version might be that the motive for obeying God's commands is not fear but love. He loves you, and you should love Him, and should wish to obey His commands in order not to offend Him.

But however we interpret the religious motivation, there are three objections to this type of answer. First, plenty of people who don't believe in God still make judgments of right and wrong, and think no one should kill another for his wallet even if he can be sure to get away with it. Second, if God exists, and forbids what's wrong, that still isn't what *makes* it wrong. Murder is wrong in itself, and that's *why* God forbids it (if He does). God couldn't make just any old thing wrong—like putting on your left sock before your right—simply by prohibiting it. If God would punish you for doing that it would be inadvisable to do it, but it wouldn't be wrong. Third, fear of punishment and hope of reward, and even love of God, seem not to be the right motives for morality. If you think it's wrong to kill, cheat, or steal, you should want to avoid doing such things because they are bad things to do to the victims, not just because you fear the consequences for yourself, or because you don't want to offend your Creator.

This third objection also applies to other explanations of the force of morality which appeal to the interests of the person who must act. For example, it may be said that you should treat others with consideration so that they'll do the same for you. This may be sound advice, but it is valid only so far as you think what you do will affect how others treat you. It's not a reason for doing the right thing if others won't find out about it, or against doing the wrong thing if you can get away with it (like being a hit and run driver).

There is no substitute for a direct concern for other people as the basis of morality. But morality is supposed to apply to everyone; and can we assume that everyone has such a concern for others? Obviously not: some people are very selfish, and even those who are not selfish may care only about the people they know, and not about everyone. So where will we find a reason that everyone has not to hurt other people, even those they don't know?

Well, there's one general argument against hurting other people which can be given to anybody who understands English (or any other language), and which seems to show that he has *some* reason to care about others, even if in the end his selfish motives are so strong that he persists in treating other people badly anyway. It's an argument that I'm sure you've heard, and it goes like this: "How would you like it if someone did that to you?"

It's not easy to explain how this argument is supposed to work. Suppose you're about to steal someone else's umbrella as you leave a restaurant in a rainstorm, and a bystander says, "How would you like it if someone did that to you?" Why is it supposed to make you hesitate, or feel guilty?

Obviously the direct answer to the question is supposed to be, "I wouldn't like it at all!" But what's the next step? Suppose you were to say, "I wouldn't like it if someone did that to me. But luckily no one *is* doing it to me. I'm doing it to someone else, and I don't mind that at all!"

This answer misses the point of the question. When you are asked how you would like it if someone did that to you, you are supposed to think about all the feelings you would have if someone stole your umbrella. And that includes more than just "not liking it"—as you wouldn't "like it" if you stubbed your toe on a rock. If someone stole your umbrella you'd *resent* it. You'd have feelings about the umbrella thief, not just about the loss of the umbrella. You'd think, "Where does he get off, taking my umbrella that I bought with my hard-earned money and that I had the foresight to bring after reading the weather report? Why didn't he bring his own umbrella?" and so forth.

When our own interests are threatened by the inconsiderate behavior of others, most of us find it easy to appreciate that those others have a reason to be more considerate. When you are hurt, you probably feel that other people should care about it: you don't think it's no concern of theirs, and that they have no reason to avoid hurting you. That is the feeling that the "How would you like it?" argument is supposed to arouse.

Because if you admit that you would *resent* it if someone else did to you what you are now doing to him, you are admitting that you think he would have a reason not to do it to you. And if you admit that, you have to consider what that reason is. It couldn't be just that it's *you* that he's hurting, of all the people in the world. There's no special reason for him not to steal *your* umbrella, as opposed to anyone else's. There's nothing so special about you. Whatever the reason is, it's a reason he would have against hurting anyone else in the same way. And it's a reason anyone else would have too, in a similar situation, against hurting you or anyone else.

But if it's a reason anyone would have not to hurt anyone else in this way, then it's a reason *you* have not to hurt someone else in this way (since *anyone* means *everyone*). Therefore it's a reason not to steal the other person's umbrella now.

This is a matter of simple consistency. Once you admit that another person would have a reason not to harm you in similar circumstances, and once you admit that the reason he would have is very general and doesn't apply only to you, or to him, then to be consistent you have to admit that the same reason applies to you now. You shouldn't steal the umbrella, and you ought to feel guilty if you do.

Someone could escape from this argument if, when he was asked, "How would you like it if someone did that to you?" he answered, "I wouldn't resent it at all. I wouldn't *like* it if someone stole my umbrella in a rainstorm, but I wouldn't think there was any reason for him to consider my feelings about it." But how many people could honestly give that answer? I think most people, unless they're crazy, would think that their own interests and harms matter, not only to themselves, but in a way that gives other people a reason to care about them too. We all think that when we suffer it is not just bad *for us,* but *bad, period.*

The basis of morality is a belief that good and harm to particular people (or animals) is good or bad not just from their point of view, but from a more general point of view, which every thinking person can understand. That means that each person has a reason to consider not only his own interests but the interests of others in deciding what to do. And it isn't enough if he is considerate only of some others—his family and friends, those he specially cares about. Of course he will care more about certain people, and also about himself. But he has some reason to consider the effect of what he does on the good or harm of everyone. If he's like most of us, that is what he thinks others should do with regard to him, even if they aren't friends of his.

Even if this is right, it is only a bare outline of the source of morality. It doesn't tell us in detail how we should consider the interests of others, or how we should weigh them against the special interest we all have in ourselves and the particular people close to us. It doesn't even tell us how much we should care about people in other countries in comparison with our fellow citizens. There are many disagreements among those who accept morality in general, about what in particular is right and what is wrong.

For instance: should you care about every other person as much as you care about yourself? Should you in other words love your neighbor as yourself (even if he isn't your neighbor)? Should you ask yourself, every time you go to a movie, whether the cost of the ticket could provide more happiness if you gave it to someone else, or donated the money to famine relief?

Very few people are so unselfish. And if someone were that impartial between himself and others, he would probably also feel that he should be just as impartial *among* other people. That would rule out caring more about his friends and relatives than he does about strangers. He might have special feelings about certain people who are close to him, but complete impartiality would mean that he won't *favor* them—if for example he has to choose between helping a friend or a stranger to avoid suffering, or between taking his children to a movie and donating the money to famine relief.

This degree of impartiality seems too much to ask of most people: someone who had it would be a kind of terrifying saint. But it's an important question in moral thought, how much impartiality we should try for. You are a particular person, but you are also able to recognize that you're just one person among many others, and no more important than they are, when looked at from outside. How much should that point of view influence you? You do matter somewhat from outside—otherwise you wouldn't think other people had any reason to care about what they did to you. But you don't matter as much from the outside as you matter to yourself, from the inside—since from the outside you don't matter any more than anybody else.

Not only is it unclear how impartial we should be; it's unclear what would make an answer to this question the right one. Is there a single correct way for everyone to strike the balance between what he cares about personally and what matters impartially? Or will the answer vary from person to person depending on the strength of their different motives?

This brings us to another big issue: Are right and wrong the same for everyone?

Morality is often thought to be universal. If something is wrong, it's supposed to be wrong for everybody; for instance if it's wrong to kill someone because you want to steal his wallet, then it's wrong whether you care about him or not. But if something's being wrong is supposed to be a reason against doing it, and if your reasons for doing things depend on your motives and people's motives can vary greatly, then it looks as though there won't be a single right and wrong for everybody. There won't be a single right and wrong, because if people's basic motives differ, there won't be one basic standard of behavior that everyone has a reason to follow.

There are three ways of dealing with this problem, none of them very satisfactory.

First, we could say that the same things *are* right and wrong for everybody, but that not everyone has a reason to do what's right and avoid what's wrong: only people with the right sort of "moral" motives—particularly a concern for others—have any reason to do what's right, for its own sake. This makes morality universal, but at the cost of draining it of its force. It's not clear what it amounts to to say that it would be wrong for someone to commit murder, but he has no reason not to do it.

Second, we could say that everyone has a reason to do what's right and avoid what's wrong, but that these reasons don't depend on people's actual motives. Rather they are reasons to change our motives if they aren't the right ones. This connects morality with reasons for action, but leaves it unclear what these universal reasons are which do not depend on motives that everyone actually has. What does it mean to say that a murderer had a reason not to do it, even though none of his actual motives or desires gave him such a reason?

Third, we could say that morality is not universal, and that what a person is morally required to do goes only as far as what he has a certain kind of reason to do, where the reason depends on how much he actually cares about other people in general. If he has strong moral motives, they will yield strong reasons and strong moral requirements. If his moral motives are weak or nonexistent, the moral requirements on him will likewise be weak or nonexistent. This may seem psychologically realistic, but it goes against the idea that the same moral rules apply to all of us, and not only to good people.

The question whether moral requirements are universal comes up not only when we compare the motives of different individuals, but also when we compare the moral standards that are accepted in different societies and at different times. Many things that you probably think are wrong have been accepted as morally correct by large groups of people in the past: slavery, serfdom, human sacrifice, racial segregation, denial of religious and political freedom, hereditary caste systems. And probably some things you now think are right will be thought wrong by future societies. Is it reasonable to believe that there is some single truth about all this, even though we can't be sure what it is? Or is it more reasonable to believe that right and wrong are relative to a particular time and place and social background?

There is one way in which right and wrong are obviously relative to circumstances. It is usually right to return a knife you have borrowed to its owner if he asks for it back. But if he has gone crazy in the meantime, and wants the knife to murder someone with, then you shouldn't return it. This isn't the kind of relativity I am talking about, because it doesn't mean morality is relative at the basic level. It means only that the same basic moral principles will require different actions in different circumstances.

The deeper kind of relativity, which some people believe in, would mean that the most basic standards of right and wrong—like when it is and is not all right to kill, or what sacrifices you're required to make for others—depend entirely on what standards are generally accepted in the society in which you live.

This I find very hard to believe, mainly because it always seems possible to criticize the accepted standards of your own society and say that they are morally mistaken. But if you do that, you must be appealing to some more objective standard, an idea of what is *really* right and wrong, as opposed to what most people think. It is hard to say what this is, but it is an idea most of us understand, unless we are slavish followers of what the community says.

There are many philosophical problems about the content of morality—how a moral concern or respect for others should express itself; whether we should help them get what they want or mainly refrain from harming and hindering them; how impartial we should be, and in what ways. I have left most of these questions aside because my concern here is with the foundation of morality in general—how universal and objective it is.

I should answer one possible objection to the whole idea of morality. You've probably heard it said that the only reason anybody ever does anything is that it makes him feel good, or that not doing it will make him feel bad. If we are really motivated only by our own comfort, it is hopeless for morality to try to appeal to a concern for others. On this view, even apparently moral conduct in which one person seems to sacrifice his own interests for the sake of others is really motivated by his concern for himself: he wants to avoid the guilt he'll feel if he doesn't do the "right" thing, or to experience the warm glow of self-congratulation he'll get if he does. But those who don't have these feelings have no motive to be "moral."

Now it's true that when people do what they think they ought to do, they often feel good about it; similarly if they do what they think is wrong, they often feel bad. But that doesn't mean that these feelings are their motives for acting. In many cases the feelings result from motives which also produce the action. You wouldn't feel good about doing the right thing unless you thought there was some other reason to do it, besides the fact that it would make you feel good. And you wouldn't feel guilty about doing the wrong thing unless you thought that there was some other reason not to do it, besides the fact that it made you feel guilty: something which made it *right* to feel guilty. At least that's how things should be. It's true that some people feel irrational guilt about things they don't have any independent reason to think are wrong—but that's not the way morality is supposed to work.

In a sense, people do what they want to do. But their reasons and motives for wanting to do things vary enormously. I may "want" to give someone my wallet only because he has a gun pointed at my head and threatens to kill me if I don't. And I may want to jump into an icy river to save a drowning stranger not because it will make me feel good, but because I recognize that his life is important, just as mine is, and I recognize that I have a reason to save his life just as he would have a reason to save mine if our positions were reversed.

Moral argument tries to appeal to a capacity for impartial motivation which is supposed to be present in all of us. Unfortunately it may be deeply buried, and in some cases it may not be present at all. In any case it has to compete with powerful selfish motives, and other personal motives that may not be so selfish, in its bid for control of our behavior. The difficulty of justifying morality is not that there is only one human motive, but that there are so many.

## READING COMPREHENSION QUESTIONS

1. Toward the beginning of his essay, Nagel considers people who do not care about morality. Is there any reason why such a person *should* care? If you think there is, what is that reason? If you think there isn't, then are those people exempt from morality?

2. Nagel distinguishes what he calls a "crude version" of a religious foundation for morality from a "more appealing version." Describe these two versions and how they differ. (Be sure you are clear about what question both versions are meant to address.)

3. Describe the three objections Nagel raises against the religious foundation for morality. Do you think these objections are good ones? Why or why not?

4. Nagel claims that an argument based on the question, "What if someone did that to you?" can be used to show that almost all people (if not all) must admit that they have reason not to hurt others. What are the steps in Nagel's argument? Do you find the argument plausible? (You may want to review the discussion of evaluating arguments from the first chapter.)

5. In discussing the universality of morality—the idea that the same basic ethical requirements apply to everyone—Nagel considers an argument that has as one of its premises the claim that people's motives differ, and concludes with the claim that there isn't a single standard of right and wrong that applies to everyone. What are the other steps in that argument? Evaluate the argument.

6. Nagel proceeds to consider three ways of responding to the argument mentioned in question 5. What are they? What does Nagel say about each of them?

7. Nagel considers the claim that right and wrong are relative to one's circumstances and distinguishes this claim from "a deeper kind of relativism." What is this deeper kind of relativism? Why isn't the claim about right and wrong being relative to one's circumstances equivalent to this deeper form of relativism?

8. What objections does Nagel raise against deep relativism? Based on the reading from Benedict, how do you think she would reply to Nagel?

9. Toward the end of his essay, Nagel considers what was identified in the introduction to ethics as *psychological egoism*. Why does Nagel think this view is a threat to morality? What does Nagel say in response to this threat? Do you find his response convincing? Why or why not?

# 37

# In Defense of Utilitarianism

## J. S. MILL

*John Stuart Mill (1806–1873), a British philosopher, was a leading intellectual of the nineteenth century. In the following excerpt from his book* Utilitarianism *(1863), Mill considers three objections to the utilitarian theory. First, some opponents charge that the emphasis on the pursuit of pleasure makes utilitarianism "a doctrine worthy of only swine." Mill responds by distinguishing higher from lower pleasures. Because utilitarianism considers pursuit of higher, distinctively human pleasures (such as enjoying great literature) as especially important, it is, Mill asserts, a doctrine worthy of human beings. Second, some argue that utilitarian moral theory sets standards that are "too high for humanity." Third, still others object that in ordinary circumstances that call for a moral decision, we lack the time needed for calculating the utility of actions. Mill argues that these latter two objections are based on misunderstandings of the utilitarian theory. After answering these objections, Mill offers what he calls an "indirect proof" of the principle of utility.*

The creed which accepts as the foundation of morals, Utility, or the Greatest Happiness Principle, holds that actions are right in proportion as they tend to promote happiness, wrong as they tend to produce the reverse of happiness. By happiness is intended pleasure, and the absence of pain; by unhappiness, pain, and the privation of pleasure. To give a clear view of the moral standard set up by the theory, much more requires to be said; in particular, what things it includes in the ideas of pain and pleasure; and to what extent this is left an open question. But these supplementary explanations do not affect the theory of life on which this theory of morality is grounded—namely that pleasure, and freedom from pain, are the only things desirable as ends; and that all desirable things (which are as numerous in the utilitarian as in any other scheme) are desirable either for the pleasure inherent in themselves, or as means to the promotion of pleasure and the prevention of pain.

Now, such a theory of life excites in many minds, and among them in some of the most estimable in feeling and purpose, inveterate dislike. To suppose that life has (as they express it) no higher end than pleasure—no better and nobler object of desire and pursuit—they designate as utterly mean and grovelling; as a

SOURCE: Reprinted from *Utilitarianism* (1863).

doctrine worthy only of swine, to whom the followers of Epicurus were, at a very early period, contemptuously likened; and modern holders of the doctrine are occasionally made the subject of equally polite comparisons by its German, French, and English assailants.

When thus attacked, the Epicureans have always answered, that it is not they but their accusers, who represent human nature in a degrading light; since the accusation supposes human beings to be capable of no pleasures except those of which swine are capable. If this supposition were true, the charge could not be gainsaid, but would then be no longer an imputation; for if the sources of pleasure were precisely the same to human beings and to swine, the rule of life which is good enough for the one would be good enough for the other. The comparison of the Epicurean life to that of beasts is felt as degrading, precisely because a beast's pleasures do not satisfy a human being's conceptions of happiness. Human beings have faculties more elevated than the animal appetites, and when once made conscious of them, do not regard anything as happiness which does not include their gratification. I do not, indeed, consider the Epicureans to have been by any means faultless in drawing out their scheme of consequences from the utilitarian principle. To do this in any sufficient manner, many Stoic, as well as Christian, elements require to be included. But there is no known Epicurean theory of life which does not assign to the pleasures of the intellect, of the feelings and imagination, and of the moral sentiments, a much higher value as pleasures than to those of mere sensation. It must be admitted, however, that utilitarian writers in general have placed the superiority of mental over bodily pleasures chiefly in the greater permanency, safety, uncostliness, etc., of the former—that is, in their circumstantial advantages rather than in their intrinsic nature. And on all these points utilitarians have fully proved their case; but they might have taken the other, and, as it may be called, higher ground, with entire consistency. It is quite compatible with the principle of utility to recognize the fact, that some *kinds* of pleasure are more desirable and more valuable than others. It would be absurd that while, in estimating all other things, quality is considered as well as quantity, the estimation of pleasures should be supposed to depend on quantity alone.

If I am asked, what I mean by difference of quality in pleasures, or what makes one pleasure more valuable than another, merely as a pleasure, except its being greater in amount, there is but one possible answer. Of two pleasures, if there be one to which all or almost all who have experience of both give a decided preference, irrespective of any feeling of moral obligation to prefer it, that is the more desirable pleasure. If one of the two is, by those who are competently acquainted with both, placed so far above the other that they prefer it, even though knowing it to be attended with a greater amount of discontent, and would not resign it for any quantity of the other pleasure which their nature is capable of, we are justified in ascribing to the preferred enjoyment a superiority in quality, so far outweighing quantity as to render it, in comparison, of small account.

Now it is an unquestionable fact that those who are equally acquainted with, and equally capable of appreciating and enjoying, both, do give a most marked preference to the manner of existence which employs their higher faculties. Few human creatures would consent to be changed into any of the lower animals, for a promise of the fullest allowance of a beast's pleasures; no intelligent human being would consent to be a fool, no instructed person would be an ignoramus, no person of feeling and conscience would be selfish and base, even though they should be persuaded that the fool, the dunce, or the rascal is better satisfied with his lot than they are with theirs. They would not resign what they possess more than he for the most complete satisfaction of all the desires which they have in common with him. If they ever fancy they would, it is only in cases of unhappiness so extreme, that to escape from it they would exchange their lot for almost any other, however undesirable in their own eyes. A being of higher faculties requires more to make him happy, is capable probably of more acute suffering, and is certainly accessible to it at more points than one of an inferior type; but in spite of these liabilities, he can never really wish to sink into what he feels to be a lower grade of existence. We may give what explanation we please of this unwillingness; we may attribute it to pride, a name which is given indiscriminately to some of the most and to some of the least estimable feelings of which mankind are capable; we may refer it to the love of liberty and personal independence, an appeal to which was with the Stoics one of the most effective means for the inculcation of it; to the love of power, or to the love of excitement, both of which do really enter into and contribute to it: but its most appropriate appellation is a sense of dignity, which all human beings possess in one form or other, and in some, though by no means in exact, proportion to their higher faculties, and which is so essential a part of the happiness of those in whom it is strong, that nothing which conflicts with it could be, otherwise than momentarily, an object of desire to them. Whoever supposes that this preference takes place at a sacrifice of happiness—that the superior being, in anything like equal circumstances, is not happier than the inferior—confounds the two very different ideas, of happiness, and content. It is indisputable that the being whose capacities of enjoyment are low, has the greatest chance of having them fully satisfied; and a highly-endowed being will always feel that any happiness which he can look for, as the world is constituted, is imperfect. But he can learn to bear its imperfections, if they are at all bearable; and they will not make him envy the being who is indeed unconscious of the imperfections, but only because he feels not at all the good which those imperfections qualify. It is better to be a human being dissatisfied than a pig satisfied; better to be Socrates dissatisfied than a fool satisfied. And if the fool, or the pig, is of a different opinion, it is because they only know their own side of the question. The other party to the comparison knows both sides. . . .

. . . The objectors to utilitarianism cannot always be charged with representing it in a discreditable light. On the contrary, those among them who entertain anything like a just idea of its disinterested character, sometimes find fault with its standard as being too high for humanity. They say it is exacting too much to require that people shall always act from the inducement of promoting the general interests of society. But this is to mistake the very meaning of a standard of morals, and to confound the rule of action with the motive of it. It is the business of ethics to tell us what are our duties, or by what test we may know them; but no system of ethics requires that the sole motive of all we do shall be a feeling of duty; on the contrary, ninety-nine hundredths of all our actions are done from other motives, and rightly so done, if the rule of duty does not condemn them. It is the more unjust to utilitarianism that this particular misapprehension should be made a ground of objection to it, inasmuch as utilitarian moralists have gone beyond almost all others in affirming that the motive has nothing to do with the morality of the action, though much with the worth of the agent. He who saves a fellow creature from drowning does what is morally right, whether his motive be duty, or the hope of being paid for his trouble: he who betrays the friend that trusts him, is guilty of a crime, even if his object be to serve another friend to whom he is under greater obligations. But to speak only of actions done from the motive of duty, and in direct obedience to principle: it is a misapprehension of the utilitarian mode of thought, to conceive it as implying that people should fix their minds upon so wide a generality as the world, or society at large. The great majority of good actions are intended, not for the benefit of the world, but for that of individuals, of which the good of the world is made up; and the thoughts of the most virtuous man need not on these occasions travel beyond the particular persons concerned, except so far as is necessary to assure himself that in benefiting them he is not violating the rights—that is, the legitimate and authorized expectations— of any one else. The multiplication of happiness is, according to the utilitarian ethics, the object of virtue: the occasions, on which any person (except one in a thousand) has it in his power to do this on an extended scale, in other words, to be a public benefactor, are but exceptional; and on these occasions alone is he called on to consider public utility; in every other case, private utility, the interest or happiness of some few persons, is all he has to attend to. Those alone the influence of whose actions extends to society in general, need concern themselves habitually about so large an object. In the case of abstinences indeed— of things which people forbear to do, from moral considerations, though the consequences in the particular case might be beneficial—it would be unworthy of an intelligent agent not to be consciously aware that the action is of a class which, if practiced generally, would be generally injurious, and that this is the ground of the obligation to abstain from it. The amount of regard for the public interest implied in this recognition, is no greater than is demanded by every system of morals; for they all enjoin to abstain from whatever is manifestly pernicious to society. . . .

. . . Again, defenders of utility often find themselves called upon to reply to such objections as this—that there is not time, previous to action, for calculating and weighing the effects of any line of conduct on the general happiness. This is exactly as if any one were to say that it is impossible to guide our conduct by Christianity, because there is not time, on every occasion on which anything has to be done, to read through the Old and New Testaments. The answer to the objection is, that there has been ample time, namely, the whole past duration of . . . the human species. During all that time mankind have been learning by experience the tendencies of actions; on which experience all the prudence, as well as all the morality of life, is dependent. People talk as if the commencement of this course of experience had hitherto been put off, and as if, at the moment when some man feels tempted to meddle with the property or life of another, he had to begin considering for the first time whether murder and theft are injurious to human happiness. Even then I do not think that he would find the question very puzzling; but, at all events, the matter is now done to his hand. It is truly a whimsical supposition that if mankind were agreed in considering utility to be the test of morality, they would remain without any agreement as to what *is* useful, and would take no measures for having their notions on the subject taught to the young, and enforced by law and opinion. There is no difficulty in proving any ethical standard whatever to work ill, if we suppose universal idiocy to be conjoined with it, but on any hypothesis short of that, mankind must by this time have acquired positive beliefs as to the effects of some actions on their happiness; and the beliefs which have thus come down are the rules of morality for the multitude, and for the philosopher until he has succeeded in finding better. That philosophers might easily do this, even now, on many subjects; that the received code of ethics is by no means of divine right; and that mankind have still much to learn as to the effects of actions on the general happiness, I admit, or rather, earnestly maintain. The corollaries from the principle of utility, like the precepts of every practical art, admit of indefinite improvement, and, in a progressive state of the human mind, their improvement is perpetually going on. But to consider the rules of morality as improvable, is one thing; to pass over the intermediate generalizations entirely, and endeavor to test each individual action directly by the first principle, is another. It is a strange notion that the acknowledgment of a first principle is inconsistent with the admission of secondary ones. To inform a traveller respecting the place of his ultimate destination, is not to forbid the use of landmarks and direction-posts on the way. The proposition that happiness is the end and aim of morality, does not mean that no road ought to be laid down to that goal, or that persons going thither should not be advised to take one direction rather than another. Men really ought to leave off talking a kind of nonsense on this subject, which they would neither talk nor listen to in other matters of practical concernment. Nobody argues that the art of navigation is not founded on astronomy, because sailors cannot wait to calculate the Nautical Almanack. Being rational creatures, they go to sea with it ready calculated; and all rational creatures go out upon the sea of life with their minds made up on the common questions of right and wrong, as well as on many of the far more difficult questions of wise and foolish. And this, as long as foresight is a human quality, is to be presumed they will continue to do. Whatever we adopt as the fundamental principle of morality, we require subordinate principles to apply it by: the impossibility of doing without them, being common to all systems, can afford no argument against any one in particular: but gravely to argue as if no such secondary principles could be had, and as if mankind had remained till now, and always must remain, without drawing any general conclusions from the experience of human life, is as high a pitch, I think, as absurdity has ever reached in philosophical controversy. . . .

## OF WHAT SORT OF PROOF THE PRINCIPLE OF UTILITY IS SUSCEPTIBLE

It has already been remarked, that questions of ultimate ends do not admit of proof, in the ordinary acceptation of the term. To be incapable of proof by reasoning is common to all first principles; to the first premises of our knowledge, as well as to those of our conduct. But the former, being matters of fact, may be the subject of a direct appeal to the faculties which judge of fact—namely, our senses, and our internal consciousness. Can an appeal be made to the same faculties on questions of practical ends? Or by what other faculty is cognizance taken of them?

Questions about ends are, in other words, questions about what things are desirable. The utilitarian doctrine is, that happiness is desirable, and the only thing desirable, as an end; all other things being only desirable as means to that end. What ought to be required of this doctrine—what conditions is it requisite that the doctrine should fulfill—to make good its claim to be believed?

The only proof capable of being given that an object is visible, is that people actually see it. The only proof that a sound is audible, is that people hear it: and so of the other sources of our experience. In like manner, I apprehend, the sole evidence it is possible to produce that anything is desirable, is that people do actually desire it. If the end which the utilitarian doctrine proposes to itself were not, in theory and in practice, acknowledged to be an end, nothing could ever convince any person that it was so. No reason can be given why the general happiness is desirable, except that each person, so far as he believes it to be attainable, desires his own happiness. This, however, being a fact, we have not only all the proof which the case admits of, but all which it is possible to require, that happiness is a good: that each person's happiness is a good to that person, and the general happiness, therefore, a good to the aggregate of all persons. Happiness has made out its title as *one* of the ends of conduct, and consequently one of the criteria of morality.

But it has not, by this alone, proved itself to be the sole criterion. To do that, it would seem, by the same rule, necessary to show, not only that people desire happiness, but that they never desire anything else. Now it is palpable that they do desire things which, in common language, are decidedly distinguished from happiness. They desire, for example, virtue, and the absence of vice, no less really than pleasure and the absence of pain. The desire of virtue is not as universal, but it is as authentic a fact, as the desire of happiness. And hence the opponents of the utilitarian standard deem that they have a right to infer that there are other ends of human action besides happiness, and that happiness is not the standard of approbation and disapprobation.

But does the utilitarian doctrine deny that people desire virtue, or maintain that virtue is not a thing to be desired? The very reverse. It maintains not only that virtue is to be desired, but that it is to be desired disinterestedly, for itself. Whatever may be the opinion of utilitarian moralists as to the original conditions by which virtue is made virtue; however they may believe (as they do) that actions and dispositions are only virtuous because they promote another end than virtue; yet this being granted, and it having been decided, from considerations of this description, what *is* virtuous, they not only place virtue at the very head of the things which are good as means to the ultimate end, but they also recognize as a psychological fact the possibility of its being, to the individual, a good in itself, without looking to any end beyond it; and hold, that the mind is not in a right state, not in a state conformable to Utility, not in the state most conducive to the general happiness, unless it does love virtue in this manner—as a thing desirable in itself, even although, in the individual instance, it should not produce those other desirable consequences which it tends to produce, and on account of which it is held to be virtue. This opinion is not, in the smallest degree, a departure from the Happiness principle. The ingredients of happiness are very various, and each of them is desirable in itself, and not merely when considered as swelling an aggregate. The principle of utility does not mean that any given pleasure, as music, for instance, or any given exemption from pain, as for example health, are to be looked upon as a means to a collective something termed happiness, and to be desired on that account. They are desired and desirable in and for themselves; besides being means, they are a part of the end. Virtue, according to the utilitarian doctrine, is not naturally and originally part of the end, but it is capable of becoming so; and in those who love it disinterestedly it has become so, and is desired and cherished, not as a means to happiness, but as a part of their happiness. . . .

## READING COMPREHENSION QUESTIONS

1. State in your own words Mill's Greatest Happiness Principle.

2. What is Mill's view of happiness? Do you find his view plausible? Explain.

The next four questions refer to the three objections to the Greatest Happiness Principle and Mill's replies.

3. In the second paragraph of the excerpt, Mill considers what is often referred to as the "doctrine of swine" objection to the Greatest Happiness Principle. What are the steps (the premises and conclusion) of this argument?

4. Mill's reply to the argument depends on the idea that in addition to the quantity of pleasure (their "how muchness"), pleasures may differ in *quality*. What does Mill mean by the quality of pleasures? How does Mill think that differences in quality can be determined? Do you find what he says plausible? Why or why not?

5. A second objection that Mill considers is the "too high for humanity" objection. Explain the objection in your own words. How does Mill respond to this objection? (Hint: It helps to state Mill's principle as clearly as possible because he claims that the objection is based on a misunderstanding of his principle.) Do you find his response plausible? Why or why not?

6. The third objection may be called the "lack of time" objection. State the objection and Mill's reply to it. Do you find Mill's reply plausible? Explain.

7. After defending his theory against objections, Mill proceeds to give what he calls a proof of the principle of utility. What exactly is the claim that Mill attempts to prove? (Note: It is actually a two-part claim.) How is this claim related to the Greatest Happiness Principle with which Mill begins?

8. Try your hand at stating the premises of Mill's proof. Because Mill is trying to establish a two-part claim, his proof is really a combination of two arguments.

9. As it is often interpreted, Mill's proof involves the fallacy of equivocation because the term "desirable" has two senses. (Readers may want to consult Chapter 1, in which this fallacy is discussed.) One of the senses is suggested by Mill's example of what is visible. What is the other sense? Can you spot the fallacy of equivocation in Mill's argument?

# 38

# The Moral Law and Autonomy
# of the Will

IMMANUEL KANT

*Kant (1724–1804) is one of the most important philosophers of the Western world. He wrote three major ethical works:* Groundwork (Foundations) of the Metaphysics of Morals *(1785),* Critique of Practical Reason *(1788), and* The Metaphysics of Morals *(1797). Included below are selections from the first and third of these works. In the first selection, which I have entitled, "Foundations," Kant presents and defends what he takes to be the fundamental moral principle, the categorical imperative, which serves as a law for the behavior of all rational agents. He argues that this principle can be discovered by reflecting on the idea of a good will and that it can be formulated in different ways—in terms of the idea of* universal law *and in terms of the idea of* humanity *as an end in itself. He proceeds to explain how this principle (in its different formulations) can be used to derive a variety of moral duties, including the negative duties to refrain from suicide and false promises and the positive duties to develop one's talents and to help others (often referred to as a duty of beneficence).*

*In the second selection, "Casuistical Questions," taken from his final work in moral philosophy, Kant briefly explores certain questions of detail and casuistry (the art of applying principles to particular cases) that arise in connection with the four duties featured in the* Foundations.

## I. FOUNDATIONS

### The Good Will

Nothing can possibly be conceived in the world, or even out of it, which can be called good, without qualification, except a Good Will. Intelligence, wit, judgment, and the other *talents* of the mind, however they may be named, or

SOURCE: Part I, "Foundations," is reprinted from *The Foundations of the Metaphysic of Morals*, translated by T. K. Abbott (first published in 1873). Part II, "Casuistical Questions," is reprinted from *The Metaphysics of Morals*, translated by James W. Ellington and published in *Ethical Philosophy*, 2nd ed. (Indianapolis, IN: Hackett, 1984). Reprinted by permission of Hackett Publishing Company, Inc. All rights reserved.

courage, resolution, perseverance, as qualities of temperament, are undoubtedly good and desirable in many respects; but these gifts of nature may also become extremely bad and mischievous if the will which is to make use of them, and which, therefore, constitutes what is called *character,* is not good. It is the same with the *gifts of fortune.* Power, riches, honor, even health, and the general well-being and contentment with one's condition which is called *happiness,* inspire pride, and often presumption, if there is not a good will to correct the influence of these on the mind, and with this also to rectify the whole principle of acting, and adapt it to its end. The sight of a being who is not adorned with a single feature of a pure and good will, enjoying unbroken prosperity, can never give pleasure to an impartial rational spectator. Thus a good will appears to constitute the indispensable condition even of being worthy of happiness.

There are even some qualities which are of service to this good will itself, and may facilitate its action, yet which have no intrinsic unconditional value, but always presuppose a good will, and this qualifies the esteem that we justly have for them, and does not permit us to regard them as absolutely good. Moderation in the affections and passions, self-control, and calm deliberation are not only good in many respects, but even seem to constitute part of the intrinsic worth of the person; but they are far from deserving to be called good without qualification, although they have been so unconditionally praised by the ancients. For without the principles of a good will, they may become extremely bad; and the coolness of a villain not only makes him far more dangerous, but also directly makes him more abominable in our eyes than he would have been without it.

A good will is good not because of what it performs or effects, not by its aptness for the attainment of some proposed end, but simply by virtue of the volition, that is, it is good in itself, and considered by itself is to be esteemed much higher than all that can be brought about by it in favor of any inclination, nay, even of the sum-total of all inclinations. Even if it should happen that, owing to special disfavor of fortune, or the niggardly provision of a step-motherly nature, this will should wholly lack power to accomplish its purpose, if with its greatest efforts it should yet achieve nothing, and there should remain only the good will (not, to be sure, a mere wish, but the summoning of all means in our power), then, like a jewel, it would still shine by its own light, as a thing which has its whole value in itself. Its usefulness or fruitlessness can neither add to nor take away anything from this value....

... Thus the moral worth of an action does not lie in the effect expected from it, nor in any principle of action which requires to borrow its motive from this expected effect. For all these effects—agreeableness of one's condition, and even the promotion of the happiness of others—could have been also brought about by other causes, so that for this there would have been no need of the will of a rational being; whereas it is in this alone that the supreme and unconditional good can be found. The pre-eminent good which we call moral can therefore consist in nothing else than *the conception of law* in itself, *which certainly is only possible in a rational being,* in so far as this conception, and not the expected effect, determines the will. This is a good which is already present in the person who acts accordingly, and we have not to wait for it to appear first in the result.

## The Supreme Principle of Morality: The Categorical Imperative

But what sort of law can that be, the conception of which must determine the will, even without paying any regard to the effect expected from it, in order that this will may be called good absolutely and without qualification? As I have deprived the will of every impulse which could arise to it from obedience to any law, there remains nothing but the universal conformity of its actions to law in general, which alone is to serve the will as a principle, i.e. I am never to act otherwise than *so that I could also will that my maxim should become a universal law.* Here, now, it is the simple conformity to law in general, without assuming any particular law applicable to certain actions, that serves the will as its principle, and must so serve it, if duty is not to be a vain delusion and a chimerical notion. The common reason of men in its practical judgments perfectly coincides with this, and always has in view the principle here suggested. Let the question be, for example: May I when in distress make a promise with the intention not to keep it? I readily distinguish here between the two significations which the question may have: Whether it is prudent, or whether it is right, to make a false promise? The former may undoubtedly often be the case. I see clearly indeed that it is not enough to extricate myself from a present difficulty by means of this subterfuge, but it must be well considered whether there may not hereafter spring from this lie much greater inconvenience than that from which I now free myself, and as, with all my supposed *cunning,* the consequences cannot be so easily foreseen but that credit once lost may be much more injurious to me than any mischief which I seek to avoid at present, it should be considered whether it would not be more *prudent* to act herein according to a universal maxim, and to make it a habit to promise nothing except with the intention of keeping it. But it is soon clear to me that such a maxim will still only be based on the fear of consequences. Now it is a wholly different thing to be truthful from duty, and to be so from apprehension of injurious consequences. In the first case, the very notion of the action already implies a law for me; in the second case, I must first look about elsewhere to see what results may be combined with it which would affect myself. For to deviate from the principle of duty is beyond all doubt wicked; but to be unfaithful to my maxim of prudence may often be very advantageous to me, although to abide by it is certainly safer. The shortest way, however, and an unerring one, to discover the answer to this question whether a lying promise is consistent with duty, is to ask myself, Should I be content that my maxim (to extricate myself from difficulty by a false promise) should hold good as a universal law, for myself as well as for others? and should I be able to say to myself, "Every one may make a deceitful promise when he finds himself in a difficulty from which he cannot otherwise extricate himself"? Then I presently become aware that while I can will the lie, I can by no means will that lying should be a universal law. For with such a law there would be no promises at all, since it would be in vain to allege my intention in regard to my future actions to those who would not believe this allegation, or if they over-hastily did so, would pay me back in my own coin. Hence my maxim, as soon as it should be made a universal law, would necessarily destroy itself. . . .

## Imperatives: Hypothetical and Categorical

Everything in nature works according to laws. Rational beings alone have the faculty of acting according *to the conception of laws,* that is according to principles, i.e., have a *will.* Since the deduction of actions from principles requires *reason,* the will is nothing but practical reason. If reason infallibly determines the will, then the actions of such a being which are recognized as objectively necessary are subjectively necessary also, i.e., the will is a faculty to choose *that only* which reason independent of inclination recognizes as practically necessary, i.e., as good. But if reason of itself does not sufficiently determine the will, if the latter is subject also to subjective conditions (particular impulses) which do not always coincide with the objective conditions; in a word, if the will does not *in itself* completely accord with reason (which is actually the case with men), then the actions which objectively are recognized as necessary are subjectively contingent, and the determination of such a will according to objective laws is *obligation,* that is to say, the relation of the objective laws to a will that is not thoroughly good is conceived as the determination of the will of a rational being by principles of reason, but which the will from its nature does not of necessity follow.

The conception of an objective principle, in so far as it is obligatory for a will, is called a command (of reason), and the formula of the command is called an Imperative.

All imperatives are expressed by the word *ought* [or *shall* ], and thereby indicate the relation of an objective law of reason to a will, which from its subjective constitution is not necessarily determined by it (an obligation). They say that something would be good to do or to forbear, but they say it to a will which does not always do a thing because it is conceived to be good to do it. That is practically *good,* however, which determines the will by means of the conceptions of reason, and consequently not from subjective causes, but objectively, that is on principles which are valid for every rational being as such. It is distinguished from the *pleasant,* as that which influences the will only by means of sensation from merely subjective causes, valid only for the sense of this or that one, and not as a principle of reason, which holds for every one.

A perfectly good will would therefore be equally subject to objective laws (viz., laws of good), but could not be conceived as *obliged* thereby to act law- fully, because of itself from its subjective constitution it can only be determined by the conception of good. Therefore no imperatives hold for the Divine will, or in general for a *holy* will; *ought* is here out of place, because the volition is already of itself necessarily in unison with the law. Therefore imperatives are only formulae to express the relation of objective laws of all volition to the subjective imperfection of the will of this or that rational being, e.g., the human will.

Now all *imperatives* command either *hypothetically* or *categorically.* The former represent the practical necessity of a possible action as means to something else that is willed (or at least which one might possibly will). The categorical imperative would be that which represented an action as necessary of itself without reference to another end, i.e., as objectively necessary....

## First Formulation of the Categorical Imperative: Universal Law

There is therefore but one categorical imperative, namely, this: *Act only on that maxim whereby thou canst at the same time will that it should become a universal law.*

Now if all imperatives of duty can be deduced from this one imperative as from their principle, then, although it should remain undecided whether what is called duty is not merely a vain notion, yet at least we shall be able to show what we understand by it and what this notion means.

Since the universality of the law according to which effects are produced constitutes what is properly called *nature* in the most general sense (as to form), that is the existence of things so far as it is determined by general laws, the imperative of duty may be expressed thus: *Act as if the maxim of thy action were to become by thy will a universal law of nature.*

**Four Illustrations**    We will now enumerate a few duties, adopting the usual division of them into duties to ourselves and to others, and into perfect and imperfect duties.

1. A man reduced to despair by a series of misfortunes feels wearied of life, but is still so far in possession of his reason that he can ask himself whether it would not be contrary to his duty to himself to take his own life. Now he inquires whether the maxim of his action could become a universal law of nature. His maxim is: From self-love I adopt it as a principle to shorten my life when its longer duration is likely to bring more evil than satisfaction. It is asked then simply whether this principle founded on self-love can become a universal law of nature. Now we see at once that a system of nature of which it should be a law to destroy life by means of the very feeling whose special nature it is to impel to the improvement of life would contradict itself, and therefore could not exist as a system of nature; hence that maxim cannot possibly exist as a universal law of nature, and consequently would be wholly inconsistent with the supreme principle of all duty.

2. Another finds himself forced by necessity to borrow money. He knows that he will not be able to repay it, but sees also that nothing will be lent to him, unless he promises stoutly to repay it in a definite time. He desires to make this promise, but he has still so much conscience as to ask himself: Is it not unlawful and inconsistent with duty to get out of a difficulty in this way? Suppose, however, that he resolves to do so, then the maxim of his action would be expressed thus: When I think myself in want of money, I will borrow money and promise to repay it, although I know that I never can do so. Now this principle of self-love or of one's own advantage may perhaps be consistent with my whole future welfare; but the question now is, Is it right? I change then the suggestion of self-love into a universal law, and state the question thus: How would it be if my maxim were a universal law? Then I see at once that it could never hold as a universal law of nature, but would necessarily contradict itself. For supposing it to be a universal law that everyone when he thinks himself in a difficulty should be able to promise whatever he pleases, with the purpose of not keeping his promise, the promise itself would become impossible, as well as the end that one might have in view in it, since no one would consider that anything was promised to him, but would ridicule all such statements as vain pretenses.

3. A third finds in himself a talent which with the help of some culture might make him a useful man in many respects. But he finds himself in comfortable circumstances, and prefers to indulge in pleasure rather than to take pains in enlarging and improving his happy natural capacities. He asks, however, whether his maxim of neglect of his natural gifts, besides agreeing with his inclination to indulgence, agrees also with what is called duty. He sees then that a system of nature could indeed subsist with such a universal law although men (like the South Sea islanders)

should let their talents rust, and resolve to devote their lives merely to idleness, amusement, and propagation of their species—in a word, to enjoyment; but he cannot possibly *will* that this should be a universal law of nature, or be implanted in us as such by a natural instinct. For, as a rational being, he necessarily wills that his faculties be developed, since they serve him, and have been given him, for all sorts of possible purposes.

4. A fourth, who is in prosperity, while he sees that others have to contend with great wretchedness and that he could help them, thinks: What concern is it of mine? Let everyone be as happy as Heaven pleases, or as he can make himself; I will take nothing from him nor even envy him, only I do not wish to contribute anything to his welfare or to his assistance in distress. Now no doubt if such a mode of thinking were a universal law, the human race might very well subsist, and doubtless even better than in a state in which everyone talks of sympathy and good-will, or even takes care occasionally to put it into practice, but, on the other side, also cheats when he can, betrays the rights of men, or otherwise violates them. But although it is possible that a universal law of nature might exist in accordance with that maxim, it is impossible to *will* that such a principle should have the universal validity of a law of nature. For a will which resolved this would contradict itself, inasmuch as many cases might occur in which one would have need of the love and sympathy of others, and in which, by such a law of nature, sprung from his own will, he would deprive himself of all hope of the aid he desires. . . .

## Second Formulation of the Categorical Imperative: Humanity as an End in Itself

. . . Now I say: man and generally any rational being *exists* as an end in himself, *not merely as a means* to be arbitrarily used by this or that will, but in all his actions, whether they concern himself or other rational beings, must be always regarded at the same time as an end. All objects of the inclinations have only a conditional worth; for if the inclinations and the wants founded on them did not exist, then their object would be without value. But the inclinations themselves being sources of want are so far from having an absolute worth for which they should be desired, that, on the contrary, it must be the universal wish of every rational being to be wholly free from them. Thus the worth of any object which is *to be acquired* by our action is always conditional. Beings whose existence depends not on our will but on nature's, have nevertheless, if they are nonrational beings, only a relative value as means, and are therefore called *things;* rational beings, on the contrary, are called *persons,* because their very nature points them out as ends in themselves, that is as something which must not be used merely as means, and so far therefore restricts freedom of action (and is an object of respect). These, therefore, are not merely subjective ends whose existence has a worth *for us* as an effect of our action, but *objective ends,* that is things whose existence is an end in itself: an end moreover for which no other can be substituted, which they should subserve *merely* as means, for otherwise nothing whatever would possess *absolute worth;* but if all worth were conditioned and therefore contingent, then there would be no supreme practical principle of reason whatever.

If then there is a supreme practical principle or, in respect of the human will, a categorical imperative, it must be one which, being drawn from the conception of that which is necessarily an end for everyone because it is *an end in itself,* constitutes an *objective* principle of will, and can therefore serve as a universal practical law. The foundation of this principle is: *rational nature exists as an end in itself.* Man necessarily conceives his own existence as being so: so far then this is a *subjective* principle of human actions. But every other rational being regards its existence similarly, just on the same rational principle that holds for me: so that it is at the same time an objective principle from which as a supreme practical law all laws of the will must be capable of being deduced. Accordingly the practical imperative will be as follows: *So act as to treat humanity, whether in thine own person or in that of any other, in every case as an end withal, never as means only....*

We will now inquire whether this can be practically carried out.

To abide by the previous examples:

*Firstly,* under the head of the necessary duty to oneself: He who contemplates suicide should ask himself whether his action can be consistent with the idea of humanity *as an end in itself.* If he destroys himself in order to escape from painful circumstances, he uses a person merely as *a means* to maintain a tolerable condition up to the end of life. But a man is not a thing, that is to say, something which can be used merely as a means, but must in all his actions be always considered as an end in himself. I cannot, therefore, dispose in any way of a man in my own person so as to mutilate him, to damage or kill him. (It belongs to ethics proper to define this principle more precisely so as to avoid all misunderstanding, e.g., as to the amputation of the limbs in order to preserve myself; as to exposing my life to danger with a view to preserve it, &c. This question is therefore omitted here.)

*Secondly,* as regards necessary duties, or those of strict obligation, towards others; he who is thinking of making a lying promise to others will see at once that he would be using another man *merely as a mean,* without the latter containing at the same time the end in himself. For he whom I propose by such a promise to use for my own purposes cannot possibly assent to my mode of acting towards him, and therefore cannot himself contain the end of this action. This violation of the principle of humanity in other men is more obvious if we take in examples of attacks on the freedom and property of others. For then it is clear that he who transgresses the rights of men, intends to use the person of others merely as means, without considering that as rational beings they ought always to be esteemed also as ends, that is, as beings who must be capable of containing in themselves the end of the very same action.

*Thirdly,* as regards contingent (meritorious) duties to oneself; it is not enough that the action does not violate humanity in our own person as an end in itself, it must also *harmonize with* it. Now there are in humanity capacities of greater perfection which belong to the end that nature has in view in regard to humanity in ourselves as the subject: to neglect these might perhaps be consistent with the *maintenance* of humanity as an end in itself, but not with the *advancement* of this end.

*Fourthly,* as regards meritorious duties towards others: the natural end which all men have is their own happiness. Now humanity might indeed subsist, although no one should contribute anything to the happiness of others, provided he did not intentionally withdraw anything from it; but after all, this would only harmonize negatively not positively with *humanity as an end in itself,* if everyone does not also endeavor, as far as in him lies, to forward the ends of others. For the ends of any subject which is an end in himself, ought as far as possible to be *my* ends also, if that conception is to have its *full* effect with me.

... Looking back now on all previous attempts to discover the principle of morality, we need not wonder why they all failed. It was seen that man was bound to laws by duty, but it was not observed that the laws to which he is subject are *only those of his own giving,* though at the same time they are *universal,* and that he is only bound to act in conformity with his own will; a will, however, which is designed by nature to give universal laws. For when one has conceived man only as subject to a law (no matter what), then this law required some interest, either by way of attraction or constraint, since it did not originate as a law from *his own* will, but this will was according to a law obliged by *something else* to act in a certain manner. Now by this necessary consequence all the labor spent in finding a supreme principle of *duty* was irrevocably lost. For men never elicited duty, but only a necessity of acting from a certain interest. Whether this interest was private or otherwise, in any case the imperative must be conditional, and could not by any means be capable of being a moral command. I will therefore call this the principle of *Autonomy* of the will, in contrast with every other which I accordingly reckon as *Heteronomy.*

## The Kingdom of Ends

The conception of every rational being as one which must consider itself as giving in all the maxims of its will universal laws, so as to judge itself and its actions from this point of view—this conception leads to another which depends on it and is very fruitful, namely, that of a *kingdom of ends.*

By a *kingdom* I understand the union of different rational beings in a system by common laws. Now since it is by laws that ends are determined as regards their universal validity, hence, if we abstract from the personal differences of rational beings, and likewise from all the content of their private ends, we shall be able to conceive all ends combined in a systematic whole (including both rational beings as ends in themselves, and also the special ends which each may propose to himself), that is to say, we can conceive a kingdom of ends, which on the preceding principles is possible.

For all rational beings come under the *law* that each of them must treat itself and all others *never merely as means,* but in every case *at the same time as ends in themselves.* Hence results a systematic union of rational beings by common objective laws, *i.e.,* a kingdom which may be called a kingdom of ends, since what these laws have in view is just the relation of these beings to one another as ends and means. ...

## II. CASUISTICAL QUESTIONS

### [Suicide]

Is it self-murder to plunge oneself into certain death (like Curtius) in order to save one's country? Or is martyrdom—the deliberate sacrifice of oneself for the good of mankind—also to be regarded, like the former case, as a heroic deed?

Is committing suicide permitted in anticipation of an unjust death sentence from one's superior? Even if the sovereign permitted such a suicide (as Nero permitted of Seneca)?

Can one attribute a criminal intention to a great, recently deceased monarch [Frederick the Great] because he carried a fast-acting poison with him, presumably so that if he was captured in war (which he always conducted personally), he might not be forced to submit to conditions of ransom which might be harmful to his country? (For he can be credited with such a purpose without one's being required to presume that he carried the poison out of mere arrogance.)

Bitten by a mad dog, a man already felt hydrophobia coming upon him. He declared that since he had never known anybody cured of it, he would destroy himself in order that, as he said in his testament, he might not in his madness (which he already felt gripping him) bring misfortune to other men too. The question is whether or not he did wrong.

Whoever decides to let himself be inoculated against smallpox risks his life on an uncertainty, although he does it to preserve his life. Accordingly, he is in a much more doubtful position with regard to the law of duty than is the mariner, who does not in the least create the storm to which he entrusts himself. Rather, the former invites an illness which puts him in the danger of death. Consequently, is smallpox inoculation allowed?

## [Lying]

Can an untruth from mere politeness (e.g., "your most obedient servant" at the end of a letter) be taken as lying? Nobody is deceived by it. An author asks one of this readers, "How do you like my work?" To be sure, the answer might be given in an illusory way inasmuch as one might jest concerning the captiousness of such a question. But who always has his wits about him? The slightest hesitation with the answer is already a mortification for the author. May one flatter him, then?

If I utter an untruth in actual business affairs, which come to questions of mine and thine, must I answer for all the consequences that might spring from it? For instance, a householder has instructed his servant that, if a certain person should ask for him, the servant should deny knowing anything about him. The servant does this, but in doing so is the occasion of the master's slipping away and committing a great crime, which would otherwise have been prevented by the watchman who was sent out to take him. Upon whom (according to ethical principles) does the blame fall? To be sure, also upon the servant, who here violates a duty to himself by lying, the consequence of which will now be imputed to him by his own conscience.

## [Self-Perfection: Natural and Moral]

It is a duty of man to himself to cultivate his natural powers (of the spirit, of the mind, and of the body) as means to all kinds of possible ends. Man owes it to himself (as an intelligence) not to let his natural predispositions and capacities (which his reason can use some day) remain unused, and not to leave them, as it were, to rust. Let it even be supposed that he is satisfied with the inborn range of his capacities for meeting his natural needs. Nevertheless, it is his reason which, by means of principles, points out to him this satisfaction with the meager compass of his capacities; for he (as a being capable of having ends or of making objects ends for himself) must owe the use of his powers not merely to natural instinct, but also to the freedom with which he determines their scope. It is thus not for the advantage which the cultivation of his capacity (for all kinds of ends) can provide that man should concern himself with such cultivation, even though, in view of the roughness of nature's requirements, this advantage would perhaps (according to Rousseau's principles) turn out to be profitable. But it is a command of morally practical reason and a duty of man to himself to build up his capacities (one more than another according to the variety of his ends), and to be a man fit (in a pragmatic sense) for the end of his existence.

Powers of the spirit are those whose exercise is possible only through reason. They are creative as far as their use is not obtained from experience but is derived a priori from principles. Such are mathematics, logic, and the metaphysics of nature. The latter two can also be counted as theoretical philosophy, which, to be sure, does not literally mean wisdom, but only science. However, philosophy can be favorable to the end of wisdom.

Powers of the mind are those which are at the disposal both of the understanding and of the rule which the understanding uses to satisfy purposes of its own liking, and in this they follow the lead of experience. Such are memory, imagination, and the like, upon which learnedness, taste (internal and external beautification), and so on can be established. These latter offer tools for many purposes.

Finally, the cultivation of the powers of the body (the true gymnastics) is care for that which constitutes the stuff (the matter) of man, without which the ends of man would remain unfulfilled. Consequently, the continual deliberate stimulation of the animal in man is a duty of man to himself.

Which of these natural perfections may be preferable, and in what proportions, in comparison with one another, it may be man's duty to himself to make them his aim, are matters left to one's own rational reflection upon his desire for a certain mode of life, and his evaluation of the powers requisite for it. This reflection and evaluation are necessary in order to choose what his mode of life should be, e.g., a handicraft, commerce, or a learned profession. For apart from the necessity of self-preservation, which in itself can establish no duty, man owes it to himself to be a useful member of the world, because being one belongs also to the worth of the humanity in his own person, which he should not degrade.

However, man's duty to himself regarding his physical perfection is only a broad and imperfect duty. This is so because such a duty contains, to be sure, a law for the maxim of actions, but determines nothing so far as the actions themselves are concerned—nothing as to their kind and degree. Rather, it allows a latitude for free choice.

[Moral] perfection consists subjectively in the purity (puritas moralis) of one's disposition toward duty: when, without any admixture of aims taken from sensibility, the law is its own incentive, and one's actions occur not only in accordance with duty but also from duty. "Be holy" [I Peter 1:16] is here the command. Secondly, such perfection consists objectively in doing one's full duty and in attaining the completeness of one's moral end regarding himself. "Be perfect!" [Matthew 5:48] For man, striving for this goal is always only a progression from one stage of perfection to another. "If there is any virtue, if there is any praise, aspire to it" [Philippians 4:8].

This duty to oneself is in quality strict and perfect, though in degree it is broad and imperfect because of the frailty *(fragilitas)* of human nature.

Such perfection, which it is indeed a duty to strive after but not to attain (in this life)—the obedience to this duty consisting thus only in a constant progression toward this perfection—is in reference to the object (the idea whose fulfillment one must make his end) a strict and perfect duty, but in reference to the subject, a broad and only imperfect duty to oneself.

The depths of the human heart are unfathomable. Who knows himself well enough, when he feels an incentive for observing duty, to tell whether the incentive arises wholly from the representation of the law, or whether many other sensible impulses contribute to it? Such impulses aim at advantage (or aim at preventing disadvantage) and might well, on another occasion, also serve vice. But as for what concerns perfection as a moral end, there is indeed in idea (objectively) only one virtue (as moral strength of one's maxims); but in fact (subjectively) there is a multitude of virtues of heterogeneous qualities, among which, if one wanted to look for it, one might possibly discover some lack of virtue (although this would not bear the name of vice since it is in the company of many virtues). However, a sum of virtues, whose completeness or deficiency our self-knowledge never lets us adequately discern, can establish nothing but an imperfect duty to be perfect.

Thus, all the duties to oneself regarding the end of the humanity in one's own person are only imperfect duties.

## [Beneficence]

How far should one push the expenditure of his means in beneficence? Certainly not to the point where he would finally need the beneficence of others. How valuable is the benefit which one bestows impersonally (as when, in departing from his life, he leaves a will)? Can he who exercises a legal power over another deprive this other of freedom by acting according to his own option as to what will make this other person happy (a serf of his estate, for instance)? I say, can this man regard himself as a benefactor when he looks after such a person paternally, as it were, according to his own concepts of happiness? Or, rather, is not the unrighteousness of depriving someone of his freedom something so contrary to juridical duty in general, that to count upon the beneficence of one's master and to surrender oneself to it on such conditions would be the greatest throwing away of one's humanity? And, further, would not then the greatest care of the master for such a person be no beneficence at all? Or can the merit of such beneficence perhaps be so great that the rights of humanity might be outweighed by comparison with it? I can benefit no one (with the exception of minors and the mentally deranged) according to my own concepts of happiness, but only according to the concepts of him whom I think of benefiting; I actually do not benefit him when I urge a gift upon him.

The wherewithal for doing good, which depends upon the gifts of fortune, is for the most part a result of the patronage of various men owing to the injustice of government, which introduces an inequality of wealth that makes beneficence necessary. Under such circumstances, does the assistance which the rich render the needy deserve at all the name of beneficence, with which one so gladly plumes himself as merit?

## READING COMPREHENSION QUESTIONS

1. According to Kant, the only conceivable thing that is "good without qualification" is what he calls a "good will." Kant attempts to defend this claim by
   considering other candidates that might be considered good without qualification. What are they? And how does Kant argue that none of them are
   good without qualification?

2. What is Kant's conception of a good will and what does he think is the source
   of its goodness?

3. The universal law formulation of the categorical imperative involves testing
   maxims, which Kant proceeds to illustrate with four examples. For each of his
   examples, try explaining in your own words how Kant's test is supposed to
   work in showing that certain maxims cannot be consistently willed as universal law.

4. Kant also applies the "humanity as an end in itself" formulation to the same
   four examples. For each of these examples, explain how Kant uses his principle to establish claims about the morality of the type of action in question?

5. For each of Kant's examples, he raises various "casuistical questions." How
   would you answer these questions? What reasons would you give for your
   answers?

# 39

---

# An Ethic of Caring

### NEL NODDINGS

*Nel Noddings is professor of philosophy and education at Teachers College,
Columbia University, and Lee L. Jacks Professor of Child Education emerita at
Stanford University. Her books include* Caring: A Feminine Approach to
Ethics and Moral Education *(1984),* Awakening the Inner Eye: Intuition
and Education *(with Paul J. Shore, 1984), and* Women and Evil *(1989).
According to Noddings, moral obligation is rooted in a sentiment or feeling
of "natural care"—a sentiment typified by the care a woman has for her
infant. Natural caring together with one's reflective evaluation of the caring relation*

*as good gives rise to a second, specifically moral, sentiment experienced as an obligation to respond to anyone in need with whom we come into contact in concrete, real-life situations. Furthermore, two criteria govern our obligation to care: (1) the existence of or potential for presently being related to another, and (2) the potentiality of the cared-for individual to reciprocate the care of the one caring. After examining the implications of this ethic of care for the case of making an abortion decision, Noddings considers the role of judgments of right and wrong in an ethic of care and what sort of justification one can provide for such an ethic.*

## FROM NATURAL TO ETHICAL CARING

David Hume long ago contended that morality is founded upon and rooted in feeling—that the "final sentence" on matters of morality, "that which renders morality an active virtue—. . . this final sentence depends on some internal sense or feeling, which nature has made universal in the whole species. For what else can have an influence of this nature?"[1]

What is the nature of this feeling that is "universal in the whole species"? I want to suggest that morality as an "active virtue" requires two feelings and not just one. The first is the sentiment of natural caring. There can be no ethical sentiment without the initial, enabling sentiment. In situations where we act on behalf of the other because we want to do so, we are acting in accord with natural caring. A mother's caretaking efforts in behalf of her child are not usually considered ethical but natural. Even maternal animals take care of their offspring, and we do not credit them with ethical behavior.

The second sentiment occurs in response to a remembrance of the first. Nietzsche speaks of love and memory in the context of Christian love and Eros, but what he says may safely be taken out of context to illustrate the point I wish to make here:

> There is something so ambiguous and suggestive about the word love, something that speaks to memory and to hope, that even the lowest intelligence and the coldest heart still feel something of the glimmer of this word. The cleverest woman and the most vulgar man recall the relatively least selfish moments of their whole life, even if Eros has taken only a low flight with them.[2]

This memory of our own best moments of caring and being cared for sweeps over us as a feeling—as an "I must"—in response to the plight of the other and our conflicting desire to serve our own interests. There is a transfer of feeling analogous to transfer of learning. In the intellectual domain, when I read a certain kind

---

[1]David Hume, "An Enquiry Concerning the Principles of Morals," in *Ethical Theories,* ed. A. I. Melden (Englewood Cliffs, N.J.: Prentice-Hall, Inc., 1967), p. 275.

[2]Friedrich Nietzsche, "Mixed Opinions and Maxims," in *The Portable Nietzsche,* ed. Walter Kaufmann (New York: The Viking Press, Inc., 1954), p. 65.

of mathematical puzzle, I may react by thinking, "That is like the sailors, monkey, and coconuts problem," and then, "Diophantine equations" or "modulo arithmetic" or "congruences." Similarly, when I encounter an other and feel the natural pang conflicted with my own desires—"I must—I do not want to"—I recognize the feeling and remember what has followed it in my own best moments. I have a picture of those moments in which I was cared for and in which I cared, and I may reach toward this memory and guide my conduct by it if I wish to do so.

Recognizing that ethical caring requires an effort that is not needed in natural caring does not commit us to a position that elevates ethical caring over natural caring. Kant has identified the ethical with that which is done out of duty and not out of love, and that distinction in itself seems right. But an ethic built on caring strives to maintain the caring attitude and is thus dependent upon, and not superior to, natural caring. The source of ethical behavior is, then, in twin sentiments—one that feels directly for the other and one that feels for and with that best self, who may accept and sustain the initial feeling rather than reject it.

We shall discuss the ethical ideal, that vision of best self, in some depth. When we commit ourselves to obey the "I must" even at its weakest and most fleeting, we are under the guidance of this ideal. It is not just any picture. Rather, it is our best picture of ourselves caring and being cared for. It may even be colored by acquaintance with one superior to us in caring, but, as I shall describe it, it is both constrained and attainable. It is limited by what we have already done and by what we are capable of, and it does not idealize the impossible so that we may escape into ideal abstraction. . . .


## OBLIGATION

There are moments for all of us when we care quite naturally. We just do care; no ethical effort is required. "Want" and "ought" are indistinguishable in such cases. I want to do what I or others might judge I ought to do. But can there be a "demand" to care? There can be, surely, no demand for the initial impulse that arises as a feeling, an inner voice saying "I must do something," in response to the need of the cared-for. This impulse arises naturally, at least occasionally, in the absence of pathology. We cannot demand that one have this impulse, but we shrink from one who never has it. One who never feels the pain of another, who never confesses the internal "I must" that is so familiar to most of us, is beyond our normal pattern of understanding. Her case is pathological, and we avoid her.

But even if I feel the initial "I must," I may reject it. I may reject it instantaneously by shifting from "I must do something" to "Something must be done," and removing myself from the set of possible agents through whom the action should be accomplished. I may reject it because I feel that there is nothing I can do. If I do either of these things without reflection upon what I might do in behalf of the cared-for, then I do not care. Caring requires me to respond to the initial impulse with an act of commitment: I commit myself either to overt action on behalf of the cared-for (I pick up my crying infant) or I commit myself to thinking about what I might do. In the latter case, as we have seen, I may or may not act overtly in behalf of the cared-for. I may abstain from action if I believe that anything I might do would tend to work against the best interests of the cared-for. But the test of my caring is not wholly in how things turn out; the primary test lies in an examination of what I considered, how fully I received the other, and whether the free pursuit of his projects is partly a result of the completion of my caring in him.

But am I obliged to embrace the "I must"? In this form, the question is a bit odd, for the "I must" carries obligation with it. It comes to us as obligation. But accepting and affirming the "I must" are different from feeling it, and these responses are what I am pointing to when I ask whether I am obliged to embrace the "I must." The question nags at us; it is a question that has been asked, in a variety of forms, over and over by moralists and moral theorists. Usually, the question arises as part of the broader question of justification. We ask something of the sort: Why must I (or should I) do what suggests itself to reason as "right" or as needing to be done for the sake of some other? We might prefer to supplement "reason" with "and/or feeling." This question is, of course, not the only thorny question in moral theory, but it is one that has plagued theorists who see clearly that there is no way to derive an "I ought" statement from a chain of facts. I may agree readily that "things would be better"—that is, that a certain state of affairs commonly agreed to be desirable might be attained—if a certain chain of events were to take place. But there is still nothing in this intellectual chain that can produce the "I ought." I may choose to remain an observer on the scene.

Now I am suggesting that the "I must" arises directly and prior to consideration of what it is that I might do. The initial feeling is the "I must." When it comes to me indistinguishable from the "I want," I proceed easily as one-caring. But often it comes to me conflicted. It may be barely perceptible, and it may be followed almost simultaneously by resistance. When someone asks me to get something for him or merely asks for my attention, the "I must" may be lost in a clamor of resistance. Now a second sentiment is required if I am to behave as one-caring. I care about myself as one-caring and, although I do not care naturally for the person who has asked something of me—at least not at this moment—I feel the genuine moral sentiment, the "I ought," that sensibility to which I have committed myself.

Let me try to make plausible my contention that the moral imperative arises directly. And, of course, I must try to explain how caring and what I am calling the "moral imperative" are related. When my infant cries in the night, I not only feel that I must do something but I want to do something. Because I love this child, because I am bonded to him, I want to remove his pain as I would want to remove my own. The "I must" is not a dutiful imperative but one that accompanies the "I want." If I were tied to a chair, for example, and wanted desperately to get free, I might say as I struggled, "I must do something; I must get out of these bonds." But this "must" is not yet the moral or ethical "ought." It is a "must" born of desire.

The most intimate situations of caring are, thus, natural. I do not feel that taking care of my own child is "moral" but, rather, natural. A woman who allows her own child to die of neglect is often considered sick rather than immoral; that is, we feel that either she or the situation into which she has been thrust must be pathological. Otherwise, the impulse to respond, to nurture the living infant, is overwhelming. We share the impulse with other creatures in the animal kingdom. Whether we want to consider this response as "instinctive" is problematic, because certain patterns of response may be implied by the term and because suspension of reflective consciousness seems also to be implied (and I am not suggesting that we have no choice), but I have no difficulty in considering it as innate. Indeed, I am claiming that the impulse to act in behalf of the present other is itself innate. It lies latent in each of us, awaiting gradual development in a succession of caring relations. I am suggesting that our inclination toward and interest in morality derives from caring. In caring, we accept the natural impulse to act on behalf of the present other. We are engrossed in the other. We have received him and feel his pain or happiness, but we are not compelled by this impulse. We have a choice; we may accept what we feel, or we may reject it. If we have a strong desire to be moral, we will not reject it, and this strong desire to be moral is derived, reflectively, from the more fundamental and natural desire to be and to remain related. To reject the feeling when it arises is either to be in an internal state of imbalance or to contribute willfully to the diminution of the ethical ideal.

But suppose in a particular case that the "I must" does not arise, or that it whispers faintly and disappears, leaving distrust, repugnance, or hate. Why, then, should I behave morally toward the object of my dislike? Why should I not accept feelings other than those characteristic of caring and, thus, achieve an internal state of balance through hate, anger, or malice?

The answer to this is, I think, that the genuine moral sentiment (our second sentiment) arises from an evaluation of the caring relation as good, as better than, superior to, other forms of relatedness. I feel the moral "I must" when I recognize that my response will either enhance or diminish my ethical ideal. It will serve either to increase or decrease the likelihood of genuine caring. My response affects me as one-caring. In a given situation with someone I am not fond of, I may be able to find all sorts of reasons why I should not respond to his need. I may be too busy. He may be undiscerning. The matter may be, on objective analysis, unimportant. But, before I decide, I must turn away from this analytic chain of thought and back to the concrete situation. Here is this person with this perceived need to which is attached this importance. I must put justification aside temporarily. Shall I respond? How do I feel as a duality about the "I" who will not respond?

I am obliged, then, to accept the initial "I must" when it occurs and even to fetch it out of recalcitrant slumber when it fails to awake spontaneously. The source of my obligation is the value I place on the relatedness of caring. This value itself arises as a product of actual caring and being cared-for and my reflection on the goodness of these concrete caring situations.

Now, what sort of "goodness" is it that attaches to the caring relation? It cannot be a fully moral goodness, for we have already described forms of caring that are natural and require no moral effort. But it cannot be a fully nonmoral goodness either, for it would then join a class of goods many of which are widely separated from the moral good. It is, perhaps, properly described as a "premoral good," one that lies in a region with the moral good and shades over into it. We cannot always decide with certainty whether our caring response is natural or ethical. Indeed, the decision to respond ethically as one-caring may cause the lowering of barriers that previously prevented reception of the other, and natural caring may follow.

I have identified the source of our obligation and have said that we are obligated to accept, and even to call forth, the feeling "I must." But what exactly must

I do! Can my obligation be set forth in a list or hierarchy of principles? So far, it seems that I am obligated to maintain an attitude and, thus, to meet the other as one-caring and, at the same time, to increase my own virtue as one-caring. If I am advocating an ethic of virtue, do not all the usual dangers lie in wait: hypocrisy, self-righteousness, withdrawal from the public domain? We shall discuss these dangers as the idea of an ethical ideal is developed more fully.

Let me say here, however, why it seems preferable to place an ethical ideal above principle as a guide to moral action. It has been traditional in moral philosophy to insist that moral principles must be, by their very nature as moral principles, universifiable. If I am obligated to do X under certain conditions, then under sufficiently similar conditions you also are obligated to do X. But the principle of universifiability seems to depend, as Nietzsche pointed out, on a concept of "sameness."[3] In order to accept the principle, we should have to establish that human predicaments exhibit sufficient sameness, and this we cannot do without abstracting away from concrete situations those qualities that seem to reveal the sameness. In doing this, we often lose the very qualities or factors that gave rise to the moral question in the situation. That condition which makes the situation different and thereby induces genuine moral puzzlement cannot be satisfied by the application of principles developed in situations of sameness.

This does not mean that we cannot receive any guidance from an attempt to discover principles that seem to be universifiable. We can, under this sort of plan, arrive at the doctrine of "prima facie duty" described by W. D. Ross.[4] Ross himself, however, admits that this doctrine yields no real guidance for moral conduct in concrete situations. It guides us in abstract moral thinking; it tells us, theoretically what to do, "all other things being equal." But other things are rarely if ever equal. A and B, struggling with a moral decision, are two different persons with different factual histories, different projects and aspirations, and different ideals. It may indeed be right, morally right, for A to do X and B to do not-X. We may, that is, connect "right" and "wrong" to faithfulness to the ethical ideal. This does not cast us into relativism, because the ideal contains at its heart a component that is universal: Maintenance of the caring relation. . . .

Our obligation is limited and delimited by relation. We are never free, in the human domain, to abandon our preparedness to care; but practically, if we are meeting those in our inner circles adequately as ones-caring and receiving those linked to our inner circles by formal chains of relation, we shall limit the calls upon our obligation quite naturally. We are not obliged to summon the "I must" if there is no possibility of completion in the other. I am not obliged to care for starving children in Africa, because there is no way for this caring to be completed in the other unless I abandon the caring to which I am obligated. I may still choose to do something in the direction of caring, but I am not obliged to do so. . . .

---

[3]Friedrich Nietzsche, *The Will to Power,* trans. Walter Kaufmann (New York: Random House, 1957), pp. 476, 670. For a contemporary argument against strict application of universalizability, see Peter Winch, *Ethics and Action (London: Routledge & Kegan Paul, 1972).*

[4]W. D. Ross, *The Right and the Good* (Oxford: Clarendon Press, 1930).

Now, this is very important, and we should try to say clearly what governs our obligation. On the basis of what has been developed so far, there seem to be two criteria: the existence of or potential for present relation, and the dynamic potential for growth in relation, including the potential for increased reciprocity and, perhaps, mutuality. The first criterion establishes an absolute obligation and the second serves to put our obligations into an order of priority.

If the other toward whom we shall act is capable of responding as cared-for and there are no objective conditions that prevent our receiving this response—if, that is, our caring can be completed in the other—then we must meet that other as one-caring. If we do not care naturally, we must call upon our capacity for ethical caring. When we are in relation or when the other has addressed us, we must respond as one-caring. The imperative in relation is categorical. When relation. has not yet been established, or when it may properly be refused (when no formal chain or natural circle is present), the imperative is more like that of the hypothetical: I must if I wish to (or am able to) move into relation.

The second criterion asks us to look at the nature of potential relation and, especially, at the capacity of the cared-for to respond. The potential for response in animals, for example, is nearly static; they cannot respond in mutuality, nor can the nature of their response change substantially. But a child's potential for increased response is enormous. If the possibility of relation is dynamic—if the relation may clearly grow with respect to reciprocity—then the possibility and degree of my obligation also grows. If response is imminent, so also is my obligation. This criterion will help us to distinguish between our obligation to members of the nonhuman animal world and, say, the human fetus. We must keep in mind, however, that the second criterion binds us in proportion to the probability of increased response and to the imminence of that response. Relation itself is fundamental in obligation.

I shall give an example of thinking guided by these criteria, but let us pause for a moment and ask what it is we are trying to accomplish. I am working deliberately toward criteria that will preserve our deepest and most tender human feelings. The caring of mother for child, of human adult for human infant, elicits the tenderest feelings in most of us. Indeed, for many women, this feeling of nurturance lies at the very heart of what we assess as good. A philosophical position that has difficulty distinguishing between our obligation to human infants and, say, pigs is in some difficulty straight off. It violates our most deeply cherished feeling about human goodness. This violation does not, of course, make the position logically wrong, but it suggests that especially strong grounds will be needed to support it. . . .

Now, let's consider an example: the problem of abortion. Operating under the guidance of an ethic of caring, we are not likely to find abortion in general either right or wrong. We shall have to inquire into individual cases. An incipient embryo is an information speck—a set of controlling instructions for a future human being. Many of these specks are created and flushed away without their creators' awareness. From the view developed here, the information speck is an information speck; it has no given sanctity. There should be no concern over the waste of "human tissue," since nature herself is wildly prolific, even profligate. The one-caring is concerned not with human tissue but with human consciousness—with pain, delight, hope, fear, entreaty and response.

But suppose the information speck is mine, and I am aware of it. This child-to-be is the product of love between a man deeply cared-for and me. Will the child have his eyes or mine? His stature or mine? Our joint love of mathematics or his love of mechanics or my love of language? This is not just an information speck; it is endowed with prior love and current knowledge. It is sacred, but I—humbly, not presumptuously—confer sacredness upon it. I cannot, will not destroy it. It is joined to loved others through formal chains of caring. It is linked to the inner circle in a clearly defined way. I might wish that I were not pregnant, but I cannot destroy this known and potentially loved person-to-be. There is already relation albeit indirect and formal. My decision is an ethical one born of natural caring.

But suppose, now, that my beloved child has grown up; it is she who is pregnant and considering abortion. She is not sure of the love between herself and the man. She is miserably worried about her economic and emotional future. I might like to convey sanctity on this information speck; but I am not God—only mother to this suffering cared-for. It is she who is conscious and in pain, and I as one-caring move to relieve the pain. This information speck is an information speck and that is all. There is no formal relation, given the breakdown between husband and wife, and with the embryo, there is no present relation; the possibility of future relation—while not absent, surely—is uncertain. But what of this possibility for growing response? Must we not consider it? We must indeed. As the embryo becomes a fetus and, growing daily, becomes more nearly capable of response as cared-for, our obligation grows from a nagging uncertainty—an "I must if I wish"—to an utter conviction that we must meet this small other as one-caring.

If we try to formalize what has been expressed in the concrete situation described so far, we arrive at a legal approach to abortion very like that of the Supreme Court: abortions should be freely available in the first trimester, subject to medical determination in the second trimester, and banned in the third, when the fetus is viable. A woman under the guidance of our ethic would be likely to recognize the growing possibility of relation; the potential is clearly dynamic. Further, many women recognize the relation as established when the fetus begins to move about. It is not a question of when life begins but of when relation begins.

But what if relation is never established? Suppose the child is born and the mother admits no sense of relatedness. May she commit infanticide? One who asks such questions misinterprets the concept of relatedness that I have been struggling to describe. Since the infant, even the near-natal fetus, is capable of relation—of the sweetest and most unselfconscious reciprocity—one who encounters the infant is obligated to meet it as one-caring. Both parts of this claim are essential; it is not only the child's capability to respond but also the encounter that induces obligation. There must exist the possibility for our caring to be completed in the other. If the mother does not care naturally, then she must summon ethical caring to support her as one-caring. She may not ethically ignore the child's cry to live....

Our ethic of caring—which we might have called a "feminine ethic"—begins to look a bit mean in contrast to the masculine ethics of universal love or universal justice. But universal love is illusion. Under the illusion, some young people retreat to the church to worship that which they cannot actualize; some write lovely poetry extolling universal love; and some, in terrible disillusion, kill to establish the very principles which should have entreated them not to kill. Thus are lost both principles and persons.

## RIGHT AND WRONG

How are we to make judgments of right and wrong under this ethic? First, it is important to understand that we are not primarily interested in judging but, rather, in heightening moral perception and sensitivity. But "right" and "wrong" can be useful.

Suppose a mother observes her young child pulling the kitten's tail or picking it up by the ears. She may claim, "Oh, no, it is not nice to hurt the kitty," or, "You must not hurt the kitty." Or she may simply say, "Stop. See—you are hurting the kitty," and she may then take the kitten in her own hands and show the child how to handle it. She holds the kitten gently, stroking it, and saying, "See? Ah, ah, kitty, nice kitty. . . ." What the mother is supposing in this interaction is that the realization that his act is hurting the kitten supplemented by the knowledge of how to avoid inflicting hurt, will suffice to change the child's behavior. If she believes this, she has no need for the statement, "It is wrong to hurt the kitty." She is not threatening sanctions but drawing dual attention to a matter of fact (the hurting) and her own commitment (I will not hurt). Beyond this, she is supposing that her child, well-cared-for-himself, does not want to inflict pain. . . .

The one-caring, clearly, applies "right" and "wrong" most confidently to her own decisions. This does not, as we have insisted before, make her a relativist. The caring attitude that lies at the heart of all ethical behavior is universal. . . .

. . .[I]n general the one-caring evaluates her own acts with respect to how faithfully they conform to what is known and felt through the receptivity of caring. But she also uses "right" and "wrong" instructively and respectfully to refer to the judgments of significant others. If she agrees because the matter at hand can be assessed in light of caring, she adds her personal commitment and example; if she has doubts—because the rule appealed to seems irrelevant or ambiguous in the light of caring—she still acknowledges the judgment but adds her own dissent or demurrer. Her eye is on the ethical development of the cared-for and, as she herself withholds judgment until she has heard the "whole story," she wants the cared-for to encounter others, receive them, and reflect on what he has received. Principles and rules are among the beliefs he will receive, and she wants him to consider these in the light of caring.

But is this all we can say about right and wrong? Is there not a firm foundation in morality for our legal judgments? Surely, we must be allowed to say, for example, that stealing is wrong and is, therefore, properly forbidden by law. Because it is so often wrong—and so easily demonstrated to be wrong—under an ethic of caring, we may accede that such a law has its roots *partly* in morality. We may legally punish one who has stolen, but we may not pass moral judgment on him until we know why he stole. An ethic of caring is likely to be stricter in its judgment, but more supportive and corrective in following up its judgment, than ethics otherwise grounded. For the one-caring, stealing is almost always wrong:

Ms. A talks with her young son. *But, Mother,* the boy pleads, *suppose I want to make you happy and I steal something you want from a big chain store. I haven't hurt anyone, have I? Yes, you have,* responds his mother, and she points to the predicament of the store managers who may be accused of poor stewardship and to the higher prices suffered by their neighbors. *Well, suppose I steal from a rich, rich person? He can replace what I take easily, and . . . Wait,* says Ms. A. *Is someone suffering? Are you stealing to relieve that suffering, and will you make certain that what you steal is used to relieve it? . . . But can't I steal to make someone happy?* her son persists. Slowly, patiently, Ms. A explains the position of one-caring. *Each one* who comes under our gaze must be met as one-caring. When I want to please X and I turn toward Y as a means for satisfying my desire to please X, I must now meet Y as one-caring. I do not judge him for being rich—for treasuring what I, perhaps, regard with indifference. I may not cause him pain by taking or destroying what he possesses. *But what if I steal from a bad guy—someone who stole to get what he has?* Ms. A smiles at her young son, struggling to avoid his ethical responsibility: *Unless he is an immediate threat to you or someone else, you must meet him, too, as one-caring.*

The lessons in "right" and "wrong" are hard lessons—not swiftly accomplished by setting up as an objective the learning of some principle. We do not say: It is wrong to steal. Rather, we consider why it was wrong or may be wrong in this case to steal. We do not say: It is wrong to kill. By setting up such a principle, we also imply its exceptions, and then we may too easily act on authorized exceptions. The one-caring wants to consider, and wants her child to consider, the act itself in full context. She will send him into the world skeptical, vulnerable, courageous, disobedient, and tenderly receptive. The "world" may not depend upon him to obey its rules or fulfill its wishes, but you, the individual he encounters, may depend upon him to meet you as one-caring.

## THE PROBLEM OF JUSTIFICATION

. . .Why should I be committed to not causing pain? Now, clearly, in one sense, I cannot answer this better than we already have. When the "Why?" refers to motivation, we have seen that the one-caring receives the other and acts in the other's behalf as she would for herself; that is, she acts with a similar motive energy. Further, I have claimed that, when natural caring fails, the motive energy in behalf of the other can be summoned out of caring for the ethical self. We have discussed both natural caring and ethical caring. Ethical caring, as I have described it, depends not upon rule or principle but upon the development of an ideal self. It does not depend upon just any ideal of self, but the ideal developed in congruence with one's best remembrance of caring and being cared-for.

So far, in recommending the ethical ideal as a guide to ethical conduct, I have suggested that traditional approaches to the problem of justification are mistaken. When the ethical theorist asks, "Why should I behave thus-and-so?" his question is likely to be aimed at justification rather than motivation and at a logic that resides outside the person. He is asking for reasons of the sort we expect to find in logical demonstration. He may expect us to claim that moral judgments can be tested as claims to facts can be tested, or that moral judgments are derived from divine commandment, or that moral truths are intuitively apprehended. Once started on this line of discussion, we may find ourselves arguing abstractly about the status of relativism and absolutism, egoism and altruism, and a host of other positions that, I shall claim, are largely irrelevant to moral conduct. They are matters of considerable intellectual interest, but they are distractions if our primary interest is in ethical conduct.

Moral statements cannot be justified in the way that statements of fact can be justified. They are not truths. They are derived not from facts or principles but from the caring attitude. Indeed, we might say that moral statements come out of the moral view or attitude, which, as I have described it, is the rational attitude built upon natural caring. When we put it this way, we see that there can be no justification for taking the moral viewpoint—that in truth, the moral viewpoint is prior to any notion of justification.

## READING COMPREHENSION QUESTIONS

1. According to Noddings, what two "sentiments" are fundamental to morality? Give an example of each. *How* are they fundamental to morality in Noddings's view?

2. What is Noddings's answer to the question (that she raises in the section on "Obligation"): "Why should I behave morally toward [someone who is] the object of my dislike?"

3. What does Noddings mean by one's "ideal self"? What role does this ideal play in her ethic of care?

4. According to Noddings, how are we to determine *to whom* we have obligations?

5. According to Noddings, why aren't our obligations to nonhuman animals as strong as our obligations to human beings?

6. According to Noddings, what does the ethic of care imply about the morality of abortion? Do you find this view plausible? Why or why not?

7. At the very end of her essay, Noddings claims "there can be no justification for taking the moral viewpoint." How does she defend this claim? Do you find her claim and its defense plausible? Why or why not?

# 40

# Virtue and Character

ARISTOTLE

*Aristotle (384–322 B.C.E.) is one of the most important philosophers ever to have lived. The son of a physician, he was a student of Plato and served as tutor to Alexander the Great. He contributed important works on logic, the sciences, and virtually every area of philosophy.*

*In the following selection from his* Nicomachean Ethics, *Aristotle begins by arguing that a happy or good life essentially involves a life of activity in accordance with virtue. He then goes on to define virtue as a disposition to avoid extremes in feeling and action. For example, in matters relating to money, the virtue of generosity stands between the extremes of extravagance and stinginess.*

## CHARACTERISTICS OF THE GOOD

**1. The Good Is the End of Action**   But let us return once again to the good we are looking for, and consider just what it could be, since it is apparently one thing in one action or craft, and another thing in another; for it is one thing in medicine, another in generalship, and so on for the rest.

What, then, is the good in each of these cases? Surely it is that for the sake of which the other things are done; and in medicine this is health, in generalship victory, in house-building a house, in another case something else, but in every action and decision it is the end, since it is for the sake of the end that everyone does the other things.

And so, if there is some end of everything that is pursued in action, this will be the good pursued in action; and if there are more ends than one, these will be the goods pursued in action.

Our argument has progressed, then, to the same conclusion [as before, that the highest end is the good]; but we must try to clarify this still more.

**2. The Good Is Complete**   Though apparently there are many ends, we choose some of them, e.g., wealth, flutes and, in general, instruments, because of

SOURCE: From *Nicomachean Ethics*, trans. Terence Irwin (Hackett, 1974). Reprinted by permission of Hackett Publishing Company, Inc. All rights reserved.

something else; hence it is clear that not all ends are complete. But the best good is apparently something complete. Hence, if only one end is complete, this will be what we are looking for; and if more than one are complete, the most complete of these will be what we are looking for.

## CRITERIA FOR COMPLETENESS

An end pursued in itself, we say, is more complete than an end pursued because of something else; and an end that is never choiceworthy because of something else is more complete than ends that are choiceworthy both in themselves and because of this end; and hence an end that is always [choiceworthy, and also] choiceworthy in itself, never because of something else, is unconditionally complete.

**3. Happiness Meets the Criteria for Completeness, but Other Goods Do Not**   Now happiness more than anything else seems unconditionally complete, since we always [choose it, and also] choose it because of itself, never because of something else. Honor, pleasure, understanding and every virtue we certainly choose because of themselves, since we would choose each of them even if it had no further result, but we also choose them for the sake of happiness, supposing that through them we shall be happy. Happiness, by contrast, no one ever chooses for their sake, or for the sake of anything else at all.

**4. The Good Is Self–Sufficient; So Is Happiness**   The same conclusion [that happiness is complete] also appears to follow from self-sufficiency, since the complete good seems to be self-sufficient.

Now what we count as self-sufficient is not what suffices for a solitary person by himself, living an isolated life, but what suffices also for parents, children, wife and in general for friends and fellow–citizens, since a human being is a naturally political [animal]. Here, however, we must impose some limit; for if we extend the good to parents' parents and children's children and to friends of friends, we shall go on without limit; but we must examine this another time.

Anyhow, we regard something as self-sufficient when all by itself it makes a life choiceworthy and lacking nothing; and that is what we think happiness does.

**5. The Good Is Most Choiceworthy; So Is Happiness**   Moreover, [the complete good is most choiceworthy, and] we think happiness is most choiceworthy of all goods, since it is not counted as one good among many. If it were counted as one among many, then, clearly, we think that the addition of the smallest of goods would make it more choiceworthy; for [the smallest good] that is added becomes an extra quantity of goods [so creating a good larger than the original good], and the larger of two goods is always more choiceworthy. [But we do not think any addition can make happiness more choiceworthy; hence it is most choiceworthy.]

Happiness, then, is apparently something complete and self-sufficient, since it is the end of the things pursued in action.

**A Clearer Account of the Good: The Human Soul's Activity Expressing Virtue**   But presumably the remark that the best good is happiness is apparently something [generally] agreed, and what we miss is a clearer statement of what the best good is.

**1. If Something Has a Function, Its Good Depends on Its Function**    Well, perhaps we shall find the best good if we first find the function of a human being. For just as the good, i.e., [doing] well, for a flautist, a sculptor, and every craftsman, and, in general, for whatever has a function and [characteristic] action, seems to depend on its function, the same seems to be true for a human being, if a human being has some function.

**2. What Sorts of Things Have Functions?**    Then do the carpenter and the leatherworker have their functions and actions, while a human being has none, and is by nature idle, without any function? Or, just as eye, hand, foot and, in general, every [bodily] part apparently has its functions, may we likewise ascribe to a human being some functions besides all of theirs?

**3. The Human Function**    What, then, could this be? For living is apparently shared with plants, but what we are looking for is the special function of a human being; hence we should set aside the life of nutrition and growth. The life next in order is some sort of life of sense-perception; but this too is apparently shared, with horse, ox and every animal. The remaining possibility, then, is some sort of life of action of the [part of the soul] that has reason.

**Clarification of "Has Reason" and "Life"**    Now this [part has two parts, which have reason in different ways], one as obeying the reason [in the other part], the other as itself having reason and thinking. [We intend both.] Moreover, life is also spoken of in two ways [as capacity and as activity], and we must take [a human being's special function to be] life as activity, since this seems to be called life to a fuller extent.

**4. The Human Good Is Activity Expressing Virtue**    (a) We have found, then, that the human function is the soul's activity that expresses reason [as itself having reason] or requires reason [as obeying reason]. (b) Now the function of F, e.g., of a harpist, is the same in kind, so we say, as the function of an excellent F, e.g., an excellent harpist. (c) The same is true unconditionally in every case, when we add to the function the superior achievement that expresses the virtue; for a harpist's function, e.g., is to play the harp, and a good harpist's is to do it well. (d) Now we take the human function to be a certain kind of life, and take this life to be the soul's activity and actions that express reason. (e) [Hence by (c) and (d)] the excellent man's function is to do this finely and well. (f) Each function is completed well when its completion expresses the proper virtue. (g) Therefore [by (d), (e) and (f)] the human good turns out to be the soul's activity that expresses virtue.

**5. The Good Must Also Be Complete**    And if there are more virtues than one, the good will express the best and most complete virtue. Moreover, it will be in a complete life. For one swallow does not make a spring, nor does one day; nor, similarly, does one day or a short time make us blessed and happy. . . .

# VIRTUES OF CHARACTER IN GENERAL

## How a Virtue of Character Is Acquired

Virtue, then, is of two sorts, virtue of thought and virtue of character. Virtue of thought arises and grows mostly from teaching, and hence needs experience and time. Virtue of character [i.e., of *ethos*] results from habit [*ethos*]; hence its name "ethical," slightly varied from *"ethos."*

**Virtue Comes About, Not by a Process of Nature, but by Habituation**
Hence it is also clear that none of the virtues of character arises in us naturally.

**1. What Is Natural Cannot Be Changed by Habituation**  For if something is by nature [in one condition], habituation cannot bring it into another condition. A stone, e.g., by nature moves downwards, and habituation could not make it move upwards, not even if you threw it up ten thousand times to habituate it; nor could habituation make fire move downwards, or bring anything that is by nature in one condition into another condition.

Thus the virtues arise in us neither by nature nor against nature, but we are by nature able to acquire them, and reach our complete perfection through habit.

**2. Natural Capacities Are Not Acquired by Habituation**  Further, if something arises in us by nature, we first have the capacity for it, and later display the activity. This is clear in the case of the senses; for we did not acquire them by frequent seeing or hearing, but already had them when we exercised them, and did not get them by exercising them.

Virtues, by contrast, we acquire, just as we acquire crafts, by having previously activated them. For we learn a craft by producing the same product that we must produce when we have learned it, becoming builders, e.g., by building and harpists by playing the harp; so also, then, we become just by doing just actions, temperate by doing temperate actions, brave by doing brave actions.

**3. Legislators Concentrate on Habituation**  What goes on in cities is evidence for this also. For the legislator makes the citizens good by habituating them, and this is the wish of every legislator; if he fails to do it well he misses his goal. [The right] habituation is what makes the difference between a good political system and a bad one.

**4. Virtue and Vice Are Formed by Good and Bad Actions**  Further, just as in the case of a craft, the sources and means that develop each virtue also ruin it. For playing the harp makes both good and bad harpists, and it is analogous in the case of builders and all the rest; for building well makes good builders, building badly, bad ones. If it were not so, no teacher would be needed, but everyone would be born a good or a bad craftsman.

It is the same, then, with the virtues. For actions in dealings with [other] human beings make some people just, some unjust; actions in terrifying situations and the acquired habit of fear or confidence make some brave and others cowardly. The same is true of situations involving appetites and anger; for one or

another sort of conduct in these situations makes some people temperate and gen-
tle, others intemperate and irascible.

**Conclusion: The Importance of Habituation**    To sum up, then, in a single
account: A state [of character] arises from [the repetition of] similar activities.
Hence we must display the right activities, since differences in these imply corresponding differences in the states. It is not unimportant, then, to acquire one sort
of habit or another, right from our youth; rather, it is very important, indeed all-
important. . . .

But our claims about habituation raise a puzzle: How can we become good
without being good already?

However, someone might raise this puzzle: "What do you mean by saying that
to become just we must first do just actions and to become temperate we must first
do temperate actions? For if we do what is grammatical or musical, we must
already be grammarians or musicians. In the same way, then, if we do what is
just or temperate, we must already be just or temperate."

**First Reply: Conformity Versus Understanding**    But surely this is not so even
with the crafts, for it is possible to produce something grammatical by chance or
by following someone else's instructions. To be a grammarian, then, we must both
produce something grammatical and produce it in the way in which the grammarian produces it, i.e., expressing grammatical knowledge that is in us.

**Second Reply: Crafts versus Virtues**    Moreover, in any case what is true of
crafts is not true of virtues. For the products of a craft determine by their own
character whether they have been produced well; and so it suffices that they are
in the right state when they have been produced. But for actions expressing virtue
to be done temperately or justly [and hence well] it does not suffice that they are
themselves in the right state. Rather, the agent must also be in the right state when
he does them. First, he must know [that he is doing virtuous actions]; second, he
must decide on them, and decide on them for themselves; and, third, he must also
do them from a firm and unchanging state.

As conditions for having a craft these three do not count, except for the
knowing itself. As a condition for having a virtue, however, the knowing counts
for nothing, or [rather] for only a little, whereas the other two conditions are very
important, indeed all-important. And these other two conditions are achieved by
the frequent doing of just and temperate actions.

Hence actions are called just or temperate when they are the sort that a just or
temperate person would do. But the just and temperate person is not the one who
[merely] does these actions, but the one who also does them in the way in which
just or temperate people do them.

It is right, then, to say that a person comes to be just from doing just actions
and temperate from doing temperate actions; for no one has even a prospect of
becoming good from failing to do them.

**Virtue Requires Habituation, and Therefore Requires Practice, Not Just
Theory**    The many, however, do not do these actions but take refuge in arguments, thinking that they are doing philosophy, and that this is the way to become

excellent people. In this they are like a sick person who listens attentively to the doctor, but acts on none of his instructions. Such a course of treatment will not improve the state of his body; any more than will the many's way of doing philosophy improve the state of their souls.

# A VIRTUE OF CHARACTER IS A STATE INTERMEDIATE BETWEEN TWO EXTREMES, AND INVOLVING DECISION

## The Genus

**Feelings, Capacities, States**   Next we must examine what virtue is. Since there are three conditions arising in the soul—feelings, capacities and states—virtue must be one of these.

By feelings I mean appetite, anger, fear, confidence, envy, joy, love, hate, longing, jealousy, pity, in general whatever implies pleasure or pain.

By capacities I mean what we have when we are said to be capable of these feelings—capable of, e.g., being angry or afraid or feeling pity.

By states I mean what we have when we are well or badly off in relation to feelings. If, e.g., our feeling is too intense or slack, we are badly off in relation to anger, but if it is intermediate, we are well off; and the same is true in the other cases.

**Virtue Is Not a Feeling** ...   First, then, neither virtues nor vices are feelings. (a) For we are called excellent or base in so far as we have virtues or vices, not in so far as we have feelings. (b) We are neither praised nor blamed in so far as we have feelings; for we do not praise the angry or the frightened person, and do not blame the person who is simply angry, but only the person who is angry in a particular way. But we are praised or blamed in so far as we have virtues or vices. (c) We are angry and afraid without decision; but the virtues are decisions of some kind, or [rather] require decision. (d) Besides, in so far as we have feelings, we are said to be moved; but in so far as we have virtues or vices, we are said to be in some condition rather than moved.

**Or a Capacity** ...   For these reasons the virtues are not capacities either; for we are neither called good nor called bad in so far as we are simply capable of feelings. Further, while we have capacities by nature, we do not become good or bad by nature; we have discussed this before.

**But a State**   If, then, the virtues are neither feelings nor capacities, the remaining possibility is that they are states. And so we have said what the genus of virtue is.

## The Differentia

But we must say not only, as we already have, that it is a state, but also what sort of state it is.

**Virtue and the Human Function**   It should be said, then, that every virtue causes its possessors to be in a good state and to perform their functions well; the virtue of eyes, e.g., makes the eyes and their functioning excellent, because it makes us see well; and similarly, the virtue of a horse makes the horse excellent, and thereby good at galloping, at carrying its rider and at standing steady in the face of the enemy. If this is true in every case, then the virtue of a human being will likewise be the state that makes a human being good and makes him perform his function well. . . .

**The Numerical Mean and the Mean Relative to Us**   In everything continuous and divisible we can take more, less and equal, and each of them either in the object itself or relative to us; and the equal is some intermediate between excess and deficiency.

By the intermediate in the object I mean what is equidistant from each extremity; this is one and the same for everyone. But relative to us the intermediate is what is neither superfluous nor deficient; this is not one, and is not the same for everyone.

If, e.g., ten are many and two are few, we take six as intermediate in the object, since it exceeds [two] and is exceeded [by ten] by an equal amount, [four]; this is what is intermediate by numerical proportion. But that is not how we must take the intermediate that is relative to us. For if, e.g., ten pounds [of food] are a lot for someone to eat, and two pounds a little, it does not follow that the trainer will prescribe six, since this might also be either a little or a lot for the person who is to take it—for Milo [the athlete] a little, but for the beginner in gymnastics a lot; and the same is true for running and wrestling. In this way every scientific expert avoids excess and deficiency and seeks and chooses what is intermediate—but intermediate relative to us, not in the object.

**Virtue Seeks the Mean Relative to Us: Argument from Craft to Virtue**   This, then, is how each science produces its product well, by focusing on what is intermediate and making the product conform to that. This, indeed, is why people regularly comment on well-made products that nothing could be added or subtracted, since they assume that excess or deficiency ruins a good [result] while the mean preserves it. Good craftsmen also, we say, focus on what is intermediate when they produce their product. And since virtue, like nature, is better and more exact than any craft, it will also aim at what is intermediate.

**Arguments from the Nature of Virtue of Character**   By virtue I mean virtue of character; for this [pursues the mean because] it is concerned with feelings and actions, and these admit of excess, deficiency and an intermediate condition. We can be afraid, e.g., or be confident, or have appetites, or get angry, or feel pity, in general have pleasure or pain, both too much and too little, and in both ways not well; but [having these feelings] at the right times, about the right things, towards the right people, for the right end, and in the right way, is the intermediate and best condition, and this is proper to virtue. Similarly, actions also admit of excess, deficiency and the intermediate condition.

Now virtue is concerned with feelings and actions, in which excess and deficiency are in error and incur blame, while the intermediate condition is correct and wins praise, which are both proper features of virtue. Virtue, then, is a mean, in so far as it aims at what is intermediate.

Moreover, there are many ways to be in error, since badness is proper to what is unlimited, as the Pythagoreans pictured it, and good to what is limited; but there is only one way to be correct. That is why error is easy and correctness hard, since it is easy to miss the target and hard to hit it. And so for this reason also excess and deficiency are proper to vice, the mean to virtue; "for we are noble in only one way, but bad in all sorts of ways."

**Definition of Virtue**    Virtue, then, is (a) a state that decides, (b) [consisting] in a mean, (c) the mean relative to us, (d) which is defined by reference to reason, (e) i.e., to the reason by reference to which the intelligent person would define it. It is a mean between two vices, one of excess and one of deficiency.

It is a mean for this reason also: Some vices miss what is right because they are deficient, others because they are excessive, in feelings or in actions, while virtue finds and chooses what is intermediate.

Hence, as far as its substance and the account stating its essence are concerned, virtue is a mean; but as far as the best [condition] and the good [result] are concerned, it is an extremity.

**The Definition Must Not Be Misapplied to Cases in Which There Is No Mean**    But not every action or feeling admits of the mean. For the names of some automatically include baseness, e.g., spite, shamelessness, envy [among feelings], and adultery, theft, murder, among actions. All of these and similar things are called by these names because they themselves, not their excesses or deficiencies, are base.

Hence in doing these things we can never be correct, but must invariably be in error. We cannot do them well or not well—e.g., by committing adultery with the right woman at the right time in the right way; on the contrary it is true unconditionally that to do any of them is to be in error.

[To think these admit of a mean], therefore, is like thinking that unjust or cowardly or intemperate action also admits of a mean, an excess and a deficiency. For then there would be a mean of excess, a mean of deficiency, an excess of excess and a deficiency of deficiency.

Rather, just as there is no excess or deficiency of temperance or of bravery, since the intermediate is a sort of extreme [in achieving the good], so also there is no mean of these [vicious actions] either, but whatever way anyone does them, he is in error. For in general there is no mean of excess or of deficiency, and no excess or deficiency of a mean.

## THE DEFINITION OF VIRTUE AS A MEAN APPLIES TO THE INDIVIDUAL VIRTUES

However, we must not only state this general account but also apply it to the particular cases. For among accounts concerning actions, though the general ones are common to more cases, the specific ones are truer, since actions are about particular cases, and our account must accord with these. Let us, then, find these from the chart.

## Classification of Virtues of Character

**Virtues Concerned with Feelings.**     1. First, in feelings of fear and confidence the mean is bravery. The excessively fearless person is nameless (and in fact many cases are nameless), while the one who is excessively confident is rash; the one who is excessively afraid and deficient in confidence is cowardly.

2. In pleasures and pains, though not in all types, and in pains less than in pleasures, the mean is temperance and the excess intemperance. People deficient in pleasure are not often found, which is why they also lack even a name; let us call them insensible.

**Virtues Concerned with External Goods.**     3. In giving and taking money the mean is generosity, the excess wastefulness and the deficiency ungenerosity. Here the vicious people have contrary excesses and defects; for the wasteful person spends to excess and is deficient in taking, whereas the ungenerous person takes to excess and is deficient in spending. At the moment we are speaking in outline and summary. . . .

4. In questions of money there are also other conditions. Another mean is magnificence; for the magnificent person differs from the generous by being concerned with large matters, while the generous person is concerned with small. The excess is ostentation and vulgarity, and the deficiency niggardliness, and these differ from the vices related to generosity. . . .

5. In honor and dishonor the mean is magnanimity, the excess something called a sort of vanity, and the deficiency pusillanimity.

6. And just as we said that generosity differs from magnificence in its concern with small matters, similarly there is a virtue concerned with small honors, differing in the same way from magnanimity, which is concerned with great honors. For honor can be desired either in the right way or more or less than is right. If someone desires it to excess, he is called an honor-lover, and if his desire is deficient he is called indifferent to honor, but if he is intermediate he has no name. The corresponding conditions have no name either, except the condition of the honor-lover, which is called honor-loving.

This is why people at the extremes claim the intermediate area. Indeed, we also sometimes call the intermediate person an honor-lover, and sometimes call him indifferent to honor; and sometimes we praise the honor-lover, sometimes the person indifferent to honor. . . .

**Virtues Concerned with Social Life.**     7. Anger also admits of an excess, deficiency and mean. These are all practically nameless; but since we call the intermediate person mild, let us call the mean mildness. Among the extreme people let the excessive person be irascible, and the vice be irascibility, and let the deficient person be a sort of inirascible person, and the deficiency be inirascibility.

There are three other means, somewhat similar to one another, but different. For they are all concerned with association in conversations and actions, but differ in so far as one is concerned with truth-telling in these areas, the other two with sources of pleasure, some of which are found in amusement, and the others in daily life in general. Hence we should also discuss these states, so that we can better observe that in every case the mean is praiseworthy, while the extremes are neither praiseworthy nor correct, but blameworthy. Most of these cases are also nameless, and we must try, as in the other cases also, to make names ourselves, to make things clear and easy to follow.

8. In truth-telling, then, let us call the intermediate person truthful, and the mean truthfulness; pretense that overstates will be boastfulness, and the person who has it boastful; pretense that understates will be self-deprecation, and the person who has it self-deprecating.

9. In sources of pleasure in amusements let us call the intermediate person witty, and the condition wit; the excess buffoonery and the person who has it a buffoon; and the deficient person a sort of boor and the state boorishness.

10. In the other sources of pleasure, those in daily life, let us call the person who is pleasant in the right way friendly, and the mean state friendliness. If someone goes to excess with no [further] aim he will be ingratiating; if he does it for his own advantage, a flatterer. The deficient person, unpleasant in everything, will be a sort of quarrelsome and ill-tempered person.

**Mean States that Are Not Virtues**    11. There are also means in feelings and concerned with feelings: shame, e.g., is not a virtue, but the person prone to shame as well as the virtuous person we have described receives praise. For here also one person is called intermediate, and another—the person excessively prone to shame, who is ashamed about everything—is called excessive; the person who is deficient in shame or never feels shame at all is said to have no sense of disgrace; and the intermediate one is called prone to shame.

12. Proper indignation is the mean between envy and spite; these conditions are concerned with pleasure and pain at what happens to our neighbors. For the properly indignant person feels pain when someone does well undeservedly; the envious person exceeds him by feeling pain when anyone does well, while the spiteful person is so deficient in feeling pain that he actually enjoys [other people's misfortunes].

## READING COMPREHENSION QUESTIONS

1. How does Aristotle defend the claim that the good for human beings is happiness?

2. In explaining what the good or happy life for a human being consists in, Aristotle gives what has come to be known as the "function" argument. What are the steps (the premises and conclusion) of his argument? Do you find it plausible? Explain.

3. According to Aristotle, how is virtue acquired?

4. How does Aristotle define virtue? What role does the idea of a "mean" play in his definition?

5. Are there any traits of character or mind that you think are missing from Aristotle's discussion?

6. Which of the virtues and vices Aristotle discusses strike you as distinctively ethical or moral virtues and vices? If you think that some of the virtues and vices are not ethical, what is the basis for distinguishing ethical from other types of virtue and vice?

# Glossary

**agnosticism:** The general belief that we don't have sufficient reason either to affirm or to deny any god's existence.

**a posteriori justification:** A justification for a belief or position making reference to experience, i.e., an empirical justification. For example, one is justified in believing other people exist because one can *see* them.

**a posteriori knowledge:** Knowledge of some proposition that is based wholly or partly on experience (which includes sensory experience and introspection). Contrasted with a priori knowledge.

**a priori justification:** A justification for a belief or position making no reference to experience, i.e., a non-empirical justification. For example, one is justified in believing that all triangles have three sides just by consideration of the concept of a triangle alone.

**a priori knowledge:** Knowledge of some proposition that is "prior to" or independent of experience (which includes sensory experience and introspection).

**argument:** In philosophy, an argument is a collection of statements, called **premises**, that together are intended to provide support for another statement, called a **conclusion**.

**argument by analogy:** A type of **inductive argument** that provides a comparison between two or more things in order to draw a conclusion about one of them, e.g., "Your sweater is 100 percent wool, just like mine, and since mine is scratchy, yours must be too."

**argument from design:** An argument for the existence of God, inferring from the occurrence of irreducible complexity or design in nature that there was an intelligent designer of it all, called God. The most famous advocate of this argument was William Paley, who compared the universe to a watch. Also known as the **teleological argument**.

**argument from miracles:** An argument for the existence of God, maintaining that the only explanation for the occurrence of various miracles throughout history is God's intervention in nature.

**atheism:** The belief that there is no god(s) of any kind.

**begging the question:** An argument flaw in which one either assumes without **argument** the very thing one is trying to prove or one answers a question with a variation of the very question asked. To beg the question is to undermine the very point of argumentation, which is to provide reasoned support for a **conclusion**.

**behaviorism:** See **philosophical behaviorism**.

**Body Criterion (of personal identity):** X at one time is the same person as Y at some later time if and only if Y has the same body as X.

**Brain Criterion (of personal identity):** X at one time is the same person as Y at some later time if and only if Y has the same brain as X.

**Cartesian conception of knowledge:** The view that **propositional knowledge** consists in having a justified true belief where one's justifying evidence guarantees that the belief is true.

**Cartesian dualism:** A version of **substance dualism** according to which (a) minds are nonphysical, nonspatial substances or entities whose essential nature is the activity of thinking and (b) minds and bodies are capable of causally interacting with one another.

**Cartesian skepticism:** The view that denies knowledge in some or all domains. Also called **theoretical skepticism**.

**categorical imperative:** The fundamental principle in Kant's ethical theory, which states that one ought only to act on maxims (policies) that one can consistently will that everyone adopt and act on. This is called the **universal law formulation** of the categorical imperative. Kant also provided what is known as the **humanity formulation** of the categorical imperative.

**central-state identity theory:** The view that mental states and events are **numerically identical** to brain states and events. Also called the identity theory of mind.

**circular reasoning:** Another name for the argumentative flaw known as **begging the question**.

**compatibilism:** The theory that **determinism** is, or could be, true, and yet, regardless, it is compatible with **free agency** and **moral responsibility**. Also known as **soft determinism**.

**conclusion:** A statement in an **argument** that one intends to support with various reasons (called **premises**).

**correspondence theory of truth:** The view that what makes a proposition true is that there exists a fact to which the proposition corresponds.

**cosmological argument:** An argument for the existence of God, positing God as the only explanation for the existence of the universe. In a version offered by Thomas Aquinas, he focuses on one key feature of the universe—causation—to argue for the conclusion that a first cause, called God, must exist in order for anything else to exist at all.

**counterexample:** An exception to a universal claim or principle. A counterexample to the abstract claim "All X's are Y's" would just be an example of an X that isn't a Y. Finding a counterexample to an **argument** undermines its **soundness**.

**cultural relativism:** See **ethical relativism**.

**deductive argument:** A kind of **argument** in which the aim is to prove a conclusion in the strongest possible way, providing for it a logical guarantee. If a deductive argument is done correctly, then if the premises are true, the conclusion has to be true as well.

**deep agnosticism:** The belief that we don't have sufficient reason either to affirm or to deny God's existence *because the very concept of God is incoherent*.

**deism:** The belief in an "absentee" God, i.e., one who long ago set things in motion but thereafter left it alone.

**determinism:** The theory that the state of the universe at any point in time is entirely fixed by the state of the universe at a prior time, in combination with the laws of nature.

**divine command theory:** An **ethical theory** according to which what makes actions right or wrong are the commands of God.

**dualism:** A family of theories about mind and body according to which the essential nature of the mind or of what is mental is something nonphysical (nonmaterial). Thus, according to dualism, human beings are composites of two fundamentally different kinds of things: nonphysical minds and physical bodies. The two main versions of dualism are **substance dualism** and **property dualism**.

**epiphenomenalism:** A version of **property dualism** according to which physical brain events cause mental events; however, mental events are causally impotent.

**epistemological criterion:** One sense of the term "criterion," referring to *how we might know that* something is as it is. So X is an epistemological criterion of Y if and only if X provides an explication of how we can know what Y's nature consists in.

**epistemology:** The field of philosophy that inquires into the nature, possibility, and scope of knowledge. Also called *theory of knowledge*.

**equivocation:** An argumentative flaw in which a key word or phrase in an argument shifts its meaning within the course of that argument.

**ethical egoism:** An **ethical theory** according to which what is right or wrong for *you* to do is really just a matter of what will be good *for you*—what will best promote your self-interest.

**ethical principles:** Very general ethical statements that purport to specify what makes actions right or wrong or what makes something (including persons) good or bad.

**ethical relativism:** An **ethical theory** according to which what's right or wrong for one to do depends on the ethical norms one's culture happens to accept. Also called **cultural relativism**.

**ethical theory:** Addresses fundamental ethical questions about the nature of right and wrong, good and bad.

**ethics:** The branch of philosophy that inquires into questions about right and wrong, good and bad.

**ethics of care:** An **ethical theory** according to which considerations of *care* are central in what makes actions right and wrong.

**exclusion principle:** In order to know some proposition *p*, one must be able, on the basis of one's evidence, to rule out or exclude (and thus know to be false) any proposition that one knows to be incompatible with *p*.

**explanatory reason:** A consideration providing an explanation for some state of affairs, usually a causal story. An explanatory reason for X's belief B provides an explanation for why X came to believe B.

**extrinsic value:** The value (positive or negative) that something X possesses in virtue of being related to something else Y that has **intrinsic value**. For instance, money and power, while not intrinsically valuable, can nevertheless possess extrinsic value when they are used to bring about or contribute to something that has intrinsic value, such as happiness.

**false analogy:** An argumentative flaw of certain **arguments by analogy** that is due to the fact that there are important *disanalogies* between the items that are the basis of the analogy and the item the conclusion is about.

**free agency:** Refers to the ability to act freely. One is a free agent to the extent one's actions are free, whatever that consists in.

**functionalism:** A view about the mind according to which the nature or essence of a mental state is its causal role in relation to (a) *environmental inputs to the body,* (b) *other mental states,* and (c) *behavioral outputs.*

**global skepticism:** A version of **skepticism** that refuses to grant knowledge in *all* domains or areas of inquiry.

**golden rule:** Do unto others as you would have them do unto you.

**hard determinism:** The theory that **determinism** is true, and so we never act freely (because all our actions are entirely caused), and we are never morally responsible for our actions.

**hard indeterminism:** The theory that **indeterminism** is true, and so we never act freely (because our actions are really just the product of random events), and we are never morally responsible for our actions.

**hasty generalization:** An argumentative flaw of some **inductive arguments**, in which a sweeping conclusion is drawn from either a severely small or an unrepresentative sample size.

**henotheism:** The belief that there are many gods, but only one to which the believer owes his or her allegiance.

**humanity formulation:** A formulation of Kant's **categorical imperative**, which states that one ought always to treat humanity, both in oneself and others, never as a mere means but as an end in itself.

**identity theory:** See **central-state identity theory**.

**ignorance:** Lack of knowledge.

**indeterminism:** The theory that the state of the universe at any point in time is *not* entirely fixed by the state of the universe at a prior time in combination with the laws of nature.

**inductive argument:** A kind of **argument** in which the aim is to provide reasons (premises) that strongly support, but do not guarantee, the truth of a conclusion. Arguments in which the aim is to provide reasons that guarantee the truth of the conclusion are **deductive arguments**.

**inductive generalization:** A type of **inductive argument** that moves from a "sample" to a general conclusion about a population, e.g., "Every swan I've ever seen is white, so therefore all swans are (probably) white."

**inductively strong:** A term of evaluation for an **inductive argument**, applying to it if its premises provide strong support for the conclusion. In other words, an argument is inductively strong if we can say of it that if its premises are true, it is probable that the conclusion is also true.

**inductively weak:** A term of evaluation for an **inductive argument**, applying to it if its premises don't provide very strong support for the conclusion. This doesn't mean the argument's conclusion is false, however; instead, it just means that the conclusion isn't made much more probable by *this* argument.

**intentionality:** That feature by which our mental states are *about* or *directed toward* something. For instance, the belief that Chicago is in Illinois is about the city of Chicago, the state of Illinois, and their spatial relationship to one another.

**interactionistic property dualism:** A version of **property dualism** according to which the mental and the physical causally interact. That is, mental properties are caused by physical properties of the brain, and mental properties in turn are causes of certain physical properties of the brain.

**intrinsic value:** The value (positive or negative) possessed by something in virtue of its own inherent nature. For example, some philosophers claim that pleasure has positive intrinsic value—its value derives from the nature of pleasurable experiences.

**justifying reason:** A consideration providing a justification for some state of affairs. A justifying reason for X's belief B provides a justification for X's believing B, i.e., a consideration in favor of X's *continued belief* in B.

**Kant's ethical theory:** The theory developed and defended by German philosopher Immanuel Kant that features the **categorical imperative** as the fundamental **ethical principle** governing right and wrong.

**libertarianism:** The theory that **determinism** is incompatible with **free agency**, but that determinism is false, and we may indeed be free agents as a result.

**local skepticism:** A version of **skepticism** that refuses to grant knowledge in some but not all domains or areas of inquiry. For example, one sort of local skeptic refuses to grant knowledge in the domain of religious belief but grants it in the domain of science.

**logical behaviorism:** See **philosophical behaviorism**.

**materialism:** (also called **physicalism**) is the view that human beings, as well as non-human animals with a mental life, are thoroughly material or physical beings. So on this view there is no special mental mind "stuff" or special mental properties.

**Memory Criterion (of personal identity):** X at one time is the same person as Y at some later time if and only if Y remembers the thoughts and experiences of X.

**metaphysical criterion:** One sense of the term "criterion," referring to *what makes it the case that* something is as it is. So X is a metaphysical criterion of Y if and only if X provides an explication of what Y consists in, an explication of Y's nature.

**monotheism:** The belief that there is only one Supreme Being, who is both personal and moral.

**moral responsibility:** Being appropriately subject to praise or blame.

**naturalism:** The theory that everything can be wholly explained in terms of natural phenomena (i.e., no supernatural explanations needed).

**necessary condition:** X is a necessary condition for Y when X must obtain for Y to obtain. For example, light is a necessary condition for unaided visual perception in humans.

**nonskepticism (about knowledge):** The view in **epistemology** that affirms the possibility of knowledge in at least some domains. Most nonskeptical views not only affirm the possibility of knowledge in one or more domains but claim that humans currently have at least some knowledge in those domains.

**numerical identity:** See **quantitative identity**.

**ontological argument:** An argument attempting to prove the existence of God solely through consideration of the concept of God. This is a purely **a priori justification** for belief in God, and its most famous advocate was St. Anselm.

**Pascal's wager:** An argument for why belief in God is prudentially rational, offered by Blaise Pascal. Pascal noted that the payoff for belief in a God who turned out to exist was infinite (eternal happiness), whereas one lost nothing if one believed in a God that didn't exist, so it was overwhelmingly in one's best interests to be a believer.

**philosophical behaviorism:** The view that mental terms can be defined in terms that refer exclusively to behavior and dispositions to behave. Also called **logical behaviorism**.

**physicalism:** See **materialism**.

**polytheism:** The belief in a multitude of personal gods, each responsible for a different department of life.

**popular dualism:** A version of **substance dualism** according to which the mind is a spiritual nonphysical substance *located in*, and capable of interacting with, the body. This view is like **Cartesian dualism** except that it claims that minds are located *inside* bodies and hence that they have spatial location.

**practical skepticism (about knowledge):** The view in **epistemology** that neither affirms nor denies knowledge in some or all domains. Also called **Pyrrhonian skepticism**.

**premise:** A statement in an **argument** that is being used to provide support for some **conclusion**. Premises are usually identified by tip-off words, like "because," "since," "for," and "for the reason that."

**principle of utility:** The fundamental principle of ethics in **utilitarianism** according to which (roughly) morality requires that we produce as much overall happiness (also called *utility*) as possible. J. S. Mill, one of the founding fathers of utilitarianism, called this the "greatest happiness" principle.

**principles of right conduct: Ethical principles** that purport to explain what makes an action right or wrong.

**principles of value:** Principles that purport to indicate what it is that makes something intrinsically good or intrinsically bad.

**property dualism:** A version of mind-body dualism according to which there are two fundamentally different types of properties: physical properties and mental properties. Human brains, for example, have physical properties such as mass and weight, but they also possess mental properties such as the properties of having a pain, having a visual sensation, believing something, and so on. This view contrasts with **substance dualism** in denying that what is called the "mind" is an entity or substance.

**propositional knowledge:** Knowledge having to do with *knowing that* some proposition is true.

**psychological egoism:** A psychological thesis according to which all human actions are done solely for the sake of self-interest. This thesis should not to be confused with **ethical egoism**.

**Pyrrhonian skepticism:** See **practical skepticism**.

**qualia:** The subjective what-it-is-likeness of experiences. For instance, the taste of a peach, the visual experience of vivid blue, the sound of a siren, and the way touching a smooth surface feels are all qualia—*qualitative* features of one's experiences.

**qualitative identity:** One sense of the term "identity" referring to exact similarity. An object is qualitatively identical to another if and only if their qualities are exactly alike.

**quantitative identity:** One sense of the term "identity" meaning *one and the same thing as*. So X is quantitatively identical to Y if and only if whatever is true of X is true of Y and vice versa. Also known as **numerical identity**.

**reductio ad absurdum (or just plain "reductio"):** Latin name for the argumentative flaw in which some portion of one's **argument** may be shown to imply either a contradiction or a patent absurdity. If a claim in one's argument implies a contradiction, then it is *false;* if it implies an absurdity, then it is *implausible*.

**reductive materialism:** The proposal that mental states can be reduced to (are nothing but) brain states. This proposal is an implication of the **central-state identity theory** of the mind.

**running a reductio:** A strategy in which one shows that someone's argument is subject to a **reductio ad absurdum**.

**skepticism:** A view in **epistemology** that refuses to grant that there is knowledge. **Local skepticism** refuses to grant knowledge in some but not all domains or areas of inquiry, while **global skepticism** refuses to grant any knowledge. The two main varieties of skepticism about knowledge are **theoretical skepticism** and **practical skepticism**. (Note: some skeptics go further than skeptics about knowledge and refuse to grant that any beliefs are *justified*.)

**Socrates:** A famous ancient Greek philosopher (469–400 B.C.E.), eventually executed by the state, allegedly for not worshipping the gods of the city and "corrupting the youth" with his philosophizing.

**soft determinism:** See **compatibilism**.

**soul criterion (of personal identity):** X at one time is the same person as Y at some later time if and only if Y has the same soul as X.

**sound:** A term of evaluation for a **deductive argument**, applying to it if it is **valid** and it has all true **premises**. A sound argument is one whose conclusion, therefore, must be true.

**structuralism:** The theory that the ability to do otherwise is not a necessary condition of **free agency** and **moral responsibility**, and that one may be a free agent and morally responsible just in case one's will is structured so that one's actions depend on one's choices, and one's choices are truly "one's own."

**substance dualism:** A version of **dualism** about mind and body according to which minds are non-physical substances whose nature is completely different from the nature of physical, material substances, and thus completely different from physical bodies. There are different versions of this type of dualism including **Cartesian dualism** and **popular dualism**.

**sufficient condition:** X is a sufficient condition for Y when X's being the case is enough for Y's being the case. Having ten dimes is a sufficient condition (but not a **necessary condition**) for having a dollar.

**sufficient evidence doctrine:** One ought only to believe what one has sufficient evidence or justification for believing.

**superficial agnosticism:** The belief that, while the concept of God is perfectly coherent, we nevertheless don't have sufficient reason either to affirm or to deny God's existence *because there's insufficient evidence either way.*

**syllogism:** A type of **deductive argument** wherein a conclusion is inferred from two premises.

**teleological argument:** See **argument from design**.

**theism:** The belief in the existence of god(s).

**theodicies:** Attempts to justify the presence of evil in the world, while also maintaining God's power and goodness. Theodicies provide possible **justifying reasons** for why God allows all the evil in the world to take place.

**theoretical skepticism (about knowledge):** The view in **epistemology** that denies knowledge in some or all domains. Also called **Cartesian skepticism**.

**theory of knowledge:** See **epistemology**.

**theory of right conduct:** That branch of **ethics** featuring **principles of right conduct** whose aim is to explain what makes actions right or wrong.

**theory of value:** That branch of **ethics** featuring **principles of value** whose aim is to explain what it is that makes something intrinsically good or intrinsically bad.

**universal law formulation:** See **categorical imperative**.

**utilitarianism:** An **ethical theory** based on the **principle of utility**, according to which what makes an action right or wrong is how much net happiness (also called **utility**) it will bring about (if performed) where everyone's happiness (and unhappiness) is considered equally.

**valid:** A term of evaluation for a **deductive argument**, applying to it if the **premises** logically guarantee the truth of the **conclusion**. In other words, a deductive argument is valid if the rules of inference have been applied correctly, so that *if* the premises are true, the conclusion must be true as well. Notice that assessing validity has nothing whatsoever to do with assessing whether or not the premises really *are* true. A valid argument may have all true premises and conclusion, all false premises and conclusion, or a mixture of the two.

**vice:** A trait of character or mind that involves dispositions to act, feel, and think in certain ways, and that is central in the *negative* evaluation of persons. Examples include dishonesty, stinginess, and cowardice.

**virtue:** A trait of character or mind that involves dispositions to act, feel, and think in certain ways and that is central in the *positive* evaluation of persons. Examples include honesty, generosity, and courage.

**virtue ethics:** An approach to **ethics** that takes considerations of **virtue** and **vice** as central in thinking about how to live one's life.

# Index